UNDERSTANDING THE TIMES

Revised 2nd Edition

David A. Noebel

Summit Press
P.O. Box 207
Manitou Springs, CO 80829

Published by Summit Press, a division of Summit Ministries, P.O. Box 207, Manitou Springs, Colorado 80829
© 1991, 1995, 2006 by David A. Noebel and Summit Ministries
All rights reserved.
First unabridged edition published 1991. First abridged edition 1995. Second abridged and revised edition 2006.

Eighth printing (2014), Printed by Bang Printing, Brainerd, MN USA

ISBN (hc): 0–936163–00–3

Library of Congress Cataloging-in-Publication Data
Noebel, David A.
    Understanding the Times : The Collision of Today's Competing Worldviews / David A. Noebel
        p.   cm.
    Includes glossary and index
    ISBN 0–936163–00–3
    1. Apologetics.   2. Christianity.   3. Islam.   4. Humanism.   5. Marxism.   6. New Age Movement.
7. Postmodernism   I. Title

This book is dedicated once again to every student who attended the Summit Ministries' one or two-week programs over the past 45 years either in Colorado, Tennessee, Ohio, Canada, South Africa, Australia or New Zealand. It is also dedicated to my son Brent who literally died persuading young lives what one blind guy and a bunch of teenagers could do for Jesus and the Body of Christ in the Sudan; and to Ronald H. Nash who left this world to be united with his Savior, and who told me many times how much he enjoyed working with and teaching our Summit students over the years.

Comparing Competing Worldviews

	CHRISTIANITY	ISLAM	SECULAR HUMANISM	MARXISM-LENINISM	COSMIC HUMANISM	POST-MODERNISM
	Bible	Qur'an, Hadith, Sunnah	Humanist Manifestos I, II, III	Marx, Engels, Lenin, Mao	MacLaine, Spangler, Chopra, Walsch	Nietzsche, Foucault, Derrida, Rorty
THEOLOGY	Theism (Trinitarian)	Theism (Unitarian)	Atheism	Atheism	Pantheism	Atheism
PHILOSOPHY	Supernaturalism (Faith and Reason)	Supernaturalism (Faith and Reason)	Naturalism	Dialectical Materialism	Non-Naturalism	Anti-Realism
ETHICS	Moral Absolutes	Moral Absolutes	Moral Relativism	Proletariat Morality	Moral Relativism (Karma)	Cultural Relativism
BIOLOGY	Creationism	Creationism	Neo-Darwinian Evolution	Punctuated Evolution	Cosmic Evolution	Punctuated Evolution
PSYCHOLOGY	Mind/Body Dualism (Fallen)	Mind/Body Dualism (Un-fallen)	Monism (Self-Actualization)	Monism (Behaviorism)	Higher Consciousness	Socially-Constructed Selves
SOCIOLOGY	Traditional Family, Church, State	Polygamy, Mosque, Islamic State	Non-Traditional Family, Church, State	Classless Society	Non-Traditional Family, Church, State	Sexual Egalitarianism
LAW	Divine/Natural Law	Shari'ah Law	Positive Law	Proletariat Law	Self-Law	Critical Legal Studies
POLITICS	Justice, Freedom, Order	Islamic Theocracy (Global Islam)	Liberalism (Secular World Gov't)	Statism (Communist World Gov't)	Self-Government (New World Order)	Leftism
ECONOMICS	Stewardship of Property	Stewardship of Property	Interventionism	Socialism	Universal Enlightened Production	Interventionism
HISTORY	Creation, Fall, Redemption	Historical Determinism (Jihad)	Historical Evolution	Historical Materialism	Evolutionary Godhood	Historicism

Introduction

Part One

"Where is the philosopher? Where is the scholar? Where is the debater of the age? Hasn't God made the world's wisdom foolish?"[1]

— PAUL THE APOSTLE

0.1.1 INTRODUCTION

Perusing the offerings at a well-stocked newsstand in downtown Chicago, I discovered a microcosm of the modern world in front of me. Headlines, box scores, still pictures, weird pictures, war pictures, pictures of beautiful people. I saw articles on an array of topics—beheadings, gay marriage, a murdered judge, date rape, a "no rules" restaurant, a child molester—and this was just the beginning.

As I scanned further, I discovered even more disturbing phenomena: The sexual revolution is ongoing; grass, LSD, and homemade meth are the latest therapeutic techniques for relieving depression; teen pregnancy affects 14- to 16-year-olds; porn everywhere; rich denounced, poor praised; school shot up, students dead; teen suicide; a third of all children in the U.S. born out of wedlock; world to end early next week; those who believe in truth are the root of all evil; concept of absolute values is for morons; there is no evil or good; no right or wrong; witness lies in court; husband kills wife, dumps body in neighbors' trash bin, gets six years in slammer; twentieth century bloodiest of all centuries; man clones self; world is overpopulated . . . .

---

[1] 1 Corinthians 1:20 (Holman Christian Standard Bible).

0.1.2 FROM NEWSSTAND TO CLASSROOM

University of Chicago law professor Albert W. Alschuler holds that "[a]lmost every measure confirms that America's youth are in trouble."[2] To support his claim, he cites Perry Farrell, the lead singer of Porno for Pyros, who "shouts the central lyrics of twentieth-century American jurisprudence, 'Ain't no wrong, ain't no right, only pleasure and pain.'"[3] Alschuler laments these signs of cultural discouragement and decay, saying, "One should expect to hear this lyric from orange-headed, leather-clad rock stars as well as Richard Rorty and Richard Posner."[4]

Why would he say that? What does Postmodernist intellectual Richard Rorty's worldview have to do with the worldview of an orange-headed rock star?

0.1.3 WORLDVIEWS IN COLLISION

Competing worldviews are breaking out everywhere if only we have eyes to see, ears to hear, and minds to think true thoughts. They are propagated at newsstands and on the evening news and played out at the United Nations, in the halls of Congress, and most assuredly at Harvard, Yale, Princeton, Duke, UC Berkeley, and yes, even the local community college.

When we consider the tug-of-war between and among worldviews that currently rages in America and around the world, we tend to think of the battle mostly in terms of political and ethical issues that divide those who hold traditional Christian ideas and values from those who hold various liberal/radical Humanist views (i.e., Secular, Marxist, Cosmic, and Postmodern) or who espouse the beliefs and practices of historical Islam.

> This battle for the minds and hearts of young people encompasses much more than politics and ethics.

But this battle for the minds and hearts of young people encompasses much more than politics and ethics. As believers in and followers of Jesus Christ, we need to consider how our commitment to Him affects not only our political and ethical convictions, but also the way we think and act about theology, philosophy, ethics, biology, psychology, sociology, law, politics, economics, and history. This collection of convictions is what we call a worldview. And it is in the arena of worldviews that one of the greatest battles of our time is now being waged 24/7 in each of the ten areas of thought listed above.

This book is about these competing worldviews. Its goal is to help Christian students recognize the significance of some of the most influential ideas and values prevalent in our non-Christian culture and to understand the unbiblical, unrealistic, and, yes, even irrational assumptions about reality from which they arise. If we understand the real differences between the Biblical Christian worldview and the Secular Humanist, Marxist, Cosmic Humanist (New Age), Postmodern, and Islamic worldviews, we will be better prepared to love, live, and defend God's truth as revealed in the Bible and in His Creation. A clear understanding of these six worldviews will not only help protect us from deception by grounding us more firmly in the Christian faith, but it will also give us tools to more effectively witness for Christ in these conflicting times.

---

[2] Albert W. Alschuler, *Law Without Values: The Life, Work, and Legacy of Justice Holmes* (Chicago, IL: University of Chicago Press, 2000), 189. My opening paragraphs were inspired by Alschuler's "politics of resentment" survey of American life (188).

[3] Ibid., 189–190.

[4] Ibid., 190.

0.1.4 MAKING SENSE OF THE WORLD

Making sense of the world and figuring out what is happening around us is fun! A basic understanding of the six worldviews listed above, each divided into ten significant disciplines, will give students a firm grasp of what, indeed, is going on both around them and around the world. In other words, six worldviews times ten disciplines will provide students with sixty ideas/beliefs/values to help them gain an "understanding of the times," which is exactly what the Bible exhorts us to do (1 Chronicles 12:32).[5]

> We cannot remain silent and concede everything away.

C.S. Lewis says that Christians "are tempted to make unnecessary concessions to those outside the Faith." We give in too much, he says. "We must show our Christian colours, if we are to be true to Jesus Christ. We cannot remain silent and concede everything away."[6]

0.1.5 JESUS CHRIST AND WESTERN CULTURE

As Christians, our worldview should be based on the Bible and constructed around the person of Jesus Christ (2 Corinthians 10:5). What would Jesus think? What would Jesus do?

An article in *Newsweek* magazine observes that "for Christians, Jesus is the hinge on which the door of history swings." But the *Newsweek* writer is quick to point out that our faith commitment affects more than just our view of history. He goes on to say that by "any secular standard, Jesus is also the dominant figure of Western culture. Like the millennium itself, much of what we now think of as Western ideas, inventions and values finds its source of inspiration in the religion that worships God in his name. Art and science, the self and society, politics and economics, marriage and the family, right and wrong, body and soul—all have been touched and often radically transformed by Christian influence."[7]

What *Newsweek* notes here is the pervasive influence of Christian faith and thinking upon every area of life, not only on how we act and the kind of life we live, but also on how we think and the things we hold most important. As Christians, our basic assumptions about life are formed by our central beliefs in the person and message of Jesus Christ. Those who do not hold biblically-based beliefs will usually come to very different conclusions about life and what makes it worthwhile.

> As Christians, our basic assumptions about life are formed by our central beliefs in the person and message of Jesus Christ.

As C.S. Lewis notes, "We are now getting to the point at which different beliefs about the universe lead to different behavior. Religion involves a series of statements about facts, which must be either true or false. If they are true, one set of conclusions will follow about the right sailing of the human fleet, if they are false, quite another set."[8]

Behavior that follows beliefs is exactly what Paul is talking about when he says that part of our responsibility as Christians is to cast down or overthrow arguments and every high thing (including naturalistic science and humanistic psychology) that exalts itself against the

---

[5] In fact, we need to understand fewer than 60 ideas/beliefs/values because many humanistic worldviews have similar views.

[6] C.S. Lewis, *God in the Dock* (Grand Rapids, MI: Eerdmans, 2002), 262.

[7] *Newsweek* (March 29, 1999), 54. For further information on the influence of Christ on Western culture see Alvin J. Schmidt, *How Christianity Changed the World* (Grand Rapids, MI: Zondervan, 2004) and D. James Kennedy and Jerry Newcombe, *What If Jesus Had Never Been Born* (Nashville, TN: Nelson, 2005).

[8] C.S. Lewis, *Mere Christianity* (New York, NY: Macmillan, 1972), 58.

knowledge of God, "bringing every thought [or idea] into captivity to the obedience of Christ" (2 Corinthians 10:5).

Paul wants God's people to have their minds and hearts renewed so they can discern right from wrong and good from evil (Romans 12:2) and to have the spirit of their minds discern the truth found in Jesus (Ephesians 4:21–22). The writer of Hebrews also underscores the importance of this point when he says, "For the word of God is living and powerful, and sharper than any two-edged sword, piercing even to the division of soul and spirit, and of joints and marrow, and is a discerner of the thoughts and intents of the heart" (Hebrews 4:12). The heart, as well as the mind, has the ability to discern good ideas from bad ideas.

The current conflict of worldviews engulfing Western culture is designed to dethrone Jesus Christ (Psalm 2) and replace the Biblical Christian worldview with the ideas of fallible but very clever human beings. The conflict pits the wisdom of God against the wisdom of the world. As Paul says, "Where is the philosopher? Where is the scholar? Where is the debater of this age? Hasn't God made the world's wisdom foolish? ...God's foolishness is wiser than human wisdom, and God's weakness is stronger than human strength" (1 Corinthians 1:20, 25, HCSB).[9]

> "Lord Acton was convinced that there were 'some twenty or thirty predominate currents of thought or attitudes of mind' that provided the structure of modern history and held the key to explaining it. The majority of these ideas were either religions or substitutes for religion."*
>
> ROBERT SCHUETTINGER

0.1.6 WAGING SPIRITUAL WARFARE

Richard Rorty outlines the Postmodernist battle plan in the struggle for students' allegiance: "The fundamentalist parents [i.e., Christian parents] of our fundamentalist students [i.e., Christian students] think that the entire 'American liberal establishment' is engaged in a conspiracy. These parents have a point. When we American college teachers encounter religious fundamentalists, we do not consider the possibility of reformulating our own practices of justification so as to give more weight to the authority of the Christian scriptures. Instead, we do our best to convince these students of the benefits of [humanistic] secularization. Rather, I think these students are lucky to find themselves under the benevolent *Herrschaft* [teaching] of people like me, and to have escaped the grip of their frightening, vicious, dangerous parents."[10]

Rorty further defines his teaching goal as enticing students to read Darwin and Freud "without disgust and incredulity" and to "arrange things so that students who enter as bigoted, homophobic, religious fundamentalists [i.e., Christian students] will leave college with views more like our own."[11] Because of views like Rorty's, which are antithetical to the goals of Christian education, this book has become necessary.

---

[9] An excellent example of human wisdom involves a discussion of the evolution of the eye. The conclusion was reached that it would take approximately 300 million years for a fully functioning eye to evolve by chance and accident (to which a wit quipped that a father and a mother can produce a fully functioning eye in nine months!).

[10] Robert B. Brandom, ed., *Rorty and His Critics* (Malden, MA: Blackwell Publishers, 2001), 21–22.

[11] Ibid., 21.

* Robert Schuettinger, *Lord Acton: Historian of Liberty* (LaSalle, IL: Open Court, 1976), 174.

Attacks on Christian ideas come from a variety of directions. Here are a few examples:

- Jesus taught that God created human beings male and female (Mark 10:6). Darwin, Marx, Freud, Nietzsche, Huxley, Russell, Rorty, and their legions of disciples disagree, insisting that humankind is a product of chance, spontaneous generation, and evolution. S. Matthew D'Agostino states it more colorfully: "We're not absolutely sure what life looked like once the process [of evolution] was fully underway: something like algae, the biologists suggest, a foamy blue-green pond scum."[12]

- Jesus warns that we are not to fear those who kill the body, but rather those who can destroy body and soul in hell (Matthew 10:28). But Wundt, Watson, Skinner, and all other atheistic psychologists have developed various psychologies based on their conviction that we have no soul and that there is no hell to shun. These psychologists define us as evolving, physical, sexual animals with no spiritual dimension. We are atoms in motion. We are, to put it bluntly, animals in heat seeking pleasure and avoiding pain.

- Jesus claims that He and the Father are one (John 10:30). But Freud, Nietzsche, Rorty, Dewey, and their followers say that there is no eternal Father, that faith in God is a mark of weakness or insanity, and that persons and cultures create their own reality and morality.

- Jesus says we should love God with our heart, mind, soul, and strength, and our neighbors as ourselves (Mark 12:30–31). But Marx and Lenin assert that there is no God and that we must eliminate the bourgeois class, by violence if necessary. In another arena, the Qur'an teaches that non-Muslims (Christians and Jews) are the enemies of Allah and may be killed.[13]

- Jesus tells us He is the resurrection and the life (John 11:25). But Dewey, Rorty, Foucault, and their followers insist there is no resurrection and that life itself is an accident of nature.

- Jesus promises that He will prepare a place in heaven for those who love Him (John 14). But Freud, Marx, Nietzsche, and their disciples believe that all religion is an illusion, wishful thinking, an opiate of the masses, or a chasing after 'pie in the sky.'

- Jesus teaches His followers to render unto Caesar (government) "the things that are Caesar's, and to God the things that are God's" (Matthew 22:21). No Humanist believes this because no Humanist believes anything belongs to God.

- Jesus teaches that people love darkness rather than light because their deeds are evil (John 3:19). Richard Dawkins maintains that "the universe we observe has precisely the properties we should expect if there is at bottom no design, no purpose, no evil, no good, nothing but blind, pitiless indifference."[14]

0.1.7 THE BATTLE FOR HEARTS AND MINDS

Clearly a vast chasm divides Christianity and the worldviews with which it battles for the allegiance of the hearts and minds of the human race. But where do these other worldviews manifest themselves?

Dr. James Dobson says, "The [Secular] Humanist system of values has now become the predominant way of thinking in most of the power centers of society. It has outstripped

---

[12] *Free Inquiry* (Winter 2001/02): 39.

[13] Qur'an 2:191; 9:123. Cited in Serge Trifkovic, *The Sword of the Prophet* (Boston, MA: Regina Orthodox, 2002), 87–88.

[14] *Claremont Review of Books* (Winter 2004): 50.

Judeo-Christian precepts in the universities, in the news media, in the entertainment industry, in the judiciary, in the federal bureaucracy, in business, medicine, law, psychology, sociology, in the arts, in many public schools and, to be sure, in the halls of Congress."[15]

The influence of the Secular Humanist worldview is prevalent in every sector of our lives. Consider, for example, the way atheistic evolutionary thinking has become the accepted and undisputed truth within the scientific establishment and for those who are teaching

> The [Secular] Humanist system of values has now become the predominant way of thinking in most of the power centers of society.
>
> — JAMES DOBSON

the next generation of young people. Although the overwhelming majority of Americans believes in the existence of God, 94 percent of the leadership of the National Academy of Science consider themselves atheists.[16] Their atheistic dogma reaches into every public school in America via naturalistic evolutionary propaganda. Evolution is not treated as a theory, but as an unquestioned scientific fact. Ironically, a Chinese paleontologist writes, "In China we can criticize Darwin, but not the government; in America you can criticize the government, but not Darwin."[17]

As Christians, we were happy to learn that at least one peer-reviewed scientific journal has recently published an anti-Darwinian study: "In the last decade or so a host of scientific essays and books have questioned the efficacy of [natural] selection and mutation [genetic mistakes] as a mechanism for generating morphological novelty, as even a brief literature survey will establish. . . . Genetics might be adequate for explaining microevolution, but micro-evolutionary changes in gene frequency were not seen as able to turn a reptile into a mammal or to convert a fish into an amphibian. Microevolution looks at adaptations that concern the survival of the fittest, not the arrival of the fittest. As Goodwin (1995) points out, 'the origin of species—Darwin's problem—remains unsolved' (p. 361)."[18]

We were not happy to learn, however, that the editor of this Smithsonian publication was forced to leave his position in spite of the fact that he possesses two earned Ph.D.s in science. Humanists cannot tolerate any opinion that weakens Darwin's hold on their worldview.

Michael Ruse would surely agree with his Chinese counterpart quoted above. Such mean-spirited action by the Smithsonian only reinforces Ruse's contention that evolution itself is a religion. Ruse, an atheistic evolutionist, admits, "Evolution is a religion. This was true of evolution in the beginning and it is true still today. . . . One of the most popular books of the era was *Religion Without Revelation* by Julian Huxley, grandson of Thomas Huxley. . . . As always evolution was doing everything expected of religion, and more."[19] Secular Humanism would crumble under its own weight if evolution were removed as a building block.

0.1.8 MORAL VALUES AWASH

Notwithstanding the importance of the evolutionary underpinning of Secular Humanist beliefs, the atheistic premise in and of itself has had a frightening effect on the moral values of

---

[15] James C. Dobson and Gary L. Bauer, *Children At Risk* (Dallas, TX: Word, 1990), 22.

[16] Phillip E. Johnson, *The Wedge of Truth: Splitting the Foundations of Naturalism* (Downers Grove, IL: InterVarsity Press, 2000), 86.

[17] Quoted in Jonathan Wells, *Icons of Evolution: Science or Myth?* (Washington, DC: Regnery Publishing, 2000), 58. Under Wells' analysis, the 10 most popular arguments favoring evolution are systematically destroyed with scientific data.

[18] Stephen C. Meyer, "The Origin of the Biological Information and the Higher Taxonomic Categories," Proceedings of the Biological Society of Washington, D.C., August 28, 2004.

[19] *National Post*, (Canadian edition; May 13, 2000): B3.

our culture, leaving America awash in cultural and ethical relativism.[20] Atheistic thinking has left many feeling unsure that they can hold any moral values with certainty.

In the current politically correct environment, in which all cultures are created equal and beyond criticism (except Nazi culture, which is selectively condemned), the Christian commitment to moral absolutes has been attacked and undermined, especially in the area of sexuality. As Richard John Neuhaus suggests, most of our major current cultural issues are based upon changing (declining) values in the area of human sexuality. Neuhaus notes the comment by Modris Eksteins (in *Rites of Spring*, his historical study of the rise of modernism) that the issue of sexual morality became a "vehicle of rebellion against bourgeois [Christian] values." The newfound power of homosexual and feminist activists yields a shift away from a Biblical Christian perspective of sexual morality.

For nearly two centuries, Secular Humanist/Atheist thinkers have sought to replace Christian moral values with ideas they envision will enhance human development and social progress. The ideas and philosophies of men and women such as Marx, Freud, Darwin, Nietzsche, Lenin, Stalin, Russell, Heidegger, Adorno, Lukacs, Gramsci, Sanger, Dewey, Kinsey, Sagan, Derrida, Foucault and others have led to an array of practices and lifestyles contrary to biblical values. These practices include free love, pornography, aberrant sex education, homosexuality, shacking up, teen pregnancy, abortion, assisted suicide, euthanasia, unrestricted embryonic stem cell research, cloning, out of wedlock children, irresponsible parenting, etc.

Clearly the moral values espoused by Secular Humanist thinkers have recently exerted a much greater impact on our culture than has the traditional Christian worldview and its system of ethical values that, to a large degree, have been eradicated from the public square. Secular Humanists have cleverly and methodically gained ascendancy over Christianity in the past two to three generations.

0.1.9 SECULAR RELIGION

Years ago, Russian novelist Alexander Solzhenitsyn pointed to the weakness and danger of the humanistic agenda for humanity: "There is a disaster which has already been under way for quite some time. I am referring to the calamity of a despiritualized and irreligious humanistic consciousness. . . . If humanism were right in declaring that man is born to be happy, he would not be born to die. Since his body is doomed to die, his task on earth evidently must be of a more spiritual nature."[21]

In spite of the wisdom of thinkers like Solzhenitsyn, Humanists proceed with their own agenda. What they offer is essentially their own religious alternative to the Christian faith—a fully-constructed worldview that ignores the reality of God. Indeed, the three Humanist worldviews discussed in this book (Secular, Marxist, Cosmic Humanism) are religious worldviews, each possessing a defining theology.

In our book *Mind Siege*, Tim LaHaye and I prove that Secular Humanism, for example, is a religious worldview.[22] John Dewey, one of the founders of the Secular Humanist movement, admits as much in *A Common Faith*: "Here are all the elements for a religious faith. . . . Such a faith has always been implicitly the common faith of mankind."[23] As Christians, we cannot afford to ignore the implications of such a confession.

[20] Francis J. Beckwith and Gregory Koukl, *Relativism: Feet Firmly Planted in Mid-Air* (Grand Rapids, MI: Baker Book House, 1998).

[21] Alexander Solzhenitsyn, "A World Split Apart." 1978 Harvard University graduation address.

[22] Tim LaHaye and David Noebel, *Mind Siege: The Battle for Truth in the New Millennium* (Nashville, TN: Word, 2001), 155f.

[23] John Dewey, *A Common Faith* (1934, repr., New Haven, CT: Yale University Press, 1962), 87.

In light of these concerted efforts to replace the Christian understanding of reality, we must take the time to understand the beliefs of our adversaries in the battle for minds and hearts and search out what the Bible teaches about each of the major areas of human thought and culture. A deep understanding of biblical truth is certainly one of our greatest weapons in this battle.

0.1.10 OUT OF THE DESERT

Though the vast forces of humanism and anti-humanism are already ranged mightily against Christ and His followers, another powerful worldview that we must take seriously has claimed center stage. "Islam is not only a religious doctrine," says Serge Trifkovic, "it is also a self-contained world outlook, and a way of life that claims the primary allegiance of all those calling themselves 'Muslim.'"[24] A Muslim, says Trifkovic, "is first and foremost the citizen of Islam, and belongs morally, spiritually, and intellectually, and in principle totally to the world of belief of which Muhammad is the Prophet, and Mecca is the capital."[25] Today, Islam is the fastest growing religion in the world, and its more radical elements have bonded with the radical Left in the United States and Europe.[26]

"Radical Muslims," says Trifkovic, "dominate the Islamic life in the United States to the point that moderates hardly have a voice. Radical Muslims control every major Muslim organization, including the Islamic Association for Palestine, the Islamic Circle of North America, the Islamic Committee for Palestine, the Islamic Society for North America, the Muslim Arab Youth Association, the Muslim Public Affairs Council, and the Muslim Students Association. They also control a growing majority of mosques, weekly newspapers, and communal organizations. They are funded by the Iranians, Libyans, and Saudis, who have for years helped the most extreme groups."[27]

David Horowitz agrees with Trifkovic in his analysis of the situation. "In word and deed," says Horowitz, "both of these allies [radical Islamists and radical Leftists] make it plain that they consider everything about the United States to be evil and unworthy of preservation, that they wish to see American society and its way of life crushed by any means necessary, including violent revolution."[28]

Therefore, this book explains the Islamic worldview and the basic differences between Christianity and Islam. We will look at what Christianity and Islam teach about God, the universe, society, and the human condition. We will contrast what we consider Islam's erroneous conclusions with the truths found in the Bible, the revelational basis of Christianity. We will be challenged to decide what is true and what is not, remembering John's admonition, "And we know that the Son of God has come and has given us an understanding, that we may know Him who is true; and we are in Him who is true, in His Son Jesus Christ. This is the true God and eternal life" (1 John 5:20).

---

[24] Trifkovic, 7.

[25] Ibid.

[26] David Horowitz, *Unholy Alliance: Radical Islam and the American Left* (Washington, DC: Regnery Publishing, 2004).

[27] Trifkovic, 270.

[28] David Horowitz and John Perazzo, "Unholy Alliance: The 'Peace Left' and the Islamic Jihad Against America," FrontPageMagazine.com., April 13, 2005, http://www.frontpagemag.com/Articles/ ReadArticle.asp?ID=17702. Horowitz and Perazzo identify the campus Communist groups including Workers World Party, International ANSWER, etc.

0.1.11 MARX ALIVE AND WELL

Some of you may question whether or not Marxism should still be included in our list of influential worldviews, believing as many do that Marxism came crashing down with the Berlin Wall in 1989. Unfortunately, this is not the case. Although the political and institutional forms of Marxism may have changed, Marxism still exerts a huge influence in the academic world and in various political and economic ideologies. *U.S. News and World Report* as late as September 2003 published a lengthy article entitled "Where Marxism Lives Today," which states, "But Marxism is so entrenched in courses ranging from literature to anthropology, and addressing topics on everything from class systems of Victorian England to the alienation expressed by hip-hop culture, says Joseph Childers, English professor at the University of California, Riverside, that today's students are virtually bathed in Marx's ideas."[29]

The harsh reality is that the major elements of the Marxist worldview (atheism, materialism, evolution, positive law, denial of soul and spirit, sexual liberation or free love, socialism, etc.) are alive and flourishing in American universities as well as in parts of Eastern and Western Europe, Russia, China, Cuba, and Latin America.

David Horowitz writes about his experience with Marxism in the academic world in *Radical Son: A Generational Odyssey*. He says, "The Marxists and socialists who had been refuted by historical events were now the tenured establishment of the academic world. . . . [M]ore Marxists could be found on the faculties of American colleges than in the entire former Communist bloc. The American Historical Association was run by Marxists, as was the professional literature association, whose field had been transformed into a kind of pseudo sociology of race-gender-class oppression."[30] Serious students, therefore, must continue to consider the influence of the Marxist worldview.

0.1.12 THE ANTI-WORLDVIEW WORLDVIEW

The one worldview covered in this book that denies being a worldview is Postmodernism. Postmodernism's word for worldview is **metanarrative**. A metanarrative is a single overarching objective interpretation or narrative of reality. French Postmodernist Lyotard refers to it as "A Big Story" or "The Grand Narrative."[31] Postmodernists deny the existence of all metanarratives and grand narratives.

> **METANARRATIVE:** a single overarching objective interpretation or narrative of reality

Postmodernists insist there is no eternal truth or truth that is true around the world. Truth for some Postmodernists is what their community allows each member to say is true, or as Rorty famously stated, truth is whatever his colleagues or peers allow him to get away with believing or saying.

Each Postmodernist included in this work (Foucault, Derrida, Barthes, Lyotard, Baudrillard, Rorty, etc.) is theologically atheist, philosophically skeptical, ethically relativist, biologically evolutionist, psychologically soul-less, legally pragmatist, and politically leftist.

Postmodernists may contend that all truth is relative to one's peers or community, but they nevertheless insist that atheism, skepticism, relativism, and evolution are true around the world. Postmodernists in China and Postmodernists in New York believe that punctuated equilibrium

---

[29] *U.S. News and World Report*, September 2, 2003, Special Collection Edition, 86.

[30] David Horowitz, *Radical Son: A Generational Odyssey* (New York, NY: The Free Press, 1997), 405.

[31] Jean-Francois Lyotard, *The Postmodern Condition: A Report on Knowledge* (Minneapolis, MN: University of Minnesota Press, 1989), 37.

should be taught as absolute truth. The only truths Postmodernists see as relative are truths supporting Christianity. They treat their own published works as universally true.

You cannot read Richard Rorty, a leading Postmodernist, without concluding that what he says he actually believes. When he says that "the United States of America will someday yield up sovereignty to what Tennyson called 'the Parliament of Man, the Federation of the World,'"[32] he seems not to be talking relativistically. Rather, he is talking the politics of universal government and the suspension of America's national sovereignty. When he says that Americans should follow in the footsteps of Walt Whitman[33] and John Dewey[34] and abandon belief in God, rendering America a secular state, clearly he believes he is speaking absolute truth.

Therefore, this book treats Postmodernism as a complete worldview, examining what it says in all ten of the disciplines that make up a worldview.

0.1.13 NO MORE CHRISTIAN COWARDS

I agree with C.S. Lewis that we must not remain neutral in this titanic struggle for the hearts and minds of the human race. Elijah, for example, was not neutral when he confronted the prophets of Baal and Asherah at Mount Carmel (1 Kings 18). Jesus was not neutral when He took on the Greek and Roman gods at Mount Hermon (Matthew 16–17). Paul was not neutral when he confronted the Secular and Cosmic Humanists of his own day, the Stoics and Epicureans, at Mount Mars (Acts 17). The apostle to the Gentiles (Romans 11:13) clearly understood their belief systems and stood against them by demonstrating their weaknesses (2 Corinthians 10:5). He took on the Humanists with the resurrection of Jesus Christ, the creation of heaven and earth, and the judgment to come. Ideas have not changed a great deal. The spiritual and intellectual battlefield itself has remained relatively unchanged over the centuries. God is still the Hound of Heaven, pursuing the human race to live as He planned for us to live.

> We must not remain neutral in this titanic struggle for the hearts and minds of the human race.

We must do no less than Elijah, Jesus, and Paul did as they withstood those seeking to destroy the wisdom and knowledge of God. If we fail, we will lose every idea and belief that Christians hold dear, as well as the institutions based on them (i.e., home, church, state, education, occupation). It is no accident that wherever Christians establish themselves they build homes, churches, and schools and then work hard for the glory of God. In fact, it is safe to say that Christians founded the first 150 colleges and universities in the United States and all the major universities across Europe.

Regarding the influence of Christ, most of these institutions have been lost. The One who is most responsible for Western Civilization and culture has been shut out and replaced with the follies of humanity. We cannot afford to lose any more territory and, indeed, we must begin

---

[32] Richard Rorty, *Achieving Our Country: Leftist Thought in Twentieth Century America* (Cambridge, MA: Harvard University Press, 1998), 3.

[33] See Richard J. Ellis, *The Dark Side of the Left: Illiberal Egalitarianism in America* (Lawrence, KS: University Press of Kansas, 1998) for a look at Whitman's influence on American radicals, e.g., "Whitman profoundly shaped a host of left-wing literary radicals of the early twentieth century, from Randolph Bourne and Van Wyck Brooks to John Reed and Max Eastman, who tellingly identified himself as an 'American lyrical Socialist—a child of Walt Whitman reared by Karl Marx'" (p. 79, 80). Whitman, himself, was heavily involved in the eugenics movement desirous to create a new master race (p. 79).

[34] John Dewey was the voice of the League for Industrial Democracy (LID), which was the American counterpart to the British Fabian Society. The LID also birthed the Students for a Democratic Society (SDS), a radical student organization. See Ellis, pages 116f, for details.

reclaiming what we have lost. James Russell Lowell wrote, "Once to every man and nation, Comes the moment to decide, In the strife of Truth with Falsehood, For the good or evil side, Then it is the brave man chooses, While the coward stands aside."

According to Hebrews 11:32–40, God wants His sons and daughters to be brave men and women rather than cowards, men and women who understand the times and know what needs to be done. To summarize Lowell's poetic call, each of us must choose. Fortunately, millions have chosen to stand firm for Jesus Christ.

My hope is that this book will help prepare thousands more Christian young people to stand firm in the spiritual and intellectual battle of their life—a battle that encompasses body, soul, mind, heart, and spirit. This battle has eternal consequences if, indeed, Christianity's declarations are true: God created the heavens and the earth (Genesis 1); God created Adam and Eve (Genesis 1–2); Adam and Eve (and all humanity) disobeyed God and fell into sin (Genesis 3); God sent His only Son into the world (John 3:16); our salvation is through Jesus Christ's death on the cross and His literal physical resurrection (1 Corinthians 15); and heaven and hell exist as part of a final judgment of the entire human race (Revelation 20).

I have enjoyed the privilege of helping educate thousands of young men and women in the Christian worldview. I have watched them use resources such as this book to help others stand fast in their Christian faith and not fall prey to the wisdom of the world (1 Corinthians 1:19ff) or the subtlety of the Evil One (2 Corinthians 11:3).

The youth ministry I have been associated with for over forty years[35] receives letters and e-mails every day from former students or their parents, sharing how materials such as this have affected their lives by equipping them to fight the good fight of faith (2 Timothy 4:7).

May our Lord, therefore, use this book to instruct many more students in how to fight the spiritual and intellectual battles of the twenty-first century and grow stronger in their Christian faith. May none of us grow weary in doing good, loving mercy, and walking humbly with our God (Micah 6:8).

---

[35] Summit Ministries, Manitou Springs, CO 80829, http://www.summit.org.

Introduction

Part Two

"Finding one's way through unfamiliar terrain," John Lewis Gaddis also wisely observed, "generally requires a map of some sort.". . . World views and causal theories are indispensable guides. . . "[1]

— Samuel Huntington

0.2.1 INTRODUCTION

"A few years ago, the eminent Harvard political scientist Samuel Huntington published in *Foreign Affairs* a widely noted article called 'The Clash of Civilizations.' Looking at contemporary international relations from a geopolitical vantage point, he predicted a clash of the world's major civilizations: the West, the Islamic world, and the Confucian East. Huntington's article provoked a response from one of his own most brilliant former students—Swarthmore's James Kurth. In an article in the *National Interest* entitled 'The Real Clash,' Kurth argued persuasively that the clash that is coming—and that has, indeed, already begun—is not so much among the world's great civilizations as it is within the civilization of the West, between those who claim the Judeo-Christian worldview and those who have abandoned that worldview in favor of the 'isms' of contemporary American life—feminism, multiculturalism, gay liberation, lifestyle liberation—what I have lumped together as a family called the secularist orthodoxy."[2]

In this brief paragraph from Princeton's Robert George we have the major players vying for the hearts and minds of Christian young people today: Christians, Muslims, Marxists, Secular

---

[1] Samuel P. Huntington, *The Clash of Civilizations,* (New York, NY: Touchstone, 1996), 30.
[2] Robert George, *The Clash of Orthodoxies* (Wilmington, DE: ISI Books, 2001), 3.

Humanists, and Postmodernists. The only worldview George doesn't mention is Cosmic Humanism. Needless to say, his "secularist orthodoxy" is standard fare in American public schools.[3]

Back in the early 1990s, Dr. James C. Dobson and Gary Bauer sought to identify what they saw happening to Christian young people in the United States. Their conclusion was that "nothing short of a great Civil War of Values rages today throughout North America. Two sides with vastly differing and incompatible worldviews are locked in a bitter conflict that permeates every level of society."[4]

This textbook is an in-depth account of this "Great Civil War"—an account of the war for this and succeeding generations. The war, as Dobson and Bauer put it, is a struggle "for the hearts and minds of people. It is a war over ideas."[5] While the word "war" may strike some as too drastic a word, one or two semesters in higher education will convince any alert student that it is indeed a battle for his or her mind and heart.[6]

> Nothing short of a great Civil War of Values rages today throughout North America. Two sides with vastly differing and incompatible worldviews are locked in a bitter conflict that permeates every level of society.
>
> — JAMES DOBSON AND GARY BAUER

To be more precise, it is a battle between and among worldviews. On one side is clearly the Christian worldview. On the other side are Secular Humanism, Marxism-Leninism, Cosmic Humanism (the New Age movement) and Postmodernism. While these worldviews don't agree in every detail, they unanimously concur on one point—their opposition to Biblical Christianity. In this context we will seek to understand them while presenting a strong, honest, truthful, and intelligent defense of the Biblical Christian worldview.

Since September 11, 2001, and the destruction of the Twin Towers in New York City, however, another worldview has come to the forefront of our consciousness—Islam. Therefore, this study will also look at the Islamic worldview and note its similarities and differences with Biblical Christianity.

"Someday soon," Dobson and Bauer say, "a winner [in the battle for our children's hearts and minds] will emerge and the loser will fade from memory. For now, the outcome is very much in doubt."[7] Christians must quickly arrive at an understanding of the times and "know what [they] ought to do" (1 Chronicles 12:32).

0.2.2 WHAT IS A WORLDVIEW?

Ideas have consequences. Sometimes the consequences are good, but sometimes they are deadly. Whether the result is hopelessness arising from a philosophy that claims God does not exist, or pain and oppression arising from the philosophy of a despotic ruler, ideas *do* have consequences.

Each of us bases our decisions and actions on a worldview. We may not be able to

---

[3] For a detailed account of how the philosophy of education in America has changed from a biblical orientation to a secular foundation, see B.K. Eakman's *Cloning of the American Mind: Eradicating Morality Through Education* (Lafayette, LA: Huntington House, 1998).

[4] James C. Dobson and Gary L. Bauer, *Children at Risk: The Battle For the Hearts and Minds of Our Kids* (Dallas, TX: Word, 1990), 19.

[5] Ibid., 19–20.

[6] Nancy Pearcey, *Total Truth: Liberating Christianity from its Cultural Captivity* (Wheaton, IL: Crossway Books, 2004); Jim Nelson Black, *Freefall of the American University* (Nashville, TN: WND, 2004).

[7] Dobson and Bauer, 20.

articulate our worldview, and worldviews are often inconsistent, but we all have one. *But what is a worldview?* Essentially, a worldview is the way we view our world and our place in it.

A worldview answers fundamental questions such as *Why are we here? What is the meaning and purpose of life? Is there a difference between right and wrong? Is there a God? Are humans merely highly evolved animals?*

We all have ideas that attempt to answer these questions. Our ideas naturally give rise to some sort of system of beliefs, a system that forms the basis for our decisions and actions. Our worldview does not merely determine what we think the world is like; it determines what we think the world *should be* like. In other words, our worldview determines how we act and respond to every aspect of life. Because our ideas *do* determine how we behave, the bottom line is that our ideas *do* have consequences.

If we were to ask an average person about his or her philosophy of life, we would probably get a blank stare. But if we were to

> ## The Pop Culture Connection
>
> *The Truman Show* (a 1998 film, starring Jim Carey)–Truman, who is the subject of a 24/7 TV program, has spent his entire life on a stage without knowing it. As the story unfolds, Truman begins to realize something is not right in his "world" and he determines to walk off the set. As he approaches an exit door, the director, with a booming voice coming out of the clouds, addresses Truman. Truman asks a series of three questions: "Who are you?," "Who am I?," and "Was nothing real?" As it turns out, these are the real-life questions everyone must ask, since these questions deal with foundational issues that affect every worldview—theology, psychology, and philosophy.*

ask this average person about *how life began*, he or she would probably give some sort of answer, even if the answer were not completely coherent. If we were to continue the conversation by asking *why* she believes what she claims to believe, we would most likely discover that she, like most people, simply does not have reasons for what she believes. Often people get their beliefs like they catch colds—by being around other people! We often adopt other people's beliefs even if we do not realize we are doing so. Such is the power of friends, family, movies, television, books, magazines, etc.

Many of us do not think very deeply about why we believe the things we do. Even when we want to examine our beliefs, we do not really know how. Sometimes we do not even know the questions to ask.

0.2.3 THE HEART OF A WORLDVIEW

What is a worldview? Norman Geisler and William Watkins explain that "a worldview is a way of viewing or interpreting all of reality. It is an interpretive framework through which or by which one makes sense of the data of life and the world."[8]
To say that a worldview is "an interpretive framework" is to say

> A worldview is a way of viewing or interpreting all of reality. It is an interpretive framework through which or by which one makes sense of the data of life and the world.
>
> — NORMAN GEISLER AND WILLIAM WATKINS

---

[9] Norman L. Geisler and William D. Watkins, *Worlds Apart* (Grand Rapids, MI: Baker Book House, 1989), 11.
* Note: Our use of a particular film in the "Pop Culture Connection" throughout this text does not mean we endorse the film. We include these to illustrate how others in society communicate similar ideas through their artistic works. A rationale for using popular movies, music, and art is found in the article "Worldviews in Popular Culture" by Chuck Edwards in the Resources section of our website (www.summit.org).

that a worldview is like a pair of glasses—it is something through which you view everything. And the fact is, everyone has a worldview, a way he or she looks at the world.

Have you ever put on someone else's glasses? If you have, then you know that they do not always help your sight. In fact, putting on someone else's glasses can give you a headache, a throbbing pain in your eyes, or simply make you dizzy. If the prescription for the glasses is not the right one for you, what you see through the glasses will be a distorted view of reality. In other words, without the proper prescription, glasses will not help you see the world more clearly; rather, they will keep you from seeing the world as it truly is.

It is the same with worldviews. Just as a prescription for glasses will either help or hinder your eyes, your worldview will either help or hinder your mind as it tries to understand the world. If your worldview is an expression of the truth of God's Word, then that worldview will help you see the world as it truly is. But if your worldview says that there is no God, then when you look at the design in nature, you see something other than design. You see an accident that happens to look like design.

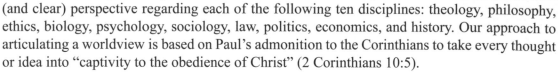

Another way of understanding what a worldview is would be for you to think about a tree. If you were to draw a tree on a piece of paper right now, you would probably draw a trunk and some fluffy branches. But what part of the tree keeps it from falling over? What part of the tree channels nutrients to the trunk so that the tree can live? What part of the tree do we usually *not* see? The roots, of course. Your worldview is like a tree's roots—it is essential to your life and stability. Just as we cannot see the roots of a tree, we cannot see your worldview. We see only the exposed part of it—your actions.

The term *worldview*, as used in this textbook, refers to any set of ideas, beliefs, convictions, or values that provides a framework or map to help you understand God, the world, and your relationship to God and the world. Specifically, a worldview should contain a particular (and clear) perspective regarding each of the following ten disciplines: theology, philosophy, ethics, biology, psychology, sociology, law, politics, economics, and history. Our approach to articulating a worldview is based on Paul's admonition to the Corinthians to take every thought or idea into "captivity to the obedience of Christ" (2 Corinthians 10:5).

The writer of Hebrews declares "the word of God is living and powerful, and sharper than any two-edged sword, piercing even to the division of soul and spirit, and of joints and marrow, and is a discerner of the thoughts and intents of the heart" (4:12). We contend that *mind* and *heart* are both cognitive elements of our personhood. Scripture uses them interchangeably many times (see 2 Corinthians 3:13, 15). We do not, however, deny the possibility that the heart may well see further than the mind regarding knowledge and understanding. For example, when we think of the heavens declaring the glory of God and pouring out speech night after night, communicating knowledge (Psalm 19:1–2), we could understand this as the heart interpreting God's wisdom and knowledge apart from words.

0.2.4 WHAT CONSTITUTES A WORLDVIEW?

Many people, including many Christians, do not realize that the Bible addresses all ten disciplines listed above. Therefore, according to this definition of a worldview, Biblical Christianity is a worldview. Because it contains a theology, it is also a religious worldview.

As this study will show, Secular Humanism and Marxism-Leninism are also religious worldviews—although from an atheistic perspective. That is because Secular Humanism has a theology and Marxism-Leninism has a theology. Further, both directly address the nine other disciplines, so they conform to our definition of a worldview. The New Age movement (Cosmic Humanism), although less tightly organized as a worldview, and Postmodernism, even more loosely held together, are classified and studied here as worldviews. In contrast to them, Islam constitutes a tightly knit and highly organized worldview.

Each worldview offers a particular perspective from which to approach each discipline. Conversely, each discipline is value-laden with worldview implications. Christian students must understand that these various disciplines are not value-free. Each discipline is built on certain basic assumptions about the nature of reality in order to grant meaning to specific approaches to it.

This text analyzes the six worldviews' perspectives on each of the ten disciplines, but it does so without losing sight of how each system of thought integrates its various presuppositions, categories, and conclusions. We are not out to "over-analyze." Rather, we are attempting to understand each discipline and how it fits into each worldview. Dissecting is artificial; integration is real. No discipline stands alone. The worldview disciplines are like grapes—they come in bunches. Each affects all others in one way or another. The line separating theology and philosophy is fragile; the line separating theology, philosophy, ethics, law, and politics is more so. In fact, there is no ultimate line of demarcation, since the convictions held in one area have implications for all the other areas.

Thus, the arrangement of the categories is, to some degree, arbitrary; but we have tried to place them in their most logical sequence. Clearly, theological and philosophical assumptions color every aspect of a worldview. Disciplines such as sociology and psychology are related; but other relations and distinctions are less recognizable. Therefore, one reader may feel that we have done law an injustice by distancing it from ethics, and another may feel history to be almost as foundational to a worldview as philosophy. There is no correct order according to which these chapters must be read.

Regardless of the approach you choose, keep in mind that you are studying the six worldviews that exert the most influence over the whole world. Other worldviews exist, but they wield much less influence. Confucianism, Buddhism, Taoism, Hinduism, Vedantism, Jainism, or Shintoism, for example, may profoundly influence some Eastern countries, but hardly sway the whole world. The major ideas and belief systems influencing and/or controlling the world, and especially the West, are contained in the following six worldviews.

0.2.5 WHY STUDY THE CHRISTIAN WORLDVIEW?

This text focuses on Christianity because it is the one worldview that provides a consistent and truthful explanation of all the facts of reality (including personal experiences, history, reason, intuition, science, revelation, and imagination) with regard to theology, philosophy, ethics, economics, or anything else. Furthermore, the author is Christian and is writing primarily to help Christian young people strengthen their faith by understanding their worldview. As Carl F.H. Henry says, "The Christian belief system, which the Christian knows to be grounded in divine revelation, is relevant to all of life."[9]

This relevance results from the fact that Christianity is, we believe, the one worldview based on truth. "Christianity is true," says George Gilder, "and its truth will be discovered anywhere you look very far."[10] Gilder, who is not only an outstanding economic philosopher but also a sociologist, found Christ while seeking sociological truth.

---

[9] Carl F.H. Henry, *Toward a Recovery of Christian Belief* (Westchester, IL: Crossway Books, 1990), 113.

[10] L. Neff, "Christianity Today Talks to George Gilder," *Christianity Today* (March 6, 1987): 35.

Philosopher C.E.M. Joad found Christ because he was seeking ethical truth. "I now believe," he wrote, "that the balance of reasoned considerations tells heavily in favor of the religious, even of the Christian view of the world."[11] Joad recognized the need for absolute truth, rather than a truth that evolves with each new discovery: "A religion which is in constant process of revision to square with science's ever-changing picture of the world might well be easier to believe, but it is hard to believe it would be worth believing."[12]

> The Christian belief system, which the Christian knows to be grounded in divine revelation, is relevant to all of life.
>
> — CARL F.H. HENRY

Christianity is the embodiment of Christ's claim that He is "the way, the truth, and the life" (John 14:6). When we say "this is the Christian way," we mean "this is the way Christ would have us act in such a situation." It is no small matter to think and act as Christ instructs. The Christian agrees with Humanist Bertrand Russell's admission that "[w]hat the world needs is Christian love or compassion."[13] Such love and compassion are a direct result of following in the footsteps of Christ Himself, who is the epitome of love and compassion. No one else has been willing to die for the sins of the world and able to return from the dead to place a period at the end of the event.

America is often described as a Christian nation. Over one hundred and fifty years ago Alexis de Tocqueville wrote, "There is no country in the whole world, in which the Christian religion retains a greater influence over the souls of men than in America; and there can be no greater proof of its utility, and of its conformity to human nature, than that its influence is most powerfully felt over the most enlightened and free nation of the earth."[14] Unfortunately, however, America—and the rest of Western Civilization—is turning away from its heritage. Western nations are eradicating large chunks of Christianity from the public square.

We contend that America should be moving in the opposite direction—embracing the Christian worldview rather than running from it. Christian philosopher Francis Schaeffer blames America's drift toward secularism and injustice on the Christian community's failure to apply its worldview to every facet of society: "The basic problem of the Christians in this country . . . in regard to society and in regard to government, is that they have seen things in bits and pieces instead of totals."[15]

Schaeffer goes on to say that Christians have very gradually "become disturbed over permissiveness, pornography, the public schools, the breakdown of the family, and finally abortion. But they have not seen this as a totality—each thing being a part, a symptom of a much larger problem. They have failed to see that all of this has come about due to a shift in the world view—that is, through a fundamental change in the overall way people think and view the world and life as a whole."[16]

> The basic problem of the Christians in this country in regard to society and in regard to government, is that they have seen things in bits and pieces instead of totals.
>
> — FRANCIS SCHAEFFER

[11] C.E.M. Joad, *The Recovery of Belief* (London, UK: Faber and Faber, 1955), 22.

[12] Ibid., 240.

[13] Bertrand Russell, *Human Society in Ethics and Politics* (New York, NY: Mentor, 1962), viii.

[14] Alexis de Tocqueville, *Democracy in America*, 2 vols. (New Rochelle, NY: Arlington House, n.d.), 1:294. Elsewhere he declared, "The Americans combine the notions of Christianity and of liberty so intimately in their minds, that it is impossible to make them conceive the one without the other" (p. 297).

[15] Francis A. Schaeffer, *A Christian Manifesto* (Westchester, IL: Crossway Books, 1981), 17.

[16] Ibid.

This study is intended to provide a wake-up call for America in particular, but for members of Western Civilization as well. A country seeking to promote human rights (including the right to be born) and human liberty must adhere to the only worldview that can account for their existence and their dignity—Christianity. We contend that human rights come from the fact that human beings are created in the very image of God, a uniquely Biblical perspective. Unfortunately, countless Americans are embracing other worldviews—most notably Secular Humanism, Marxism, Cosmic Humanism, Postmodernism, and even Islam.

0.2.6 WHY STUDY THE ISLAMIC WORLDVIEW?

While most Christians place the beginnings of Christianity at the Cross or Resurrection of Jesus Christ sometime between 29 and 33 A.D., Islam claims its origin as September 24, 622 A.D.

On this date seventy muhajirun, including Zaid, Ali, and Abu-Bakr, pledged their loyalty to Muhammad, and Medina became the city of the Prophet. Muhammad, born ca. 570 A.D., was an Arabian trader from Mecca whose flight to Medina marked the beginnings of his special revelations from Allah. In fact, the first revelation was permission to fight the Meccans! Muhammad's submission to God's revelations gave Islam its name, meaning "submission." Those who submit to Allah and Muhammad are called Muslims. Hence, the cry of the Muslims is "There is no God but Allah, and Mohammad is His Prophet." Muslims believe that Muhammad is the last of God's prophets, superseding even Abraham, Moses, and Jesus Christ Himself.

"Islam," says Serge Trifkovic, "is not a 'mere' religion; it is a complete way of life, an all-embracing social, political and legal system that breeds a worldview peculiar to itself."[17]

Norman L. Geisler posits five basic Muslim articles of faith that make up its worldview and five more basic pillars of Islamic practice. The five articles of faith entail (a) There is only one God (monotheism); (b) Muhammad is God's latest prophet, following Noah, Abraham, Moses, and Christ; (c) God created angels both good and bad; (d) The Qur'an is God's full and final revelation; and (e) A final day of judgment is coming with either heaven or hell the final resting place of each person. The five pillars of Islamic practice include (a) All that is necessary to become a Muslim is to repeat "There is no God but Allah, and Muhammad

> Islam is not a "mere" religion; it is a complete way of life, an all-embracing social, political and legal system that breeds a worldview peculiar to itself.
>
> — SERGE TRIFKOVIC

is his prophet;" (b) One must pray the salat usually five times a day; (c) One must fast during the month of Ramadan; (d) One gives 1/40th of one's income to the needy; and (e) Every able Muslim makes a trip to Mecca during pilgrimage.[18]

While Christianity and Islam have some teachings in common (including creation of the material universe, angels, immortality of the soul, heaven, hell, judgment of sin, etc.), the major difference is Islam's rejection of the death of Jesus Christ for the sins of the world. Muslims likewise reject Christ's physical resurrection from the dead and His claim to be the Son of God, although they do accept Christ as a prophet, His virgin birth, physical ascension, second coming, sinlessness, miracles, and even messiahship.[19]

One major difference between the founder of Christianity and the founder of Islam is the fact that Jesus Christ lived a sinless life and Muhammad had many flaws. "Muhammad's

---

[17] Serge Trifkovic, *The Sword of the Prophet* (Boston, MA: Regina Orthodox, 2002), 55.

[18] Norman L. Geisler, *Baker Encyclopedia of Christian Apologetics* (Grand Rapids, MI: Baker Book House, 1999), 368–9.

[19] Ibid., 369.

practice and constant encouragement of bloodshed are unique in the history of religions. Murder, pillage, rape, and more murder as depicted in the Koran and in the Traditions "seem to have impressed his followers with a profound belief in the value of bloodshed as opening the gates of Paradise."[20] This translates into how the average Muslim views the world as "an open-ended conflict between the Land of Peace (Dar al-Islam) and the Land of War (Dar al-Harb)."[21]

Islam has not had a positive attitude toward Christians and Jews. In fact, all non-Muslims have been under the gun for centuries. The history of Islam from 622 A.D. to the present has been a history of violence and war toward infidels.

In more recent years, the Islamic worldview has been growing exponentially in power and influence, and, therefore, it is worthy of our study. Muslims' belief that "tomorrow belongs to Islam" provides an additional incentive to understand its beliefs and goals.

0.2.7 WHY STUDY THE SECULAR HUMANIST WORLDVIEW?

In this study the term Secular Humanism refers primarily to the ideas and beliefs outlined in the *Humanist Manifestoes* of 1933, 1973, and 2000. It will quickly become apparent that humanists have plenty to say in all ten disciplines of a worldview. Secular Humanism is the dominant worldview in our secular colleges and universities. It has also made gains in many Christian colleges and universities (especially in the areas of biology, sociology, politics, and history). Christians considering a college education must be well versed in the Secular Humanistic worldview or risk losing their own Christian perspective by default. In her book *Walking Away From the Faith*, Ruth Tucker, professor at Calvin Seminary, makes it very clear that Christian students *are* walking away from their faith because of Secular Humanist teaching.

Secular Humanists recognize the classroom as a powerful context for indoctrination. Since they understand that many worldviews exist and are competing for adherents, they believe they must use the classroom to flush out "unenlightened" worldviews and to encourage students to embrace their worldview. Secular Humanism, operating under the educational buzz word "liberalism," controls the curriculum in America's public schools thanks to the National Education Association, the National Academy of Sciences, and a host of foundations, including the Ford Foundation. Christianity has been deliberately, some would say brilliantly, erased from America's educational system. The same has been the case in all Western nations for a number of years.

Regarding American, the direction of education can be seen as a descent from Jonathan Edwards (1750) and the Christian influence, through Horace Mann (1842) and the Unitarian influence, to John Dewey (1933) and the Secular Humanist influence.

Notes William F. Buckley, "The most influential educators of our time—John Dewey, William Kilpatrick, George Counts, Harold Rugg, and the lot—are out to build a New Social Order. There is not enough room, however, for the New Social Order and religion [Christianity]. It clearly won't do, then, to foster within some schools a respect for an absolute, intractable, unbribable God, a divine intelligence who is utterly unconcerned with other people's versions of truth and humorless inattentive to majority opinion. It won't do to tolerate a competitor for the allegiance of man. The State prefers a secure monopoly for itself. It is intolerably divisive to have God and the State scrapping for disciples. Religion [Christianity], then, must go….The fight is being won. Academic freedom is entrenched. Religion [Christianity] is outlawed in the public schools. The New Social Order is larruping along."[22]

---

[20] Trifkovic, 51.

[21] Ibid.

[22] William F. Buckley, *Let Us Talk Of Many Things* (Roseville, CA: Forum, 2000), 9–10.

But we contend that Christian theologians and scholars such as Jonathan Edwards or Timothy Dwight have better things to say than John Dewey, William Kilpatrick, George Counts, and Harold Rugg, and that Christians should get back into the public square and influence educational policy. The Christian worldview is a fitting competitor to Dewey's religious view (as summarized in his book *A Common Faith*). But since most Christian teenagers accept their older, "wiser" professors' teachings uncritically and may therefore find themselves subject to Secular Humanistic viewpoints, this study becomes necessary to equalize the battle for the mind.

Hosea's statement, "My people are destroyed for lack of knowledge" (4:6), applies in spades to college-bound Christian students. Many never recover from their educational befuddlement, lapsing instead into atheism, materialism, "new" morality, evolutionism, globalism, and other non-Biblical views. Others suffer for years from their near loss of faith. Those who are prepared, however, can not only survive, but thrive as capable ambassadors for Christ.

America's colleges and universities are not the only areas of Secular Humanist influence, however. The mass media continually publish and broadcast the Secular Humanist worldview. The 1990 Humanist of the Year was Ted Turner, former chief executive officer of Turner Broadcasting System, which now owns TBS Super Station, CNN, CNN Headline News, and Turner Network Television (TNT). In 1985, Turner founded the Better World Society; presently he is willing to present $500,000 to anyone able to invent a new worldview suitable for the new, peaceful earth. According to Turner, Christianity is

> Christianity is a "religion for losers," and Christ should not have bothered dying on the cross. I don't want anybody to die for me. I've had a few drinks and a few girlfriends, and if that's gonna put me in hell, then so be it.
>
> —— TED TURNER

a "religion for losers," and Christ should not have bothered dying on the cross. "I don't want anybody to die for me," said Turner. "I've had a few drinks and a few girlfriends, and if that's gonna put me in hell, then so be it."[23]

Turner also maintains that the Ten Commandments are "out of date." He wants to replace them with his Ten Voluntary Initiatives, which include the following statements: "I promise to have love and respect for the planet earth and living things thereon, especially my fellow species—humankind. I promise to treat all persons everywhere with dignity, respect, and friendliness. I promise to have no more than two children, or no more than my nation suggests. I reject the use of force, in particular military force, and back United Nations arbitration of international disputes. I support the United Nations and its efforts to collectively improve the conditions of the planet."[24]

Still another reason for examining the Secular Humanist worldview is that many Humanists have gained positions of influence in our society. B.F. Skinner, Abraham Maslow, Carl Rogers, and Erich Fromm, all former Humanists of the Year, have powerfully affected psychology. Scientist Carl Sagan, another Humanist of the Year, preached his Humanism on a widely heralded television series. Norman Lear has produced and otherwise influenced a number of shows on television. Ethical decisions are made for us by Humanist of the Year Faye Wattleton, former director of Planned Parenthood. Humanist science fiction writer Isaac Asimov wrote tirelessly for his causes. Clearly, Humanists are willing to support their worldview—often more faithfully than Christians. For these and other reasons, we will give the Secular Humanist worldview close attention.

---

[23] Cal Thomas, "Turner's Takeover Tender," *The Washington Times* (November 6, 1989): F2.
[24] Julie Lanham, "The Greening of Ted Turner," *The Humanist* (Nov./Dec. 1989): 6.

0.2.8 WHY STUDY THE MARXIST-LENINIST WORLDVIEW?

Marxism-Leninism is an atheistic, materialistic worldview. It has developed a perspective regarding each of the ten disciplines—usually in great detail. Often, Marxism produces a "champion" of its perspective in the various fields—for example, I.P. Pavlov in psychology or T.D. Lysenko in biology. In addition, Marxism-Leninism is responsible for the death of over 100 million people during the twentieth century alone.[25] But the main reason Christians need to understand Marxism is that it has been one of Christianity's most vocal detractors. All these things make mainstream Marxism worthy of study.

Based on the writings of Karl Marx in the late 1800s, Marxism has flourished and developed into several different strands, including Leninism (from the influence of Vladimir Lenin, the leader of the 1917 Bolshevik revolution in Russia), Maoism (based on the writings of the Chinese revolutionary, Mao Tse-tung), and Trotskyism (after the Russian Marxist, Leon Trotsky), as well as other offshoots. While Marxism has taken on some new looks in recent years—including debasing culture as a form of revolutionary activity[26]—its presence continues to be felt around the world. The latest Communist Manifesto, titled *Empire*, was published in 2000 by Harvard University Press in spite of the fact that one of its authors is in an Italian prison. The other author teaches Marxism at Duke University.

This becomes all the more sinister when we realize that some Christian groups have attempted to combine their Christianity with Marxism. Evangelical voices, often referred to as the "Christian Left," are known to support some aspects of Marxism, and one of its influential proponents has compared Karl Marx to the prophet Amos. Another voice of the "Christian Left" actually cheered on the Communist forces of North Vietnam during the Vietnam War. One can find both men lecturing widely on Christian college campuses.

The World Council of Churches saw no inconsistency in holding its meetings behind the Iron Curtain before it disintegrated. The editors of *National Review* note that "substantial parts of various American churches . . . have been active on the side of communist insurrection. The Maryknoll priests, the liberation theologians, Episcopal and Methodist groups and Jesuits have placed themselves in direct alliance with totalitarianism . . . With an enormous Christian rebirth taking place in Eastern Europe, it is ironic that so much of the American church is decadent."[27]

The liberal churches' position regarding Marxism does not, of course, take into account the profound incompatibility of their faith with the Marxist worldview. Alexander Solzhenitsyn, before the fall of the Iron Curtain, described this incompatibility in concrete terms: "The Soviet Union [under Marxist rule] is a land where churches have been leveled, where triumphant atheism has rampaged uncontrolled for two-thirds of a century, where the clergy is utterly humiliated and deprived of all independence, where what remains of the Russian Orthodox Church as an institution is tolerated only for the sake of propaganda directed at the West, where even today, people are sent to labor camps for their faith, and where, within the camps themselves, those who gather to pray at Easter are clapped into punishment cells."[28]

---

[25] Stephane Courtois, ed., *The Black Book Of Communism: Crimes, Terror, Repression* (Cambridge, MA: Harvard University Press, 1999); R.J. Rummel, *Death By Government* (New Brunswick, NJ: Transaction, 1994).

[26] Paul Edward Gottfried, *The Strange Death of Marxism: The European Left in the New Millennium* (Columbia, MO: University of Missouri Press, 2005); David Horowitz, *Unholy Alliance: Radical Islam and the American Left* (Washington, DC: Regnery Publishing, 2004); Michael Hardt and Antonio Negri, *Empire* (Cambridge, MA: Harvard University Press, 2000); Rolf Wiggershaus, *The Frankfurt School: Its History, Theories, and Political Significance* (Cambridge, NY: MIT, 1998); Raymond Aron, *The Opium of the Intellectuals* (third printing; New Brunswick, NJ: Transaction, 2003).

[27] "No One Here But Us Church Mice," *National Review* (December 31, 1989): 15.

[28] Reed Irvine, "Soviet Religious Propaganda," *The Washington Times* (April 3, 1984): 9A.

This text delineates the insurmountable differences between Marxism and Christianity. By addressing both worldviews, this study highlights their incompatibility.

0.2.9 MARXISM STILL A THREAT?

Some may point out that the downfall of communist countries all around the world proves that the Marxist-Leninist worldview is a failure, completely incompatible with reality. Why, in light of these historical events, should we still study the Marxist-Leninist perspective? Is Marxist ideology not dead?

Two words should suffice: **Tiananmen Square**. Marxism-Leninism hates resistance and will crush believers in rival worldviews any way possible, even with tanks. While Marxism has crumbled in many countries, it still encompasses others in its death grip. Marxism is the dominant worldview in some African and Latin American countries.

> TIANANMEN SQUARE refers to the June 4, 1989, event where the Chinese government sent heavily armed troops into Tiananmen Square located in Beijing, China, and massacred 11,000 students and adults—the protesters were killed for insisting that the Communist government grant its citizens basic human freedoms

And, incredibly, Marxism predominates on many American university campuses. In an article entitled "Marxism in U.S. Classrooms,"[29] *U.S. News and World Report* reported that there are ten thousand Marxist professors on America's campuses. Georgie Anne Geyer says that "the percentage of Marxist faculty members can range from an estimated 90 percent in some Midwestern universities."[30] Arnold Beichman says that "Marxist academics are today's power elite in the universities."[31] As noted in Part I, *U.S. News and World Report's* Special Collector's Edition contained an article entitled "Where Marxism Lives Today," which confirms that Marxism in the United States is doing very well indeed.[32]

"The strides made by Marxism at American universities in the last two decades are breathtaking," says New York University's Herbert London, writing in 1987. "Every discipline has been affected by its preachment, and almost every faculty now counts among its members a resident Marxist scholar."[33] Duke University Slavic Languages professor Magnus Krynski describes the increasing Marxist presence on his campus—a presence actively encouraged by the university administration, which, he says, is "faddishly" luring Marxist literary critics to Duke with large salaries. In March 1987, Duke University hosted the Southeast Marxist Scholars Conference. Dr. Malcolm Gillis, former vice provost of Duke University, thanked some one hundred Marxist professors, graduate students, and activists for gathering at Duke, saying, "When I left this campus twenty years ago, there were very few Marxists here. When I returned in 1984, I saw Marxists in many parts of the social science faculty."[34] The conference was sponsored by the Marxist Educational

> The strides made by Marxism at American universities in the last two decades are breathtaking. Every discipline has been affected by its preachment, and almost every faculty now counts among its members a resident Marxist scholar.
>
> — HERBERT LONDON

---

[29] David B. Richardson, "Marxism in U.S. Classrooms," *U.S. News and World Report* (January 25, 1982): 42–5.
[30] Georgie Anne Geyer, "Marxism Thrives on Campus," *The Denver Post* (August 29, 1989): B7.
[31] Ibid.
[32] *U.S. News and World Report* (September 2, 2003): 86–87.
[33] Herbert London, "Marxism Thriving on American Campuses," *The World and I* (January 1987): 189.
[34] *Accuracy in Academia Campus Report* (April 1987): 1.

Press (based at the University of Minnesota) and Duke's own Program on Perspectives in Marxism and Society.

The Marxist, or "Politically Correct," influence has reached its most alarming heights in American universities' humanities departments. "With a few notable exceptions," says former Yale professor Roger Kimball, "our most prestigious liberal arts colleges and universities have installed the entire radical menu at the center of their humanities curriculum at both the undergraduate and the graduate level."[35]

William S. Lind is not bashful in identifying the Marxist influence in the United States. Says Lind, "In the United States of America our traditional Western, Judeo-Christian culture is collapsing. It is not collapsing because it failed. On the contrary, it has given us the freest and most prosperous society in human history. Rather, it is collapsing because we are abandoning it."[36]

Lind explains how this planned attack hit American shores: "Starting in the mid-1960s, we have thrown away the values, morals, and standards that define traditional Western culture. In part, this has been driven by cultural radicals, people who hate our Judeo-Christian culture. Dominant in the elite, especially in the universities, the media, and the entertainment industry (now the most powerful force in our culture and a source of endless degradation), the cultural radicals have successfully pushed an agenda of moral relativism, militant secularism, and sexual and social 'liberation.' This agenda has slowly codified into a new ideology, usually known as 'multiculturalism' or 'political correctness,' that is in essence Marxism translated from economic into social and cultural terms."[37]

0.2.10 GRAMSCI AND LUKACS

In a radio talk on December 13, 1998, Lind traced the Marxist influence of Antonio Gramsci (Italy) and George Lukacs (Hungary) and their planned assault on Western culture. They reasoned that the proletariat (the property-less class) of the world would never rise up in a world revolution while steeped in Christian culture, including Christian marriage and sexual values. Their goal: destroy Christian culture to advance the Marxist cause. Lukacs was responsible for establishing a Marxist think tank called the Institute for Social Research, but more popularly known as The Frankfurt School. This Marxist think tank has had great influence throughout Europe and the United States with its goal to subvert traditional Western culture.

Gramsci referred to his assault on Western culture as "a long march through the institutions," meaning subverting schools, churches, media, entertainment, and then taking political power to establish a global, socialist paradise.

Such well-known personalities as Max Horkehimer, Theodore Adorno, and Herbert Marcuse were involved in remaking traditional Christian sexual morality into the permissive society. Marcuse, a philosophy professor at the University of California (San Diego), is largely responsible for what today is labeled "political correctness." The idea behind political correctness is the notion of oppression. Women, blacks, Hispanics, and homosexuals are viewed as oppressed minorities due to the influence of Christianity and capitalism, bringing about the need for a revolution to overthrow their white, male, heterosexual, Euro-centric oppressors.[38]

---

[35] Roger Kimball, *Tenured Radicals* (New York, NY: Harper and Row, 1990), xiii. Christian young people should read Kimball's book, then Allan Bloom's *The Closing of the American Mind* (New York, NY: Simon & Schuster, 1987), and finally Ronald Nash's *The Closing of the American Heart: How Higher Education has Failed Democracy and Impoverished the Souls of Today's Students* (Brentwood, TN: Wolgemuth & Hyatt, 1990) to grasp what Christian students face in America's colleges and universities.

[36] *The Marine Corps Gazette* (December 1994): 37.

[37] Ibid.

[38] Alvin Schmidt, *The Menace of Multiculturalism: The Trojan Horse in America* (Westport, CT: Praeger, 1997).

One voice in the wilderness seeking to expose the Marxist influence in America, but especially on her campuses, is David Horowitz. His book *Unholy Alliance: Radical Islam and the American Left* is not only a "good read," as former CBS newsman Bernard Goldberg says, but "it's a must read." Horowitz spends nearly 300 pages exposing and explaining the Marxist agenda for America. He notes that *A People's History of the United States,* by popular historian Howard Zinn, "is a raggedly conceived Marxist caricature that begins with Columbus and ends with George Bush."[39] "Zinn's book," says Horowitz, "has been embedded by leftist academics in the collegiate and secondary schools' curricula."[40]

> The New Age is the ultimate eclectic religion of self: Whatever you decide is right for you is what's right, as long as you don't get narrow-minded and exclusive about it.
>
> — JOHANNA MICHAELSEN

The Marxist worldview is alive and well in the American classroom. As worldview expert on Marxism-Leninism Dr. Fred Schwarz says, "The colleges and universities are the nurseries of communism."[41] Christian students must be aware not only of their prevalence, but also of the subversive goals of Marxist-thinking professors.

0.2.11 WHY STUDY THE COSMIC HUMANIST WORLDVIEW?

Commonly referred to as the New Age movement, this worldview is more accurately described by its real name, Cosmic Humanism. Because it professes a marked disdain for dogma, this worldview is more vaguely defined than the others, except perhaps Postmodernism. Indeed, some members of the New Age movement go so far as to claim that their worldview "has no religious doctrine or teachings of its own."[42]

This attitude results from the New Age belief that truth resides within each individual and, therefore, no one can claim a corner on the truth or dictate truth to another. "The New Age," explains Christian writer Johanna Michaelsen, "is the ultimate eclectic religion of self: Whatever you decide is right for you is what's right, as long as you don't get narrow-minded and exclusive about it."[43]

The assumption that truth resides within each individual, however, becomes the cornerstone for a worldview. Granting oneself the power to discern all truth is a facet of theology, and this theology has ramifications that many members of the New Age movement have already discovered. Some have grudgingly begun to consider their movement a worldview. Marilyn Ferguson, author of *The Aquarian Conspiracy* (a book referred to as "The New Age watershed classic"), says the movement ushers in a "new mind—the ascendance of a startling worldview."[44]

This worldview is summed up in its skeletal form, agreeable to virtually every Cosmic Humanist, by Jonathan Adolph: "In its broadest sense, New Age thinking can be characterized as a form of utopianism, the desire to create a better society, a 'New Age' in which humanity lives in harmony with itself, nature, and the cosmos."[45]

---

[39] David Horowitz, *Unholy Alliance: Radical Islam and the American Left* (Washington, DC: Regnery Publishing, 2004), 102.

[40] Ibid.

[41] Newsletter of the Christian Anti-Communism Crusade, P.O. Box 129, Manitou Springs, CO 80829, February 1, 1988.

[42] Jonathan Adolph, "What is New Age?" *New Age Journal* (Winter 1988): 11.

[43] Johanna Michaelsen, *Like Lambs to the Slaughter* (Eugene, OR: Harvest House, 1989), 11.

[44] Marilyn Ferguson, *The Austrian Conspiracy* (Los Angeles, CA: J.P. Tarcher, 1980), 23.

[45] Adolph, 11.

While the New Age movement still appears fragmented and without strong leadership, it has grown at a remarkable rate. The Stanford Research Institute estimates that "the number of New Agers in America could be as high as 5 to 10 percent of the population—12 million or more people."[46] Others have put the figure as high as 60 million, although this includes people who merely believe in reincarnation and astrology. John Randolph Price, a world leader of the New Age movement, says, "There are more than half a billion New Age advocates on the planet at this time, working among various religious groups."[47]

Further, people adhering to the Cosmic Humanist worldview are gaining converts in the West and around the world. Malachi Martin lists dozens of organizations that are either New Age or New Age sympathetic. Barbara Marx Hubbard, a spokeswoman for the New Age, made a bid for the 1984 Democratic vice presidential nomination. Clearly, Cosmic Humanism, a transplant from the East, is becoming a presence throughout the Western hemisphere.

0.2.12 WHY STUDY THE POSTMODERN WORLDVIEW?

The sixth and final worldview in our study is Postmodernism, or better, Postmodern*isms*. The Book of Judges concludes with a description of the moral compass of the Israelites of that day—everyone did what was right in his (or her) own eyes (Judges 21:25). So it is with Postmodern adherents—each one holds his or her own definition of the term.

Much of this study concentrates on the thinking of what we consider mainstream Postmodernists—Lyotard, Baudrillard, Derrida, Foucault, Lacan, Macherey, Mandelbrot, Barthes, DeBord, Deleuze, Guattari, and Rorty. We will study these philosophers and literary critics in more detail in the coming chapters. Although there is scant consensus among these individuals, their writings provide a sampling of the Postmodern worldview.

Forced to face the inhumanity, destruction, and horror brought about by the Third Reich and the Soviet Gulag, a substantial group of Enlightenment humanists and neo-Marxists abandoned their worldview to create one they believed more fitting with reality, resulting in the Postmodern turn. Though Postmodernism comes in many forms, there are three unifying values: (1) a commitment to relativism; (2) an opposition to rationalism; and (3) the promotion of culturally created realities, all of which are designed to deny any true worldview or belief system for which we would be willing to kill or to die.

Postmodernism's most effective methodological tool is known as Deconstructionism, which means (1) that words do not represent reality, and (2) that concepts expressed in sentences in any language are arbitrary. Some Postmodernists go so far as to deconstruct humanity itself. Thus, along with the death of God, truth, and reason, humanity is also obliterated. Paul Kugler notes the ironic twist: "Today, it is the speaking subject who declared God dead one hundred years ago whose very existence is now being called into question."[48]

The Pop Culture Connection

A short list of movies that exhibit generally Cosmic Humanist subtexts or major themes include the *Star Wars* series, *Poltergeist, Indiana Jones and the Temple of Doom, The Dark Crystal, Solarbabies, Mulan, The Exorcist, What Dreams May Come,* and *Sixth Sense.* Cosmic Humanist education with a more neo-pagan flair, specifically animism and ancestor worship, are on display in notable children's films such as *Pocahontas,* where the main character sings "I know every rock and tree and creature has a life, has a spirit, has a name," and *The Lion King,* particularly in its theme song, "The Circle of Life."

---

[46] Ray A. Yungen, *For Many Shall Come in My Name* (Salem, OR: Ray Yungen, 1989), 34.

[47] John Randolph Prince, *The Superbeings* (Austin, TX: Quartus, 1981), 51.

[48] Walter Truett Anderson, *The Future of the Self: Exploring the Post-Identity Society* (New York, NY: Tarcher/

Earlier we defined a worldview as any set of ideas or beliefs that provides a framework for understanding the world, including a particular perspective on ten disciplines—theology, philosophy, ethics, etc. When we ask whether Postmodernism is a worldview under this definition, we find that the primary writings of the core Postmodernists are atheistic, showing us that Postmodernism does, indeed, contain a perspective on theology. A closer look reveals that while Postmodernists in general insist that all truth is socially constructed by local communities, they insist that their atheistic theology is true for all communities around the world!

This study will show that Postmodernists have a perspective, more or less, on all ten disciplines. Their perspective on ethics is relativistic. Their perspective on biology sees humans as merely clever animals. As Richard Rorty puts it, humans are able to "take charge of [their] own evolution, take ourselves in directions which have neither precedent nor justification in either biology or history."[49] Many adhere to the theory of punctuated evolution.

Myron B. Penner says, "Postmodernism is a Zeitgeist[50], or a worldview; it is a total cognitive interpretation and affects one's general outlook. In some respects Postmodernism is more descriptive of a personal and social reality than a philosophy—although it quite obviously entails certain philosophical theses."[51]

Kevin J. Vanhoozer seconds Penner's view that Postmodernism is a worldview when he says, "Postmodernity is more of a condition than a distinct position, a mood rather than a metaphysics; it nonetheless communicates something about human being-in-the-world. It is a world and life view, not in the sense that it yields a system of propositions, but in the sense that it creates an ethos. Postmodernity may be more than a philosophy, but it is not less; it is a world and life view that is in a relation of codependency with modernity."[52]

0.2.13 HISTORICAL AND PHILOSOPHICAL ROOTS OF POSTMODERNISM

Historically speaking, we would expect Postmodernism to be something that came after the modern era (modernity). However, many Postmodernists find their roots in thinkers such as Nietzsche and Marx who were associated with modernity. J.P. Moreland notes that Postmodernism refers to a philosophical approach primarily in the area of epistemology, or what counts as knowledge or truth. Broadly speaking, Moreland says "Postmodernism represents a form of cultural relativism about such things as truth, reality, reason, values, linguistic meaning, the 'self' and other notions."[53]

Perhaps the most descriptive delineation of Postmodernism is this: "Truth is a short-term contract here. You cannot speak in the name of universal human principles and expect them to form a fixed standard by which to judge other people's perspectives. You can no longer look to ideas like morality, justice, enlightenment or human nature and expect them to form a globally agreed basis for your own point of view. It is impossible to draw up a complete map [worldview] of the world in such a way that everybody would be able to recognize it as representing their own knowledge and experience. Postmodernists argue that it is no longer possible to write a 'theory of everything'; you can only take the pragmatic and relativist line that some truths are more useful than others in specific circumstances."[54]

Putnam, 1997), 32.

[49] Robert B. Brandom, ed., *Rorty and His Critics* (Malden, MA: Blackwell Publishers, 2001), 3.

[50] *Weltanschauung* would have been the correct German word.

[51] Myron B. Penner, *Christianity and the Postmodern Turn* (Grand Rapids, MI: Brazos Press, 2005), 17.

[52] Ibid., 77.

[53] See J.P. Moreland's website for his article "Postmodernism and the Christian Life." Also, J. P. Moreland and William Lane Craig, *The Philosophical Foundation of a Christian Worldview*.

[54] Ibid., 175.

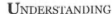

Such is the essence of mainstream Postmodernism—a worldview that claims there are no worldviews. We like to think of it as an "anti-worldview" worldview, one that certainly merits our attention. To complicate matters even further, we must acknowledge that there even exists a variety of Postmodernism called "Christian Postmodernism."[55] This, too, we will examine.

0.2.14 CONCLUSION

As you go through this study, you will see that Marxism, Postmodernism, and Secular Humanism have a number of similarities. You will, however, also learn how they differ. Secular Humanism is the mother (Humanists trace their heritage to the Greeks 400 years before Christ), while Marxism and Postmodernism are the daughters of Humanism. From a comprehensive point of view, the differences between Secular Humanism and Marxism are real, but minor. Both Karl Marx and Humanist Paul Kurtz recognize the truth of these assertions. Marx puts it like this: "Communism, as fully developed naturalism, equals humanism."[56] And Kurtz says Marx "is a humanist because he rejects theistic religion and defends atheism."[57]

> Too many Christian young people are ill prepared to take the lead in proclaiming and defending the Gospel of Jesus Christ throughout society.

Furthermore, Cosmic Humanism and Secular Humanism are closely related. The New Age movement is little more than spiritualized Secular Humanism. Cosmic Humanism claims to meet our spiritual needs—something Marxism and Secular Humanism cannot claim—but it is stuck with a vague, impersonal, pantheistic god. Practically speaking, there is little difference between claiming no god exists and claiming everything is god.

We cannot overstate the significance of the similarities between these anti-Christian views. Public schools in America are immersed in many of the same ideas that caused Marxism to crumble in Eastern Europe and today cause suffering to the men and women in India because of their society's acceptance of a version of Cosmic Humanism. The basis for much of what is taught in the public classroom today comes from Secular and Postmodern thinking, taking on a variety of labels: liberalism, multiculturalism, political correctness, deconstructionism, or self-esteem education. Or, in its more sinister form, the labels are dropped and courses are taught from Secular/Marxist/Postmodern/Cosmic assumptions without the students being told the worldview that is being expressed.

Young people will flourish in the light of truth only when the emphasis shifts to a Christian perspective. This dramatic shift in emphasis *can* be brought about through the leadership of thousands of informed, confident Christian students who will become the future leaders in education, business, science, and government.

Our desire to bring about this shift in emphasis to a Christian perspective in education is, then, our fundamental reason for preparing *Understanding the Times*. Too many Christian young people are ill prepared to take the lead in proclaiming and defending the Gospel of Jesus Christ throughout society. The vast majority have no concept of the components of their worldview and will stand intellectually naked before their liberal or left-wing professors. Carl F.H. Henry says that evangelical students know more about God than their secular counterparts, but "with some few gratifying exceptions, neither home nor church has shaped a comprehensive and consistent faith

[55] See D.A. Carson, *The Gagging of God: Christianity Confronts Pluralism* (Grand Rapids, MI: Zondervan, 1996); Myron B. Penner, ed., *Christianity and the Postmodern Turn* (Grand Rapids, MI: Brazos Press, 2005); and D.A. Carson, *Becoming Conversant with the Emerging Church* (Grand Rapids, MI: Zondervan, 2005).
[56] Karl Marx and Friedrich Engels, *Collected Works*, 40 vols. (New York, NY: International, 1976), 3:296.
[57] Paul Kurtz, *The Fullness of Life* (New York, NY: Horizon, 1974), 36.

that stands noon-bright amid the dim shadows of spiritual rebellion and moral profligacy."[58]

Christ's teachings impart just such a noon-bright faith to all Christians who master their worldview, who truly *understand the times*. The foundational Bible verse for this book is 1 Chronicles 12:32, which announces that just two hundred individuals who understood the times provided the leadership for an entire nation because they knew "what Israel ought to do."

The first chapter of the Book of Daniel explains how Daniel and his friends prepared themselves to survive and flourish amid the clash of worldviews of their day. We believe that Christian young people equipped with a comprehensive knowledge and understanding of the Christian worldview and its rivals can become "Daniels" who will not stand on the sidelines, but will participate in the great collision of worldviews in the twenty-first century.

[58] Carl F.H. Henry, *Twilight of a Great Civilization* (Wheaton, IL: Crossway Books, 1988), 94.

UNDERSTANDING
THE TIMES

Introduction

Part Three

"There are not two realities, but only one reality, and that is the reality of God, which has become manifest in Christ in the reality of the world."[1]

— DIETRICH BONHOEFFER

0.3.1 INTRODUCTION

Many believe that when Christians confront or challenge other worldviews and attempt to speak to such "worldly" disciplines as politics, economics, biology, and law, they are overstepping their bounds. Jesus taught His followers, "You are not of the world, but I chose you out of the world" (John 15:19).

How, then, can Christians justify their claim to a worldview that speaks to every facet of life? Should Christians stick to spiritual matters and allow non-Christians to concentrate on the practical matters of running the world? In short, isn't there a vast chasm between the secular and the sacred? Not according to Dietrich Bonhoeffer, who says that we should not distinguish between the two: "There are not two realities, but only one reality, and that is the reality of God, which has become manifest in Christ in the reality of the world."[2]

---

[1] *Baker's Dictionary of Christian Ethics* (Grand Rapids, MI: Baker Book House, 1973), 67.
[2] Ibid.

0.3.2 CREATIVE AND REDEMPTIVE ORDER

From the Biblical Christian perspective, the ten disciplines addressed in this text reflect various aspects of God and His creative and redemptive orders. God created humankind with theological, philosophical, ethical, biological (and so on) dimensions. We live and move and have our being (our very essence and existence) within and about these categories. Why? Because that is the way God created us.

The Christian views these ten categories as sacred, not secular. They are sacred because they are imprinted in the creative order. For example, consider these texts from Genesis in light of the ten disciplines:

Theology and Philosophy: "In the beginning God created the heavens and the earth" (1:1)
Ethics: "knowledge of good and evil" (2:9)
Biology: "according to its kind" (1:21)
Psychology: "a living being" (2:7)
Sociology (and Ecology): "be fruitful and multiply; fill the earth" (1:28)
Law: "I commanded you" (3:11)
Politics (and Law again): "whoever sheds man's blood" (9:6)
Economics: "it shall be for food" (1:29)
History: "enmity between you and the woman" (3:15)

All ten disciplines are addressed in just the first few chapters of the Bible because they manifest and accent certain aspects of the creative order.

Further, God manifests Himself in the person of Jesus Christ in such a way as to underline the significance of each discipline. Consider how the following references describe Him:

Theology: "the fullness of the Godhead" (Colossians 2:9)
Philosophy: the Logos of God (John 1:1)
Ethics: "the true Light" (John 1:9, 3:19–20)
Biology: "the life" (John 1:4, 11:25; Colossians 1:16)
Psychology: "Savior" (Luke 1:46–47; Titus 2:13)
Sociology: "Son" (Luke 1:30–31; Isaiah 9:6)
Law: "lawgiver" (Genesis 49:10; Isaiah 9:7)
Politics: "KING OF KINGS AND LORD OF LORDS" (Revelation 19:16; 1 Timothy 6:15; Isaiah 9:6; Luke 1:33)
Economics: Owner of all things (Psalm 24:1; 50:10–12; 1 Corinthians 10:26)
History: "the Alpha and the Omega" (Revelation 1:8)

> The Bible and the life of Jesus Christ provide the Christian with the basis for a total life worldview.

The integration of these various categories into society has come to be known as Western Civilization and previous to that Christendom or the Holy Roman Empire.[3]

The Bible and the life of Jesus Christ provide the Christian with the basis for a total life worldview. Indeed, Christians gain a perspective so comprehensive that they are commanded to "take captive every thought to make it obedient to Christ" (2 Corinthians 10:5).

---

[3] Alvin J. Schmidt, *How Christianity Changed the World* (Grand Rapids, MI: Zondervan, 2004).

0.3.3 CONFRONTING DECEPTIVE PHILOSOPHIES

Once we have captured every idea and made it obedient to Christ, we are to use these thoughts to "demolish arguments and every pretension [scientific naturalism, ethical relativism, biological evolution, etc.] that sets itself up against the knowledge of God" (2 Corinthians 10:4–5). When nations and men forget God[4] they experience what mankind experienced in the twentieth century. Nazism and communism, two major movements bereft of the knowledge of God, cost the human race tens of millions of lives. Whittaker Chambers says that communism's problem is not a problem of economics, but of atheism: "Faith is the central problem of this age."[5] Alexander Solzhenitsyn echoes him: "Men have forgotten God."

In Colossians 2, the Apostle Paul insists that those who have "received Christ Jesus the Lord" (Colossians 2:6) are to be rooted and built up in Him, strengthened in the faith as they were taught (Colossians 2:7). While Christians work to strengthen their faith, they must see to it that no one takes them "captive through hollow and deceptive philosophy, which depends on human tradition and the basic principles of this world rather than on Christ" (Colossians 2:8, NIV).

From the Christian point of view, Islam, Secular, Cosmic, Postmodern and Marxist Humanism fall within the confines of "the basic principles of this world." They are based on the wisdom of this world (1 Corinthians 1:19f) and not upon Christ. And Paul says that God has made the world's wisdom foolishness. Only fools can tell themselves "there is no God." Only fools can scan the heavens and argue for chance and accident. Only fools can examine the human body and not see intelligent design. Only the fool can experience the seasons of life and never sense the witness of God. Only fools can listen to Handel's Messiah and actually think they are listening to evolving monkeys making music.

These were not empty ideas for Paul. He practiced what he preached. In Acts 17, Paul confronted the vain and deceitful philosophies of the atheistic Epicureans and pantheistic Stoics—the professional Humanists of his day. The Apostle countered their ideas with Christian ideas, he reasoned and preached, and he accented three truths—the resurrection of Jesus Christ (Acts 17:18), the creation of the universe by God (Acts 17:24), and the judgment to come (Acts 17:31).

Can we do less? We, too, must fearlessly proclaim the good news of the gospel: God created the universe and all things in it; humankind rebelliously smashed the image of God through their sin; Jesus Christ died for our sin, was raised from the dead, and is alive forevermore (1 Corinthians 15:1–4). And we must stand fast in the context of the same worldview as Paul: creation, resurrection, and judgment.

> And we must stand fast in the context of the same worldview as Paul: creation, resurrection, and judgment.

0.3.4 THE RELIGION OF MARXISM-LENINISM

Paul recognized that we cannot compartmentalize aspects of our life into boxes marked "sacred" and "secular." He understood not only that Christianity was both a worldview and a religion, but also that all worldviews are religious by definition. Indeed, he went so far as to tell the Epicureans and Stoics that they were religious—they just worshiped an "unknown God" (Acts 17:22, 23).

Most people have no problem recognizing that certain non-Christian worldviews are

---

[4] See Psalm 2.
[5] Whittaker Chambers, *Witness* (New York, NY: Random House, 1952), 17.

religious. Cosmic Humanists talk about god, so they must practice a religion. But how can the "religious" label apply to atheists like Marxists or Secular Humanists? It applies because all worldviews contain a theology—that is, all begin with a religious declaration. Christianity and Islam begin with, "In the beginning God." Marxism-Leninism, Postmodernism, and Secular Humanism begin with, "In the beginning no God." Cosmic Humanism or New Age begins with the declaration, "Everything is God."

The Marxist view is religious in a number of other ways as well. Marxism's philosophy of dialectical materialism grants matter god-like attributes, as Gustav A. Wetter acknowledges in *Dialectical Materialism*:

> [T]he atheism of dialectical materialism is concerned with very much more than a mere denial of God. . . . [I]n dialectical materialism . . . the higher is not, as such, denied; the world is interpreted as a process of continual ascent, which fundamentally extends into infinity. But it is supposed to be matter itself which continually attains to higher perfection under its own power, thanks to its indwelling dialectic. As Nikolai Berdyaev very rightly remarks, the dialectical materialist attribution of "dialectic" to matter confers on it, not mental attributes only, but even divine ones.[6]

The Pop Culture Connection

Based on the memoirs of World War II veteran Ernest Gordon and accounts from other POWs, the major motion picture ***To End All Wars*** (2001, starring Kiefer Sutherland) tells the story of four Allied prisoners who endure harsh treatment from their Japanese captors while being forced to build a railroad through the Burmese jungle. Ultimately, they find true freedom by forgiving their enemies. In weaving the story together, Christian screenwriter Brian Godawa clearly contrasts the worldviews of secularism, the imperial Japanese warrior code, and Biblical Christianity.[8]*

We will discuss this further in the Marxist philosophy chapter. For now, it is enough to understand that Wetter perceives communism as religious in character.

Even Secular Humanists such as Bertrand Russell recognize the religiosity of Marxism: "The greatest danger in our day comes from new religions, communism and Nazism. To call these religions may perhaps be objectionable both to their friends and to their enemies, but in fact they have all the characteristics of religions. They advocate a way of life on the basis of irrational dogmas; they have a sacred history, a Messiah, and a priesthood. I do not see what more could be demanded to qualify a doctrine as a religion."[7]

0.3.5 THE RELIGION OF SECULAR HUMANISM

Secular Humanism is more openly religious than Marxism. Charles Francis Potter, a signatory of the first *Humanist Manifesto*, wrote a book in 1930 entitled *Humanism: A New Religion*. Potter claims to have organized a religious society—the First Humanist Society of New York.

The first Humanist Manifesto (1933) describes the agenda of "religious" Humanists. The 1980 preface to the *Humanist Manifestoes I & II*, written by Paul Kurtz, says, "Humanism is a philosophical, religious, and moral point of view." John Dewey, a signatory of the 1933 Manifesto, wrote *A Common Faith*, in which he says, "Here are all the elements for a religious

---

[6] Gustav A. Wetter, *Dialectical Materialism* (Westport, CT: Greenwood, 1977), 558.
[7] Bertrand Russell, *Understanding History* (New York, NY: Philosophical Library, 1957), 95.
[8] *Visit Godawa's website to order his commentary of the film: www.godawa.com

faith that shall not be confined to sect, class or race. . . . It remains to make it explicit and militant."[9]

While the *Humanist Manifesto II* (written primarily by Kurtz and published in 1973) drops the expression "religious humanism," it nevertheless contains religious implications and even religious terminology, including the statement that "no deity will save us; we must save ourselves."[10]

Lloyd L. Morain, a past president of the American Humanist Association, wrote a book with his wife Mary entitled *Humanism as the Next Step* (1954). In this work the authors describe Humanism as the fourth religion. The Morains were co-winners of the 1994 Humanist of the Year award.

The U.S. Supreme Court's decision in Torcaso v. Watkins (June 19, 1961) declared, "Among religions in this country which do not teach what would generally be considered a belief in the existence of God are Buddhism, Taoism, Ethical Culture, Secular Humanism and others."[11] A few years later (1965) the Supreme Court allowed Daniel Seeger conscientious objector status because of his religious beliefs. He claimed to be a Secular Humanist. Building on both Supreme Court decisions, the Seventh Court of Appeals on August 19, 2005, decreed atheism to be a religion.[12]

Auburn University's *Student, Faculty and Staff Directory* contains a section entitled "Auburn Pastors and Campus Ministers." Included in the listing is a Humanist Counselor, Delos McKown, who also happens to be the head of Auburn's philosophy department. This is not an isolated example. The University of Arizona lists Humanism under religious ministries. Harvard University has a Humanist chaplain who is one of 34 full or part-time chaplains that comprise the United Ministry at Harvard and Radcliffe. He is sponsored by the American Humanist Association, the American Ethical Union, the Fellowship of Religious Humanists, and, until his death, "generous gifts from [Secular Humanist] Corliss Lamont."

In fact, the American Humanist Association "certifies humanist counselors who enjoy the legal status of ordained priests, pastors, and rabbis."[13] In its preamble, the Association states that one of it functions is to extend its principles and operate educationally. Toward this end it publishes books, magazines, and pamphlets; engages lecturers; selects, trains, and "accredits humanistic counselors as its ordained ministry of the movement."[14]

0.3.6 SECULAR HUMANISM AS A RELIGIOUS ORGANIZATION

Kurtz—who has written a book that denies that Humanism is a religion throughout its first half and, in the second half, encourages the establishment of Humanist churches, calling them Eupraxophy Centers—admits that the organized Humanist movement in America is put in a quandary over whether Humanism is a religion. Why? Simply because "the Fellowship of Religious Humanists (300 members), the American Ethical Union (3,000 members), and the Society for Humanistic Judaism (4,000 members) consider themselves to be religious. Even the American Humanist Association," says Kurtz, "has a [501(c)3] religious tax exemption."[15]

[9] John Dewey, *A Common Faith* (New Haven, CT: Yale University Press, 1934), 87.

[10] Paul Kurtz, ed., *Humanist Manifestos I and II* (Buffalo, NY: Prometheus, 1980), 87.

[11] *United States v. Seeger*, 380 U.S. 163. Also see *Welsh v. United States*, 398 U.S. 333 (1970).

[12] In The United States Court of Appeals for the Seventh Circuit No. 04–1914, August 19, 2005, *Kaufman v. McCaughtry*, the Court decided that "Atheism is Kaufman's religion, and the group that he wanted to start was religious in nature even though it expressly rejects a belief in a supreme being" (8).

[13] See *American Education on Trial: Is Secular Humanism a Religion?* (Cumberland, VA: Center for Judicial Studies, 1987), 34.

[14] Ibid.

[15] Paul Kurtz, "Is Secular Humanism a Religion?" *Free Inquiry* (Winter 1986/87): 5.

Kurtz's recent denial that Secular Humanism is a religion is not based on truth; it is a calculated political maneuver. Kurtz seeks to dodge the all-important question: If Secular Humanism is a religion, then what is it doing in the public schools? If Christianity is thrown out of secular schools under the guise of separation of church and state, why shouldn't we banish Secular Humanism as well? Kurtz understands this, admitting that if Secular Humanism is a religion, "then we would be faced with a violation of the First Amendment to the United States Constitution."[16]

Christians who have seen their worldview effectively eliminated from the public schools are rightfully outraged by Humanists' violations of the present interpretation of the First Amendment. They are angered that a mere 15 million Humanists can control the content of American public schooling while the country's Christians provide the lion's share of students and bear the majority of the cost through their tax dollars.

Humanists attempt to downplay their violation of the present interpretation of the First Amendment by claiming that they present a neutral viewpoint. But no educational approach is neutral, as Richard A. Baer notes: "Education never takes place in a moral and philosophical vacuum. If the larger questions about human beings and their destiny are not being asked and answered within a predominantly Judeo-Christian framework [worldview], they will be addressed with another philosophical or religious framework—but hardly one that is 'neutral.'"[17]

In 1954, Archie J. Bahm organized the Southwestern Regional American Humanist Association. At that time he was professor of philosophy at the University of New Mexico. In 1964 he wrote a book published by Southern Illinois University entitled *The World's Living Religions*. Included in the religions were Hinduism, Jainism, Buddhism, Vedantism, Yoga, Taoism, Confucianism, Shintoism, Judaism, Christianity, Islam, and Humanism. The first four words in his chapter on Humanism: "Humanism is a religion."[18]

In 1996, Ian S. Markham edited a book entitled *A World Religions Reader*. In this work, used in many colleges and seminaries, Markham lists the following religions: Secular Humanism, Buddhism, Chinese Religions, Shintoism, Judaism, Christianity, Islam, and Sikhism. His definition of religion: "Religion, for me, is a way of life (one which embraces a total worldview, certain ethical demands, and certain social practices) that refuses to accept the secular view that sees human life as nothing more than complex bundles of atoms in an ultimately meaningless universe."[19] Secular Humanism, in contrast to Secularism, has an ethical dimension, observes certain social practices, and embraces a total worldview.

> Secular Humanism, in contrast to Secularism, has an ethical dimension, observes certain social practices, and embraces a total worldview.

Clearly, both Secular Humanism and Marxism are religious worldviews. Thus, in order to provide a just educational system for our young people, we must recognize that all worldviews have religious implications and that it is discriminatory to bar some worldviews and not others from the public classroom.

0.3.7 AN EVEN-HANDED APPROACH

After many years of study, contemplation, and teaching, we believe that the Biblical Christian worldview is spiritually, intellectually, emotionally, and practically far superior to

---

[16] Paul Kurtz, *Eupraxophy: Living Without Religion* (Buffalo, NY: Prometheus, 1989), 80.

[17] Richard A. Baer, "They are Teaching Religion in Public Schools," *Christianity Today* (February 17, 1984): 15.

[18] Archie J. Bahm, *The World's Living Religions* (Fremont, CA: Jain Publishing, 1992), 335.

[19] Ian S. Markham, *A World Religions Reader* (Oxford, UK: Blackwell Publishers, 1996, 2000), 5.6.

all other worldviews. Christianity is something that, as C.S. Lewis said, we "could not have guessed," but that, once revealed, is recognizable as indisputable truth. Therefore, we believe that if students are given the opportunity to study and seriously think through creation versus evolution, for example, the vast majority will choose the creationist, or Christian, position.

This book represents an effort to allow individuals such opportunities by comparing the ideas and beliefs of six dominant worldviews. We present these views and their approach to the ten disciplines as accurately as possible. We do not represent non-Christians as either stupid or insane, despite their tendency to describe Christians in such unflattering terms. While Humanists such as Albert Ellis call Christians "emotionally disturbed: usually neurotic but sometimes psychotic,"[20] this text resists such name-calling and treats Secular Humanists, Marxists, Postmodernists, New Agers, and followers of Islam simply as individuals who have not yet recognized the inconsistent and erroneous nature of their worldviews.

No Muslim, Marxist, Humanist, or Postmodernist, upon reading this text, should feel that we deliberately misrepresent their ideas, values, beliefs, or positions. We quote the exact words of adherents to each worldview in their corresponding chapters, so that Cosmic Humanists describe the New Age position, Marxists the Marxist position, and so on. When we say Secular Humanism is atheistic, we believe students should hear what the Secular Humanists say about the issue themselves. When we contend that Marxism-Leninism relies biologically on punctuated equilibrium, students should hear that from the Marxist. Further, no quote is purposely taken out of context. In the best tradition of Christian scholarship, we allow competing non-Christian worldviews to have their say as they wish to say it.

We contend that by seeing these worldviews contrasted with each other, Christian students will have a clearer picture of both their own worldview and the alternatives and will be able to enunciate and defend their position more persuasively and intelligently. Many young people do not know what they believe; our duty as Christians is to share our faith with such a spiritually and intellectually rootless generation. The Apostle Peter says as much when he exhorts believers in Jesus Christ to "be ready to give a defense to everyone who asks you a reason for the hope that is in you" (1 Peter 3:15).

0.3.8 A Word about Sources

There is no lack of resources for each worldview we have chosen to analyze, and we have focused on the best of these materials. Whether we are describing the Islamic, Marxist, or Postmodern position, we quote their ideological leaders.

The most important source for Islam is the Qur'an, considered by devoted Muslims to be the most accurate and final revelation from God (Allah). Muslims also derive their worldview from the words and actions of Mohammed as recorded in the Hadith, as well as the opinions of Muslim scholars found in the Sunna. These sources, as well as the writings of current Muslim theologians, form the bulk of our assessment of the Islamic worldview.

The primary Secular Humanist publishing house is Prometheus Books, located in Buffalo, New York. Their leaders include John Dewey, Roy Wood Sellars, Corliss Lamont, Paul Kurtz, Isaac Asimov, Sidney Hook, Carl Sagan, Julian Huxley, and Erich Fromm. The list of signatories of the *Humanist Manifestoes* includes scores of men and women who endorse the Secular Humanist position. Those chosen as "Humanist of the Year" also provide a rich source of Humanistic viewpoints, as do contributing authors in *The Humanist* and *Free Inquiry* magazines. Through strict adherence to these resources, we are able to describe Secular Humanism without distortion.

[20] Albert Ellis, "The Case Against Religiosity," from a section reprinted in "Testament of a Humanist," *Free Inquiry* (Spring 1987). 21.

Marxism-Leninism is even easier to document. None deny the major roles Karl Marx, Friedrich Engels, V.I. Lenin, and Joseph Stalin played in formulating the Marxist position. International Publishers, in New York City, prints and distributes hundreds of books from the Marxist-Leninist point of view. English translations of works published in the former Soviet Union are easily accessible, thanks to various distribution centers located in the United States.

The New Age worldview fills entire bookstores in America today. Cosmic Humanist leaders include Shirley MacLaine, David Spangler, Neale Donald Walsch, Joseph Campbell, John Denver, and Robert Muller. Many feminist leaders, including Marianne Williamson and Gloria Steinem, have begun to embrace the New Age movement. Many publishers woo New Age authors; the Bantam Doubleday Dell Publishing Group has a special New Age Books imprint.

There are a handful of individuals who stand out as the founders and advocates of Postmodernism. Among them are French philosophers Gilles Deleuze, Michel Foucault, and Jean Baudrillard; French literary critics Pierre Macherey, Roland Barthes, Jean-François Lyotard, and Jacques Derrida; French psychoanalyst Jaques Lacan; and American Professor of Comparative Literature, Richard Rorty. The works of these men undermined the foundations of modernism and laid the groundwork for the emergence of Postmodernism. For this reason, they are our main sources.

The Bible, of course, is the primary source for the Christian worldview. We contend that Christianity explains the facts of reality better than any other worldview because it relies upon divine inspiration, observation, reason, personal experience, history, and intuition. If the Bible is truly God's special revelation to humanity, as we believe it is, then the only completely accurate view of the world must be founded on Scripture.

The divine inspiration of Scripture explains not only its miraculous coherency but also the incredible power of the figure of Christ. Atheist historian W.E.H. Lecky admits that the character of Jesus "has been not only the highest pattern of virtue but the strongest incentive to its practice; and has exercised so deep an influence that it may be truly said that the simple record of three short years of active life has done more to regenerate and to soften mankind than all the disquisitions of philosophers, and all the exhortations of moralists."[21]

> Christianity explains the facts of reality better than any other worldview because it relies upon divine inspiration, observation, reason, personal experience, history, and intuition.

Jesus Christ is the cornerstone of the Christian worldview. When the Samaritan woman at the well spoke to Him about the coming Messiah, Jesus told her, "I who speak to you am He" (John 4:26). His claim was fundamental truth. The truths Jesus spoke about Himself, the Father, the human condition, and the only way to eternal salvation constitute the central precepts of the Christian worldview. Christ is the way, the truth, and the life (John 14:6).

Even Leonard Sweet, who considers himself "a Postmodern pilgrim," concedes the power and influence of the life and legacy of Jesus Christ: "In a world of Cheshire-cat absolutes, one absolute remains absolute. That absolute is Jesus: the Way, the Truth, and Life, and a cornucopia of 117 other scriptural names like The Bright Morning Star, The Dayspring from on High, The Sun of Righteousness, The Light of the World, The Lily of the Valley, The Rose of Sharon, The Bread of Life, The Door of the Sheepfold, The Good Shepherd, The Horn of Salvation, The Lamb of God, The Lion of Judah, The Root of David. . . ."[22]

---

[21] W.E.H. Lecky, *History of European Morals (from Augustus to Charlemagne),* 2 vols. (New York, NY: George Braziller, 1955), 2:8–9.

[22] Leonard Sweet, *Postmodern Pilgrims: First Century Passion For The 21ˢᵗ Century World* (Nashville, TN: Broadman & Holman, 2000), 155.

0.3.9 TAKING THE BIBLE LITERALLY?

When presenting the Christian worldview, then, we take the Bible at face value. Call it "literal" interpretation if you wish, but it is difficult to see how else the writers of the Old and New Testaments meant to be taken. Figures of speech, yes; typologies, yes; analogies, yes; but overall they wrote in simple, straightforward terms. When a writer says, "In the beginning God created the heavens and the earth," we understand him to say that there is a God, there was a beginning to creation, that heaven and earth exist, and that God made them.

It does not take a Ph.D. or a high IQ to comprehend the basic message of the Bible. God's special revelation is open to everyone. There is no room for an "intellectual elite" in Christianity; only one "high priest" need intercede between God and us: Jesus Christ. For this reason, each of us may "come boldly to the throne of grace" (Hebrews 4:14–16).

This text also relies on Christian men and women to describe the Christian worldview; their words, however, must always conform to the truth of Scripture. "If we receive the witness of men, the witness of God is greater; for this is the witness of God which He has testified of His Son." (1 John 5:9). The Christian worldview stands or falls on the accuracy of the Bible.

Perhaps after reading this text, you will decide that the Bible is not right, and that another worldview most conforms to the truth. If the facts support such a conclusion, personal integrity demands that you adopt that view. We have examined the facts and wrestled with the possibilities, and we have found that intellectual integrity demands adherence to Biblical Christianity.

Most social ills, problems of every kind, and sins are ultimately matters of the mind, soul, and spirit. Materialistic and pantheistic worldviews are unable to solve these ills; instead they contribute more problems. Only the worldview based on Jesus Christ—a worldview that promotes and sustains the proper attitudes toward family, church, and state—can effectively speak to these areas. However, we cannot force our conclusion on others. All we can do is encourage you to "taste and see that the LORD is good." We believe the Lord is good, His ways are good, and His teachings form a consistent, truthful, well-rounded Christian worldview.

0.3.10 APPROACHES TO THIS TEXT

Background reading suggestions: If you wish to build a foundation for thinking about worldviews before reading this text, we recommend the following: James Orr's *A Christian View of God and the World* (1989); James W. Sire's *The Universe Next Door* (1976); Francis Schaeffer's *A Christian Manifesto* (1981); Karl Marx and Frederick Engel's *Communist Manifesto* (1848); and the three *Humanist Manifestos* (1933, 1973, 2000). Read these texts with the notion in mind that *ideas have consequences*.

Following Albert Einstein's dictum that everything should be made as simple as possible but not simpler, this text attempts to paint the categorical positions of each worldview with broad and general strokes. We do not address every subtlety of each position. Rather we attempt to capture the kernel of each of the six worldviews' perspectives on each of the ten disciplines. As C.S. Lewis in *Mere Christianity* (1952) attempted to capture the essence of Christianity that all Christians could agree upon, so we attempt to capture the essence of mere Cosmic Humanism, Marxism, Secular Humanism, Postmodernism, Islam, and of course Christianity. For example, the heart of Christian theology will always be theism, just as the heart of Humanist ethics will always be relativism and the heart of Marxist biology will always be evolution. By examining the core of each worldview, we hope that this text will not become outdated.

We envision two possible approaches to this text. You may wish to proceed section by section, examining one discipline at a time and how each of the six worldviews approaches that discipline. Or you may wish to examine one worldview at a time, examining how it approaches each of the ten disciplines. We trust that the final outcome will be the same regardless of your approach—that you will gain helpful insight through the comparative analysis of the various ideas central to each worldview.

0.3.11 SHUT NO DOOR?

Sometimes we gain insight from examining the complaints of earlier decades in relation to current controversies. In 1925, evolutionists in America were bemoaning the fact that they were not allowed to teach their viewpoint in the public schools. John Scopes' attorney, Dudley Field Malone, arguing in favor of the teaching of evolution, said, "For God's sake, let the children have their minds kept open—close no doors to their knowledge; shut no door from them."[23] Today the situation is reversed. Teaching creationism in public schools is barred by law. Displaying the Ten Commandments and using the words "In God We Trust" are in jeopardy, and even Christian crosses on tombstones in federal and state cemeteries are threatened. Christianity rarely receives a fair hearing in the public square, Jesus Christ is ridiculed, and His name is profaned.

New challenges to the Biblical Christian worldview arise each day. How can you determine truth when certain worldviews cannot be discussed in public classrooms? How can you develop a consistent worldview without comparing and contrasting it with other worldviews? We believe that you will improve your overall conceptual skills by learning to compare and contrast the merits of different worldviews. Perhaps some feel that Christians should be shielded from non-Christian views. We disagree. Knowing and understanding what others believe is essential preparation for facing the world, especially the world of the university. Jesus sent His followers out as sheep among wolves (Matthew 10:16). We believe that as sheep, you should be prepared!

0.3.12 FACING THE CHALLENGE

The Apostle Paul faced the religious humanists of his day, and Christians must be alert and faithful in facing the humanists of our day—whether they be Secular or Cosmic Humanists, Postmodernists, or Marxists. Preparation to do so requires hard work!

Although this study does require work, the result can be that you understand the ideas that make the world turn as well as the differences among them: theism, atheism, pluralism, agnosticism, supernaturalism, teleology, naturalism, materialism, dialectics, relativism, deconstruction, spontaneous generation, evolution, creationism, biblical morality, class morality, new morality, freedom, totalitarianism, private property, socialism, capitalism, Eurocentrism, heterocentrism, globalism, mind, soul, spirit, self-actualization, sin, law, etc. The invaluable reward of struggling with complex and conflicting ideas is this: "an all-encompassing belief system, grander than the individual and larger than the family, to explain disparate facts and to furnish meaning in life."[24]

We believe that the Christian worldview is the only proper "all-encompassing belief system" and that it is larger than both the individual and the family, but it destroys neither. Christianity

---

[23] W.R. Bird, *The Origin of Species Revisited: The Theories of Evolution and of Abrupt Appearance*, 2 vols. (Nashville, TN: Thomas Nelson, 1991), 2:367.

[24] Ken Adelman, "Beyond Ideology," *The Washington Times* (December 25, 1989): D4.

not only gives your life meaning, it also best fits the facts of history, science, reason, and the experience of the real world—a world described by the Bible, Dante, Shakespeare, Milton, and other literary giants.

Humanist Will Durant says, "The greatest question of our time is not communism versus individualism, not Europe versus America, not even the East versus the West—it is whether man can live without God."[25] The goal of this resource is to demonstrate a theistic worldview so comprehensive that it renders all questions of atheism obsolete. Christianity is so

> Christianity not only gives your life meaning, it also best fits the facts of history, science, reason, and the experience of the real world.

consistent and faithful to the truth that we should ask instead why we would *want* to live without God. Indeed, loving God and our fellow human beings summarizes the Christian worldview, bringing to mind the confession of Secular Humanist Bertrand Russell who said that what the world needs is more Christian love.

We pray that this resource will help you recognize the value, truthfulness, and superiority of the Christian worldview, to grow in the grace and knowledge of your Lord and Savior Jesus Christ, and to share His love with those in the world who need it so badly.

> And can it be that I should gain
> An interest in the Savior's blood?
> Died He for me, who caused His pain?
> For me, who Him to death pursued?
> Amazing love! How can it be
> That Thou my God shouldst die for me?
> — Charles Wesley

[25] Quoted in Charles Colson, *Kingdoms in Conflict* (Grand Rapids, MI: Zondervan, 1987), 225.

Theology

Christianity

Theism, the belief that God is, and atheism, the belief
that God is not, are not simply two beliefs . . . .
They are two fundamental ways of seeing the whole of
existence. The one, theism, sees existence as ultimately
meaningful, as having a meaning beyond itself; the other
sees existence as having no meaning beyond itself.[1]

— STEPHEN D. SCHWARZ

1.1.1 INTRODUCTION

The Christian worldview affirms **theism**, the belief in the existence of a supernatural God. Christian theism rests primarily on two solid foundations: special revelation (the Bible) and general revelation (the created order). While the Bible reveals the character and personality of God page after page, the "whole workmanship

> **THEISM:** The belief in a supernatural God

of the universe," according to John Calvin, reveals and discloses God day after day. The Psalmist says, "The heavens declare the glory of God" (Psalm 19).

James Orr explains that the theistic position is established not by any single clue or evidence, but by "the concurrent forces of many, starting from different and independent standpoints."[2] Christians see evidences of God everywhere. It is the Christian position that history, theology,

---

[1] Roy Abraham Varghese, *The Intellectuals Speak Out About God* (Dallas, TX: Lewis and Stanley, 1984), 98.
[2] James Orr, *The Christian View of God and the World* (Edinburgh, Scotland: Andrew Elliot, 1897), 111.

philosophy, science, mathematics, logic, and personal experience all point to the existence of a Creator and Redeemer.

1.1.2 SPECIAL REVELATION

Christian theists believe that God has revealed Himself to people in a general way through creation and in a special (personal) way evidenced by His divine words and acts contained in the Bible and especially in the person of Jesus Christ. Millard Erickson defines the two forms of revelation this way: "On the one hand, **general revelation** is God's communication of Himself to all persons, at all times, and in all places. **Special revelation** on the other hand, involves God's particular communications and manifestations which are available now only by consultation of certain sacred writings."[3]

> **GENERAL REVELATION:** God's communication—through nature and conscience—regarding His existence
>
> **SPECIAL REVELATION:** God's more specific communication—through the Bible and Jesus Christ—about salvation and His nature

General revelation has been viewed consistently throughout church history by a variety of Christian theists as a necessary but insufficient means for providing knowledge about the Creator and His character. It is better theology and philosophy to begin with the God of the Bible to explain the universe than to begin with the universe to explain God.

According to the Christian view, the destiny of created humanity involves both salvation and judgment. It is not general revelation but special revelation (the Bible) that answers such questions as *How can I be saved? From what must I be saved? Why will judgment occur?* Special revelation, then, is "special" because it is the key that opens the door to both heaven and earth.

One of the most basic tenets of Christian belief is the divine inspiration of the Bible. When you accept Scripture as the Word of God, the teachings and events described in the Bible become the most important basis for understanding all reality. Without faith that the Bible is God's Word, you are left adrift—forced to trust your own (unfounded) thought processes as the ultimate criteria for discerning truth. No one can deny the Bible's divine inspiration and still claim to be a Biblical Christian for the simple reason that Scripture proclaims itself to be God-breathed (2 Timothy 3:16–17). If you believe the Bible to be a true and accurate document, then you must accept its claim to be divinely inspired.

The evidence for the Christian's belief in the divine inspiration of the Bible is convincing. For example, the unity of teaching in the Bible is startling in light of the fact that its books were authored by different men in very different circumstances over many centuries. Further, the astounding ability of the Bible to metamorphose the lives of individuals (for the better) who accept its authority strengthens its claim to be special revelation from God. The degree of moral truth contained in the Bible also supports its divine inspiration. All these arguments support the belief that the Bible is God's Word; however, the most convincing witness for divine inspiration is the Bible itself. Those hesitant to accept Scripture as God's special revelation are most often convinced by a thorough, open-minded study of the Bible.

In studying the Bible, the reader meets God's most direct form of special revelation: the person of Jesus Christ. "In Jesus of Nazareth," writes Carl F.H. Henry, "the divine source of revelation and the divine content of that revelation converge and coincide."[4] Christ's teachings, actions, and most significantly, His resurrection, as revealed in the Bible, provide the cornerstone for special revelation and a solid foundation for Christian theism.

---

[3] Millard J. Erickson, *Christian Theology*, 3 vols. (Grand Rapids, MI: Baker Book House, 1983), 1:153.

[4] Carl F.H. Henry, *God, Revelation and Authority*, 6 vols. (Waco, TX: Word Books, 1976ff), 2:11.

The purpose of divine revelation lies in its communication to the Christian of the significance of Christ's teachings and actions. The third member of the Trinity, the Holy Spirit, plays an important role in this dialogue. Henry explains: "Scripture itself is given so that the Holy Spirit may etch God's Word upon the hearts of his followers in ongoing sanctification that anticipates the believer's final, unerring conformity to the image of Jesus Christ, God's incarnate Word."[5] This is the ultimate reason God chose to reveal Himself and His plan for us in the Bible.

> Christ's teachings and actions as revealed in the Bible provide the cornerstone for special revelation and a solid foundation for Christian theism.

For this reason, the Christian's reliance on the Bible should be profound and constantly renewed—the Christian doesn't read the Bible once and set it aside; rather, we study it as the living Word of God and seek constantly to conform ourselves to its teachings. We spend our lives studying to understand the powerful message of the Bible.

1.1.3 DESIGN AND GENERAL REVELATION

Special revelation, then, is the linchpin of Christianity, while general revelation serves as a prod that encourages us to recognize the ultimate truths set down in Scripture and embodied in Jesus Christ.

Although God's revelation through nature, in and of itself, fails to bring us to a saving knowledge of God, it is capable of bringing us to a general knowledge of God. A great majority of intellectuals agree that the concepts of purpose and design, for example, have validity in regard to the question of the existence of God.

Anglican clergyman William Paley argued in *Natural Theology* (a book about which Charles Darwin admitted, "I do not think I hardly ever admired a book more . . ."[6]) that a person chancing upon a watch in the wilderness could not conclude that the watch had simply always existed; rather, the obvious design of the watch—not only its internal makeup but also the fact that it clearly exists for a purpose—would necessarily imply the existence of its designer. Paley went on to substitute the universe for the watch and contended that a mechanism so obviously designed as the universe necessitated the existence of a grand Designer.[7] This is most often referred to as the **argument from design** and is an excellent example of the way in which the created order reveals the existence of God.

The universe forces its sense of design (and thus a Designer) on all people who are open to such a possibility. Antony Flew, the legendary British philosopher and champion of atheism, now in his eighties, describes his personal odyssey from atheism to theism and the central place the design argument had in his journey. Flew currently believes ". . . the most impressive arguments for God's existence are those that are supported by recent scientific discoveries." He came to this conclusion because "the findings of more than fifty years of DNA research have provided materials for a new and enormously powerful argument to design."[8]

> ARGUMENT FROM DESIGN: Argument that purports that if something exists that is designed then it has a designer

Many discover God through the general revelation of a structured universe; many more

---

[5] Ibid., 15.

[6] Charles Darwin, *Autobiography* (New York, NY: Dover Publishing, 1958), 59.

[7] See Geoffrey Simmons, *What Darwin Didn't Know* (Eugene, OR: Harvest House, 2004) for an up to date argument for creation from design.

[8] Taken from an interview at http://www.biola.edu/antonyflew/.

C.E.M. Joad

encounter God in the general revelation of the purposeful nature of reality. **C.E.M. Joad**, who was an atheist for much of his professional career, shortly before his death wrote a book entitled *The Recovery of Belief*. This book traces his gradual advance toward God and Jesus Christ. Joad was largely convinced by his observation of human nature—his realization that a moral law exists, and that we often flaunt that law.

C.S. Lewis presents still another twist on the argument for the general revelation of God's existence. Suppose there were no intelligence behind the universe, says Lewis. In that case nobody designed my brain for the purpose of thinking. Thought is merely the by-product of some atoms within my skull. "But if so, how can I trust my own thinking to be true?" asks Lewis. "But if I can't trust my own thinking, of course, I can't trust the arguments leading to atheism, and therefore have no reason to be an atheist, or anything else. Unless I believe in God, I can't believe in thought; so I can never use thought to disbelieve in God."[9]

The evidence points to what Christians believe—that a personal God has revealed Himself through a created world, and that He has a plan and ultimate destiny for that world.

1.1.4 WHAT DOES REVELATION TELL US ABOUT GOD?

The Christian is concerned not only with the existence of God in general, but also with the relationship that exists between God and us, and particularly with the redemption of all people. While Humanists declare in the *Humanist Manifesto II* that no God can save us—"we must save ourselves"—Christian theism echoes Thomas, who referred to Jesus as "My Lord and My God" (John 20:28), and Peter, who said to Jesus, "You alone have the words of eternal life" (John 6:68). God, as revealed throughout the Bible and especially in the person of Christ, is clearly knowable and desires to be known.

To say that God is knowable is also to say that God "relates" or has personality—that He is "personal." God's self-awareness, His emotions, and His self-determining will make up the core of His divine personality. The Bible is emphatic in describing God as a person aware of Himself. In Isaiah 44:6, God says, "I am the first and I am the last, and there is no God besides me." In Exodus 3:14, God says to Moses, "I Am Who I Am."

Besides possessing a sense of self-awareness, the God of the Bible (like people) has sensibilities. At times God is portrayed as being sorrowful (Genesis 6:6), angry (Deuteronomy 1:37), compassionate (Psalm 111:4), jealous (Exodus 20:5), and able to show satisfaction (Genesis 1:4). Theologians do not feel that such scriptures suggest that God is limited, but rather that God is willing to reveal Himself in an anthropomorphic, personal way to us.

1.1.5 CHARACTERISTICS OF THE PERSONAL GOD

Besides believing that God is a personal God and has communicated His nature to us, Christians believe that God is self-determining—that is, sovereign in regard to His will. God's self-determination is described in Daniel 4:35: "And all the inhabitants of the earth are

---

[9] C.S. Lewis, *Broadcast Talks* (London, UK: G. Bles, 1944), 37–8.

accounted as nothing, but He does according to His will in the host of heaven and among the inhabitants of the earth; and no one can ward off His hand or say to Him, 'What hast Thou done?'"

In addition to being self-determining, the God of the Bible is moral. Proverbs 15:3 warns us that God distinguishes between good and evil, and that He is concerned with our morality. (See also Proverbs 5:21.) God's uncompromisingly moral character is one of the most crucial aspects of His being. A true understanding of God's absolute goodness leads us unerringly to the conclusion that each of us has an acute need for a Redeemer.

> **TRINITARIAN THEISM:** The belief in one God who exists as three separate persons—Father, Son, and Spirit

Long-suffering patience and faithfulness are also personality traits of God. God's willingness to delay His judgment upon the Israelites when they worshipped the golden calf (Exodus 32:11–14) and His faithful promise to save the believer from eternal judgment (John 10:28) are prime examples of His patience and faithfulness.

Perhaps the most astounding characteristic of God's personality is that He is triune. The Christian believes that God is three co-existent, co-eternal persons in one, who are equal in purpose and in essence, but who differ in function, a doctrine known as **trinitarian theism**.

The God of the Christian is also a God of power, evidenced by His works in creation and providence. Hebrews 1:10 declares, "In the beginning, O Lord, you laid the foundations of the earth, and the heavens are the works of your hands." Christian theology asserts that God is the source of all things and that He created the cosmos out of His own mind, according to His plan. "Christianity," says C.S. Lewis, "thinks God made the world—that space and time, heat and cold, and all the colors and tastes, and all the animals and vegetables, are things that God 'made up out of his head' as a man makes up a story. But it also thinks that a great many things have gone wrong with the world that God made and that God insists, and insists very loudly, on our putting them right again."[10]

> Each created thing has an appointed destiny God has a plan for His world, and nothing takes Him by surprise.

God also demonstrates His power by moving His world to its purposeful end. Each created thing has an appointed destiny—God has a plan for His world, and nothing takes Him by surprise. The Bible is emphatic on this point. Romans 9:25–26 says, "I will call those who were not my people, My people, and her who was not beloved, beloved. And it shall be that in the place where it was said to them 'you are not my people,' there they shall be called sons of the living God." Scripture makes it clear that God manifests His power by a sovereign and holy plan—a plan that generally collides with our plans, but a sovereign plan that includes human choice and human responsibility.[11]

"Remember this, fix it in mind, take it to heart, you rebels [transgressors]. Remember the former things, those of long ago; I am God, and there is no other; I am God, and there is none like me. I make known the end from the beginning, from ancient times, what is still to come. I say: My purpose will stand, and I will do all that I please. From the east I summon a bird of prey; from a far-off land, a man to fulfill my purpose. What I have said, that will I bring about; what I have planned, that will I do" (Isaiah 46: 8–11).

---

[10] C.S. Lewis, *Mere Christianity* (New York, NY: Macmillan Publishing, 1974), 45.

[11] Norman L. Geisler, *Systematic Theology*, 4 vols. (Minneapolis, MN: Bethany House, 2003), 2:543, 574.

1.1.6 GOD AS JUDGE

The judgment of God is not a popular subject—even among Christians. A great majority of people abhor the thought that the "God of love" could also be the "God of wrath." One cannot read the Bible, however, without encountering the judgment of God.[12]

The holiness of God necessitates the judgment of God. Christian theists agree that God must be a judge because His holy nature is antithetical to sin. Such acts in the Bible as the great flood (Genesis 6:17–7:24), the destruction of Sodom and Gomorrah (Genesis 19), the deaths of Nadab and Abihu (Leviticus 10:1–7), the fall of the Canaanites (Leviticus 18–20), and indeed the fall of Israel (2 Kings 17) and Judah (2 Chronicles 36) are all demonstrations of God's judgment as motivated by His holy nature.

Christianity teaches that God is fair and always right, because His nature is perfect. God is not a giant bully or a cosmic killjoy brooding in the heavens, waiting for every opportunity to spoil our fun. The Bible teaches that God is truly interested in good winning over evil, and in holiness being the victor over moral depravity. In short, God is the judge of people because all people are sinners. The Bible is clear in communicating that God does not take pleasure in the judgment of the wicked (Ezekiel 33:11), but the wicked must be judged because God is holy (Jude 15).

1.1.7 GOD AS REDEEMER

Only one thing can protect us from God's justice on the Day of Judgment: God's mercy. In His mercy, God has provided an advocate for every individual—an advocate so righteous that He washes away the sin that should condemn us. God as the Redeemer, in the person of Christ, saves humanity from His wrath.

The central theme of redemption is the love of God. John 3:16 tells us, "God so loved the world, that He gave His only begotten Son, that whoever believes in Him should not perish, but have eternal life." Using John 3:16 as a text for portraying God's love, theologian Floyd Barackman points out the following characteristics of this love:

- God's love is universal. God loves every nation, tribe, race, class, and sex (male/female) equally. There were no social prejudices when God offered His Son. Christ died for the rich and for the poor; for the free and for the enslaved; for the old and for the young; for the beautiful and for the ugly.
- God's love is gracious. God loves sinners even when they hate Him and are undeserving of His love. Romans 5:8 clearly outlines the nature of God's love: "But God demonstrates His own love toward us, in that while we were yet sinners, Christ died for us." How could God love the sinner? This question is answered by the Christian doctrine of grace. Christianity declares that God's love and mercy are so awesome that He can love the sinner while hating the sin. He expects His children to do likewise (Jude 22, 23).
- God's love is sacrificial. God did not send His only Son to earth just to be a good example or simply to be a teacher, but to be a perfect and atoning sacrifice for humanity's sin. Christ's substitutionary death was sacrificial and closely resembles the Old Testament concept of atonement. The main difference between the Old Testament concept of atonement and the New Testament concept is that atonement in the Old Testament was temporary, whereas in the New Testament Christ atoned for sins once and for all (I

[12] Ibid., 3:398.

* http://www.pluggedinonline.com/movies/movies/a0002447.cfm

John 2:2). Through the death of Christ, God has reconciled the world to Himself, and offered a way for His wrath to be appeased (Colossians 1:20)—humanity now must be reconciled to God through faith in Christ (2 Corinthians 5:20).

- God's love is beneficial. For all those who receive Christ (John 1:12), for all those who are born from above (John 3:3), for all those who believe (John 3:16), there await certain eternal benefits given by God. Scripture declares that through God's grace, the believer will not be condemned (Romans 3:24) and will not be captive to sin (Romans 6:11). Further, the believer is a new creation (2 Corinthians 5:17) who has been declared righteous (2 Corinthians 5:21), redeemed (1 Peter 1:18), forgiven (Ephesians 1:7), and the recipient of the gift of eternal life (John 3:16).

1.18 CONCLUSION

Christian theology is Christ-centered. The God who "so loved the world that He gave His only Son" has allowed for a personal relationship between Himself and fallen humanity. Theoretical atheistic possibilities belittle the God who has revealed Himself propositionally through His creation and His word and has sacrificed His incarnate and holy Son. If this story is true, then anyone who lives in unbelief should be fearful, for he or she sits under the judgment of God until recognizing and experiencing the ever-faithful promise of Jesus: "Behold, I stand at the door and knock; if anyone hears My voice and opens the door, I will come in to him, and will dine with him, and he with Me" (Revelation 3:20).

The Pop Culture Connection

The Lion, The Witch, and the Wardrobe (a 2006 film based C.S. Lewis' classic work)—In this film Aslan serves as a Christ figure and allegory for Christ's suffering, death, and resurrection—Aslan serves the Emperor Beyond the Sea (God the Father) and yet is also creator of Narnia (compare Colossians 1:16). Even though Aslan clearly has power over the White Witch, he chooses to work through human beings to accomplish his will to free Narnia. And he offers his own innocent blood to pay for Edmund's sin (Romans 5:8).*

Theology

Islam

La ilaha illa Allah, Muhammadu Rasool Allah. [There is no God but God and Muhammad is the Messenger of God.]

THE ESSENTIAL MUSLIM PROFESSION OF FAITH

1.2.1 INTRODUCTION

There are several sources for the study of Islam. Of foremost importance is the Qur'an itself. The Qur'an, (from the verb qara'a "to read" or "to recite"), is the holy book of Islam. Muslims believe that the Qur'an is the literal word of God (Arabic Allah) and the culmination of God's revelation to mankind as revealed to Muhammad, the final prophet of humanity, over a period of twenty-three years through the angel Jibril. In this text we use primarily the translation of A. Yusuf Ali.[1] While it is an older translation (sounding much like the King James Version of the Bible), it is well respected and widely known.

Ranking second to the Qur'an are the Hadith. The Hadith record the teachings, rulings, and actions of Muhammad as recounted by his early associates. Muslims believe that the Hadith are inspired by God, and thus are to be obeyed. Unlike the Qur'an, the Hadith enjoy a diversity of sources and divergence of readings. It is not uncommon to find a variety of forms of particular sayings or recollections of Muhammad's actions. Different Muslim factions have different collections or highlight different actions or sayings recorded in the Hadith.

---

[1] Abdullah Yusuf Ali, *The Holy Qur'an: Text, Translation, and Commentary* (Washington, DC: The American International Printing Company, 1946). In some quotations from Ali's translation, we have taken the liberty of smoothing out the text, removing unnecessary punctuation and poetic capitalization of letters.

ISLAMIC HOLY BOOKS

QUR'AN: Muslims believe that the Qur'an is the literal word of God (Arabic Allah) and the culmination of God's revelation to mankind as revealed to Muhammad (the final prophet of humanity) over a period of twenty-three years through the angel Jibril

HADITH: The traditions of the teachings, rulings, and actions of Muhammad and his early and chief companions. From these traditions are derived the Sunna, which are the actions of Muhammad that are viewed as exemplary

In addition to the Qur'an and the Hadith, we also turn to the works of noted scholars of Islam, whether Muslim or non-Muslim, as well as works popularly promoted by Islamic organizations. Throughout our presentation of Islam, we strive to be fair to the central features of the worldview, as well as to the diversity found among Muslims.

1.2.2 CENTRAL BELIEFS

There are several central beliefs of Islam. First, Muslims believe in **Unitarian theism**. They reject the Christian doctrine of the Trinity and deny the deity of Jesus Christ. The one unforgivable sin is *shirk*, associating partners with God (i.e., polytheism). God is viewed as sovereign over humans and history, which has led to a discussion of the relationship between God's sovereignty and human responsibility that parallels the same discussion among Christians.

Muslims also affirm the existence of angels and *jinn*, the latter being mischievous spirits made from fire. The angels exist in a hierarchy, with Gabriel at the top. Some believe that two angels attend each person, one recording good deeds and the other recording bad deeds.

The Qur'an teaches that God has sent prophets to every nation under heaven, though the final prophet is Muhammad. Also, while God gave special books to Moses, David, Jesus, and Muhammad, only the one given to Muhammad, the Qur'an, has been preserved without error, and is thus the ultimate authoritative scripture.

UNITARIAN THEISM: The belief in one God in one person (i.e. no trinity)

Capping off the central beliefs of Islam is the Day of Judgment, a day when every human being will face a weighing of deeds, both good and evil. Only if the weight of one's good deeds surpasses that of one's bad deeds can each person hope to enter into Paradise rather than descending into Hell.

1.2.3 PRACTICE

Building upon the central beliefs of Islam (meaning "submission"), a devout Muslim ("one who submits") is expected to practice the following five (or six) "pillars" of their religion:

1. The first pillar of Islam is the confession of faith: *There is no God but Allah and Muhammad is his prophet*. If a person pronounces this confession with sincerity of mind and heart, then he or she is a Muslim.
2. The second pillar is prayer. Muslims are expected to engage in prayer five times a day, facing Mecca. On Friday, Muslim men (and, in some cases, women) are expected to meet at a mosque to engage in noon prayer.
3. The third pillar is fasting during Ramadan. This involves refraining from food, smoking, and sexual relations during daylight hours, though these may be enjoyed after sundown.
4. The fourth pillar is almsgiving. Muslims are expected to give 2.5 percent of their annual capital to the poor, either directly or through Muslim charitable organizations.

5. The fifth pillar is pilgrimage. All Muslims are expected to make a pilgrimage to Mecca at least once in their lifetime, if their finances and health permit.

6. Some would add a sixth pillar, that of *jihad*, which has two facets. First, it is the battle against temptation and sin for the sake of self-control. Second, it is the battle against any and all who oppose Islam.[2]

1.2.4 REVELATION

Christians and Muslims believe that God exists, that He has revealed His will through prophets, and that all humans are accountable to Him. But the similarities largely cease here, for while Muslims affirm that God has revealed His will through prophets and enclosed that revelation in scripture, they deny that the Bible is a trustworthy source of that revelation, and instead affirm other sources of revelation.

Muslims believe that God graciously sent messengers to every nation to teach them submission to God and to warn them against false religious teachings and practices (Qur'an 16:36; 35:24). Moses and Jesus are considered prophets of Islam, as well as Ishmael, Isaac, and Jacob (3:67; 61:6; 2:136). Muslims are expected to honor these prophets and their respective books (4:136). The religions that predated Muhammad are understood as having been originally Islamic and their prophets Muslims (15:10).

Muhammad is seen as the successor of the prophets of old (Qur'an 61:6), their books containing prophecies about him (7:157). Many Muslims even believe the Bible contains prophecies regarding Muhammad, most significantly Deuteronomy 18:15–18 and John 14:16. These prophets' missions were geographically and temporally limited, while Muhammad is considered to be *the one prophet for all humankind* (7:158; 34:28), and the last of the prophets (33:40). As a well-known Hadith illustrates: "Allah's Apostle said, 'My similitude in comparison with the other prophets before me, is that of a man who has built a house nicely and beautifully, except for a place of one brick in a corner. The people go about it and wonder at its beauty, but say: "Would that this brick be put in its place!" So I am that brick, and I am the last of the Prophets.'"[3]

Not only do Muslims ascribe superlative status to Muhammad, they ascribe such status to the Qur'an as well. The Qur'an is the incomparable, infallible, and final revelation from God (Qur'an 17:88–89), confirming all previous revelations (10:37; 46:12). Unlike the previous revelations, such as the Bible—deemed to be textually corrupted and confused by human interpretations—the Qur'an is inscribed on a tablet in heaven (85:21–22) and is kept incorruptible by God: "We have, without doubt, sent down the Message [the Qur'an]; and We will assuredly guard it (from corruption)" (15:9).

The other primary source for Islamic theology today is the Hadith. The Hadith are traditions of the teachings, rulings, and actions of Muhammad and his early and chief companions. From these traditions are derived the Sunna, which are the actions of Muhammad that are viewed as

---

[2] The notion of *opposition* varies among Muslims. Some attempt to limit it to actual aggression, primarily of a military variety, and thus view *jihad* as exclusively defensive in posture. The history of Islam relegates this perspective to a minority view—in its early years, Islam spread through conquest. Many contemporary Muslims understand "defense" as the response needed against anything or anyone who would seek to inhibit Islam from becoming a global civilization. Additionally, since Muslims believe that the world originally was Islamic, and that every person is born a Muslim, they can easily move toward holding any and all non-Muslims as inherently in opposition to Islam.

[3] Sahih al-Bukhari, Volume 4, Book 56, Hadith 735. http://www.usc.edu/dept/MSA/fundamentals/ hadithsunnah/ bukhari/056.sbt.html#004.056.735 (accessed August 14, 2004).

exemplary.[4] Muslims believe these two sources are inspired and authoritative. They provide the two lenses through which Muslims see all of reality.

Khurshid Ahmad describes the Qur'an and the Hadith as follows: ". . . [T]he teachings of Islam have been preserved in their original form and God's Guidance is available without adulteration of any kind. The Qur'an is the revealed book of God which has been in existence for the last fourteen hundred years and the Word of God is available in its original form. Detailed accounts of the life of the Prophet of Islam and his teachings are available in their pristine purity. There has not been an iota of change in this unique historic record. The sayings and the entire record of the life of the Holy Prophet have been handed down to us with unprecedented precision and authenticity in the works of the *Hadith* . . ."[5]

1.2.5 MONOTHEISM

Muslims believe that God exists, that He created the world, and that all humans will one day give an account before Him at the judgment. On these basics (though not in all details), the three monotheistic religions of the world—Judaism, Christianity and Islam—agree. The 112th Sura (chapter) of the Qur'an, though only four verses long, summarizes the Islamic understanding of the unity and nature of God: "In the name of God, the Most Gracious, Most Merciful. Say: He is God, the One and Only; God, the Eternal, Absolute; He begetteth not, nor is He begotten; and there is none like unto Him."[6]

Though God has ninety-nine names in the Qur'an (see 59:22–24 for some examples), every Muslim affirms **monotheism**. It is encased in their fundamental creed: "There is no God but God and Muhammad is his prophet."

Muslims affirm that God created the universe. The Qur'an often appeals to the grandeur and order of the world as evidence of God's existence and His creative intelligence, but the

MONOTHEISM: The belief in one God

Qur'an itself is held as the most important proof of God's existence. Sura 2:22–23 not only attributes the multiplicity of good things throughout creation to God's creative power, but challenges anyone who doubts the Qur'an to produce something comparable. "Who has made the earth your couch, and the heavens your canopy; and sent down rain from the heavens; and brought forth therewith fruits for your sustenance; then set not up rivals unto God when ye know (the truth). And if ye are in doubt as to what We have revealed from time to time to Our servant [Muhammad], then produce a Sura like thereunto; and call your witnesses or helpers (if there are any) besides God, if your (doubts) are true."

Muslims firmly believe that the Qur'an is the best and most beautiful book on earth. There is no equal, and nothing surpasses it in content or quality.[7]

Muslims believe that theirs is the original faith, the faith of Adam, Noah, Abraham, Moses, David, John the Baptist, and Jesus. They also believe that Christians have distorted and denied

---

[4] Faslur Rahman, *Islam*, 2nd ed. (Chicago, IL: University of Chicago Press, 1979): "The difference between the two is that whereas a Hadith as such is a mere report . . . the Sunna is the very same report when it acquires a normative quality and becomes a practical principle for the Muslim" (45); "this authority of Muhammad refers to the verbal and performative behavior of the Prophet outside the Qur'an" (50); and "to his Companions his life was a religious paradigm and as such normative" (52).

[5] Khurshid Ahmad, ed., *Islam: Its Meaning and Message*, 3rd ed. (Leicester, UK: The Islamic Foundation, 1999), 43.

[6] We have updated punctuation and decreased the frequency of capital letters. Different versions of the Qur'an vary not only in translation but also in versification. Thus the chapters and verses we use, from Ali's translation, may differ somewhat from other versions.

[7] These assertions are addressed in some detail in Norman L. Geisler and Abdul Saleeb's book, *Answering Islam: The Crescent in Light of the Cross*, rev. ed. (Grand Rapids, MI: Baker Book House, 2002). See chapter 9, "An Evaluation of the Qur'an," 183–210.

that original faith, especially in relation to the doctrine of the Trinity. The Qur'an denounces the Trinity in no uncertain terms:

> O People of the Book! Commit no excesses in your religion; nor say of God aught but the truth. Christ Jesus the son of Mary was (no more than) an Apostle of God, and His Word, which He bestowed on Mary, and a Spirit proceeding from Him; so believe in God and His apostles. Say not "Trinity"; desist: for God is One God: Glory be to Him: (far Exalted is He) above having a son. To Him belong all things in the heavens and on earth. And enough is God as a Disposer of affairs. (4:171)

> They do blaspheme who say, "God is Christ the son of Mary." But said Christ, "O Children of Israel! Worship God, my Lord and your Lord." Whoever joins other gods with God, God will forbid him the Garden, and the Fire will be his abode. There will for the wrong-doers be no one to help. They do blaspheme who say "God is one of three in a Trinity," for there is no god except One God. If they desist not from their word (of blasphemy), verily a grievous penalty will befall the blasphemers among them. (5:75–76)

> And behold! God will say, "O Jesus the son of Mary! Didst thou say unto men, 'Worship me and my mother as gods in derogation of God'?" He will say, "Glory to Thee! Never could I say what I had no right (to say). Had I said such a thing, Thou wouldst indeed have known it. Thou knowest what is in my heart, though I know not what is in Thine, for Thou knowest in full all that is hidden. (5:119)

Muslims also deny that Jesus was crucified. Sura 4 in the Qur'an (vv. 157–158) says the following: "They that said (in boast), "We killed Christ Jesus the son of Mary, the Apostle of God"; but they killed him not, nor crucified him, but so it was made to appear to them, and those who differ therein are full of doubts, with no (certain) knowledge, but only conjecture to follow, for a surety they killed him not: nay, God raised him up unto Himself; and God is Exalted in Power, Wise . . ."

1.2.6 ISLAM AND OTHER RELIGIONS

Because Muhammad was the final prophet and the Qur'an God's final revelation, Muslims reject all claims to new divine revelation or inspired prophets. Thus they are highly critical of groups branching off of Islam, such as the Baha'i,[8] the Ahmadiyyah,[9] and the Nation of Islam (i.e., "Black Muslims"),[10] which assert prophetic continuation past Muhammad.

Even though there was a time when Muslims embraced adherents of other monotheistic faiths (such as Jews and Christians), this came to an end with the finished work of Muhammad and the full revelation of the Qur'an. Now only Muslims are accepted by God: "If anyone desires a religion other than Islam (submission to God), never will it be accepted of him; and in the Hereafter he will be in the ranks of those who have lost (all spiritual good)" (3:85).[11]

---

[8] See www.bahai.org and www.us.bahai.org. For Christian interactions with the Baha'i faith, see, Francis J. Beckwith, *Baha'i* (Minneapolis, MN: Bethany House, 1985) and William M. Miller, *The Baha'i Faith: Its History and Teachings* (South Pasadena, CA: William Carey Library Publications, 1984).

[9] See John Gilchrist, "A Study of the Ahmadiyyah Movement," found at http://www.answering-islam.org/Gilchrist/Vol1/9c.html

[10] See C. Eric Lincoln, *The Black Muslims in America*, 3rd ed. (Grand Rapids, MI: Eerdmans, 1994) and Steven Tsoulkas, *The Nation of Islam: Understanding the 'Black Muslims'* (Phillipsburg, NJ: Presbyterian and Reformed, 2001).

[11] See Jane Dammen McAuliffe, *Qur'anic Christians: An Analysis of Classical and Modern Exegesis* (Cambridge, UK: Cambridge University Press, 1991).

1.2.7 CRITIQUE OF ISLAMIC THEOLOGY

Since the tragic events of September 11, 2001, it has become increasingly common to hear that "Christians, Jews, and Muslims worship the same God," even from government leaders. But to claim that these three monotheistic faiths worship the same God is misleading. For example, even if they worship the same God, does each religion teach the same basic things about that God? In point of fact, careful examination uncovers significant theological differences.

One major difference between Muslim and Christian theology is found in their respective views on the nature of God. While we affirm that only one God exists (monotheism), we also affirm that this one God has revealed Himself as triune: Father, Son, and Holy Spirit. Muslims deny the doctrine of the Trinity, viewing it as the greatest of sins (Jews also reject the Trinity).[12] Unfortunately, many Muslims are quite confused about the doctrine of the Trinity. This is probably due to how the Qur'an misrepresents it. A careful reading of Sura 5:119 (cited above) reveals how the Qur'an defines the Trinity as essentially *polytheistic*, that is, affirming the existence of more than one true God.

Even though there was a time when Muslims embraced adherents of other monotheistic faiths (such as Jews and Christians), this came to an end with the finished work of Muhammad and the full revelation of the Qur'an.

Because these misrepresentations are encased in the Qur'an, and Muslims attribute absolute authority to the Qur'an, despite our appeals to Scripture[13] and our explanations of the doctrine, it is extremely difficult to persuade Muslims that Christianity is unwaveringly and unqualifiedly *monotheistic*.

Regarding Jesus' death on a cross, Muslims find repugnant the idea that God would allow one of His holy prophets to die such an ignominious death. Yet both the Bible (e.g., 2 Chronicles 36:16; Matthew 5:12; 23:31; Acts 7:52) and the Qur'an (4:155) testify that the prophets often faced persecution and terrible deaths. In addition, the Bible presents the crucifixion not as an illustration of the weakness of God or Christ, but rather as an expression of His power (1 Corinthians 1:18). Indeed, it was Jesus' desire to lay down His life (John 10:14–18) in fulfillment of God's promises (Matthew 26:53–54; Isaiah 53). Without this submission of His will, no one *could* have killed Him (Matthew 26:54; John 10:18). Jesus' resurrection from the dead illustrates that He is the Son of God (Romans 1:4) and has power over death (1 Corinthians 15:23–26).

One of the most profound Islamic claims is that *Islam fulfills Christianity as Christianity fulfills Old Testament religion*. This can be seen in the Muslim view that all the prophets taught Islam, each in succession, with Muhammad being the final and ultimate prophet. Yet if one religion is to fulfill another, there must be significant *continuity* between the two. In other words, essential elements of the first must not be denied by the second; there must be continuity of essence, though not necessarily of form. It is here that the Islamic claim to have fulfilled Christianity faces the greatest difficulties.

We already noted some commonalities between Islam, Christianity, and Old Testament Judaism—that there is only one God; that He created the universe; that He is sovereign, that He is our judge; that He is maximally powerful; that He interacts with His creation; that He has spoken to humanity through messengers; and that He inscripturated His message in holy books.

[12] We recommend the works of Michael L. Brown, *Answering Jewish Objections to Jesus: General and Historical Objections* (Grand Rapids, MI: Baker Book House, 2000); Michael L. Brown, *Answering Jewish Objections to Jesus: Theological Objections* (Grand Rapids, MI: Baker, 2000); and *idem, Answering Jewish Objections to Jesus: Messianic Prophecy* (Grand Rapids, MI: Baker Book House, 2003).

[13] E.g. Deuteronomy 4:35, 39; Isaiah 44:6–8; 43:10–11; 1 Corinthians 8:5–6; Ephesians 4:4–6.

Even with such substantial agreements, several distinct differences exist. Here we will address only the issue of revelation, as the infallibility and authority of Scripture are foundational to Christianity.

Muslims hold that the biblical prophets of the Old and New Testaments originally taught Islam, though Muslims are forced to deny the reliability of the Old and New Testament scriptures as they stand today for the simple reason that the Bible does not teach Islam. Yet, they have never successfully shown that the Bible is corrupted.

In contrast to Muslim criticism, the New Testament affirms the entire Old Testament as inspired by God, even providing wisdom for salvation through Christ Jesus (2 Timothy 3:14–17). The Old Testament prophets are acknowledged to have been inspired (1 Peter 1:21; cf. 2 Samuel 23:2). Furthermore, both the Old and New Testaments contain divine declarations that God's Word will not pass away (Isaiah 40:6–8; 1 Peter 1:24–25). Jesus confirmed the truthfulness of the Old Testament in the Sermon on the Mount (Matthew 5–7, especially 5:17–18) and elsewhere (Luke 16:31; 24:27; John 10:35; 17:17).[14] This is significant because we have portions of Old Testament texts, dating to and before the first century AD, which illustrate that the texts we have are substantially the same as those Jesus and Paul had. Thus Muslims cannot prove that the Old Testament was corrupted and cleansed of Islamic teachings sometime after Jesus' death.[15] We are compelled to ask our Muslims acquaintances, "If God can sustain the Qur'an throughout the ages, can He not sustain the biblical texts?" The evidence shows that He has preserved His Word.[16]

In addition to these straightforward statements regarding the Word of God, throughout the New Testament we find regular appeals to the Old Testament as the source and confirmation of Christianity. For example, consider some of the numerous affirmations and teachings of the apostle Paul in the book of Romans.[17]

Paul both introduces and concludes his letter to the Romans by noting how the gospel he proclaims stems from the Old Testament (1:1–2; 16:25–27; see Galatians 3:6–8). Paul also noted that the law and the prophets testified to the heart of the gospel—the righteousness of God (3:21). He taught that his ministry and message of Christ confirmed God's promises to the Patriarchs: "For I tell you that Christ has become a servant of the circumcised on behalf of the truth of God in order that he might confirm the promises given to the patriarchs so that the Gentiles may glorify God for his mercy" (15:8–9a).

Even though some of his contemporaries charged Paul with being unlawful (Romans 3:8; see 6:1, 15), he denied their accusations: "Do we, then, nullify the law by this faith? Not at all! Rather, we uphold the law" (3:31). He even viewed himself and his congregations as accountable to the Old Testament scriptures, noting that they have a continuing validity for the Church as the people of God. "For whatever was written in former days was written for our instruction, so that by steadfastness and by the encouragement of the scriptures we might have hope" (15:4; cf. 4:23–24 and 1 Corinthians 10:1ff). Paul's dependence upon the Old Testament is amply verified by the many explicit quotations he culled from the law, the writings, and the prophets (3:10–18; 10:5–21; 15:8–12), as well as his innumerable allusions to the Old Testament.[18]

---

[14] See John W. Wenham, *Christ and the Bible* (Grand Rapids, MI: Baker Book House, 1984).

[15] See Walter Kaiser, *Are the Old Testament Documents Reliable and Relevant?* (Downers Grove, IL: InterVarsity Press, 2001).

[16] See Norman L. Geisler and William E. Nix, *A General Introduction to the Bible*, rev. ed. (Chicago, IL: Moody Press, 1986).

[17] Some critics, including Muslims, assert that the teachings of the apostle Paul are different than the teachings of Jesus. In response, see David Wenham, *Paul: Follower of Jesus or Founder of Christianity?* (Grand Rapids, MI: Eerdmans, 1995), David Wenham, *Paul and Jesus: The True Story* (Grand Rapids, MI: Eerdmans, 2002).

[18] Gerald F. Hawthorne and Ralph P. Martin, eds., *Dictionary of Paul and His Letters*, (Downers Grove, IL:

1.2.8 CONCLUSION

Rather than denying that the Old Testament is the Word of God, Christians affirm—in direct contrast to Muslim criticisms of the Bible—that it is God's inspired Word and is useful for teaching, correction, rebuke, and instruction in godliness (1 Timothy 3:16–17). Islam is *not* to Christianity as Christianity is to the Old Testament. We can begin to illustrate the truthfulness of God's Word to Muslims by showing the New Testament's appeals to, dependence upon, and development from the Old Testament, as well as demonstrating our own high regard for the *whole* Bible—both Old and New Testaments.

InterVarsity Press, 1993), 630–642; Ben Witherington, *Paul's Narrative Thought World: The Tapestry of Tragedy and Triumph* (Nashville, TN: Westminster/John Knox, 1994); and the relevant discussions in *Right Doctrine from the Wrong Texts?: Essays on the Use of the Old Testament in the New*, Gregory K. Beale, ed. (Grand Rapids, MI: Baker Book House, 1996).

Theology

Secular Humanism

Humanism cannot in any fair sense of the word apply to one who still believes in God as the source and creator of the universe.[1]

— PAUL KURTZ

1.3.1 INTRODUCTION

After thinking about religion and the supernatural for three years, **Bertrand Russell** abandoned the notion of God. He later admitted, "I believed in God until I was just eighteen."[2] Russell, one of Secular Humanism's most famous international voices, maintained that the whole idea of God was a conception derived from the ancient Oriental despotisms, and therefore concluded, "I am not a Christian . . . I do not believe in God and in immortality; and . . . I do not think that Christ was the best and wisest of men, although I grant Him a very high degree of moral goodness."[3]

While eighteen might seem a tender age to determine whether or not God exists, Miriam Allen deFord, an American

Bertrand Russell

[1] Paul Kurtz, ed., *The Humanist Alternative* (Buffalo, NY: Prometheus Books, 1973), 177.
[2] Robert E. Egner and Lester E. Denonn, *The Basic Writings of Bertrand Russell* (New York, NY: Simon and Schuster, 1961), 40.
[3] Ibid., 586.

Humanist, had already concluded by age thirteen that there was sufficient evidence for denying the existence of all gods. Furthermore, she was convinced that people possessed no soul and that immortality (life after death) was a hoax. "To put it bluntly and undiplomatically," deFord says, "Humanism, in my viewpoint, must be atheistic or it is not Humanism as I understand it."[4]

ATHEISM: The denial of the existence of a supernatural God

Corliss Lamont, author of *The Philosophy of Humanism*, insists that Humanism, "rejecting supernaturalism" and "seeking man's fulfillment in the here and now of this world," has a long honored tradition of **atheism**, beginning with Democritus in ancient Greece and Lucretius in ancient Rome and continuing through history to John Dewey and Bertrand Russell in the twentieth century.

1.3.2 THEOLOGICAL BELIEFS OF LEADING HUMANISTS

The theology of the Humanist is surprisingly unshakeable in its dogmatic belief that the supernatural—including God, Satan, angels, demons, and souls—does not exist, a theology which is spelled out in all its certitude by various Humanist leaders.

Lamont believes that the fundamental principle of **Humanism**, which distinguishes it from all other worldviews, is that "Humanism . . . considers all forms of the supernatural as myth."[5] The supernatural—that is, anything outside nature—"does not exist."[6] Lamont says, "Humanism, "in its most accurate philosophical sense, implies a worldview in which

HUMANISM: The belief that humanity is the highest of all beings and truth and knowledge rest in science and human reason

Nature is everything, in which there is no supernatural."[7]

Lamont asserts that "intellectually, there is nothing to be gained and much to be lost for philosophy by positing a supernatural Creator or First Cause behind the great material universe."[8] There is no place in the Humanist worldview for God and, insists Lamont, instead of the gods creating the cosmos, "the cosmos, in the individualized form of human beings giving rein to their imagination, created the gods."[9]

Some years earlier than Lamont's first edition of *The Philosophy of Humanism* (1949), many Humanists, including John Dewey and Roy Wood Sellars, published *Humanist Manifesto I* (1933). It described the universe as "self-existing and not created." Further, the Manifesto declared, "the time has passed for theism . . . ."[10]

Forty years after the 1933 *Manifesto*, the Humanists published *Humanist Manifesto II* and reiterated, "We find insufficient evidence for belief in the existence of a supernatural; it is either meaningless or irrelevant to the question of the survival and fulfillment of the human race. As non-theists, we begin with humans not God, nature not deity." Again, ". . . we can discover no divine purpose or providence for the human species. While there is much that we do not know, humans

HUMANIST MANIFESTO: The title of three manifestoes laying out a Secular Humanist worldview. They are *Humanist Manifesto I* (1933), *Humanist Manifesto II* (1973), and *Humanist Manifesto III* (2000), although the latter is actually titled *Planetary Humanism*. The central theme of all three is the elaboration of a philosophy and value system that does not include belief in God.*

---

[4] Kurtz, *The Humanist Alternative*, 82.

[5] Corliss Lamont, *The Philosophy of Humanism* (New York, NY: Frederick Ungar, 1982), 145.

[6] Ibid., 14.

[7] Ibid., 22.

[8] Ibid., 123.

[9] Ibid., 145.

[10] *Humanist Manifesto I* (Buffalo, NY: Prometheus Books, 1980), 8.

* http://en.wikipedia.org/wiki/Humanist_Manifesto

are responsible for what we are or will become. No deity will save us; we must save ourselves."[11] Hundreds of Humanists signed this declaration of atheism, as did hundreds more the subsequent *Humanist Manifesto 2000.*

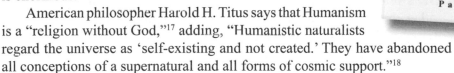

> No deity will save us; we must save ourselves.
>
> HUMANIST MANIFESTO II

Isaac Asimov served as the director of the American Humanist Association from 1989 to 1992. Writing in *Free Inquiry*, Asimov leaves no doubt regarding his personal theology: "I am an atheist, out and out. It took me a long time to say it. I've been an atheist for years and years, but somehow I felt it was intellectually unrespectable to say one was an atheist, because it assumed knowledge that one didn't have. Somehow it was better to say one was a humanist or an agnostic. I finally decided that I'm a creature of emotion as well as reason. Emotionally I am an atheist. I don't have the evidence to prove that God doesn't exist, but I so strongly suspect he doesn't that I don't want to waste my time."[12]

Bold atheism is proclaimed by every orthodox Humanist, including **Paul Kurtz**. Kurtz is the long-time editor of *Free Inquiry,* the quarterly magazine for skeptics and atheists. He declares, "Humanism cannot in any fair sense of the word apply to one who still believes in God as the source and creator of the universe. Christian Humanism would be possible only for those who are willing to admit that they are atheistic Humanists. It surely does not apply to God-intoxicated believers."[13]

For Kurtz, "God himself is man deified."[14] Such theology, of course, is quite close to the Marxist point of view. In fact, Kurtz refers to Marx as "one of history's great humanist thinkers." Kurtz says Marx is a Humanist because "he rejects theistic religion and defends atheism."[15] British biologist and author Julian Huxley said, "I disbelieve in a personal God in any sense in which that phrase is ordinarily used." He went on to say, "For my own part, the sense of spiritual relief which comes from rejecting the idea of God as a supernatural being is enormous."[16]

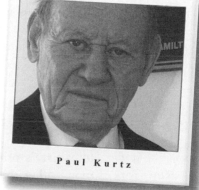

Paul Kurtz

American philosopher Harold H. Titus says that Humanism is a "religion without God,"[17] adding, "Humanistic naturalists regard the universe as 'self-existing and not created.' They have abandoned all conceptions of a supernatural and all forms of cosmic support."[18]

1.3.3 JOHN DEWEY: GURU TO THE PUBLIC SCHOOLS

The atheism of leading Humanist **John Dewey** has had such an impact on American culture that it requires more intense scrutiny. Because of Dewey's status as an educator, and especially because he had such a profound influence on America's public school system, his theological views must be understood by everyone seeking to understand modern education.

---

[11] *Humanist Manifesto II* (Buffalo, NY: Prometheus, 1980), 16.
[12] Isaac Asimov, "An Interview with Isaac Asimov," *Free Inquiry*, (Spring 1982), no. 2, 9.
[13] Kurtz, *The Humanist Alternative*, 178.
[14] Paul Kurtz, *The Fullness of Life* (New York, NY: Horizon Press, 1974), 35–6.
[15] Ibid.
[16] Julian Huxley, *Religion Without Revelation* (New York, NY: Mentor, 1957), 32.
[17] Harold H. Titus, "Humanistic Naturalism," *The Humanist* (1954), no. 1, 33.
[18] Ibid., 30.
[19] *Photo by Gary Wiepert. Copyright 2006 Center for Inquiry.

In his work *A Common Faith*, Dewey distinguishes between the words "religion" and "religious." He reserves the term "religion" for the supernatural while maintaining the term "religious" for the world of the natural (especially as it involves human relations, welfare, and progress). Dewey rejects the supernatural and a supernatural God. He accepts only evolving nature, with all of its "religious" ramifications. "I cannot understand," says Dewey, "how any realization of the democratic ideal as a vital moral and spiritual ideal in human affairs is possible without surrender of the conception of the basic division to which supernatural Christianity is committed."[20] For Dewey, democracy cannot ingest the Christian notions of saved and lost. He considers such notions "spiritual aristocracy" and contrary to the ideals of democracy. A democratic church must include both believer and unbeliever.

John Dewey

Dewey makes it clear that he believes science has largely discredited Biblical Christianity. "Geological discoveries," he says, "have displaced Creation myths which once bulked large."[21] Biology, says Dewey, has "revolutionized conceptions of soul and mind which once occupied a central place in religious beliefs and ideas."[22] He also says that biology has made a "profound impression" on the ideas of sin, redemption, and immortality. Anthropology, history, and literary criticism have furnished a "radically different version of the historic events and personages upon which Christian religions have built."[23] And psychology is already opening up "natural explanations of phenomena so extraordinary that once their supernatural origin was, so to say, the natural explanation."[24] For Dewey, science and the scientific method have exiled God and the supernatural to the dustbins of history.

1.3.4 HUMANISTIC THEOLOGICAL LITERATURE

Secular Humanism's primary publishing arm is Prometheus Books, located in Buffalo, New York. Among other things, Prometheus publishes atheistic children's books, including *What About Gods?* by Chris Brockman. This book is designed to indoctrinate children with dogmatic atheistic sentiments like, "Many people say they believe in a god. Do you know what a god is? Do you know what it means to believe in a god? A god is a mythical character. Mythical characters are imaginary, they're not real. People make them up. Dragons and fairies are two of many mythical characters people have made up. They're not real. . . ."[25]

Prometheus also publishes atheistic literature geared toward adult audiences. Paul Blanshard's *Classics of Free Thought* was published, "to keep atheism before the public." *Critiques of God*, edited by Peter Angeles, contains 371 pages supporting Humanist theology's denial of the existence of God.

In *Critiques*, Angeles explains that belief in the supernatural has all but vanished from our culture. He says that God has lost His spatial location as a monarch in heaven and His temporal precedence to the universe as its Creator ex nihilo. "It is not that God is being relegated to a remote region," Angeles insists. "It is not that God has become a bodiless abstraction (a sexless

---

[20] John Dewey, *A Common Faith* (New Haven, CT: Yale University Press, 1934, renewed 1962), 84.

[21] Ibid., 31.

[22] Ibid.

[23] Ibid.

[24] Ibid.

[25] Chris Brockman, *What About Gods?* (Buffalo, NY: Prometheus Books, 1978).

> Without God, what is left? Man and the Universe. That should be enough. That has to be enough because that is all there is.
> — PETER ANGELES

It). It is the realization that there is no God left to which to relate. Without God, what is left? Man and the Universe. That should be enough. That has to be enough because that is all there is."[26]

The Secular Humanists' 1980 declaration does not diverge from their earlier *Manifestoes* (1933, 1973) or their latest published in 2000. Written by Kurtz and published in *Free Inquiry*, it contends that "Secular Humanists may be agnostics, atheists, rationalists, or skeptics, but they find insufficient evidence for the claim that some divine purpose exists for the universe. They reject the idea that God has intervened miraculously in history or revealed himself to a chosen few, or that he can save or redeem sinners."[27]

Humanist theology, start to finish, is based on the denial of God and the supernatural. This denial, however, leads the Humanist to another necessary theological conclusion: humanity is the Supreme Authority. (It is possible that Humanism's deification of humanity preceded its atheistic assumptions because the existence of God becomes a decided nuisance after one has declared oneself sovereign.)

1.3.5 CONCLUSION

Ultimately, it is of little importance whether the dethroning of God or the deification of man was Humanism's first theological presupposition. The crux of their theology remains anti-God. This is the heart and soul of Secular Humanism: man setting himself up in place of God. Unfortunately for the Humanist, this theology often strips him of all sense of purpose. As Ernest Nagel explains, atheism "can offer no hope of personal immortality, no threats of divine chastisement, no promise of eternal recompense for injustices suffered, no blueprints to sure salvation . . . A tragic view of life is thus [an undeniable] . . . ingredient in atheistic thought."[28]

Perhaps it was this "tragic view of life" that finally caught up to Antony Flew, one of *Free Inquiry's* contributing editors. At 81 years of age Dr. Flew abandoned his atheism and joined the ranks of the theists (he claims some form of Deism[29]).

The Pop Culture Connection

Contact—a 1997 film adapted from the novel by Carl Sagan, in which SETI (Search for Extraterrestrial Intelligence) researcher and atheist, Ellie Arroway (Jodi Foster) identifies a coded message from an alien source, including plans to build a machine to take humans to other civilizations in distant galaxies. Sagan's beliefs about God and humanity are revealed in the following statements:

Ellie: So what's more likely? That an all-powerful, mysterious God created the Universe, and decided not to give any proof of his existence? Or, that he simply doesn't exist at all, and that we created him, so that we wouldn't have to feel so small and alone?

Ellie: For as long as I can remember, I've been searching for something, some reason why we're here. What are we doing here? Who are we? If this is a chance to find out even just a little part of that answer...I don't know, I think it's worth a human life. Don't you?

Alien to Ellie: You're an interesting species, an interesting mix. You're capable of such beautiful dreams and such horrible nightmares. You feel so lost, so cut off, so alone, only you're not. See, in all our searching, the only thing we've found that makes the emptiness bearable is each other.

---

[26] Peter Angeles, ed., *Critiques of God* (Buffalo, NY: Prometheus Books, 1976), xiii.

[27] Paul Kurtz, "A Secular Humanist Declaration," *Free Inquiry* (Winter 1980/81), no. 1, 5.

[28] Angeles, *Critiques of God*, 17.

[29] Deism is the belief that God exists and created the universe, but then vacated it for humanity to manage by itself without any external interference.

Richard Ostling describes his spiritual journey this way: "A British philosophy professor who has been a leading champion of atheism for more than a half-century has changed his mind. He now believes in God more or less based on scientific evidence and says so on a video. At age 81, after decades of insisting belief is a mistake, Antony Flew has concluded that some sort of intelligence or First Cause must have created the universe."[30]

The important point is that science and reason drove Flew to this conclusion, not revelation or history. Secular Humanists continue to stress that science and reason will drive one from the Christian point of view of creation. Dr. Flew more than answers this claim. As it turns out, biology and science in general are not confining the supernatural to any dustbin of history, as Dewey claimed.[31]

---

[30] Richard Ostling, *The Associated Press* (December 9, 2004).
[31] See Stephen C. Meyer, "The Origin of the Biological Information and the Higher Taxonomic Categories," Proceedings of the Biological Society of Washington, August 28, 2004; John Angus Campbell and Stephen C. Meyer, *Darwinism, Design, and Public Education* (East Lansing, MI: Michigan State University Press, 2003); Geoffrey Simmons, *What Darwin Didn't Know* (Eugene, OR: Harvest House, 2004); Michael J. Behe, *Darwin's Black Box: The Biochemical Challenge To Evolution* (New York, NY: The Free Press, 1996).

Theology

Marxism-Lenism

> Religion is opium for the people. Religion is a sort of spiritual booze. . . .[1]
>
> — V.I. LENIN

1.4.1 INTRODUCTION

"We Communists are atheists,"[2] declared Chou En-lai at the Bandung, Indonesia Conference in April 1955. This Chinese communist leader captured the fundamental theological ingredient of Marxism-Leninism in one word: atheism. Today, Marxists-Leninists prefer two words: scientific atheism.

From the university days of Karl Marx to the present, official spokesmen for Marxism have been consistent about the content of their theology—that God, whether known as a Supreme Being, Creator, or Divine Ruler, does not, cannot, and must not exist.[3]

God is considered an impediment, even an enemy, to a scientific, materialistic, socialistic outlook. The idea of God, insists Lenin, encourages the working class (the proletariat) to drown its terrible economic plight in the "spiritual booze" of some mythical heaven ("pie in the sky by and by"). Even a single sip of this intoxicant decreases the revolutionary fervor necessary to exterminate the oppressing class (the bourgeois), causing the working class to forfeit its only chance of creating a truly human heaven on earth: global communism.

---

[1] V.I. Lenin, *Complete Collected Works*, 45 vols. (Moscow, USSR: Progress Publishers, 1978), 10:83.
[2] James D. Bales, *Communism: Its Faith and Fallacies* (Grand Rapids, MI: Baker Book House, 1962), 37.
[3] See David B.T. Aikman's Ph.D. dissertation entitled "The Role of Atheism in the Marxist tradition." (Ann Arbor, MI: UMI Dissertation Services, 1979). Aikman covers all aspects of Marxist atheism in his 500+ page dissertation.

Karl Marx

1.4.2 MARX'S THEOLOGICAL BELIEFS

Religion as the opium of the masses, however, was a later development in the mind of **Karl Marx**. His atheism was conceived in the heady arena of philosophy, not economics or sociology. When Marx became an atheist at the University of Berlin, he was not thinking about surplus value or the dictatorship of the proletariat. He was thinking about the philosophies of Prometheus, Georg W. F. Hegel, Bruno Bauer, David Strauss, and Ludwig Feuerbach.

"Philosophy makes no secret of it," said Marx. "Prometheus's admission: 'In sooth all gods I hate' is its own admission, its own motto against all gods, heavenly and earthly, who do not acknowledge the consciousness of man as the supreme divinity. There must be no god on a level with it."[4]

In a circle of radical Young Hegelians that included Ludwig Feuerbach and Frederick Engels, Marx became an atheist. Atheism was embraced by the group, with Feuerbach proclaiming, "It is clear as the sun and evident as the day that there is no God; and still more, that there can be no God."[5]

Accepting Feuerbach's conclusion that God is a projection of humanity's own making, Marx boasted, "Man is the highest being for man." Indeed, Marx explains that this view signals the demise of all religion: "The criticism of religion ends with the teaching that man is the highest being for man. . . ."[6]

For Marx, then, humanity is God. We created God in our own image. We created religion in order to worship ourselves. The notion that God is merely our projection is contained in Marx's assertion that man "looked for a superhuman being in the fantastic reality of heaven and found nothing there but the reflection of himself."[7]

THE COMMUNIST MANIFESTO was first published on February 21, 1848, and is one of the world's most influential political tracts. Commissioned by the Communist League and written by communist theorists Karl Marx and Friedrich Engels, it laid out the League's purposes and program. The *Manifesto* suggested a course of action for a proletarian revolution to overthrow capitalism and, eventually, to bring about a classless society.

Because Marx believes that we are God, he also believes we must seize control of reality and shape it to our specifications. "The philosophers have only interpreted the world, in various ways," says Marx; "the point, however, is to change it."[8] Because the institutions of society rested on a foundation of theism, Marx determined to change all social institutions and re-establish them on atheistic foundations.

To this end, Marx and Engels, in the *Communist Manifesto*, called for the "forcible overthrow" of all existing social conditions.

---

[4] Karl Marx and Frederick Engels, *On Religion* (New York, NY: Schocken Books, 1974), 15.

[5] See Richard Wurmbrand, *My Answer to the Moscow Atheists* (New Rochelle, NY: Arlington House, 1975), 16. Also, see Wurmbrand's *Marx & Satan* (Bartlesville, OK: Voice of the Martyrs Publishers, 1990), 13, for Marx stating, "Then I will be able to walk triumphantly, Like a god, through the ruins of their kingdom. Every word of mine is fire and action. My breast is equal to that of the Creator." Wurmbrand contends that Marx was involved in Satanism.

[6] Karl Marx and Fredrick Engels, *Collected Works*, 40 vols. (New York, NY: International Publishers, 1976), 3:175.

[7] Ibid., 3:182.

[8] Karl Marx, *On Historical Materialism* (New York, NY: International Publishers, 1974), 13.

This call was based on Marx's dogmatic atheism, and not on dispassionate societal observation. Marx's economic theories—and, indeed, his entire worldview—were tailored to fit his theology.

1.4.3 SIGNIFICANCE OF THEOLOGY IN MARXIST THEORY

While some attempts have been made to minimize atheism's role in Marxist theory (especially in recruiting naive Christians and other religious people to participate in Marxist-Leninist activity, such as the Liberation Theology movement), Marxists are privately aware of their fundamental need for an atheistic foundation.

Marx's search for "scientific truths" to bolster his atheism led him to conclusions that shaped his communist theory. As he moved from the philosophical basis for atheism into the socioeconomic realm, he reached the conclusion (based upon his atheistic assumptions) that religion is merely an anti-depressant for the oppressed working class. His summary of this explanation has been quoted throughout the world, even though it was not his original basis for atheism. "Religion," said Marx, "is the sigh of the oppressed creature, the sentiment of a heartless world, as it is the spirit of spiritless conditions. It is the opium of the people."[9]

> We have once and for all declared war on religion and religious ideas and care little whether we are called atheists or anything else.
>
> — FREDERICK ENGELS

Marx's friend and fellow atheist, Engels, declared, "We want to sweep away everything that claims to be supernatural and superhuman, for the root of all untruth and lying is the pretension of the human and the natural to be superhuman and supernatural. For that reason we have once and for all declared war on religion and religious ideas and care little whether we are called atheists or anything else."[10]

As with Marx, Engels foresaw a time when all religion would cease. He contended that when society adopts socialism, i.e., when society takes possession of all means of production and uses them on a planned basis (thus eliminating the working class's economic bondage), religion itself will vanish.

1.4.4 LENIN'S THEOLOGICAL CONTRIBUTIONS TO MARXISM

Some years later, V.I. Lenin affirmed the conclusions of Marx and Engels: "The philosophical basis of Marxism, as Marx and Engels repeatedly declared, is . . . a materialism which is absolutely atheistic and positively hostile to all religion."[11] Elsewhere, Lenin made it clear that fighting religion was an essential ingredient in a materialistic reality. "We must combat religion," he said, "that is the ABC of all materialism, and consequently of Marxism."[12]

In his "Socialism and Religion" address, Lenin insists that the communist program is based on a scientific, materialistic world outlook and therefore "our propaganda necessarily includes the propaganda of atheism."[13] Lenin went on to urge his fellow communists to follow Engels' advice and translate and widely disseminate the atheistic literature of the eighteenth-century French Enlightenment.

Lenin made it clear that any idea of God was taboo, claiming, "Every religious idea, every idea of God, even flirting with the idea of God, is unutterable vileness . . . vileness of the most

---

[9] Marx and Engels, *Collected Works*, 3:175.
[10] Ibid., 3:463.
[11] Lenin, *Selected Works*, 15:402.
[12] Ibid., 405.
[13] Ibid., 10:86.

dangerous kind, 'contagion' of the most abominable kind. Millions of sins, filthy deeds, acts of violence and physical contagions . . . are far less dangerous than the subtle, spiritual idea of a God decked out in the smartest 'ideological' costumes. . . . Every defense or justification of the idea of God, even the most refined, the best intentioned, is a justification of reaction."[14]

Clearly, Lenin's theology unerringly corresponds with that of Marx and Engels. Together they established the foundations for future communist declarations of atheism.[15]

1.4.5 ATHEISM IN THE FORMER SOVIET UNION

Marxist theology has remained consistent throughout the history of communism. From Marx's time to the present, communists everywhere have vehemently denied the existence of God. This becomes especially obvious when one considers the theological stance of the former U.S.S.R. The Great Soviet Encyclopedia, published in Moscow in 1950, called on the Communist Party to oppose religion and "to fight for the 'full victory' of atheism."[16] The Young Communist League's list of Ten Commandments contains the declaration "If you are not a convinced atheist, you cannot be a good Communist. . . . Atheism is indissolubly bound to Communism."[17]

In 1955, Soviet premier Nikita Khrushchev said, "Communism has not changed its attitude of opposition to religion. We are doing everything we can to eliminate the bewitching power of the opium of religion."[18]

The Atheist's Handbook was published in Moscow in 1959 in conjunction with Khrushchev's campaign to eliminate the remaining traces of religion in the U.S.S.R. This text attacks the Bible, the Qur'an, Christianity, and Islam. "Science," says the *Handbook*, "has long since established that Jesus Christ never existed, that the figure of the alleged founder of Christianity is purely mythical."[19] And according to the *Handbook,* the Apostle Paul, too, turns out to be "a mythical figure."[20]

1.4.6 THE MARXIST ASSAULT ON THE CHURCH

This Marxist hatred of anything supernatural—and especially anything Christian—is most often vented on religious peoples and institutions in Marxist countries.

Although the July 10, 1918 Constitution of the former U.S.S.R. recognized freedom of both "religious and anti-religious propaganda" as the right of every citizen, the Soviet state constantly worked to suppress theistic religion. Article 65 of the 1918 Constitution declared priests and clerics to be "servants of the bourgeoisie" and had them disenfranchised. This meant, among other things, that priests were denied ration cards and their children were barred from attending school above the elementary grades. Paul Kurtz, a Secular Humanist, points out that from 1918 to 1921 "religious persecution continued unabated. . . . All church property was nationalized, and it is estimated that tens of thousands of bishops, clerics, and laymen were killed or imprisoned."[21]

In the former Soviet Union, church after church was declared counter-revolutionary and shut down.[22] Churches were turned into cinemas, radio stations, granaries, museums, machine repair

[14] Ibid., 35:122.

[15] Aikman, for an in-depth look at Lenin's atheism and its influence in the U.S.S.R.

[16] *The Great Soviet Encyclopedia* (Moscow, USSR: 1950), quoted in Bales, *Communism*, 37.

[17] Young Communist League's "Ten Commandments of Communism," quoted in Bales, *Communism*, 37.

[18] Nikita Khrushchev, speech, September 22, 1955, quoted in Bales, *Communism*, 165–6.

[19] *The Atheist's Handbook*, [Sputnik Ateista], (Moscow, USSR: Gos. Izd. Politicheskoi Literatury, 1961), reproduced in English by U.S. Joint Publications Research Service (Washington, DC), 117.

[20] Ibid., 69.

[21] Paul Kurtz, "Militant Atheism Versus Freedom of Conscience," *Free Inquiry* (Fall 1989): 28.

[22] See Stephane Courtois, et al., *The Black Book Of Communism* (Cambridge, MA: Harvard University Press, 1999). Also, see R. J. Rummel, *Death By Government* (New Brunswick, NJ: Transaction Publishers, 1994), 79f.

shops, etc. Before the revolution, Moscow had 460 Orthodox churches. On January 1, 1930, the number was down to 224, and by January 1, 1933, the figure was about 100.

Even though the 1936 Soviet Constitution again guaranteed "freedom of religion," Marxist attacks on religious peoples continued unabated. In the days following the new Constitution, some Christians attempted to conform to laws by registering with the government. The Soviet government required these believers to collect fifty signatures. When the Christians presented the signatures to the government officials, all fifty "conspirators" would be deemed "members of a secret counter-revolutionary organization"[23] and arrested.

Such persecution will continue as long as the Marxist worldview rules any country. Modern times have not made Marxists more tolerant of religion. In 1993, in the People's Republic of China, Marxist leaders tore down an Islamic mosque, ostensibly because it was not "government sanctioned." The Marxist government can sanction only one religion: the religion of atheism—the "ABC of Marxism."

1.4.7 CONCLUSION

In theory and practice, Marxism reflects its atheistic base. To be a Marxist demands adherence to atheism. To be a good Marxist entails being a propagator of atheism. To be the *best* Marxist is to see atheism as part of the scientific, materialistic, socialistic outlook and to strive to eradicate all religious sentiment.

From the heady days of Marx and Engels through the era of Lenin and Stalin and on to the Frankfurt School (Adorno, Marcuse, etc.), the Red Brigades, Herbert Aptheker, William Z. Foster, Paul Robeson (winner of the Stalin Peace Prize), the Communist Party USA, Gerda Lerner, Eric Foner, Howard Zinn, International ANSWER, Antonio Gramsci, Gyorgy Lukacs, Walter Benjamin, Eric Hobsbawn—the trial of Marxism continues along its atheistic theology.

From *The Communist Manifesto* (1848)[24] to the latest manifesto entitled *Empire* (2000), the quest for a godless world continues. *Empire* was written by Michael Hardt of Duke University and Antonio Negri and published by the Harvard University Press. Negri, associated with the Red Brigades, was responsible for much mayhem across Europe. He and Hardt instruct us, "Our pilgrimage on earth, however, in contrast to Augustine's has no transcendent telos beyond [purpose beyond this world]; it is and remains absolutely immanent [here and now]. Its continuous movement, gathering aliens in community, making this world its home, is both means and end, or rather a means without an end." [25]

National Review referred to *Empire* as "the Communist 'hot, smart book of the moment'"[26] and *Foreign Affairs* magazine referred to it as "[a] sweeping neo-Marxist vision of the coming world order."[27]

Theists everywhere recognize, as did Feodor Dostoevsky, that "[t]he problem of Communism is not an economic problem. The problem of Communism is the problem of atheism."[28]

Chapter four is entitled, "61,011,000 Murdered—The Soviet Gulag State."

[23] Robert Conquest, *Harvest of Sorrow* (Oxford, UK: Oxford University Press, 1986), 209. Many of the facts concerning the closing of the churches are found in Conquest's chapter "The Churches and the People."

[24] The latest American edition of *The Communist Manifesto* was published by Haymarket Books (Chicago, 2005), and edited by Phil Gasper, a professor of philosophy at Notre Dame de Namur University in northern California.

[25] Michael Hardt and Antonio Negri, *Empire* (Cambridge, MA: Harvard University Press, 2000), 207.

[26] *National Review*, September 17, 2001, 28.

[27] Hardt, back cover.

[28] Whittaker Chambers, *Witness* (New York, NY: Random House, 1952), 712.

Theology

Cosmic Humanism

What is God? God is the interlinking of yourself with the whole.[1]

— KEVIN RYERSON

I've investigated a number of religions. I was into Zen Buddhism for a while. But voodooism is the one that stuck more. It's very interesting. Not that I practice it or anything.[2]

— ACTRESS KRISTANNA LOKEN

1.5.1 INTRODUCTION

Like every other worldview, Cosmic Humanism's theology forms the foundation for all other aspects of its worldview. However, Cosmic Humanism (the New Age movement) differs from Christianity, Islam, and the secular worldviews in that it embraces neither theism nor atheism.

Cosmic Humanism begins by denying the preeminence of any purported special revelation over any other. That is, Cosmic Humanists believe that the Bible is no more the word of God than is the Qur'an, or the teachings of Confucius. New Age advocate David Spangler says,

---

[1] Kevin Ryerson, *Spirit Communication: The Soul's Path* (New York, NY: Bantam Books, 1989), 106.
[2] *Rolling Stone*, July 24, 2003, 46.

> We can take all the
> scriptures, and all the
> teachings, and all the
> tablets, and all the laws,
> and all the marshmallows
> and have a jolly good
> bonfire and marshmallow
> roast, because that is all
> they are worth.
>
> — DAVID SPANGLER

"We can take all the scriptures, and all the teachings, and all the tablets, and all the laws, and all the marshmallows and have a jolly good bonfire and marshmallow roast, because that is all they are worth."[3]

Obviously, if the Bible is valuable only as fuel, this nullifies the significance of the life, death, and resurrection of Jesus Christ. The Cosmic Humanist sees Christ's life as important only in the sense that it showed humanity to be capable of achieving perfection, even godhood. An article in the New Age publication *Science of Mind* states, "The significance of incarnation and resurrection is not that Jesus was a human like us but rather that we are gods like him—or at least have the potential to be."[4]

This interpretation of Christ allows the New Age theologian to postulate, as John White does, that "The Son of God . . . is not Jesus but our combined Christ consciousness."[5] Jesus is looked on as one of a select company, having achieved Christ consciousness. Every person is encouraged to acquire this same level of consciousness.

How can anyone hope to achieve such a divine consciousness? Because everyone is a part of God. Cosmic Humanists believe that we and God are ontologically one.

1.5.2 EVERY PERSON IS GOD

"Each of us has access to a supraconscious, creative, integrative, self-organizing, intuitive mind whose capabilities are apparently unlimited," says John Bradshaw. "This is the part of our consciousness that constitutes our God-likeness."[6]

Shirley MacLaine

Most Cosmic Humanists state the case more forcefully. Ruth Montgomery supposedly channeled a spirit that spoke through her, claiming, "We are as much God as God is a part of us . . . each of us is God . . . together we are God . . . this all-for-one-and-one-for-all . . . makes us the whole of God."[7] White states that "sooner or later every human being will feel a call from the cosmos to ascend to godhood."[8]

Meher Baba declares, "There is only one question. And once you know the answer to that question there are no more to ask. . . . Who am I? And to that question there is only one answer—I am God!"[9] **Shirley MacLaine** recommends that every person should begin each day by affirming his or her own godhood. "You can use I am God or I am that I am as Christ often did, or you can extend the affirmation to fit your own needs."[10]

Special revelation need not exist in books or in any other form outside of us, because each

[3] David Spangler, *Reflections on the Christ* (Forres, Scotland: Findhorn Publications, 1982), 73.
[4] *Science of Mind* (October 1981): 40–2. Cited in Ray A. Yungen, *For Many Shall Come in my Name* (Salem, OR: Ray Yungen, 1989), 164.
[5] John White, "A Course in Miracles: Spiritual Wisdom for the New Age," *Science of Mind* (March 1986): 10.
[6] John Bradshaw, *Bradshaw on the Family* (Pompono Beach, FL: Health Communications, 1988), 230.
[7] Ruth Montgomery, *A World Beyond* (New York, NY: Ballantine/Fawcett Crest Books, 1972), 12.
[8] John White, ed., *What is Enlightenment?* (Los Angeles, CA: J.P. Tarcher, 1984), 126.
[9] Meher Baba, quoted in Allan Y. Cohen, "Meher Baba and the Quest of Consciousness." Cited in White, *What is Enlightenment?*, 87.
[10] F. LaGard Smith, *Out On a Broken Limb* (Eugene, OR: Harvest House, 1986), 181.

of us has our own special revelation in our higher consciousness, our own ability to get in touch with the part of us that is God. Inner soul-searching becomes the only significant means of discovering truth. By asserting that man is God, the Cosmic Humanist grants each individual the power of determining reality by creating or co-creating truth.

1.5.3 ALL IS ONE

It is important to understand that the belief that every individual is God and God is every individual is tied inextricably to the concept of consciousness. Because Cosmic Humanists have this "all is one" mentality, they necessarily believe that humanity can become attuned to all the powers of its godhood by achieving unity of consciousness. "Once we begin to see that we are all God," says Beverly Galyean, "that we all have the attributes of God, then I think the whole purpose of human life is to reown the Godlikeness within us; the perfect love, the perfect wisdom, the perfect understanding, the perfect intelligence, and when we do that, we create back to that old, that essential oneness which is consciousness."[11] Robert Muller says, "Only the unity of all can bring the well-being of all."[12]

The concept of humanity's unity, the idea that all is one, tends to support the theological concept of rein-carnation. Virtually every "orthodox" adherent of the New Age movement believes that each individual's soul was present in other material forms earlier in history and that it will manifest itself in still other forms after its present body dies. The body may pass away, but the soul will continue its quest for godhood in other bodies. This belief in reincarnation caused MacLaine, when recalling her daughter's birth, to muse, "When the doctor brought her to me in the hospital bed on that afternoon in 1956, had she already lived many, many times before, with other mothers? Had she, in fact, been one herself? Had she, in fact, ever been my mother? Was her one-hour-old face housing a soul perhaps millions of years old?"[13]

The Pop Culture Connection

Mentor of Modern Mythologies: Joseph Campbell (d. 1987), American professor and writer, is best known for his work in comparative mythology and comparative religion and for mentoring a generation of Hollywood directors and screenwriters. In his influential book, *The Hero with a Thousand Faces* (1949), Campbell discusses the "monomyth" cycle of the hero's journey, a pattern, he claims, found in many cultures. The monomyth involves the hero receiving a "call to adventure" and passing "threshold guardians" (often with the aid of a wise mentor or spirit guide) before entering a dreamlike world. There, after a series of trials, the hero achieves the object of his quest—often an atonement with the father, a sacred marriage, or an apotheosis (elevation to divine status). He then returns home. Campbell wrote that almost all hero myths, religious and secular, throughout history and across cultures, contain at least a subset of these patterns. Thus, Campbell concluded that all religions tell the same story. George Lucas was the first Hollywood filmmaker to publicly credit Campbell's influence on his own work. Lucas stated that the *Star Wars* series re-invented mythology for today's generation. Campbell's influence also is seen in a number of other successful Hollywood films, including Disney's 1993 film, *The Lion King*, and blockbuster series such as *The Matrix* and *The Legend of Bagger Vance*. More recently, computer game companies have used Campbell's ideas for developing storyboarding techniques and new products.

---

[11] Cited in Francis Adeney, "Educators Look East," *Spiritual Counterfeits Journal* (Winter 1981): 29. SCP Journal is published by Spiritual Counterfeits Project, P.O. Box 4308, Berkeley, CA 94704.

[12] Benjamin B. Ferencz and Ken Keyes, Jr., *Planethood* (Coos Bay, OR: Vision Books, 1988), 92.

[13] Quoted in Smith, 12.

In order to understand oneself (and one's path to godhood), a person must be cognizant of at least some of his or her past lives. Gary Zukav explains: "If your soul was a Roman centurion, an Indian beggar, a Mexican mother, a nomad boy, and a medieval nun, among other incarnations, for example, . . . you will not be able to understand your proclivities, or interests, or ways of responding to different situations without an awareness of the experiences of those lifetimes."[14] Reincarnation can serve little purpose unless people can know about and learn from their past lives.

1.5.4 EVERYTHING IS GOD

Reincarnation, however, is not the only logical consequence of a theology based on the unity of God and man and the concept that all is one. If we cannot delineate between God and ourself, how can we be certain that we can delineate between other living or dead things and God? Indeed, if all is one, perhaps everything that exists is God.

And so it is. Stars are God, water is God, plants are God, trees are God, the earth is God, whales and dolphins are God, everything is God. Cosmic Humanists worship the creation and the creator at the same time. For them, there is no difference.

The belief that everything is God and God is everything is known as **pantheism**. This ancient concept forms the theological foundation of the New Age movement. "Everything has divine power in it," says Roman Catholic New Ager Matthew Fox, and this divine force is what gives the planet its "sacredness."[15] An example of pantheistic theology occurs in a New Age children's book entitled *What is God?*: "There are many ways to talk about God. Does that mean that everything that everybody ever says about God is right? Does that mean that God is everything? Yes! God is everything great and small! God is everything far away and near! God is everything bright and dark! And God is everything in between! If everything is God, God is the last leaf on a tree, if everything is God, God is an elephant crashing through the jungle."[16]

> **PANTHEISM:** The belief that god is everything and everything is god

The god-as-cosmic-energy concept has been popularized in George Lucas' now classic film series, *Star Wars*. In a 1999 interview with Bill Moyers, Lucas explained why he made the series, "With *Star Wars*, I consciously set about to re-create myths and the classic mythological motifs. I wanted to use those motifs to deal with issues that exist today. . . . I see *Star Wars* as taking all the issues that religion represents and trying to distill them down into a more modern and easily accessible construct . . . . I'm telling an old myth in a new way." What Lucas fails to mention is "the old myth" he refers to is Eastern religion, not western Christianity. In this way, New Age mysticism was thrust from the big screen into the consciousness of countless viewers, young and old.[17] Weaving pantheistic religion throughout *Star Wars* was not an accident. While most viewers enjoyed this film saga for its entertainment value, producer Lucas sees his role as an educator as well as entertainer. He notes, "I've always tried to be aware of what I say in my films because all of us who make motion pictures are teachers, teachers with very loud voices."[18] Likewise, Irvin Kershner revealed his religious intention for directing *The Empire Strikes Back*. Kershner stated in one interview, "I wanna introduce some Zen here because I

---

[14] Gary Zukav, *The Seat of the Soul* (New York, NY: Simon and Schuster, 1999), 29.

[15] Matthew Fox, in an interview with Laura Hagar, "The Sounds of Silence," *New Age Journal* (March/April 1989): 55.

[16] Etan Boritzer, *What is God?* (Willowdale, CA: Firefly Books, 1990), 26.

[17] "Of Myth and Men: A Conversation between Bill Moyers and George Lucas on the meaning of the Force and the true theology of *Star Wars*," *Time*, April 26, 1999, 92.

[18] Quote attributed to George Lucas in www.pbs.org/wnet/americanmasters/database/lucas_g.html.

don't want the kids to walk away just feeling that everything is shoot-em-up . . . but that there's also a little something to think about here in terms of yourself and your surroundings."[19]

1.5.5 CONCLUSION

The all-encompassing God of the Cosmic Humanist is not a personal God,[20] but merely *a* cosmic force. There is no transcendent God "out there" apart from His creation. God is the creation. Marilyn Ferguson states, "In the emergent spiritual tradition God is not the personage of our Sunday School mentality. . . . God is experienced as flow, wholeness . . . the ground of being. . . . God is the consciousness that manifests as Lila, the play of the universe. God is the organizing matrix we can experience but not tell, that which enlivens matter."[21]

Unlike the Marxist and the Secular Humanist, the Cosmic Humanist believes in a supernatural realm consisting of spiritual relationships. However, the New Age version of God differs infinitely from the Christian concept of God. While the Christian believes that God created us and all that exists and that we can know His will only through the general revelation of nature and conscience and the special revelation of the Bible, the Cosmic Humanist believes that every person and all reality is God, and therefore that any "truth" our inner self discovers is God's truth. If we fail to realize our godhood in this lifetime, never fear! We'll soon have another incarnation and another chance to achieve Christ consciousness.

> ## The Pop Culture Connection
>
> In the 1977 original episode of **Star Wars**, Obi-wan Kenobi explains the nature of the god-force as he tells Luke Skywalker, "The Force is what gives the Jedi his power. It's an energy field created by all living things. It surrounds us and penetrates us and binds the galaxy together." In four other scenes throughout the film, Obi-wan gives Luke additional information about the Force.
>
> During an extended scene in **The Empire Strikes Back** (1980), Yoda, the Jedi master, takes Luke as an apprentice and instructs him more fully in the ways of the Force. In true guru fashion, Yoda tells Luke, "For my ally is the Force, and a powerful ally it is. Life breeds it, makes it grow. Its energy surrounds us and binds us. Luminous beings are we, not this crude matter. You must feel the force around you, here between you, me, the tree, the rock, everywhere, yes, even between land and ship."
>
> Talk about the Force takes place in other scenes throughout the *Star Wars* series, providing a comprehensive initiation into Cosmic Humanist theology.

Ultimately, every person will achieve godhood, and total unity will be restored. New Age theology, like fairy tales, guarantees a happy ending.

---

[19] Irvin Kershner, *Rolling Stone*, July 24, 1980, 37.

[20] One of India's Swamis, A.C. Bhaktivedanta Prabhupada (d. 1977), has cast the *Bhagavad-Gita* into a "theistic science" mould and identifies Lord Sri Krsna (Hare Krishna) as the Supreme Personality of the Godhead. According to Prabhupada, Hare Krishna (or God) descends to earth once every eight trillion, six hundred million years. See A.C. Prabhupada, *Bhagavad-Gita: As It Is* (Los Angeles, CA: Bhaktivedanta Book Trust International, 2004), xviii, 33.

[21] Marilyn Ferguson, *The Aquarian Conspiracy* (Los Angeles, CA: J.P. Tarcher, 1980), 383.

Theology

Postmodernism

I might have written an account of how even atheists
like myself are impressed, improved and morally
instructed by [reading] Pilgrim's Progress.[1]

— RICHARD RORTY

1.6.1 INTRODUCTION

Atheism is the theological belief that there is no God, no supernatural Creator, no Divine moral lawgiver, and no ultimate Judge of man's actions. It is the theological backbone of not only Secular Humanism and Marxism, but it is also the predominant theological view of classical Postmodernism.

Although more subtle in some ways than their fellow atheists,[2] Postmodernists have their theological underpinnings in atheism. Kevin J. Vanhoozer says, "Postmodernists agree with Nietzsche that 'God'—which is to say, the supreme being of classical theism—has become unbelievable, as have the autonomous self and the meaning of history."[3]

---

[1] Robert B. Brandom, ed., *Rorty and His Critics* (Oxford, UK: Blackwell Publishers, 2001), 344.

[2] See Mark Goldblatt's article "Can Humanists Talk to Poststructuralists?" in *Academic Questions* 18, no. 2 (Spring 2005): 59. "In *Dissemination* Derrida states: 'It is thus not simply false to say that Mallarme is a Platonist or a Hegelian. But it is above all not true. And vice versa." As Goldblatt says, "the 'vice versa' undermines any attempt to get at what Derrida means." Derrida also regularly employs terminology that simultaneously affirms and denies. Says Goldblatt, "the only way to read Derrida on his own terms is mentally to insert the phrase 'or not' after every one of his statements."

[3] Kevin J. Vanhoozer, ed., *Postmodern Theology* (Cambridge, UK: Cambridge University Press, 2005), 12.

1.6.2 MARXIST INFLUENCE

According to Glen Ward, the vast majority of mainstream Postmodernists emerged from the Marxist atheistic tradition.[4] Michel Foucault, for example, was at one time a member of the French Communist Party and one other Maoist organization.[5] Jean Baudrillard's writings were "within a loosely Marxist framework,"[6] thinking it was his responsibility to "bring Marx up to date."[7] Pierre Macherey was "a Marxist critic . . . concerned with how texts act to reproduce the values of capitalism."[8] A sympathetic critic defined Postmodernism as Marxism-lite dressed in a French tuxedo, sippin' French wine in a French café on the campus of the *College International de Philosophie*. A less sympathetic critic referred to Postmodernism as linguistic sophistry seeking to save Marxism's irrelevant posterior.

During its early years Marxism promised a this-world salvation for the enlightened irreligious. However, with the passage of time and countless body bags, the idea of a Marxist utopia was eventually revealed for what it was—a mirage. As a result, Postmodernism was birthed as a "wayward stepchild of Marxism, and in a sense a generation's realization that it is orphaned."[9]

Thus, Postmodernism became a reaction against Marxist dogma of violent revolutions, Marxist dialectical logic, and the Marxist worldview itself. On the other hand, Postmodernism is a continuation of other Marxist ideas, namely atheism, socialism, punctuated evolution, and the socially constructed self, among others.

1.6.3 NIETZSCHE'S INFLUENCE

Friedrich Nietzsche

In the pre-modern era God, revelation, and the clergy were the ultimate sources for truth about reality. However, in the modern era science and reason became the key resources for truth about reality. Well into the age of modernism, **Friedrich Nietzsche** stated the obvious from a modernist perspective: "God is dead; we have killed him." By this statement Nietzsche did not mean to imply that humanity killed God or that God was once alive and had died. Rather Nietzsche meant that *belief in* God was no longer necessary.

Foucault later checked the vital signs of modernity and discovered a corpse as cold as Nietzsche's God. He discovered that the modernist era had given way to another— Postmodernism. With this coming new era both Nietzsche and Foucault predicted a period of violence, death, destruction, and ultimately the end of humanity itself. Nietzsche put it down as follows:

Have you not heard of that madman who lit a lantern in the bright morning hours, ran to the market place, and cried incessantly: "I seek God! I seek God!"—

As many of those who did not believe in God were standing around just then, he provoked much laughter. Has he got lost? asked one. Did he lose his way like a child? asked another. Or is he

---

[4] See Glen Ward's *Teaching Yourself Postmodernism* (Chicago, IL: McGraw-Hill, 2003), 78f.

[5] Mark Lilla, *The Reckless Mind: Intellectuals in Politics* (New York, NY: New York Review Books, 2001), 150.

[6] Ward, *Teaching Yourself Postmodernism*, 78.

[7] Ibid.

[8] Ibid., 97.

[9] Lawrence E. Cahoone, ed., *From Modernism to Postmodernism: An Anthology*, 2nd ed. (Malden, MA: Blackwell Publishers, 2003), 4–5. Also see Gene Edward Veith, *Postmodern Times: A Christian Guide to Contemporary Thought and Culture* (Wheaton, IL: Crossway Books, 1994), 75–76.

hiding? Is he afraid of us? Has he gone on a voyage? emigrated?—Thus they yelled and laughed. The madman jumped into their midst and pierced them with his eyes.

"Whither is God?" he cried; "I will tell you. *We have killed him*—you and I. All of us are his murderers. But how did we do this? How could we drink up the sea? Who gave us the sponge to wipe away the entire horizon? What were we doing when we unchained this earth from its sun? Whither is it moving now? Whither are we moving? Away from all suns? Are we not plunging continually? Backward, sideward, forward, in all directions? Is there still any up or down? Are we not straying, as through an infinite nothing? Do we not feel the breath of empty space? Has it not become colder? Is not night continually closing in on us? Do we not need to light lanterns in the morning? Do we hear nothing as yet of the noise of the gravediggers who are burying God? Do we smell nothing as yet of the divine decomposition? Gods, too, decompose. God is dead. God remains dead. And we have killed him

"How shall we comfort ourselves, the murderers of all murderers? What was holiest and mightiest of all that the world has yet owned has bled to death under our knives: who will wipe this blood off us? What water is there for us to clean ourselves? What festivals of atonement, what sacred games shall we have to invent? Is not the greatness of this deed too great for us? Must we ourselves not become gods simply to appear worthy of it? There has never been a greater deed; and whoever is born after us—for the sake of this deed he will belong to a higher history than all history hitherto."

Here the madman fell silent and looked again at his listeners; and they, too, were silent and stared at him in astonishment. At last he threw his lantern on the ground, and it broke into pieces and went out. "I have come too early," he said then; "my time is not yet. This tremendous event is still on its way, still wandering; it has not yet reached the ears of men. Lightning and thunder require time; the light of the stars requires time; deeds, though done, still require time to be seen and heard. This deed is still more distant from them than most distant stars—*and yet they have done it themselves*.

It has been related further that on the same day the madman forced his way into several churches and there struck up his *requiem aeternam deo*. Led out and called to account, he is said always to have replied nothing but: "What after all are these churches now if they are not the tombs and sepulchers of God?"[10]

Foucault elaborates: ". . . Nietzsche indicated the turning-point from a long way off; it is not so much the absence or the death of God that is affirmed as the end of Man . . . it becomes apparent, then, that the death of God and the last man are engaged in a contest with more than one round: is it not the last man who announces that he has killed God, thus situating his language, his thought, his laughter in the space of that already dead God, yet positing himself also as he who has killed God and whose existence includes the freedom and the decision of that murder? Thus, the last man is at the same time older and yet younger than the death of God; since he has killed God, it is he himself who must answer for his own finitude; but since it is in the death of God that he speaks, thinks, and exists, his murder itself is doomed to die; new gods, the same gods, are already swelling the future Ocean; Man will disappear."[11]

Both Nietzsche and Foucault agree that after humanity kills God, they sign their own death certificate. A worldview perspective reveals how theological beliefs have implications for other areas of life. Nietzsche and Foucault understand the connection.

[10] Friedrich Wilhelm Nietzsche, *The Gay Science: With a Prelude in Rhymes and an Appendix of Songs*, trans. and comm. by Walter Arnold Kaufmann (New York, NY: Random House, 1974), 181. For a clear and understandable analysis of Nietzsche's anti-God and anti-Christ positions, see chapter nine of Will Durant, *The Story of Philosophy* (New York, NY: Simon and Schuster, 1983).

[11] Michel Foucault, *The Order of Things: An Archaeology of the Human Sciences* (New York, NY: Vintage Books, 1994), 385. Students reading Foucault need to keep in mind his own admission, "I am fully aware that I have never written anything other than fictions." Quoted in Dreyfus and Rabinow's *Michel Foucault: Beyond Structuralism and Hermeneutics*, 2nd ed. (Chicago, IL: University of Chicago Press, 1983), 204. Cited in Myron B. Penner, ed., *Christianity and the Postmodern Turn* (Grand Rapids, MI: Brazos Press, 2005), 30.

1.6.4 ATHEISM . . . POSTMODERN STYLE

The classical Postmodern theological spectrum stretches from militant atheism to village atheist. All the major Postmodern writers were atheists, including Foucault, Derrida, Lyotard, Bataille, Barthes, Baudrillard, Macherey, Deleuze, Guattari, and Lacan.

Charlotte Allen noted that Jacques Derrida, Michel Foucault, "and their [followers] . . . were all militant atheists, with all the intolerance and totalitarian tendencies of that breed."[12]

Yet at times Derrida himself was more cryptic about his atheism. Speaking before a convention of the American Academy of Religion in 2002, Derrida commented, "I rightly pass for an atheist."[13] However, when asked why he would not say more plainly 'I am an atheist,' he replied, "Maybe I'm not an atheist."[14] How can Derrida claim to be and not be an atheist? Both the existence or nonexistence of God requires a universal statement about reality, but Derrida is unwilling to make such an absolute claim. In this regard Derrida's theology is consistent with his Postmodern inclination for ambiguity.[15]

Likewise, Richard Rorty at one time admitted he was an atheist,[16] but in a subsequent work, *The Future of Religion,* he says he now agrees with Gianni Vattimo that "atheism (objective evidence for the nonexistence of God) is just as untenable as theism (objective evidence for the existence of God)."[17] Thus, Rorty insists that atheism, too, must be abandoned in favor of something he labels "anti-clericalism." Ecclesiastical institutions are dangerous, but not necessarily the local congregation of believers. "Religion," he says, "is unobjectionable as long as it is privatized."[18]

1.6.5 DECONSTRUCTION AND "THE DEATH OF GOD" THEOLOGIANS

If God is dead, the belief that there is no ultimate reality or eternal truth becomes a philosophical necessity. A firm believer in this, Derrida concluded further that words and sentences have no inherent meaning. He insisted that human beings construct reality through their use of language. In other words, as you read this page, you will construct your own meaning shaped by your culture and life experiences. The author's meaning is thus "deconstructed" or altered by the reader. In other words, the author's meaning becomes captive to the reader. As Ward says, "Deconstruction is a [literary] method of reading which effectively turns texts against themselves."[19]

For example, according to Derrida's theory of deconstruction, the Bible is merely a book written by men who were locked in their own culture, experiences, and language. Thus, the Biblical authors were writing about their own subjective experiences, not communicating objective or eternal truths about God and humanity. Therefore, when someone reads the Bible today, he or she brings a personal interpretive grid to the text. The theory of deconstruction can thus be used to explain how some cultures can read the Bible and proceed to slaughter

---

[12] *National Review*, September 13, 2004, 52.

[13] See Simon Barrow's "Derrida's Enduring Legacy" on the FaithInSociety weblog.

[14] Ibid.

[15] Millard J. Erickson, *Truth or Consequences: The Promise & Perils of Postmodernism* (Downers Grove, IL: InterVarsity Press, 2001), 131: "Derrida's own statements are seldom unequivocal [having one meaning]. He either makes a statement and conjoins it with its contradictory, or makes a statement and then in another place says something very different on the subject."

[16] Brandom, *Rorty and His Critics*, 344.

[17] Richard Rorty and Gianni Vattimo, *The Future of Religion* (New York, NY: Columbia University Press, 2005), 33, quoted in *Philosophia Christi* 7, no. 2 (2005): 525.

[18] Ibid.

[19] Ward, *Teaching Yourself Postmodernism*, 211.

another race, while other cultures reading the same Bible build hospitals, schools, orphanages, and homeless shelters.

> **DEATH OF GOD THEOLOGY:** A movement that flourished in the 1960s and 1970s, essentially promoting the idea that religion did not need to invoke "God" in the area of theology

Derrida's theory of deconstruction influenced a group of theologians in 1960s England. Bishop John A.T. Robinson in his book *Honest to God* sought to explain what it meant to be a Christian in the Postmodern world. This group became known as the "**Death of God**" theologians. According to Graham Ward, these theologians[20] saw "the potential of [Derrida's] deconstruction for furthering their project of announcing the end of theology [the death of God]."[21]

The "death of God" theologians fastened onto Derrida's idea that words refer only to other words in a textual setting and cannot be used to describe external realities such as God. They therefore claimed that God is not the Supreme Being who is literally "up there" in heaven somewhere, but instead we should think of God as being "out there" in a spiritual sense. God is "there" when we love another person, and this becomes the main Christian message. In this sense, the traditional concept of God ruling over His Creation is lifeless.[22]

Alister McGrath in *The Twilight of Atheism* speaks of the relationship between Postmodernism, atheism, and deconstruction. He says, "Many Postmodern writers are, after all, atheist (at least in the sense of not actively believing in God). The very idea of deconstruction seems to suggest that the idea of God ought to be eliminated from Western culture as a power play on the part of churches and others with vested interests in its survival."[23]

Derrida also supposed that the Western powers, because of their belief in the existence of God, went off the edge toward violence. However, this notion is far off base. The three "isms" of the 20th century responsible for the slaughter of tens of millions[24] (Communism, Nazism, and Fascism) were not exactly bastions of theism and Christianity. As a matter of fact, all three were grounded in atheism, evolution, and socialism—the very stuff of Postmodernism.

1.6.6 RELIGIOUS PLURALISM

The Postmodern idea that religious beliefs are private preferences has filtered down from the academy to the "unenlightened" commoner, many of whom now embrace pluralism.

Religious pluralism is the belief that one must be tolerant of all religious beliefs because no one religion can be true.[25] This notion agrees with the defining tenets of the Postmodern mood—skepticism of absolute truth, skepticism of a discernable foundation for knowledge, and, in the end, skepticism of all metanarratives (any overarching story that defines reality).[26] As such, many of those immersed in the present Postmodern culture deny religious truth claims.[27]

---

[20] Besides Robinson, other "death of God" theologians included William Hamilton, Thomas J. J. Altizer, Mark C. Taylor, Robert Scharlemann, Charles Winquist, Max Meyer, and Carl Raschke.

[21] Graham Ward, "Deconstructive Theology." Cited in Kevin J. Vanhoozer, ed., *Postmodern Theology* (Cambridge, UK: Cambridge University Press, 2003), 76.

[22] A good example of "Death of God theology" can found in Mark C. Taylor, "A Postmodern Theology," in Cahoone, *From Modernism to Postmodernism*, 435–46.

[23] Alister McGrath, *The Twilight of Atheism* (New York, NY: Doubleday, 2004), 227.

[24] R. J. Rummel, *Death By Government* (New Brunswick, NJ: Transaction Publishers, 1994).

[25] D.A. Carson, "Christian Witness in an Age of Pluralism," in D.A. Carson and John Woodbridge, eds., *God and Culture: Essays in Honor of Carl F.H. Henry* (Grand Rapids, MI: Eerdmans, 1993).

[26] A more complete list of what Postmodernism is against can be found in Robert Audi, *The Cambridge Dictionary of Philosophy*, 2nd ed. (Cambridge, UK: Cambridge University Press, 2001), 725.

[27] The logic of this position is very similar to the religious pluralism championed by some liberal theologians—John Hick, William Cantwell Smith, and S. Wesley Ariarajah. We must be careful not to equate these liberal theologians with outright Postmodernists. David S. Dockery, ed., *The Challenge of Postmodernism: An Evangeli-*

This trend can be seen in how our present society often thinks about religious claims in general. In the pre-modern and modern eras, religious claims were judged to be either true or false. For example, either there is a God or there is not. Either Jesus is Savior or He is not. Either miracles happen or they do not.

> **RELIGIOUS PLURALISM:** The conviction that we should be tolerant of all religious beliefs because no one religion can be true

However, in our Postmodern climate where truth is denied, religious claims are based on *preference* rather than on objective standards. For example, either you prefer the notion of the existence of God or you do not. Either you like the idea of Jesus being Savior or you do not. Either miracles appeal to you or they do not.[28] This attitude accommodates *all* religious preferences.

A problem arises when certain religions claim to go beyond personal preferences and convey objective truth, such as Judaism, Christianity, and Islam. But making exclusive truth claims runs counter to the Postmodern condition. For that reason, the only religions *not* tolerated are Judaism, Christianity, and Islam.

1.6.7 POST-CONSERVATIVE CHRISTIANS

Another theological trend is that of Postmodern Christianity or post-conservatism, or the **emergent church.**[29] A small yet influential group of Christian thinkers make up the leadership of this group—Stanley Grenz, Nancy Murphey, Roger Olson, Robert Webber, James K. A. Smith, Merold Westphal, and **Brian McLaren**. These "Postmodern" thinkers should not be identified with such atheistic thinkers as Nietzsche, Derrida, Foucault, Lyotard, or Rorty. [30] McLaren makes it clear that although he and his followers accept the term "Postmodern,"

> **POST-CONSERVATIVE CHRISTIANITY [OR EMERGENT CHURCH]:** A relatively new movement of Christians who are incorporating elements of Postmodernism within their theology

they are not "nihilistic, relativistic, anti-Christian, and otherwise slimy and bad."[31] Most in this camp believe the term best applies to their disposition rather than their dogma.

Although the movement is young, a number of common characteristics are emerging: (1) a critique of the negative aspects of modernism;[32] (2) a strong emphasis on community;[33] (3) a strong emphasis on putting one's faith into action;[34] and (4) a reminder that not all truth is propositional[35]—e.g. the *story* of "the good Samaritan" expresses the same truth that is found within the *proposition* "love your neighbor."

---

cal Engagement, 2nd ed. (Grand Rapids, MI: Baker Academic Books, 2001), 135, 142.

[28] Walter Truett Anderson, *Reality Isn't What It Used to Be: Theatrical Politics, Ready-to-Wear Religion, Global Myths, Primitive Chic, and Other Wonders of the Postmodern World* (San Francisco, CA: Harper & Row, 1990).

[29] The term "Post-conservative" is used by Roger Olson; Brian McLaren uses the term "emergent church;" Robert Webber uses the term "younger evangelicals;" and "Post-evangelical" has also been mentioned as a fitting label.

[30] Merold Westphal, *Overcoming onto-Theology: Toward a Postmodern Christian Faith*, Perspectives in Continental Philosophy No. 21 (New York, NY: Fordham University Press, 2001), xi.

[31] Brian McLaren, "Why I Still Use the Word Postmodern," http://www.emergingchurch.info/reflection/brianmclaren/index.htm.

[32] Stanley J. Grenz and John R. Franke, *Beyond Foundationalism: Shaping Theology in a Postmodern Context* (Louisville, KY: Westminster/John Knox, 2001), 10.

[33] John R. Franke, *The Character of Theology: An Introduction to Its Nature, Task, and Purpose* (Grand Rapids, MI: Baker Academic Books, 2005), 165–198.

[34] Ibid.

[35] See Kevin J. Vanhoozer, "The Semantics of Biblical Literature: Truth and Scripture's Diverse Literary Forms," in D.A. Carson and John D. Woodbridge, eds., *Hermeneutics, Authority, and Canon* (Grand Rapids, MI: Zondervan, 1986), 53–104.

On the other hand, several troubling traits are also emerging: (1) a denial of the Bible's inerrancy;[36] (2) a skepticism of foundational knowledge;[37] and (3) an orthodoxy that is perhaps *too* generous.[38] Thus, although they claim to be evangelical,[39] the jury of orthodoxy is still in deliberation.[40]

Brian McLaren

Myron B. Penner contends that culturally and philosophically the West is "in the throes of Postmodernity."[41] His suggestion: "Christians must come to terms with and work through the Postmodern turn and its implications for faith, not ignore or retreat from it. Above all, Christians must persevere in our faith through hope and love."[42] Penner warns Christians flirting with Postmodernism to be careful not to get caught up in the subjectivity of language to the point where words become emptied of all truth.[43]

1.6.8 CONCLUSION

We recognize that some individuals become atheists because they think Darwin solved the question of life's ultimate origins. Others become atheists because they look upon God's moral order as "too restrictive." Still others believe because they agree with Freud that, "God was a projection. When children have problems, they run to their father for protection. When adults have problems, they project their earthly father into the skies, and they run to this entity for comfort."[44] Some look at all the evil in the world and decide that no loving God could allow such a situation.[45] In the end, however, Postmodernists offer no new rationale for defending their brand of atheism. Our critique of atheism has been presented in other sections of this work, so it will not be repeated here.

In response to religious pluralism, we contend that the problem with this system in particular is the problem with Postmodernism in general—namely that neither our perspectives nor our preferences can dictate reality. Real people may end up in a literal Hell regardless

> R. Scott Smith, Truth and the New Kind of Christian: The Emerging Effects of Postmodernism in the Church (Wheaton, IL: Crossway Books, 2005) offers a fair and balanced treatment of the Emergent Church movement.

---

[36] Stanley J. Grenz, *Renewing the Center: Evangelical Theology in a Post-Theological Era* (Grand Rapids, MI: Baker Book House, 2000), 34, 70–84.

[37] Ibid. Also, see Nancey C. Murphy, *Anglo-American Postmodernity: Philosophical Perspectives on Science, Religion, and Ethics* (Boulder, CO: Westview, 1997), 27.

[38] Brian D. McLaren, *A Generous Orthodoxy: Why I Am a Missional, Evangelical, Post/Protestant, Liberal/Conservative, Mystical/Poetic, Biblical, Charismatic/Contemplative, Fundamentalist/Calvinist, Anabaptist/Anglican, Methodist, Catholic, Green, Incarnational, Depressed-yet-Hopeful, Emergent, Unfinished Christian* (El Cajon, CA; Grand Rapids, MI: Emergent YS; Zondervan, 2004). Also, see Jeremy Green's online book review in the 2005 Volume 8 Denver Seminary Journal: http://www.denverseminary.edu/dj/articles2005/0400/0406.php

[39] Stanley E. Porter and Anthony R. Cross, eds., "Post-Conservative Evangelical Theology and the Theological Pilgrimage of Clark Pinnock," in *Semper Refromandum: Studies in Honour of Clark H. Pinnock* (Carlisle, PA: Paternoster, 2003), 20.

[40] Millard J. Erickson, Paul Kjoss Helseth, and Justin Taylor, eds., *Reclaiming the Center: Confronting Evangelical Accommodation in Postmodern Times* (Wheaton, IL: Crossway Books, 2004).

[41] Ibid.

[42] Ibid.

[43] Penner, *Christianity and the Postmodern Turn*, 30.

[44] Ian S. Markham, ed., *A World Religious Reader* (Malden, MA: Blackwell Publishers, 2000), 24.

[45] McGrath, *The Twilight of Atheism*, 229.

of whether or not they prefer the doctrine of eternal punishment.[46] In the end, *reality is what it is* whether one prefers that reality or not. For example, many may not prefer a number of Christianity's tenets—creation, fall, salvation, judgment, abstinence, sobriety, etc. However, our preferences about Christianity or even reality itself cannot change the true nature of reality.

The Bible, of course, has a descriptive term for a person who says in his or her heart there is no God (Psalm 14:1). We will explore in later chapters the consequences of atheism as lived out in the areas of ethics, psychology, sociology, and each of the other disciplines. In these chapters we will find that those who embrace this theology have followed a foolish path indeed.

In the final analysis, atheism is a belief system of the intellectual elite ("the people of fashion") because only they possess enough faith to believe in it. The common, everyday working man cannot believe that everything in the universe is a result of random chance. As Mary Midgley says, "It may simply not be within our capacity—except of course by just avoiding thought—to think of [the universe] as having no sort of purpose or direction whatever."[47]

---

[46] Veith, *Postmodern Times*, 193–4.

[47] Mary Midgley, *Evolution as a Religion* (London, UK: Routledge Classics, 2002), 159–160.

Philosophy

Christianity

A little philosophy inclineth man's mind to atheism, but depth in philosophy bringeth men's minds about to religion.[1]

— SIR FRANCIS BACON

2.1.1 INTRODUCTION

Because it requires faith in biblical revelation, you might assume that the Christian worldview cannot possibly have a philosophy of its own. According to the secular worldviews, naturalism and materialism are grounded firmly in modern scientific methodology and enlightened human experience. How can we as Christians, who are required to postulate existence or reality outside the material realm, ever hope to prove that our beliefs are true, reasonable, rational, and worth living and dying for?

Unfortunately, some Christians adopt just such an attitude, concluding that their faith is indefensible. They attempt to avoid the whole problem by stating that what they believe is "beyond reason." These Christians point to Colossians 2:8, where Paul writes "See to it that no one takes you captive through hollow and deceptive philosophy . . . " and from this they draw the conclusion that God does not want us to meddle in such a vain and deceitful discipline as philosophy. However, people who use this verse as an anti-philosophical proof-text often omit its ending, in which Paul describes the kind of philosophy he is warning against—philosophy "which depends on human tradition and the basic principles of this world rather than on Christ."

---

[1] Hugh G. Dick, ed., *Select Writings of Francis Bacon* (New York, NY: Random House, 1955), 44.

The Bible does not ask us to abandon reason in order to accept its truth. "Come now," records Isaiah, "and let us reason together, saith the Lord: though your sins be as scarlet, they shall be white as snow" (Isaiah 1:18). The Apostle Peter encourages Christians to present logical, compelling reasons for their hope in Christ (1 Peter 3:15). But is this possible? Is Christian faith, and more specifically Christian philosophy, defensible?

C.E.M. Joad, who lived most of his life believing that the concept of God was unacceptable, finally concludes, "It is because . . . the religious view of the universe seems to me to cover more of the facts of experience than any other that I have been gradually led to embrace it."[2] He concluded his long personal pilgrimage by admitting "I now believe that the balance of reasonable considerations tells heavily in favor of the religious, even of the Christian view of the world."[3] This is the same Joad who appeared on BBC radio with Humanist Bertrand Russell attacking Christianity.

> It is because . . . the religious view of the universe seems to me to cover more of the facts of experience than any other that I have been gradually led to embrace it.
>
> — C.E.M. JOAD

Many who finally begin to reflect on the deeper things of life—"How did I get here? Why am I here? Where am I going?"—simply discover that Christianity answers these questions more completely than any other worldview. Those who earnestly seek truth will ultimately find themselves face-to-face with the God of the Bible. While some may enjoy debating about whether or not God exists, for the average person such debate is irrelevant—he or she is aware of His existence on a soul-deep level. Even today the vast majority of people (some polls place the figure as high as 95 percent) believe in a God, a fact Paul also found to be true in the Athens of his day (Acts 17:23).

2.1.2 FAITH AND EPISTEMOLOGY

The basic tenets of Christian philosophy are rational because they are held by average, rational men and women. But surely Christianity must still run into an epistemological problem—how does the Christian "know" without clashing with science and experience? How can the knowledge we gain through faith in Biblical revelation compare to knowledge gained by a scientific investigation of the universe?

The answer is not as difficult as you might imagine. All knowing requires faith. Faith precedes reason or, as W.J. Neidhardt puts it, "Faith correctly viewed is that illumination by which true rationality begins."[4] In other words, every worldview begins with a basic assumption about the nature of reality that cannot be proven by using the scientific method or logical deduction. This becomes the starting point from which to build a total view of life.

EPISTEMOLOGY: The study of knowledge

While Marxists and Humanists wish to portray science as primary knowledge and faith in biblical revelation as blind second-class **epistemology** or even superstition, the fact remains that all methods of knowing ultimately rely on certain assumptions. Edward T. Ramsdell writes, "The natural man is no less certainly a man of faith than the spiritual, but his faith is in the ultimacy of something other than the Word of God. The spiritual man is no less certainly a man of reason than the natural, but his reason, like

---

[2] C.E.M. Joad, *The Recovery of Belief* (London, UK: Faber and Faber Limited, 1955), 16.

[3] Ibid., 22.

[4] Carl F.H. Henry, *God, Revelation and Authority*, 6 vols. (Waco, TX: Word Books, 1976), 1:169. Henry mentions W.J. Neidhardt's work "Faith, the Unrecognized Partner of Science and Religion" as the source for his comments.

that of every man, functions within the perspective of his faith."[5]

The basic problem of philosophy is not the problem of faith versus reason. "The crucial problem," says Warren C. Young, "is that some thinkers place their trust in a set of assumptions in their search for truth, while other thinkers place their trust in a quite different set of assumptions."[6] That is, Humanists and Marxists place their trust in certain findings of science and experience, neither of which can be rationally demonstrated as the source of all truth.

Christians also appeal to science, history, and personal experience, but they know such avenues for discovering truth are not infallible. Christians know that scientists make mistakes and scientific journals can practice discrimination against views considered dangerous. Christians know that history can be perverted, distorted, or twisted and that personal experience is not a good source of fact or knowledge. On the other hand, Christians believe that Biblical revelation is true and that God would not mislead His children.

Christian philosophy does not reject reason or tests for truth. Christianity says the New Testament is true because its truths can be tested. Christians do not ask non-believers to put their faith in a revelation of old wives' tales or fables, but instead to consider certain historical evidences that reason itself can employ as an attorney building a case uses evidences in the law to determine questions of fact. Christian epistemology is based on special revelation, which in turn is based on history, the law of evidence, and the science of archaeology.

Philosophical naturalists also make assumptions that they, by definition, accept on faith. All naturalists agree that there is no supernatural. "This point," says Young, "is emphasized by the naturalists themselves without seeming to be at all troubled by the fact that it is an emotional rather than a logical conclusion."[7]

The Pop Culture Connection

In **Revolutions**, the third of the Matrix trilogy, the final scene shows a girl asking the Oracle if she always knew Neo was "the One." "Oh no," replies the Oracle. "But I believed, I believed." The Oracle's statement reflects a common misconception about the nature of belief, or faith. Many people think faith refers to a strong belief apart from any reason or evidence to back it up. Yet, the Bible does not use "faith" in that way. According to Hebrews 11:1, faith "is being sure of what we hope for and certain of what we do not see." The Greek terms used for "sure" and "certain" mean assurance and proof or conviction. Thus, the Bible defines faith as a sure conviction based on evidence, not a blind emotional state devoid of rational thought and evaluation.

Faith is critical in every philosophy. When developing a philosophy, we must be extremely careful to base our case on the most truthful assumptions—otherwise, should one of the assumptions prove to be untrue (as it appears the assumptions of the theory of evolution will be), the whole philosophy will crumble. If evolution crumbles (which is quite possible—Dr. Karl Popper believes evolution does not fit the definition of "a scientific theory"), Marxism and Humanism are intellectually dead.

So far, we have established two things regarding Christian philosophy: many hold it to be the most rational of all worldviews, and it requires no more faith than any other philosophy. Indeed, we could argue that it takes a great deal *more* faith to believe in the spontaneous generation of Darwinian evolution or the randomness of all nature (i.e., that the universe happened by accident) than it does to accept the Christian doctrine of Creator/Creation.

[5] Edward T. Ramsdell, *The Christian Perspective* (New York, NY: Abingdon-Cokesbury Press, 1950), 42.
[6] Warren C. Young, *A Christian Approach to Philosophy* (Grand Rapids, MI: Baker Book House, 1975), 37.
[7] Ibid., 182.

2.1.3 RECONCILING SCIENCE AND CHRISTIAN PHILOSOPHY

People tend to believe in the most likely solution to a problem. That is why most people believe that "In the beginning God created the heavens and the earth" (Genesis 1:1) and "all things therein" (Acts 17:24). Jean Piaget, a child psychologist, has found that a seven-year-old believes almost instinctively that everything in the universe has a purpose.

> It has often been represented that the conclusions of science are hostile to the tenets of religion. Whatever grounds there may have been for such a view in the past, it is hard to see with what good reason such a contention could be sustained today.
>
> — C.E.M. JOAD

Believing the truth of Genesis 1:1 makes more sense than believing that a series of cosmic accidents brought about the orderly, beautiful, meaningful cosmos. Two skeptics, Peter D. Ward and Donald Brownlee, wrote a work entitled *Rare Earth* [8] in which they detail a number of incredibly precise measurements related to the elements and parameters of the earth that had to be exactly correct in order to sustain life on this planet. Yet they concluded that it all happened by accident. On the other hand, the producers of "The Privileged Planet" cannot accept the notion that the earth "got it just right" as a mark of chance. The God of the universe is responsible for such a magnificent creation. [9]

The wise Christian philosopher recognizes the scientific method as a limited but valuable ally. In addition to lending support for the teleological argument (that design in the universe implies a Designer), science also shores up the cosmological argument (that God is the "first cause" of the universe). Joad reinforces the idea that science does not threaten Christianity, stating, "It has often been represented that the conclusions of science are hostile to the tenets of religion. Whatever grounds there may have been for such a view in the past, it is hard to see with what good reason such a contention could be sustained today." [10]

Stephen D. Schwarz cites four particular scientific discoveries that support the conclusion that God exists: the Second Law of Thermodynamics (stating that the universe is running out of usable energy and cannot be infinitely old), [11] the impossibility of spontaneous generation of life from non-life (verified by Pasteur over 150 years ago), genetic information theory (which postulates that specified complexity, like that found in DNA, comes from a mind, never by chance), [12] and the Anthropic Principle (that the universe as well as planet earth are specifically "fine-tuned" to accommodate life).

For the Christian, then, science need not be an enemy—indeed, science should be accepted as a somewhat successful method of obtaining knowledge about God's design in the universe. As **C.S. Lewis** says, "In science we have been reading only the notes to a poem; in Christianity we find the poem itself." [13]

---

[8] Peter D. Ward and Donald Brownlee, *Rare Earth: Why Complex Life is Uncommon in the Universe* (New York, NY: Copernicus, 2000).

[9] "The Privileged Planet" was produced by Illustra Media (www.illustramedia.com).

[10] Joad, *The Recovery of Belief*, 107.

[11] J.P. Moreland and William Lane Craig, *Philosophical Foundations For A Christian Worldview* (Downers Grove, IL: InterVarsity Press, 2003): "According to the second law of thermodynamics, processes taking place in a closed system always tend toward a state of equilibrium . . . The universe is, on a naturalistic view, a gigantic closed system, since it is everything there is there is nothing outside it. This seems to imply that, given enough time, the universe and all its processes will run down, and the entire universe will come to equilibrium. This is known as the heat death of the universe."

[12] See Michael J. Behe, *Darwin's Black Box: The Biochemical Challenge to Evolution* (New York, NY: The Free Press, 1996) for the workings of DNA.

[13] Clyde S. Kilby, ed., *A Mind Awake: An Anthology of C.S. Lewis* (New York, NY: Harcourt, Brace & World, 1968), 240.

2.1.4 THE ORIGIN OF SCIENCE

An examination of the history of modern science reaffirms the supernaturalist's premise that science is not hostile to the Christian position. Modern science was founded by those who viewed the world from a Christian perspective. Francis Schaeffer writes, "Since the world had been created by a reasonable God, [scientists] were not surprised to find a correlation between themselves as observers and the thing observed—that is, between subject and object. . . . Without this foundation, modern Western science would not have been born."[14]

C.S. Lewis

Christianity was "the mother of modern science."[15] Norman L. Geisler and J. Kerby Anderson's *Origin Science* contains a chapter titled "The Supernatural Roots of Modern Science." Both Alfred North Whitehead and J. Robert Oppenheimer defended this view. Philosopher and historian of science Stanley L. Jaki notes that historically the belief in creation and the Creator was the moment of truth for science: "This belief formed the bedrock on which science rose."[16] Jaki powerfully defends this position in the *Origin of Science* and the *Savior of Science*. Rodney Stark comes to the same conclusion.[17]

Re-examine the statements by Schaeffer and Jaki for a moment. Notice that each claim is grounded on the fact that science assumed an orderly universe. If we believe the universe is disorderly or chaotic, we would not have the philosophical basis for modern science, which assumes matter will behave in certain meaningful ways under controlled conditions. On earth, we always expect an apple to fall down rather than up because we believe in consistent law—the Law of Gravity. Lewis says people became scientific because they expected Law in Nature and "they expected Law in Nature because they believed in a Legislator."[18] In other words, the origin of modern science itself provides grounds for the teleological argument—the argument from design to Designer.

2.1.5 METAPHYSICS: ONTOLOGY/COSMOLOGY

The Christian view of **metaphysics**—of ultimate reality (**ontology** and **cosmology**)—is part of what C.S. Lewis termed "Mere Christianity." There are certain things virtually all Christians believe, and one is that God is the supreme source of all being and reality. He is the ultimate reality. Because of this, we and the entire space-time creation, says Carl F.H. Henry, depend on the Creator-God "for its actuality, its meaning and its purpose."[19] This creation is intelligible because God is intelligent and we can understand the creation and Creator because He made us in His image with the capacity to understand Him and His intelligent order.

> METAPHYSICS: The study of ultimate reality
>
> COSMOLOGY: The study of the structure, origin, and design of the universe
>
> ONTOLOGY: The study of the existence of being

The Christian view of metaphysics is clearly spelled out in Scripture: "In the beginning [of the cosmos] was the Word [Logos, mind, reason, thought, wisdom, intelligence, idea, law,

---

[14] Francis A. Schaeffer, *How Should We Then Live?* (Old Tappan, NJ: Fleming H. Revell, 1976), 134.

[15] Ibid.

[16] Stanley L. Jaki, *The Road of Science and the Ways to God* (South Bend, IN: Regnery Gateway, 1979).

[17] Rodney Stark, *For The Glory Of God* (Princeton, NJ: Princeton University Press, 2003).

[18] Kilby, *A Mind Awake*, 234.

[19] Henry, *God, Revelation and Authority*, 5:336.

order, purpose, design], and the Word was with God, and the Word was God. The same [Word] was in the beginning with God. All things were made by him; and without him was not anything made that was made. In him was life; and the life was the light of men" (John 1:1–4).

The flow of this passage sets the parameters of Christian philosophy—mind before matter; God before people; plan and design before creation; life from life; and enlightenment from the Light. The orderly universe was conceived in the orderly and rational mind of God before it was created. Without the Logos there would be no cosmos. From the Christian perspective it is no surprise to see philosophers and scientists refer to the universe as a manifestation of mathematical law, order, design, and beauty.

It is no accident that at every level of the cosmos—sub-atomic, atomic, organic, inorganic, sub-human, human, earth, moon, sun, stars, galaxies—all things manifest amazing order and rationality that can be reasonably explained only as the result of a deliberate, creative act of God.

The current theory of evolution declares the cosmos to be the result of a series of random accidents. Christianity considers this view an entirely irrational notion. Such a position is tantamount to claiming that a skyscraper can come together without an architect, plan, or engineer. It doesn't happen that way in the real world; only in the minds of those who assume there is no supernatural Designer.

2.1.6 MIND/BODY PROBLEM AND THE MENTAL PROOF

The supernaturalist believes that the mind, or consciousness, exists as a separate entity from the purely physical. As Christians, we believe that our mind is a reflection of the Universal Mind, and we see the mind as an additional proof for the existence of the supernatural.

We perceive that our thinking process is something different from the material world. Young says, "Man is so made that his spirit may operate upon and influence his body, and his body is so made that it may operate upon his mind or spirit."[20] This distinction between brain and mind implies a distinction about the whole order of things: matter exists (i.e., the brain), and something other than matter exists (i.e., the mind). "We find in the created universe an important difference between beings which think, and beings which are spatially extended, or spiritual beings and material beings. . . . In the body and mind of man we see integrated interaction between the spiritual thinking being, and the material extended being."[21]

MIND/BODY PROBLEM: The study of the relationship of the mind (e.g. mental events, mental functions, mental properties, and consciousness) to the physical body

MIND/BODY DUALISM: Contends that the body is material in substance while the mind is immaterial

MIND/BODY MONISM: Contends the body and mind are both purely material substances

Many Christian thinkers believe this distinction between the brain and the mind is intuitively obvious, and this is the beginning of the mental proof for the existence of a Higher Mind responsible for our minds. Other Christian thinkers begin with the untenability of the materialist position that the mind is only a material phenomenon and draw the conclusion that because the materialist explanation is irrational, the supernatural explanation must be the acceptable position.

Young says, "Christian realists are contingent dualists but not eternal dualists. They hold that there are two kinds of substance: Spirit (or God) and matter which was created by God ex nihilo as Augustine suggested. Matter is not spirit, nor is it reducible to spirit, but its existence

---

[20] Ibid., 120.

[21] James Oliver Buswell, Jr., *A Christian View of Being and Knowing* (Grand Rapids, MI: Zondervan, 1960), 8.

is always dependent upon God Who created it out of nothing."[22] Young chooses to use the term Christian **realism** to represent the Christian philosophy. In an effort to stress the existence of something other than the material, we employ the term **supernaturalism**.

> REALISM: The belief that what one encounters in the world exists independently of human thought

At this juncture, science aids the Christian philosopher in undermining the materialist worldview. Writes Buswell, "The mind is not the brain. The 'brain track' psychology has failed. . . . It is a known fact that if certain parts of the brain are destroyed, and the functions corresponding to those parts impaired, the functions may be taken up by other parts of the brain. There is no exact correspondence between mind and brain."[23]

Sir John Eccles has made a voluminous contribution to this discussion in recent years. His three works, *The Self and Its Brain* (with Karl Popper), *The Human Mystery*, and *The Human Psyche* are considered classics in the field. Eccles maintains that having a mind means one is conscious, and that consciousness is a mental event, not a material event. He further contends that there are two distinct, different orders, i.e., the brain is in the material world and the mind is in the "world of subjective experience."

Lewis cuts to the heart of the materialist and naturalist dilemma when he writes, "The Naturalists have been engaged in thinking about Nature. They have not attended to the fact that they were thinking. The moment one attends to this it is obvious that one's own thinking cannot be merely a natural event, and that therefore something other than Nature exists. The Supernatural is not remote and abstruse: it is a matter of daily and hourly experience, as intimate as breathing."[24]

D. Elton Trueblood believes that supernaturalism is unavoidable: "How can nature include mind as an integral part unless it is grounded in mind? If mind were seen as something alien or accidental, the case would be different, but the further we go in modern science the

> SUPERNATURALISM: The belief that reality is more than nature; that a transcendent agent intervenes in the course of natural law

clearer it becomes that mental experience is no strange offshoot. Rather it is something which is deeply rooted in the entire structure."[25] Implied, then, is the existence of a God who could create an entire structure with mind as an integral part. Once an individual grants the existence of an orderly mind separate from the physical universe, belief in the Ultimate Mind becomes the only rational option.

We must remember, however, that God is much more than an "Ultimate Mind." The mental proof may help to establish the existence of God, but the God of rational "proofs" alone is unworthy of worship—only the Christian God, in all His power and holiness, elicits awe and love in their proper proportion.

[22] Young, *A Christian Approach to Philosophy*, 37.
[23] Ibid., 142.
[24] Kilby, *A Mind Awake*, 205.
[25] D. Elton Trueblood, *Philosophy of Religion* (Grand Rapids, MI: Baker Book House, 1957), 206.

2.17 CONCLUSION

Supernaturalism is more than a philosophy in the narrow sense. Christian philosophy represents an entire worldview, a view that is consistent with the Bible throughout. In the end, you must choose between a materialist/naturalist worldview and a supernaturalist worldview—and your choice will create repercussions throughout every aspect of your life.

The Christian philosophy embraces the meaningful, purposeful life, a life in which you shape your beliefs according to a coherent, reasonable, truthful worldview. As a Christian with such a worldview, you will not be tossed to and fro by every secularist doctrine. "In the same way," says Dr. Young, "it can be said that the Christian philosopher and theologian must be acquainted with the contending world-views of his age. Philosophy after all is a way of life, and the Christian believes that he has the true way—the true pattern for living. It is the task of the Christian leader to understand the ideologies of his day so that he may be able to meet their challenges. The task is a never-ending one, for, although the Christian's worldview does not change, the world about him does. Thus the task of showing the relevance of the Christian realistic philosophy to a world in process is one which requires eternal vigilance. To such a task, to such an ideal, the Christian leader must dedicate himself."[26], [27]

[26] Young, *A Christian Approach to Philosophy*, 228–9.

[27] See Ronald H. Nash, *Life's Ultimate Questions: An Introduction to Philosophy* (Grand Rapids, MI: Zondervan, 1999); J.P. Moreland and William Lane Craig, *Philosophical Foundations For A Christian Worldview* (Downers Grove, IL: InterVarsity Press, 2003); and Alvin Plantinga, *Warranted Christian Belief* (Oxford, UK: Oxford University Press, 2000).

Philosophy

Islam

Belief in angels originates from the Islamic principle that knowledge and truth are not entirely confined to the sensory knowledge or sensory perception alone.[1]

— HAMMUDA ABDALATI

2.2.1 INTRODUCTION

Islamic and Christian philosophies agree in some ways because both are theistic and share some biblical roots. Both affirm the supernatural and miracles. Both also use faith and reason to support their religious beliefs. Thoughtful Muslims would agree with most of what J.P. Moreland and William Lane Craig say in *Philosophical Foundations for a Christian Worldview*.[2] In tandem with it, a fuller treatment of Islamic philosophy is available in Oliver Leaman's *An Introduction to Classical Islamic Philosophy*.[3]

---

[1] Hammuda Abdalati, *Islam in Focus* (Indianapolis, IN: Amana Publications, 1975), 13.

[2] J.P. Moreland and William Lane Craig, *Philosophical Foundations For A Christian Worldview* (Downers Grove, IL: InterVarsity Press, 2003).

[3] Oliver Leaman, *An Introduction to Classical Islamic Philosophy* (Cambridge, UK: Cambridge University Press, 2002). Also, a good summary of Islamic philosophy is in Gordon H. Clark, *Thales to Dewey: A History of Philosophy* (Grand Rapids, MI: Baker Book House, 1980), 265f.

2.2.2 TRADITIONS OF ISLAMIC PHILOSOPHY

The history of Islam contains significant examples of Islamic philosophers, who sought to appropriate what they could of various philosophical traditions: Al-Farabi (872–950); Avicenna (980–1037); Averroes (1126–1198); and Al-Ghazali (1058/1111).[4]

Islamic philosophers were greatly influenced by Greek philosophy and sought to use it to understand, defend, and further their faith. However, their theorizing often led them astray from orthodox Islamic teachings. For example, some of them believed, following Aristotle, that the material world was eternal, though they also affirmed that it existed only because God made it to exist. Others denied physical resurrection, substituting the continued existence of the soul. Still others proposed a replacement body that looked like the original, but actually was not. Most philosophers advocated the idea that God was a Necessary Being (a being who could not *not* exist) and that the world was dependent upon God for its existence.[5]

> **KALAM COSMOLOGICAL ARGUMENT:** A rational reflection of three exhaustive dilemmas regarding the origin of the cosmos: 1) Did the universe have a beginning or has it always existed? 2) Was the beginning caused or uncaused? 3) Is the agent of cause personal or impersonal?

The **Kalam Cosmological Argument** for the existence of God was developed by Islamic philosophers and is both commended and employed by Christian philosophers today. The cosmological argument, for example, is the argument from creation to a Creator. "It argues *a posteriori*, from effect to cause, and is based on the principle of causality. This states that every event has a cause, or that every thing that begins has a cause. The Kalam (Arabic: 'eternal') argument is a horizontal (linear) form of the cosmological argument. The universe is not eternal, so it must have had a Cause. That Cause must be considered God. This argument has a long and venerable history among such Islamic philosophers as Alfarabi, Al Ghazali, and Avicenna. Some scholastic philosophers also used it, especially Bonaventure."[6]

Some Islamic philosophers ventured into mysticism. Rahman asserts that much of the Islamic philosophic tradition fell away from orthodox Islam, but was retained and furthered in Sufism, a semi-mystic sect of Islam.

Though some traditionalist Muslims believe such ventures into philosophy inherently conflict with the Qur'an and the Hadith, many others believe such attempts to explain and defend Islam with philosophical tools are entirely appropriate (though they would not be able to affirm *all* that Islamic philosophers have concluded).

2.2.3 AFFIRMING SUPERNATURALISM

Islam argues for the existence of entities beyond the natural world; affirmation of the existence of God, for example, illustrates that Islam denies naturalism in favor of super-naturalism. Islam also affirms the existence of the human spirit beyond death, as well as the existence of angels and jinn.

Abdalati writes, "The true Muslim also believes in the angels of God. They are purely spiritual and splendid beings whose nature requires no food or drink or sleep. They have no physical desires of any kind nor material needs. They spend their days and nights in the service of God. There are many of them, and each is charged with a certain duty. If we cannot see the angels with our naked eyes, it does not necessarily deny their actual existence . . . Belief in

---

[4] Al-Ghazali was a brilliant Muslim scholar, a Sufi, who challenged the philosophers and sought to defend orthodox Islamic theology.

[5] See the discussion in Fazlur Rahman, *Islam*, 2nd ed. (Chicago, IL: University of Chicago Press, 1979), 117–127, as well as the full-scale survey and discussion in Leaman.

[6] Norman L. Geisler, *Baker Encyclopedia of Christian Apologetics* (Grand Rapids, MI: Baker Book House, 1999), 399.

angels originates from the Islamic principle that knowledge and truth are not entirely confined to the sensory knowledge or sensory perception alone . . ."[7]

In admitting the existence of angels, Abdalati also alludes to the Islamic view of epistemology: not all things may be known through human senses, nor may we limit the field of existence to what our senses perceive.

2.2.4 LIFE AFTER DEATH AND RESURRECTION

Fundamental to Islam is the belief in final judgment, necessitating an implied belief in life after death. Muslims further affirm the bodily resurrection of the dead (though they deny that Jesus died and was resurrected). "See thee not that God, Who created the heavens and the earth . . . is able to give life to the dead? Yea, verily He has power over all things (Qur'an 46:33). And he [unbelieving man] makes comparisons for Us, and forgets his own (origin and) Creation: He says, 'Who can give Life to (dry) bones and decomposed ones (at that)?' Say, 'He will give them Life Who created them for the first time! For He is well-versed in every kind of creation'" (36:78–79).

2.2.5 MIRACLES

The story of Islam begins with Muhammad receiving divine visions and communicating with the angel Gabriel, indicating an acceptance of the supernatural. Indeed, the Qur'an affirms that prophets of old performed many miracles. Consider some passages regarding Moses:

> (Pharaoh) said: 'If indeed thou hast come with a Sign, show it forth, if thou tellest the truth.' Then (Moses) threw his rod, and behold, it was a serpent, plain (for all to see)! And he drew out his hand, and behold, it was white to all beholders! (7:106–107)

> Said Moses [to the sorcerers of Pharaoh's court]: 'Throw ye (first).' So when they threw, they bewitched the eyes of the people, and struck terror into them: for they showed a great (feat of) magic. We put it into Moses' mind by inspiration: 'Throw (now) thy rod': and behold, it swallows up straightaway all the falsehoods which they fake! Thus truth was confirmed and all that they did was made of no effect. (7:116–118)

> 'Then we sent Moses and his brother Aaron, and with Our Signs and Authority manifest.' (23:45; see, 7:106 108)

The miracles Jesus performed are also acknowledged.

> Then will God say: 'O Jesus the son of Mary! Recount My favour to thee and to they mother . . . and thou healest those born blind, and the lepers, by My leave. And behold, thou bringest forth the dead by My leave. And behold, I did restrain the Children of Israel from (violence to) thee when thou didst show them the Clear Signs. . . . (5:113)

These stories presuppose a view of supernaturalism wherein God intervenes in the world (miracles) and seeks to convey His will to human beings (revelation). Orthodox Islamic philosophy affirms the occurrence of miracles and the existence of supernatural beings.

2.2.6 MUHAMMAD'S LACK OF MIRACLES

Oliver Leaman observes that despite a stated belief in miracles, "it is worth emphasizing that Islam as a religion does not make much use of miracles."[8] Leaman is referring to the fact

---

[7] Abdalati, *Islam in Focus*, 13.
[8] Leaman, *An Introduction to Classical Islamic Philosophy*, 102.

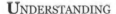

that the Qur'an records Muhammad performing no miracles in support of his claim to be a prophet, a lack that led people to challenge his claims.

> And the unbelievers say: 'Why is not a Sign sent down to him [Muhammad] from his Lord?' But thou art truly a warner and to every people a guide. (13:7)

> God hath heard the taunt of those who say, 'Truly, God is indigent and we are rich!' We shall surely record their word and (their act) of slaying the Prophets in defiance of right, and We shall say: 'Taste yet the Penalty of scorching Fire! This is because of the (unrighteous deeds) which your hands sent on before ye: For God never harms those who serve Him.'

> They also said: 'God took our promise not to believe in an apostle unless He showed us a sacrifice consumed by fire (from heaven).' Say: 'There came to you Apostles before me [Muhammad] with Clear Signs and even with what ye ask for: why then did ye slay them, if ye speak the truth?'

> Then if they reject thee, so were rejected apostles before thee, who came with Clear Signs, Books of dark prophecies, and the Book of Enlightenment. (3:181–184)

We could suppose that "the greatest of the prophets" of Islam would perform the greatest of miracles. Jesus was the greatest prophet in the Bible and He walked on water, multiplied loaves of bread and fishes to feed thousands, and was resurrected from the dead (though Muslims deny it). Throughout His lifetime, Jesus performed great and wondrous signs to support His claim to be Israel's Messiah. Paul notes that even the apostles performed miracles ("The things that mark an apostle—signs, wonders, and miracles—were done among you with great perseverance." 2 Corinthians 12:12). Muhammad not only claimed to be a prophet of God, he also claimed to be greater than Jesus. In this light, the conclusion of the Christian philosopher Blaise Pascal is apropos: "Any man can do what Mahomet has done; for he performed no miracles . . . No man can do what Christ has done."[9]

> Any man can do what Mahomet has done; for he performed no miracles . . . No man can do what Christ has done.
>
> — BLAISE PASCAL

2.2.7 MUHAMMAD AND BIBLICAL PROPHECY

Christianity and Islam conflict not on the *possibility* of the miraculous, but on the content and competing claims attending such miracles. For instance, the Muslim convictions that Muhammad is a prophet and the Qur'an is divine revelation are convictions with which Christians disagree. Given Muhammad's denial of the deity, death, and resurrection of Jesus, Christians simply cannot see Muhammad as a reliable source of information, let alone a prophet of God.

Muslims believe that the Qur'an is only one of several holy books (including the Torah of Moses, the Psalms of David, and the Gospel of Jesus). However, Muslims' belief that the Qur'an is the only holy book preserved through time without error conflicts sharply with the Christian belief in God's preservation of the Bible (a belief confirmed by impressive historical evidence). Muslim apologists join forces with critics of the Bible, asserting that biblical miracles and narratives are merely legends.

One of the best ways to illustrate the contrasts between Muslim and Christian belief relates to the Muslim belief that passages in the Bible foretell Muhammad's coming. If these Islamic claims were true, then Christians would be obligated to become Muslims. But if these claims

---

[9] Blaise Pascal, *Pensées*, #600, http://www.ccel.org/ccel/pascal/pensees.x.html (Accessed May 12, 2006).

are not true, then an important support of the Islamic worldview is lost. Muslims appeal to Deuteronomy, Psalms, Isaiah, Habakkuk, and the Gospel of John. Most prominent among these references are Deuteronomy 18:15,18 and John 14:16.

2.2.8 DEUTERONOMY 18:15,18

Muslims believe the promised prophet in the following Old Testament verses is Muhammad rather than Jesus: "The LORD your God will raise up for you a prophet like me [Moses] from among your own brothers. You must listen to him . . . I [God] will raise up for them a prophet like you [Moses] from among their brothers; I will put my words in his mouth, and he will tell them everything I command him" (Deuteronomy 18:15, 18).

Moses says in these verses that God will raise up (1) a prophet, (2) like Moses, (3) from among the Israelites, that (4) He will put His words in his mouth, and (5) he will proclaim to the Israelites everything God commands him. The earliest Christians believed that this prophecy was fulfilled in Jesus Christ, who was a prophet, as well as God incarnate.

Several Bible passages record that Jesus describes Himself as a prophet: "And they took offense at him. But Jesus said to them, 'Only in his hometown and in his own house is a prophet without honor'" (Matthew 13:57; cf. Mark 6:4 and John 4:44). "'In any case, I must keep going today and tomorrow and the next day—for surely no prophet can die outside Jerusalem!'" (Luke 13:33).

Not only does Jesus describe Himself as a prophet, but some of the people of Israel do as well. John writes about Jesus miraculously feeding five thousand people: "After the people saw the miraculous sign that Jesus did, they began to say, 'Surely this is the Prophet who is to come into the world'" (John 6:14). Matthew writes about Jesus' triumphal entry into Jerusalem: the crowds proclaimed, "This is Jesus, the prophet from Nazareth in Galilee" (Matthew 21:11). Luke records part of a conversation between Jesus and some of His followers after His crucifixion. While their eyes were temporarily blinded to the fact that they were actually talking to Jesus, their description of Him as a prophet remains: "One of them, named Cleopas, asked [Jesus], 'Are you only a visitor to Jerusalem and do not know the things that have happened there in these days?' 'What things?' [Jesus] asked. 'About Jesus of Nazareth,' they replied. 'He was a prophet, powerful in word and deed before God and all the people'" (Luke 24:18–19).

Peter and Stephen also proclaimed the same message, specifying that Jesus was the promised prophet like Moses: "Repent, then, and turn to God, so that your sins may be wiped out, that times of refreshing may come from the Lord, and that he may send the Christ, who has been appointed for you—even Jesus. He must remain in heaven until the time comes for God to restore everything, as He promised long ago through His holy prophets. For Moses said, 'The Lord your God will raise up for you a prophet like me from among your own people; you must listen to everything he tells you. Anyone who does not listen to him will be completely cut off from among his people'" (Acts 3:19–23). Here Peter quotes the prophecy from Deuteronomy 18, applying it to Jesus (see also Stephen's speech in Acts 7:37–53).

These passages show that according to the New Testament authors, including Jesus Himself, Jesus fulfilled the prophecy of Deuteronomy 18 long before Muhammad arrived.

2.2.9 JESUS AND MOSES

Muslims contend that Jesus could not have fulfilled the prophecy of Deuteronomy 18 because He did not proclaim the law like Moses. However, the biblical account clearly shows that Jesus sought to restore the people of God to the purity of the law. This is seen most clearly in the Sermon on the Mount (Matthew 5–7). Consider Jesus' thesis statement in Matthew

5:17–20: "Do not think that I have come to abolish the Law or the Prophets; I have not come to abolish them but to fulfill them. I tell you the truth, until heaven and earth disappear, not the smallest letter, not the least stroke of a pen, will by any means disappear from the Law until everything is accomplished. Anyone who breaks one of the least of these commandments and teaches others to do the same will be called least in the kingdom of heaven, but whoever practices and teaches these commands will be called great in the kingdom of heaven. For I tell you that unless your righteousness surpasses that of the Pharisees and the teachers of the law, you will certainly not enter the kingdom of heaven."

In proclaiming the endurance of the law, as well as the importance of obeying the law, Jesus surely sounds like Moses (see Deuteronomy 30:11–16). In addition, Jesus gave laws to His people. In John 14:34, Jesus says, "A new command I give you: Love one another. As I have loved you, so you must love one another." Later New Testament authors even speak of "the law of Christ" (Galatians 6:2; 1 Corinthians 9:21).

So, Jesus is a prophet and, like Moses, a proclaimer of the law, but Muslims do not agree that the phrase "from among their brothers" refers to an Israelite prophet. They believe the passage refers to non-Israelites, as it does in Deuteronomy 2:4 and 2:8, which refers to the descendants of Esau.

Yet within the context of Deuteronomy 18:15, 18 "brethren" cannot be taken to mean anything other than a reference to fellow Israelites. For example, Deuteronomy 17:15 provides the stipulation for the installment of a king over Israel. He was to be "from among your own brothers," not "a foreigner" (and Muhammad definitely was a foreigner to Israel). The king was to write a copy of the law for himself and read it all the days of his life, so he will not "consider himself better than his brothers" (17:20). Deuteronomy 18:2 explains that the Levites would not be granted an allotment of the promised land, having "no inheritance among their brothers." And as the Israelites prepare for the battles they will face as they enter the promised land, they are told that if one of them is fearful, "Let him go home so that his brothers will not become disheartened too" (20:8). Thus Jesus fulfills completely this aspect of the prophecy, for He (in contrast to Muhammad) was an Israelite (see the genealogies of Matthew 1 and Luke 3).

In addition to the evidence that Jesus, His disciples, and other New Testament authors agree that Deuteronomy 18:15, 18 was fulfilled in Jesus, John says that the words Jesus spoke were from God and that He proclaimed them to Israel: "Jesus answered, 'My teaching is not my own. It comes from him [God] who sent me'" (John 7:16). "So Jesus said, 'When you have lifted up the Son of Man, then you will know that I am the one I claim to be and that I do nothing on my own but speak just what the Father has taught me'" (John 8:28). "For I did not speak of my own accord, but the Father who sent me commanded me what to say and how to say it" (John 12:49).

That Jesus proclaimed the Word of God to Israel is a truth evident in even a cursory reading of the New Testament gospels. The weight of the evidence supports the Christian conviction that the promise of Deuteronomy 18:15, 18 was fulfilled in Jesus, not in Muhammad. Thus Jesus' challenge rings true, "If you believed Moses, you would believe me, for he wrote about me" (John 5:46).

2.2.10 JOHN 14:16—ANOTHER COUNSELOR: MUHAMMAD?

Muslims also believe the promised Counselor or Comforter in the following New Testament verse is Muhammad rather than the Holy Spirit: "And I will ask the Father, and he will give you another Counselor to be with you forever" (John 14:16). Yusuf Ali makes the case in a footnote to Qur'an 3:81:

That argument is: You (People of the Book) are bound by your own oaths, sworn solemnly in the presence of your own Prophets. In the Old Testament as it now exists, Muhammad is foretold in Deut. xviii. 18; and the rise of the Arab nation in Isaiah, xlii. 11, for Kedar was a son of Ismail and the name is used for the Arab nation: in the New Testament as it now exists, Muhammad is foretold in the Gospel of St. John, xiv. 16, xv. 26, and xvi.7: the *future* Comforter cannot be the Holy Spirit as understood by Christians, because the Holy Spirit already was present helping and guiding Jesus. The Greek word translated 'Comforter' is 'Paracletos', which is an easy corruption from 'Periclytos', which is almost a literal translation of 'Muhammad' or 'Ahmad'. . . .[10]

Yusuf Ali goes further in a footnote to Qur'an 61:6:

'Ahmad,' or *'Muhammad,'* the Praised One, is almost a translation of the Greek word *Periclytos*. In the present Gospel of John, xiv. 16, xv. 26, and xvi. 7, the word 'Comforter' in the English version is for the Greek word *'Paracletos,'* which means 'Advocate,' 'one called to the help of another, a kind friend' rather than 'Comforter.' Our doctors contend that Paracletos is a corrupt reading for Periclytos, and that in their original saying of Jesus there was a prophecy of our holy Prophet *Ahmad* by name.[11]

Simply put, the argument is that in New Testament Greek manuscripts the word *paracletos* is a corruption of *periclytos*. But there is absolutely no manuscript evidence to support this claim. Of the over 5,000 manuscripts now available, not one witnesses to *periclytos*, making the charge of textual corruption in this example without historical or textual support.

Further, while Muslims claim that identifying the promised Counselor with the Holy Spirit is a misinterpretation, Jesus states this exact connection in the context of John 14:16: "But the Counselor, the Holy Spirit, whom the Father will send in my name, will teach you all things and will remind you of everything I have said to you" (John 14:26). Muslims can claim that this statement was made up by later Christians, but such an accusation would need at least *some* evidence.

Numerous other difficulties attend the Muslim attribution of John 14:16 to Muhammad. The Counselor was to be with Jesus' early disciples "forever" (14:16), but Muhammad was *never* with them, nor is the answer that the message of Muhammad has continued to this day in the Qur'an a sufficient response. Jesus also said the Counselor would be "in you" (14:17), which harmonizes perfectly with the role of the Holy Spirit, but not Muhammad. The Counselor would also be sent in Jesus' name (14:26), but Muhammad was not.

We hope that any Muslim who would seek to accredit the prophecy of John 14:16 to Muhammad would first read John 14–16 in its entirety. As these chapters clearly demonstrate, the qualities of the Counselor cannot be plausibly attributed to Muhammad.

Muslims use additional Bible passages to support their claim that the Bible prophesies the coming of Muhammad, but the same difficulties that accompany their attempts to use Deuteronomy 18:15, 18 and John 14:16 in this way trouble the other (less significant) passages.

---

[10] A. Yusuf Ali, *The Holy Qur'an*, 144, n. 416.
[11] Ibid., 1540, n. 5438.

Philosophy

Secular Humanism

Humanism is naturalistic and rejects the supernaturalistic stance with its postulated Creator-God and cosmic Ruler.[1]

— ROY WOOD SELLARS

2.3.1 INTRODUCTION

Secular Humanists list a variety of philosophical positions that fit their worldview: **naturalism**, physicalism, materialism, organicism, or other theories "based upon science." But this choice is not as broad as it sounds—each doctrine listed holds to the same core tenet: the material world is all that exists. In fact, each option presented is really little more than a synonym for naturalism, the philosophical view of Secular Humanism.

> NATURALISM [OR MATERIALISM]: The philosophical belief that reality is composed solely of matter and that all phenomena can be explained in terms of natural causes e.g., law of gravity

This dogmatic position is summarized in *Humanist Manifesto II*: "Nature may indeed be broader and deeper than we now know; any new discoveries, however, will but enlarge our knowledge of the natural."[2] The essence of naturalism, then, is this—whatever exists can be explained by natural causes. Thus, in a Humanist's mind, the supernatural cannot exist. While some Humanists prefer to call themselves organicists or materialists (or "scientific"

---

[1] Paul Kurtz, ed., *The Humanist Alternative* (Buffalo, NY: Prometheus Books, 1973), 135.
[2] Paul Kurtz, *Humanist Manifesto II* (Buffalo, NY: Prometheus Books, 1980), 16.

Corliss Lamont

materialists), the name makes little difference. As **Corliss Lamont** notes, "Materialism denotes the same general attitude toward the universe as Naturalism."[3]

2.3.2 DENIAL OF THE SUPERNATURAL

The key tenet of naturalism is its denial of the supernatural. People either believe that only the supernatural exists, or that some supernatural things and some natural things exist, or that only natural things exist. By "supernatural," philosophers generally mean things that are not material, such as the soul, personality, or God. Naturalists deny everything that is not made up of matter or that does not exist in nature.

This current of thought runs throughout Humanist beliefs. Sellars writes, "Christianity, for example, had a supernaturalistic framework in a three-tier universe of heaven, earth and hell. . . . The Humanist argues that the traditional Christian outlook has been undercut and rendered obsolete by the growth of knowledge about man and his world."[4] Humanists rely on this "growth of knowledge" to provide a more accurate worldview. Naturalism insists that an object be observable and measurable to be believable.

Naturalists are especially unwilling to believe in a universe that exudes too much design, because this design could be construed as evidence for a Designer.[5] The naturalist cannot accept a Designer or a personal First Cause. Henry Miller plainly states, "To imagine that we are going to be saved by outside intervention, whether in the shape of an analyst, a dictator, a savior, or even God, is sheer folly."[6]

Naturalistic Humanism, then, is a complete philosophy. Corliss Lamont puts it this way: "To define naturalistic Humanism in a nutshell: it rejects all forms of supernaturalism, pantheism, and metaphysical idealism, and considers man's supreme aim as working for the welfare and progress of all humanity in this one and only life, according to the methods of reason, science and democracy."[7] This definition is important from a philosophical perspective because it outlines both the metaphysics and epistemology of naturalism. This chapter will focus on the metaphysics (specifically the cosmology) of naturalism first, and then explore its epistemology.

2.3.3 METAPHYSICS: COSMOLOGY

Cosmology refers to the philosophical study of the universe, especially its origin. Secular Humanists believe that the physical universe came into being by accident and that it is all that exists. Denying the existence of a supernatural Creator, Secular Humanists instead believe that eternal matter spontaneously generated life, and ultimately the human mind, through an evolutionary process.

---

[3] Corliss Lamont, *The Philosophy of Humanism* (New York, NY: Frederick Ungar, 1982), 28.

[4] Kurtz, *The Humanist Alternative*, 133.

[5] Paul Amos Moody, *Introduction to Evolution* (New York, NY: Harper & Row, Publishers, 1970), 497: "The more I study science the more I am impressed with the thought that this world and universe have a definite design—and a design suggests a designer. It may be possible to have design without a designer, a picture without an artist, but my mind is unable to conceive of such a situation." Also, William A. Dembski, *The Design Inference: Eliminating Chance Through Small Probabilities* (Cambridge, UK: Cambridge University Press, 1999). High school students will enjoy observing "The Privileged Planet" distributed by Illustra Media at www.illustramedia.com.

[6] Roger E. Greeley, ed., *The Best of Humanism* (Buffalo, NY: Prometheus Books, 1988), 149.

[7] Ibid.

Carl Sagan, the 1981 recipient of the Humanist of the Year award, sums up the cosmology of naturalism: "The Cosmos is all that is or ever was or ever will be."[8] For Secular Humanists, no personal First Cause exists—only the cosmos. "Nature is but an endless series of efficient causes. She cannot create but she eternally transforms. There was no beginning and there can be no end."[9]

Carl Sagan

Secular Humanists have no need for a God in order to explain the origin of the cosmos. Humanists assign a different basis for reality to the universe, a non-sequential group of first causes, avoiding God as the First Cause. Lamont calls these the "ultimate principles of explanation and intelligibility."[10] These ultimate principles are a sufficient cause for the rest of reality. Interestingly, Paul Kurtz, editor of *Free Inquiry,* pays his respects to science, saying that "the discoveries of astronomy, physics, relativity theory, and quantum mechanics have increased our understanding of the universe,"[11] but he never mentions the "Big Bang" metaphor. Acknowledging such a metaphor suggests a creative point like that in Genesis 1:1, which is outside the purview of Secular Humanist cosmology.

Worth noting, in contrast, is the controversy among Christians about the age of the universe, not whether a Big Bang occurred (if a Big Bang refers to the moment of Creation).[12]

Also worth noting is Einstein's conclusion regarding the origin of the cosmos: "The harmony of natural law . . . reveals an intelligence of such superiority that, compared with it, all the systematic thinking and acting of human beings is an utterly insignificant reflection."[13] More recently, Robert Jastrow startled his fellow scientists with a similar conclusion: "The **Anthropic principle** is the most interesting development next to the proof of the creation, and it is even more interesting because it seems to say that science itself has proven, as a hard fact, that this universe was made, was designed, for man to live in. It is a very theistic result."[14]

> **ANTHROPIC PRINCIPLE:** Either of two principles in cosmology: (a) conditions that are observed in the universe must allow the observer to exist; (b) the universe must have properties that make inevitable the existence of intelligent life

[8] Carl Sagan, *Cosmos* (New York, NY: Random House, 1980), 4. For an in-depth look at how Sagan faired in his confrontation with Immanuel Velikovsky, see Charles Ginenthal, *Carl Sagan & Immanuel Velikovsky* (Tempe, AZ: New Falcon Publications, 1995).

[9] Greeley, *The Best of Humanism*, 162.

[10] Lamont, *The Philosophy of Humanism*, 170–1.

[11] Paul Kurtz, *Humanist Manifesto 2000: A Call For A New Planetary Humanism* (Amherst, NY: Prometheus Books, 2000), 15.

[12] See Normal L. Geisler, *Systematic Theology*, 4 vols. (Minneapolis, MN: Bethany House), 2:632f, for a good summary of the issue. *Creation and Time* by Hugh Ross presents the case for an older universe, while *Refuting Compromise* by Jonathan Sarfati presents the case for a younger universe, along with Walter Brown, *In The Beginning* (Phoenix, AZ: Center for Scientific Creation, 2003) and volumes 1 and 2 of Larry Vardiman, Andrew A. Snelling, Eugene F. Chaffin, *Radioisotopes: And The Age Of The Earth* (El Cajon, CA: Institute for Creation Research, 2005).

[13] Albert Einstein, *Ideas and Opinions* (New York, NY: Crown, 1982), 40, quoted in Geisler, *Systematic Theology*, 2:666.

[14] Robert Jastrow, "A Scientist Caught Between Two Faiths," *Christianity Today*, August 6, 1982, quoted in Geisler, *Systematic Theology*, 2:591.

2.3.4 METAPHYSICS AND EPISTEMOLOGY

Epistemology refers to our theory of knowledge and answers the questions *How much can we know about reality?* and *How do we obtain this knowledge?* Secular Humanist naturalism answers that we can know everything in the physical world (which is the extent of what exists) through science. According to Roy Wood Sellars, "The spirit of naturalism would seem to be one with the spirit of science itself."[15]

Most Secular Humanists agree with Sellars. The *Humanist Manifesto II* states, "Any account of nature should pass the tests of scientific evidence,"[16] eliminating the possibility of the supernatural, which is neither measurable nor observable. Naturalists, whose epistemology is grounded in science, find truth in what they can see with their eyes—that is, only the physical universe.

The epistemology of Secular Humanism shapes its metaphysics. A worldview consistent with the belief that the physical universe is all that exists and that science is our only source of knowledge precludes the existence of knowledge about anything supernatural. However, belief in science as the ultimate means to knowledge (truth) requires as much faith as belief in the existence and truth of the supernatural. Admitting this self-contradiction, Carl Sagan announced, "[S]cience has itself become a kind of religion."[17]

Lamont rationalizes the Secular Humanist position of placing faith in science rather than in religion: "It is sometimes argued that since science, like religion, must make ultimate assumptions, we have no more right to rely on science in an analysis of the idea of immortality than on religion. Faith in the methods and findings of science, it is said, is just as much a faith as faith in the methods and findings of religion. In answer to this we can only say that the history of thought seems to show that reliance on science has been more fruitful in the progress and extension of the truth than reliance on religion."[18]

The epistemology of the naturalist is inseparable from science. In order to properly know and understand the world around us, Secular Humanist naturalism requires that we apply science to every aspect of life, including the social and the moral.

2.3.5 THE MIND/BODY PROBLEM

The epistemology and metaphysics of naturalism create a specific problem for Secular Humanist philosophy. This dilemma is traditionally referred to as the mind-body problem, which asks *Does the mind exist solely within nature, just as the body does, or is the mind more than matter?*

Humanists believe that the mind (also referred to as consciousness, personality, or soul) is simply a manifestation of the brain. The mind is an extension of the natural world, explainable in purely physical terms. This stance arises from the Secular Humanist epistemological belief that knowledge comes from science and science supports the belief that life arose spontaneously and has evolved to its present state. Since matter is all that exists, the mind is a strictly physical phenomenon. The belief that the mind is no more than a conglomeration of matter is called *monism*. The opposing view, that the mind supersedes mere matter, is called *dualism*.

Secular Humanist philosophy thus concludes that the amazingly complex human mind is the result of evolutionary processes. According to Lamont, "Naturalistic Humanism . . . take[s]

---

[15] Roy Wood Sellars, *Evolutionary Naturalism* (Chicago, IL: Open Court, 1922), 5.

[16] *The Humanist Manifesto II*, 16.

[17] Carl Sagan, *UFO's-A Scientific Debate* (Ithaca, NY: Cornell University Press, 1972), xiv.

[18] Corliss Lamont, *The Illusion of Immortality* (New York, NY: Frederick Ungar, 1965), 124–5.

the view that the material universe came first and that mind emerged in the animal man only after some two billion years of biological evolution upon this material earth."[19]

2.3.6 IMPLICATIONS OF THE MONISTIC VIEW

Based on the Secular Humanist belief in a monistic view of the mind, two further implications are exposed. The first deals with the question of humanity's immortality. Lamont's answer is the only one open to the naturalist: "If . . . the monistic theory of psychology is true, as Naturalism, Materialism, and Humanism claim, then there is no possibility that the human consciousness, with its memory and awareness of self-identity intact, can survive the shock and disintegration of death. According to this view, the body and personality live together; they grow together; and they die together."[20]

Therefore, denial of life after death is inherent in the Secular Humanist worldview. Lamont goes further in stating that a belief in mortality is the first step to becoming a Humanist. "The issue of mortality versus immortality is crucial in the argument of Humanism against supernaturalism. For if men realize that their careers are limited to this world, that this earthly existence is all that they will ever have, then they are already more than half-way on the path toward becoming functioning Humanists."[21]

The second implication of the monistic view of the mind arises from the belief that the mind arose through evolutionary processes. If this is so, the mind is still evolving, and a better mutation is likely. Some Humanists believe that this more efficient mind is arising today in the form of computer technology. Victor J. Stenger, author of *Not By Design*, claims, "Future computers will not only be superior to people in every task, mental or physical, but will also be immortal." He believes it will become possible to save human "thoughts which constitute consciousness" in computer memory banks, as well as program computers in such a way as to give them the full range of

> ## The Pop Culture Connection
>
> ***I, Robot*** (a 2004 film based on novelist Isaac Asimov's 1950 seminal sci-fi work "I, Robot")—The original collection consisted of a series of short stories detailing a world where humans and robots coexisted—the latter operated under a preset series of laws that prevented them from harming or allowing harm to occur to their human counterparts. The 2004 film by the same name, starring Will Smith and James Cromwell, offers bits and pieces of Asimov's original work and thinking.
>
> Stephen Spielberg's 2001 film ***A.I.*** is a story about a highly advanced robotic boy (Haley Joel Osment) longing to become "real" so that he can regain the love of his human mother.

human thought. He says, "If the computer is 'just a machine,' so is the human brain." Stenger also foresees the possibility of computers becoming the next step in the evolutionary chain—the new higher consciousness. He concludes, "Perhaps, as part of this new consciousness, we will become God."[22]

Such speculations are not mere science fiction for the Secular Humanist. In their naturalistic, monistic worldview, the human mind resulted from the evolution of matter and natural selection is still at work to improve the mind through evolution.

---

[19] Corliss Lamont, *Voice in the Wilderness* (Buffalo, NY: Prometheus, 1975), 82.
[20] Lamont, *The Philosophy of Humanism*, 82–3.
[21] Ibid., 82.
[22] Victor J. Stenger, *Not By Design* (Buffalo, NY: Prometheus Books, 1988), 188–9.

2.3.7 CONCLUSION

Secular Humanist philosophy's denial of the supernatural and reliance on science as its source of knowledge necessitates specific conclusions about our mortality, our mind, and the very nature of our humanity. The resulting worldview may seem to elevate our importance in terms of our ability to control our fate. However, this responsibility becomes a burden resulting in a pessimistic view, for without God or an eternal soul, we are left without hope or purpose in life. E.A. Burtt believes "the ultimate accommodation necessary in a wise plan of life is acceptance of a world not made for man, owing him nothing, and in its major processes quite beyond his control."[23] This pessimism is voiced more dramatically by Clarence Darrow: "The purpose of man is like the purpose of the pollywog—to wiggle along as far as he can without dying; or, to hang to life until death takes him."[24]

---

[23] Edwin Arthur Burtt, *Types of Religious Philosophy* (New York, NY: Harper and Brothers, 1939), 353. Clearly, the Humanist has no patience with the Anthropic Principle, which contends that the world was tailored for man's existence. For an excellent defense of this principle, see Roy Abraham Varghese, ed., *The Intellectuals Speak Out About God* (Dallas, TX: Lewis and Stanley, 1984), 102ff.

[24] Greeley, *The Best of Humanism*, 154.

Philosophy

Marxism-Leninism

> The real unity of the world consists in its materiality,
> and this is proved . . . by a long and protracted
> development of philosophy and natural science. . . . But
> if the . . . question is raised: what then are thought
> and consciousness, and whence they come, it becomes
> apparent that they are products of the human brain and
> that man himself is a product of nature, which has been
> developed in and along with its environment.[1]
>
> — FREDERICK ENGELS

2.4.1 INTRODUCTION

The philosophy of dialectical materialism is the Marxist-Leninist approach to understanding and changing the world. Many of the attributes we as Christians ascribe to God—eternality, infinitude, an uncreated being, indestructibility, the Lawgiver, the Life, and the Mind—Marxists-Leninists ascribe to dialectical matter. Marxist philosophy affirms matter as ultimately real, rather than God. Thus it is a godless philosophy.

Karl Marx wrote in a letter to Frederick Engels, "[A]s long as we actually observe and think, we cannot possibly get away from materialism."[2] Engels explained his epistemology by writing, "The materialist world outlook is simply the conception of nature as it is."[3] Marxist-Leninist philosophy holds that the matter we see in nature is all that exists. This

---

[1] V.I. Lenin, *The Teachings of Karl Marx* (New York, NY: International Publishers, 1976), 14.
[2] Ibid., 15.
[3] Joseph Stalin, *Dialectical and Historical Materialism* (New York, NY: International Publishers, 1977), 15.

materialistic interpretation of the world is an essential ingredient of Marxist thought.

Lenin wrote, "Matter is primary nature. Sensation, thought, consciousness are the highest products of matter organized in a certain way. This is the doctrine of materialism, in general, and Marx and Engels, in particular."[4] Lenin further contended that matter is a philosophical category denoting objective reality—people, plants, animals, stars, and so on. "Matter is the objective reality given to us in sensation."[5]

When Lenin says that matter is primary, he means that matter is eternal and uncreated, that life spontaneously emerged from non-living, non-conscious matter billions of years ago, and that mind, thought, and consciousness eventually evolved from it.

2.4.2 MARXIST EPISTEMOLOGY

Science plays a crucial role in the Marxist theory of knowledge. According to Lenin, "The fundamental characteristic of materialism arises from the objectivity of science, from the recognition of objective reality, reflected by science."[6] Marxist epistemology, like that of the Secular Humanists, places faith in the truth of science and denies all religious truth claims. Putting their faith in science as the infallible source of all knowledge logically follows from Marxist beliefs about reality. According to Lenin, "Perceptions give us correct impressions of things. We directly know objects themselves."[7] The objects Lenin speaks of are strictly material—"Matter is . . . the objective reality given to man in his sensations, a reality which is copied, photographed, and reflected by our sensations."[8]

In contrast, anything supernatural lacks objective, material reality, so according to Marxism we have no means of perceiving it or of gaining knowledge about it. Thus, Marxists deny the supernatural. They distinguish between knowledge of the material world and what they term *true belief* in an attempt to allow for scientific speculation while ignoring speculation about God. "What we call 'knowledge' must also be distinguished from 'true belief.' If, for example, there is life on Mars, the belief that there is life on Mars is true belief. But at the same time we certainly, as yet, know nothing of the matter. True belief only becomes knowledge when backed by some kind of investigation and evidence. Some of our beliefs may be true and others false, but we only start getting to know which are true and which are false when we undertake forms of systematic investigation. . . . For nothing can count as 'knowledge' except in so far as it has been properly tested."[9]

Therefore, Marxist epistemology declares that we can never know belief in the supernatural as "true belief" because we cannot test it scientifically or empirically. We can determine as true beliefs only our speculations about the material world because only these can undergo systematic investigation. Thus, knowledge can apply only to the material world.

Marxists believe that practice—testing knowledge throughout history—is also a valuable tool for gaining knowledge. We can test knowledge by applying it to our lives and society, and this application will eventually determine its truth or falsity. By examining history, we can determine which beliefs are true and which are not.

Marxist epistemology is inextricably tied to Marxist dialectics. In fact, it is virtually impossible to separate Marxist materialism, dialectics, and epistemology. This is true

---

[4] V.I. Lenin, *Materialism and Empirio-Criticism* (New York, NY: International Publishers, 1927), 21.

[5] Ibid., 145.

[6] Ibid., 252.

[7] Ibid., 81.

[8] Ibid., 102.

[9] Maurice Cornforth, *The Open Philosophy and the Open Society* (New York, NY: International Publishers, 1968), 82.

largely because Marxists claim that dialectics operates in the place of metaphysics in their philosophy.

2.4.3 DIALECTICAL MATERIALISM

The notion of *dialectical process* was modified and polished into a broad-based philosophy by Georg Wilhelm Friedrich Hegel, who died when Marx was thirteen years old. The dialectical process is not a creation of Marxist philosophy. Instead, Marxists combine the theory with materialism, creating a hybrid philosophy—**dialectical materialism**. Marx and Engels simply adopted Hegel's ideas (which were built on an idealistic foundation—that is, the dialectic was thought to be a mental construct) and redesigned them to fit into a materialistic scheme of reality. Thus Lenin could write of the "great Hegelian dialectics which Marxism made its own, having first turned it right side up."[10]

> DIALECTICAL MATERIALISM: The dialectic says that in everything there is a thesis (the way things are) and an antithesis (an opposition to the way things are), which must inevitably clash. The result of the struggle and merging that comes from the clash is the synthesis, which becomes the new thesis. This new thesis will eventually attract another antithesis, and produce a new synthesis.

Gustav A. Wetter summarizes the Hegelian dialectic: "In Hegel's sense of the term, dialectic is a process in which a starting-point [a thesis, e.g., Being] is negated [the antithesis, e.g., Non-Being], thereby setting up a second position opposed to it. This second position is in turn negated i.e., by negation of the negation, so as to reach a third position representing a synthesis [e.g., Becoming] of the two preceding, in which both are 'transcended,' i.e., abolished and at the same time preserved on a higher level of being. This third phase then figures in turn as the first step in a new dialectical process [i.e., a new thesis], leading to a new synthesis, and so on."[11]

Frederick Engels best sums up the fundamental perspective with regard to dialectics: "The world is not to be comprehended as a complex of ready-made [created] things, but as a complex of [evolutionary] processes."[12] This notion is inherent to the dialectic, which views all of life as a constantly evolving process resulting from the clash of opposing forces.

In the dialectical process, the thesis must always attract an antithesis, and this tension must always result in a synthesis, which in turn becomes a new thesis. This new thesis is always more advanced than the last thesis, because dialectics perceives the developmental process as an upward spiral. Simply stated, dialectics sees change or process due to conflict or struggle as the only constant, and this change and conflict always lead to a more advanced level.

Marxists believe the proof for dialectics is all around us. Engels notes, "When we reflect on Nature, or the history of mankind, or our own intellectual activity, the first picture presented to us is an endless maze of relations and interactions."[13] These interactions are always in the process of thesis/antithesis/synthesis. This constant development or process of evolution implies that the world (indeed, the universe) is always in motion—always moving, always changing.

Frederick Engels

Now we can begin to see how dialectics affects the

[10] V.I. Lenin, *Collected Works*, 45 vols. (Moscow, USSR: Progress Publishers, 1977), 7:409.

[11] Gustav A. Wetter, *Dialectical Materialism* (Westport, CT: Greenwood Press, 1977), 4.

[12] Frederick Engels, *Ludwig Feuerbach* (New York, NY: International Publishers, 1974), 44.

[13] Lenin, *The Teachings of Karl Marx*, 27.

materialist view. In Marxist philosophy, we can understand matter only when we understand that it is constantly involved in an eternal process of change. The evolutionary process best illustrates this idea—life on earth has been undergoing changes throughout time, beginning with simple living forms and evolving onward and upward to more advanced states. Engels says, "Nature is the proof of dialectics."[14]

Marxist philosophy fixes evolutionary theory as a universal law for both organic and inorganic matter, as Engels makes clear: "All nature, from the smallest thing to the biggest, from a grain of sand to the sun, from the protista [the primary living cell] to man, is in a constant state of coming into being and going out of being, in a constant flux, in a ceaseless state of movement and change."[15]

2.4.4 DIALECTICS OPPOSED TO METAPHYSICS

Dialectics is a means of understanding the processes of life. Marxism took this system of thought and applied it to its own philosophy, which is foundational for its entire worldview. Marxists hasten to point out, however, that dialectics is a method directly opposed to metaphysics, which they claim is an outdated mode of viewing the world.

Yet in making this delineation, Marxists define metaphysics in a peculiar way. Normally understood, metaphysics is "the branch of philosophy that deals with first principles and seeks to explain the nature of being or reality (ontology) and of the origin and structure of the world (cosmology),"[16] questions that every philosophy must confront sooner or later. Marxists, however, attempt to dodge this branch of philosophy by claiming that metaphysics assumes that nature and being are stagnant and unchanging, while dialectics views life as a constant process, and that metaphysics views reality in disjointed parts, while dialectics views reality as an interconnected whole.

If we grant the Marxists their definition of metaphysics, then we cannot argue with their conclusion that dialectics is directly opposed to it. In the strict sense of the word, however, Marxists most definitely do maintain metaphysics, and they are not shy about articulating it. Because understanding any philosophy's beliefs about the nature of being and the origin and structure of the universe is crucial to understanding the philosophy as a whole, we will now examine Marxist metaphysics (in the traditional sense of the word), beginning with its cosmology and moving on to its ontology.

2.4.5 MARXIST METAPHYSICS

As previously noted, Marxist theology and philosophy deny the supernatural. The universe is all that exists and all that ever will exist. "Materialism gives a true picture of the world, without any irrelevant adjuncts in the shape of spirits, of a god who created the world, and the like. The materialists do not await the help of supernatural powers, they believe in man, in his capacity to transform the world by his own hand."[17]

Whether Marxists choose to admit it or not, their philosophy includes a metaphysical cosmology. They are far from bashful about declaring the absence of a God or anything supernatural in the universe, just as they are more than willing to proclaim that the material universe is all that exists and that it has always existed and always will.

---

[14] Frederick Engels, *Socialism: Utopian and Scientific* (New York, NY: International Publishers, 1935), 48.

[15] Frederick Engels, *Dialectics of Nature* (New York, NY: International Publishers, 1976), 13.

[16] *Webster's New Twentieth Century Dictionary of the English Language*, 2nd ed., unabridged (New York, NY: Collins & World, 1977), 1132.

[17] Raymond S. Sleeper, ed., A *Lexicon of Marxist-Leninist Semantics* (Alexandria, VA: Western Goals, 1983), 168.

Marxist philosophy relies on a specific ontology, as well. For Marxists, the ultimate substance and the ultimate cause is ever-changing dialectical matter. Perhaps this is why they choose to avoid metaphysics—it is difficult, in the face of modern physics, to argue that matter is the ultimate substance. Nonetheless, Marxist philosophy holds tenaciously to the view that matter is all that exists, that it is eternal, and that it is the ultimate substance or reality.

> Matter is the only existing objective reality: the cause, foundation, content and substance of all the diversity of the world.
>
> — ALEXANDER SPIRKIN

Alexander Spirkin, a modern Marxist author, writes that "matter is the only existing objective reality: the cause, foundation, content and substance of all the diversity of the world."[18] Engels says we know from experience and theory "that both matter and its mode of existence, motion, are uncreatable."[19]

Marxist dialectics, then, is not opposed to metaphysics in the traditional sense of the word. In truth, Marxist philosophy relies on its metaphysics (ontology and cosmology), which it assumes in its entirety without rational defense, to provide a basis and explanation for being, the nature of the universe, and ultimately humanity itself.

2.4.6 THE MIND/BODY PROBLEM

Like every philosophy, dialectical materialism must address the mind-body problem. Marxists rely on the key word *reflect* when addressing this issue. They contend that our mind reflects matter in a way that makes our perception accurate. For Marx, "the ideal is nothing else than the material world reflected by the human mind, and translated into forms of thought."[20] However, Marx does not address the origin of this *ideal*. Lenin echoes Marx: "The existence of the mind is shown to be dependent upon that of the body, in that the mind is declared to be secondary, a function of the brain, or a reflection of the outer world."[21] To avoid calling consciousness supernatural, Marxists rely on the notion that consciousness is just a subjective reflection of objective reality.

For the dialectical materialist, everything must have proceeded from matter, even societal interrelationships and the mind. Maurice Cornforth writes, "Mental functions are functions of highly developed matter, namely, of the brain. Mental processes are brain processes, processes of a material, bodily organ."[22] Although Marxists may refer to thought as a *reflection* of objective reality, they must admit that in their view the mind is simply a function of matter.

2.4.7 CONCLUSION

Dialectical materialism, the philosophy of Marxism, contains an epistemology, a cosmology, an ontology, and an answer to the mind-body problem. For the Marxist, science and practice refine knowledge; the universe is infinite and all that will ever exist; matter is eternal and the ultimate substance; life is a product of this non-living matter; and the mind is a reflection of this material reality. But the Marxist philosophy embraces an even broader view of the world than is generally meant by the term *philosophy*. In truth, dialectical materialism is an entire method for viewing the world — it colors the Marxist perception of everything from ethics to history.

---

[18] Alexander Spirkin, *Dialectics and Materialism* (Moscow, USSR: Progress Publishers, 1983), 66.

[19] Engels, *Dialectics of Nature*, 337.

[20] Karl Marx, *Introduction to Capital*, 3 vols. (London, UK: Progress Publishers, 1889), vol. 1.

[21] Lenin, *Materialism and Empirio-Criticism*, 66.

[22] Maurice Cornforth, *The Theory of Knowledge* (New York, NY: International Publishers, 1963), 22.

Marxist philosophy as a worldview must be understood by anyone who claims to support the Marxist cause. "One cannot become a fully conscious, convinced Communist without studying Marxist philosophy. This is what Lenin taught."[23] Why? Because, according to Marxism, the dialectic can explain every process and change that occurs. Marxist philosophy is process philosophy. This process is written not only within the metaphysical make-up of our matter, but also in the evolution of humanity and the evolving social and historical context of our existence. This materialist belief affects the Marxist view of history, causing Marxists to view the bourgeoisie and the proletariat as thesis and antithesis, clashing to form a synthesis. This clash is in essence an evolutionary struggle. While evolutionists believe that animals evolved certain physical characteristics to aid in their survival, Marxists believe their philosophy of dialectical materialism evolved to meet the needs of the proletariat.

Every knowledgeable Marxist recognizes this and is prepared to act in accordance with dialectical materialism. While many philosophies are chiefly theoretical, Marxism is concerned with theory and practice. Dialectical materialism is a worldview and a philosophy of evolution and revolution—the call to action is implicit in its makeup. Every good Marxist understands his philosophy and is prepared to act upon it, because Marx himself requires it: "The philosophers have only interpreted the world in various ways; the point, however, is to change it."[24]

Unfortunately from a Marxist point of view, all such change is merely transitory, because each new synthesis (including the long-anticipated communist classless society) inevitably becomes a new thesis in the never-ending process of dialectical materialism. Even the victorious dictatorship of the proletariat will be but a brief moment in evolutionary history. Communist dialectics decrees that communism itself is transitory. The synthesis of communism today will become the new thesis of tomorrow, and new struggles will evolve according to the laws of dialectical materialism.

[23] F.V. Konstantinov, ed., *The Fundamentals of Marxist-Leninist Philosophy* (Moscow, USSR: Progress Publishers, 1982), 78.

[24] Karl Marx, *Collected Works*, 40 vols. (New York, NY: International Publishers, 1976), 5:8.

Philosophy

Cosmic Humanism

The mystery of life is beyond all human conception. .
. . We always think in terms of opposites. But God, the
ultimate, is beyond the pairs of opposites, that is all
there is to it.[1]

— JOSEPH CAMPBELL

All things are One Thing. There is only One Thing, and
all things are part of the One Thing That Is.[2]

— NEALE DONALD WALSCH

2.5.1 INTRODUCTION

The contemporary Cosmic Humanist movement has its roots in the Romantic poets of the 1800s, such as Ralph Waldo Emerson, Walt Whitman, and Henry David Thoreau. These men rejected the God of the Bible, instead writing at length about a transcendent quality of spirituality experienced purely through personal introspection. These ideas did not attract a broad audience until the 1960s, when popular recording artists, movie stars, and Eastern gurus began trumpeting their New Age views across the nation. More recently, well-known recording artists such as Madonna and Alanis Morissette have identified themselves with Hinduism, while popular personalities such as Tiger Woods, Phil Jackson, and Richard Gere openly embrace **Zen Buddhism**. Other luminaries, such as Tom Cruise and John Travolta, express a belief in scientology.

---

[1] Joseph Campbell, *The Power of Myth* (New York, NY: Doubleday, 1988), 49.
[2] Neale Donald Walsch, *The New Revelations: A Conversation with God* (New York, NY: Atria Books, 2002), 360.

ZEN: **ZEN:** A branch of Mahayana Buddhism that believes enlightenment can be attained through meditation, self-contemplation

As a result, Cosmic Humanist ideas are being widely disseminated through movies, television, and burgeoning book sales. Since its publication in 1993, *The Celestine Prophecy* has sold over 8 million copies in more than 32 countries, achieving distinction as the bestselling American hardcover book in the world for two consecutive years. Author James Redfield wrote in the 1997 afterword, "[W]e are manifesting nothing less than a new world view that will flourish in the next millennium." Another "modern day spiritual messenger" is **Neale Donald Walsch**, the author of fifteen books on spirituality in everyday life. His first five books in the *Conversations with God* series all made the *New York Times* bestseller list (the first book remained there for well over two years). His books have been translated into 27 languages, selling more than 7 million copies worldwide.

Because of this extensive New Age influence, it is important that Christians are equipped to counter New Age beliefs. This begins with understanding Cosmic Humanism's answers to the questions of theology and philosophy.

2.5.2 WHAT IS REAL?

Cosmic Humanists reject naturalistic and materialistic philosophies because such explanations deny the all-pervasive supernatural. David Spangler says, "From a very early age I was aware of an

Neale Donald Walsch

extra dimension or presence to the world around me, which as I grew older I came to identify as a sacred or transcendental dimension."[3] If Spangler's perspective is correct, and if (as pantheism declares) every aspect of existence is sacred, then everything must have a spiritual nature.

If the spiritual aspects of life lead to higher consciousness and inner truth, we should view all reality from a supernatural perspective. This perspective leads Cosmic Humanists to a philosophy of **non-naturalism**—nothing is natural, everything is supernatural. The philosophical stance of Cosmic Humanism is that ultimate reality is in the spiritual dimension.

Cosmic Humanists believe that all reality is God—from a grain of sand to the Milky Way. Their philosophy reflects this belief by focusing on such principles as the Gaia hypothesis, which

NON-NATURALISM: The belief that everything is a part of God and in essence, spiritual. The things that we can see and feel are only a manifestation of spirit, and all matter will melt away when universal consciousness is achieved

views planet Earth, and indeed, the whole universe, as a living organism. (Gaia is sometimes referred to as Mother Earth.) According to Fritjof Capra, "The universe is no longer seen as a machine, made up of a multitude of objects, but has to be pictured as one indivisible, dynamic whole whose parts are essentially interrelated and can be understood only as patterns of a cosmic process."[4]

2.5.3 COSMIC HUMANIST EPISTEMOLOGY: HOW DO WE KNOW?

The Cosmic Humanist philosophy of non-naturalism affects both its epistemology and its ontology. In terms of epistemology (theory of knowledge), proponents of the New Age movement emphasize the importance of getting in touch with our higher self. When we get in

[3] David Spangler, *Emergence: The Rebirth of the Sacred* (New York, NY: Delta/Merloyd Lawrence, 1984), 12.

[4] Fritjof Capra, *The Turning Point* (Toronto, ON: Bantam, 1982), 77–8.

touch with the God-force within, we can intuitively *know* truth without limits. Shakti Gawain says, "When we consistently suppress and distrust our intuitive knowingness, looking instead for [external] authority, validation, and approval from others, we give our personal power away."[5]

Joseph Campbell

When we look within, we will find truth, but this is not *truth* as it is commonly understood. New Age truth is emotive rather than descriptive. **Joseph Campbell**, in one of the New Age movement's most influential books, says, "What's the meaning of the universe? What's the meaning of a flea? It's just there. That's it. And your own meaning is that you're there. We're so engaged in doing things to achieve purposes of outer value that we forget that the inner value, the rapture that is associated with being alive, is what it's all about."[6] To Cosmic Humanists, truth—what we can know—is a feeling or an experience. Knowledge does not contain the meaning of life.

Each of us creates our own truth according to the principle *if it feels like truth to you, it is*. All knowledge exists in the God-force within us, and if we connect with that power, we tap into knowledge. Jack Underhill explains what would happen if everyone in the world were to connect with his or her godhood, "They can turn off the sun and turn it back on. They can freeze oceans into ice, turn the air into gold, talk as one with no movement or sound. They can fly without wings and love without pain, cure with no more than a thought or a smile. They can make the earth go backwards or bounce up and down, crack it in half or shift it around. . . . There is nothing they cannot do."[7]

2.5.4 COSMIC HUMANIST ONTOLOGY: WHAT IS ULTIMATE REALITY?

The Cosmic Humanist ontology also stems from a non-naturalistic philosophy. Ultimate reality or substance is the God-force or Christ-consciousness. God is "the essence of existence, the life force within all things."[8] Cosmic Humanist philosophy, like Secular Humanism and Marxism-Leninism, is monistic—all reality is one—but in a very different sense. In Cosmic Humanism, ultimate reality is spiritual rather than material. Robert Muller suggests this when he says, "Oh God, I know that I come from you, that I am part of you, that I will return to you, and that there will be no end to my rebirth in the eternal stream of your splendid creation."[9]

Whereas Muller's statement only implies that God is the essence of humanity, Spangler more accurately describes New Age ontology: "This worldview encourages us to treat all things not only as ourselves, as the holistic view would see it, but as honored and precious manifestations of God."[10]

This ontological perspective may prove problematic since it does not specify the substance that makes up the God-force. However, Cosmic Humanists seem unconcerned with this question since each of us arrives at our own truth and our interpretations will differ. To Gary Zukav, consciousness is ultimate reality: "All that is can form itself into individual droplets of consciousness. Because you are part of all that is, you have literally always been, yet there

---

[5] Shakti Gawain, *Living in the Light* (San Rafael, CA: New World Library, 1986), 69.

[6] Campbell, *The Power of Myth*, 6.

[7] Jack Underhill, "My Goal in Life," *Life Times Magazine*, Winter 1986/1987, 90.

[8] Dean C. Halverson, *Crystal Clear: Understanding and Reaching New Agers* (Colorado Springs, CO: NavPress, 1990), 91.

[9] Robert Muller, *The New Genesis: Shaping a Global Spirituality* (New York, NY: Image Books, 1984), 189.

[10] Spangler, *Emergence*, 83.

was the instant when that individual energy current that is you was formed. Consider that the ocean is God. It has always been. Now reach in and grab a cup full of water. In that instant, the cup becomes individual, but it has always been, has it not? This is the case with your soul. There was the instant when you became a cup of energy, but it was of an immortal original Being. You have always been because what it is that you are is God, or Divine Intelligence, but God takes on individual forms, droplets, reducing its power to small particles of individual consciousness."[11]

The Pop Culture Connection

Lost (ABC TV, premiered September, 2004)—"Why are we here? Is there an intelligent force controlling our destiny? How am I connected to others in the grand scheme of things? Rarely does a network TV series ponder such existential issues. But on the Emmy-winning drama *Lost*, those questions haunt every castaway who survived the crash of Oceanic Air flight 815 . . . For its compelling characters and cryptic sci-fi sleight of hand, *Lost* has been called 'the next great cult-pop sensation.' . . . [T]the creators of *Lost* seem intent on exploring faith in the supernatural sense. Miracles. Visions. Chance encounters that aren't random after all. Is it fate? Karma? Divine intervention? It's hard to say what the writers believe or want loyal followers to accept since the show's spirituality lacks context. And it's all over the map . . . Episodes . . . have incongruously featured depictions of the staunch faith of a martyred African priest *and* the heretical assertion by one (influential) character that Jesus' baptism by John was orchestrated to absolve Christ of His 'sins.'"*

Other Cosmic Humanists may answer the question differently based on their own personal *experience* of the truth, preferring to acknowledge their godhood without insisting on dogmatic views of its ultimate nature. Marilyn Ferguson states, "We need not postulate a purpose for this Ultimate Cause nor wonder who or what caused whatever Big Bang launched the visible universe. There is only the experience."[12]

2.5.5 ZEN PHILOSOPHY IN POPULAR CULTURE

Cosmic Humanist philosophy finds its way into popular culture through music and movies. For example, in *The Matrix,* Neo goes to see the Oracle. While waiting, he focuses on a boy in Buddhist robes sitting cross-legged on the floor, bending metal spoons simply by staring at them. The boy explains to Neo, "Don't try to bend the spoon. That's impossible. Only understand the truth . . . there is no spoon." The boy's statement reflects a classic Hindu/Buddhist conception of reality—that what we see is an illusionary world. There is no objective world, only the reality of our mental state.

Larry and Andy Wachowski, the writing/directing team behind *The Matrix*, are candid about their purpose in bringing a Cosmic Humanist dimension into their film: "We think the most important sort of fiction attempts to answer some of the big questions. One of the things that we had talked about when we first had the idea of *The Matrix* was an idea that I believe philosophy and religion and mathematics all try to answer . . . a reconciling between a natural world and another world that is perceived by our intellect."[13] In the same interview, the Wachowskis admit Buddhism plays a major role in their understanding of religion.

As pop culture commentator Roberto Rivera observes, "You can see Zen's fingerprints everywhere, including the way Morpheus talks to Neo. Instead of answering Neo's questions in a straightforward manner, he insists on [Buddhist-style] koans such as, 'I can only show you the

---

[11] Gary Zukav, *The Seat of the Soul* (New York, NY: Simon and Schuster), 85–6.

[12] Marilyn Ferguson, *The Aquarian Conspiracy* (Los Angeles, CA: J.P. Tarcher, 1980), 383.

* From a review on http://www.pluggedinonline.com/tv/television/a0001947.cfm.

[13] Interview with Larry and Andy Wachowski, November 6, 1999, http://www.dvdwb.com/matrixevents/wachowski.html.

door, you must walk through,' and 'when the time comes, you won't need to dodge the bullet.' Or my favorite, '[the Oracle] didn't lie, she told you exactly what you needed to hear.'"[14]

2.5.6 CONCLUSION

In Cosmic Humanist philosophy, all is one, so only one type of ultimate reality can exist. This ultimate reality must be spiritual because God, which is everything, is ultimately spiritual. Spirit is the only substance that exists, and matter is only a manifestation of spirit.

The purpose of knowing is not to explain or describe reality; rather, knowledge is useful only as experience, and experience is getting in touch with our godhood. Each of us may experience different truth because truth resides in the individual and manifests itself in our godhood.

Cosmic Humanist philosophy is a useful tool to help us think thoughts that lead to feelings of unity rather than a system for discovering and interpreting reality. Marianne Williamson, a popular New Age feminist author, says that although most people do not think this way, they should: "To say, 'God, please help me,' means, 'God, correct my thinking.' 'Deliver me from hell,' means 'Deliver me from my insane thoughts.'"[15] The best thoughts are not necessarily logical, but they are *sane* in that they remind us to feel at one with God.

[14] Roberto Rivera, "So, What is The Matrix? Rethinking Reality," http://www.boundless.org/1999/departments/atplay/a0000115.html.

[15] Marianne Williamson, *A Return to Love: Reflections on the Principles of "A Course in Miracles"* (New York, NY: Harper Collins, 1992), 22.

Philosophy

Postmodernism

> We . . . [should] give up the correspondence theory of truth, and start treating moral and scientific beliefs as tools for achieving greater human happiness, rather than as representations of the intrinsic nature of reality.[1]
>
> — RICHARD RORTY

2.6.1 INTRODUCTION

The philosophical ideas of Postmodernism divide modern-day academia. Today's college students will find Postmodernism ruling the day in their humanities and social studies courses, but will also find Modernism still prevalent in their science, engineering, and mathematics courses.[2] As well, there is little acceptance of the Postmodern approach to knowledge and truth in America's philosophy departments. The Postmodern notion that truth is community-oriented likewise appeals to few Christian theologians.[3]

While there is no single cohesive Postmodern philosophy (rather, there are several), a few consistent themes emerge from each mainstream Postmodern writer.

---

[1] Richard Rorty, *Achieving Our Country: Leftist Thought In Twentieth-Century America* (Cambridge, MA: Harvard University Press, 1998), 96.

[2] Nancy Pearcey, *Total Truth: Liberating Christianity from Its Cultural Captivity* (Wheaton, IL: Crossway Books, 2004), 107, 113.

[3] Myron B. Penner, ed., *Christianity and the Postmodern Turn: Six Views* (Grand Rapids, MI: Brazos Press, 2005), 210f.

2.6.2 SUBJECTIVE TRUTH

One of these themes is a denial of universal, objective truth. This is clearly declared in **Jean-Francois Lyotard**'s famous statement "incredulity towards metanarrative."[4] A metanarrative refers to a unifying story that seeks to explain how the world is—in other words a metanarrative

is a worldview. Lyotard suggests that we should be skeptical of such broad explanations. For example, the statement "God so loved the world" is nonsensical to Postmodernists for two reasons: (1) they deny the existence of God, and (2) statements reflecting the whole world (metanarratives) are impossible.

For Postmodernists, since there is no universal Truth (capital "T"), there are only "truths" (small "t") that are particular to a society or group of people and limited to individual perception. Written or verbal statements can reflect only a particular localized culture or individual point of view. A well-worn catchphrase we hear in this regard is, "That may be true for you, but not for me."

Jean-Francois Lyotard

Yet, by making the universal statement that there are no metanarratives, Postmodernists have put themselves in the position of creating a metanarrative. Their story that explains the world is that there are no explanations of the world, only local stories told by various cultures. For this reason, we refer to Postmodernism as the anti-worldview worldview.

2.6.3 LANGUAGE AND DECONSTRUCTION

Regarding literature, Postmodernists are highly concerned with the language of written texts. The term defining the major literary methodology of Postmodernists is **deconstruction**. Associated with the work of the French philosopher **Jacques Derrida**, deconstruction involves reading a text to

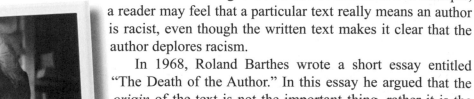

DECONSTRUCTION: A means of textual criticism that considers a text open to the reader's interpretation and laden with hidden bias, assumptions, and prejudices

ferret out its hidden or multiple meanings (polysemy). In this way, a reader's interpretation of the text becomes more important than the text itself. Also significant is the subjectivity of the

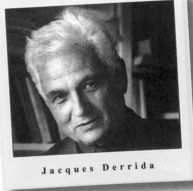

reader in determining what the author intended. For example, a reader may feel that a particular text really means an author is racist, even though the written text makes it clear that the author deplores racism.

In 1968, Roland Barthes wrote a short essay entitled "The Death of the Author." In this essay he argued that the *origin* of the text is not the important thing, rather it is the *destination*—the reader. By allowing the reader to invent new meanings, the text is freed from the tyranny of the author's single intended meaning.

For example, there is no reason to assume "that a Shakespearean play means exactly the same thing today as

Jacques Derrida

---

[4] Jean-Francois Lyotard, *The Postmodern Condition: A Report on Knowledge* (Minneapolis, MN: University of Minnesota Press, 1984), xxiv.

it did when first performed."[5] Each author (or artist) is the product of his or her own cultural setting and uses language to fit his or her condition. Thus, Postmodern literary criticism claims that words never describe the objective world but only refer to other words.[6] Therefore, no matter how a writer constructs a sentence, it can never tell us about the real world, but only about the world as understood by the reader. This concept is summed up in the phrase, "That's just *your* interpretation."

The Pop Culture Connection

Mona Lisa Smile (a 2003 film set in the year 1953)—an art-history professor, Katherine Watson (Julia Roberts), hopes to open the minds of her students at conservative Wellesley College. In class she shows a slide of the painting *Carcass* by Suteen (1925) and asks, "Is it any good? Come on, ladies. There's no wrong answer. There's also no textbook telling you what to think. It's not that easy, is it?" While some of her students defend accepted standards for determining good art, others claim personal preference as the overarching guide. Watson's approach promotes the assumption that there are no standards of truth, beauty, or goodness.

2.6.4 ANTI-REALISM AND THE CONSTRUCTION OF REALITY

This concept of deconstruction is taken far beyond the area of literature. Just as you, the reader, are creating the meaning of this text, you also construct the world according to your culture and experiences. In other words, there is no "real world" out there—only six billion constructions of the world, a belief known as **anti-realism**.[7]

> **ANTI-REALISM:** The belief that reality is subjectively constructed by human thought

Traditionally, Truth (with a capital "T") was understood as the relationship between the real, objective world and statements that correspond to the real world. This view is called the **correspondence theory of truth**. However, Postmodernists claim this kind of Truth is impossible to achieve. There is no universal "Truth," only personal, subjective truths that exist only in a particular situation or cultural surrounding. Thus, according to the Postmodernist paradigm of anti-realism, there is no real world to which truth can correspond. Rather, our words correspond only to other words and, in the end, create our understanding of reality. If words signify only other words, then words can never be used in the pursuit of Truth.

A classic example of the concept that words do not refer to reality is found in Foucault's essay entitled, "This Is Not a Pipe." In this essay, he analyzes a 1966 painting by Magritte that shows a picture of a pipe on a blackboard with the written phrase "This is not a pipe." Above the blackboard is an abstraction of a pipe hanging in the air. Foucault insists that none of these is a pipe, but merely a text that simulates a pipe.[8]

> **CORRESPONDENCE THEORY OF TRUTH:** belief that truth corresponds to reality

The primary idea behind this "word play" is the Postmodern insistence that all human beings are conditioned by their culture and language—their situation in life—and that no one is able to break through his or her situation to engage a universe with objectively true statements of fact. 'Water wets' is true for only a small community of individuals locked in their own language and culture. In addition, it is true only as long as this community agrees upon this

---

[5] Glen Ward, *Postmodernism* (Chicago, IL: McGraw-Hill, 2003), 162.

[6] What the very first words refer to is never explained because there were no other words to which to refer.

[7] For a more complete definition of "anti-realism," see Robert Audi, ed., *The Cambridge Dictionary of Philosophy*, 2nd ed. (Cambridge, UK: Cambridge University Press, 1999), 33.

[8] See Foucault's *This Is Not a Pipe* (Berkeley, CA: University of California Press, 1983), 49.

particular usage. In fact, the community determines what is truth through the words it chooses to use.

Richard Rorty has said that truth for him is whatever his community of scholars allows him to get away with. If Rorty says the moon is made of green cheese and his community does not disagree with him, then for him the moon is made of green cheese. Again, reality is not what objectively exists; reality is produced by our agreement of what it is. We do not discover true facts about the real world—we create it.

The Pop Culture Connection

The Matrix (the 1999 Wachowski brothers film)—gives a nod to Jean Baudrillard. In an early scene, Neo reaches into a hidden compartment in a book to retrieve a computer disk. The book's title is *Simulacra and Simulation*, the title of Baudrillard's 1981 book where he discusses how we create reality from the signs of culture and the media. Later in the film, Morpheus introduces Neo to "the desert of the real," a phrase taken from Baudrillard.

French cultural theorist Jean Baudrillard took this concept to its logical conclusion. In 1991 he claimed that the Gulf War was not real, but merely simulated for CNN television. The truth that real people were killed did not seem to enter the equation. In actuality, not all Postmodernists take the concept of language and reality to Baudrillard's extreme. Yet, as Glenn Ward notes, this piece has been used ". . . to discredit not only Baudrillard, but Postmodernism's abandonment of truth and evaluation."[9]

2.6.5 RORTY AND HIS CONVERSATIONS

Rorty also thinks we need to abandon the search for objective truth and instead concentrate on areas where we can all agree. He refers to this quest as "hermeneutic conversation." Rorty invites his opponents to dialogue with him to see if they can reach agreement, or at least a fruitful disagreement. He says that the "hope of agreement is never lost as long as the conversation lasts."[10]

But does truth result from such a conversation? Not really. Rorty's insistence on give and take and final agreement only sets the stage for another round of conversations where give and take results in further agreement or disagreement. Truth is never the result of continuing conversation, because the conversation will never be finished.[11]

For Rorty, this use of language and dialogue is "edifying philosophy"—a chance to create some type of reality with the realization that we can never discover true or objective reality outside the boundaries of language, culture, and locality. Since there is no objective, universal Truth, Rorty suggests that perhaps we can reach some type of agreeable truth (small "t") in order to get along with others.

2.6.6 SUMMARY OF POSTMODERN PHILOSOPHY

Kevin J. Vanhoozer, Research Professor of Systematic Theology at Trinity Evangelical Divinity School, is a shrewd observer of the Postmodern scene and a somewhat sympathetic critic. In addition, he understands the important role Nietzsche played in expressing the foundational ideas for Postmodernism.[12] He writes, "Nietzsche, the patron saint of postmodernity, prophesied

[9] Ward, *Postmodernism*, 77. For a systematic analysis and critique of Postmodernism, we recommend Christopher Norris' *The Truth About Postmodernism* (Oxford, UK: Blackwell Publishers, 1996).

[10] Richard Rorty, *Philosophy and the Mirror of Nature* (Princeton, NJ: Princeton University Press, 1980), 318.

[11] This is reminiscent of the Marxist dialectic (thesis, antithesis, and synthesis) in which the synthesis of agreement becomes a new thesis, disagreement is the antithesis, and the process is never-ending.

[12] See Arthur Herman, *The Idea of Decline in Western History* (New York, NY: The Free Press, 1997), Will Du-

accurately: if God is dead, then it's interpretation 'all the way down.'. . . [O]ne word only points to another word and never to reality itself. No one interpretation can ever be regarded as final. As in interpretation, so in life: everything becomes undecidable."[13]

Vanhoozer points us to the late C.S. Lewis, who foresaw the shift toward Postmodernist thinking. Lewis' term for this movement is "bulverism" after its imaginary inventor Ezekiel Bulver. Vanhoozer explains: "Lewis imagines the moment that bulverism was born, when five-year-old Ezekiel heard his mother say to his father, 'Oh, you say that because you are a man.' Bulver intuitively grasped the stunning implication: arguments need not be refuted, only situated. One rebuts a thought simply by calling attention to the genealogy or location of its thinker."[14] Probably nothing in Postmodernism today would surprise Lewis.

Vanhoozer offers a concise summary of Postmodern philosophy:

a) The mark of the Postmodern condition of knowledge is a move away from the authority of universal science toward narratives of local knowledge.[15]

b) Postmodernists reject the notion of universal rationality; reason is always situated within particular narratives, traditions, institutions, and practices.

c) Postmodernists reject unifying, totalizing, universal schemes in favor of new emphases on difference, plurality, fragmentation, and complexity.

d) Postmodernists reject the notion that the person is an autonomous individual with a rational consciousness that transcends his or her particular place in culture, language, history, and gendered body.

e) Postmodernists agree with Nietzsche that "God" (that is to say, the supreme being of classical theism) has become unbelievable, as have the autonomous self and the meaning of history.

f) What we know about things is linguistically, culturally, and socially constructed.

g) Language stands for the socially constructed order within which we think and move and have our being.[16]

2.6.7 SUBJECTIVE TRUTH, DECONSTRUCTION, AND ANTI-REALISM

Postmodernists have difficulty living with their view of reality. They claim that "reality" is constructed by language. On one level we can agree that the statement "The train is coming" may convey a multitude of interpretations to different people. To some it may even simulate a train. But we contend that if people fail to get off the tracks, the result of their interpretation could prove fatal. There are indeed objective, non-verbal referents to words and texts. Real life, however, is not open to infinite interpretations. At any particular moment in time, either a train is coming down the track or a train is not coming down the track. This real-world fact is not a matter of our personal interpretation. Regardless of the word games Postmodernists play there is a reality. Postmodernists have a hard time escaping the correspondence theory of truth.

---

rant's *The Story of Philosophy*, and John P. Koster, *The Atheist Syndrome* (Brentwood, TN: Wolgemuth & Hyatt Publishers, 1989) for background material on Nietzsche.

[13] Penner, *Christianity and the Postmodern Turn: Six Views*, 78.

[14] Ibid., 76.

[15] Postmodernists were not the first to offer such a view of knowledge. Bertrand Russell held a similar view "all truths are particular truths." See Mary Midgley, *Evolution as a Religion* (London, UK: Rutledge Classics, 2002), 127. Midgley offers a classic critique of this position, quoting Wittgenstein that "particular propositions cannot always be prior to general ones. Both are elements in language, which is itself an element in our whole system of behaviour. In a crucial sense, the whole is always prior to its parts. And unquestionably this kind of belief in a law-abiding universe . . . is a precondition of any possible physical science."

[16] Kevin J. Vanhoozer, ed., *Postmodern Theology* (Cambridge, UK: Cambridge University Press), 10–13.

Consider also the Postmodern phrase, "That's just *your* interpretation." As D. A. Carson points out, this view is problematic. Carson says he has never met a deconstructionist who would be pleased if a reviewer misinterpreted his work. He notes, ". . . in practice deconstructionists implicitly link their own texts with their own intentions."[17] In other words, deconstructionists believe in authorial intent when they are the authors, but deny authorial intent when it comes to works by anyone else.

Likewise, we recognize a dilemma with the well-worn Postmodern slogan, "That may be true for you, but not for me." If the person making that statement means that it applies only to him, then who cares what he says—he is only talking to himself. On the other hand, if the person means to apply his statement also to *you*, then you can properly respond, "I get the impression that you think I should believe what you just said. If that is the case, why are you trying to impose your concept of what is true on me?" Either way, the Postmodernist has made a statement he cannot live with himself. It is a position that is self-defeating and ultimately absurd. If you try to apply the Postmodernist view of truth in day-to-day life, the result is a total breakdown of your ability to communicate.

Another serious problem arises from a Postmodern philosophy of language: if each community determines what is true through its use of language, which community gets to decide between rival communities when it comes to conflicting ideas? Take for example such disputed ideas as suttee (the Hindu practice of burning widows on their deceased husband's pyre), exterminating the Jewish race, or abolishing private ownership of property. Since no community can claim to be "right" on these or other issues, the result is an increased competition for which group will dominate the others. We are witnessing this kind of escalation between warring factions in many areas of society, from the college campus to the political arena to the international scene.

Elaborating on this problem is Jurgen Habermas, a German philosopher speaking from a Secular Humanist point of view. Ward explains: "Habermas sees Postmodernism's apparent embrace of irrationality as morally bankrupt and believes, contrary to Lyotard, that some sort of universally agreed-upon framework is both possible and necessary in order to ensure that freedom and justice are achieved. Habermas disputes the claims of some Postmodern thinkers that human identity is unstable, fragmented, or 'in process:' for him we all, deep down, share eternal human needs and desires. The failure of the Postmodernists is that they refuse to propose a route towards the fulfillment of these."[18]

Paul Kurtz, in *Humanist Manifesto 2000,* agrees with Habermas and says that Postmodernism—"a philosophical-literary movement"—is nihilistic (the view that nothing can be known or communicated). In contrast to the idea that objective truth is unknowable, Kurtz declares that science offers "reasonably objective standards for judging its truth claims." He says, "Science has become a universal language, speaking to all men and women no matter what their cultural backgrounds."[19]

Kurtz fails, however, to acknowledge Christianity's role in the foundation and development of modern science.[20] Also, while Kurtz is correct in his statement that scientific knowledge can lead to Truth concerning the physical world, the Biblical Christian philosophy of knowledge also emphasizes revealed truth as a means for understanding other Truths, including our relationship to God.

---

[17] D.A. Carson, *The Gagging of God: Christianity Confronts Pluralism* (Grand Rapids, MI: Zondervan Publishing House, 1996), 103.

[18] Ward, *Postmodernism*, 179.

[19] Kurtz, *Humanist Manifesto 2000*, 22.

[20] See the chapter on Biblical Christian Biology.

Yet far more significant than these criticisms is the negative consequences of a Postmodern approach to language. For a telling example, look at the results of applying deconstruction to law revealed by the 1973 *Roe v. Wade* case. In handing down their decision, the majority of the Supreme Court justices chose to look at the Constitution as a "living document"—that is, open to many interpretations (polysemy). As a result, they invented new meanings from the original text—meanings that were not openly stated—and came up with a novel interpretation regarding a woman's reproductive rights that has apparently gone unnoticed for almost 200 years. One consequence of that reinterpretation is that since 1973 over forty million unborn children have been murdered at the request of their mothers.

Postmodernists are correct about one thing—interpretation is important. Confucius is quoted as saying, "When words lose their meanings, people lose their freedom."[21] However, it is worse than that. In reality, when words lose their meaning, people not only lose their freedom, but their lives as well.

2.6.8 CONCLUSION

Christian students need to understand that according to the Christian worldview "Truth" exists. Nearly everything about Christianity is *universal* in scope and application. God created the whole universe, including men and women. Sin is a *universal* condition affecting every human being. God loved the *whole world*, including every human being. Christ died for the sins of the *whole world*, not just one or two particular communities. Christians are to love God with all their heart and mind and their fellow human beings around the *world*.

Most importantly, God chose to communicate the Truth about Himself and His world by words contained in the Scriptures and the language of the heavens (Psalm 19). God's words do not depend upon a reader's interpretation. Instead, the reader is to interpret the Bible according to God's intention. The Apostle Peter is clear when he writes, "Above all, you must understand that no prophecy of Scripture came about by the prophet's own interpretation. For prophecy never had its origin in the will of man, but men spoke from God as they were carried along by the Holy Spirit" (2 Peter 1:19–21).

To correctly understand the meaning of any text of Scripture, we should heed Paul's advice to Timothy: "Do your best to present yourself to God as one approved, a workman who does not need to be ashamed and who correctly handles the word of truth." (2 Timothy 2:15) By acknowledging that God has communicated in language Truth about the real world, and by diligently studying the Bible, you can know the Truth that sets you free (John 8:32).

---

[21] F.A. Hayek, *The Fatal Conceit: The Errors of Socialism* (Chicago, IL: University of Chicago Press, 1989), 106.

125

Ethics

Christianity

Love must be sincere. Hate what is evil; cling to what is good.

ROMANS 12:9 (NIV)

Therefore, whatever you want others to do for you, do also the same for them—this is the Law and the Prophets.

MATTHEW 7:12

3.1.1 INTRODUCTION

Ethics is the study of good and evil, right and wrong. Biblical Christian ethics is inseparable from theology because it is grounded in the character of God. The task of Christian ethics, then, is to determine what conforms to God's character and what does not. Francis Schaeffer explains the uniqueness of Christian ethics: "One of the distinctions of the Judeo-Christian God is that not all things are the same to Him. That at first may sound rather trivial, but in reality it is one of the most profound things one can say about the Judeo–Christian God. He exists; He has a character; and not all things are the same to Him. Some things conform to His character, and some are opposed to His character."[1]

> Biblical Christian ethics is inseparable from theology because it is grounded in the character of God.

---

[1] Francis Schaeffer, "Christian Faith and Human Rights," *Simon Greenleaf Law Review*, 2 (1982-3), 5. Cited in

Muslims believe that moral norms are arbitrary, a product of God's decree, and therefore can change as God chooses. Marxists and Secular Humanists rely almost exclusively on their economic or naturalistic philosophy to determine ethics. Postmodernists argue for a morality based on shared "community" values and Cosmic Humanists assume that everyone acts morally by following inner truth determined on an individual basis. Christians, on the other hand, believe that moral norms come from God's nature or essence. Rather than believing in some passing fancy bound to society's ever-changing whims, as Christians we are committed to a specific moral order revealed to us through both general and special revelation.

> The human mind, has no more power of inventing a new value than of imagining a new primary color, or, indeed, of creating a new sun and a new sky for it to move in.
>
> — C.S. LEWIS

We know that God's ethical order is the only true source of morality, and, in fact, the only possible morality; there can be no other. "The human mind," says C.S. Lewis, "has no more power of inventing a new value than of imagining a new primary color, or, indeed, of creating a new sun and a new sky for it to move in."[2] For the Christian, the moral order is as real as the physical order—some would say even more real. The Apostle Paul says the physical order is temporary, but the order "not seen" is eternal (2 Corinthians 4:18). This eternal moral order is a reflection of the character and nature of God Himself.

3.1.2 REVELATION AND OUR COMMON MORAL HERITAGE

Christian ethics, in one sense, is simply an expansion of a moral order that is generally revealed to everyone. Despite some disagreement regarding the morality of specific actions, Calvin D. Linton comments on the consistency of the moral code within all people everywhere: ". . . [T]here is a basic pattern of similarity among [ethical codes]. Such things as murder, lying, adultery, cowardice are, for example, almost always condemned. The universality of the ethical sense itself (the 'oughtness' of conduct), and the similarities within the codes of diverse cultures indicate a common moral heritage for all mankind which materialism or naturalism cannot explain."[3]

We may define this common moral heritage as anything from an attitude to a conscience, but however we define it, we are aware that some **moral absolutes** do exist outside ourselves. According to this universal moral code, whenever we pass judgment we are relying upon a yardstick that measures actions against an absolute set of standards. Without a standard, justice could not exist; without an ethical absolute, morality could not exist.

MORAL ABSOLUTES: The belief that an absolute ethical standard exists for all individuals regardless of era or culture

This objective, absolute standard is apparent throughout humanity's attitudes toward morality. According to a secular philosophy, we should treat all morals as relative—but in practice, even secular society treats some abstract values (such as justice, love, and courage) as consistently moral. Secular society also cringes at the Nazi holocaust, the Russian prison system of Siberian gulags, and the abuse of children. We cannot explain this phenomenon unless we accept the notion that certain value judgments apply universally and are somehow inherent to all mankind.

Christian morality is founded on the conviction that an absolute moral order exists outside of, and yet somehow is inscribed into, our very being. It is a morality flowing from the nature of the Creator through the nature of created things, not a construction of the human mind. It is part

---

John Montgomery, *Human Rights and Human Dignity* (Dallas, TX: Probe Books, 1986), 113.

[2] C.S. Lewis, *The Abolition of Man* (New York, NY: Macmillan, 1973), 56–7.

[3] Carl F.H. Henry, ed., *Baker's Dictionary of Christian Ethics* (Grand Rapids, MI: Baker, 1973), 620.

of God's general revelation. "At the core of every moral code," says Walter Lippman, "there is a picture of human nature, a map of the universe, and version of history. To human nature (of the sort conceived), in a universe (of the kind imagined), after a history (so understood), the rules of the code apply."[4]

This moral light is what the Apostle John refers to as having been lit in the hearts of all men and women—"The true light that gives light to every man" (John 1:9, NIV). It is what the Apostle Paul calls "the work of the law written in their hearts, their conscience" (Romans 2:15).

This morality is not arbitrarily handed down by God to create difficulties for us. God does not make up new values according to whim. Rather, God's innate character is holy and cannot tolerate evil or moral indifference—what the Bible calls sin. Therefore, if we wish to please God and prevent sin from separating us from Him, we must act in accordance with His moral order.

Christians are assured of these truths about God's nature and judgment as a result of special revelation. Whereas general revelation has informed all people of the existence of a moral order, special revelation—the Bible—discloses specifics regarding that order. In the final analysis, Christians rely on God and His Word for a full explanation of the moral order.

3.1.3 THE CHRISTIAN RESPONSE TO SECULAR ETHICS

Christians need to recognize secular ideas regarding ethics and the flaws inherent in these ideas. For the Christian, morality is a lifestyle of glorifying God, and it is crucial for our moral health to stay away from the hazy thinking that creates less–than–absolute moral values. Rejecting moral absolutes in favor of "situational ethics" is nothing but an excuse to do as we please under the banner of morality. Although history clearly shows that the consequences of such a morality are deadly, thousands today continue to perish as a direct result of their immoral behavior.

Secular moralities are based on a belief that our own ideas about right and wrong are sufficient for an ethical code. Yet, this leaves us without a clear standard for judging moral actions and attitudes. Schaeffer insists that there must be an absolute if there is to be a moral order and real values. "If there is no absolute beyond man's ideas, then there is no final appeal to judge between individuals and groups whose moral judgments conflict. We are merely left with conflicting opinions."[5]

> Rejecting moral absolutes in favor of "situational ethics" is nothing but an excuse to do as we please under the banner of morality.

This is the Achilles' heel of ethical relativism—it leaves us with no standards, only conflicting opinions and subjective value judgments. The ethical vacuum created by relativism allows leaders to misuse their power. "Those who stand outside all judgments of value cannot have any ground for preferring one of their own impulses to another except the emotional strength of that impulse,"[6] writes Lewis.

For the Christian, God is the ultimate source of morality, and it is nothing short of blasphemy when we assume His role. And yet, if we do not submit entirely to the moral absolutes established in God's character, logically the only ethical authority presiding over us is our own impulses. Christians need to understand the fallacies of secular ethics so we can avoid the inconsistencies of unfounded ethical ideals. We must recognize all secular ethical codes as aberrations of God's code.

---

[4] Walter Lippman, *Public Opinion* (New York, NY: The Free Press, 1965), 80, quoted in Thomas Sowell, *A Conflict of Visions* (New York, NY: William Morrow and Company, 1987), 18.

[5] Francis A. Schaeffer, *How Should We Then Live?* (Old Tappan, NJ: Fleming H. Revell, 1976), 145.

[6] Lewis, *The Abolition of Man*, 78.

3.1.4 CHRISTIAN ETHICS AND SPECIAL REVELATION

As Christians, we embrace the concept of moral absolutes and believe we should teach them to our children. But what specific absolutes make up the moral order we profess? What should we do? How should we live?

Absolutes are revealed to us in the Bible. While it is impossible for every situation requiring moral decisions to be addressed in the Bible, sufficient guidelines are provided to give us a sense of what is right in each circumstance. The most obvious moral absolutes, of course, are the Decalogue (the Ten Commandments), which establish the basic moral law for humanity. Much of the Old and New Testaments is dedicated to describing and explaining God's moral order. For example, the New Testament books of Romans and Galatians contain a number of moral directives for us to follow.

The Bible also introduces us to God Incarnate, Jesus Christ, and describes His ministry and teachings so that we might better understand the implications of living a moral life. The apex of Christ's ethical teaching is found in the Sermon on the Mount (Matthew 5–7). In addition, Jesus Christ provides the perfect role model for virtuous living. W.E.H. Lecky, who never claimed to be a Christian, admits, "The character of Jesus has not only been the highest pattern of virtue, but the strongest incentive to its practice . . . ."[7]

In fact, the call to follow Jesus is the simplest summation of Christian ethics, and at the same time, the most difficult thing for us to do. Dietrich Bonhoeffer, a Christian who died for his faith at the hands of the Nazis during World War II, notes, "On two separate occasions Peter received the call, 'Follow me.' It was the first and last word Jesus spoke to his disciple (Mark 1:17, John 21:22)."[8] Christ asks but one thing of all Christians: follow Me!

3.1.5 RESPONSIBILITY IN CHRISTIAN ETHICS

We are called to "love the Lord your God with all your heart and with all your soul and with all your strength and with all your mind, and love your neighbor as yourself" (Luke 10:27). This command, like all other commands in the Bible, implies that Christians have responsibilities.

This responsibility to love others requires not only compassion but also a servant attitude. At its most basic level, loving God means serving others. Carl F.H. Henry summarizes our Christian duty: "The Apostle John appeals to the explicit teaching of the Redeemer to show the inseparable connection between love of God and love of neighbor: 'If a man says, I love God, and hateth his brother, he is a liar: for he that loveth not his brother whom he hath seen, how can he love God whom he hath not seen? And this commandment have we from him, that he who loveth God love his brother also' (1 John 4:20f). 'God is love, and he that dwelleth in love dwelleth in God, and God in him' (4:16). The love of God is the service of man in love."[9]

This duty toward our neighbors requires more than serving their spiritual needs. "[M]an is more than a soul destined for another world," says Norman Geisler; "he is also a body living in this world. And as a resident of this time-space continuum man has physical and social needs which cannot be isolated from spiritual needs. Hence, in order to love man as he is—the whole man—one must exercise a concern about his social needs as well as his spiritual needs."[10] As Christians, we cannot claim that our faith in God exempts us from worldly concerns such as

---

[7] W.E.H. Lecky, *History of European Morals (from Augustus to Charlemagne)*, 2 vols. (New York, NY: George Braziller, 1955), 2:8–9.

[8] Norman L. Geisler, *Ethics: Alternatives and Issues* (Grand Rapids, MI: Zondervan, 1979), 156.

[9] Carl F.H. Henry, *Christian Personal Ethics* (Grand Rapids, MI: Eerdmans, 1957), 221–2.

[10] Geisler, *Ethics*, 179.

feeding the hungry or caring for the sick. Jesus tells us in Matthew 25:31–46 that when we serve others we serve Him; and that when we fail to serve others we fail to serve Him. Furthermore, He will judge us on the basis of our service to those who are in need.

As Christians, our responsibility to love our neighbor entails an even more fundamental obligation: our duty to love God. "The moral end, or highest good, is the glory of God," writes William Young. "In declaring by word and deed the perfections, especially the moral perfections of the Most High, man finds true happiness."[11] Carl Henry describes the heart and soul of Christian ethics: "Hebrew-Christian ethics unequivocally defines moral obligation as man's duty to God."[12]

The Pop Culture Connection

Les Miserables (the 1979 film version based on the book by Victor Hugo)—The pivotal scene illustrates the dramatic change in a person who experiences God's grace. After being imprisoned under hard labor for 19 years for stealing a loaf of bread, Valjean makes an escape. On the run and desperate, he is taken in by a kindly Bishop, but in the night steals the Bishop's silver and flees. Upon being caught and returned to the scene of the crime, the Bishop unexpecedly gives him a pair of expensive candlesticks to have along with the silverware. Valjean, weeping in repentance over the kindness of the Bishop, leaves a changed man.

3.1.6 THE INEVITABILITY OF SIN

The Bible not only defines the moral order, it also announces that God will judge our character and conduct. Revelation 22:11–15 warns that at the judgment many will be left outside the city of God. This warning has staggering implications. "Christianity declares that God is more than the ground and goal of the moral order," explains Henry. "Unequivocally it lays stress on the reality of God's judgment of history. It affirms, that is, the stark fact of moral disorder and rebellion: 'the whole world lieth in wickedness' (1 John 5:19). By emphasizing the fact of sin and the shattered moral law of God, the dread significance of death, the wiles of Satan and the hosts of darkness, Christian ethics sheds light on the treacherous realities of making moral choices."[13]

The reality is, of course, that we "all have sinned and fall short of the glory of God" (Romans 3:23). This is a unique aspect of the Christian ethical system. "When a person makes up his own ethical code," D. James Kennedy says, "he always makes up an ethical system which he thinks he has kept. In the law of God, we find a law which smashes our self-righteousness, eliminates all trust in our own goodness, and convinces us that we are sinners. The law of God leaves us with our hands over our mouths and our faces in the dust. We are humbled before God and convinced that we are guilty transgressors of his law."[14]

Acknowledging our guilt before a Holy God is crucial if we are to understand the incredible sacrifice God made when He sent His Son to die for us. The Christian ethical code calls for perfection, and no one other than Christ has ever achieved it. Thus, the ethical code itself points us first to our own sinful nature and then to the realization that the only One who can save us is the Man who has not transgressed that code, Jesus Christ. The absolute moral code shows us our absolute dependence on Him. Put more simply, "The law is given to convince us that we fail to keep it."[15] When we realize this truth, we are driven for salvation to the One who has not failed.

[11] Henry, *Baker's Dictionary of Christian Ethics*, 432–3.
[12] Henry, *Christian Personal Ethics*, 209.
[13] Ibid., 172.
[14] D. James Kennedy, *Why I Believe* (Waco, TX: Word Books, 1980), 91.
[15] Ibid., 90.

We cannot, however, simply rely on Christ to save us and then continue in our sinful ways. Rather, once we understand the ultimate sacrifice God made for us, we cannot help but respond with a grateful desire to please God by adhering to His moral order. This does not mean that it becomes easy to do what is morally right—it simply means we desire to do God's will. As Lewis says, "There is nowhere this side of heaven where one can safely lay the reins on the horse's neck. It will never be lawful simply to 'be ourselves' until 'ourselves' have become sons of God."[16] Obeying the laws of Christian ethics requires a firm commitment and an unflagging zeal for doing what is right and good in the Lord's sight. Paul says Christians must "[h]ate what is evil; cling to what is good" (Romans 12:9, NIV). In the chapters that follow, he defines what he means by "the good."

3.1.7 CONCLUSION

The Christian ethical system is both like and unlike any other system ever postulated. Every ethical system contains some grain of the truth found in the Christian code, but no other system can claim to be the whole truth, handed down as an absolute from God to humanity.

As Christians who recognize the truth of God's law, we must dedicate our lives to obeying it. This dedication is far too rare today. Bonhoeffer asks, "Who stands fast? Only the man whose final standard is not his reason, his principles, his conscience, his freedom, or his virtue, but who is ready to sacrifice all this when he is called to obedient and responsible action in faith and in exclusive allegiance to God—the responsible man, who tries to make his whole life an answer to the question and call of God. Where are these responsible people?"[17]

Such Christians are those who are willing to treat God's moral order with the same respect they show His physical order; who love God with their whole body, soul, spirit, mind, and strength; who treat others as they desire to be treated. They may be in the halls of government, standing firm against tyranny and slavery, or in the mission field, sacrificing everything for the sake of the gospel. More often they are quite ordinary Christians living extraordinary lives, showing the world that Christ's truth is worth believing and living. (For biblical examples of ethically responsible men and women, see Hebrews 11:32–12:3.)

[16] C.S. Lewis, *God in the Dock* (Grand Rapids, MI: Eerdmans, 1972), 286.
[17] Joan Winmill Brown, ed., *The Martyred Christian* (New York, NY: Macmillan, 1985), 157.

Islam

> There is no division of ethics and law in Islam.[1]
>
> — S. PARVEZ MANZOOR

3.2.1 INTRODUCTION

Because of the linkage between Islamic ethics and law, this chapter touches briefly on certain elements of Islamic ethics. A study of Islamic ethics is more fruitful when done in conjunction with a study of Islamic law.

3.2.2 MUHAMMAD AS EXEMPLAR

Historically, Muslims derive their ethics from the Qur'an and the Hadith. The Qur'an contains several commands Muhammad's followers must obey. The Hadith presents Muhammad as *the* exemplary human whom Muslims must imitate in all respects. "Muhammad was only a mortal being commissioned by God to teach the word of God and lead an exemplary life," writes Hammuda Abdalati. "He stands in history as the best model for man in piety and perfection. He is a living proof of what man can be and of what he can accomplish in the realm of excellence and virtue."[2]

Ram Swarup explains how the actions and judgment of Muhammad recorded in the Hadith are perceived by Muslims:

---

[1] "Islamic Conceptual Framework," section on "Shari'ah: The Ethics of Action," http://www.islamonline.net/english/Contemporary/2002/05/Article23.shtml.

[2] Hammuda Abdalati, *Islam in Focus* (Indianapolis, IN: Amana Publications, 1978), 8.

The Prophet is caught as it were in the ordinary acts of his life—sleeping, eating, mating, praying, hating, dispensing justice, planning expeditions and revenge against his enemies. The picture that emerges is hardly flattering, and one is left wondering why in the first instance it was reported at all and whether it was done by admirers or enemies. One is also left to wonder how the believers, generation after generation, could have found this story so inspiring.

The answer is that the [Muslim] believers are conditioned to look at the whole thing through the eyes of faith. An infidel in his fundamental misguidance may find the Prophet rather sensual and cruel—and certainly many of the things he did do not conform to ordinary ideas of morality—but the believers look at the whole thing differently. To them morality derives from the Prophet's actions; the moral is whatever he did. Morality does not determine the Prophet's actions, but his actions determine and define morality. Muhammad's acts were not ordinary acts; they were Allah's own acts [i.e., acts empowered, guided and approved by Allah].

It was in this way and by this logic that Muhammad's opinions became the dogmas of Islam and his personal habits and idiosyncrasies became moral imperatives: Allah's commands for all believers in all ages and climes to follow.[3]

We will detail some of these traditions regarding Muhammad's life and teachings in other chapters.

3.2.3 MORAL ABSOLUTES

The Islamic worldview, like the Christian worldview, affirms ethical absolutes. Whereas the Bible grounds morality in God's essential character, the Qur'an teaches that God cannot ultimately be known. Certain actions are good not because they derive from God's character, but because God chooses to call them good. God could have decreed a different set of moral principles. Therefore, Muslims know moral goodness by God's decree. Islam and Christianity agree to some of the same moral standards although significant differences exist.

> The Bible grounds morality in God's essential character; the Qur'an teaches that God cannot ultimately be known.

Hammudah Abdalati summarizes Islamic morality as follows:

The concept of morality in Islam centers around certain basic beliefs and principles. Among these are the following: (1) God is the Creator and Source of all goodness, truth, and beauty. (2) Man is a responsible, dignified, and honorable agent of his Creator. (3) God has put everything in the heavens and the earth in the service of mankind. (4) By His Mercy and Wisdom, God does not expect the impossible from man or hold him accountable for anything beyond his power. Nor does God forbid man to enjoy the good things of life. (5) Moderation, practicality, and balance are the guarantees of high integrity and sound morality. (6) All things are permissible in principle except what is singled out as obligatory, which must be observed, and what is singled out as forbidden, which must be avoided. (7) Man's ultimate responsibility is to God and his highest goal is the pleasure of his Creator.[4]

[3] Ram Swarup, *Understanding Islam Through Hadis* (Delhi, India: Voice of India, 1983), xv–xvi, as quoted in George W. Braswell, *Islam: Its Prophet, Peoples, Politics and Power* (Nashville, TN: Broadman and Holman, 1996), 83.

[4] Abdalati, *Islam in Focus*, 40.

3.2.4 THE FIVE PILLARS OF PRACTICE

The **Five Pillars** of Islam encompass the basic moral obligations for Muslims. The first pillar of Islam is the confession of faith: *There is no God but Allah and Muhammad is his prophet*. Under this pillar all other obligations are subsumed, for to believe in God and Muhammad as His prophet is to obey their teachings and the example of Muhammad's life.

FIVE PILLARS
1. Confession
2. Prayer
3. Fasting
4. Almsgiving
5. Pilgrimage

The second pillar is prayer: Muslims are expected to engage in prayer five times a day, facing Mecca. Prayer provides a daily rhythm to Muslim life. Muslims hope to please God by remembering him constantly with regulated prayer. Muslims also hope that systematic praying will help them avoid temptations to immorality.

The third pillar is fasting during Ramadan. Fasting involves refraining from such things as food, tobacco, and sexual relations during daylight hours, though they are not prohibited after sundown. These periods of fasting are to encourage and enable Muslims to develop self-control, to squelch bad habits, and to refocus their minds toward personal spiritual progress.

The fourth pillar is almsgiving wherein Muslims are required to give at least 2.5 percent of their annual capital to the poor, either directly or through Muslim charitable organizations. Giving to the poor is intended to achieve a generous lifestyle and a sense of caring for the Muslim community, especially those lacking physical and financial means.

The fifth pillar is pilgrimage. All Muslims are expected to make a pilgrimage to Mecca at least once in their lifetime, if their finances and health permit. During their pilgrimage, Muslims don white garments and remove all indicators of status or class. This practice is intended to help Muslims recognize that before God they are all equal. Racial, gender, and economic differences are muted as masses of Muslims from many nations bow together to worship Allah.

A sixth pillar, *jihad*, is sometimes added as an obligation for Muslims. *Jihad* has two facets: first is the battle against temptation and sin for the sake of self-control and the development of virtue. The second is the battle against any and all who oppose Islam. *Jihad* is seen as the most self-sacrificing action Muslims can undertake. Indeed, Muslims who die in *jihad* are guaranteed entrance into Paradise, where men have access to scores of perpetual virgins. Women, however, are not told what awaits them.

The Pop Culture Connection

Paradise Now (2005)—Made by a Palestinian director, Hany Abu-Assad, this film "tells the story of two (potential) Palestinian suicide bombers, from the start of their mission to its sad end. The film humanizes the bombers in ways that are probably repugnant to Israeli families affected by such attacks. But it possesses something valuable...an honest, local perspective on one aspect of violence in the Middle East....This is not to say that the film's outlook on the conflict is the right one—Israel is portrayed without nuance as an occupier, oppressor, and villain. The film fails to question this perspective, although it does question the ongoing violent response to Israel's stance. More than religious zeal, even, a sense of indignity and inferiority motivates Mr. Abu-Assad's characters. *Paradise Now* paints a sad, fascinating portrait of two young men who think that death (their own, and, although this integral element is skirted, of the Israeli civilians they blow up) is better than that indignity."[5]*

---

[5] * Andrew Coffin, "Syriana and Paradise Now," WORLD Magazine, December 24, 2005, Vol. 20, No. 50, http://worldmag.com/articles/11381.

3.2.5 SOME PROHIBITIONS FOR MUSLIMS

Along with positive commands (ethical imperatives) Muslims are ruled by a number of ethical prohibitions. The Qur'an prohibits drinking wine (Qur'an 2:219; 4:43; 5:93–94; some Muslims apply this prohibition by analogy to all alcoholic beverages and intoxicating drugs). The Qur'an prohibits eating pork, animals who kill with claws, teeth, or fangs, birds of prey, rodents, reptiles, worms, and dead animals (2:172–173; 5:4–6). Muslims may not eat meat that has not been properly slaughtered, which includes a prayer to Allah at the time of the slaughter. The Qur'an also prohibits gambling (2:219) and sexual immorality.

3.2.6 THE DAY OF JUDGMENT

Muslims believe in a day of final judgment when all humanity will be judged and their deeds weighed in the balance. Muslims are motivated toward ethical behavior on several fronts: to develop personal virtue and spirituality; to better the state of others; to strengthen relationships; and to anticipate the coming judgment.

> Then those whose balance (of good deeds) is heavy, they will attain salvation: But those whose balance is light, will be those who have lost their souls, in Hell will they abide. (Qur'an 23:102–103)

Fear of an eternity in hell is the strongest motivation of all.

> This world will come to an end some day, and the dead will rise to stand for their final and fair trial. Everything we do in this world, every intention we have, every move we make, every thought we entertain, and every word we say, all are counted and kept in accurate records. On the Day of Judgment they will be brought up. People with good records will be generously rewarded and warmly welcomed to the Heaven of God, and those with bad records will be punished and cast into Hell . . . However, the Muslim believes that there definitely will be compensation and reward for the good deeds, and punishment for the evil ones. That is the Day of justice and final settlement of all accounts. [6]

3.2.7 CONCLUSION

Muslims see Muhammad as the exemplary human being, the one all people should seek to imitate. Along with more general virtues, the Five Pillars of Practice form a core of Islamic ethics. In addition to many motivations for ethical behavior, anticipation of final judgment is the strongest.

---

[6] Abdalati, *Islam in Focus*, 13.

Ethics

Secular Humanism

The fundamental question of ethics is, who makes the
rules? God or men? The theistic answer is that God makes
them. The humanistic answer is that men make them.
This distinction between theism and humanism is the
fundamental division in moral theory.[1]

— MAX HOCUTT

3.3.1 INTRODUCTION

Atheistic theology presents a special problem for Secular Humanists— namely, choosing a code of ethics. Humanists reject the unchanging moral codes posited by the Christian religion. In fact, Paul Kurtz, author of *Humanist Manifesto II*, states, "The traditional supernaturalistic moral commandments are especially repressive of our human needs. They are immoral insofar as they foster illusions about human destiny [heaven] and suppress vital inclinations."[2] Humanists find religious ethical codes such as the Ten Commandments too restrictive in that such codes do not allow us to fulfill our conception of the good life.

Humanists are working toward a "science of ethics" specifically in keeping with their beliefs in atheism, naturalism, and evolution. Kurtz, in *The Humanist Alternative*, calls for Secular Humanism to be "interpreted as a moral point of view."[3] Indeed, in the preface to *Humanist Manifestoes I & II*, Kurtz defines Humanism "as a philosophical, religious, and moral point of

---

[1] Morris B. Storer, ed., *Humanist Ethics* (Buffalo, NY: Prometheus Books, 1980), 137.

[2] Paul Kurtz, ed., *The Humanist Alternative* (Buffalo, NY: Prometheus Books, 1973), 50.

[3] Ibid., 179.

view."[4] Later in *Humanist Manifesto 2000* Kurtz redefines Humanism as "an ethical, scientific, and philosophical outlook that has changed the world."[5]

Can morality be achieved without the foundation of absolute religious beliefs? Humanists hope so, but they have difficulty agreeing what morality means without God. The need for a consistent Humanist ethical standard gave rise to a book edited by Morris B. Storer, entitled simply *Humanist Ethics*. Storer sums up the multitude of Humanist ethical views in his preface: "Is personal advantage the measure of right and wrong, or the advantage of all affected: Humanists differ. Is there truth in ethics? We differ. Are 'right' and 'wrong' expressions of heart or head? Do people have free wills? Do you measure morality by results or by principles? Do people have duties as well as rights? We have our differences on all these and more."[6]

3.3.2 THE FOUNDATION OF HUMANIST ETHICS

These differences among Humanists result largely from their disagreement over the foundation of morality. Kurtz believes in "a limited number of basic values and principles,"[7] but he does not point to a specific foundation for ethical principles, saying only that they are "naturalistic and empirical phenomena."[8]

Mihailo Markovic, another Humanist writing in Storer's collection of essays, takes exception to Kurtz's assumption about the origin of these principles, pointing out that Humanists have no unchanging standard that requires people to act in a certain way: "It remains quite unclear where this 'ought' comes from. It is one thing to describe a variety of actual historical patterns of conduct and moral habits. It is a completely different thing to make a choice among them and to say that we 'ought' to observe some of them. Why some and not others?"[9]

> I can find no ultimate basis for 'ought'.
>
> — MIHAILO MARKOVIC

Markovic cuts to the heart of the problem Humanists face when discussing ethics. If we are is going to decide what we "ought" to do, then we must refer to a moral code, or foundation, which dictates this "ought." Kurtz, when challenged by Markovic, admits, "I can find no ultimate basis for 'ought.'"[10]

These differences over the foundation of ethical standards divide Humanists regarding the "absolute" nature of ethics. The problem according to Humanist Max Hocutt is that "[t]he nonexistence of God makes more difference to some of us than to others. To me, it means that there is no absolute morality, that moralities are sets of social conventions devised by humans to satisfy their need. To [Alistair] Hannay, it means that we must postulate an alternative basis for moral absolutism."[11]

This lack of consensus about the foundation of ethics is problematic for the whole concept of Humanist ethics. Without a God who sets forth an absolute moral code, Humanists must believe either that the code is subjective and should be applied differently to changing situations, or that an absolute code exists, somehow outside of ourselves, but within the whole evolutionary scheme of things.

---

[4] Paul Kurtz, ed., *Humanist Manifestoes I & II* (Buffalo, NY: Prometheus Books, 1980), 3.

[5] Paul Kurtz, *Humanist Manifesto 2000: A Call for a New Planetary Humanism* (Amherst, NY: Prometheus Books, 2000), 7.

[6] Storer, *Humanist Ethics*, 3.

[7] Ibid., 13.

[8] Ibid., 22.

[9] Ibid., 33.

[10] Ibid., 35.

[11] Ibid., 191.

Hocutt maintains that an absolute moral code cannot exist without God, and God does not exist. "Furthermore, if there were a morality written up in the sky somewhere but no God to enforce it, I see no good reason why anybody should pay it any heed, no reason why we should obey it. Human beings may, and do, make up their own rules."[12] This view is more consistent with the Humanist view that life evolved by chance—otherwise, the Humanist has a difficult time explaining where an external absolute code originated. If we are the highest beings in nature and did not develop the absolute moral code ourselves, then what creature or force in nature did?

> Human beings may, and do, make up their own rules.
> — MAX HOCUTT

Some Humanists have gone so far as to cast doubt on the idea that we can even perceive what is right or wrong. Kai Nielsen, a signatory to *Humanist Manifesto II*, proposed a "no-truth thesis" that states that no question of the truth or falsity of moral values can sensibly arise. Nielsen's thesis appears to be the logical conclusion for Humanists since they are unwilling to grant the existence of an absolute moral code. Without an absolute moral code, what standard do we have for judging actions as right or wrong, or moral beliefs as true or false? Humanists recognize the dilemma of being unable to determine the difference between right and wrong and have attempted to explain away the "no-truth thesis" in a number of ways.

Most Humanists dodge the "no-truth thesis" by claiming that they use reason to determine right and wrong in the context of ethical relativism. A general statement of policy issued by the British Humanist Association states, "Humanists believe that man's conduct should be based on humanity, insight, and reason. He must face his problems with his own moral and intellectual resources, without looking for supernatural aid."[13]

Many other Humanists echo this call for the use of reason and experience as a guide for moral conduct. Lamont says that as long as we pursue "activities that are healthy, socially useful, and in accordance with reason, pleasure will generally accompany [us]; and happiness, the supreme good, will be the eventual result."[14]

Lamont's optimism, significantly, is based on the "hope" provided by evolutionary theory. We can reason our way to the good and to happiness because evolution is constantly improving things, even humanity. Assuming that morals do not arise from God or exist independently of nature, evolution provides a plausible explanation for the source of ethics and is consistent with other Humanist concepts.

A serious problem is created, however, by Humanism's desire to wed ethics to biology—this view allows Darwin's concept of the struggle for existence to become the absolute on which moral decisions are based. Such a morality allows men like Friedrich von Bernhardi, in his work *Germany and the Next War*, to insist, "War is a biological necessity; it is as necessary as the struggle of the elements of Nature; it gives a biologically just decision, since its decisions rest on the very nature of things."[15] Most Humanists would rather avoid this conclusion, but it lurks in the background under the guise of social or ethical Darwinism.

Weikart explains the inevitable results of basing ethics in evolution: "Many argued that by providing a naturalistic account of the origin of ethics and morality, Darwinism delivered a death-blow to the prevailing Judeo-Christian ethics, as well as Kantian ethics and any other fixed moral code. If morality was built on social instincts that changed over evolutionary time, then morality must be relative to the conditions of life at any given time. Darwinism—together

[12] Ibid., 137.

[13] Annual General Meeting of the British Humanist Association, July 1967.

[14] Corliss Lamont, *The Philosophy of Humanism* (New York, NY: Frederick Ungar, 1982), 253

[15] Bolton Davidheiser, *Evolution and Christian Faith* (Philadelphia, PA: Presbyterian and Reformed, 1969), 352.

with other forms of historicism ascendant in the nineteenth century—thus contributed to the rise of moral relativism."[16]

3.3.3 MORAL RELATIVISM

By rejecting the existence of purpose behind the evolutionary basis for a code of ethics, we necessarily reject any code that exists outside ourselves. This done, all ethics are relative to our interpretation of right and wrong in any given situation. **Moral relativism** consists of little more than experimenting with ethics in every new scenario. Mason Olds says, "Of course, humanism has no single ethical theory, therefore ethical theory and moral subject must be chosen, examined, and even debated."[17]

> MORAL RELATIVISM: The belief that morals are relative to the individual and the

These ideas about Humanist ethics are not just the radical ideas of a few Humanists on the fringe. Rather, ethical relativism is the generally accepted morality for Humanists. "The morality or immorality of any behavior," says Dr. Arthur E. Gravatt, "including sexual behavior, has been put in the context of 'situation ethics.' In this approach moral behavior may differ from situation to situation. Behavior might be moral for one person and not another or moral at one time and not another."[18]

Joseph Fletcher says that "rights and wrongs are determined by objective facts or circumstances, that is, by the situations in which moral agents have to decide for the most beneficial course open to choice."[19] Herbert W. Schneider calls morality "an experimental art," saying it is the "basic art of living well together. Moral right and wrong must therefore be conceived in terms of moral standards generated in a particular society."[20] Kurtz says "moral principles should be treated as hypotheses," tested by their practical worth and judged by what they cause to happen.[21]

Joseph Fletcher

3.3.4 PROBLEMS WITH ETHICAL RELATIVISM

Secular Humanists recognize that ethical relativism has the potential to create problems among people. Although they believe that dogma unnecessarily restricts our pursuit of happiness, they do address the question of whether or not people will act responsibly in a society without rules and corresponding penalties.

Kurtz addresses the dilemma with these words: "Nevertheless, the humanist is faced with a crucial ethical problem: Insofar as he has defended an ethic of freedom, can he develop a basis for moral responsibility? Regretfully, merely to liberate individuals from authoritarian social institutions, whether church or state, is no guarantee that they will be aware of their moral responsibility to others. The contrary is often the case. Any number of social institutions regulate conduct by some means of norms and rules, and sanctions are

---

[16] Richard Weikart, *From Darwin to Hitler: Evolutionary Ethics, Eugenics, and Racism in Germany* (New York, NY: Palgrave-Macmillan, 2004), 230.

[17] Mason Olds, "Ethics and Literature," *The Humanist* (Sept./Oct. 1985): 36.

[18] Arthur E. Gravatt, quoted in William H. Genne, "Our Moral Responsibility," *Journal of the American College Health Association* vol. 15 (May 1967): 63.

[19] Joseph Fletcher, "Humanist Ethics: the Groundwork," quoted in Storer, *Humanist Ethics*, 255.

[20] Storer, *Humanist Ethics*, 99–100.

[21] Kurtz, ed., *The Humanist Alternative*, 55.

imposed for enforcing them. . . . Once these sanctions are ignored, we may end up with [a man] concerned with his own personal lust for pleasure, ambition, and power, and impervious to moral constraints.[22]

Secular Humanists refute the religious doctrine of original sin (because it is part of the religious myth), but most recognize that there is no guarantee we will behave responsibly once all laws and dogma are removed.

The biggest problem with ethical relativism is that anything can be construed as *good* or *bad* under the assumption that the judgment is relative to the situation in which we find ourselves. Even if we are striving to do the right thing, we may honestly disagree among ourselves what the right thing is if there is no absolute standard by which to judge. Baier explains, "Plainly, it is not easy to determine in an objective way what conduct is morally ideal. Hence even among people of good will, that is, among people perfectly willing to do what is morally ideal, there may be sincere disagreement."[23]

Lamont acknowledges another aspect of ethical relativism, which in turn leads to another problem. "For the Humanist," he says, "stupidity is just as great a sin as selfishness; and 'the moral obligation to be intelligent' ranks always among the highest of duties."[24] The implication of this statement is that only intelligent people are capable of making correct

The Pop Culture Connection

Chocolat (a 2000 film directed Lasse Hahlstrom)—The bonus section of the DVD states, "This is a story about temptation and not denying yourself the good things in life." The main character, Vianne (Juliet Binoche), is sweet, kind, and all-embracing, but has an obvious disdain for Christianity. Throughout the film Christians are shown as weak and having little positive influence. For example, Anouk asks her mother, "Why can't we go to church?" Vianne replies, "You can if you want. But it won't make things easier." A defining moment in the film comes on Easter Sunday, as the priest says, "Do I want to speak of the miracle of our Lord's divine transformation? Not really. I don't want to talk about His divinity. I'd rather talk about His humanity—how He lived His life here on earth, His kindness, His tolerance. I think we can't go around measuring our goodness by what we don't do, by what we deny ourselves, what we resist, and who we exclude. I think we've got to measure goodness by what we embrace, what we create, and who we include." Following the sermon, the voiceover says, "It was certainly not the most fiery or eloquent sermon. But the parishioners felt a new sensation that day—a lightening of the spirit, a freedom from the old tradition."

moral choices, leading to the assumption that intelligent people are to act as the moral compass for the rest of society. This amounts to giving power to a select few to create a dogma that all others must follow. And this is precisely what Humanists try to avoid when they disassociate themselves from absolute moral codes.

[22] Paul Kurtz, "Does Humanism Have an Ethic of Responsibility?" Cited in Storer, *Humanist Ethics*, 15.
[23] Storer, *Humanist Ethics*, 81.
[24] Lamont, *The Philosophy of Humanism*, 248.

3.3.5 FROM THEORY TO PRACTICE

The theoretical foundation of Secular Humanist ethics, therefore, is moral relativism based on a belief in evolutionary change. Now we will examine how theory translates into practice, especially in the area of human sexuality.

Earlier in this chapter we noted Kurtz's contention that a code of ethics derived from a supernatural or religious base is repressive and immoral in that it "suppress[es] vital inclinations." Kirkendall identifies some of these inclinations in *A New Bill of Sexual Rights and Responsibilities* as homosexuality, bisexuality, pre- and extra-marital sexual relations, and "genital association."

Secular Humanists believe that homosexuality is a legitimate lifestyle because of scientific proof that some men are born homosexual. Alfred Kinsey concluded that homosexuality is biologically determined at birth. Pedophilia (man/boy sex) and incest may also be biologically determined according to Vern Bullough, historian of the homosexual movement.

> Three Humanists of the year Margaret Sanger, Mary Calderone, and Faye Wattleton have held key positions in Planned Parenthood.

The sexual revolution has been furthered by agencies such as Planned Parenthood, where three Humanists of the Year—Margaret Sanger, Mary Calderone, and Faye Wattleton—have served in key positions. One of its goals is to stop teenage pregnancy through education rather than to discourage teenage sexual activity. Planned Parenthood campaigns for easier access to condoms for teens and school-based health clinics "that provide contraceptives as part of general health care." According to one staff member, one goal of Planned Parenthood is to help "young people obtain sex satisfaction before marriage. By sanctioning sex before marriage, we will prevent fear and guilt."[25]

Corliss Lamont also calls for sex without guilt for those who are contemplating marriage. He advocates an experimental period of living together "for at least six months." Lamont reasons, "Historically, a primary reason for the enormous importance given to genital faithfulness and unfaithfulness was the lack of reliable birth-control techniques. Now that those techniques, including abortion, are generally available, this importance has more and more diminished."[26] Thus in this view, scientific advances and legal precedent give a whole new look to marital fidelity or infidelity.

Another good example of theory translating into practice was Margaret Sanger's involvement with the eugenics[27] movement to create a master race. This illustrates how the ethics of Secular Humanism is enmeshed in the evolutionary concept of survival of the fittest. We should note that many of her fellow humanists distanced themselves from this project. .

3.3.6 CONCLUSION

Because Secular Humanists disagree with each other so often, defining their ethical ideas as a conceptual whole is problematic. To remain consistent with their theology and philosophy, most Secular Humanists take the side of ethical relativism, but it remains difficult to standardize

---

[25] Lena Levine, "Psycho-sexual Development," *Planned Parenthood News* (Summer 1953): 10.

[26] Corliss Lamont, *Voice in the Wilderness* (Buffalo, NY: Prometheus Books, 1974), 97.

[27] See Edwin Black, *War against the Weak: Eugenics and America's Campaign to Create a Master Race* (New York, NY: Thunder's Mouth Press, 2003) for details regarding Sanger's eugenics connections. Also, see Jonah Goldberg, *Liberal Fascism: The Secret History of the American Left from Mussolini to the Politics of Meaning* (New York, NY: Doubleday, 2007), 243f.

what exactly that entails. Because Secular Humanists are aware of their logical inconsistencies and the dangers inherent in an ethics of relativism, their inability to make ethical assertions may be a mixed blessing. For example, Paul Kurtz insists that Secular Humanists accept the Golden Rule and even the biblical injunction to "accept the aliens within our midst, respecting their differences."[28] Kurtz likewise insists that Secular Humanists "ought to tell the truth, keep promises, be honest, sincere, beneficent, reliable, dependable, show fidelity, appreciation, gratitude, be fair-minded, just, tolerant, should not steal, injure, maim or harm other persons."[29] Christians have no difficulty agreeing with him in these dogmas or values. What Kurtz and his fellow Secular Humanists fail to address, however, is why these values are worth defending as moral declarations.

---

[28] Kurtz, *Humanist Manifesto 2000*, 32.
[29] Ibid.

Ethics

Marxism-Leninism

Is there such a thing as communist morality? Of course, there is. It is often suggested that we have no ethics of our own; very often the bourgeoisie accuse us Communists of rejecting all morality. This is a method of confusing the issue, of throwing dust in the eyes of the workers and peasants.[1]

— V.I. LENIN

3.4.1 INTRODUCTION

Marxist ethics proceeds out of Marxist theology, philosophy, biology, economics, and history. Whereas Secular Humanists have a difficult time reaching a consensus regarding their ethical beliefs, Marxists do not—mainly because of their single-minded approach to all five aforementioned disciplines. This approach is rooted in dialectical materialism and the class struggle. While there is no absolute foundation for Marxist ethical ideals, most Marxists believe the dialectical view of the class struggle is foundation enough.

According to the Marxist dialectic, everything in the universe—including society—is in a state of constant change. These changes are moving society upward toward the elimination of all social and economic class distinctions. The next social advance in history will be the move from capitalism to socialism, which will inevitably result in changes in society's moral ideals.

The dialectical view of history dictates the clash of thesis and antithesis—in this historical

---

[1] V.I. Lenin, *Collected Works*, 45 vols. (Moscow, USSR: Progress Publishers, 1982), 31:291.

context, the relentless clash between the proletariat and the bourgeoisie. Marxist-Leninists believe that the morality of these two classes is totally different, and when the proletariat finally destroys the bourgeoisie, a new morality will reign—a new morality for the new social system.

Marxists believe that "old morality"—the morality of the reigning capitalist class—exploits the working class. According to this view, old religious moral codes must be abandoned. For Karl Marx and Frederick Engels "Thou shalt not steal" establishes a society in which some have property and some do not; such an establishment is the root of the problem.

"It must be constantly borne in mind," says Howard Selsam, "that Marx and Engels denied that moral ideals, moral considerations, are central in human life and social evolution."[2] Rather, it is biological and social evolution that determines morality. What is right or wrong is determined by what is best for this evolution. If the bourgeois class hinders either biological or social evolution, nature dictates the removal of that class.

3.4.2 THE EVOLUTION OF MORALITY

The inevitability of change is the cornerstone of the Marxist ethical code. Marx writes in the *Manifesto* of the Communist Party, "Does it require deep intuition to comprehend that man's ideas, views and conceptions, in one word, man's consciousness, changes with every change in the conditions of his material existence, in his social relations and in his social life?"[3] By Marx's definition, our social and economic status is always changing according to the laws of the dialectic, so our ideas about morality must also be in a state of continual change.

V.I. Lenin answers the charge that the inevitability of change in both history and ethics precludes the existence of a moral code in Marxist philosophy: "Is there such a thing as communist morality? Of course there is. It is often suggested that we have no ethics of our own; very often the bourgeoisie accuse us Communists of rejecting all morality. This is a method of confusing the issue, of throwing dust in the eyes of the workers and peasants. In what sense do we reject ethics, reject morality? In the sense given to it by the bourgeoisie, who based ethics on God's commandments. On this point we, of course, say that we do not believe in God, and that we know perfectly well that the clergy, the landowners and the bourgeoisie invoked the name of God so as to further their own interests as exploiters."[4] In Lenin's view, Communist morality had to evolve beyond that morality of outdated Christian myth used by the exploiting class to suppress the exploited class.

When all class distinctions are erased, however, the Marxist moral view necessarily must change again because promoting class struggle will no longer be the immediate moral necessity. We say "immediate" because the dialectic is an eternal process that entails a continuing thesis/antithesis struggle. The ever-changing nature of history will dictate a new moral view for Marxists. When Marxists say there is no system of morality that fits all times, they include the future in their philosophy, realizing that history will change our perceptions of life again after our present aims are attained. Something can be morally right only in its context in history. Today the morally right action is the one necessary to attain the victory of the proletariat over the bourgeoisie.

The new classless society will determine the new morality, just as this evolution toward a classless society is dictating today's morality. For Marxists, morality is conduct that is in harmony with history as it flows in the direction of a classless society and beyond.

[2] Ibid.
[3] Karl Marx and Frederick Engels, *Collected Works*, 40 vols. (New York, NY: International Publishers, 1977), 6:503.
[4] Lenin, *Collected Works*, 31:291.

3.4.3 OLD MORALITY

Marxists wholeheartedly reject moral codes that are founded in religious beliefs, including traditional universal moral ideals. They reject and label such ideals as "old morality," as products of the bourgeoisie invented and used by the propertied class to oppress the propertyless proletariat. G.L. Andreyev, in *What Kind of Morality Does Religion Teach?*, states, "In the reigning morality under capitalism that act is considered moral which promotes the preservation and strengthening of the system of exploitation and the acquirement of profits. Religion merely justifies this unjust and oppressive, bloody, and inhuman system in the name of God."[5]

Marxists believe that what is generally regarded by society as moral directly contradicts the Marxist goal of a classless society. Nikita Khrushchev states, "So long as classes exist on the earth, there will be no such thing in life as something good in the absolute sense. What is good for the bourgeoisie, for the imperialists, is disastrous for the working class, and, on the contrary, what is good for the working people is not admitted by the imperialists, by the bourgeoisie."[6] This, then, is the whole problem with the old morality as perceived by Marxists—the old morality is simply a tool used by the oppressing classes to maintain their position in society. Christian ethics is the means by which the rich control the working class poor.

Marx says that for the proletariat, "Law, morality, religion, are . . . so many bourgeois prejudices, behind which lurk in ambush just as many bourgeois interests."[7] Lenin agrees with Marx: "The old society was based on the principle: rob or be robbed; work for others or make others work for you; be a slave-owner or a slave."[8]

3.4.4 PROLETARIAT MORALITY

The proper Marxist morality for the present historical period is a class morality—specifically, the morality of the proletariat, the propertyless masses. According to *Scientific Communism: A Glossary*, "Devotion to the cause of the

> **PROLETARIAT MORALITY:** The ethical belief that whatever advances the proletariat and the cause of communism is morally good and whatever hinders the proletariat or communism is morally evil

working class, collectivism, mutual aid, comradely solidarity, hatred toward the bourgeoisie and toward traitors to the common cause, internationalism, and stoicism in struggle are traits which not only define the content of proletarian ethics, but also characterize the moral image of the typical representatives of the working class."[9] This is the code of ethics Marxists hold and promote.

Hatred of the bourgeoisie is fundamental to the Marxist ethical code. Robert Conquest's *The Harvest of Sorrow*, a documentation of the inhumanity of applied Marxist theory, contains illustration after illustration of "class hatred" or communist class morality in practice. According to Marxist ethics, hatred is moral as long as it is directed toward the proper institution, class, or enemy. Hatred thus becomes a necessary ingredient in the clash between the proletariat and the bourgeoisie. It follows, then, that society's generally accepted moral principles (which Marxists

[5] G.L. Andreyev, *What Kind of Morality Does Religion Teach?* (Moscow, USSR: 1959). Cited in Raymond S. Sleeper, *A Lexicon of Marxist-Leninist Semantics* (Alexandria, VA: Western Goals, 1983), 174.

[6] Nikita Khrushchev, "The Great Strength of Soviet Literature and Art," *Soviet Booklet*, no. 108, (London: UK: Farleigh Press, 1963), 30. Cited in James Bales, *Communism and the Reality of Moral Law* (Nutley, NJ: The Craig Press, 1969), 5.

[7] Marx and Engels, *Collected Works*, 6:494.

[8] Lenin, *Collected Works*, 31: 293.

[9] Cited in Sleeper, *A Lexicon of Marxist-Leninist Semantics*, 106.

claim are bourgeois tools) are in direct opposition to the moral principles of the proletariat. If this is true, no one in the bourgeoisie can do right or act morally. Unless members of the propertied class became proletarian, anything they do, no matter how moral by their standards, will be contemptible to Marxists.

3.4.5 UTILITARIANISM

To Marxists, the acceptable action in class morality is whatever it takes to accomplish the ultimate goal—namely, a classless communist society. In other words, **utilitarianism**—the end justifies the means. Freedom can be achieved only when all class barriers are erased, and therefore anything that serves that end is judged as moral. "Ethics, in short," says Selsam, "is good only as anything else is good, for what it can accomplish, for the direction in which it takes men."[10]

UTILITARIANISM: An ethical framework that posits that all action should be directed toward achieving the greatest utility for the greatest number of people (that the end justifies the means)

The problem, of course, is that we can justify mistreating our neighbor by claiming that it will serve the "higher good" in the long run. Ivan Bahryany, a Ukrainian citizen who estimates that the Soviets killed 10 million of his countrymen between 1927 and 1939, states the problem this way: "The party clique which follows the slogan expressed by the saying 'the end justifies the means' is actually always ready to use any means."[11] In the case of the Ukrainians, the "means" included shooting, starvation, and slave labor in Siberia. **Joseph Stalin** referred to this action as the liquidation of the kulak class. Lenin admitted that the proletariat would be willing to work with the "petty bourgeois proprietors" as long as their work furthered the Marxist cause, "[b]ut after that our roads part. Then we shall have to engage in the most decisive, ruthless struggle against them."[12]

3.4.6 MORAL REVOLUTION

Revolution is the most efficient means for creating a society without class distinctions. According to Marxists, revolution is unavoidable and it is the only way to overthrow the bourgeoisie and lift up the proletariat.

Communists believe their revolution is unquestionably moral. Andreyev says, "From the point of view of communist morality the struggle against everything which hinders the cause of communist construction is moral and humane and for this reason we consider the struggle against the enemies of communism to be of a moral nature."[13]

Joseph Stalin

This class struggle is not peaceful just as the struggle for survival in nature is not peaceful. According to Marxists, critics of the elimination of the bourgeoisie for social evolutionary reasons fail to remember the cost in death and suffering caused by biological evolution. Nature accumulates the good and disposes of

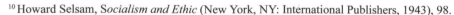

[10] Howard Selsam, *Socialism and Ethic* (New York, NY: International Publishers, 1943), 98.
[11] S.O. Pidhainy, ed., *The Black Deeds of the Kremlin* (Toronto, ON: The Basilian Press, 1953), 14. Robert Conquest in *The Harvest of Sorrow* (Oxford, UK: Oxford University Press, 1986*)*, 305, places the figure at 14.5 million.
[12] Lenin, *Collected Works*, 36:255, 265.
[13] Sleeper, *A Lexicon of Marxist-Leninist Semantics*, 175.

the bad. The fit must survive both biologically and socially. The unfit, along with their social institutions, must perish.

Marx states, "The Communists disdain to conceal their views and aims. They openly declare that their ends can be attained only by the forcible overthrow of all existing social conditions."[14] They perceive this forcible overthrow as morally right. It is right because it destroys hindrances to a communist society. Morally speaking, Communists have an ethical duty to work toward the forcible overthrow of capitalism.

The obligation to work toward the overthrow of the bourgeoisie may very well include the duty to kill. Khrushchev explains, "Our cause is sacred. He whose hand will tremble, who will stop midway, whose knees will shake before he destroys tens and hundreds of enemies, he will lead the revolution into danger. Whoever will spare a few lives of enemies, will pay for it with hundreds and thousands of lives of the better sons of our fathers.[15]

Communists cannot know if their revolutionary actions are the right ones to accomplish Marxist goals. According to Lenin, they will make mistakes, but the cause is worth the risk: "Even if for every hundred correct things we committed 10,000 mistakes, our

> ## The Pop Culture Connection
>
> ***The Motorcycle Diaries*** (a 2004 film directed by Walter Salles and produced by Robert Redford)—depicts Ernesto Guevara and his friend Alberto's eight-month road-trip of introspection and personal discovery through South America. Ernesto (soon to become 'Che') Guevara, Fidel Castro's right hand man during the bloody Marxist revolution in Cuba, went from a nice middle class medical student to one of history's most famous revolutionaries. The film rationalizes his radical change with a glimpse into this transformative period of his life. Traveling across South America, Ernesto witnesses first-hand the plight of the lower class and identifies with their dire situation.
>
> Columnist Paul Berman sets the record straight on Che. He writes, "The cult of Ernesto Che Guevara is an episode in the moral callousness of our time. Che was a totalitarian. He achieved nothing but disaster. . . . Che presided over the Cuban Revolution's first firing squads. He founded Cuba's 'labor camp' system. . . . The present-day cult of Che—the T-shirts, the bars, the posters—has succeeded in obscuring this dreadful reality . . . . Che was an enemy of freedom, and yet he has been erected into a symbol of freedom. He helped establish an unjust social system in Cuba and has been erected into a symbol of social justice. He stood for the ancient rigidities of Latin-American thought, in a Marxist-Leninist version, and he has been celebrated as a free-thinker and a rebel. And thus it is in Salles' *Motorcycle Diaries*."*

revolution would still be—and it will be in the judgment of history—great and invincible. . . ."[16]

Stalin took Lenin's philosophy to heart, stating, "To put it briefly: the dictatorship of the proletariat is the domination of the proletariat over the bourgeoisie, untrammeled by the law and based on violence and enjoying the sympathy and support of the toiling and exploited masses."[17] Consistent with his rhetoric, Stalin announced on December 27, 1929, "the liquidation of the kulaks as a class."[18] British journalist D.G. Stewart-Smith estimates that international communism is responsible for 83 million deaths between 1917 and 1964. From a Marxist-

[14] Marx and Engels, *Collected Works*, 6:519.

[15] Nikita Khrushchev, *Ukrainian Bulletin* (August 1–August 15, 1960): 12, quoted in Bales, *Communism and the Reality of Moral Law*, 121.

[16] Lenin, *Collected Works*, 28:72.

* See "The Cult of Che: Don't applaud *The Motorcycle Diaries*," by Paul Berman, http://www.slate.com/id/2107100/.

[17] Joseph Stalin, *J. Stalin Works* (Moscow, USSR: Foreign Languages Publishing House, 1953), 6:118.

[18] Conquest, *The Harvest of Sorrow*, 117.

Leninist perspective, if 83 million people died to abolish social classes and private property, it was worth the price—even morally just. Marxists judge the results, not the methods.

Stalin, therefore, acted always within the Marxist-Leninist ethical code. He used means that he assumed would serve his ends—the destruction of the class enemy—and should those ends ever be accomplished, Marxists would have to applaud Stalin as a Marxist with the proper concept of morality. But Stalin was not alone in his morality; Lenin, too, advocated the elimination of the kulaks as a class, insisting that they were not 'human beings"[19] and that it was necessary to have recourse to "economic terror."[20]

3.4.7 CONCLUSION

Many uncertainties surround Marxist ethics. While virtually all Marxists agree on the dialectical materialist foundation for morality and the inevitability of the evolution of moral precepts, they cannot predict what the ethics of a classless society would look like. Marxists label Christian ethics "immoral" because it theoretically maintains the domination of the bourgeoisie over the proletariat; but Marxists cannot conceive of a moral scheme other than the vague idea of the "creation of a new moral man."

An ethical ideology that includes the inevitability of change and the evolution of morals leaves Marxists free to abandon generally accepted moral standards in pursuit of a greater good—the creation of a classless communist society. This pursuit requires Marxists to dedicate themselves to the cause and to use whatever action they believe will bring about a classless society. Any course of action then, no matter how immoral it appears to a world that believes in an absolute or universal moral standard, is morally good within the Marxist-Leninist worldview.

---

[19] Ibid., 129.
[20] Ibid., 60.

Ethics

Cosmic Humanism

It's taking everything you've learned from your parents and school and finding out what works for you and what you have to offer. The important question is, 'What feels right for you?'[1]

— ACTOR BRAD PITT

It [is] not possible to judge another's truth.[2]

— SHIRLEY MACLAINE

3.5.1 INTRODUCTION

Cosmic Humanism's ethical perspective is based on its theological pantheism and philosophical monism. If each of us is God, then final authority resides in us, and we must seek the freedom to act in harmony with our inner truth. "Free will," says Shirley MacLaine, "is simply the enactment of the realization you are God, a realization that you are divine; free will is making everything accessible to you."[3]

Individual autonomy is the one ethical absolute promoted by the New Age movement. This autonomy places the authority for judging values squarely within the soul of each human being. **Marilyn Ferguson** writes, "Most importantly, when people become autonomous, their values

---

[1] Brad Pitt answering a question about what defines the teenage years, *Teen People*, August 2003, 112.

[2] F. LaGard Smith, *Out On a Broken Limb* (Eugene, OR: Harvest House, 1986), 33.

[3] Quoted in William Goldstein, "Life on the Astral Plane," *Publishers Weekly*, March 18, 1983, 46.

Marilyn Ferguson

become internal."[4] Internalized values allow us to seek higher consciousness, whereas any external limit or authority blocks our ability to get in touch with our inner truth. Thus, Vera Alder tells us, "We should search ourselves very carefully to see if we have any fixed ideas, any great shyness or self-consciousness. If we have, we must seek freedom."[5]

Shakti Gawain provides us with a practical application of total freedom in relation to our sexuality: "If you're setting limits on your sexual energy, it becomes distorted. If you believe it is something to be hidden, ignored, and controlled, then you learn to hold back completely or act sexually only at certain safe moments."[6] According to the Cosmic Humanist worldview, such limitations sap our personal power and deny our godhood. We must not acknowledge outside boundaries—especially the boundaries of the Ten Commandments, which are an external authority and, as such, hinder our evolutionary growth.

3.5.2 MORAL RELATIVISM

When we choose to ignore all outside authority and all rational restrictions, boundless moral relativism results. Ferguson admits as much: "Autonomous human beings can create and invent. And they can change their minds, repudiating values they once held."[7]

This kind of relativism means that no one may decide whether another's actions are right or wrong. Ferguson believes that once we achieve the higher consciousness of the New Age, "There is less certainty about what is right for others. With an awareness of multiple realities, we lose our dogmatic attachment to a single point of view."[8]

In other words, we must not judge other people's beliefs or actions. Tolerance is the key: Cosmic Humanists must tolerate all other views regarding morality because ethics is relative to the truth within each of us. "Adam and Eve," says Marianne Williamson, "were happy until she 'ate of the knowledge of good and evil.' What that means is that everything was perfect until they began to judge—to keep their hearts open sometimes, but closed at others . . . . Closing our hearts destroys our peace. It's alien to our real nature."[9]

Randall Baer, a former Cosmic Humanist who converted to Christianity, states the basic New Age credo: "create your own reality according to what feels right for you." Whether you choose to be homosexual, bisexual, monogamous, polygamous, etc.—any choice you make is acceptable as long as "It's right for me" or "It's done with love, and no one's hurt." This is a kind of relativistic, human-founded ethics (or design-your-own ethics). In effect, New Age followers pick and choose from the multitudes of options in each area of life according personal preferences.[10]

---

[4] Marilyn Ferguson, *The Aquarian Conspiracy* (Los Angeles, CA: J.P. Tarcher, 1980), 327.

[5] Verar Alder, *When Humanity Comes of Age* (New York, NY: Samuel Weiser, 1974), 48–9.

[6] Shakti Gawain, *Living in the Light* (San Rafael, CA: New World Library, 1986), 128.

[7] Ferguson, *The Aquarian Conspiracy*, 331.

[8] Ibid., 192.

[9] Marianne Williamson, *A Return to Love: Reflections on the Principles of "A Course in Miracles"* (New York, NY: Harper Collins, 1992), 22.

[10] Randall N. Baer, *Inside the New Age Nightmare* (Lafayette, LA: Huntington House, 1989), 88.

3.5.3 Karma and the Unity of Good and Evil

According to the Cosmic Humanist, we must simply assume that everyone acts morally by following inner truth. Gawain, in fact, absolves Adolf Hitler and every other human being of moral responsibility by claiming that everyone is following the shortest path to higher consciousness and is, therefore, acting morally: "I believe that every being chooses the life path and relationships that will help him or her to grow the fastest."[11]

> **KARMA:** The total effect of a person's actions and conduct during each phase of existence, determining the person's destiny

Moral relativism leads Cosmic Humanists to a point where the distinction between good and evil becomes hopelessly blurred. No absolute right or wrong exists, only what is right or wrong according to each individual's truth. If everything is one, it is difficult to distinguish between good and evil. What may appear evil in this life could be the reverse in a reincarnated existence.

This concept involves what New Age devotees refer to as **karma**, which Shirley MacLaine defines this way: "Whatever action one takes will ultimately return to that person—good and bad—maybe not in this life embodiment, but sometime in the future. And no one is exempt. . . . For every act, for every indifference, for every misuse of life, we are finally held accountable. And it is up to us to understand what those accounts might be.[12]

Unfortunately, because there is no standard by which to judge what may be "an act of indifference," or "a misuse of life," we cannot know if there is any difference between them or, for that matter, if there is any difference between cruelty and non-cruelty. This is an alarming conclusion, but one Cosmic Humanists accept. This acceptance results from the New Age concept of unity—if all is one, then good and evil are one, and so are right and wrong.

> Christ is the same force as Lucifer. . . . Lucifer prepares man for the experience of Christhood. . . . Lucifer works within each of us to bring us to wholeness as we move into the New Age.
>
> — DAVID SPANGLER

Ferguson explains unity this way: "This wholeness unites opposites. . . . In these spiritual traditions [that form the basis for New Age thought] there is neither good nor evil. There is only light and the absence of light . . . wholeness and brokenness . . . flow and struggle."[13]

David Spangler echoes this view, but in more startling language: "Christ is the same force as Lucifer. . . . Lucifer prepares man for the experience of Christhood. . . . Lucifer works within each of us to bring us to wholeness as we move into the New Age."[14] What the world considers evil—war, murder, etc.—becomes a part of the evolutionary flow and struggle of reality as supraconsciousness strives to be born on a higher level.

3.5.4 Conclusion

For the Cosmic Humanist, morality is a nebulous thing. Each of us must listen to the "God within" to determine our own ethical system, but we may never hold others accountable to our system. Ironically, nothing is ever really wrong except judging other people's moral beliefs

---

[11] Gawain, *Living in the Light*, 60.

[12] Shirley MacLaine, *Out On a Limb* (Toronto, ON: Bantam, 1984), 96, 111.

[13] Ferguson, *The Aquarian Conspiracy*, 381.

[14] David Spangler, *Reflections of the Christ* (Forres, Scotland: Findhorn, 1977), 40–44.

The Pop Culture Connection

Screenwriter and producer David Franzoni (*Amistad, King Arthur,* and *Gladiator*) knows exactly why he is involved in making movies. He said, "That's the whole point of writing to me: to change the world through your art . . ." Referring to *Gladiator* (2000, Best Picture and Best Actor: Russell Crowe winner), Franzoni said, "The film is about a hero who has morality, but that morality is a secular morality that transcends conventional religious morality. In other words, I believe there is room in our mythology for a character who is deeply moral, but who's not traditionally religious: I loved that he was a pagan, not Christian or any other traditional/ established religion."[16]*

and actions.

Yet judging cannot be completely bad either because it is part of the unity of reality. If "all is one," then even horrible mistakes, like judgmental actions, are manifestations of God. Thus, by individualizing both good and evil, difficulties multiply like dandelions in Cosmic Humanist ethics. Such a skewed worldview leads to drastically skewed thinking.

Kevin Ryerson's thoughts on karma give us a telling example of this truth: "Criminals and murderers sometimes come back around to be murdered themselves, or perhaps to become a saint. For instance, Moses was a murderer. . . . He beat the fellow to death out of rage, which was not exactly the most ethical decision. But he went on to become a great intellect, a great law-giver, and is considered a saint by many people. So basically, you get many chances. Your karma is your system of judgment. There is justice."[15]

[15] Kevin Ryerson, *Spirit Communication: The Soul's Path* (New York, NY: Bantam Books, 1989), 84.
[16] * WGA.org's "Exclusive Interview with David Franzoni" by John Soriano, http://www.wga.org/craft/interviews/franzoni2001.html.

Ethics

Postmodernism

> I suggest that the novelty of the postmodern approach
> to ethics consists first and foremost in . . . the
> rejection of the typically modern ways of going about
> its moral problems (that is . . . the philosophical
> search for absolutes, universals and foundations in
> theory).[1]
>
> — ZYGMUNT BAUMAN

> [U]niversal moral principles must be eradicated and
> reverence for individual and cultural uniqueness
> inculcated.[2]
>
> — ADAM PHILLIPS

3.6.1 INTRODUCTION

Postmodern ethics is not based on universal or unchanging principles. Christians and Muslims embrace ethical codes of moral absolutes based on God's character or moral decree; Secular Humanists, Marxists, and Postmodernists ground their ethical systems in atheism, naturalism, and evolution. Despite springing from the same roots, however, Postmodern ethics differ significantly from Secular Humanist and Marxist ethics.

---

[1] Zygmunt Bauman, *Postmodern Ethics* (Oxford, UK: Blackwell Publishers, 1993), 3–4.
[2] *The Weekly Standard*, November 14, 2005, 41.

The Pop Culture Connection

Match Point (a 2006 film written and directed by Woody Allen)—Chris, a tennis pro turned tennis instructor, is "a middle class Englishman [who] falls in love and marries a woman from a wealthy family, but continues in a passionate adulterous affair with [Nola,] an American actress . . . Chris realizes that if Nola reveals the adultery to Chris's family, he would lose his entire life of wealth and comfort and live in poverty with his passionate mistress. So he takes the only way out for a pragmatic nihilist: kill the mistress and return to normal life. Chris is shown early on reading *Crime and Punishment* by Dostoevsky, which is about Raskolnikov, a student who kills someone as an expression of his belief in the Uberman of Nietzsche, the man who is 'above society's petty constructed moralities'. . . . After Chris kills Nola and successfully makes it look like a drug killing, he muses to himself that 'you learn to push the guilt under the rug. The innocent are slain to make way for a grander scheme'. . . . Odd, this is exactly how the Nazis thought, and would have cremated Allen himself were he around Germany at the time."*

From a worldview perspective, ethics is the logical outgrowth of a prior commitment to a particular theology. Richard Rorty makes this connection in his work *Achieving Our Country*, where he denigrates the existence of God and God's place in the moral scheme of the universe. To illustrate this perspective, Rorty calls upon the poetry of Walt Whitman, who expresses his view of God in the following lines: "And I call to mankind, Be not curious about God. For I who am curious about each am not curious about God."[3] Embracing Whitman's idea, Rorty states: "Whitman thought there was no need to be curious about God because there is no standard, not even a divine one, against which the decisions of a free people can be measured. Americans, [Whitman] hoped, would spend the energy that past human societies had spent on discovering God's desires on discovering one another's desires."[4]

Rorty insists that for both Whitman[5] and John Dewey, there was "no room for obedience to a nonhuman authority [i.e., God]." In fact, creating the new conception of what it means to be human was "a matter of forgetting about eternity."[6] Rorty and his fellow Postmodernists construct the ethical portion of their worldview from this foundation of atheism.

3.6.2 CULTURAL MORAL RELATIVISM

After denying the existence of God, Rorty moves on to deny the existence of a universal moral reality "to which our moral judgments might hope to correspond, as our physical science supposedly corresponds to physical reality."[7] At this stage, we might ask, *If there is no objective moral reality, why concern ourselves with ethical issues?* While this seems a reasonable next step, Postmodernists are not comfortable with abandoning ethics completely and instead are driven to search within their worldview for a standard of right and wrong.

---

[3] Richard Rorty, *Achieving Our Country: Leftist Thought in Twentieth-Century America* (Cambridge, MA: Harvard University Press, 1998), 16.

[4] Ibid.

[5] Richard J. Ellis, *The Dark Side of the Left: Illiberal Egalitarianism in America* (Lawrence, KS: University Press of Kansas, 1998), 79–80: "Whitman profoundly shaped a host of left-wing literary radicals of the early twentieth century, from Randolph Bourne and Van Wyck Brooks to John Reed and Max Eastman, who tellingly identified himself as an 'American lyrical Socialist—a child of Walt Whitman reared by Karl Marx.'"

[6] Rorty, *Achieving Our Country*, 18.

[7] Robert B. Brandom, ed., *Rorty and his Critics* (Oxford, UK: Blackwell Publishers, 2001), 4–5.

* Brian Godawa, http://www.chalcedon.edu/movieblog/blog.php.

Vanhoozer reveals how Postmodernist Jean-François Lyotard "acknowledges that the central issue of Postmodernity is the possibility of ethics, that is, right action." [8] The next question becomes, *How is right action determined?* Vanhoozer explains, "Lyotard, for his part, is content to live with 'little narratives.'"

If philosophical truth (what we can know about reality) resides in the local community, it follows that moral truth (how we should behave) resides in the same community. This is what Lyotard means when he says he is content to live with "little narratives." Since there is no "grand narrative" telling us what is real and how to behave, each community develops its own "little narratives" to fulfill those needs. This is Lyotard's way of expressing what is called **cultural relativism**.

However, Postmodernists are hesitant to use the term "relativism." Rorty, for example, tries to soften the word 'relative.' He comments, "This view is often referred to as 'cultural relativism.' But it is not relativistic, if that means saying that every moral view is as good as every other. *Our* moral view is, I firmly believe, much better than any competing view, even though there are a lot of people whom you will never be able to convert to it. It is one thing to say, falsely, that there is nothing

> **CULTURAL RELATIVISM:** The belief that truth and morals are relative to one's culture

to choose between us and the Nazis. It is another thing to say, correctly, that there is no neutral, common ground to argue our differences. That Nazi and I will always strike one another as begging all the crucial questions, arguing in circles."[9]

Here, Rorty says that while there is no objective basis for determining what is right, he still insists that his view is right when compared with Nazi morality. But while making this claim, he also admits there is no way to judge between the two views. Still, he will fight for his moral view.

In the final analysis, each community places moral standards on its members' actions. In other words, for a Postmodernist, the members of a particular community govern the moral choices its members are allowed to make. In that light, even Rorty insists that he can do whatever his particular community allows him to get away with.

3.6.3 EVOLVING MORALITY WITH A PUSH

For Postmodernists, community moral standards are decided by both coercion and consensus. Morality is not connected to God or dictated by any type of natural laws; rather, ethical systems are constructed within societies. Every culture, thus, has its own set of moral standards arising from the various influences within each particular group. Moreover, morality is not stagnant; it changes, adapts, and is constantly evolving according to the dictates of the group.[10]

To demonstrate that moral standards are both set by culture and evolve with society, consider the example of abortion. In the past, most civilized Western societies, under the influence of Christian persuasion, detested the practice of abortion. However, in our current society, secular government and its citizens are more comfortable with this practice.

Why do Postmodernists such as Richard Rorty speak and write about moral issues if morality does not actually exist? Quite simply, because Rorty is a consistent atheist and Darwinist. Since there is no God, no absolute morality, and ultimately no truth, then we get to construct the world in a way that best helps us survive. Rorty, therefore, advocates the subjective "ethical standards" that he prefers, standards he is personally comfortable with. For Rorty, words are

---

[8] Kevin J. Vanhoozer, *Postmodern Theology* (Cambridge, UK: Cambridge University Press, 2005), 10.

[9] Richard Rorty, *Philosophy and Social Hope* (New York, NY: Penguin Books, 1999), 15.

[10] This concept of morality is explored in the essay "Ethics Without Principles" quoted in Ibid., 72–88.

merely "tools" of persuasion.[11] There is no need to be logically consistent with words because words are instruments that, if used properly or creatively, invoke individuals to change. In the end, Rorty hopes that he will be able to persuade others (you) to view the world the way he does and even adopt his ideas and his moral standards.

In a very real sense, Rorty is trying to "push" the evolution of society's moral standards into line with his own. In the end, morality and society operate like an unconscious negotiation—everyone in a community is presenting the beliefs he or she prefers; these ideas are considered, debated, and adapted; and in the end, consensus emerges—although the consensus is in a constant state of arbitration.

Think of it this way: morality is like a reality TV show challenge. The contestants are forced to work together in order to obtain what they personally desire. Everyone must work together or else no one gets anywhere. However, along the way Rorty wants to persuade others to adopt his ethical principles, and if he can, he wins. However, if someone who has a different set of values can persuade the others in the group, then Rorty's ideas will lose favor, and he will be sidelined or even kicked off the island!

Not all Postmodernists agree with Rorty's assessment. Postmodern psychiatrist Adam Phillips insists *any* ethical boundaries are "a form of pontification and imperial self-aggrandizement. . . . No adult can know what's best for another adult; and, by the same token, no group or society can know what's best for another group or society."[12] Phillips' stance seems more in keeping with the overall Postmodern mindset, which does not allow anyone to be "right" on any particular issue, including ethics.

3.6.4 CONCLUSION

The following narrative poignantly illustrates the consequences of the breakdown of ethical values and social obligations, what happens when people actually put into practice the Postmodern idea of "it's right for me."

For over 15 years, British physician and psychiatrist Theodore Dalrymple cared for the poorest of the poor in London's slums. From that experience, Dalrymple notes that the intellectuals of the twentieth century "sought to free our sexual relations of all social, contractual or moral obligations and meaning whatsoever, so that henceforth only raw sexual desire itself would count in our decision making." When these ideas are adopted "both literally and wholesale in the lowest and most vulnerable social class," he illustrates the real-life results: "If anyone wants to see what sexual relations are like, freed of contractual and social obligations, let him look at the chaos of the personal lives of members of the underclass. Here are abortions procured by abdominal kung fu; children who have children, in numbers unknown before the advent of chemical contraception and sex education; women abandoned by the father of their child a month before or a month after delivery; insensate jealousy, the reverse of the coin of general promiscuity, that results in the most hideous oppression and violence; serial stepfatherhood that leads to sexual and physical abuse of children on a mass scale; and every kind of loosening of the distinction between the sexually permissible and the impermissible.[13]

While it may sound broadminded to argue that we should allow people to live as they please, the real world comes crashing in to reveal the consequences of flaunting the universal moral order. We know from Romans 1–2 that God clearly reveals not only His existence, but

---

[11] A theme throughout Rorty's *Philosophy and Social Hope* is the use of words, ideas, and philosophies as tools rather than true things, especially in chapters 22–26.

[12] *The Weekly Standard*, 41.

[13] Theodore Dalrymple, *Life at the Bottom: The Worldview That Makes the Underclass* (Chicago, IL: Ivan R. Dee, 2001), xi.

also His moral laws and the consequences we can expect when we disregard them. After reading Dalrymple's graphic portrayal of the consequences of creating our own moral standards, we need to reevaluate the wisdom of the world in light of the wisdom of God in discovering the differences between right and wrong, good and evil.

God does not care what actions or philosophies any particular community or culture declare to be right and good if, according to His standards, they are wrong and evil. God does care that we know the truth He makes plain to us and that we understand the consequences of turning a blind eye to His standards of righteous thought and behavior.

Biology

Christianity

And God created great whales, and every living
creature that moveth, which the waters brought forth
abundantly, after their kind, and every winged fowl
after his kind.

GENESIS 1:21

4.1.1 INTRODUCTION

Perhaps no other aspect of Christianity has troubled believers more in the last century than the question of the origin of life.[1] Because many biologists (both Christian and non-Christian) treat evolution as a scientific fact, Christians have struggled to reconcile their faith in the Bible with the "facts" of science.

For example, the Bible states that God created our first parents (Adam and Eve) fully formed, yet evolutionary science claims that all living things evolved from a single speck of life. In addition, evolutionary theory posits a very old universe, somewhere between 13 and 15 billion years old. On the other hand, a straight-forward reading of Genesis 1 seems to indicate that the original creation event took place much more recently. We acknowledge that within the Christian community the age of the universe is a controversial subject, yet for the purposes of this chapter, we will focus our attention on defending the "fact" of creation, not necessarily its timing.[2]

---

[1] David Berlinski's article "On the Origins of Life" in *Commentary* (February 2006) indicates that believing and unbelieving Jews are also extremely interested in the subject.

[2] See Normal L. Geisler, *Systematic Theology*, 4 vols. (Minneapolis, MN: Bethany House), 2:632f, for a good

Because the positions of creation and evolution are poles apart, it seems that reconciliation is impossible. However, some Christians have proposed a middle ground, seeking to combine elements of both sides of the debate. This middle ground is called theistic evolution.

4.1.2 THEISTIC EVOLUTION

The belief that God created the first speck of life on earth and then directed its evolution to generate man is called **theistic evolution**. To hold this position, Christians must take substantial liberties in interpreting the Bible. They also face most of the same weaknesses as proponents of atheistic evolution. In truth, there is no difference between theistic and atheistic evolution, except that theistic evolutionists argue that God used evolution to generate the diversity of life throughout Earth's history.

> **THEISTIC EVOLUTION:** The belief that God works through the natural process of evolution

Theistic evolutionists interpret the Bible in accordance with their view of evolution. For example, Jesus Christ declares in Mark 10:6, "But at the beginning of creation God 'made them male and female.'" Theistic evolutionists interpret this verse and others like it (Luke 11:50; Acts 3:21) to support the evolutionary position that the term *creation* simply means God created the first spark of life and then continually directed His creation through the vehicle of evolution from that first spark to human beings.

Thus, some Christians believe that the Bible can support evolutionary theory as an explanation for origins. This may be a tenable position when discussing only verses concerned strictly with the question of origins. However, when we examine the entire message of the Bible, the theory of theistic evolution severely undermines the Christian understanding of God's place and our place in His universe.

While it is true that God is all powerful—so that He could have used evolution to generate all species—we contend that He did not employ such an inefficient (and often totally ineffective) mechanism. If God designed the world to operate according to specific natural laws requiring minimal interference, why would He use an evolutionary mechanism that would require Him to constantly meddle with the development of life? Further, such a mechanism seems an especially cruel method for creating humans, since it involves a "survival of the fittest" or "destruction of the weak and unfit" mentality. As Jacques Monod notes, natural selection is the "blindest and most cruel way of evolving new species."[3]

4.1.3 ADAM AND CHRIST

More important, if evolution is true, then we must view the story of the Garden of Eden and original sin as nothing more than allegory. This viewpoint, however, severely undermines the significance of Christ's sinless life and sacrificial death on the cross because the Bible presents Jesus as analogous to Adam. The condemnation and corruption brought on by Adam's

summary of the issue. Geisler says, "There are many scientific arguments for an old universe, some of which one may find persuasive. However, none of these is foolproof, and all of them may be wrong" (649). Those advocating an older universe include: Hugh Ross, *Creator and the Cosmos*; Norman Geisler, *When Skeptics Ask*; Walter Kaiser, *Hard Sayings of the Bible*; Don Stoner, *A New Look at an Old Earth*; Francis A. Schaeffer, *No Final Conflict* and C.I. Scofield, *Rightly Dividing the Word of Truth*. Presenting a younger earth: Walt Brown, *In the Beginning*; Larry Vardiman, et. al. *Radioisotopes and the Age of the Earth*; Jonathan Sarfati, *Refuting Compromise*; Henry Morris, *The Long War Against God*; Duane Gish, *Creation Scientists Answer Their Critics* and Don Batten, ed., *The Revised and Expanded Answers Book*.

[3] Australian Broadcasting Co., June 10, 1976, quoted in Henry Morris, *The Long War against God* (Grand Rapids, MI: Baker Book House, 1990), 58.

sin are the counterparts of the justification and sanctification made possible for us by Christ's righteousness and death (Romans 5:12–19). If Adam were not a historical individual, and if his fall into sin were not literally true, then the biblical doctrines of sin and redemption collapse. This conclusion is unacceptable to Christians.

Thus, the proper Christian worldview requires a belief in the Creator as He is literally portrayed in Genesis. A thoughtful reading of Genesis 1 depicts a very literal-sounding creation story, although we often hear the caveat "you can't take Genesis literally." Genesis 1 mentions sun, moon, and stars along with birds in the air and fish in the sea—these physical objects and living creatures are literal. The mention of day, month, and year seem literal in the context of Genesis 1. Adam and Eve are depicted as literal people whose descendants continue through the history of the biblical narrative up to the birth of Jesus. If Adam and Eve were mythical, it would be difficult to determine where myth ends and history begins in the genealogy of the human race.

Because evolution appears to be unassailably scientific, Christians who continue to believe in **creationism** seemed

> ## The Pop Culture Connection
>
> ***Inherit the Wind*** (a 1960 film staring Frederic March and Spencer Tracy)—This classic film is a thinly disguised story about the real 1925 "Scopes Monkey Trial." The film shows the triumph of reason over fundamentalist religion as the attorney for Scopes (Clarence Darrow) exposes the prosecuting attorney (William Jennings Bryan) as an ignorant buffoon. This film adaptation of the 1955 play by the same name, along with the later TV versions, is the storyline that everyone thinks of when the question of teaching the concept of a Intelligent Design is introduced into public school biology classes. However, *Inherit the Wind* turns out to be all wind and very little fact, with most of the details shown in the film being opposite from the actual events. For example, an opening scene shows an angry mob arresting Scopes for teaching evolution, throwing him in jail and shouting to lynch him. In real life, Scopes was never jailed and had a friendly relationship with the people of the town throughout the trial. In the film, Bryan is shown as a defeated, narrow-minded ignoramus. In reality, Bryan was jovial, well-informed, and an articulate defender of biblical creationism.[4]

to be taking a radical, almost backward stance. Understandably, many Christians turn to theistic evolution as the only means of reconciling science with their Christian faith. However, more recent scientific discoveries have undermined the foundations of evolutionary theory and provided a rich soil for the development of a robust theory of creation. For example, Jonathan Wells has examined the ten most popular "proofs" for the theory of evolution (peppered moths, Darwin's Finches, fossil record, Haeckel's embryos, ape to human, etc.) and found that each one lacks scientific rigor.[5] With so much new and compelling information coming to light, Christians who wish to integrate science and their Christian faith would do well to abandon evolution as a rational explanation for the origin of species and explore instead the creation model.

> **CREATIONISM:** The scientific theory proposing that each living organism was created separately (in much their present forms) by a supernatural being

---

[4] For a detailed account of the differences between the film and actual events, see Carol Iannone's excellent article, "The Truth About Inherit the Wind," *First Things* (February 1997): 28–33, available online at http://www.firstthings.com/ftissues/ft9702/iannone.html.

[5] Jonathan Wells, *Icons of Evolution: Science Or Myth?* (Washington, DC: Regnery Publishing, 2000). Judith Hooper, in *An Evolutionary Tale of Moths and Men: The Untold Story of Science and the Peppered Moth* (New York, NY: W.W. Norton & Company, 2002), spends a whole book on the peppered moth, the insect that has been used as scientific proof for evolution. Few could read what really happened and call this science.

4.1.4 FRAMING THE DEBATE

Before examining the latest scientific discoveries related to the origin of life, we need to make a distinction between two aspects of evolutionary theory. The idea that living things incorporate small, adaptive changes over time is termed "**microevolution**." These minor changes within a species have produced a wide variety of dogs and breeds of cows that produce more milk. These are well-established, observable facts of science.

However, scientists extrapolate on this theory to posit that micro-adaptive changes can produce novel features and new species. This is called "**macroevolution**"—the idea that a first speck of life that emerged from non-living material slowly evolved into one-celled organisms,

> MICROEVOLUTION: Small changes within the species of a gene pool
>
> MACROEVOLUTION: The origin, over time, of fundamentally new organisms from prior life forms

which in turn, through eons of genetic mutations and natural selection, eventually turned into *homo sapiens*. This grand scheme of amoeba-to-man (or better yet, of spontaneous generation-to-man) is what is commonly understood when we use the term "evolution." Yet, large-scale changes leading to new species have never been observed and, therefore, cannot technically support a "scientific" theory, much less fact, as the evolutionists would have us believe. Rather, evolution is an extrapolation from microevolution based on naturalistic assumptions.

Failure to distinguish (or to understand the distinction) between micro- and macroevolution in public discussion can make Christians look foolish if we give the impression that we do not agree with microevolution, a clearly established fact. To clarify the issue, throughout this book when we use the term "evolution," we are referring to macroevolution, commonly called Darwinian evolution or Neo-Darwinism.[6] In reality, evolution as it is taught today in most public schools teaches spontaneous generation to the human race within a period of 3.5 billion years.

With these distinctions in mind, we turn our attention to developing a scientific view of life's origins consistent with the biblical account described in Genesis 1 and 2.

4.1.5 TELEOLOGY SUPPORTS CREATIONISM

One line of scientific reasoning that points to a Creator is the intricate design found in all living organisms. This is known as the teleological argument. William Paley presented one of the most famous versions of this argument—that of the watch and the watchmaker.[7] Since the nineteenth century, however, it has been widely believed that Paley's argument for a universal Designer was effectively answered by the philosopher David Hume. Hume claimed that Paley's analogy between living things and machines was unfounded and unrealistic in that life does not need an intelligent designer as machines do.

In addition to his philosophical argument, Hume advanced a theory of natural selection similar to Darwin's, which he claimed could account for the apparent design seen in nature. Atheist Richard Dawkins writes in *The Blind Watchmaker*, "Biology is the study of complicated things that give the appearance of having been designed for a purpose."[8] Dawkins goes on to explain that there is no need to postulate God as the Designer since natural selection can perform the miracles.

---

[6] Neo-Darwinism is merely mutations added on to Darwin's Natural Selection theory. Since Natural Selection cannot produce new species, it is thought that harmful mutations can.

[7] Christians need to remember that it was the Psalmist who said the heavens declare the glory of God and His handiwork (Psalm 19)—a teleological observation.

[8] Robert T. Pennock, *Intelligent Design: Creationism and its Critics* (Cambridge, MA: The MIT Press, 2001), 644. Dawkins spends 300 pages in *The Blind Watchmaker* trying to show that design is only appearance, not fact.

However, in spite of Dawkins' claims, scientists can no longer ignore the idea of design. Recent discoveries reveal that life is indeed analogous to the most complex machinery, thereby reinforcing Paley's argument. Michael Denton, a molecular biologist, states, "Paley was not only right in asserting the existence of an analogy between life and machines, but was also remarkably prophetic in guessing that the technological ingenuity realized in living systems is vastly in excess of anything yet accomplished by man."[9]

Science is re-learning an old lesson: the more we uncover details about the universe and living organisms, the more we discover design. Many notable scientists inadvertently support Paley's arguments as they describe the design in nature revealed to them through science. Physicist Paul Davies, who does not profess to be a Christian, supports **teleology**—and ultimately creationism—when he says, "Every advance in fundamental physics seems to reveal yet another facet of order."[10] Albert Einstein said, "The harmony of natural law . . . reveals an intelligence of such superiority that, compared with it, all the systematic thinking and acting of human beings is an utterly insignificant reflection."[11] And Robert Jastrow, an agnostic, shook up his fellow scientists when he said, "The Anthropic principle is the most interesting development next to the proof of the creation, and it is even more interesting because it seems to say that science itself has proven, as a hard fact, that this universe was made, was designed, for man to live in. It is a very theistic result."[12]

Evolution assumes that the universe came into existence and continues to run by chance rather than

> **TELEOLOGY:** The study of design and purpose in nature

laws designed by a Law-maker. When world-class non-Christian scientists like these declare that the universe cannot be viewed as a product of chance, they strike a severe blow to materialistic evolutionary theory.

Michael Behe details in his book, *Darwin's Black Box,* a number of molecular "machines" (such as the bacterial flagellum) and chemical pathways (such as the process for blood clotting) that are essential components for particular organisms. He coined the phrase "**irreducible complexity**" to highlight the fact that these features cannot be reduced to simpler parts and still perform their required function. The theory of irreducible complexity thus eliminates the possibility of these features arising through a gradual evolutionary process.

When we truly understand the ordered complexity of life,[13] it is hard to imagine chance producing even bacterial cells, the simplest living systems. Denton explains, "Although the tiniest bacterial cells are incredibly small, weighing less than $10^{(-12)}$ gms, each is in effect a veritable micro-miniaturized factory containing thousands of exquisitely designed pieces of intricate molecular machinery, made up altogether of one hundred thousand million atoms, far more complicated than any machine built by man and absolutely without parallel in the non-living world."[14]

[9] Michael Denton, *Evolution: A Theory in Crisis* (Bethesda, MD: Adler and Adler, 1986), 340.

[10] Paul Davies, *Superforce* (New York, NY: Simon and Schuster, 1984), 223.

[11] Albert Einstein, *Ideas and Opinions* (New York, NY: Crown, 1982), 40, quoted in Geisler, *Systematic Theology*, 2:666.

[12] Robert Jastrow, "A Scientist Caught Between Two Faiths," *Christianity Today*, August 6, 1982, quoted in Geisler, *Systematic Theology*, 2:591. Clearly, the Humanist has no patience with the Anthropic Principle, which states that the world was tailored for our existence. For an excellent defense of this principle, see Roy Abraham Varghese, ed., *The Intellectuals Speak Out About God* (Dallas, TX: Lewis and Stanley, 1984), 102ff.

[13] See Michael J. Behe's *Darwin's Black Box: The Biochemical Challenge to Evolution* (New York, NY: The Free Press, 1996) for a full discussion on the complexity of the cell. Also, David Berlinski's article "On the Origins of Life" in *Commentary* (February 2006). "Darwinian evolution," says Berlinski, "begins with self-replication, and self-replication is precisely what needs to be explained" (29).

[14] Denton, *Evolution*, 250.

IRREDUCIBLE COMPLEXITY: The philosophical concept that considers the complexity of living organisms—if any part is removed, the system loses function

As Paley pointed out almost two centuries ago, this kind of complexity requires an intelligent mind—chance processes cannot produce such intricate order. Norman L. Geisler and Frank Turek make the same argument in *I Don't Have Enough Faith to Be an Atheist*.[15] And while David Berlinski's article "On the Origins of Life" does not argue for an intelligent mind, it does describe the complexity of life in great detail.[16]

4.1.6 EVIDENCE FOR CREATION: THE GENETIC CODE

The existence and properties of deoxyribonucleic acid (**DNA**) support creationism both through the teleological argument and by demonstrating evolution's inability to explain crucial aspects of life. DNA contains the genetic information code and is a crucial part of all living matter, yet evolutionary theory is powerless to explain how it came into existence, let alone why DNA evinces such phenomenal design.

The teleological quality of DNA is overwhelming. Charles Thaxton believes DNA is the most powerful indicator of intelligent design: "Is there any basis in experience for an intelligent cause for the origin of life? Yes! It is the analogy between the base sequences in DNA and

alphabetical letter sequences in a book . . . there is a structural identity between the DNA code and a written language."[17] That is, we can assume DNA is the product of intelligence because it is analogous to human languages, which are, without exception, products of intelligent minds.

Even excluding the teleological nature of DNA, its very existence assumes an intelligent beginning. Walter Brown points out, "DNA can only be produced with the help of at least 20 different types of proteins. But these proteins can only be produced at the direction of DNA. Since each requires the other, a satisfactory explanation for the origin of one must also explain the origin of the other. Apparently, this entire manufacturing system came into existence simultaneously. This implies Creation."[18]

4.1.7 THE GENE POOL AND THE LIMITS TO CHANGE

A third line of scientific evidence supporting an Intelligent Designer is found in the fact that mutations do not produce unlimited changes in a species. In fact, animals and plant breeders have consistently found that there is a barrier beyond which they can no longer produce change in succeeding generations. Evolutionists believe that no limits to breeding exist because life forms must ultimately break these "species barriers" to create new species. Indeed, evolutionists see beneficial mutations as breaking all barriers to change, because these mutations supposedly can produce a vast array of structures—even a human eye—given enough time.

---

[15] Norman L. Geisler and Frank Turek, *I Don't Have Enough Faith to Be an Atheist* (Wheaton, IL: Crossway Books, 2004).

[16] *Commentary* (February 2006).

[17] Charles Thaxton, "In Pursuit of Intelligent Causes: Some Historical Background," an unpublished essay presented at an Interdisciplinary Conference in Tacoma, Washington, June 23–26, 1988, 13.

[18] Walter T. Brown, Jr., *In the Beginning* (Phoenix, AZ: Center for Scientific Creation, 1986), 6.

Unfortunately for evolutionists, science simply has not been able to demonstrate that mutations can break these limits to change. Pierre Paul Grasse, after studying mutations in bacteria and viruses, concludes, "What is the use of their unceasing mutations if they do not change? In sum, the mutations of bacteria and viruses are merely hereditary fluctuations around a median position; a swing to the right, a swing to the left, but no final evolutionary effect."[19]

If indeed such limits exist, then evolution is a meaningless explanation. If a species can only evolve so far before it hits a barrier and is forced to remain the same species, then no macroevolution occurs. This notion of the gene pool limiting the possible variation of species has troubled a great number of evolutionists, including Alfred Russell Wallace, one of the founders of the theory of natural selection. Wallace grew to doubt his theory later in life, largely because he became aware of Gregor Mendel's genetic laws and could not reconcile the apparent limits to change with evolution's need for boundless development.

Incredibly, Edward Deevey, Jr. also recognizes these limitations, yet remains an evolutionist: "Some remarkable things have been done by crossbreeding and selection inside the species barrier, or within a larger circle of closely related species, such as the wheats. But wheat is still wheat, and not, for instance, grapefruit; and we can no more grow wings on pigs than hens can make cylindrical eggs."[20] Believing in virtually unlimited change when limits abound within species is irrational. Creationists believe the evolutionary position lacks reason, logic, and meaningful observation and therefore reject it.

> What is the use of their unceasing mutations if they do not change? In sum, the mutations of bacteria and viruses are merely hereditary fluctuations around a median position; a swing to the right, a swing to the left, but no final evolutionary effect.
>
> — PIERRE PAUL GRASSE

4.1.8 EVIDENCE FOR CREATION: THE IMPOSSIBILITY OF SPONTANEOUS GENERATION

It has been scientifically demonstrated that life only comes from pre-existing life. This accords with Creationism and is yet another disproof of evolution. Evolutionists must postulate that for life to have arisen by naturalistic, random processes, at some point in time non-living matter must have come alive. The late George Wald (Harvard University and Nobel Prize winner) admitted that the "reasonable" view was to believe in spontaneous generation because it was the only alternative to believing "in a single, primary act of supernatural creation." There is no third position. He also said, "One has only to contemplate the magnitude of this task to concede that the spontaneous generation of a living organism is impossible. Yet, here we are—as a result, I believe, of spontaneous generation."[21]

In 1996, the National Academy of Sciences framed the issue as follows: "For those who are studying aspects of the origin of life, the question no longer seems to be whether life could have originated by chemical processes involving non-biological components, but rather what pathway might have been followed."[22] This statement of the National Academy of Sciences is anti-Darwinian since Darwin rejected the concept of spontaneous generation, arguing instead for a Creator who "originally breathed" life into "a few forms or into one."[23]

[19] Pierre Paul Grasse, *Evolution of Living Organisms: Evidence for a New Theory of Transformation* (New York, NY: Academic Press, 1977), 87.

[20] Edward S. Deevey, Jr., "The Reply: Letter from Birnham Wood," *Yale Review* vol. 61, 1971-72: 636.

[21] George Wald, "The Origin of Life," *Scientific American* vol. 190 (August 1954): 46, quoted in Brown, *In the Beginning*, 37.

[22] *Commentary* (February 2006): 22.

[23] Charles Darwin, *The Origin of Species By Means of Natural Selection Or The Preservation Of Favored Races In*

Many evolutionists point to the work of Alexander Oparin in defense of spontaneous generation. Oparin described a theory that supposedly allowed for chance processes working in a prebiotic soup to give rise to life. Unfortunately for evolutionists, this theory is rapidly being refuted by science.[24]

In fact, the further science progresses, the more unlikely spontaneous generation seems. Dean Kenyon, a biochemist and a former chemical evolutionist, now concedes, "When all relevant lines of evidence are taken into account, and all the problems squarely faced, I think we must conclude that life owes its inception to a source outside of nature."[25] Kenyon based this conclusion on four premises: (1) the impossibility of the spontaneous origin of genetic information; (2) the fact that most attempts to duplicate the conditions necessary for chemical evolution yield non-biological material; (3) the unfounded nature of the belief (necessary for the chemical evolutionists) that prebiotic conditions encourage a trend toward the formation of L amino acids; and (4) the geochemical evidence that O_2 or oxygen existed in significant amounts in the Earth's early atmosphere (organic compounds decompose when oxygen is present).

> When all relevant lines of evidence are taken into account, and all the problems squarely faced, I think we must conclude that life owes its inception to a source outside of nature.
>
> — DEAN KENYON

Brown also believes the existence of oxygen creates an insurmountable problem for chemical evolutionists: "If the earth, in its alleged evolution, had oxygen in its atmosphere, the chemicals needed for life to begin would have been removed by oxidation. But if there had been no oxygen, then there would have been no ozone in the upper atmosphere. Without this ozone life would be quickly destroyed by the sun's ultraviolet radiation."[26] Ozone and life, therefore, must have originated simultaneously at the time of creation.

4.1.9 EVIDENCE FOR CREATION: THE SECOND LAW OF THERMODYNAMICS

The **Second Law of Thermodynamics** states that, "[A]lthough the total energy in the cosmos remains constant, the amount of energy available to do useful work is always getting smaller."[27]

J.P. Moreland and William Lane Craig describe the law as follows: "According to the second law of thermodynamics, processes taking place in a closed system always tend toward a state of equilibrium. Now our interest in the law concerns what happens when it is applied to the universe as a whole. The universe is, on a naturalistic view, a gigantic closed system, since it is everything there is and there is nothing outside it. This seems to imply that given enough time, the universe and all its processes will run down, and the entire universe will come to equilibrium. This is known as the heat death of the universe."[28]

The second law of thermodynamics does not just contradict evolutionary theory—it also reinforces the creationist explanation of origins. First, the second law suggests that the

The Struggle For Life, 2 vols. (New York, NY: D. Appleton and Company 1898), 2:306.

[24] Walter T. Brown, *In The Beginning*, 7th ed. (Phoenix, AZ: Center for Scientific Creation, 2001), 5, 42: "Spontaneous generation (the emergence of life from nonliving matter) has never been observed. All observations have shown that life only comes from life" (5).

[25] Ibid.

[26] Ibid., 5.

[27] A.E. Wilder-Smith, *Man's Origin, Man's Destiny* (Wheaton: IL: Harold Shaw Publishers, 1968), 55.

[28] J.P. Moreland and William Lane Craig, *Philosophical Foundations for a Christian Worldview* (Downers Grove, IL: InterVarsity Press, 2003), 478.

universe had a beginning. "If the entire universe," says Brown, "is an isolated system, then, according to the Second Law of Thermodynamics, the energy in the universe that is available for useful work has always been decreasing. However, as one goes back in time, the amount of energy available for useful work would eventually exceed the total energy in the universe that, according to the First Law of Thermodynamics, remains constant. This is an impossible condition. Therefore, it implies that the universe had a beginning."[29]

> SECOND LAW OF THERMODYNAMICS: A natural law that states that although the total energy in the cosmos remains constant, the amount of energy available to do useful work is always decreasing

Second, the second law of thermodynamics suggests that the universe began as a highly ordered system. Wilder-Smith says, "The second law of thermodynamics seems thus to describe the whole situation of our present material world perfectly and the Bible very clearly confirms this description. For example, Romans 8:22–23 teaches us that the whole creation is subjected to 'vanity' or to destruction. Everything tends to go downhill to chaos and destruction as things stand today."[30]

The creationist position in this regard is far more in harmony with modern science than is evolutionary theory.

4.1.10 FOSSIL GAPS AND INTERMEDIATE FORMS

Another problem with macroevolution is the lack of fossil evidence. Over one hundred years ago, Darwin wrote, "The geological record is extremely imperfect . . . [and this fact] will to a large extent explain why . . . we do not find intermediate varieties, connecting together all the extinct and existing forms of life by the finest graduated steps. . . . He who rejects these views on the nature of the geological record, will rightly reject my whole theory."[31]

When Darwin made this claim, he was correct in asserting that the geological record, as scientists knew it then, was imperfect. After a century of careful scrutiny of the geological record, it fails to support Darwin's theories. One reason the fossil record does not support evolutionary theory is that many complex life forms appear in the very earliest rocks without any indication of forms from which they could have evolved.[32] Creatures without ancestors cannot help but imply special creation. As Brown puts it, "The evolutionary tree has no trunk."[33]

When scientists discover trilobites in lower Cambrian strata with magnificent body and eye structure without any ancestors leading up to them—there are no monobites—they know that evolutionary theory is hurting. No wonder Richard Dawkins said it was as though they "were just planted there, without any evolutionary history."[34] The problem at the present time is that "paleontologists lack clear ancestral precursors for the representatives of not just one new phylum but virtually all the phyla represented in **Cambrian explosion**."[35]

---

[29] Brown, *In the Beginning*, 9.

[30] Wilder-Smith, *Man's Origin, Man's Destiny*, 72.

[31] Darwin, *The Origin of Species*, 2:124–5.

[32] See Walter L. Starkey, *The Cambrian Explosion: Evolution's Big Bang? Or Darwin's Dilemma?* (Dublin, OH: WLS Publishing, 1999) and John Angus Campbell and Stephen C. Meyer, ed., *Darwinism, Design, and Public Education* (East Lansing, MI: Michigan State University Press, 2003). Also, see volume 2 of Larry Vardiman, Andrew A. Snelling and Eugene F. Chaffin, *Radioisotopes and the Age of the Earth* (El Cajon, CA: Institute For Creation Research, 2005).

[33] Brown, *In the Beginning*, 3.

[34] John Angus Campbell and Stephen C. Meyer, ed., *Darwinism, Design, and Public Education* (East Lansing, MI: Michigan State University Press, 2003), 340.

[35] Ibid., 342.

CAMBRAN EXPLOSION: THE SUDDEN GEOLOGICAL APPEARANCE OF MOST MAJOR GROUPS OF ANIMALS

The term Cambrian explosion "describes the geologically sudden appearance of animals in the fossil record during the Cambrian period of geologic time. During this event, at least nineteen, and as many as thirty-five (of forty total), phyla made their first appearance on earth. Phyla constitute the highest biological categories in the animal kingdom, with each phylum exhibiting a unique architecture, blueprint, or structural body plan."[36]

This explosion of complex life is not the only way in which the fossil record condemns evolution. The lack of fossils supporting the transitional phases between species is perhaps the single most embarrassing topic for evolutionists, yet their absence is undeniable.

This fact is grudgingly recognized by leading evolutionists. The late paleontologist Stephen Jay Gould admitted, "The extreme rarity of transitional forms in the fossil record persists as the trade secret of paleontology."[37] Paleontologist George Gaylord Simpson wrote, "Nearly all categories above the level of families appear in the [fossil] record suddenly and are not led up to by known, gradual, completely continuous transitional sequences."[38] And David Raup, a geologist, confesses, "The record of evolution is still surprisingly jerky and, ironically, we have even fewer examples of evolutionary transition than we had in Darwin's time."[39]

The systematic lack of transitional fossils remains a major problem for evolutionists. This is made clear by Brown: "If [Darwinian] evolution happened, the fossil record should show continuous and gradual changes from the bottom to the top layers and between all forms of life. Actually, many gaps and discontinuities appear throughout the fossil record."[40] An evolutionary tree with no trunk (no life forms earlier than the already very complex ones in Cambrian rocks) and no branches (no transitional forms) can hardly be called a tree at all.

Not only are transitional forms not to be found in the fossil beds, but the very concept of specific transitional forms are even hard to imagine. Evolutionists are unable to present a reasonable explanation for the survival of any hypothetical transitional forms in nature because most novel features in their developmental phases would be useless until fully formed. Half-developed organs or appendages provide no clear advantage; on the contrary, they are more likely to be handicaps. Once again, Brown elaborates, "If a limb were to evolve into a wing, it would become a bad limb long before it became a good wing."[41]

> The lack of fossils supporting the transitional phases between species is perhaps the single most embarrassing topic for evolutionists.

4.1.11 CONCLUSION

The teleological argument provides the best critique of evolutionary theory and the strongest support for creationism. It is clear that God-as-Designer provides a much better explanation for the design evidenced by life than does a theory that requires transitional forms guided by natural selection.

The fossil record and the teleological nature of numerous living organisms both testify to the impossibility of gradual change. Yet gradual change is absolutely critical to traditional evolutionary theory. Darwin himself admits, "If it could be demonstrated that any complex

---

[36] Ibid., 324–5.

[37] Pennock, *Intelligent Design*, 133.

[38] Ibid., 143.

[39] David Raup, "Conflicts Between Darwin and Paleontology," *Field Museum of Natural History Bulletin* (January 1979): 25.

[40] Brown, *In the Beginning*, 3.

[41] Ibid.

organ existed, which could not possibly have been formed by numerous, successive, slight modifications, my theory would absolutely break down."[42]

This is precisely what creationists have claimed for years—that Darwin's evolutionary theory is bankrupt. Reason requires that biologists abandon evolution and embrace creation as a more rational explanation.

The belief that God created all things, including men and women, in His own image requires faith. But evolutionary theory requires more faith because evolution runs contrary to science (e.g., spontaneous generation) and history (e.g., the fossil record). Still, many evolutionists hold desperately to their theory, simply because it is the only explanation of origins that begins with nature, not God. Scientists who believe that everything can be explained in natural terms cannot tolerate the concept of a supernatural Being. In fact, one scientist said, "Science must be provisionally atheistic or cease to be itself."[43] For Christian biologists, however, the world is comprehensible only in light of God's existence. As a piece of art suggests an artist, the orderly universe and every living thing suggest a Designer.

[42] Darwin, *The Origin of Species*, 1:229.
[43] Pennock, *Intelligent Design*, 144.

Biology

Islam

The basic Islamic concept is that the entire universe
was created by God, whom Islam calls Allah and who is
the Lord and Sovereign of the Universe. He is the Lord
of the universe which He alone sustains.[1]

— KHURSHID AHMAD

4.2.1 INTRODUCTION

The Islamic worldview affirms that God created the universe. Thus Christians and Muslims
part company with atheistic worldviews that deny the existence of God and assert a naturalistic
origin and evolution of the world. "Muslims, like Christians, do witness that God is the Creator.
As Creator, he is other than creation. He is not nature; he is above and beyond his creation
(transcendent). Muslims believe that God's creation is perfect."[2]

4.2.2 CREATIONISM

According to Islam, God has always existed. He is eternal and self-existent. He created
everything and set the universe in order. Echoing Genesis 1, we read in the Qur'an that when
God spoke, the world was created. "To Him is due the primal origin of the heavens and the
earth: when He decreeth a matter, He saith to it: 'Be,' and it is" (2:117). When the virgin Mary

---

[1] Khurshid Ahmad, *Islam: Its Meaning and Message*, 3rd ed. (Leicester, UK: The Islamic Foundation, 1999), 29.
[2] Badru D. Kateregga and David W. Shenk, *Islam and Christianity: A Muslim and a Christian in Dialogue*, electronically available on *The World of Islam: Resources for Understanding* CD-ROM, published by Global Mapping International, 5350.

found herself with child, she inquired as to how it could be so. "She said, 'O my Lord! How shall I have a son when no man has touched me?' He said: 'Even so: God createth what He willeth: when He hath decreed a Plan, He but saith to it, "Be," and it is!'" (3:47).

4.2.3 CREATION IN SIX OR EIGHT DAYS?

Though Christians and Muslims share some common convictions regarding the existence of God and the creation of the world, the Islamic view of creation differs from biblical revelation. For instance, while the Bible describes creation in six days (with God's Sabbath on the seventh day), the Qur'an asserts otherwise. In some passages creation is said to have taken six days:

> Your Guardian-Lord is God, Who created the heavens and the earth is six Days, and is firmly established on the Throne . . . (7:54)

> It is God Who has created the heavens and the earth, and all between them, in six Days, and is firmly established on the Throne . . . (32:4)

> We created the heavens and the earth and all between them in Six Days, nor did any sense of weariness touch Us. (50:38)

But another passage describes the creation as taking eight days (two plus four plus two):

> Say: It is that ye deny Him Who created the earth in *two Days*? And do ye join equals with Him? He is the Lord of (all) the Worlds. He set on the (earth) mountains standing firm, high above it, and bestowed blessings on the earth, and measured therein all things to give them nourishment in due proportion, in *four Days*, in accordance with (the needs of) those who seek (sustenance). Moreover He comprehended in His design the sky, and it had been (as) smoke: He said to it and to the earth: "Come ye together, willingly or unwillingly." They said: "We do come (together), in willing obedience." So He created them as seven firmaments in *two Days*, and He assigned to each heaven its duty and command… (41:9–12, emphasis added)

4.2.4 TWENTY-FOUR HOUR DAYS OR AGES?

As the Christian community is divided over whether to advocate an old or young earth, Muslims are divided as well. While many more traditional Muslims take the reference to days as twenty-four hours in duration, some contemporary Muslim spokesmen hold that the days of creation were long periods of time (though they do not normally advocate evolutionary theories). "The earth and universe were created by God through a long step-by-step process," writes Badru Kateregga. "The Qur'anic witness further testifies that God created the heavens and the earth and what is between them in six 'periods,' and no weariness touched him (Qur'an 50:38). God created the universe and the earth in an orderly step-by-step progression."[3]

4.2.5 CREATION AND THE FALL

Muslims deny the significance of the fall of Adam and Eve. The Bible describes the significance of the fall not only upon human beings but also upon the world itself. Due to Adam and Eve's rebellion, the ground is cursed (Genesis 3:17) and has been "groaning" ever since,

---

[3] Ibid., 5273.

awaiting the day of the resurrection of humans and the renewal of the earth (Romans 8:19–23). Muslims reject "the Christian view that God in fact 'cursed' the ground (Gen. 3:14–24)," writes Katterega. "All that God tells man in relation to the ground after the descent of Adam to earth is as quoted: 'Therein Ye shall live and therein Ye shall die, and therein Ye shall be brought forth [in the resurrection]' (Qur'an 7:25)."[4]

4.2.6 DESIGN POINTS TO GOD

The Qur'an describes the universe as finely ordered, illustrating God's magnificent mind in designing it.

> It is He who hath created for you all things that are on earth; moreover His design comprehended the heavens, for He gave order and perfection to the seven firmaments; and of all things He hath perfect knowledge. (2:29)

> Blessed is He Who made Constellations in the skies, and placed therein a Lamp and a Moon giving light; and it is He Who made the Night and the Day to follow each other. (25:61)

> He has created man: He has taught him speech (and Intelligence). The sun and the moon follow courses (exactly) computed; and the herbs and the trees—both (alike) bow in adoration. And the Firmament has He Raised high. (55:3–7)

As do Christians, Muslims regularly appeal to the order of the universe as evidence of God's existence and creative activity. Ahmad writes,

> How can one observe the inexhaustible creativity of nature, its purposefulness, its preservation of that which is morally useful and destruction of that which is socially injurious, and yet fail to draw the conclusion that behind nature there is an All-Pervading Mind of whose incessant creative activity the processes of nature are but an outward manifestation? The stars scattered through the almost infinite space, the vast panorama of nature with its charm and beauty, the planned waxing and waning of the moon, the astonishing harmony of the seasons—all point towards one fact; there is a God, the Creator, the Governor. We witness a superb, flawless plan in the universe—can it be without a Planner? We see great enchanting beauty and harmony in its working—can it be without a Creator? We observe wonderful design in nature—can it be without a Designer? We feel a lofty purpose in physical and human existence—can it be without a Will working behind it? We find that the universe is like a superbly written fascinating novel—can it be without an Author?[5]

4.2.7 ISLAM AND MODERN SCIENCE

Although Muslim scholars agree that God is the Creator of the universe, it is also historically true that modern science did not grow out of an Islamic worldview, but instead, flourished in the soil of Biblical Christianity. If both worldviews affirm a Creator, why did modern science not develop within Islam nations as it did in Western culture?

Sociology scholar Rodney Stark suggests the answer to the above question rests with the Muslim concept of God and the role of philosophy. Regarding Muslim theology, Stark writes,

---

[4] Ibid., 5350.
[5] Khurshid Ahmad, *Islam*, 29–30.

"Allah is not presented as a lawful creator but has been conceived of as an extremely active God who intrudes on the world as he deems it appropriate. Consequently, there soon arose a major theological bloc within Islam that condemned all efforts to formulate natural laws as blasphemy insofar as they denied Allah's freedom to act."[6]

Validating this concept is a verse in the Qur'an that states, "Verily, God will cause to err whom he pleaseth, and will direct whom he pleaseth." Although this statement refers specifically to God's direction in the lives of individuals, it has also been interpreted more broadly. Stark continues, "if God does as he pleases, and what he pleases is variable, then the universe may not be lawful."[7] Thus, Muslim theology did not provide the necessary fundamental assumptions for erecting the concept of science based on observations leading to formulate natural laws.

In addition, devout Muslim and historian Caesar E. Farah mentions a second reason that Muslim scientific inquiry was stunted. He writes that Muslim philosophy sought *"to assimilate* rather than *to generate,* with the conscious striving to adapt the results of Greek thinking to Muslim philosophical conceptions…"[8] This means that Muslim philosophers tied their understanding of reality to Greek concepts of the ideal to the point of tipping the scales toward the realm of ideas and away from experimental science. The result, Muslim science could travel only so far before stagnating, the same as the ancient Greeks. To be sure, both the Greeks and Muslims had "a theoretical collection of facts, and isolated crafts and technologies," but "they never broke through to real science."[9]

4.2.8 ISLAM AND EVOLUTION

Though some modern Muslims have been persuaded that evolutionary theories accurately describe the history of the world and the origin of species, the majority of Muslims reject evolutionary theories on both religious and scientific grounds. Orthodox Muslim scholars lament that other Muslims have adopted evolutionary theories and attempted to merge them with Islam. "For a notable segment of modernized Muslims evolution remains practically like a religious article of faith whose overt contradiction of the teachings of the Qur'an they fail to realize," writes Seyyed Hossein Nasr. "Those who think they are rendering a service to Islam by incorporating evolutionary ideas into Islamic thought are in fact falling into a most dangerous pit and are surrendering Islam to one of the most insidious pseudo-dogmas of modern man, created in the eighteenth and nineteenth centuries to enable men to forget God."[10]

By and large, it seems that Muslims who have adopted evolutionary theory have done so due to the influence of humanist education in the West or the importation of such theories into Muslim lands. In this regard, Muslim evolutionists have been influenced much like Christian evolutionists have been. But as we have shown, there are compelling reasons (biblical, scientific, and philosophical) to reject such theories, based as they are on atheistic premises. The contemporary Intelligent Design movement, (ID) movement, comprised of Christians and non-Christians, has drawn the attention of some Muslims scientists and theorists. Mustafa Akyol, a Muslim writer based in Turkey, writes

> "ID presents a new perspective on science, one that is based solely on scientific evidence yet is fully compatible with faith in God. That's why William Dembski, one of its leading theorists, defines ID as a bridge between science and theology. As the history of the cultural

[6] Rodney Stark, *For the Glory of God* (Princeton, NJ: Princeton University Press, 2003), 154.

[7] *Ibid.,* 155.

[8] Cited in Stark, *For the Glory of God*, 155.

[9] Ibid., 152.

[10] Ibid., 228–230.

conflict between the modern West and Islam shows, ID can also be a bridge between these two civilizations. The first bricks of that bridge are now being laid in the Islamic world. In Turkey, the current debate over ID has attracted much attention in the Islamic media. Islamic newspapers are publishing translations of pieces by the leading figures of the ID movement, such as Michael J. Behe and Phillip E. Johnson. The Discovery Institute is praised in their news stories and depicted as the vanguard in the case for God…. Now, for the first time, Muslims are discovering that they share a common cause with the believers in the West….[11]

Akyol goes on to say, "Of course, Darwinians have the right to believe in whatever they wish, but it is crucial to unveil that theirs is a subjective faith, not an objective truth, as they have been claiming for more than a century. This unveiling would mark a turning point in the history of Western civilization, by reconciling science and religion and letting people become intellectually fulfilled theists."[12]

4.2.9 Conclusion

Muslims affirm the existence of God and His creation of the universe. They do not equate God with the creation. They maintain a Creator-creature distinction, as do Christians. They also believe that the design of the universe points to the existence of the Designer. While some modernized Muslims have adopted evolutionary theories (as have some Christians), orthodox Muslims know that such naturalistic theories conflict with the teachings of the Qur'an and Muhammad. While Christians and Muslims hold several beliefs in common, the Qur'an presents confusion on the number of days of creation—though many Muslims read these days in a non-literal fashion—and they deny that the fall of Adam and Eve brought God's curse upon the earth.

[11] Mustafa Akyol, "Under God or Under Darwin? Intelligent Design could be a bridge between civilizations," *National Review Online,* December 02, 2005, http://www.nationalreview.com/comment/akyol200512020813.asp. Mustafa Akyol is a Muslim writer based in Istanbul, Turkey, and one of the expert witnesses who testified to the Kansas State Education Board during the hearings on evolution.
[12] Ibid.

Biology

Secular Humanism

"Man is the result of a purposeless and natural process
that did not have him in mind. He was not planned. He is
a state of matter, a form of life, a sort of animal, and
a species of the Order Primates, akin nearly or remotely
to all of life and indeed to all that is material."[1]

— GEORGE GAYLORD SIMPSON

4.3.1 INTRODUCTION

Belief in evolution is as crucial to Humanism's worldview as are its atheistic theology and naturalistic philosophy. In fact, the Humanist's ideas about the origin of life can be considered a special dimension of these disciplines. Without the theory of evolution, the Humanist would have to rely on God as the explanation for life, which would necessarily destroy his atheism. Therefore, every Secular Humanist embraces the theory of evolution.

The *Humanist Manifesto I* states, "Humanism believes that man is a part of nature and that he has emerged as the result of a continuous process."[2] This belief is echoed in the *Humanist Manifesto II*, which claims that "science affirms that the human species is an emergence from natural evolutionary forces."[3] And in *Humanist Manifesto 2000* Kurtz says, "The theory of

---

[1] George Gaylord Simpson, *The Meaning of Evolution* (New Haven, CT: Yale University Press, 1971), 345.

[2] *Humanist Manifesto I* (Buffalo, NY: Prometheus Books, [1933] 1980), 8.

[3] *Humanist Manifesto II* (Buffalo, NY: Prometheus Books, [1973] 1980), 17.

evolution and the standards of ecology should also be studied."[4]

For the Humanist, atheistic evolution is not one option among many, but rather the only option compatible with their worldview. Creationism, or Intelligent Design, is considered an enemy of science.

4.3.2 THE ROLE OF SCIENCE

Humanists rely on science as the basic source of knowledge. They claim that a true definition of science excludes any supernatural explanation for any event occurring in nature, including the origin of life. For Humanists, the scientist must only study what takes place in nature and arrive at naturalistic explanations for all events. In this way, the supernatural is ruled out of bounds.

Obviously, when one assumes that science is the best method of obtaining knowledge and that science must exclude the supernatural, one cannot accept supernatural explanations for the origin of life. Julian Huxley sums it up: "Modern science must rule out special creation or divine guidance."[5]

Why must "modern" science rule out creation? Because, as we have noted, science cannot observe or measure the supernatural and therefore is incapable of obtaining any knowledge about it. But by this definition science cannot render judgment on the theory of evolution, either. That is because one-time-only historical events, such as the origin of life, fall outside the parameters of the scientific method. The reason: such events cannot be repeated, observed, tested, or falsified.[6] Accordingly, neither creationism nor evolution is strictly "scientific."

> ## The Pop Culture Connection
>
> **Flatliners** In the 1990 sci-fi thriller starring Kiefer Sutherland and Julia Roberts, viewers are presented with the notion that knowledge is found only through the five senses—the realm of scientific inquiry. The story involved a number of young doctors willing to die temporarily to find out what was on the other side.
>
> Doctor #1: *"Wait a minute! Wait! Quite simply, why are you doing this?"*
>
> Doctor #2: *"Quite simply to see if there is anything out there beyond death. Philosophy failed! Religion failed! Now it's up to the physical sciences. I think mankind deserves to know!"* (Scene 19)
>
> Likewise, science is shown to be a distinctly *human* endeavor in Stephen Spielberg's 1993 film adaptation of Michael Crichton's, **Jurassic Park**. However, in this story viewers witness an example of mankind's manipulation of technology run amuck.

Still, Humanists insist that evolutionary theory is scientific and the idea of a Grand Designer is not. Just how closed-minded the Humanists are toward creation is summed up by Isaac Asimov: "To those who are trained in science, creationism seems like a bad dream, a sudden reliving of a nightmare, a renewed march of an army of the night risen to challenge free thought and enlightenment."[7]

---

[4] Paul Kurtz, *Humanist Manifesto 2000* (Amherst, NY: Prometheus Books, 2000), 43.

[5] Julian Huxley, *Evolution: The Modern Synthesis* (New York, NY: Harper and Brothers Publishers, 1942), 457.

[6] However, Humanists accept both the Big Bang, a one-time event, and spontaneous generation as science.

[7] Ashley Montagu, ed., *Science and Creationism* (Oxford, UK: Oxford University Press, 1984), 183. For an in-depth study on the politicization of science and how Humanists use science to stifle dissent see Tom Bethel's *The Politically Incorrect Guide to Science* (Washington, DC: Regnery Publishing, 2005).

UNDERSTANDING
THE TIMES

4.3.3 EVOLUTION AS "FACT"

Carl Sagan states simply, "Evolution is a fact, not a theory."[8] Huxley claims, "The first point to make about Darwin's theory is that it is no longer a theory, but a fact . . . Darwinianism has come of age so to speak. We do no longer have to bother about

> Evolution is a fact, not a theory.
>
> — CARL SAGAN

establishing the fact of evolution."[9] Antony Flew is scandalized by the notion that there was a time, "unbelievably," when the Vatican questioned "the fact of the evolutionary origin of the species."[10]

Thus, Humanists claim that the fact of evolution relates to changes within a species (microevolution) as well as macroevolution, or the transmutation of species. In other words, Humanists are not just claiming that science has proven that dogs can evolve into faster or bigger breeds; they also are claiming that all dogs, indeed all mammals, evolved from reptiles, and reptiles evolved from amphibians, amphibians evolved from fish, and so on back to the first speck of life. They wholeheartedly believe Darwin's conclusion that because microevolutionary changes occur among species, these changes can accumulate over time to produce macro-changes.

4.3.4 SPONTANEOUS GENERATION

But in order to change from one species to another, Humanists must first have a theory of how life initially appeared on the planet. Their answer is that life arose spontaneously from non-living matter. However, as we covered in some detail in the section on Biblical Christian biology, the idea of **spontaneous generation** was *scientifically* demonstrated to be false through the experiments of Redi and Pasteur in the mid 1800s. Yet, because of their commitment to philosophical naturalism, Humanists assume that life must have come from non-living matter, they have just not yet discovered how that happened. They also assume that features of the "early" earth were

> SPONTANEOUS GENERATION: The theory that non-living matter gave rise to living organisms

different from today, and would thereby allow for the emergence of the first life.

Ironically, not even Charles Darwin was willing to postulate a theory that hinged on the idea of spontaneous generation. Rather, he wrote, "Probably all the organic beings which have ever lived on this earth have descended from some one primordial form, into which life was first breathed."[11] Even though Darwin felt the need to postulate a supernatural force to explain the appearance of first life, the Humanist cannot afford such a concession. As Harvard paleontologist Richard Lewontin protests, "Materialism is absolute, for we cannot allow a Divine Foot in the door."[12]

---

[8] Carl Sagan, *Cosmos* (New York, NY: Random House, 1980), 27.

[9] Julian Huxley, "At Random," a television preview on Nov. 21, 1959. Also, Sol Tax, *Evolution of Life* (Chicago, IL: University of Chicago Press, 1960), 1.

[10] Paul Kurtz, ed., *The Humanist Alternative* (Buffalo, NY: Prometheus Books, 1973), 110. Two interesting developments since Flew made these remarks: (a) Dr. Flew has left his atheistic position for some form of Deism, (b) the Roman Catholic Church since the death of Pope John Paul II has staked out a more creationist position.

[11] Charles Darwin, *The Origin of Species By Means of Natural Selection Or The Preservation Of Favored Races In The Struggle For Life*, 2 vols. (New York, NY: D. Appleton and Company 1898), 2:306, cited in Sagan, *Cosmos*, 23.

[12] Richard Lewontin, "Billions and Billions of Demons," *The N.Y. Review of Books*, January 9, 1997.

4.3.5 NATURAL SELECTION

The second idea Humanists embrace in biology is natural selection. Natural selection is the mechanism proposed by Darwin that, through competition and other factors such as predators, geography, and time, only those life forms best suited to survive will live and reproduce. Tied up in this theory is the notion of "survival of the fittest, "or the struggle for existence." Carl Sagan insists that "natural selection is a successful theory devised to explain the fact of evolution."[13]

Charles Darwin relied on natural selection as the mechanism for his theory of evolution largely because he felt it was something man had already observed through artificial breeding. When one breeds horses to create faster offspring, one is artificially selecting a beneficial trait and, therefore, engaging in a microevolutionary process. Darwin was convinced that, given enough time, nature does the selecting to evolve new forms of life. Indeed, Darwin believed that "natural selection is daily and hourly scrutinizing . . . every variation, even the slightest; rejecting that which is bad, preserving and adding up all that is good; silently and insensibly working. . . at the improvement of each organic being."[14]

Charles Darwin

While a breeder *purposely* controls the selection process so that each generation contains the best improvements, Darwin believed that *random* variations were responsible for such improvements in nature. Current evolutionary scientists agree, even stating more forcefully that natural selection is a mindless process that does not have an ultimate goal or purpose in view. Cornell University Professor William Provine, a leading historian of science, writes, "Modern science directly implies that the world is organized strictly in accordance with mechanistic principles. There are no purposive principles whatsoever in nature."[15] In the words of Richard Dawkins, "Natural section, the blind, unconscious, automatic process which Darwin discovered . . . has no purpose in mind. It has no mind and no mind's eye. It does not plan for the future. It has no vision, no foresight, no sight at all. If it can be said to play the role of a watchmaker in nature, it is the *blind* watchmaker."[16]

4.3.6 STRUGGLE FOR EXISTENCE AND SURVIVAL

Inherent in natural selection is the notion that those life forms best equipped to survive will win the struggle for existence. This explains why living organisms have become better equipped to survive as time passes. Corliss Lamont, explains, "The processes of natural selection and survival of the fittest, with the many mutations that occur over hundreds of millions of years, adequately account for the origin and development of the species."[17]

However, some Humanists are more cautious than Lamont about expressing their views on "survival of the fittest." That is because of the ethical implications: the only moral good

[13] Carl Sagan, *The Dragons of Eden* (New York, NY: Random House, 1977), 6.
[14] Charles Darwin, *The Origin of Species*, 1:103.
[15] Cited in Phillip E. Johnson's *Darwin on Trial* (Downers Grove, IL: InterVarsity Press, 1991), 124.
[16] Richard Dawkins, *The Blind Watchmaker* (New York, NY: W.W. Norton & Company, 1996), 5.
[17] Corliss Lamont, *The Philosophy of Humanism*, rev. ed. (New York, NY: Frederick Ungar, [1949] 1982), 120.
For the counter point on whether or not mutations can carry Darwin's theory see Stephen C. Meyer, "The Origin of the Biological Information and the Higher Taxonomic Categories" in *Proceedings of the Biological Society of Washington* (August 28, 2004).

becomes survival. Survival of the fittest is bloodthirsty; it does not care for the weak or the poor. As one would expect, survival of the fittest became the framework for both Engels' Marxism and Hitler's Aryan policies.[18]

There is also another problem with survival of the fittest. Asimov describes it this way: "In the first place, the phrase 'the survival of the fittest' is not an illuminating one. It implies that those who survive are the 'fittest,' but what is meant by 'fittest'? Why, those are 'fittest' who survive. This is an argument in a circle."[19] In other words, when you say "survival of the fittest," you really aren't saying anything of consequence. It is a tautology—an explanation that includes its own definition.

Obviously, Humanists would like to avoid discussing the struggle for existence whenever possible—but at the same time, there is a need to explain natural selection as a mechanism for evolution, so it seems they are stuck with it.

4.3.7 MUTATIONS AND ADAPTATIONS

Another important aspect of evolutionary theory involves combining natural selection with genetic mutations to provide an explanation for adaptation. Adaptation explains why life evolved specialized abilities that allow it to survive in particular niches in the environment. During the 1930's evolutionary scientists combined Darwin's idea of natural selection with that of the newly discovered science of genetics and called it **Neo-Darwinism**.

Of course, in accepting adaptation as part of the mechanism of evolution, the Humanist must overlook (or explain away) all the apparently meaningless adaptations existing in our world. Darwin admits, "I did not formerly consider sufficiently the existence of structures which, as far as we can . . . judge, are neither beneficial nor injurious, and this I believe to be one of the greatest oversights as yet detected in my work."[20]

> **NEO-DARWINISM:** The theory that new species arise from natural selection acting over vast periods of time on chance genetic mutations in reproductively isolated populations

Huxley attempts to solve this problem for Darwin by explaining seemingly harmful or meaningless adaptations in such a way that they could rightly be labeled beneficial. His attempt becomes absurd, however, when he tries to describe schizophrenia as a useful adaptation. He claims that "genetic theory makes it plain that a clearly disadvantageous genetic character like this cannot persist in this frequency in a population unless it is balanced by some compensating advantage. In this case it appears that the advantage is that schizophrenic individuals are considerably less sensitive than normal persons to histamine, are much less prone to suffer from operative and wound shock, and do not suffer nearly so much from various allergies."[21] Huxley does not say whether he would rather be schizophrenic or suffer from allergies.

4.3.8 THE FOSSIL RECORD

The final plank on which the theory of evolution rests is the claim that the fossil record provides an accurate historical account of the process of transmutation of the species, or macroevolution. "Evolution is a fact," says Sagan, "amply demonstrated by the fossil record."[22]

---

[18] See Richard Weikart, *From Darwin to Hitler: Evolutionary Ethics, Eugenics, and Racism in Germany* (New York, NY: Palgrave-Macmillan, 2004).
[19] Isaac Asimov, *The Wellsprings of Life* (London, UK: Abelard-Schuman, 1960), 57.
[20] Charles Darwin, as cited in Norman Macbeth, *Darwin Retried* (Boston, MA: Gambit, 1971), 73.
[21] Julian Huxley, *Essays of a Humanist* (New York, NY: Harper and Row, 1964), 67.
[22] Sagan, *The Dragons of Eden*, 6.

The fossil record is the only means available to the scientist to observe steps in the evolutionary process.

In Darwin's day, the actual evidence was missing. There was no fossil evidence that any of the major divisions of nature (fish, amphibians, reptiles, and mammals) had been crossed. But without convincing evidence from fossils, the theory of evolution would have no basis for grounding itself in the scientific method and would be left in the realm of faith. The problem is, as demonstrated in the Christian Biology section, the needed "transitional" fossils are systematically missing.

4.3.9 PUNCTUATED EQUILIBRIUM

If the fossil record is the only means for observing macroevolution, and if that record provides nothing that corresponds with the theory, then the evolutionist is left holding a groundless theory. This is intolerable for the Humanist—so a theory has been proposed that forces the fossil record to fit into the evolutionary mold. This theory is referred to as punctuated equilibrium. "Equilibrium" refers to the fact that species manifest a stubborn stability (stasis) in nature. "Punctuated" refers to the dramatic changes deemed necessary to explain how the gaps are bridged in the fossil record between the major divisions in nature.

Chris McGowan, after admitting that the fossil record does not contain evidence of macroevolution, jumps to the conclusion that punctuated equilibrium is the answer. He states, "New species probably evolve only when a segment of the population becomes isolated from the rest. Speciation occurs relatively rapidly, probably in a matter of only a few thousand years and possibly less."[23]

That is, punctuated equilibrium claims that science cannot discover the links between species in the fossil record because the change from one species to another occurs too rapidly, geologically speaking, to leave accurate fossil documentation.[24]

How does punctuated evolution mesh with the theory of evolution as presented by Darwin? Not as well as one might expect—in fact, it clashes directly with Darwin's ideas. He writes, "If it could be demonstrated that any complex organ existed, which could not possibly have been formed by numerous, successive, slight modifications, my theory would absolutely break down."[25] Apparently, some evolutionists are willing to "break down" Darwin's theory in an effort to make a new form of evolution fit the facts.

4.3.10 CONCLUSION

Secular Humanist biology rests its case for evolution on six specific planks: spontaneous generation, natural selection, struggle for existence, beneficial mutations, adaptations, and the fossil record. However, over the past thirty years, the fossil record has only hindered attempts to prove macroevolution. Therefore, some evolutionists have been forced to abandon Darwin's original theory of gradual change and postulate punctuated equilibrium in order to salvage the last plank of their theory.

Humanism relies on evolution for much more than a theory about the origin of life. The theory of evolution has significant implications for ethics, sociology, law, and politics. Humanists consider evolution the correct foundation for every individual's worldview and believe that a proper understanding of the world comes only from this perspective.

---

[23] Chris McGowan, *In the Beginning* (Buffalo, NY: Prometheus Books, 1984), 29.

[24] See Walter James ReMine, *The Biotic Message: Evolution Versus Message Theory* (St. Paul, MN: St Paul Science Publishers, 1993) for a discussion on punctuated equilibrium.

[25] Darwin, *Origin of Species*, 1:229, cited in Macbeth, *Darwin Retried*, 76.

For this reason, Humanists encourage teaching evolution as "fact" throughout our educational system—thereby relegating the supernatural, especially God, to the world of literary mythology. Humanists do not just expect evolution to be taught as fact in the biology classroom, but rather believe, in the words of Julian Huxley, that "it is essential for evolution to become the central core of any educational system, because it is evolution, in the broad sense, that links inorganic nature with life, and the stars with earth, and matter with mind, and animals with man. Human history is a continuation of biological evolution in a different form."[26]

> Humanists consider evolution the correct foundation for every individual's worldview and believe that a proper understanding of the world comes only from this perspective.

Since Huxley, however, a lot of discussion in the scientific community has been unfavorable for Darwin. As Stephen Meyer writes,

> In the last decade a host of scientific essays and books have questioned the efficacy of [natural] selection and [genetic] mutation as a mechanism for generating morphological novelty, as even a brief literature survey will establish. Thomson (1992:107) expressed doubt that large-scale morphological changes could accumulate via minor phenotypic changes at the population genetic level. Miklos (1993:29) argued that neo-Darwinism fails to provide a mechanism that can produce large-scale innovations in form and complexity. Gilbert et. al. (1996) attempted to develop a new theory of evolutionary mechanisms to supplement classical neo-Darwinism, which, they argued, could not adequately explain macroevolution.[27]

The reason there is neo-Darwinism (natural selection plus mutations or genetic mistakes) is because Darwinism (natural selection by itself) could not carry the evolutionary theory. The reason there is punctuated equilibrium is because neo-Darwinism can't either. Now, the entire edifice is beginning to crumble under the latest scientific investigations. It appears this major category of the Secular Humanist worldview is beginning to disintegrate before their eyes.

---

[26] Julian Huxley, "At Random," a television preview on Nov. 21, 1959.

[27] Stephen C. Meyer, "Intelligent Design: The Origin of Biological Information and the Higher Taxonomic Categories," *Proceedings of the Biological Society of Washington* vol. 117, no. 2 (November 30, 2005): 213–239. Available online at http://www.discovery.org/scripts/viewDB/index.php?command=view&id=2177.

Biology

Marxism-Leninism

"Darwin's [Origin of Species] is very important and provides me with the basis in natural science for the class struggle in history."[1]

— Karl Marx

4.4.1 INTRODUCTION

While Karl Marx and Frederick Engels were developing their communistic worldview, Charles Darwin was presenting his theory of evolution and creating quite a stir among the intellectuals of the nineteenth century. Many people perceived that Darwin's theory could provide the foundation for an entirely materialistic perspective on life. Marx and Engels were among those who recognized the usefulness of Darwin's theory as just such a foundation for their theory of dialectical materialism.

In a letter to Engels, Marx writes, "During . . . the past four weeks I have read all sorts of things. Among others Darwin's work on Natural Selection. And though it is written in the crude English style, this is the book which contains the basis in natural science for our view."[2]

John Hoffman tells us that Marx so admired Darwin's work that he "sent Darwin a complimentary copy of Volume I of *Capital* and tried unsuccessfully to dedicate Volume II to him."[3] Darwin's wife insisted he not have any relationship with "that atheist."

[1] Karl Marx and Frederick Engels, *Selected Correspondence* (New York, NY: International Publishers, 1942), 125.

[2] Charles J. McFadden, *The Philosophy of Communism* (Kenosha, WI: Cross, 1939), 35–6. Also, see Jacques Barzun's *Darwin, Marx and Wagner* (Chicago, IL: University of Chicago Press, 1981) for additional material on this point.

[3] John Hoffman, *Marxism and the Theory of Praxis* (New York, NY: International Publishers, 1976). 69.

4.4.2 DARWIN, MARX, AND SOCIETY

Marx believed that Darwin's evolutionary theory could be extended naturally to answer questions about human society. Marx felt that society, like life itself, had gone through an evolutionary process and must continue to undergo such a process until a classless society evolved. Marx integrated this notion of evolution into his worldview, writing, "Darwin has interested us in the history of Nature's technology, i.e., in the formation of the organs of plants and animals, which organs serve as instruments of production for sustaining life. Does not the history of the productive organs of man, of organs that are the material basis of all social organization, deserve equal attention?"[4]

> Just as Darwin put an end to the view of animal and plant species being unconnected, fortuitous, 'created by God' and immutable, and was the first to put biology on an absolutely scientific basis . . . so Marx . . . was the first to put sociology on a scientific basis.
>
> — V.I. LENIN

Engels more straightforwardly states the link between Darwin's and Marx's theories: "Just as Darwin discovered the law of evolution in organic nature, so Marx discovered the law of evolution in human history."[5]

This claim has been reaffirmed throughout Marxism's development. V.I. Lenin echoes Marx and Engels, stressing the scientific nature of their theory: "Just as Darwin put an end to the view of animal and plant species being unconnected, fortuitous, 'created by God' and immutable, and was the first to put biology on an absolutely scientific basis . . . so Marx . . . was the first to put sociology on a scientific basis . . ."[6]

Marxists understand evolution as an essential pillar in their worldview, due largely to the fact that it complements their social and historical theory so well.

4.4.3 DARWIN AND TELEOLOGY

The founders of Marxism entertained another reason for incorporating Darwin's evolutionary theory into their system. Just as Secular Humanist theology cannot stand if it accepts the notion that God exists, so Marxist theology is directly opposed to God. Atheism is at the core of Marxist theory. This worldview is coherent and consistent only if God and the supernatural do not exist. Therefore, Marx and his followers eagerly embraced a theory of biology that makes God unnecessary for the origin of life.

Marx proclaims that Darwin's *Origin of Species* dealt the "death-blow . . . to 'teleology.'"[7] F.V. Konstantinov, in *The Fundamentals of Marxist-Leninist Philosophy*, echoes Marx: "Darwin's theory of evolution is the third great scientific discovery that took place in the middle of the 19th century. Darwin put an end to the notion of the species of animals and plants as 'divine creations,' not connected with anything else, providential and immutable, and thus laid the foundation of theoretical biology."[8]

---

[4] Karl Marx, *Capital*, 3 vols. (London, UK: Lawrence and Wishart, 1970), 1:341.

[5] Frederick Engels, *Selected Works*, 3 vols. (New York, NY: International Publishers, 1950), 2:153, quoted in R.N. Carew Hunt, *The Theory and Practice of Communism* (Baltimore, MD: Penguin Books, 1966), 64.

[6] V.I. Lenin, *Collected Works*, 45 vols. (Moscow, USSR: Progress Publishers, 1977), 1:142.

[7] Marx, *Selected Correspondence*, 125.

[8] F.V. Konstantinov, ed., *The Fundamentals of Marxist-Leninist Philosophy* (Moscow, USSR: Progress Publishers, 1982), 42.

This "great scientific discovery" is crucial. Without the theory of evolution, the design of the universe could be explained only by postulating a rational, purposeful, powerful God, and this is inconceivable for Marxists. Miracles cannot exist in a materialistic worldview, so Marxism must accept evolution unreservedly.

4.4.4 SPONTANEOUS GENERATION

The aspect of evolutionary theory that is most important to Marxists is spontaneous generation. A fervent belief in the doctrine that life arose from non-life allows Marxists to abandon God completely.

Marx uses the concept of spontaneous generation to back both his philosophy and his theology, stating, "The idea of the creation of the earth has received a severe blow . . . from the science which portrays the . . . development of the earth as a process of spontaneous generation. . . .Generatio aequivoca [spontaneous generation] is the only practical refutation of the theory of creation."[9]

> We have every reason to believe that sooner or later, we shall be able practically to demonstrate that life is nothing else but a special form of existence of matter.
>
> — A.I. OPARIN

Marxists continued to embrace spontaneous generation long after the time of Marx and Engels. A.I. Oparin, a Marxist scientist, "was the first to enunciate the theory of abiogenic origin of life."[10] Oparin claimed, "We have every reason to believe that sooner or later, we shall be able practically to demonstrate that life is nothing else but a special form of existence of matter."[11]

Modern Marxist textbooks also embrace the theory of spontaneous generation. M.V. Volkenshtein, author of *Biophysics,* declares that Oparin "presumed that the origin of life had been preceded by chemical evolution. . . . Today these ideas are widely accepted."[12]

Engels held firm his belief in spontaneous generation when other scientists were in doubt. Louis Pasteur (1822–1895) disproved the theory of spontaneous generation, but Engels was unconvinced: "Pasteur's attempts in this direction are useless; for those who believe in this possibility [of spontaneous generation] he will never be able to prove their impossibility by these experiments alone. . . ."[13]

Secular Humanists, Marxists, and Postmodernists must assume the theory of spontaneous generation in spite of its unscientific nature. Science has proven that life only comes from pre-existing life. It has not proven that non-life leads to life. Microbiology professor Michael Behe elaborates, "One of the chief advocates of the theory of spontaneous generation during the

---

[9] Cited in Francis Nigel Lee, *Communism Versus Creation* (Nutley, NJ: The Craig Press, 1969), 68. For a scientific look at the major issues involved in the theory of spontaneous generation, see David Berlinski's "The Origin of Life" *Commentary* magazine, February 2006.

[10] M.V. Volkenshtein, *Biophysics* (Moscow, USSR: Mir Publishers, 1983), 565.

[11] A.J. Oparin, *The Origin of Life* (Moscow, USSR: Foreign Languages Publishing House, 1955), 101.

[12] Karen Arms and Pamela S. Camp, *Biology,* 2nd ed. (New York, NY: CBS College Publishers, 1982), 293. Arms and Camp turn to Oparin and Haldane for confirmation of spontaneous generation: "In 1924 a Russian, Alexander Oparin, published a theory of how life could have arisen from simple molecules on the early earth. An English-man, J.B.S. Haldane, published a paper in 1929 that said essentially the same thing . . . Research since then has largely borne out the predictions made by Oparin and Haldane. Scientists have simulated prebiotic (before life existed) conditions in their laboratories; surprisingly, the nonliving systems formed in these artificial environments exhibit many properties that we consider characteristic of life" (p. 294). Haldane wrote the preface and notes for the 1940 edition of Engels' *Dialectics of Nature*. See Frederick Engels, *Dialectics of Nature* (New York, NY: International Publishers, 1976).

[13] Frederick Engels, *Dialectics of Nature* (New York, NY: International Publishers, 1976), 189.

middle of the nineteenth century was Ernst Haeckel, a great admirer of Darwin and an eager popularizer of Darwin's theory. From the limited view of cells that microscopes provided, Haeckel believed that a cell was a 'simple little lump of albuminous combination of carbon,' not much different from a piece of microscopic gelatin. So it seemed to Haeckel that such simple life, with no internal organs, could be produced easily from inanimate material. Now, of course, we know better."[14]

Marxist faith in spontaneous generation has not wavered for more than a century. But Marxist faith in Darwin's specific version of evolutionary theory of gradualism (evolution of new species by gradual accumulation of small genetic changes over long periods of time) has faltered considerably since Marx and Engels first embraced it.

4.4.5 DARWIN AND DIALECTICS

Darwin's theory of evolution seemed to mesh perfectly with Marx's interpretation of dialectics. Marx writes, "You will see from the conclusion of my third chapter . . . that in the text I regard the law Hegel discovered . . . as holding good both in history and natural science."[15] If nature is dialectical (Hegelian process of change) and Darwin's notion about the mechanism nature employed to create species was correct, then Marx believed Darwin's theory was dialectical.

Darwin's theory of evolution appeared dialectical to early Marxists because it portrayed development as a process. Engels believed that Darwin's "new outlook on nature was complete in its main features; all rigidity was dissolved, all fixity dissipated, all particularity that had been regarded as eternal became transient, the whole of nature was shown as moving in eternal flux and cyclical course."[16] The concept of eternal flux was important for the Marxist worldview, in keeping with Engel's belief: "The world is not to be comprehended as a complex of ready-made things, but as a complex of processes."[17]

Another reason Darwin's theory seemed to reinforce Marx's view of dialectics was that it called for the evolution of the simple to the more complex. Marxist dialectics states that process is always spiraling upward—that the synthesis is always a more advanced stage than the previous thesis. It appeared that Darwin's theory of natural selection relied on the same concept of change—more advanced species evolved that were better suited to live in their environment, nature accumulated the good and disposed of the bad.

At first glance, then, Darwin's theory of evolutionary change appeared to fit perfectly with Marx's notions about dialectics. Closer inspection, however, showed otherwise. Lenin hinted at a problem when he placed Marx's theories separate from and above Darwin's, claiming, "Still, this idea, as formulated by Marx and Engels on the basis of Hegel's philosophy, is far more comprehensive and far richer in content than the current idea of [Darwinian] evolution is."[18] Lenin saw a difference between Darwinian evolution and the dialectic applied to nature.

4.4.6 PUNCTUATED EVOLUTION

As it turns out, Lenin was right. When examined closely, Darwinian evolution—gradual change from species to species—actually works contrary to the dialectical method. According

---

[14] Michael J. Behe, *Darwin's Black Box: The Biochemical Challenge to Evolution* (New York, NY: The Free Press, 1996), 24.

[15] Cited in McFadden, *The Philosophy of Communism*, 36.

[16] Engels, *Dialectics of Nature*, 13.

[17] Frederick Engels, *Ludwig Feuerbach* (New York, NY: International Publishers, 1974), 54.

[18] Lenin, *Collected Works*, 24:54–5.

to dialectical materialism, whenever thesis and antithesis clash, the new synthesis created occurs rapidly, in the form of a sudden jump, rather than a long, gradual process.

Thus, according to this view, both evolution and revolution are necessary in the social sphere to move from a capitalist society to a classless, communist society. The change must occur rapidly, as did the overthrow of the Russian government. When thesis (bourgeoisie) and antithesis (proletariat) clash (through revolution), the resulting synthesis is a necessary leap resulting from the nature and flow of the dialectic. Darwin's theory of slow and gradual natural selection did not match the Marxist requirements of progress—either natural or social.

Darwin's theory emphasized gradual progress as opposed to sudden "leaps in being." Early in the twentieth century, Marxists acknowledged this difference and abandoned Darwin's natural selection theory. But Marxists did not abandon evolution. Plekhanov espoused the new Marxist attitude toward Darwin when he said, "Many people confound dialectic with the theory of evolution. Dialectic is, in fact, a theory of evolution. But it differs profoundly from the vulgar [Darwinian] theory of evolution, which is based substantially upon the principle that neither in nature nor in history do sudden changes occur, and that all changes taking place in the world occur gradually."[19]

> ### The Pop Culture Connection
>
> **X-Men 2** (a 2003 film) expresses a view of punctuated evolution in the closing monologue, as Dr. Jean Grey intones, "Mutation. It is the key to our evolution. It has enabled us to evolve from a single-celled organism into the dominant species on the planet. This process is slow and normally taking thousands and thousands of years. But every few hundred millennia, evolution leaps forward."

Marxists expect evolution to work according to the dialectic: when thesis (a species) and antithesis (some aspect of the environment) clash, the synthesis (a new species) occurs rapidly. In 1972, an evolutionary theory that better fit the dialectical process was postulated: punctuated equilibrium, or punctuated evolution. **Punctuated evolution** allows for jumps, rapid change, and chance. It speaks the language of dialectical materialism. It speaks the language of revolution within evolution.

The evolutionary model of punctuated equilibrium sees biological change "as an episodic process occurring in fits and starts interspaced with long periods of stasis [i.e., lack of change]."[20] New species are said to arise rapidly "in small peripherally isolated populations." Instead of the Darwinian gradualist model of evolution in which new species occur slowly over long periods of time, punctuated equilibrium calls for long periods marked by little change, and then short, isolated periods of rapid change. American scientists most closely associated with this theory are **Stephen Jay Gould**,[21] Richard Levins, Richard Lewontin,[22] Niles Eldredge, and Steven Stanley.

Both Gould and Eldredge agree that their theory of punctuated equilibrium coincides with a Marxist interpretation of biology: "Alternative conceptions of change have respectable pedigrees in philosophy. Hegel's dialectical laws, translated into a materialist context, have become the official

> **PUNCTUATED EVOLUTION:** The theory of evolution that proposes that evolutionary changes occur over a relatively quick period of time, followed by periods of little to no evolutionary change

[19] G. Plekhanov, *Fundamental Problems of Marxism* (London, UK: Lawrence, 1929), 145.

[20] Michael Denton, *Evolution: A Theory in Crisis* (Bethesda, MD: Adler and Adler, 1985), 192–3.

[21] Walter James ReMine, *The Biotic Message: Evolution Versus Message Theory* (St. Paul, MN: St. Paul Science Publishers, 1993), contains a strong refutation of Gould's punctuated equilibrium theory of evolution.

[22] Lewontin's textbook is entitled *The Dialectical Biologist,* published by Harvard University Press.

'state philosophy' of many socialist nations. These laws of change are explicitly punctuational, as befits a theory of revolutionary transformation in human society. In light of this official philosophy, it is not at all surprising that a punctuational view of speciation, much like our own, but devoid (so far as we can tell) of references to synthetic evolutionary theory and the allopatric model, has long been favored by many Russian paleontologists. It may also not be irrelevant to our personal preferences that one of us [Gould] learned his Marxism, literally, at his daddy's knee."[23]

Stephen J. Gould

Marxists are pleased with the theory of punctuated equilibrium and how it affirms their worldview. Volkenshtein uses the fossil record as proof for the veracity of Marxist biology, claiming, "Whereas it was believed earlier that evolution occurs slowly, by way of gradual accumulation of small changes, at present biology takes into account a multitude of facts indicating that macroevolution occurred in a jumpwise manner and was not reduced to microevolution. The absence of transient forms in the paleontological records points, in a number of cases, not to a deficiency but to the absence of such forms. Small changes are often not accumulated at all."[24] Volkenshtein cites other "proofs" for punctuated equilibrium as well, pointing out that "no gradual transition can take place between feathers and hair, etc."[25]

Creationists have cited for years these discrepancies in evolutionary theory. They take on new importance when Marxists use them as "proof" for a new theory of evolution that supports their worldview. Gould explains, "Stasis, or nonchange, of most fossil species during their lengthy geological lifespans was tacitly acknowledged by all paleontologists, but almost never studied explicitly because prevailing theory treated stasis as uninteresting nonevidence for nonevolution… The overwhelming prevalence of stasis became an embarrassing feature of the fossil record, best left ignored as a manifestation of nothing (that is, nonevolution)."[26]

4.4.7 LYSENKO AND MENDEL

Because it more closely aligns with dialectics, Marxists are delighted that punctuated equilibrium is now considered a viable scientific explanation for the origin of the species. Marxists, however, seem willing to embrace virtually any evolutionary idea as long as it fits their worldview and disallows the existence of the supernatural. This pattern can be demonstrated by examining an episode from the era after Marxists became disappointed with the gradualism of Darwin and before punctuated equilibrium theory was postulated.

During World War II, Darwin's notions about struggle for existence and survival of the fittest were unpopular with Marxists, so Marxists attempted to "customize" evolutionary theory so that it would better fit the dialectic. T.D. Lysenko, the leading Soviet biologist from the early 1930s into the 1950s and President of the Academy of Sciences, spearheaded this effort during the height of its prestige (1936–45). Lysenko claimed that **Gregor Mendel**'s discoveries about genetics were inconclusive, declaring, "It is time to eliminate Mendelism in all its varieties

[23] Niles Eldredge and Stephen J. Gould, *Paleobiology*, vol. 3 (Spring 1977): 145–6. Cited in Luther D. Sunderland, *Darwin's Enigma* (Santee, CA: Master Book Publishers, 1988), 108.

[24] Volkenshtein, *Biophysics*, 617.

[25] Ibid., 618.

[26] S. J. Gould, "Cordelia's Dilemma," *Natural History* (February 1993): 15. Cited in ReMine's *The Biotic Message*, 307.

from all courses and textbooks."[27]

With full support from the Marxist government (indeed, most Soviet biologists who disagreed with Lysenko either repented or met untimely deaths), Lysenko began to preach a biology strictly denying Mendel's genetics: "[A]ny little particle, figuratively speaking, any granule, any droplet of a living body, once it is alive, necessarily possesses the property of heredity . . ."[28]

Lysenko's notions about heredity eventually led him to embrace Lamarckism, a theory that states that acquired characteristics can be passed from one generation to the next through heredity. He did not publicly admit his Lamarckian views, however, until it came to light that Stalin, years earlier, had supported neo-Lamarckism. Once it became clear that both Stalin and Lysenko supported some form of Lamarckism, Marxist biology had no choice but to embrace this theory of acquired characteristics. On the surface, Lamarckism did seem to complement Marxist dialectics better because it called for a more consistently progressive view of evolution than Darwin's theory.

Gregor Mendel

Unfortunately for Lysenko and the Marxists, they eventually had to face two facts the rest of the world had accepted long before—Mendel's ideas about genetics were correct, and Lamarck's idea of acquired characteristics was unscientific.

4.4.8 Conclusion

The Marxist interpretation of evolution has undergone a number of changes since Marx first embraced Darwin's theory. These changes demonstrate the willingness of Marxists to revise and distort Dawin's theory of gradualism in an effort to make it more compatible with their dialectic. Marxism attempts to interpret the theory of evolution in a way that supports the dialectic and denies the supernatural.

Regardless of how scientific or unscientific the theory of evolution is, we can be certain of one thing: Marxist biology consistently declares it as factually grounded in science. Evolution provides a basis for both Marxist theology and philosophy, and without this foundation, Marxists are unable to explain the design of our universe and the phenomena of the human mind. As Engels says, "In our evolutionary conception of the universe, there is absolutely no room for either a creator or a ruler."[29]

---

[27] Cited in David Joravsky, *The Lysenko Affair* (Cambridge, MA: Harvard University Press, 1970), 211.
[28] Ibid., 210.
[29] Frederick Engels, *Socialism: Utopian and Scientific* (New York, NY: International Publishers, 1935), 21.

Biology

Cosmic Humanism

Evolution is a light illuminating all facts, a curve that all lines must follow. . . . Man discovers that he is nothing else than evolution become conscious of itself.[1]

— PIERRE TEILHARD DE CHARDIN

4.5.1 INTRODUCTION

Cosmic Humanist biology is based on a belief in positive evolutionary change over time. This approach does not focus on biological change as much as it emphasizes humanity moving upward toward an age of higher consciousness. Cosmic Humanists believe that everything is ultimately energy that will allow people to achieve unity with others in a kind of *collective consciousness*.

Collective consciousness means that the "ultimate end of the individual is to expand into the universal oneness, which really means that the individual disappears as a separate person."[2] Cosmic Humanism postulates an evolutionary theory that allows for not only individual but also collective development. Marilyn Ferguson writes, "The proven plasticity of the human brain and human awareness offers the possibility that individual evolution may lead to collective evolution. When one person has unlocked a new capacity its existence is suddenly evident to others, who may then develop the same capacity."[3]

---

[1] Pierre Teilhard de Chardin, *The Phenomenon of Man* (New York, NY: Harper and Row, 1955), 219, 221.

[2] Dean C. Halverson, *Crystal Clear: Understanding and Reaching New Agers* (Colorado Springs, CO: NavPress, 1990), 77.

[3] Marilyn Ferguson, *The Aquarian Conspiracy* (Los Angeles, CA: J.P. Tarcher, 1980), 70.

Not everyone will evolve at an even rate toward higher consciousness; rather, when enough people achieve higher consciousness, others will be absorbed (or evolved) into the enlightened collective consciousness. Thus, all people need not embrace the New Age movement before it can

> COSMIC EVOLUTION: The progression of collective humanity toward an age of higher consciousness

become a reality—dedicated Cosmic Humanists can simply act as the catalyst for an evolutionary leap into utopia. We label this approach "**Cosmic Evolution**."

4.5.2 THE EVOLUTION OF SCIENCE

Cosmic Humanists also hold a unique view of science. While Christians see the scientific method as a way of discovering God's design of the universe and Secular Humanists view science as a means for understanding the mechanics of the natural world, Cosmic Humanists believe the traditional view of science as learning to control the laws of nature has led to an assault on the balance of planetary harmony. According to William Thompson, "The conscious purpose of science is control of Nature; its unconscious effect is disruption and chaos. The emergence of a scientific culture stimulates the destruction of nature, of the biosphere of relationships among plants, animals, and humans that we have called 'Nature.'"[4] As a result, Cosmic Humanists believe the planet is in deep trouble.

Thompson and other Cosmic Humanists believe the scientific revolution that developed during the 1600s was responsible for the raping of the planet. The predominant idea of scientists such as Isaac Newton was "a description of predictable mechanical forces."[5] Marilyn Ferguson writes that this approach to science "would finally explain everything in terms of trajectories, gravity, force. It would close in on the final secrets of a 'clockwork universe.'"[6]

But this understanding of the world in terms of mechanical laws was limited in what it could accomplish and set the stage for the next development in science. New Age popularizer James Redfield introduces this theme in his best-selling novel *The Celestine Prophecy*. The main character in the story is given a short lesson in the history of science by a physics professor, who explains, "The idea was to create an understanding of the universe that makes the world seem safe and manageable . . ."

But in the early part of the twentieth century, this attitude among scientists changed. According to Redfield's fictional professor, the change occurred when two investigations "opened our eyes again to the mystery in the universe . . . those of quantum mechanics and those of Albert Einstein. The whole of Einstein's life's work was to show that what we perceive as hard matter is mostly empty space with a pattern of energy running through it. This includes ourselves. And what quantum physics has shown is that . . . when you break apart small aspects of this energy . . . the act of observation itself alters the results—as if these elementary particles are influenced by what the experimenter expects. . . . In other words, the basic stuff of the universe, at its core, is looking like a kind of pure energy that is malleable to human intention and expectation in a way that defies our old mechanistic model of the universe. . . ."[7]

Ferguson explains the shift in how science is interpreted: "Our understanding of nature shifted from a clockwork paradigm to an uncertainty paradigm, from the absolute to the relative."[8] In this way, Cosmic Humanists claim that the latest scientific investigations support pantheistic theology and non-naturalistic philosophy.

---

[4] William Irwin Thompson, "Nine Theses for a Gaia Politique," *Sustainable Habitat* (IC#14) (Autumn 1986): 58, which can be found at http://www.context.org/ICLIB/IC14/Thompson.htm.

[5] Ferguson, *The Aquarian Conspiracy*, 26–27.

[6] Ibid., 26.

[7] James Redfield, *The Celestine Prophecy* (New York, NY: Warner Books, 1993), 41–2.

[8] Ferguson, *The Aquarian Conspiracy*, 27.

4.5.3 THE NEXT EVOLUTIONARY STEP

This new view of science also provides insights into the next stage of evolution. The evolutionary change Cosmic Humanists focus on is primarily that of ourselves and humanity as a whole. Speaking of this change, David Spangler states, "In this [evolutionary] context, civilizations, like individuals, go through profound changes from time to time which represent discontinuities; that is, a jump or shift is made from one evolutionary condition to another. The New Age is such a shift."[9] Spangler is not speaking as a Secular Humanist, who views evolutionary change as a blind force of nature acting upon living organisms, and humanity as simply a part of the natural universe. Instead, Spangler uses evolution as a change in the flow of cosmic energy, resulting not in a higher form of life, but in a higher consciousness among humanity.

Cosmic Humanists believe an elite, enlightened portion of the human race will jump into this New Age as an evolutionary leap, taking the rest of humanity with it. Ferguson agrees that the New Age "requires a mechanism for biological change more powerful than chance mutation." What is necessary is the "possibility of rapid evolution in our own time, when the equilibrium of the species is punctuated by stress. Stress in modern society is experienced at the frontiers of our psychological rather than our geographical limits."[10] Ferguson uses the terms of naturalistic punctuated equilibrium, but gives these terms a New Age meaning. She is committed to the unseen cosmic force that permeates everything and here, like Spangler, she describes the rapid change of perspective that Cosmic Humanists believe will engulf humanity.

Instead of further human physical evolution determined by geography, environment, and natural selection, Cosmic Humanists believe evolution is psychological. This psychological evolution guides humanity to a higher social order—"a New One-World Order."[11]

What will we be like after the evolutionary leap into the New Age occurs? Armand Biteaux explains, "Every man is an individual Christ; this is the teaching for the New Age . . . Everyone will receive the benefit of this step in human evolution."[12]

In the New Age, Cosmic Humanists believe, we will all achieve higher consciousness or godhood. "The final appearance of the Christ will not be a man in the air before whom all must kneel," says John White. "The final appearance of the Christ will be an evolutionary event. It will be the disappearance of egocentric, subhuman man and the ascension of God-centered Man. A new race, a new species, will inhabit the Earth—people who collectively have the stature of consciousness that Jesus had."[13] Once collective higher consciousness is achieved, humanity will be at one with itself in collective godhood.

Pierre Teilhard
de Chardin

Much of the basis for Cosmic Humanist belief rests on the writings of **Pierre Teilhard de Chardin**, a paleontologist who worked to reconcile Christianity and evolution. He accomplished this reconciliation by replacing Christianity with pantheism. Teilhard believed in "a very real 'pantheism' if you like, but an absolutely legitimate pantheism."[14] Peter Russell believes, "Evolutionary trends and patterns . . . suggest a further possibility: the emergence of something beyond a single

---

[9] David Spangler, *Emergence: The Rebirth of the Sacred* (New York, NY: Delta/Merloyd Lawrence, 1984), 18.

[10] Ferguson, *The Aquarian Conspiracy*, 70.

[11] Randall N. Baer, *Inside the New Age Nightmare* (Lafayette, LA: Huntington House, 1989), 47.

[12] Armand Biteaux, *The New Consciousness* (Minneapolis, MN: The Oliver Press, 1975), 128.

[13] John White, "The Second Coming," *New Frontier Magazine*, December 1987, 45.

[14] de Chardin, *The Phenomenon of Man*, 310.

planetary consciousness or Supermind: a completely new level of evolution, as different from consciousness as consciousness is from life, and life is from matter."[15] If planetary consciousness is not attainable, however, most Cosmic Humanists are willing to settle for achieving individual divinity.

4.5.4 THE GAIA HYPOTHESIS

Another aspect of Cosmic Humanist biology is called the **Gaia Hypothesis**. The public was introduced to the Gaia Hypothesis in 1979 with the publication of James E. Lovelock's *Gaia: A New Look at Life on Earth*. His thesis was that "taken as a whole, the planet behaves not as an inanimate sphere of rock and soil . . . but more as a biological superorganism—a planetary body—that adjusts and regulates itself."[16]

The idea that all living things and planetary systems comprise a symbiotic global network is a radical departure from orthodox evolutionary thought since it undermines the central Darwinian tenet of survival of the fittest. Instead of competition and struggle for survival, the Gaia Hypothesis emphasizes the cooperative spirit of the entire biosphere. Lovelock suggests that the earth is not a "dead" habitat that happens to support life, but is itself a living, integrated system of soil, oceans, wind, and living things working together in harmony for the good of the whole.

The Gaia Hypothesis visualizes the planet as a self-regulating system, implying a purpose behind it all. This, too, runs counter to Darwinian evolution's insistence that life is a result of chance rather than purpose.

Loveland drew the name "Gaia" from the ancient Greek goddess of the earth. Although he considers himself a "positive agnostic" and has tried to distance his theory from any religious connotations, Cosmic Humanists immediately promoted the theory as the scientific basis for their worldview. The idea that the planet is a living system fits hand-in-glove with New Age theological pantheism and philosophical non-naturalism.

> **GAIA HYPOTHESIS:** The theory that all living organisms form a single and complex living organism

Gaia is also the foundation for the modern ecological movement, as well as the more radical offshoots of *deep ecology* and *ecofeminism*. Many ecologists point out that since we are seeing signs of ecological imbalance, we should listen to our Mother (Earth) and change our ways. Saving the planet is more than a moral imperative—it is our destiny.

4.5.5 CONCLUSION

Biology provides a generous guarantee for the Cosmic Humanist—leaps in being for all humanity, and the universe itself, to the status of godhood. The Garden of Eden is not a real place in the past where Adam and Eve committed the original sin; rather, the Garden is in our present and our future. Mythologist Joseph Campbell teaches that we are living in Eden today and are evolving toward the increasing awareness that we reside in paradise.

This view of evolution provides comfort for the Cosmic Humanist, largely because it promises a shared future divinity. Further, it solves the sin problem (greed, envy, gossip, slander) by denying the reality of the fall or the inherent sinfulness of human nature.

---

[15] Peter Russell, *The Global Brain* (Los Angeles, CA: J.P. Tarcher, 1983), 99.

[16] Cited in John P. Newport, *The New Age Movement and the Biblical Worldview* (Grand Rapids, MI: Eerdmans, 1998), 287.

Campbell's idea that we are now living in paradise (as opposed to a future perfected world) is problematic in light of the wars of the twentieth century and the catastrophic and unprecedented events we have experienced in the opening years of the twenty-first century. Although we have no way of knowing how he would respond to the tragic events of this century, to those of the last century he said, "That is the way it feels, but this is it, this is Eden." We need, he says, to "see not the world of solid things but a world of radiance."[17]

The Pop Culture Connection

"With wit, smarts and hope," trumpets the film's website, *An Inconvenient Truth* (2006), "ultimately brings home [Al] Gore's persuasive argument that we can no longer afford to view global warming as a political issue[;] rather, it is the biggest moral challenge facing our global civilization." However, according to UPI science writer, Hil Anderson, "the Washington lobbying machine isn't taking this cinematic exercise lying down. News releases from various think tanks have begun flying around that pan the movie not so much for its cinematic merits, but rather for giving credibility to global warming. 'The complexity of the climate and the limitations of data and computer models mean all projections of future climate change are unreliable at best,' wrote David Legates, director of the University of Delaware's Center for Climatic Research and author of a new study on global warming for the National Center for Policy Analysis . . . 'The campaign to limit carbon dioxide emissions is the single most important regulatory issue today,' summed up CEI Senior Fellow Marlow Lewis. 'It is nothing short of an attempt to suppress energy use, which in turn would be economically devastating—all to avert an alleged catastrophe whose scientific basis is dubious.' Critics of global warming argue that modest increases of a degree or two may constitute a change in the climate, but hardly one that will KO the world as we know it."*

---

[17] Joseph Campbell, *The Power of Myth* (New York, NY: Doubleday, 1988), 230.

* Hil Anderson, "Gore churns up warming debate," May 16, 2006, http://news.monstersandcritics.com / northamerica/article_1164438.php/Analysis_Gore_churns_up_warming_debate)

Biology

Postmodernism

Biology can tell us little. . . . Selfhood is really
nothing but a fleeting, unstable, incomplete and open-
ended mess of desires which cannot be fulfilled.[1]

— Jacques Lacan

[John] Dewey's idea is that we are special because we
can take charge of our own evolution, take ourselves
in directions which have neither precedent nor
justification in either biology or history.[2]

— Richard Rorty

Science and philosophy must jettison their grandiose
metaphysical claims and view themselves more modestly
as just another set of narratives.[3]

— Terry Eagleton

---

[1] Glenn Ward, *Postmodernism* (Chicago, IL: McGraw-Hill Companies, 2003), 148–9.

[2] Robert B. Brandom, ed., *Rorty and his Critics* (Oxford, UK: Blackwell Publishers, 2001), 3.

[3] Terry Eagleton, "Awakening from Modernity," *Times Literary Supplement* (20 February 1987): 194. Cited in Stanley J. Grenz, *A Primer on Postmodernism* (Grand Rapids, MI: Eerdmans, 1996), 48.

4.6.1 INTRODUCTION

Worldviews that deny the existence of a Creator, a creation event, and the supernatural must assume some form of naturalistic evolution to explain the origin of life. Evolutionary theory takes three forms:

1. Classical Darwinism theorizes a gradual process of changes in species by means of natural selection[4] or survival of the fittest,[5] Charles Darwin's original thesis.
2. Neo-Darwinism came into vogue in the 1930s, expanding Darwin's original theory of natural selection to include change by genetic mutation.
3. Punctuated equilibrium or punctuated evolution arose in the 1970s, theorizing that evolutionary change happens abruptly (geologically speaking) in small, isolated populations.[6]

While Secular Humanists believe and defend neo-Darwinism and Marxist/Leninists and Cosmic Humanists defend punctuated evolution (although not in exactly the same sense), Postmodernists have a tendency to shy away from overtly endorsing any particular theory of origins. This is the case, first of all, because Postmodernism began, not among scientists, but among literary critics and philosophers. Second, each of the three aforementioned versions of evolutionary theory is in itself a *grand story* about the origin and development of life and Postmodernists eschew all such grand stories or *metanarratives*.

To illustrate this state of affairs, Christian author Nancy Pearcey relates the following firsthand experience: "I witnessed a fascinating altercation at a conference at Boston University on science and postmodernism several years ago. Postmodernist philosophers led off by arguing that 'there are no metanarratives,' meaning no overarching, universal truths. Responding on behalf of the scientists was Nobel Prize-winning physicist Steven Weinberg, who replied: But of course there are metanarratives. After all, there's evolution—a vast metanarrative from the Big Bang to the origin of the solar system to the origin of human life. And since evolution is true, that proves there is at least *one* metanarrative. . . . To which the postmodernist philosophers responded, ever so politely: That's just *your* metanarrative. Evolution is merely a social construct, they said, like every other intellectual schema—a creation of the human mind."[7]

> That's just your metanarrative. Evolution is merely a social construct, they said, like every other intellectual schema—a creation of the human mind.

---

[4] Norman Macbeth, *Darwin Retried: An Appeal to Reason* (Boston, MA: The Harvard Common Press, 1971), 40: "Darwin never tried to define natural selection in a rigid way . . . It amounted to little more than the fact that, for various reasons, among all the individuals produced in nature some die soon and some die late. Thus natural selection for Darwin was differential mortality."

[5] Ibid., 62, "The phrase 'survival of the fittest' was not coined by Darwin. He took it over from Herbert Spencer, apparently considering it an improvement on his own natural selection. It immediately became an integral part of classical Darwinism, much to the embarrassment of modern adherents . . . a species survives because it is the fittest and is the fittest because it survives, which is circular reasoning."

[6] Walter James ReMine, *The Biotic Message: Evolution Versus Message Theory* (St. Paul, MN: St. Paul Science Publishers, 1993), 326: "Punctuated equilibria is an evolutionary theory proposed in 1972 by paleontologists Stephen Jay Gould and Niles Eldredge (and soon joined by Stephen Stanley). The theory says species are typically not evolving. Rather, species are in stasis most of their existence, a state of unchanging equilibrium. The equilibrium is punctuated occasionally by short events of rapid evolution. Most evolution is said to occur speedily during these brief punctuation events."

[7] Nancy Pearcey, *Total Truth: Liberating Christianity from Its Cultural Captivity* (Wheaton, IL: Crossway Books, 2004), 114.

4.6.2 SCIENCE AND KNOWLEDGE

Postmodernism is anti-science in many respects. Some Postmodernists argue that science is not really knowledge at all. Instead, they speak in terms of chaos theory, the unpredictability of science, indeterminacy, or uncertainty of evolution/devolution, etc. For instance, Paul Feyerabend, former philosophy professor at the University of California (Berkeley) maintains that what is called science in one culture is called voodoo in another: "To those who look at the rich material provided by history, and who are not intent on impoverishing it in order to please their lower instincts—their craving for intellectual security in the form of clarity, precision, 'objectivity,' [or]'truth'—it will become clear that there is only one principle that can be defended under all circumstances and in all stages of human development. It is the principle: anything goes."[8]

In his article "Anything Goes," Feyerabend further explains how science works. In the history of science many theories have arisen, been accepted as established, promoted as *the truth*, and then eventually discarded. When a scientist promotes scientific data in support of a theory, that bit of data is anything but neutral because the scientist has an agenda. In all fields of science questions remain open as scientific theories are regularly tweaked. And to top it off, the scientific establishment is very much politicized.[9] Thus, scientists regularly work with unproven assumptions and filter all data through their preconceived ideas.

Doubts about the objectivity and neutrality of science arose in the mid-

---

The Pop Culture Connection

"What do Christianity, Zen, and formal mathematical logic have in common? If you look closely, **The Matrix: Reloaded** will tell you. . . . Structurally, the mythology of *The Matrix* is patterned directly after a . . . mathematical logic known as the *Incompleteness Theorem*, first discovered by the Austrian logician Kurt Gödel in the early 1930s. . . . This means, in essence, that there are truths that exist within a system that are not provable using the rules of that system. . .

At heart an elaborate computer program, the Matrix is itself nothing more than another formal system. . . . As a formal system, it too is limited by Gödel's finding. The existence of the One is thus explained. . . . As the Architect explains to Neo at the end of *Reloaded*:

Your life is the sum of the remainder of an unbalanced equation inherent to the programming of the Matrix. You are the eventuality of an anomaly which is systemic, creating fluctuations in even the most simplistic equations.

Neo is a destabilizing anomaly inherent to every conceivable Matrix: he is the Gödel Sentence itself. . . . [and his] incorporation is accomplished by . . . "return[ing] to the source." This renews the Matrix and saves it from the instability introduced by his arrival. This is not a permanent fix, however, for the new version of the Matrix is susceptible to its own version of the Gödel Sentence, which will ultimately lead to the birth of yet another One and a continuing cycle of death-and-rebirth of the system, presumably ad infinitum. According to the Architect, the trilogy takes place during the fifth repetition of that cycle."*

---

[8] Paul Feyerabend, "Anything Goes," in Walter Truett Anderson, ed., *The Truth About The Truth* (New York, NY. Tarcher/Putnam Publishers, 1995), 199–200.

[9] To understand how much of science has become politicized, see Tom Bethel's *The Politically Incorrect Guide to Science* (Washington, DC: Regnery Publishing, 2005).

* *The Matrix: Reloaded, Jesus, Buddha, and Gödel: Unraveling the Matrix Mythos*, by Eric Furze, http://metaphilm.com/philm.php?id=169_0_2_0.

Thomas Kuhn

1900s from Michael Polanyi's *Personal Knowledge* [10] and **Thomas Kuhn**'s *The Structure of Scientific Revolution.* [11] Kuhn, for example, points out that science is not merely a progressive and incremental discipline that studies and records facts. So-called *facts* can be understood and interpreted in a variety of ways depending on the worldview assumptions of the scientist. [12]

In addition, Kuhn asserts that scientific theories, or paradigms, do not often fall out of favor because they are proven wrong. Rather, older theories tend to die out along with their proponents, while new and creative theories attract the attention of younger scientists who, in turn, promote their theories over the older ones. [13] A current scientific theory is just that: a *current* theory, which will be replaced by another *current* theory in the future. For that reason, science cannot tell us what is *real*, only what scientists believe to be the case at that particular time in history. This falls in line with the Postmodern concept that everyone, including the scientist, is locked into his or her particular culture and language, and thus cannot claim to have an objective picture of the world.

Even mathematics is not immune from Postmodern analysis. Doubts about the objectivity of math were brought to light with Douglas R. Hofstadter's Pulitzer prize winning book *Gödel, Escher, Bach: An Eternal Golden Braid,* published in 1979. [14] This theme has been developed in other works. In *Ethnomathematics: A Multicultural View of Mathematical Ideas,* Marcia Ascher asserts that much of mathematics education depends upon assumptions of Western culture. For example, she writes that no other culture "need share the categories triangle, right triangle, hypotenuse of a right triangle . . ." She further questions, "Is a square something that has external reality or is it something only in our minds?" [15]

However, even in light of the Postmodernist aversion to metanarratives and doubts about science being able to describe the *real* world, when pressed for an explanation concerning the origin of life Postmodernists will assume anything *but* creationism! For this reason, Postmodernists embrace the only other alternative—one of the several forms of evolution.

4.6.3 POSTMODERN LEANINGS: NEO-DARWINISM TO PUNCTUATED EVOLUTION

Regarding the origin of life, some Postmodernists tend toward neo-Darwinism. For example, Richard Rorty endorses Daniel Dennett's book *Darwin's Dangerous Idea*, a book supporting the neo-Darwinian view and harshly criticizing Gould and Eldridge's theory of punctuated evolution. Postmodern political scientist Walter Truett Anderson's *The Next Enlightenment: Integrating East and West in a New Vision of Human Evolution* approvingly cites neo-Darwinist Richard Dawkins a number of times as representing a scientific rationalist approach to truth.

[10] Michael Polanyi, *Personal Knowledge: Towards a Post-Critical Philosophy* (Chicago, IL: University of Chicago Press, 1974).

[11] Thomas S. Kuhn, *The Structure of Scientific Revolutions,* 3rd ed. (1962; Chicago, IL: University of Chicago Press, 1996).

[12] Millard J. Erickson, *Truth or Consequences: The Promise & Perils of Postmodernism* (Downers Grove, IL: InterVarsity Press, 2001), 106–7.

[13] Kuhn, *The Structure of Scientific Revolutions*, 16–19.

[14] Douglas R. Hofstadter, *Gödel, Escher, Bach: An Eternal Golden Braid*, 20th anniversary ed. (1979; New York, NY: Basic Books, 1999).

[15] Marcia Ascher, *Ethnomathematics: A Multicultural View of Mathematical Ideas* (Belmont, CA: Wadsworth, 1991), 193.

Postmodernists are drawn to evolution for at least two reasons: (1) they deny that humans are the necessary aim of evolution and (2) they believe chance is the primary catalyst of evolution. According to Michel Foucault, Hayden White, Paul deMan, and Thomas Kuhn, the notion that human beings are the *telos* or ultimate end of evolution is anthropocentric (it assumes humanity is special). Neo-Darwinist Daniel Dennett concurs. In *Darwin's Dangerous Idea*, Dennett writes of "the most common misunderstanding of Darwinism: the idea that Darwin showed that evolution by natural selection is a procedure for *producing* Us."[16]

Three reasons are generally given for holding this view. First, modern science has shattered the early religious myths of Adam and Eve, so we can no longer believe that God created humanity for some special purpose. Second, scientists already are at work evolving the next generation of humans by integrating people and computer technology, thus rendering human existence simply one small step in the total evolutionary progression. Third, considering all the species that have ever lived, *homo sapiens* is considered an insignificant species. Stephen Gould, for example, argues that "bacteria are—and always have been—the dominant form of life on Earth."[17] Therefore, Gould maintains that we are arrogant in thinking that we are a special species or that evolution somehow had humanity in mind, since there are so few of "Us" and so many of "them."[18]

In addition to this anti-teleological stance, Tony Jackson explains why the idea of chance appeals to Postmodernists. He writes about the role Stephen Gould has played in this regard. "To complete our discussion of Darwinian theory, Gould's inclusion of chance makes him the most Postmodern of contemporary Darwinists. It has led him to put forth a theory of change, called punctuated equilibrium, that stresses abruptness and discontinuity

> We are a special species or that evolution somehow had humanity in mind, since there are so few of "Us" and so many of "them" (bacteria).

rather than the more conventional gradualist story, and thus he is the Darwinian equivalent of, again, Thomas Kuhn and Michel Foucault. Kuhn, like Gould, holds that the actual historical record does not support a gradualist 'development-by-accumulation' story."[19]

Kuhn, Gould, and others insist that a gradualist history of the past is merely arbitrary. The actual fossil record does not confirm one species gradually turning into another species. On the contrary, species seem to appear in the fossil record suddenly, with little evidence of gradual transitions from one to another. Therefore, some Postmodernists opt to embrace the theory of punctuated equilibrium (or punctuated evolution) developed by Niles Eldredge and Stephen Jay Gould. (This theory is described in detail in the biology section on Marxist/Leninism.)

4.6.4 FOUCAULT'S HOPEFUL MONSTER

Also leaning toward a view of punctuated evolution is Michel Foucault. Foucault likewise denies that nature manifests the continuity necessary for Darwin's gradualist theory of evolution. He says, "Experience does not reveal the continuity of nature as such, but gives it to us both

---

[16] Daniel Dennett, *Darwin's Dangerous Idea* (New York, NY: Touchstone, 1996), 56, italics and capitalization in original.

[17] See Google (search engine), Stephen Jay Gould Archive, "Planet of the Bacteria."

[18] Gould's assertion runs counter to Darwin's claim that humanity "stands at the very summit of the organic scale." See Charles Darwin, *The Descent of Man and Selection in Relation to Sex* (New York, NY: Collier, 1902), 797, quoted in Tony E. Jackson, "Charles and the hopeful monster: postmodern evolutionary theory in 'The French Lieutenant's Woman,'" in *Twentieth Century Literature* (Summer 1997), available online at http://www.findarticles.com/p/articles/mi_m0403/is_n2_v43/ai_20563363.

[19] Jackson, "Charles and the hopeful monster."

broken up . . . and blurred, since the real, geographic and terrestrial space in which we find ourselves confronts us with creatures that are interwoven with one another, in an order which is . . . nothing more than chance, disorder, or turbulence."[20] Rather than a continuous progression from simple elements (minerals), through plants, animals, and finally human beings, Foucault sees "a confused mingling of beings that seem to have been brought together by chance."[21]

Foucault settles for a discontinuity of nature and argues for "revolutions in the history of the earth" including "geological catastrophes."[22] The elements of nature that he believes brought about the various species include the earth's relationship to the sun, climatic conditions, movements of the earth's crust, floods,[23] comets, oceans, volcanoes, and heat.

Another possibility proposed for the advent of new species is monsters. Foucault approvingly quotes J. B. Robinet to the effect that monsters are not of a different nature, but rather "we should believe that the most apparently bizarre forms . . . belong necessarily and essentially to the universal plan of being; that they are metamorphoses of the prototype just as natural as the others, even though they present us with different phenomena; that they serve as [a] means of passing to adjacent forms; that they prepare and bring about the combinations that follow them, just as they themselves were brought about by those that preceded them; that far from disturbing the order of things, they contribute to it. It is only, perhaps, by dint of producing monstrous beings that nature succeeds in producing beings of greater regularity and with a more symmetrical structure."[24] While this theory may be imaginative, it has no grounding in observable science.

4.6.5 CONCLUSION

Christians need not agree with the extreme conclusion that contemporary Postmodernists derive from Kuhn's theories of indeterminacy. Although Christians acknowledge that scientists do have biases and presuppositions, we also assert that true knowledge about reality is possible. Philosopher J.P. Moreland explains the Christian position this way: "Science (at least as most scientists and philosophers understand it) assumes that the universe is intelligible and not capricious, that the mind and senses inform us about reality, that mathematics and language can be applied to the world, that knowledge is possible, that there is a uniformity in nature that justifies inductive inferences from the past to the future and from examined cases of, say, electrons, to unexamined cases, and so forth."[25]

Saying much the same thing is Secular Humanist Paul Kurtz. In *Humanist Manifesto 2000,* Kurtz insists that rejecting objectivity is a mistake and that Postmodernism is counterproductive, even nihilistic. Kurtz writes, "Science does offer reasonably objective standards for judging its truth claims. Indeed, science has become a universal language, speaking to all men and women no matter what their cultural backgrounds."[26]

Along the same lines, Lee Campbell, chair of the Division of Natural Sciences at Ohio Dominican College, writes, "The methods used in the sciences have produced powerful explanations about how things work and innumerable useful applications, including technology

---

[20] Michel Foucault, *The Order of Things: An Archaeology of the Human Sciences* (New York, NY: Vintage Books, 1994), 147–8.

[21] Ibid., 148.

[22] Ibid., 155.

[23] Foucault does not deny the Genesis flood. See Ibid., 38, 149.

[24] Ibid., 155.

[25] J.P. Moreland, *Christianity and the Nature of Science: A Philosophical Investigation* (Grand Rapids, MI: Baker Book House, 1989), 45.

[26] Paul Kurtz, *Humanist Manifesto 2000: A Call for A New Planetary Humanism* (Amherst, NY: Prometheus Books, 2000), 22.

even its harshest critics would never be without."[27] Indeed, Postmodernists use all the comforts and conveniences that modern science and technology provide, yet at the same time deny the foundational premises on which science is established. This brings to light the contradictions within the Postmodern worldview and reveals it to be unreliable.

In contrast with Postmodernism's failed approach to science, history confirms the reality and progressive reliability of the scientific method. In fact, modern science came about because of a biblical view of reality. Campbell writes, "The rise of modern science would have been impossible without Christian presuppositions that the universe is rational because it was created by a rational God."[28]

In his book *For the Glory of God*, Rodney Stark details why Christianity (rather than Islam, Cosmic Humanism, or any of the atheistic Humanisms) is the worldview most responsible for modern science.[29] Indeed, the father of modern science, Sir Francis Bacon, was a Christian, as were many of the leading scientists who founded the disciplines of chemistry, paleontology, bacteriology, antiseptic surgery, genetics, thermodynamics, computer science, and many other fields.[30]

---

[27] Lee Campbell, "Postmodern Impact: Science," in Dennis McCallum, ed., *The Death of Truth*, (Minneapolis, MN: Bethany House, 1996), 193.

[28] Ibid.

[29] See Rodney Stark, *For the Glory of God* (Princeton, NJ: Princeton University Press, 2003).

[30] For a detailed list, see "The Worlds Greatest Creation Scientists: From Y1K to Y2K" at http://creationsafaris. com/wgcs_toc.htm.

Psychology

Christianity

"He breathed into his nostrils the breath of life and
man became a living soul."

GENESIS 2:7

5.1.1 INTRODUCTION

Christian psychology may appear at first glance to be a
contradiction in terms. Especially after you have examined
Marxist, Humanist, and Postmodern psychologies and
touched on still other theories of *secular* psychology, you
may be tempted to conclude that psychology is a discipline
unworthy of your attention. **William Kirk Kilpatrick** boldly
declares, "If you're talking about Christianity, it is much
truer to say that psychology and religion are competing
faiths. If you seriously hold to one set of values, you will
logically have to reject the other."[1]

William Kirk
Kilpatrick

What Kilpatrick says is true. But when he uses the term
psychology, he is referring specifically to secular psychology. He can make this generalization
because the secular schools of psychology (based on the work of Sigmund Freud,[2] B.F. Skinner,

---

[1] William Kirk Kilpatrick, *Psychological Seduction* (Nashville, TN: Thomas Nelson, 1983), 14.
[2] For a full discussion of Freud's psychology, see Armand M. Nicholi, Jr., *The Question of God: C. S. Lewis and Sigmund Freud Debate God, Love, Sex, and the Meaning of Life* (New York, NY: The Free Press, 2002). This work is the substance of a course at Harvard University under Dr. Armand M. Nicholi, Jr. in which he contrasts the

I.P. Pavlov, Carl Rogers, Abraham Maslow, Erich Fromm, and Jacques Lacan) comprise virtually all of modern psychology.

Just because so many falsehoods flourish in the realm of psychology (for example, that human beings are merely physical animals with no vital essence, soul, or spirit or that *mind* is merely another name for the physical brain) does not mean Christians should abandon it. Instead, Christians must bring God's truth to a deceived discipline. Psychology, true to its origin (Greek "psyche"), is the study of the soul—and no worldview other than Christianity has truer insight into the spiritual realm. As Kilpatrick says, "In short, although Christianity is more than a psychology, it happens to be better psychology than psychology is."[3]

Christianity and psychology are compatible for the simple reason that the Biblical Christian worldview contains a psychology. As Charles L. Allen aptly points out, "The very essence of religion is to adjust the mind and soul of man. . . . Healing means bringing the person into a right relationship with the physical, mental and spiritual laws of God."[4] Men and women created "in the image of God" (Genesis 1:27) require a worldview that recognizes the significance of the spiritual. Christianity maintains that God is a person, and that our personhood is somehow related to His person. Plantinga puts it this way: "How should we think about human persons? What sorts of things, fundamentally, are they? What is it to be a human, and what is it to be a human person, and how should we think about personhood? . . . The first point to note is that in the Christian scheme of things, God is the premier person, the first and chief exemplar of personhood . . . and the properties most important for an understanding of our personhood are properties we share with him."[5] In other words, as Moreland and Rae say, "There is something about the way God is that is like the way we are."[6]

It stands to reason that God's magnificent creation required thinking, planning, artistry, and execution—all qualities that men and women share with their Creator. As God reveals more of Himself apart from the creative order (general revelation) and into the redemptive order (special revelation), we find a Person with personality, love, mercy, and grace—again, qualities that are shared in limited quantities with the human race.

5.1.2 THE SOUL

Christianity acknowledges the existence of the supernatural, including a consciousness within us that is more than an **epiphenomenon** of the brain. The Bible's statements regarding body, breath of life, soul, spirit, heart, and mind suggest a dualist ontology (or study of *being*),[7] that is, the view that human nature consists of two fundamental kinds of reality: physical (material or natural) and spiritual (supernatural). Christ's statement about fearing the one who could put "both soul and body" in hell (Matthew 10:28) and Paul's statement regarding body, soul, and spirit (1 Thessalonians 5:23) enforce the distinction

> **EPIPHENOMENON:** A secondary phenomenon that results from and accompanies another, e.g., a shadow

---

worldview of C. S. Lewis with that of Sigmund Freud.

[3] Kilpatrick, *Psychological Seduction*, 15–16.

[4] Charles L. Allen, *God's Psychiatry* (Westwood, NJ: Revell, 1953), 7 (italics added).

[5] Alvin Plantinga, "Advice to Christian Philosophers," *Faith and Philosophy* 1 (July 1984): 264–5. Cited in J.P. Moreland and Scott B. Rae, *Body & Soul: Human Nature & the Crisis in Ethics* (Downers Grove, IL: InterVarsity Press, 2000), 24.

[6] Moreland and Rae, *Body & Soul*, 158.

[7] J.P. Moreland and William Lane Craig, *Philosophical Foundations for a Christian Worldview* (Downers Grove, IL: InterVarsity Press, 2003), 175: "General ontology is the most basic of metaphysics, and there are three main tasks that make up this branch of metaphysical study. First, general ontology focuses on the nature of existence itself. What is it to be or to exist? Is existence a property that something has? Etc."

between our material and spiritual qualities. The Bible does not deny body; it simply says that we are more than just a physical body.

Sir John Eccles, one of the world's most respected neuro-physiologists, believes **mind and body dualism** is the only explanation for many of the phenomena of consciousness. One of the reasons Eccles reaches this conclusion is the individual's "unity of identity." Paul Weiss explains, "[E]ven though I know I am constantly changing—all molecules are changing, everything in me is being turned over substantially—there is nevertheless my identity, my consciousness of being essentially the same that I was 20 years ago. However much I may have changed, the continuity of my identity has remained undisrupted."[8]

> **MIND/BODY DUALISM:** The belief that the mind and the body exist as separate entities, i.e. the mind is not mere matter

The point is that because the physical substance of the brain is constantly changing, no unity of identity could exist if consciousness were a condition wholly dependent on the physical brain. Something more than the physical brain—something spiritual or supernatural—must exist.

Human memory is another facet of the unity-of-identity argument that supports the existence of a supernatural soul, heart, or mind. Arthur Custance writes, "What research has shown thus far is that there is no precise one-to-one relationship between any fragment of memory and the nerve cells in which it is supposed to be encoded."[9]

Without any concept of soul, the Humanist, Marxist, and Postmodernist have difficulty explaining unity of identity and memory. Still another problem you will learn about in the chapters to come is how the materialist position accounts for free will. Only a worldview that postulates something other than the environment manipulating the human physical machine can account for free will. Christian dualism provides a better foundation for psychology because it defends the integrity of our mind and our free will.

5.1.3 FALLEN HUMAN NATURE

A proper understanding of human nature does not, however, end with affirming the existence of a spirit, soul, heart, and mind within us. The Christian position goes on to define human nature as inherently flawed because of Adam and Eve's decision to disobey God in the Garden of Eden. This understanding of our sinful bent is critical for understanding our human nature and our mental processes.

Our revolt against God caused a dramatic, reality-shattering change in our relationship to the rest of existence and even to ourselves. This change has severe ramifications for all aspects of reality, including psychology. In fact, our sinful nature—our desire to rebel against God

The Pop Culture Connection

The question of human free will is raised in *Bruce Almighty* (a 2003 film starring Jim Carrey). In the film, Bruce (Carrey), asks God how to get back his girlfriend, Grace (Jennifer Aniston). He asks, "Grace left me. . . How do you make somebody love you without affecting free will?" To which God (Morgan Freeman) replies, "Welcome to my world, son. If you come up with an answer to that one, you let me know."

and our fellow beings—is the source of all psychological problems according to the Christian view. Francis A. Schaeffer says, "The basic psychological problem is trying to be what we are

---

[8] Arthur Koestler and J.R. Smythies, eds., *Beyond Reductionism* (London, UK: Hutchinson Publishers, 1969), 251–2. For an updated discussion of identity, see Moreland and Craig, *Philosophical Foundations*, 290f.
[9] Arthur C. Custance, *Man in Adam and in Christ* (Grand Rapids, MI: Zondervan, 1975), 256. Also see Wilder Penfield, *The Mystery of the Mind* (Princeton, NJ: Princeton University Press, 1975).

References to the fall, explicit or implied, are abundant in literature, music, film, and the visual arts. Mankind's fall is depicted in classical works of Milton, Shakespeare, Rembrandt, Chopin, and Beethoven, to name a few. More recent pop culture expressions, not necessarily from a Biblical worldview, include:

- *Fallen* — a 1998 film starring Denzel Washington, John Goodman, and Donald Sutherland
- *Dear God*— a song by Sarah McLachlan from her 2003 album *Afterglow* (remake of the 1986 XTC song of the same name)
- *Fallen* — a hit 2003 musical album by Gothic rock band Evanescence
- *The Fallen* — a song by Scottish alternative rock band Franz Ferdinand from their 2005 album *You Could Have It So Much Better*

not, and trying to carry what we cannot carry. Most of all, the basic problem is not being willing to be the creatures we are before the Creator."[10] Instead, we want to be God. Creaturehood is too confining, especially when it comes to making the rules—which to a great extent is the heart of the matter. Remember, it is the heart that says there is no God (Psalm 14:1). It is the heart that is deceitful and wicked (Jeremiah 17:9).

This view is crucial for Christian theology because it allows us to understand our tremendous need for Christ's saving power. It is crucial on a lesser level, as well, for Christian psychology. In order to understand human nature properly, the psychologist must understand that we have a natural tendency to revolt against God and His laws. If the Christian view of human nature is correct, then only Christianity can develop a true, meaningful, and workable psychology because only Christianity recognizes the problem of the heart, mind, and will in relation to God. Further, only Christianity provides a framework in which we are truly held responsible for our thoughts and actions. "The great benefit of the doctrine of sin," says **Paul Vitz**, "is that it reintroduces responsibility for our own behavior, responsibility for changing as well as giving meaning to our condition."[11]

Only Christian psychology perceives human nature in a way that is consistent with reality and capable of speaking to our most difficult problems—sin problems. Christian psychology sees men and women as not only physical, but also spiritual; as morally responsible before God; as created in God's image; and as having rebelliously turned away from their Creator. Only Christianity is prepared to face the problem that necessarily arises out of our sin nature: the existence of guilt.

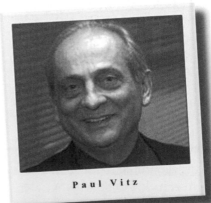

Paul Vitz

5.1.4 GUILT: PSYCHOLOGICAL OR REAL?

Both Humanists and Marxists speak only of "psychological guilt" because for them only society is evil—people do nothing individually that would incur actual guilt. For the Christian, however, each time someone rebels against God, he or she is committing a sin and the feeling of guilt that results from this rebellion is entirely justified. "Psychological guilt is actual and cruel," writes Schaeffer. "But Christians know that there is also real guilt, moral guilt before a holy God. It is not a matter only of psychological guilt; that is the distinction."[12]

---

[10] Francis Schaeffer, *The Complete Works of Francis Schaeffer*, 5 vols. (Westchester, IL: Crossway Books, 1982), 3:329.

[11] Paul Vitz, *Psychology as Religion* (Grand Rapids MI,: Eerdmans, 1985), 43.

[12] Schaeffer, *Complete Works*, 3:322.

Because Christian psychology acknowledges the existence of real, objective guilt, it alone can speak to a person who is experiencing such guilt. As Schaeffer says, "When a man is broken in these [moral and psychological] areas, he is confused, because he has the feelings of real guilt within himself, and yet he is told by modern thinkers that these are only guilt-'feelings.' But he can never resolve these feelings, because...[he] has true moral awareness and the feeling of true guilt. You can tell him a million times that there is no true guilt, but he still knows there is true guilt."[13]

Christianity understands our nature, including why this guilt arises and how to deal with it. While other schools of psychology must invent fancy terms (for example, social maladjustment) to explain away the existence of real guilt as a result of real sin, Christian psychology deals with the problem at its roots—the human heart, mind, and soul.

> Psychological guilt is actual and cruel," writes Schaeffer. "But Christians know that there is also real guilt, moral guilt before a holy God. It is not a matter only of psychological guilt; that is the distinction.
>
> — FRANCIS SCHAEFFER

5.1.5 MENTAL ILLNESS

Modern secular psychologists often speak of *mental illness*. Yet many Christian psychologists deny the existence of a large proportion of mental illnesses. Jay Adams writes, "Organic malfunctions affecting the brain that are caused by brain damage, tumors, gene inheritance, glandular or chemical disorders validly may be termed mental illnesses. But at the same time a vast number of other human problems have been classified as mental illnesses for which there is no evidence that they have been engendered by disease or illness at all."[14]

Why is Adams so suspicious of problems that cannot be directly linked to organic causes being termed *mental illness*? "The fundamental bent of fallen human nature is away from God . . . Apart from organically generated difficulties, the 'mentally ill' are really people with unsolved personal problems."[15]

This view follows logically from the Christian perception of human nature: we have rebelled against God, we have real guilt feelings about this rebellion, and so we must reconcile ourselves with God or face unsolved personal problems. Lawrence Crabb, Jr. explains, "An appreciation of the reality of sin is a critically necessary beginning point for an understanding of the Christian view of anything. A psychology worthy of the adjective 'Christian' must not set the problem of sin in parallel line with other problems or redefine it into a neurosis or psychological kink."[16]

5.1.6 THE REALISTIC APPROACH TO SIN AND GUILT

If the Christian psychologist denies the existence of most mental illnesses,[17] what good is Christian psychology? That is, how can the Christian psychologist propose to help people if he or she views their mental problems as spiritual problems caused by alienation from God? Doesn't this view place too much guilt on people and avoid any real therapy? If by the word

---

[13] Ibid.

[14] Jay E. Adams, *Competent to Counsel* (Grand Rapids, MI: Baker Book House, 1970), 28.

[15] Ibid., 29.

[16] Karl Menninger, *Whatever Became of Sin?* (New York, NY: Hawthorn Books, 1974), 48.

[17] For a secular work arguing in much the same vein, see Herb Kutchins and Stuart A. Kirk, *Making Us Crazy: DSM [Diagnostic Statistical Manual]: The Psychiatric Bible and the Creation of Mental Disorders* (New York, NY: The Free Press, 1997)

therapy we mean consciousness-raising seminars or primal scream workshops, then it is true the Christian psychologist does away with therapy. However, the Christian psychologist, and for that matter any mature Christian, still offers solutions for the troubled person.

We are bound to experience real guilt because we have a conscience and because we rebelled and continue to rebel against God. Christian psychologists acknowledge this guilt and point the hurting person toward Christ's sacrificial death and resurrection, so the guilty can know deliverance from guilt. Our sins will dog us unceasingly until they are washed away by Christ's work on the cross where God the Father declares us righteous and frees us from the penalty of sin. We no longer have to worry about the sin problem because God took care of it for us. Now we must live the life that God has ordained for us to live.

The Christian psychologist, then, must stress personal moral responsibility. Without this responsibility, we may deny any real guilt caused by our sins and thereby avoid the heart of our problem—our alienation from God. Only through recognizing our sinful nature and guilt before God can we reconcile our guilt feelings with reality.

This may seem like a rather insensitive approach to helping people with very sensitive problems. But what could be more cruel than treating merely a symptom of the problem and ignoring the actual sickness? Who would fault a doctor for giving patients a shot to fight a disease rather than a cough drop to mask a symptom? As Adams puts it, "It is important for counselors to remember that whenever clients camouflage, . . . sick treatment only makes them worse. To act as if they may be excused for their condition is the most unkind thing one can do. Such an approach only compounds the problem."[18]

The first step for the Christian psychologist in dealing with many mental and spiritual problems is to hold each client personally responsible for his or her sin. Crabb writes, "Hold your client responsible: for what? For confessing his sin, for willfully and firmly turning from it, and then for practicing the new behavior, believing that the indwelling Spirit will provide all the needed strength."[19]

This is the key for all Christian healing of *mental illnesses* that are not organically caused: confession of sin, forgiveness of sin through Christ (1 John 1:9), reconciliation with God (2 Corinthians 5:17–21), and sanctification through the disciplining work of God's Spirit (1 Thessalonians 5:23; Hebrews 12:1–11). Christian psychology, for all its fascination with human nature and the existence of guilt, leads to one simple method, summarized in James 5:16: "Therefore confess your sins to each other and pray for each other so that you may be healed. The prayer of a righteous man is powerful and effective."

5.1.7 THE PROBLEM OF SUFFERING

Most secular psychologies attempt to alleviate all suffering for the individual. Psychologists speak of methods of *successful living* that are supposed to eradicate most pain and anguish. Vitz says this "selfist" psychology "trivializes life by claiming that suffering (and by implication even death) is without intrinsic meaning. Suffering is seen as some sort of absurdity, usually a man-made mistake which could have been avoided by the use of knowledge to gain control of the environment."[20]

In contrast, Christian psychology believes that God can use suffering to bring about positive changes. This difference between secular and Christian psychology has serious implications. For the non-Christian, suffering is a harsh reality that must be avoided at all costs; for the Christian, suffering may be used by God to discipline and lead us—indeed, Christians are sometimes called

---

[18] Adams, *Competent to Counsel*, 32–3.

[19] Lawrence Crabb, Jr., *Basic Principles of Biblical Counseling* (Grand Rapids, MI: Zondervan, 1975), 102.

[20] Vitz, *Psychology as Religion*, 103.

to plunge joyously into suffering in obedience to God (Hebrews 12:7–11; Acts 6:8–7:60).

Meaning in suffering is a feature unique to Christian psychology. Kilpatrick concludes, "The real test of a theory or way of life, however, is not whether it can relieve pain but what it says about the pain it cannot relieve. And this is where, I believe, psychology lets us down and Christianity supports us, for in psychology suffering has no meaning, while in Christianity it has great meaning."[21]

Time magazine spoke to this matter of suffering with an edition titled "Special Mind & Body Issue."[22] One article in the series was entitled "The Power to Uplift: Religious people are less stressed and happier than nonbelievers. Research is beginning to explain why." After describing the setbacks in the life of 41-year-old Karen Granger (husband laid off, a miscarriage, cousin's breast cancer, two hurricanes, and best friend's brain tumor), *Time* reports, "But Granger, a devout Christian who attends Presbyterian services weekly and prays daily, doesn't allow circumstances to get her down. 'We're not in heaven yet,' she says, 'and these things happen on this earth.' Granger credits religion with helping her cope and giving her a feeling of connection and purpose. 'We're putting our lives in God's hands and trusting he has our best interests at heart,' she says. 'I've clung to my faith more than ever this year. As a consequence, I haven't lost my joy.'"[23]

Time asks the question, "So, what has science learned about what makes the human heart sing?"[24] The answer is that some things do not make the human heart sing—wealth, education, and weather. Marriage is a maybe. "Married people are generally happier than singles, but that may be because they were happier to begin with." But religious faith is a positive *yes*. "On the positive side, religious faith seems to genuinely lift the spirit, though it's tough to tell whether it's the God part or the community aspect that does the heavy lifting. Friends? A giant yes . . . [along with] strong ties to friends and family and commitment to spending time with them."[25]

> The real test of a theory or way of life, however, is not whether it can relieve pain but what it says about the pain it cannot relieve. And this is where, I believe, psychology lets us down and Christianity supports us.
>
> — WILLIAM KIRK KILPATRICK

5.18 BACK TO THEOLOGY AND PHILOSOPHY?[26]

According to *Time*, the field of psychology is rethinking and retooling. Instead of constantly dwelling on what makes people *mentally ill*, the shift is toward what makes people mentally healthy, positive, joyful, and happy to be alive. "Studies show that those who believe in life after death, for example, are happier than those who do not. 'Religion provides a unifying narrative that may be difficult to come by elsewhere in society,' says sociologist Christopher Ellison of the University of Texas at Austin."[27]

---

[21] Kilpatrick, *Psychological Seduction*, 181.

[22] *Time*, January 17, 2005.

[23] Ibid., A4–6.

[24] Ibid., A5.

[25] Ibid., A5–6.

[26] President of the Pacific Division of the American Philosophical Association, Julia Annas (University of Arizona) gave an address entitled, "Being Virtuous and Doing the Right Thing." She notes that the Virtues Project (www.virtuesproject.com) lists fifty-two virtues that have been found to be "character traits respected in seven world spiritual traditions," all of which are found in the Bible. See Proceedings & Addresses of The American Philosophical Association, Volume 78:2, November 2004.

[27] Ibid., A47–,48.

Further, reports *Time,* "It's not just what religion gives but what it takes away. 'The "thou shalt nots"—no adultery, no drugs and so on—keep people from getting addicted or otherwise increasing their level of stress,' says Koenig (that is, if they follow the rules). The strictures of religion may simplify life for adherents, and that can be a huge relief."[28]

Christian psychologist Paul Vitz says the work of Martin Seligman, former president of the American Psychological Association and professor of psychology at the University of Pennsylvania, is the catalyst for what he terms "positive psychology" i.e., emphasizing mental health instead of mental illness. "What is needed to balance our understanding of the person is recognition of positive human characteristics that can both heal many of our pathologies and help to prevent psychological problems in one's future life."[29] And what are these *positive human characteristics*? Virtues that include "wisdom, courage, humanity, justice, temperance, and transcendence."[30]

5.1.9 SIX CORE VIRTUES

Comments Vitz, "Peterson and Seligman list six core virtues, and it is not hard to provide the familiar Christian [fruit of the Spirit—Galatians 5:22,23] or Greco-Roman names for them. Their explanation of wisdom and knowledge is very close to the traditional virtue of prudence; humanity is close to charity; courage, justice, and temperance have not changed their names; and their sixth core virtue, transcendence, is not far from hope and faith."[31]

Vitz sees this move as hopeful for Christian psychology because the emphasis could be returning "to theology and philosophy" instead of toward a more secular ideal that he feels is withering on the vine along with secularism itself.

However, as Christians, we need to stay alert to so-called *self-help* psychologies that change often and that insist that to be happy, healthy, and spiritual we must forget the past, live in the present moment, abolish morality, or rearrange the marriage ceremony. For example, M. Scott Peck says in *The Road Less Traveled,* "My work with couples has led me to the stark conclusion that open marriage is the only kind of mature marriage that is healthy and not seriously destructive to the spiritual health and growth of the individual partners."[32] The truth is that *self-help* is itself an oxymoron because the individual who arrives at his or her *real self* alone, but always in conjunction with the therapist or the author of the *self-help* guide.

Christians understand that for 2000 years there has been a relationship between an individual's mental outlook (worldview) and his or her belief about God, Christ, salvation, and eternal life. We believe Christian psychology has ample incentive to focus on core virtues and what it means to be a human being with a substantive center of soul, spirit, heart, mind, and consciousness—rather than on self-improvement—because of Christianity's foundation on Scriptural principles. It is God who forgives our sins, heals our sinful human nature, and replaces our guilty consciences with the fruit of the Spirit—it is nothing that we do in our own strength. This echoes the view of Genesis 2:7: "And the Lord God formed man of the dust of the ground, and breathed into his nostrils the breath of life; and man became a living soul."

---

[28] Ibid., A48.

[29] Paul C. Vitz, "Psychology in Recovery," *First Things* (March 2005): 19.

[30] Ibid.

[31] Ibid., 20.

[32] Stewart Justman, *Fool's Paradise: The Unreal World of Pop Psychology* (Chicago, IL: Ivan R. Dee, 2005), 151. *Fool's Paradise* is a serious study of the self-help psychologies presently on the market such as M. Scott Peck, Phil McGraw, Charles Reich, Sidney Simon, Thomas Harris, John Gray, Marilyn Ferguson, Stephen Covey, and Theodore Rubin.

5.1.10 SOCIETY AND THE INDIVIDUAL

Christian psychology's view of human nature grants each individual moral responsibility, works to reconcile him or her with God, and gives meaning to suffering. An offshoot of this perspective is that Christians view society as the result of individuals' actions—that is, individuals are understood to be responsible for the evils in society. This view directly contradicts the Marxist and Humanist view that we are corrupted by evil societies.

The Pop Culture Connection

Hollywood usually portrays Christians in a negative light, as ignorant, mean-spirited, and bigoted. But in **Raising Helen** (a 2004 film), a Christian minister is given a positive character. In a leading role, Pastor Dan Parker (John Corbett) is strong, athletic, witty, wise, caring, and, oh, yes, romantic. Throughout the film he helps mold the character of Helen (Kate Hudson) as she learns to care for her recently orphaned nieces and nephew. By the end of the movie, Pastor Parker gets the girl.

As always, these views have logical consequences. For Marxists and Humanists, society must be changed, and then we can learn to do right. For the Christian, however, the individual must change for the better before society can. For the Christian, blaming individual sins on society is a cop-out. As Karl Menninger says, "If a group of people can be made to share the responsibility for what would be a sin if an individual did it, the load of guilt rapidly lifts from the shoulders of all concerned. Others may accuse, but the guilt shared by the many evaporates for the individual. Time passes. Memories fade. Perhaps there is a record, somewhere; but who reads it?"[33]

5.1.11 CONCLUSION

The Christian view of human nature or what it means to be a human being is complex because it includes such terms as soul, spirit, mind, heart, will, consciousness, and intuition.[34] Further, Christians who properly understand human nature might never need to seek professional counseling—they might maintain spiritual well-being by remaining in submission to Christ. Christians either believe God when He says He has dealt with the sin problem through the sacrifice of His Son, or do not.

Schaeffer outlines a simple approach to what he calls "positive psychological hygiene"—"As a Christian, instead of putting myself in practice at the center of the universe, I must do something else. This is not only right, and the failure to do so is not only sin, but it is important for me personally in this life. I must think after God, and I must will after God."[35] To "will after God" is not to think too highly of ourselves, "but in lowliness of mind let each esteem others better than themselves" (Philippians 2:3).

Indeed, Paul's advice in the book of Philippians is worth many a visit to the psychologist's office: Let nothing be done through strife or vain glory; let this mind be in you which was also in Christ Jesus; do all things without murmurings and disputing; rejoice in the Lord; beware of evil workers; let your moderation be known to all men; whatsoever things are true, honest, just, pure, lovely, of a good report—think on these things.

The choice between Christian psychology and all other psychological schools is clear-cut. As Kilpatrick says, "Our choice . . . is really the same choice offered to Adam and Eve: either we trust God, or we take the serpent's word that we can make ourselves into gods."[36]

---

[33] Menninger, *Whatever Became of Sin?*, 95.

[34] For an accounting of soul, spirit, mind, heart et. al., see J.P. Moreland and Scott B. Rae, *Body & Soul: Human Nature & the Crisis in Ethics* (Downers Grove, IL: InterVarsity Press, 2000).

[35] Schaeffer, *Complete Works*, 3:334.

[36] Kilpatrick, *Psychological Seduction*, 233.

Psychology

Islam

He [God] created man and appointed for each human being a fixed period of life which he is to spend upon the earth. Allah has prescribed a certain code of life as the correct one for him, but has at the same time conferred on man freedom of choice as to whether or not he adopts this code as the actual basis of his life. One who chooses to follow the code revealed by God becomes a Muslim (believer) and one who refuses to follow it becomes a Kafir (non-believer).[1]

— KHURSHID AHMAD

5.2.1 INTRODUCTION

The teachings of Islam regarding human nature, sin, and salvation may at times seem similar to the Biblical Christian worldview, but in reality they stand in very sharp distinction from it. While Islam affirms that human beings exist beyond the death of the body—thus affirming some form of psychological dualism—its view of human nature diverges from biblical teaching in the most fundamental ways.

"Islam is an Arabic word and denotes submission, surrender and obedience. As a religion, Islam stands for complete submission and obedience to Allah—that is why it is called *Islam*

---

[1] Khurshid Ahmad, ed., *Islam: Its Meaning and Message* (Leicester, UK: The Islamic Foundation, 1999), 29.

. . . Such a life of obedience brings peace of the heart and establishes real peace in society at large," writes Khurshid Ahmad. The Qur'an states: "Those who believe, and whose hearts find satisfaction in the remembrance of God: for without doubt in the remembrance of God do hearts find satisfaction. For those who believe and work righteousness, is (every) blessedness, and a beautiful place of (final) return" (13:28–29).

5.2.2 MANKIND AND THE IMAGE OF GOD

The biblical message is that we are created in the image of God (Genesis 1:26–27) and that despite the Fall we continue to bear that image (James 3:9). This feature distinguishes us from all other creatures, for not even angels were created in the image of God. The Islamic perspective differs. "The Christian witness, that man is created in the 'image and likeness of God,' is not the same as the Muslim witness. Although God breathed into man His spirit, as both Christians and Muslims believe, for Islam the only divine qualities entrusted to humans as a result of God's breath were those of knowledge, will, and power of action. If people use these divine qualities rightly in understanding God and following His law strictly, then he has nothing to fear in the present or the future, and no sorrow for the past.[2]

Muslims acknowledge that we are God's vice regents on earth but reject the idea that we are made in God's image. Muslims see us as slaves of God. Indeed, while Jesus deemed to call Christians His siblings rather than mere slaves, Islam denies that we should be called "sons and daughters of God."

5.2.3 HUMAN NATURE

Muslims believe that the original religion of humanity is Islam (Qur'an 7:172) and thus that every human being is born a Muslim (30:30). As stated in the Hadith, "Allah's Apostle said, 'Every child is born with a true faith of Islam (i.e. to worship none but Allah Alone) but his parents convert him to Judaism, Christianity or Magainism…"[3] Thus, in contrast to the biblical perspective of original sin, "[t]he true Muslim believes that every person is born free from sin," writes Abdalati.[4] "The idea of Original Sin or hereditary criminality[5] has no room in the teachings of Islam. Man, according to the Qur'an (30:30) and the Prophet, is born in a natural state of purity or *fitrah*, that is, Islam or submission to the law of God. Whatever becomes of man after birth is the result of external influence and intruding factors."[6]

In believing that we are born sinless, Islam harmonizes with Secular Humanism, Marxism, Postmodernism, and even Mormonism[7] and clashes with the biblical teaching that we are born with a sinful nature.

---

[2] Badru D. Kateregga and David W. Shenk, *Islam and Christianity: A Muslim and a Christian in Dialogue* electronically available on *The World of Islam: Resources for Understanding* CD-ROM published by Global Mapping International, 5350.

[3] Sahih Bukhari, Volume 2, Book 23, Hadith 441 (http://www.usc.edu/dept/MSA/fundamentals/hadithsunnah/bukhari/023.sbt.html#002.023.441).

[4] Hammuda Abdalati, *Islam in Focus* (Indianapolis, IN: 1975), 16.

[5] This is a caricatured way of describing the Christian understanding of original sin.

[6] Abdalati, *Islam in Focus*, 32.

[7] Dr. Ergun Mehmet Caner, Dean of Liberty Theological Seminary, contends that there are nearly two dozen similarities between Islam and Mormonism. See his website at www.erguncaner.com.

5.2.4 FREE WILL

Throughout Islamic history (as throughout the history of Judaism and Christianity) both God's sovereignty and our responsibility have been affirmed. In denying that we are born with a sinful nature, the Islamic view of the human will differs from the Christian view (which affirms that we have a real will capable of choosing good and evil, and are responsible for our thoughts and actions).

Abdalati explains the Islamic view of our free will: "Man is a free agent endowed with a free will. This is the essence of his humanity and the basis of his responsibility to his Creator. Without man's relative free will life would be meaningless and God's covenant with man would be in vain. Without human free will, God would be defeating His own purpose and man would be completely incapable of bearing any responsibility."[8]

Abdalati goes on to explain our responsibility for our own choices: "Man is a responsible agent. But responsibility for sin is borne by the actual offender alone. Sin is not hereditary, transferable, or communal in nature. Every individual is responsible for his own deeds. And while man is susceptible to corruption, he is also capable of redemption and reform. This does not mean that Islam prefers the individual to the group. Individualism means little or nothing when severed from social context. What it means is that the individual has different sets of roles to play. He must play them in such a way as to guard his moral integrity, preserve his identity, observe the rights of God, and fulfill his social obligations."[9]

The Pop Culture Connection

Hidalgo (a 2004 film set in 1890) tells the story of an ex-Pony Express courier, Frank T. Hopkins (Viggo Mortensen), who travels to Arabia with his horse, Hidalgo, to compete for a large prize in a dangerous 3,000 mile cross-country horse race. During the race Frank finds the leading Muslim rider languishing in quicksand. They have the following exchange centering on man's will versus Allah's will:

Muslim: Do not assist me, just kill me, please, use your weapon. It is God's will.
Hopkins: Tell you what, you can do whatever the **** you want when I get you out of there.
Muslim: Why did you turn back for me?
Hopkins: Ain't no prize money worth a man's life the way I see it.
Muslim: It is written that God leaves us three wishes and grants three wishes. It is God's will that I die in this race. Just as it is God's will who will win.
Hopkins: What about your will? What about your horse's will? Seems to me that's what gets you across the finish line. Only then is it written.
(The Muslim ultimately commits suicide.)

5.2.5 THE FALL

Geisler and Saleeb explain how the Islamic view of the Fall differs from biblical teaching: "Despite some general similarities to the biblical version of man's fall, there are radical differences between the Christian and the Islamic interpretations of Adam's transgression. Whereas in Christian theology man's disobedience is viewed as a fundamental turning point in his relationship to God, according to the Muslim perspective this was only a single slip on Adam and Eve's part that was completely forgiven after their repentance. It had no further effect on the nature of man and the rest of creation. Neither does the fact that man was expelled from

---

[8] Abdalati, *Islam in Focus*, 52.
[9] Ibid.

Paradise to earth (as a direct result of this transgression of divine command) play a significant role in the Islamic anthropology or soteriology."[10]

Kateregga, a Muslim scholar, further explains the differences between the Christian and Islamic view of the fall: "The Christian witness that the rebellion by our first parents has tragically distorted man, and that sinfulness pervades us individually and collectively, is very much contrary to Islamic witness. Islam teaches that the first phase of life on earth did not begin in sin and rebellion against Allah. Although Adam disobeyed Allah, he repented and was forgiven and even given guidance for mankind. Man is not born a sinner and the doctrine of the sinfulness of man has no basis in Islam."[11]

5.2.6 ISLAMIC SALVATION

Islam rejects not only the atoning work of Jesus on the cross, but also that Jesus died on a cross. As Abdalati asserts, "the Muslim cannot entertain the dramatic story of Jesus' death upon the cross just to do away with all human sins once and for all." Abdalati explains why Muslims cannot accept the truth of Jesus' sacrifice for us: "The Muslim does not believe in the crucifixion of Jesus by his enemies because the basis of this doctrine of crucifixion is contrary to Divine mercy and justice as much as it is to human logic and dignity. Such a disbelief in the doctrine does not in any way lessen the Muslim's belief in Jesus as a distinguished prophet of God. On the contrary, by rejecting this doctrine the Muslim accepts Jesus but only with more esteem and higher respect, and looks upon his original message as an essential part of Islam."[12]

If there is no Savior to deal with our sin, then we are left to our own devices to seek salvation. Abdalati says in this regard, "Each person must bear his own burden and be responsible for his own actions, because no one can expiate for another's sin."[13]

From a Christian perspective, if we do not see human nature as fundamentally flawed and inherently sinful, then such a misdiagnosis of our plight naturally results in a misconstrued understanding of our salvation. If the diagnosis is mistaken, then the cure will be too.

5.2.7 ACCOMPLISHING OUR SALVATION

As you can imagine, the Muslim view of salvation contrasts sharply with the Christian view. Muslims believe that we naturally have a good nature and that we must look to ourselves and the abilities God has given us to achieve our own salvation. According to Abdalati, "The true Muslim believes that man must work out his salvation through the guidance of God. This means that in order to attain salvation a person must combine Faith and action, belief and practice. Faith without action is as insufficient as action without Faith. In other words, no one can attain salvation until his Faith in God becomes dynamic in his life and his beliefs are translated into reality. This is in complete harmony with other Islamic articles of Faith. It shows that God does not accept lip service, and that no true believer can be indifferent as far as practical requirements of Faith are concerned. It also shows that no one can act on behalf of another or intercede between him and God (see, for example, the Qur'an, 10:9–10; 18:30; 103:1–3)."[14]

---

[10] Norman L. Geisler and Abdul Saleeb, *Answering Islam: The Crescent in Light of the Cross* (Grand Rapids, MI: Baker Book House, 1993), 44.

[11] Kateregga and Shenk, *Islam and Christianity*, 5356.

[12] Abdalati, *Islam in Focus*, 17.

[13] Ibid., 16.

[14] Ibid., 17–18. This stands in distinct contrast to biblical examples of intercession between God and sinful humans (such as Exodus 32:11–14, where Moses intercedes on behalf of sinful Israel) and the biblical teaching that the

Christians also affirm "faith without deeds is dead" (James 2:20). For Christians, however, faith always precedes obedience (Ephesians 2:8–10). We obey because we love God and place our faith in Him because He saves us. God requires good deeds, but He also enables us to accomplish them (Philippians 2:12–13). The good deeds required of Muslims (circumcision, prayer five times a day, a pilgrimage to Mecca, avoiding pork, etc.) as well as the motivation to accomplish them stand in contrast to the good deeds required of Christians.

5.2.8 FINAL JUDGMENT

The Islamic understanding of the Fall and the inherently good nature of humanity lead to an understanding of who will be saved and who will perish in the final judgment that also differs sharply from the Christian view. According to the following passages in the Qur'an, each person's good deeds will be weighed in a balance to determine who goes to paradise and who goes to hell:

> And the weighing on that day (Day of Resurrection) will be the true (weighing). So as for those whose scale (of good deeds) will be heavy, they will be the successful (by entering Paradise). And as for those whose scale will be light, they are those who will lose their own selves (by entering Hell) because they denied and rejected Our *Ayat* (proofs, evidences, verses, lessons, signs, revelations). (Qur'an 7:8–9)

> And We shall set up balances of justice on the Day of Resurrection, then none will be dealt with unjustly in anything. And if there be the weight of a mustard seed, We will bring it. And Sufficient are We to take account. (21:47)

> Then those whose balance (of good deeds) is heavy, they will attain salvation: But those whose balance is light, will be those who have lost their souls, in Hell will they abide. (23:102–103)

Although these passages refer to the balance of righteous deeds (or lack thereof) determining a Muslim's destiny, Muhammad is reported to have said, "None of you would get into Paradise because of his good deeds alone, and he would not be rescued from Fire, not even I, but because of the Mercy of Allah."[15]

5.2.9 FORGIVENESS

The Qur'an often speaks of the forgiveness of sins, instructing Muslims to counterbalance their good deeds with their bad deeds. However, any assurance of salvation is lacking.

> To those who believe and do deeds of righteousness hath Allah promised forgiveness and a great reward (5:10).

> And establish regular prayers at the two ends of the day and at the approaches of the night; for those things that are good remove those that are evil; be that the word of remembrance to those who remember (their Lord) (11:114).[16]

The Qur'an identifies in the following passage one deed that will assure Muslims of eternal

---

Holy Spirit (Romans 8:26–27) and Christ (Hebrews 7:25) intercede for us.
[15] Sahih Muslim, book 39, no. 6769.
[16] This teaching is also found in the Hadith: Bukhari 1:209; Muslim book 37; no. 6655ff.

bliss and salvation—death in jihad.

> Those who have left their homes, or been driven out therefrom, or suffered harm in My Cause, or fought or been slain, verily, I will blot out from them their iniquities, and admit them into Gardens with rivers flowing beneath; a reward from the Presence of God, and from His Presence is the best of rewards (3:195).

5.2.10 REJECTION OF JESUS AS SAVIOR

In further contrast to the Christian worldview, Muslims deny that Jesus is God incarnate, that He died on a cross as an atoning sacrifice for sin, and that He was resurrected on the third day. While the following passage contains some ambiguities (e.g., whether it denies that the Jews were those who killed Jesus or whether Jesus *did not die* on the cross), most Muslims interpret it to say that Jesus was not crucified at all.

> That they said (in boast), "We killed Christ Jesus the son of Mary, the Messenger of Allah"—but they killed him not, nor crucified him, but so it was made to appear to them, and those who differ therein are full of doubts, with no (certain) knowledge, but only conjecture to follow, for of a surety they killed him not—nay, Allah raised him up unto Himself. (Qur'an 4:157–158; cf. 3:54)

The ramifications of this denial are devastating to any claim that Islam is a continuation of the Christian faith. Not only does Islam deny Christ's death on a cross, but also His atoning work. If Jesus never died, then there would have been no resurrection from the dead. Anyone familiar with the Christian faith recognizes that if Jesus were not resurrected from the dead, then there is no hope and the Christian faith is nothing but a fraud. The apostle Paul declared, "And if Christ has not been raised, our preaching is useless and so is your faith. More than that, we are then found to be false witnesses about God, for we have testified about God that he raised Christ from the dead. But he did not raise him if in fact the dead are not raised. For if the dead are not raised, then Christ has not been raised either. And if Christ has not been raised, your faith is futile; you are still in your sins" (1 Corinthians 15:14–17).

5.2.11 CONCLUSION

Clearly, to deny Jesus' death on the cross is to renounce the gospel of Jesus Christ, which is at the core of the Christian faith. In that light, Islam offers no meaningful claim that it *confirms* the Christian faith or the gospel. In reality, Islam does not *fulfill* the Christian faith—it *replaces* it.

Muslims would disagree with the Christian belief that Islam cannot be a continuation or fulfillment of Christianity for the reasons stated above. One argument Muslims could make against the Christian view is that in the very same way Christianity is not a continuation or fulfillment of Judaism. All this argument would show (if it were true) is that both Islam and Christianity are false religions. Christians, however, could dispute this Muslim argument on several significant grounds.

A second argument Muslims could raise against Christian claims that Islam is not a continuation of Christianity is that this is just what should be expected because the biblical texts have been corrupted over time. In other words, the force of the argument is turned back on Christianity, charging Christianity with having distorted the biblical texts to the extent that they are now doctrinally and historically corrupted. Muslims have yet to provide justification

Psychology

Secular Humanism

For myself, though I am very well aware of the
incredible amount of destructive, cruel, malevolent
behavior in today's world—from the threats of war to
the senseless violence in the streets—I do not find that
this evil is inherent in human nature.[1]

— CARL ROGERS

5.3.1 INTRODUCTION

Secular Humanist psychology, like all aspects of the Secular Humanist worldview, is strongly influenced by their assumptions about theology, philosophy, and biology. Leading Secular Humanist psychologists begin with the assumption that a personal God is a myth and that we are simply products of spontaneous generation and billions of years of evolution. Naturalistic philosophy fits hand-in-hand with these first two assumptions.

Because Secular Humanists deny the existence of the supernatural—including the mind, soul, and personality in any meaningful sense—they are left

> MONISM: The belief that there is only one basic and fundamental reality

with the study of strictly material things: the brain, environmental stimuli, and tangible human responses to those stimuli. **Monism** is the belief that there is only one basic and fundamental reality, that all existence is this one reality. **Psychological monism** is the belief that the mind is part of the material body. The branch of psychology that concerns itself solely with such material data is called behaviorism. Behaviorists believe all human *thought* and *personality* are merely by-products of physical interactions of the brain. For them, psychology is a science of behavior—

---

[1] Carl Rogers, "Notes on Rollo May," *Journal of Humanistic Psychology* (Summer 1982): 8.

> **PSYCHOLOGICAL MONISM:** The belief that the mind and the body exist as part of the same entity, i.e. the mind is a part of the material body

understanding how physical stimuli encourage our physical brains and bodies to behave.

Secular Humanists who are consistent with their worldview must embrace behaviorism. If the supernatural does not exist, then psychology admits only the natural. Logically, then, Secular Humanists should be behaviorists.

In practice, however, few Secular Humanists accept behaviorism. The reason is simple: behaviorism is a stultifying theory that reduces us to mere automatons. Behaviorist theory does not allow for human freedom because ultimately personal freedom must be grounded in the will, soul, or mind. According to the behaviorist model, we are merely physical, so our behavior is dictated by our physical environment. This is not an attractive theory, nor does it seem to match our day-to-day experience. Thus, Humanist psychologists abandon logic and the consequences of their atheistic evolutionary naturalism.

Most Secular Humanists call their psychology "third force" psychology because they are unwilling to embrace behaviorism or Freudianism, the other popular model. On the one hand, they reject behaviorism because it destroys their necessary concept of freedom. On the other hand, they reject Freudianism because it focuses too much on the individual apart from society. Unsatisfied with either branch of psychology, Secular Humanists created a third.

5.3.2 ARE WE GOOD OR EVIL?

Rejecting the Christian belief that we are fallen creatures, Secular Humanist psychologists emphatically proclaim our innate goodness—we possess no fallen nature, no original sin. Abraham Maslow writes, "As far as I know we just don't have any intrinsic instincts for evil."[2] Carl Rogers says much the same thing: "I see members of the human species, like members of other species, as essentially constructive in their fundamental nature, but damaged by their experience."[3] Paul Kurtz sees us as "perfectible."[4]

This portrayal of our condition is so incompatible with the Christian view that Secular Humanists feel compelled to attack the doctrine of original sin. Some go so far as to reinterpret the Bible to distort the concept of the Fall. **Erich Fromm** claims, "The Christian interpretation

Erich Fromm

of the story of man's act of disobedience as his 'fall' has obscured the clear meaning of the story. The biblical text does not even mention the word 'sin;' man challenges the supreme power of God, and he is able to challenge it because he is potentially God."[5]

Still other Humanistic psychologists choose to attack the whole Christian view in an effort to avoid the concept of original sin. Wendell W. Watters writes, "The Christian is brainwashed to believe that he or she was born wicked, should suffer as Christ suffered, and should aspire to a humanly impossible level of perfection nonetheless."[6] According to Watters, the confusion and guilt heaped on Christians promotes mental illness: "A true Christian must

---

[2] I. David Welch, George A. Tate, and Fred Richards, ed., *Humanistic Psychology* (Buffalo, NY: Prometheus Books, 1978), 11.

[3] Rogers, "Notes on Rollo May," 8.

[4] Paul Kurtz, et al., "Credo," *The Humanist* (July/Aug. 1968): 18.

[5] Erich Fromm, *You Shall Be as Gods* (New York, NY: Holt, Rinehart and Winston, 1966), 7.

[6] Wendell W. Watters, "Christianity and Mental Health," *The Humanist* (Nov./Dec. 1987): 32.

always be in a state of torment, since he or she can never really be certain that God has forgiven him or her . . ."[7]

Clearly, Secular Humanist psychology is uneasy with the biblical concept of original sin, chiefly because the doctrine provides a reason for the existence of evil in the world. Humanist psychology, due to its insistence on the innate goodness of humanity, cannot easily answer the question of evil, yet at the same time it is unable to deny that evil exists (wars, crime, abuse, etc.).

5.3.3 WHY DO GOOD PEOPLE DO BAD THINGS?

To explain why good people do bad things, Secular Humanist psychology blames social influences rather than the individual. Maslow, for example, explains that our good impulses "are easily warped by cultures—you never find them in their pure state."[8] Virtually every Humanistic psychologist shares the view that culture provides the only means available to explain the odd fact that we are inherently good, yet still tend to commit evil acts.

Rogers notes, "Experience leads me to believe that it is cultural influences which are the major factor in our evil behaviors."[9] Humanism thus explains that evil is in the world as the result of societal influences thwarting our natural tendencies for good.

Humanist psychologist Rollo May, however, is unwilling to accept this premise. In response to claims by Rogers, May cuts to the heart of the matter when he writes, "But you say that you 'believe that it is cultural influences which are the major factor in our evil behaviors.' This makes culture the enemy. But who makes up the culture except persons like you and me?"[10] Indeed, how could culture or society ever have become evil if there were no tendency within us toward evil?

Humanist psychologists offer no solution to this dilemma. They seem to acknowledge the dichotomy, however, when they focus on treating individuals rather than society.

5.3.4 A SELF-CENTERED WORLDVIEW

Secular Humanist psychologists believe the secret to better mental health is found by getting in touch with the unspoiled inner self. When we strip ourselves of all the evil forced on us by society, we will become positive agents with virtually unlimited potential for good. Just how much potential we are assumed to have is reflected by the title of one of Fromm's most important works, *You Shall Be as Gods*.

The Humanist emphasis, then, is on self-reliance, even self-centeredness. Harold P. Marley states, "To know Humanism, first know the self in its relation to other selves. Trust thyself to stand alone; learn of others, but lean not upon a single savior."[11]

This call to trust ourselves and our natural inclinations is voiced powerfully by Maslow: "Since this inner nature is good or neutral rather than bad, it is best to bring it out and to encourage it rather than to suppress it. If it is permitted to guide our life, we grow healthy, fruitful, and happy."[12] In other words, to become good, we must focus on ourselves and what we want. In fact, Humanists believe that self-centeredness is the wave of the future—an entirely new philosophy of life. Rogers, when considering what the philosophy of the future will be

[7] Ibid., 10.

[8] Welch, Tate, and Richards, *Humanistic Psychology*, 189.

[9] Rogers, "Notes on Rollo May," 8.

[10] Rollo May, "The Problem of Evil: An Open Letter to Carl Rogers," *Journal of Humanistic Psychology* (Summer 1982): 12.

[11] Harold P. Marley, "First Know the Self," *The Humanist* (Nov./Dec. 1954): 258.

[12] Abraham Maslow, *Toward a Psychology of Being* (New York, NY: Van Nostrand Reinhold, 1968), 149.

like, guesses, "It will stress the value of the individual. It will, I think, center itself in the individual as the evaluating agent."[13]

Humanist psychologists believe this self-centered attitude is crucial for our individual mental health as well as for the eventual restructuring of society. Only when we accept the need to be completely in control can we tap the unlimited potential of being human.

5.3.5 SELF-ACTUALIZED PEOPLE

Abraham Maslow refers to those in touch with their inherent goodness as **self-actualized**. He categorizes this drive to get in touch with our inherent goodness as a need that can be attended to only after we have satisfied our lower needs—namely, physiological, safety, social, and ego needs. We must satisfy these needs as well as our need for self-actualization before we can truly be declared mentally healthy.

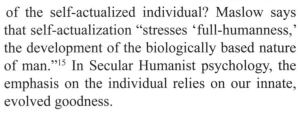

According to Maslow, few people in modern society are self-actualized. Thus, when attempting to study self-actualized individuals, he relies to some extent on historical figures as models. Maslow feels "fairly sure" that Thomas Jefferson and Abraham Lincoln "in his last days" were both self-actualized. He also singles out Albert Einstein, Eleanor Roosevelt, Jane Addams, William James, Albert Schweitzer, Aldous Huxley, and Benedict de Spinoza as "highly probable" examples of self-actualization.[14]

Abraham Maslow

What character traits mark these historical figures as being in tune with their real, creative selves? What are the characteristics of the self-actualized individual? Maslow says that self-actualization "stresses 'full-humanness,' the development of the biologically based nature of man."[15] In Secular Humanist psychology, the emphasis on the individual relies on our innate, evolved goodness.

> **SELF-ACTUALIZATION:** The highest level of a person's potential and the ultimate goal of Maslow's "hierarchy of needs" (a theory contending that as we meet our basic needs, we seek to satisfy successively higher needs)

5.3.6 HUMAN-CENTERED VALUES

This inherent goodness should not be understood as *good* in the traditional, biblical sense. Rather, it is an evolving, relative goodness. Maslow says self-actualized people's "notions of right and wrong and of good and evil are often not the conventional ones."[16] Ellis G. Olim agrees: "[M]an is constantly becoming . . . What we want, then, is not to encourage a static type of personality based on traditional notions of right and wrong, but the kind of person who is able to go forward into the uncertain future."[17]

For Secular Humanists, ethics is inseparable from psychology. Fromm believes that "values are rooted in the very conditions of human existence; hence that our knowledge of these conditions—that is, of the 'human situation'—leads us to establishing values which have

---

[13] Welch, Tate, and Richards, *Humanistic Psychology*, 223.

[14] Abraham Maslow, *Motivation and Personality* (New York, NY: Harper and Row, 1987, 127–8.

[15] Maslow, *Toward a Psychology of Being*, vi.

[16] Maslow, *Motivation and Personality*, 140–1.

[17] Welch, Tate, and Richards, *Humanistic Psychology*, 219.

objective validity; this validity exists only with regard to the existence of man; outside of him there are no values."[18]

Therefore, we must turn our eyes inward to determine what is right. Rather than help others, we should concentrate on creating a good self. Maslow describes this view succinctly: "In general, it looks as if the best way to help other people grow toward self-actualization is to become a good person yourself."[19]

Humanists embrace self-centeredness in an effort to create a better world. The call for individuals to be true to their feelings and innermost nature allows for experimentation. If we feel our innermost nature is calling us to act in a certain way, who has the authority to tell us we are misinterpreting our feelings? Humanism affirms our freedom to experiment with values and to test the aspects of morality that truly mesh with our inner nature. Self-actualized people are the final authority for Humanist ethics, regardless of the amount of scientific experimentation required to discover *the good*. However, *the good* discovered by one person is *the good* only for that person. Another person may decide something else is *the good* or that neither good nor rules even exist.

Humanist psychologists discourage this line of thinking, however, by arguing that few people are self-actualized and the non-self-actualized must look to the self-actualized for guidance. According to Maslow, people not yet self-actualized can learn what is right by watching those who are. Thus, Humanists must look to mentally healthy (self-actualized) people to determine *scientifically*, for example, if pedophilia (man/boy sex) is moral or not. Maslow says, "I propose that we explore the consequences of observing whatever our best specimens choose, and then assuming that these are the highest values for all mankind."[20]

5.3.7 IS HUMANIST PSYCHOLOGY SCIENTIFIC?

Secular Humanists believe their psychology is based on a realistic worldview grounded in science, as Maslow suggests. However, it is neither scientific nor realistic. Secular Humanists, therefore, attempt to redefine science to make it broad enough to include their psychology. They justify the new definition by pointing to the failure of existing psychological models to help us understand our nature. May complains, "Today we know a great deal about bodily chemistry and the control of physical diseases; but we know very little about why people hate, why they cannot love, why they suffer anxiety and guilt, and why they destroy each other."[21]

Secular Humanists believe their psychology explains why we act the way we do and therefore is *scientific*. Rogers believes true science "will explore the private worlds of inner personal meanings, in an effort to discover lawful and orderly relationships there. In this world of inner meanings it can investigate all the issues which are meaningless for the behaviorist— purposes, goals, values, choice, perceptions of self, perceptions of others, the personal constructs with which we build our world, the responsibilities we accept or reject, the whole phenomenal world of the individual with its connective tissue of meaning."[22]

Without meaning to do so, the Humanistic definition of *scientific* studies such as those listed by Rogers allow not only Humanist psychology to be termed scientific, but also every major religion, including Christianity. Exploring "inner personal meanings" is a goal of every major religion.

---

[18] Erich Fromm, *Man for Himself* (New York, NY: Holt, Rinehart and Winston, 1964), 17.

[19] Mildred Hardeman, "A Dialogue with Abraham Maslow," *Journal of Humanistic Psychology* (Winter 1979): 25.

[20] Maslow, *Toward a Psychology of Being*, 169.

[21] Rollo May, *Psychology and the Human Dilemma* (Princeton, NJ: D. Van Nostrand Company, 1967), 188.

[22] Arthur Koestler and J.R. Smythies, ed., *Beyond Reductionism* (New York, NY: Macmillan, 1970), 252.

5.3.8 Good Self vs. Evil Society

Secular Humanists make three assumptions about the self, mind, and mental processes: 1) we are good by nature and are therefore perfectible; 2) society and its social institutions are responsible for the evil we do; and 3) mental health can be restored to those who get in touch with their inner (good) self. While other worldviews may agree with some or all of these premises, Christians disagree with all three. Christians insist that we must admit our own sinful nature and take responsibility for our immoral acts instead of blaming someone or something else. Humanist psychology, however, allows us to intellectually deny responsibility for our behavior and moral choices.

Secular Humanists do not convincingly answer May's question of why society is evil if we are all so good. Perhaps Rogers understood the contradiction when he wrote, "I should like to make a final confession. When I am speaking to outsiders I present Humanistic psychology as a glowing hope for the future. But . . . we have no reason whatsoever for feeling complacent as we look toward the future."[23]

5.3.9 Conclusion

Joyce Milton's *The Road to Malpsychia: Humanistic Psychology and our Discontents*[24] recounts the practical failure of Secular Humanist psychology by showing how it played out in the lives of some of its major proponents and leading practitioners. The title is revealing—*malpsychia* means *bad psychology.*

For example, Milton reveals that Harvard's Timothy Leary routinely had sex with his patients, took psilocybin and LSD, pushed drugs on his own students, and entertained the goal of having four million Americans turned on to LSD. Milton says of Donald Clark that he "was fully prepared to revolutionize education, break down children's sense of modesty about their own bodies, and celebrate 'deviance.'"[25]

Milton also writes that Carl Rogers experienced so many problems with his Encounter Groups that co-worker Bill Coulson finally concluded, "humanistic psychology wasn't solving anything. In fact, it was creating new pathologies that hadn't existed before. The therapy was the disease."[26]

The book reports how Abraham Maslow had trouble accepting the existence of evil. Milton explains, "Frank Manuel, his best friend on the Brandeis faculty, had warned Maslow as early as 1960 that his inability to account for the presence of evil in the world was a potentially fatal flaw in his attempt to construct a 'religion of human nature.'"[27]

In reviewing Milton's book for *National Review*, Paul C. Vitz, professor of psychology at New York University, concludes, "The reader needs to understand that the stories of these amoral and disordered lives are not just anecdotes: They are, rather, directly relevant to the theories of these psychologists. When a theorist proposes an answer to the question of how we can live well, the theorist's life offers valuable evidence. In the case of these characters in Joyce Milton's fine book, the conclusion is as sad as it is obvious: Psychologist, heal thyself."[28]

---

[23] Welch, Tate, and Richards, *Humanistic Psychology*, 45.

[24] Joyce Milton, *The Road to Malpsychia: Humanistic Psychology and our Discontents* (San Francisco, CA: Encounter Books, 2002).

[25] Ibid., 150.

[26] Ibid., 152.

[27] Ibid., 171.

[28] *National Review* (September 2, 2002): 46.

Psychology

Marxism-Leninism

"Only science, exact science about human nature itself, and the most sincere approach to it by the aid of the omnipotent scientific method, will deliver man from his present gloom, and will purge him from his contemporary shame in the sphere of interhuman relations."[1]

— IVAN P. PAVLOV

5.4.1 INTRODUCTION

Ivan P. Pavlov

Marxist belief that human development is an inevitable march toward communism forces Marxist psychology toward a belief in behaviorism. Their deterministic view of human development seems to exclude free will, approximating the behaviorist position that our choices and actions result from our brain responding to its environmental stimuli.

The Marxist acceptance of evolution and materialism as the proper means for understanding the world affects its view of the mind/body relationship, seeing the mind as no more than the purely physical activity of the brain. Marxist denial of the supernatural categorizes the human mind, in Lenin's view, as strictly organized matter.

The behaviorism embraced by Marxists, however, differs significantly from traditional behaviorism. Marxist behaviorist theories are based on the work of **Ivan P. Pavlov**, a Russian

---

[1] Ivan P. Pavlov, *Lectures on Conditioned Reflexes* (New York, NY: International Publishers, 1963), 41.

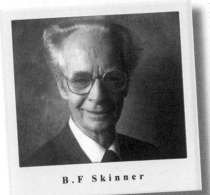

B.F Skinner

physiologist of the early twentieth century. Even though Pavlov rejected Marxist theory for most of his life, he serves as the adopted father of Marxist psychology largely because his attempts to reconcile materialism with psychology seem to fit the dialectic. An understanding of **traditional behaviorism**— through the work of **B. F. Skinner**, its most popular promoter— will help us pinpoint how Marxist behaviorism differs.

5.4.2 TRADITIONAL BEHAVIORISM DEFINED

In a behaviorist approach to psychology, human beings are seen simply as stimulus receptors, creatures that respond in one predetermined way to any given set of circumstances in our environment. According to Skinner, this is the only truly scientific approach to psychology. He says, "A scientific analysis of behavior dispossesses autonomous man and turns the control he has been said to exert over to the environment. The individual...is henceforth to be controlled by the world around him, and in large part by other men."[2]

Skinner's behaviorist psychology is rooted in an evolutionary perspective of the world: "The environment not only prods or lashes, it selects. Its role is similar to that in natural selection, though on a very different time scale . . ."[3] If the environment *selects* for us, we are not free agents, making our own decisions. "The hypothesis that man is not free is essential to the application of scientific method to the study of human behavior,"[4] according to Skinner and other behaviorists. This is consistent with the materialist belief that our brain is a bundle of nerves and synapses, capable of nothing more than responding to stimuli in ways that are outside our control.[5]

> TRADITIONAL BEHAVIORISM: A branch of psychology which asserts that human behavior can be reduced to principles that do not require consideration of unobservable mental events, such as ideas, emotions, and a mind; i.e., a form of materialism which claims that all human behavior is the result of materialistic processes and not the free will of the mind

5.4.3 PAVLOV'S ROLE IN MARXIST PSYCHOLOGY

Pavlov, like Skinner, believes that our mental processes result purely from physical causes and that behavior can be regulated. Pavlov concentrated his scientific studies on animal behavior, and he is perhaps best known for his experiments involving the salivation of dogs in response to auditory stimuli. Pavlov's dogs at first salivated when a bell was ringing because they were eating at the same time. The dogs soon *learned* to salivate when they heard the bell even without the presence of food. These canine experiments led Pavlov to propose a theory of *conditioned reflexes*—animals can learn to respond in specific, predetermined ways when exposed to certain stimuli.

Pavlov concluded that all animal activity could be accounted for in behaviorist terms and that "the whole complicated behavior of animals" is based on "nervous activity."[6] Since Pavlov

---

[2] B.F. Skinner, *Beyond Freedom and Dignity* (New York, NY: Bantam Books, 1972), 96.

[3] Ibid., 16.

[4] B.F. Skinner, *Science and Human Behavior* (New York, NY: Macmillan, 1953), 447.

[5] If the brain is a mere receptor of external stimuli, Skinner's own theories cannot be believed because "theories" are not materialistic stimuli.

[6] Pavlov, *Lectures on Conditioned Reflexes*, 42.

was an evolutionist, he believed his conclusion also applied to the highest animal—human beings. He says, "I trust that I shall not be thought rash if I express a belief that experiments on the higher nervous activities of animals will yield not a few directional indications for education and self-education in man."[7]

To this end, Pavlov, Skinner, and other behaviorists believe that similar conditioning can be applied to humans to educate, train, or control them to do only good. Shortly before his death, Pavlov told his lab assistants, "Now we can and must go forward. . . . [W]e may use all of the experimental material for the investigation of the human being, striving to perfect the human race of the future."[8]

> Now we can and must go forward. . . . [W]e may use all of the experimental material for the investigation of the human being, striving to perfect the human race of the future.
>
> — IVAN PAVLOV

5.4.4 MARXISM'S REJECTION OF TRADITIONAL BEHAVIORISM

Although Pavlov's theories harmonized well with the Marxist worldview, they did not mesh perfectly with traditional behaviorism. Where Pavlov and traditional behaviorists part company, Marxism does likewise.

Marxism rejects some of the logical conclusions that flow from traditional behaviorism. Joseph Nahem explains, "From this dialectical viewpoint, behaviorism in psychology, such as the theories of J.B. Watson or B.F. Skinner, must be criticized as mechanical, as the reduction of the psychological process of human functioning to the physiological process of behavior alone."[9]

Nahem reveals the reason Marxist psychology rejects traditional behaviorism when he says, "Marxism maintains that there are laws of social development which will lead, through conscious struggle, to a better society, socialism. Skinner believes that his 'Behavioral Engineering' will make for a better society. What kind of society will Skinner produce?"[10]

The Marxist worldview sees humanity in a *conscious struggle* to achieve a communist society. Traditional behaviorism's rejection of our free will runs counter to and would, in fact, preclude the *will* of the proletariat to revolt and overthrow the oppressive upper classes.

The conflict lies in the incompatibility of a materialist philosophy and the notion of free will. Marx, who lived before the development of behaviorist theory, recognized the conflict and tried to resolve it by claiming, "The materialist doctrine that men are the product of circumstances and education—forgets that circumstances are changed precisely by men."[11] The two conflicting ideas are made more obvious by the advent of deterministic behaviorist theory in psychology.

5.4.5 SPEECH AND STIMULI

Pavlov himself provides the solution to the Marxist dilemma of embracing many aspects of behaviorism, yet rejecting its final conclusion that we have no free will. Pavlov postulates

---

[7] Ibid., 391.

[8] Ivan Pavlov, in a statement to his assistants on Feb. 21, 1936, according to W.H. Gantt in the Introduction to *Conditional Reflexes and Psychiatry* (New York, NY: International Publishers, 1963), 14.

[9] Joseph Nahem, *Psychology and Psychiatry Today: A Marxist View* (New York, NY: International Publishers, 1981), 13.

[10] Ibid., 48.

[11] Karl Marx, "The Third Thesis on Feuerbach," in *Gesamtausgabe* (Frankfurt, GR: 1927–1932), 5:534, sec. 1.

The Pop Culture Connection

A Clockwork Orange (a 1971 Best Picture Oscar winning film) was a response to B.F. Skinner's theories of behaviorism. The movie shows a brutal criminal being subjected to a conditioning program that produces a violent physical reaction at the mere thought of harming another person. After a demonstration of the therapy's effectiveness, the following dialogue takes place between the prison warden and an Anglican clergyman, who opens the scene.

"Choice! The boy has no real choice! Has he? Self-interest! The fear of physical pain drove him to that grotesque act of self-abasement! Its insincerity was clearly to be seen. He ceases to be a wrongdoer. He ceases also to be a creature capable of moral choice."

The warden answers: "Padre, these are subtleties! We're not concerned with motives for the higher ethics. We are concerned only with cutting down crime and with relieving the ghastly congestion in our prisons! He will be your true Christian, ready to turn the other cheek! Ready to be crucified rather than crucify....The point is that it works!"

that human beings differ from the rest of the animal world in their capacity to respond to word stimuli as well as to common environmental stimuli. Nahem explains, "Pavlov identified the qualitative difference between humans and animals in the possession by humans of a second signal system, i.e., speech, which was 'the latest acquisition in the process of evolution.'"[12]

Nahem explains how Marxist psychology embraces Pavlov's "analysis of speech and language as a second signal system" as a "devastating refutation of Skinner" and a "profound contribution to psychology."[13] Thus Marxists maintain that although we are shaped by our environment and society, speech is a tool we can use to shape the stimuli that act upon us. Speech is instrumental in defining and maintaining society and allows us to shape our own environment.

5.4.6 SOCIETY AND HUMAN BEHAVIOR

In Marxist psychology, society—through speech—affects our behavior. Nahem explains further, "Most decisive in its influence on our thoughts, feelings, and behavior," says Nahem, "is society and social relations. . . . Human beings are distinguished from animals by their social labor, their social communication, their social groupings, by their social acquisition and use of language, and by their involvement in the ideas, attitudes, morality and behavior of their society."[14] According to A.R. Luria, we long for this type of societal influence and create society so as to produce more external stimuli.[15]

5.4.7 CAPITALISM'S FAILURE AND SOCIALISM'S SUCCESS

To Marxists, socialist society encourages desirable behavior better than capitalist society. The major flaw in capitalist society, they believe, is the divisive nature of social classes—the oppression of one or more classes by a ruling class creates deviant behavior. The only way to eradicate this deviant behavior is by restructuring society.

L.P. Bueva describes the problem with a capitalist society that allows religious faith: "The essence of man is presented in a mystical way, the idea of the primacy of the spirit and of a full non-acceptance of objectivity, a rejection of the real world in favor of God, the idea of 'a revolution within man' through his spiritual renaissance based on religious faith—these are

[12] Nahem, *Psychology and Psychiatry Today*, 9, quoting Pavlov's *Selected Works* (Moscow, USSR: Foreign Languages Publishing House, 1955), 537.

[13] Pavlov, *Selected Works*, 537.

[14] Nahem, *Psychology and Psychiatry Today*, 45, quoting Marx's "The Third Thesis on Feuerbach," 84.

[15] A. R. Luria, *The Nature of Human Conflicts*, (New York, NY: Grove Press, 1960), 401-2.

all ideological expressions of the crisis of capitalism's social system and of the contemporary bourgeois world's values."[16]

Bueva goes on to explain the benefits of a socialist society over a capitalist one: "Socialist social relations develop an ability of the individual for self-regulation, control over his social behavior and for developing an active attitude in relation to life."[17] Marxists hold that only socialist society can encourage and shape psychologically healthy citizens and prevent us from turning to religious faith.

5.4.8 DIALECTICS AND MARXIST PSYCHOLOGY

Marxist psychology uses dialectics to support its rejection of traditional behaviorism. In the dialectical view, our behavior is determined by the clash or struggle between our free will (thesis) and the forces in our environment and society (antithesis). The basis for this view is in Marx's declaration that "men make their own history, but they do not make it under circumstances chosen by themselves, but under circumstances directly encountered, given and transmitted from the past."[18]

Nahem summarizes the relationship between determinism and free will and between behaviorism and dialectics: "Skinner abandons freedom and dignity and espouses a rigidly determinist view, a view that Marxism calls mechanical materialism. It was only with the development of Marxism that the full relationship between freedom and determinism could be explained. Materialism needed dialectics to delineate the true meaning of freedom."[19]

5.4.9 CONCLUSION

The dialectical view of behavior and freedom is consistent with the Marxist worldview, explaining scientifically the urgency and inevitability of communism, yet maintaining the concept of free will.

The terms *freedom* or *free will* in Marxist psychology indicate our liberty to choose the type of society that will in turn determine our behavior; it does not mean we choose our own behavior. Thus, when we are not exercising our free will to choose our society, we are being controlled by our situation or environment.

Marxists hold society responsible to *regulate* us. This *regulation* exposes us to the proper stimuli that will elicit the proper behavior. This stimuli is found only in a communist society that *regulates* us to be faithful to the collective and to *internationalism*.

In this context, freedom means virtually nothing. A society that scientifically regulates human development is much like the one depicted by George Orwell in *1984*. In Marxist psychology, we are merely evolving animals that need fine-tuning before entering the perfection of the coming world order—an order where all humanity will be perfected. The new order, however, will deprive us of freedom and dignity as do Skinner and all materialist psychologies.

[16] L.P. Bueva, *Man: His Behaviour and Social Relations* (Moscow, USSR: Progress Publishers, 1979), 28.

[17] Ibid., 179.

[18] Karl Marx, *Collected Works*, 40 vols. (New York, NY: International Publishers, 1976), 11:103.

[19] Nahem, *Psychology and Psychiatry Today*, 46.

Psychology

> "Everyone anywhere who tunes into the Higher Self becomes part of the transformation. Their lives then become orchestrated from other realms."[1]
>
> — KEN CAREY

5.5.1 INTRODUCTION

Cosmic Humanist psychology is closely tied to the belief that we can hasten the progress of evolution by achieving a *higher consciousness*, which is the central goal of the New Age movement. Psychology provides the means to achieve this goal.

The psychological branch that emphasizes higher consciousness is sometimes referred to as "fourth force" psychology. According to John White, "Fourth force psychology covers a wide range of human affairs. All of them, however, are aimed at man's ultimate development—not simply a return from unhealthiness to normality—as individuals and as a species."[2]

"Ultimate development" represents the only truly healthy mindset in the New Age movement. Marilyn Ferguson explains ultimate development this way: "Well-being cannot be infused intravenously or ladled in by prescription. It comes from a matrix: the body mind. It reflects psychological and somatic harmony."[3]

Our measure of consciousness affects our body and soul, and only a constant state of higher consciousness ensures our mental and physical well-being. Psychology, therefore, plays an

[1] Ken Carey, in a speech at Whole Life Expo (Los Angeles, CA), Feb. 1987.

[2] John White, *Frontiers of Consciousness* (New York, NY: Julian Press, 1985), 7.

[3] Marilyn Ferguson, *The Aquarian Conspiracy* (Los Angeles, CA: J.P. Tarcher, 1980), 248.

important role in the Cosmic Humanist worldview for two reasons: it can hasten the realization of a collective God-consciousness and it works to ensure perfect health for each of us.

5.5.2 MIND OVER MATTER

Cosmic Humanist psychology sees health problems as mindset problems since our mindset is responsible for our health. People suffering through painful sickness or disease are doing so because they have not yet achieved **higher consciousness**. Shakti Gawain says, "Every time you don't trust yourself and don't follow your inner truth, you decrease your aliveness and your body will reflect this with a loss of vitality, numbness, pain, and eventually, physical disease."[4]

> **HIGHER CONSCIOUSNESS:** The ever-increasing awareness of one's spiritual essence and the underlying spiritual nature in all things

Vera Alder explains how failure to follow our inner truth or connect with our "God within" may even be responsible for criminal tendencies. She says, "A criminal or an idler will be recognized as a sick individual offering a splendid chance for wise help. Instead of being incarcerated with fellow unfortunates in the awful atmosphere of a prison, the future 'criminal' will be in much demand."[5] Criminals who connect with their higher consciousness are also able to lead healthy lives spiritually, physically, and ethically.

Ferguson explains the effect of achieving higher consciousness on our all-around health: "Health and disease don't just happen to us. They are active processes issuing from inner harmony or disharmony, profoundly affected by our states of consciousness, our ability or inability to flow with experience."[6]

> Health and disease don't just happen to us. They are active processes issuing from inner harmony or disharmony. . .
>
> — MARILYN FERGUSON

Shirley MacLaine explains that enlightened people who maintain higher consciousness can help others solve their problems, magnifying the importance of higher consciousness: "Somewhere way underneath me were the answers to everything that caused anxiety and confusion in the world."[7]

5.5.3 ACHIEVING HIGHER CONSCIOUSNESS

Meditation, sometimes with crystals or mantras, is often the method fourth force psychology employs to induce higher consciousness. A writer in *Life Times* magazine states emphatically, "My message to everyone now is to learn to meditate. It was through meditation that many other blessings came about."[8] Higher consciousness is one of the blessings derived from meditation, as is the ability to channel spirits. Kathleen Vande Kieft says, "Almost without exception, those who channel effectively meditate regularly. The process of channeling itself is an extension of the state of meditation . . . the best way to prepare, then, for channeling is by meditation"[9]

Channeling refers to the Cosmic Humanist belief that spirits will sometimes speak to and through a gifted person who is engaged in meditation. Elena, a spirit allegedly channeled by John Randolph Price, describes beings like herself as "angels of light—whether from earth or other

---

[4] Shakti Gawain, *Living in the Light* (San Rafael, CA: New World Library, 1986), 156.

[5] Vera Alder, *When Humanity Comes of Age* (New York, NY: Samuel Weiser, Inc., 1974), 82.

[6] Ferguson, *The Aquarian Conspiracy*, 257.

[7] Shirley MacLaine, *Out on a Limb* (Toronto, ON: Bantam, 1984), 96.

[8] "The Joys and Frustrations of Being a Healer," *Life Times* Magazine, vol. 1, no. 3, 61.

[9] Kathleen Vande Kieft, *Innersource: Channeling Your Unlimited Self* (New York, NY: Ballantine Books, 1988), 114.

worlds. They search, select and guide those men and women who may be suitable subjects."[10]

All Cosmic Humanists embrace meditation as an important tool for attaining higher consciousness, although not all consider channeling essential. New Age psychologists suggest that practices such as channeling, astrology, firewalking, Ouija boards, and aura readings are a means to enhance the state of higher consciousness achieved through meditation.

New Age psychology is based on communing with the God within. This is a fundamental difference between New Age and Christian meditation. New Age meditation focuses on the *God within*, while Christian meditation focuses on the *God without*. Christians focus on God—who is Maker, Sustainer, Provider, Redeemer, Lord, and Judge—and on His objective, external revelation of truth to us in the Bible.

The children's book *What Is God?*, which teaches Cosmic Humanist meditation to children, clearly illustrates the difference between Christian and New Age meditation. The book says, "And if you really want to pray to God, you can just close your eyes anywhere, and think about that feeling of God, that makes you part of everything and everybody. If you can feel that feeling of God, and everybody else can feel that feeling of God, then we can all become friends together, and we can really understand, 'What is God?' So, if you really want to feel God, you can close your eyes now, and listen to your breath go slowly in and out, and think how you are connected to everything, even if you are not touching everything."[11]

5.5.4 CONCLUSION

New Age psychology provides the jargon and the tools for Cosmic Humanism's relentless pursuit of higher consciousness. Before utopia or the New Age can be achieved, many more people will have to evolve past their present pain into an awareness of their godhood. Psychology's goal is to direct this effort.

Cosmic Humanist psychology provides tools to help people achieve higher consciousness, but each person chooses those applications that seem most appropriate—firewalking, séance, hypnosis, etc. Meditation, however, is required of everyone. The value of the tools is measured by the amount of pain they cure. Higher consciousness implies wellness and thus anything leading to higher consciousness will necessarily reduce physical, spiritual, and mental pain.

According to Marianne Williamson, even life-threatening disease is just a sign of an unhealthy psyche. She says, "Healing results from a transformed perception of our relationship to illness, one in which we respond to the problem with love instead of fear."[12]

If we find the right tools, Cosmic Humanists believe, we can cure the cancer by curing the mind. The tool Williamson recommends is visualization—that is, imagining events happening in the future and then willing these events to come true. Williamson suggests, "Imagine the AIDS virus as Darth Vader, and then unzip his suit to allow an angel to emerge. See the cancer cell or AIDS virus in all its wounded horror, and then see a golden light, or angel, or Jesus, enveloping the cell and transforming it from darkness into light."[13]

Cosmic Humanists believe that if we choose the right psychological tools, we can save ourselves. If we are God enough, our redemption is in our own hands.

---

[10] John Randolph Price, *The Superbeings*, (Austin, TX: Quartus Books, 1981), 51-2.

[11] Etan Boritzer, *What is God?* (Richmond Hill, ON: Firefly Books, 1990), 30.

[12] Marianne Williamson, *A Return to Love: Reflections on the Principles of "A Course in Miracles"* (New York, NY: Harpers Collins, 1989), 208.

[13] Ibid., 209.

Psychology

Postmodernism

> "[A]ll ideas about human reality are social constructions."[1]
>
> — WALTER TRUETT ANDERSON

5.6.1 INTRODUCTION

Psychology, understood as the study of the psyche, or soul, has fallen on hard times. Traditionally, we understood our personal identity as what we are born with—a stable, unified soul including mind, heart, will, and conscience. Yet, in recent years, our Postmodern condition has made the concept of a "soul" obsolete. Now, instead of being a soul, we are confronted with a multiplicity of "selves."[2]

Hazel Rose Markus, professor of psychology at the University of Michigan, calls this "the most exciting time in psychology in decades and decades." We have begun to realize, she says, that "there isn't just one answer to the 'Who am I?' question." Mitchell Stephens, a journalism professor at New York University explains that "mutating lifestyles and changing intellectual currents have led a group of increasingly influential psychologists—Postmodern psychologists seems to be the name that is sticking—to the conclusion that we have no single, separate,

---

[1] Walter Truett Anderson, *Reality Isn't What It Used To Be: Theatrical Politics, Ready-to-Wear Religion, Global Myths, Primitive Chic, and Other Wonders of the Postmodern World* (New York, NY: HarperCollins Publishers, 1990), 3.

[2] Quoted in Mitchell Stephens, "To Thine Own Selves be True," *Los Angeles Times Magazine* (August 23, 1992). Online article accessed August 10, 2005: http://www.nyu.edu/classes/stephens/Postmodern%20psych%20page. htm.

unified self. They maintain that we contain many selves and that the proper response to the suggestion 'Get in touch with yourself' or 'Be yourself' is 'Which one?'"[3]

Stephens offers the following example to clarify this point. "Consider . . . Mick Jagger. The Rolling Stones' lead singer was and, if the tabloids are to be believed, remains a classic libertine, but he is also a father and, until recently at least, a family man. Jagger is a rock'n'roller, a bohemian, whose songs and lifestyle challenge traditional standards of behavior; yet he travels in upper-class British circles, hobnobbing with dukes and princesses. Jagger can be coarse and crude, yet he knows his nonfiction and his vintages. Which is the real Mick? His answer: all of the above. 'People find it very hard to accept that you can be all these things at almost the same time,' Jagger has complained."[4]

According to philosopher Allan Bloom, "The self is the modern substitute for the soul."[5] In other words, the traditional idea of an immaterial soul as being the seat of our personal identity has been replaced with the Postmodern notion of socially constructed "selves." Reflecting historically on how this shift came about, Bloom suggests that society's earlier preoccupation with the soul "inevitably led to neglect of this world in favor of the other world,"[6] giving the priest, as the guardian of the soul, increased influence and power. This, in turn corrupted kings. "Princes were rendered ineffective by their own or their subjects' opinions about the salvation of their soul, while men slaughtered each other wholesale because of differences of such opinion. The care of the soul crippled men in the conduct of their lives."[7]

As a result, there developed a backlash against the soul. This shift was set in motion by Machiavelli (1460) and Thomas Hobbes (1651), who replaced the idea of the soul with "a feeling self." As Bloom comments, Machiavelli and Hobbes "blazed the trail to the self, which has grown into the highway of a ubiquitous psychology without the psyche (soul)."[8]

Jean-Jacques Rousseau

But the transformation did not stop there. By the time the French political theorist **Jean-Jacques Rousseau** came on the scene in the early 1700s, the self had degenerated into individual self-interest. Rousseau observed that self-interest was not a sufficient base for establishing "the common good," a necessary foundation for political life.

At the beginning of the 21st century, Postmodernism had taken the emphasis on self-interest to its logical extreme. If there is no God's-eye-view of what constitutes the individual, we are left to the changing whims of our social condition telling us who and what we are. And, as it turns out, the answers are as varied as there are people to express them.

5.6.2 THE DENIAL OF HUMAN NATURE

Elaborating on our Postmodern condition, Bloom explains, "Man is a culture being, not a natural being. What man has from nature [biology] is nothing compared to what he has acquired from culture. A culture, like the language that accompanies and expresses it, is a set of mere accidents that add up to a coherent meaning constitutive of man."[9]

---

[3] Ibid.

[4] Ibid.

[5] Allan Bloom, *The Closing of the American Mind* (New York, NY: Simon and Schuster, 1988), 173.

[6] Ibid., 174.

[7] Ibid.

[8] Ibid., 175.

[9] Bloom, *The Closing of the American Mind*, 190.

Traditionally people sensed that both nature and culture are important for human development. But once the move was set in motion to negate nature and accent culture, Postmodernists jumped to banish nature altogether. This left only culture to shape the human psyche.

For Foucault, each of us is "a being which is at least partially subjected to socially produced constraints and divisions."[10] He sees "the modern-day notion of the self [as] bound up with, and inseparable from, the workings of social structures and institutions."[11] There is, therefore, no distinction "between public and private selves implied by the concept of human nature nor can the individual be reduced to individual consciousness."[12]

Gilles Deleuze and Felix Guattari's *Anti-Oedipus: Capitalism and Schizophrenia* is an important Postmodern text. Deleuze and Guattari reject the idea that the soul is naturally whole, unified, or coherent; rather it is a harmful illusion. Instead, they see the self as a flux of desires and intensities caught up in an ongoing process of change.

With the denial of human nature complete, the stage was set for the Postmodern definition of the socially constructed self. Ward explains, "There are many sides to the unfolding story of Postmodern identity, but the starting point is that the self is fundamentally social."[13]

5.6.3 SOCIALLY CONSTRUCTED SELVES

The psychology of the socially constructed self was developed by **Jacques Lacan**, a French psychologist, who was one of four French intellectuals of the 1960s whose writings forged much of Postmodern thought.[14] "Lacan's vision of the self is outlined in his famous essay, 'The Mirror Stage as Formative of the Function of the I,' first published in 1949" writes Glenn Ward. Then, quoting Lacan, "'Selfhood is really nothing but a fleeting, unstable, incomplete and open-minded mess of desires which cannot be fulfilled.'"[15]

Jacques Lacan

Ward comments, "Lacan and Foucault propose that the stable, unified self has always been an illusion."[16] In their view, our identity is the result of social factors—"You are constructed by the social [e.g., language, geography, family, education, government, etc.] and are ultimately determined by it."[17]

Walter Truett Anderson puts it this way: "All ideas about human reality are social constructions."[18] In other words, what used to be called the soul "is replaced with a collage of social constructs."[19]

---

[10] Glen Ward, *Postmodernism* (Chicago, IL: McGraw-Hill Companies, 2003), 142.

[11] Ibid., 141.

[12] Ibid.

[13] Ibid., 118.

[14] Barbara Epstein, "Postmodernism and the Left," *New Politics* vol. 6, no. 2, Winter, 1997: "The constellation of trends that I am calling Postmodernism has it origins in the writings of a group of French intellectuals of the 60s, the most preeminently Michel Foucault, Jacques Derrida, Jacques Lacan, and Jean-Francois Lyotard. Those who developed Postmodernism tended to be associated with the radicalism of the 60s."

[15] Ward, *Postmodernism*, 149

[16] Ibid., 120.

[17] Ibid., 136. While Postmodernists are infatuated with race, gender, and class, it would appear that race and gender are not easily classified as social, but biological.

[18] Anderson, *Reality Isn't What It Used To Be*, 3.

[19] Ibid.

The Pop Culture Connection

The DaVinci Code (a 2006 film)—"Ron Howard's film version of Dan Brown's bestselling novel provides a comfortable, if remarkably flimsy, buttress for viewers looking for reasons to reject the gospel . . . [Unlike the book version of the story,] Mr. Hanks' Langdon plays much more the role of a skeptic in the film, losing some of the all-knowing academic tone that defines his character in the book. Langdon often argues with the film's version of the Holy Grail story, which involves Christ taking a bride and bearing children—regularly referring to the story as a "myth," something he doesn't do in the book . . . In place of Mr. Brown's idealized picture of ancient paganism, Mr. Howard and screenwriter Akiva Goldsman have substituted an oh-so-familiar Hollywood religion that is certainly easier to swallow for many—and a more insidious force in modern culture. This is, of course, the religion of me. Langdon's repeated advice to Sophie in a crucial final scene is, 'It's important what you believe.' Not what's true, but what's true for you. In the final analysis, Christianity isn't entirely repudiated, even if it is based on utter falsehoods, because faith (in something) is important, insofar as that faith benefits those who require it. That, more than Mr. Brown's silly, easily refuted conspiracy theories, is an all too prevalent cancer on our culture's understanding of spirituality."*

Stephens contends that "The implications of the [Postmodern] theory are large: It's not just that we each have different sides to our personality; it's that we have no central personality in relation to which all our varied behaviors might be seen as just 'sides.' We are, in other words, not absolutely anything."[20]

But there is more. Postmodern psychologists are now asserting there is no one "self," but a multiplicity of "selves." Kenneth Gergen is a psychology professor at Swarthmore College. His book, *The Saturated Self: Dilemmas of Identity in Con-temporary Life*, is considered one of the best introductions to Postmodern psychology. Gergen states, "...postmoderns are populated with a plethora of selves. In place of an enduring core of deep and indelible character, there is a chorus of invitations. Each invitation 'to be' also casts doubt on the wisdom and authenticity of the others. Further, the postmodern person senses the constructed character of all attempts at being—on the part of both self and others."[21]

Gergen's assessment of the Postmodern condition has a following among other Postmodern psychologists. Stephens writes that "a group of counselors and therapists, for example, has begun noting that we all must 'create' other selves as we leave our families in search of friendship, success and love—and then move on to new friendships, new successes and new loves. Social psychologists have begun studying not only our 'child selves,' our 'professional selves,' our 'friendship selves' and our 'parent selves,' but also what Hazel Markus labels our 'possible selves,' our 'feared possible selves,' our 'ideal selves,' our 'fleeting selves,' our 'tentative selves' and our 'chronically accessible selves.'"[22]

To illustrate our Postmodern multiplicity of selves, Gergen paints the following collage of Postmodern life: "Connie spent her childhood in New Jersey. After her parents were divorced, her mother moved with the children to San Diego. Connie's teen years were spent shuttling between father and mother on either coast. After she graduated from the University of Colorado, she moved to Alaska to work on a fishing boat, and then to Wyoming to become a ski instructor. Now Connie is working on a geological-survey vessel in the Antarctic, and is engaged to a man

[20] Stephens, "To Thine Own Selves be True."

[21] Kenneth J. Gergen, *The Saturated Self: Dilemmas of Identity in Contemporary Life* (New York, NY: Basic Books, 2000), 174. See Questia, April 19, 2006 <http://www.questia.com/PM.qst?a=o&d=30397317>.

[22] Stephens, "To Thine Own Selves be True."

* Andrew Coffin, *The DaVinci Code,* World Magazine, May 27, 2006, http://www.worldmag.com/articles/11899.

UNDERSTANDING
THE TIMES

living in Portland, Oregon. Fred is a neurologist who spends many of his spare hours working to aid families from El Salvador. Although he is married to Tina, on Tuesday and Thursday nights he lives with an Asian friend with whom he has a child. On weekends he drives his BMW to Atlantic City for gambling."[23]

Gergen is pointing out that in our technologically "saturated" society with its multiple opportunities for personal interaction, it is impossible to know which is our "real" self, since we play so many different roles at different times and with different people. This can be disorienting to some. A theory of multiple **socially constructed selves** provides a way for those living in a Postmodern world to adjust to the reality of their condition.

5.6.4 CRITIQUE OF POSTMODERN PSYCHOLOGY

A socially constructed, unstable self creates special difficulties in the area of law, crime, and punishment. For example, if a self were to "flux" quickly, a criminal act on a particular night of rape and pillage may be blamed on a previous shifting self, making it difficult to locate and punish the guilty "self." Louis Sass, a Rutgers clinical psychology professor, puts it this way, "There are clearly dangers in giving up that notion of a single self. You absolve the person of responsibility for making judgments." Imagine the excuses people might make: "Hey, it wasn't my fault. One of my other selves did it."[24]

Not only are there problems in the area of law, crime, and punishment, but there are also major problems deciding exactly what is normal and abnormal. Walter Truett Anderson addresses this problem when he says, "I have been putting words like 'abnormal' and 'deviant' in quotes, because those categorizations are under fire now, the boundary between normal and abnormal is as questionable now as all the other boundaries that once defined social reality."[25]

> **SOCIALLY-CONSTRUCTED SELVES:** The belief that one's identity is constantly changing as a result of ever-changing social factors

According to Anderson, Postmodernists are not in the boundary business. Certainly if they can't find boundaries between the biological and the cultural (nature and nurture), why should we expect them to find boundaries between the normal and abnormal? For example, Michel Foucault knowingly infected his homosexual partners with the AIDS virus. This should cause even the most devout Postmodernist to think twice before blurring the boundaries between sane and insane, normal and abnormal, and common sense and the ridiculous. If Postmodernists consider Foucault's behavior "normal," then there is no definition of abnormal worth considering.

It should also be noted that among the majority of psychologists, Postmodernist psychology is viewed as a fringe movement. At this point it seems unlikely that the Postmodern approach to psychology will have a major influence on the future direction of psychology in general.

5.6.5 CONCLUSION

Christian psychology is founded on the concept of soul (mind, heart), self-identity, and self-awareness (1 Thessalonians 5:23). In Genesis 2:7, we learn that God breathed and mankind became a living soul. In Matthew 10:28, Jesus warns us not to fear those who can kill the body, but rather fear the one who can kill the body (soma) and soul (psyche) in hell (gehenna).

J.P. Moreland summarizes the biblical concept of our identity when he says, "Human beings

---

[23] Gergen, *The Saturated Self: Dilemmas of Identity in Contemporary Life*, 171.
[24] Cited in Stephens, "To Thine Own Selves be True."
[25] Ibid.

are composed of an immaterial entity—a soul, a life principle, a ground of sentience—and a body. More specifically, a human being is a unity of two distinct entities—body and soul."[26]

Originally "psychology" meant the study of the psyche (soul). Now that we have entered into a post-Christian culture, maybe psychologists need to search for another name to describe their profession. Perhaps this is what Christian psychologist Paul C. Vitz had in mind when he wrote the article, "Psychology in Recovery." Vitz offers the following suggestion at the end of his article, "I close on a guardedly optimistic note. On the horizon I see the potential for a psychology that I call 'transmodern.' By this term I mean a new mentality that both transcends and transforms modernity. Thus, it will leave both modern and Postmodern psychology behind. It will bring in transcendent understanding that may be idealistic and philosophical (e.g., the virtues), as well as spiritual and religious. It will transform modernity by bringing in an intelligent understanding of much of premodern wisdom....In such a transmodern world, psychology would be the handmaid of philosophy and theology, as from the beginning it was meant to be."[27]

---

[26] J.P. Moreland and Scott B. Rae, *Body & Soul: Human Nature & the Crisis in Ethics* (Downers Grove, IL: Inter-Varsity Press, 2000), 17. Students are directed to Moreland and Rae's work along with editor William Dembski's work on materialism to be released in 2007. Its working title is *The End of Materialism*.

[27] Paul C. Vitz, "Psychology in Recover," *First Things* (March 2005), http://www.firstthings.com/ftissues/ft0503/articles/vitz.html.

Sociology

Christianity

"For this reason a man will leave his father and mother and be united to his wife, and the two will become one flesh."

EPHESIANS 5:31

6.1.1 INTRODUCTION

All sociologists acknowledge the existence of social institutions such as **family, church,** and **state**. They differ, however, in their description of the origin, authority, and purpose of these institutions and how each relates to the individual. These differences result from assumptions inherent in their worldview.

The Christian worldview teaches that God created men and women in His image; the atheistic worldviews, however, teach that men

> **FAMILY, CHURCH, STATE:** The Christian belief that society is divided into three God-ordained institutions

and women are evolving animals. The atheistic worldviews are the predominant views among modern sociologists, who consider God, Adam and Eve, the Garden of Eden, and the sanctity of the family to be pre-scientific myths. Christians understand that this erroneous view is responsible for many of the failures we see in contemporary society, such as drug and alcohol abuse, crime, abortion, sexual perversion, disease, and poverty.

6.1.2 FREE WILL AND SOCIETY

Christian sociology affirms the individual's free will and responsibility. There is a fundamental difference between it and atheistic sociology. Atheistic approaches claim that society determines our consciousness and actions. Christianity, on the other hand, holds that we are free to choose between right and wrong, good and evil, and that we shape society in the process (rather than being shaped by it).

> Christianity grants us control over our society, but it also requires us to be responsible for our choices.

Christianity grants us control over our society, but it also requires us to be responsible for our choices. In the Christian worldview, we face the consequences of our actions. Adam and Eve's failure to obey God in the Garden of Eden in the opening chapters of Genesis resulted not only in their expulsion from the garden paradise, but also brought a curse on the entire human race. William Stanmeyer explains, "If man's behavior were somehow conditioned by genetic code or social externals then no just judge could blame him for the evil he commits. But the scripture teaches unequivocally that God blamed Adam and Eve for succumbing to the temptation to disobedience and punished them accordingly."[1]

The Genesis account of Adam and Eve's sin not only demonstrates that we are responsible for our actions, but also teaches that we are guilty before God. One Christian author says, "The fact of guilt is one of the major realities of man's existence."[2] Christian sociology, therefore, attempts to understand society in light of our free will and the consequences of our free choice to turn away from God. The Fall has caused all societies over all time to be marked by alienation and imperfection and sin.

Some historical examples of our imperfections and state of alienation include Rousseau placing all five of his children in orphanages, the poet Shelley living in a nightmare, and the Apostle Paul calling himself chief among sinners. The history of the dark side of our human condition—a tale of degeneration and devolution rather than evolution—fills volumes. Alienation pervades all of our relationships, with God, with others, and even within ourselves. Sociologists who understand that we are alienated from God because of sin will interpret data differently than those who believe we are inherently good but have been corrupted by our society and environment.

6.1.3 THE INHERENT WORTH OF THE INDIVIDUAL

William Carey

Christian sociology does not take a pessimistic view of society even though it seems as if we always make wrong decisions and bad choices. On the contrary, Christian sociology takes an optimistic view because it accepts the fact that God grants grace to us in spite of our failures and errors. Our freedom and responsibility before God grant us far more dignity and significance than deterministic views would grant us. Francis Schaeffer explains that we are "not a cog in a machine, . . . not a piece of theater; [we] really can influence history. From the biblical viewpoint, [we are] lost, but great."[3] Christians such as **William Carey** and **William Wilberforce**, for example,

---

[1] William A. Stanmeyer, *Clear and Present Danger* (Ann Arbor, MI: Servant Books, 1983), 161.
[2] Rousas J. Rushdoony, *Politics of Guilt and Pity* (Fairfax, VA: Thoburn Press, 1978), 1.
[3] Francis A. Schaeffer, *Death in the City* (Downers Grove, IL: InterVarsity Press, 1976), 21.

were able to change their society and history by bringing an end to the slave trade.[4]

The Christian worldview sees each person as valuable and able to contribute to society. Rather than seeing the individual as helpless in the face of societal and environmental pressures, Christian sociologists view the person as more important than the social institution. C.S. Lewis explains that while atheists may think that "nations, classes, civilizations must be more important than individuals," because "individuals live only seventy odd years each and the group may last for centuries. But to the Christian, individuals are more important, for they live eternally; and races, civilizations and the like are in comparison the creatures of a day."[5]

William Wilberforce

6.1.4 THE INDIVIDUAL AS A SOCIAL BEING

Even though Christian sociology values the individual over the social order, social order is still important in the Christian worldview. We were created as social beings (Genesis 2:20) and recognize the role society plays in history

> The Christian worldview sees each person as valuable and able to contribute to society.

as well as in our relationship with God. S.D. Gaede stresses our inherent social nature when he says, "God designed the human being to be a relational creature. Note this point well. Humankind was created to relate to other beings. It was not an accident. It was not the result of sin. It was an intentional, creational given."[6] Nevertheless, because of the fall we continue to experience alienation, which Gaede refers to as the "relational dilemma." Because Christians understand the cause of this dilemma, we can work to help others not only understand its cause but its solution as well.

6.1.5 CHRISTIAN PLURALISM

The sociological concept that the individual is more important than institutions in society and that society is important because God created us as social beings is called *pluralism*. In this view, neither society nor the individual is the only true reality; both must be valued in order to correctly understand reality. This perspective ensures that we "can never be reduced to either a mere atomistic individual or a mere integer in some social whole."[7] Pluralism holds that both the individual and societal groups are accountable to God (2 Kings 17:7–23 and Acts 17:31). If each member of society acts responsibly, then each societal institution can focus on governing its realm of interest properly and allow other institutions the same freedom.

---

[4] Hugh Thomas, *The Slave Trade: The Story of the Atlantic Slave Trade: 1440–1870* (New York, NY: Simon and Schuster, 1999). Bringing the slave trade to an end was one of the great feats of human history. It was accomplished primarily by evangelical Christians. Thomas Sowell, *Black Rednecks and White Liberals* (San Francisco, CA: Encounter Books, 2005), 116, "Moreover, within Western civilization, the principal impetus for the abolition of slavery came first from very conservative religious activists—people who would today be called 'the religious right.' Clearly, this story is not 'politically correct' in today's terms. Hence it is ignored, as if it never happened."
[5] C.S. Lewis, *God in the Dock* (Grand Rapids, MI: Eerdmans, 1972), 109–110.
[6] S.D. Gaede, *Where Gods May Dwell* (Grand Rapids, MI: Zondervan, 1985), 75–6.
[7] Rockne McCarthy, Donald Oppewal, Walfred Peterson, and Gordon Spykman, *Society, State, and Schools* (Grand Rapids, MI: Eerdmans, 1982), 151.

6.1.6 BIBLICALLY PRESCRIBED INSTITUTIONS

In Christian sociology, the family, the church, and the state are God-ordained institutions. **Dietrich Bonhoeffer** and some others would include labor as a fourth God-ordained institution.

Dietrich Bonhoeffer

Realizing that God ordained these societal institutions demonstrates the relevance of Christianity to every aspect of reality. Bonhoeffer explains, "It is God's will that there shall be labor, marriage, government, and church in the world; and it is His will that all these, each in its own way, shall be through Christ, directed towards Christ, and in Christ. . . . This means that there can be no retreating from a 'secular' into a 'spiritual' sphere."[8] Bonhoeffer makes it clear that no aspect of society lies outside the realm of Christianity. All society, indeed all of life, is bound inextricably with God and His plan for the world. In Bonhoeffer's view, "the world is relative to Christ."[9]

6.1.7 MARRIAGE AND THE FAMILY

The family is ordained by God (Genesis 2:23–25) and is a fundamental social institution. The Bible strictly defines the family and its role in society. James Dobson and Gary Bauer say that a family exists when "husband and wife are lawfully married, are committed to each other for life, and [the family] adheres to the traditional values on which the family is based."[10]

George Gilder and many other Christian sociologists believe that the condition of marriage and family in any given society describes the condition of the entire society. If the family is troubled, then society is troubled. Encouraging and building up the God-ordained institution of marriage and family is, therefore, advantageous to society.

Unfortunately, society today does more to discourage marriage and family than to build it up. The many forces working against marriage and family are primarily a result of the Secular Humanist-inspired sexual revolution. For example, children in public schools are taught that homosexuality is a normal lifestyle; students are given condoms and encouraged to use them instead of practicing abstinence until marriage; teenage girls are taught about abortion and how to obtain one without their parents'

The Pop Culture Connection

Cinderella Man (a 2005 film directed by Ron Howard)—"The story of real-life Depression-era boxer James Braddock, who literally went from the soup lines to the world championship, is more than just another story about someone who overcame tremendous odds. It's a story of family and friendship, of goodness and faith. Braddock, played marvelously by Russell Crowe, is portrayed as a God-fearing man of integrity who is madly in love with his wife and kids. It's a story that illustrates the power of truly knowing what you're fighting for." Other films with a positive family message include ***The Patriot*** (2000), ***Cheaper by the Dozen*** (1950 & 2003), ***Raising Helen*** (2004), and ***Pride and Prejudice*** (2005).[11]

---

[8] Dietrich Bonhoeffer, *Ethics* (New York, NY: Macmillan 1959), 207.

[9] Ibid.

[10] James Dobson and Gary Bauer, *Children at Risk* (Dallas, TX: Word, 1990), 112.

[11] Summary excerpt from http://www.christianitytoday.com/movies/reviews/cinderellaman.html

consent or knowledge. Dobson and Bauer label these practices "a crash course in relativism, in immorality, and in anti-Christian philosophy."[12]

Attacks on the traditional family come largely from proponents of relativistic, materialistic worldviews. Humanists, Marxists, and many Postmodernists deny the existence of the soul, thereby devaluing the importance of the family. The Christian worldview recognizes marriage and family as the institution that nurtures the whole person. In this view, the family provides an environment that encourages mental, spiritual, social, and physical growth.

6.1.8 THE CHURCH IN SOCIETY

God ordained the church to serve specific functions. The church is intended to function as a community composed of individuals working together to nurture each other and going out from it to serve the larger society.

One principal role of the church is to proclaim the truth regarding sin, repentance, and salvation. The church can play a critical role in turning a society toward God by explaining that both individuals and societies are guilty of sin and will be held responsible.

Another role of the church in society is to model true community by demonstrating what it means to "love your neighbor as yourself." The church must show that God is relational and the initiator of all relations. Schaeffer is adamant about the need for community in the Christian church: "I am convinced that in the 20th century people all over the world will not listen if we have the right doctrine, the right polity, but are not exhibiting community."[13] This timeless call to serve others in love is grounded in Ephesians 4:11–16.

6.1.9 CONCLUSION

Christian sociology values both individuals and social institutions. As individuals, we are free to make choices, but our choice to turn away from God alienates us from Him and others. Society as a whole is also fallen and imperfect and responsible for its choices and attitudes. Deterministic worldviews that deny the free will of individuals and institutions deny the significance of both. There can be no meaningful judgment if forces outside our control determine all individual and corporate actions. Isaiah 46:8–11 shows us God's plan to judge our actions, as well as our ability to do what we choose.

As humans, we will face the consequences for choices we make in creating our society. God gives us the responsibility to protect and direct the societal institutions He ordains, including family, state, and church. Families are charged with reproductive responsibilities as well as training and nurturing. The state is charged with carrying out justice, primarily involving law and order. The church is charged with demonstrating Christian love within itself and in society at large.

---

[12] Ibid., 55. For an in-depth look at what is transpiring in such classroom instruction we recommend Dobson and Bauer's *Children at Risk*; Phyllis Schlafly, *Child Abuse in the Classroom* (Alton, IL: Marquette Press, 1985); Judith A. Reisman and Edward W Eichel, *Kinsey, Sex and Fraud* (Lafayette, LA: Huntington House, 1990); B.K. Eakman, *Cloning of the American Mind: Eradicating Morality Through Education* (Lafayette, LA: Huntington House, 1998); Allan Bloom, *The Closing of the American Mind* (New York, NY: Simon and Schuster, 1987); and Thomas Sowell, *Inside American Education: The Decline, The Deception, The Dogmas* (New York, NY: The Free Press, 1993).

[13] Francis A. Schaeffer, *The Church at the End of the 20th Century* (Downers Grove, IL: InterVarsity Press, 1974), 73.

We are answerable to God for the direction these institutions lead society. The same burden of responsibility, however, points to the blessing of having free will yet belonging to a loving and just God. Our freedom entails responsibilities, duties, and work. We are not free to wreak mayhem in the social order; but we are free to serve others in love and to serve and love God. Such is God's call on the human race.

Sociology

Islam

"Humanity is one single family of God and there can be no sanction for . . . barriers. Men are one—and not bourgeois or proletarian, white or black, Aryan or non-Aryan, Westerner or Easterner. Islam gives a revolutionary concept of the unity of mankind."[1]

— KHURSHID AHMAD

6.2.1 INTRODUCTION

The structures and features of society are central to the Islamic worldview. Much is said about the relationship of the individual to the society as well as the relationships of men and women, husbands and wives, and so forth.

> POLYGAMY, MOSQUE, ISLAMIC STATE: The Islamic belief that society is composed of three institutions: family (which can be polygamous), Mosque, and State

Like Christianity, the family, worship of God, and the state are central to Islamic teachings, yet there are substantial differences between the two worldviews in each area. Thus the Muslim view of sociology is summarized as revolving around the polygamous family, the mosque, and the state.

---

[1] Khurshid Ahmad, *Islam: Its Meaning and Message,* 3rd ed. (Leicester, UK: The Islamic Foundation, 1999), 30.

6.2.2 INDIVIDUAL AND SOCIETY

Muslims believe that Islam provides a perfect harmony between the individual and society, holding both in concert with each other. "Another unique feature of Islam is that it establishes a balance between individualism and collectivism. It believes in the individual personality of man and holds everyone personally accountable to God. It guarantees the fundamental rights of the individual and does not permit any one to tamper with them. It makes the proper development of the personality of man one of the prime objectives of its educational policy. It does not subscribe to the view that man must lose his individuality in society or in the state. . . . On the other hand, it also awakens a sense of social responsibility in man, organizes human beings in a society and a state and enjoins the individual to subscribe to the social good."[2]

6.2.3 MEN AND WOMEN

The Qur'an affirms that the human race originated from Adam: "O mankind! Reverence your Guardian-Lord, Who created you from a single Person, created, of like nature, his mate, and from them twain scattered (like seeds) countless men and women . . ."

The Qur'an also declares that men and women are spiritual equals before God (33:35): "For Muslim men and women, for believing men and women, for devout men and women, for true men and women, for men and women who are patient and constant, for men and women who humble themselves, for men and women who give in charity, for men and women who fast (and deny themselves), for men and women who guard their chastity, and for men and women who engage much in God's praise, for them has God prepared forgiveness and great reward."

Further, the Qur'an states the differences between men and women: "Men are the protectors and maintainers of women, because Allah has given the one more (strength) than the other, and because they support them from their means. Therefore the righteous women are devoutly obedient, and guard in (the husband's) absence what God would have them guard" (4:34).

Muslim apologists explain these passages as indicating that men are to care for women, not that women are essentially inferior. But other statements in the Qur'an seem to challenge that notion. For example, one passage says, "And get two witnesses, out of your own men, and if there are not two men, then a man and two women, such as ye choose, for witnesses" (2:282), indicating that the testimony of a woman is worth half of the testimony of a man.

Additionally, a tradition in the Sunnah describes women as having less intelligence than men: "Narrated Abu Said Al-Khudri: Once Allah's Apostle went out to the Musalla (to offer the prayer) to 'Id-al-Adha or Al-Fitr prayer. Then he passed by the women and said, 'O women! Give alms, as I have seen that the majority of the dwellers of Hell-fire were you (women).' They asked, 'Why is it so, O Allah's Apostle?' He replied, 'You curse frequently and are ungrateful to your husbands. I have not seen anyone more deficient in intelligence and religion than you. A cautious sensible man could be led astray by some of you.' The women asked, 'O Allah's Apostle! What is deficient in our intelligence and religion?' He said, 'Is not the evidence of two women equal to the witness of one man?' They replied in the affirmative. He said, 'This is the deficiency in her intelligence. Isn't it true that a woman can neither pray nor fast during her menses?' The women replied in the affirmative. He said, 'This is the deficiency in her religion.'"[3]

---

[2] Ibid., 38–39.

[3] Al-Bukhari, Vol. 1, Book 6, Number 301. See http://www.islamonline.com/cgi-bin/news_service/profile_story. asp?service_id=838

Again, while the Qur'an seems to set men and women on equal spiritual footing before Allah, some of the teaching in the Sunnah contradicts it. Muhammad said he had the opportunity to view the people in hell and recorded that the majority of its inhabitants were women! "Narrated `Imran bin Husain: The Prophet said, 'I looked at Paradise and found poor people forming the majority of its inhabitants; and I looked at Hell and saw that the majority of its inhabitants were women.'"[4]

6.2.4 MARRIAGE

The Muslim view of marriage is well developed, though diverse. Some modern Muslims are quite uncomfortable with some of Islam's teachings and practices regarding marriage. But all Muslims agree that a marriage is a contract that may be broken through divorce (though most believe that divorce may only be initiated by men). Some features of marriage noted in the Qur'an and Islamic tradition include the following:

- A Muslim man may marry up to four wives, granted that he treat them equally and provide for each of them (4:3).
- A Muslim man may have an unlimited number of concubines (including slaves) with whom he has sexual relations, though such women do not have the same rights as wives.
- A Muslim man may marry a woman *temporarily*, a marriage lasting a relatively short time (4:24).
- Muslim men may marry Jewish or Christian wives (5:5)—though not women from other religions (2:221), and, yet, Muslim women may never marry non-Muslims (2:221).[5]
- Unsubmissive women may be beaten (some say "lightly") (4:34).
- "Your wives are as a tithe unto you; so approach your tithe when or how ye will . . ." (2:223), meaning men may have sexual access to their wives whenever they please, except when the wife is menstruating (2:222).
- Adultery is severely punished (4:15–18; 17:32; 24:20), but in common practice the application of punishment often falls much harder on women than men, since the value of a woman's testimony is discounted.
- Men may divorce their wives (60:1–2; 65:1–2; 226:242), though reconciliation is to be sought (4:35). The Qur'an makes no allowance for a woman to divorce her husband, although some Muslim countries have permitted it.

6.2.5 POLYGAMY

While most Muslims practice monogamy, the Qur'an permits a man to have four wives, upon certain conditions: "If ye fear that ye shall not be able to deal justly with the orphans, marry women of your choice, two, or three, or four; but if ye fear that ye shall not be able to deal justly (with them), then only one, or (a captive) that your right hand possess. That will be more suitable, to prevent you from doing injustice" (4:3). At this time in Islam's history,

---

[4] Al-Bukhari 4:4264.

[5] The foolishness of some non-Muslim women who marry Muslim men is tragically portrayed in the movie *Not Without My Daughter* (1991, MGM). This true-to-life story portrays a Muslim man living in the United States who is caught up in the fervor of the Iranian revolution led by Ayatollah Khomeini in 1979. He returns to Iran, ostensibly for "a visit," taking his American wife and daughter with him. When he refuses to return, his wife battles Islamic law and tradition in her fight to escape back to the U.S. with her daughter.

this allowance arose because many Muslim men had been killed, leaving widows and orphans without protection or provision.

The Qur'an warns that it is unlikely that men will be able to treat various wives equally: "Ye are never able to be fair and just as between women, even if it is your ardent desire: but turn not away (from a woman) altogether, so as to leave her (as it were) hanging (in the air)" (4:129). A. Yusuf Ali notes, "Legally more than one wife (up to four) are permissible on the condition that a man can be perfectly fair and just to all. But this is a condition almost impossible to fulfill. If, in the hope that he might be able to fulfill it, a man puts himself in that impossible position, it is only right to insist that he should not discard one but at least fulfill all the outward duties that are incumbent on him in respect of her."[6]

Many modern Muslims believe that the practice of polygamy may have been acceptable in times past, but should no longer be practiced. After all, they argue, no man can treat multiple wives with equality, for not even Muhammad did that (as we will see below). While this argument does not accord with traditional Islam, the observation regarding Muhammad is instructive.

6.2.6 MUHAMMAD AND POLYGAMY

While the Qur'an limits the number of wives to four (provided that the husband can treat each woman equally), Muhammad had at least nine wives. This discrepancy is difficult to resolve, although Muhammad offered revelations that permitted him this excess. Non-Muslims, however, have a difficult time not seeing this as self-serving pretense on the part of Muhammad.

> O Prophet! We have made lawful to thee thy wives to whom thou hast paid their dowers; and those whom thy right hand possesses out of the prisoners of war whom God has assigned to thee; and daughters of thy paternal uncles and aunts, and daughters of thy maternal uncles and aunts, who migrated (from Mecca) with thee; and any believing women who dedicates her soul to the Prophet if the Prophet wishes to wed her—this is only for thee, and not for the Believers (at large); We know what We have appointed to them as to their wives and the captives whom their right hands possess—in order that there should be no difficulty for thee. And God is Oft-Forgiving, Most Merciful. (33:50)

Muslim traditions often record Muhammad's dealings with his wives, slaves, and captive women. In fact, his sex life is legendary among Muslims. As recorded in one Hadith, "'The Prophet used to visit all his wives in a round, during the day and night and they were eleven in number.' I asked Anas, 'Had the Prophet the strength for it?' Anas replied, 'We used to say that the Prophet was given the strength of thirty (men).' And Sa'id said on the authority of Qatada that Anas had told him about nine wives only (not eleven) (Bukhari 1:268)."

Muhammad's youngest wife, Aisha, was also his favored wife. She reported "that the Prophet married her when she was six years old and he consummated his marriage when she was nine years old, and then she remained with him for nine years (i.e., "till his death" (Al-Bukhari 7:64). Various traditions in the Hadith record that Muhammad showed favoritism to Aisha above his other wives (though the Qur'an speaks against such unequal treatment).

> He then said to her, "Do not hurt me regarding Aisha, as the Divine Inspirations do not come to me on any of the beds except that of Aisha." On that Um Salama said, "I repent

---

[6] *The Holy Qur'an,* A. Yusuf Ali, trans., 221, n. 639.

to Allah for hurting you." Then the group of Um Salama called Fatima, the daughter of Allah's Apostle and sent her to Allah's Apostle to say to him, "Your wives request to treat them and the daughter of Abu Bakr on equal terms." Then Fatima conveyed the message to him. The Prophet said, "O my daughter! Don't you love whom I love?" She replied in the affirmative and returned and told them of the situation. They requested her to go to him again but she refused. They then sent Zainab bin Jahsh who went to him and used harsh words saying, "Your wives request you to treat them and the daughter of Ibn Abu Quhafa on equal terms." On that she raised her voice and abused Aisha to her face so much so that Allah's Apostle looked at Aisha to see whether she would retort. Aisha started replying to Zainab till she silenced her. The Prophet then looked at Aisha and said, "She is really the daughter of Abu Bakr."[7]

Thus, instead of attempting to treat his wives equally, he told them that he loved Aisha and that revelations came to him only when he was in bed with her.

6.2.7 OF WIVES AND CONCUBINES

In addition to having up to four wives, the Muslim man is given no limit on the number of concubines he may own and have sexual relations with. Indeed, in the Hadith, discussions regarding sex with one's slave girls are common. The sexual appetites of Muslim warriors are also noted, as is Muhammad's approval of their mistreatment of female prisoners of war.

> Abu Sirma said to Abu Sa'id al Khadri (Allah be pleased with him): O Abu Sa'id, did you hear Allah's Messenger (may peace be upon him) mentioning al-'azl? He said: Yes, and added: We went out with Allah's Messenger (may peace be upon him) on the expedition to the Bi'l-Mustaliq and took captive some excellent Arab women; and we desired them, for we were suffering from the absence of our wives, (but at the same time) we also desired ransom for them. So we decided to have sexual intercourse with them but by observing 'azl (withdrawing the male sexual organ before emission of semen to avoid conception). But we said: We are doing an act whereas Allah's Messenger is amongst us; why not ask him? So we asked Allah's Messenger (may peace be upon him), and he said: It does not matter if you do not do it, for every soul that is to be born up to the Day of Resurrection will be born.[8]

Christians no doubt find the sexual practices allowed Muslim men deplorable and perverse.

6.2.8 POLYGAMY IN THE BIBLE

Polygamy occurred in biblical history, in the lives of David, Solomon, and others. Some Muslims assert that the Bible both condones and promotes polygamy and that Islam is superior to the Bible since it limits the number of wives to four. These limitations are insufficient, however, to curb problems inherent in the practice.

The biblical picture of marriage and even polygamy strikes a very different chord than that of Islam. For instance, when God created the first humans, he created a monogamous couple, Adam and Eve (Genesis 1:27; 2:21–25), a biblical ideal that Jesus noted in His teaching (Matthew 19:4).

The first instance of polygamy in the Bible is that of arrogant and sinful Lamech (Genesis 4:19,23). However, despite recording cases of polygamy throughout biblical history, the Bible

---

[7] Al-Bukhari, 3:755.
[8] Ibid., 8:3371.

clearly portrays the consequences of such a decision—*no instance in the Bible of a polygamous marriage turned out well!* God not only created our first parents as monogamous, He also prohibited the kings of Israel from "multiplying wives" (Deuteronomy 17:17), though many of them did just that, often taking wives of foreign nations along with their false gods. This was a terrible compromise that affected the entire nation. In the New Testament, leaders of the church are to be husbands "of one wife" (1 Timothy 3:2,12). Moreover, Jesus' relationship with the church is the perfect example, in that He has one bride (not "brides"), a relationship illustrated by marriage (Ephesians 5:31–32).

6.2.9 PATRIARCHALISM

Muslim societies tend to be patriarchal—that is, they tend to be dominated by men. Women are expected to have children, and those who do not have children face constant fear that the husband will seek another wife. The expectation that women must bear *male* children further aggravates the situation. Regarding "the great fear of Muslim parents that they will not have enough sons," Vivienne Stacey paints a troubling picture: "How often a wife is in distress because she has not produced a child! The wife who produces only girls will also seek religious help as well as perhaps medical help. If she has a son she will want more sons in case the child dies, as it may easily do. So a woman's importance in society in general is estimated by her ability to produce sons. This is an inequality between the sexes which the laws of a country and the efforts of family planning associations can do little about."[9]

Muslims educated in Western universities often realize that these traditions conflict with genetics and other physical concerns. Nevertheless, male expectations for their wives to bear male children, and female fears of failing to fulfill these expectations, persist widely throughout Muslim countries.

6.2.10 CONCLUSION

Islam does not distinguish between social institutions and the state. Rather, Islam is a comprehensive reality—the state is to be as much Islamic as is the local mosque. Islam is a religion; but Islam is also a government. The Muslim world today is divided between those who favor nation-states (with laws, constitutions, and boundaries distinct from other nations) and those who favor pan-Islam (the vision that the Muslim community should be united, with diminished or non-existent national boundaries). Those who favor nation-states sometimes produce Muslim nations where the population is predominantly Muslim but where the law of the land is either not Shari'ah or not purely so.[10] For example, Turkey is a Muslim nation whose constitution is not based on Shari'ah law. Although most of its population is Muslim, Turkey itself is a secular nation.

Muslims who favor a pan-Islamic community are troubled by this and tend to respond with various expressions of disapproval. Sometimes this disapproval takes the form of verbal denouncement of the nation. Sometimes it takes the form of individuals within the government seeking to reform it. The media, however, most often focuses on those who engage in armed protest and terrorist activities, such as often happens in Turkey and Egypt.

---

[9] Vivienne Stacey, *The Life of Muslim Women* (Fellowship of Faith for Muslims, 1980), 34–35.

[10] Shari'ah is the designation for Islamic law, which we discuss in the section on Law. See Chapter 7.2.

Sociology

Secular Humanism

"Essentially man is internally motivated toward positive
personal and social ends; the extent to which he is
not motivated results from a process of demotivation
generated by his relationships and/or environment."[1]

—— ROBERT TANNENBAUM AND SHELDON A. DAVIS

6.3.1 INTRODUCTION

Secular Humanist sociology and psychology are basically two sides of the same coin. Both disciplines act on the same premises—sociology concentrates on society while psychology concentrates on the individual. Thus, Secular Humanist sociologists face the unscientific nature of their discipline, just like Secular Humanist psychologists, and attempt to redefine science to fit their discipline and exclude the supernatural.

Writing about the scientific nature of social science in *The Humanist*, Read Bain says, "Supernaturalism in all its forms is dying out. Science has been slowly destroying it for over three hundred years, with rapid acceleration during the last century. Its final stronghold is in the psychosocial realm. During the last fifty years the social sciences have made great strides toward becoming natural sciences and most of the former psychosocial mysteries have become matters of rapidly developing scientific knowledge."[2]

---

[1] John F. Glass and John R. Staude, ed., *Humanistic Society* (Pacific Palisades, CA: Goodyear Publishing, 1972), 352.

[2] Read Bain, "Scientific Humanism," *The Humanist* (May 1954): 116.

In spite of Bain's optimism, Secular Humanist sociology is not on equal footing with the natural sciences, and most Humanist socialists attempt to infuse value into their discipline through means that are not purely scientific.

6.3.2 HUMANIST SOCIOLOGY AS A CATALYST

Secular Humanist sociologists adopt as their goal the betterment of society. In this sense, they work not as mere observers, but as catalysts. Patricia Hill Collins believes that "the discipline of sociology thus is highly political."[3] The concern of science is adding to our present knowledge, not through politics, but through the scientific method. In contrast, the Secular Humanist sociologist works through activism to bring about changes in society. For example, Humanist historian Vern Bullough observes "Politics and science go hand in hand. In the end it is gay activism which determines what researchers say about gay people."[4]

6.3.3 SOCIETY AS EVIL

Secular Humanists see human beings as inherently good, yet they cannot deny the existence of evil in society. Rather than blame people for it, Secular Humanists blame society and its traditional institutions. Psychologist Erich Fromm speaks of "the social process which creates man."[5] He continues, "Just as primitive man was helpless before natural forces, modern man is helpless before the social and economic forces created by himself."[6] Fromm's *The Sane Society* is based on the premise that society itself is insane and is a corrupting influence on individuals.

Secular Humanist sociology focuses on research and activism in order to restructure society and create a new social order based on Humanist values. Today's culture, the "old culture," inhibits our natural inclinations toward growth and self-betterment. Secular Humanists distrust and view as flawed the traditions in modern society that inhibit our potential and growth.

One societal tradition that Secular Humanists particularly distrust is religion. Fishman and Benello declare that Humanist sociology "seeks the concrete betterment of humankind and is opposed to theories that seek either to glorify the status quo or to march human beings lockstep into history in the interests of a vision imposed from above."[7] This view aligns with Secular Humanism's belief in evolution and denial of God or the supernatural.

6.3.4 THE FAILURE OF TRADITIONAL MARRIAGE

Secular Humanist sociologists are intolerant of the biblical view of the traditional family. They cite the institution of marriage as a prime example of the failure of Christian culture to provide freedoms that encourage human potential and growth. Heterosexual monogamy epitomizes social slavery in its restrictions and inhibitions. Lawrence Casler suggests that "marriage and family life have been largely responsible...for today's prevailing neurotic climate, with its pervasive insecurity, and it is precisely this climate that makes so difficult the acceptance

---

[3] Patricia Hill Collins, "Perceptivity and the Activist Potential of the Sociology Classroom," *Humanity and Society* (August 1986): 341.

[4] *The Washington Blade*, December 18, 1987, 19. Cited in Mark Schoofs, "International Forum Debates Treatment of Homosexuality."

[5] Erich Fromm, *Escape from Freedom* (New York, NY: Holt, Rinehart, and Winston, 1969), 12.

[6] Erich Fromm, *The Sane Society* (New York, NY: Holt, Rinehart and Winston, 1955), 362.

[7] Walda Katz Fishman and C. George Benello, *Readings in Humanist Sociology* (Bayside, NY: General Hall, 1986), 3.

of a different, healthier way of life."[8]

The concepts of biological and cultural evolution dictate that the traditional concepts of marriage and family have outlived their usefulness. As the human species and culture progress, old traditions become outdated and must be replaced by new concepts that will continue the evolutionary process.

The advent of the feminist movement within Secular Humanism provides a strong rationale for the demise of the traditional family. In this view, the family is outdated because it perpetuates the domination of women by men. Sol Gordon says, "The traditional family, with all its supposed attributes, enslaved woman; it reduced her to a breeder and caretaker of children, a servant to her spouse, a cleaning lady, and at times a victim of the labor market as well."[9] As Paul Kurtz acknowledges, "The feminist movement was begun and has been nourished by leading humanist women."[10] Elizabeth Cady Stanton, Betty Friedan,[11] Gloria Steinem, and Simone de

> ## The Pop Culture Connection
>
> Using social activism to restructure society begins by breaking down traditional moral codes, especially in the area of sexuality. This goal is best achieved by slowly introducing non-traditional themes into popular culture. Humor has been found to be especially effective in disarming the public. One of the first TV shows to introduce a gay theme was ***Three's Company*** (1977–1984). Starring John Ritter, Joyce DeWitt, and Suzanne Somers, John's character pretends to be gay so the landlord will agree to him living with the two women. Since then, numerous shows showcase gay or lesbian main characters, most notably ***Will and Grace***, which won fourteen Emmys over its first eight seasons. By 2005, Hollywood weighed in with a more serious treatment of homosexual love. ***Brokeback Mountain*** depicted the ongoing relationship between two bi-sexual cowboys and was nominated for eight Academy Awards, showing the popularity of this theme.

Beauvoir are early founders of the woman's movement, and as Kurtz concludes, "Humanism and feminism are inextricably interwoven."[12]

6.3.5 THE FAMILY ACCORDING TO HUMANIST SOCIOLOGY

Secular Humanist sociologists have suggested numerous alternative lifestyles to replace the traditional family. Robert N. Whitehurst, for example, puts forward open marriage (open to adultery), triads, cooperatives, collectives, urban communes, extended intimates, swinging and group marriage, and part-time marriage.[13] In a "New Bill of Sexual Rights and Responsibilities," Lester Kirkendall advocates similar alternative lifestyles such as homosexuality, bisexuality, pre- and extra-marital sexual relationships, and something called "genital associations."[14]

> **NON-TRADITIONAL FAMILY:** A number of alternatives to traditional marriage have been suggested, such as open marriage, triads, group marriage, same-sex marriage, part-time marriage, and premarital living arrangements

[8] Robert Rimmer, "An Interview with Robert Rimmer on Premarital Communes and Group Marriages," *The Humanist* (March/April 1974): 14.

[9] Sol Gordon, "The Egalitarian Family is Alive and Well," *The Humanist* (May/June 1975): 18.

[10] Paul Kurtz, "Fulfilling Feminist Ideals: A New Agenda," *Free Inquiry* (Fall 1990): 21.

[11] See Daniel Horowitz, *Betty Friedan and the Making of "The Feminine Mystique": The American Left, the Cold War, and Modern Feminism* (Amherst, MA: University of Massachusetts Press, 1998) for a study of Friedan's leftism and pro-Communist views.

[12] Ibid.

[13] Robert N. Whitehurst, "Alternative Life-styles," *The Humanist*, (May/June 1975): 24.

[14] Lester Kirkendall, *A New Bill of Sexual Rights and Responsibilities* (Buffalo, NY: Prometheus Books, 1976), 9.

In addition to alternatives to traditional marriage, Secular Humanist sociologists propose alternatives to traditional child rearing. Casler suggest a society where "there would be no compulsory responsibility for child-rearing."[15] He explains how children raised in institutions could retain their inherent goodness: "It is supposed that the principles of ethical, productive, and happy living will be learned more readily when children are free of the insecurities, engendered chiefly by parents, that ordinarily obstruct the internalization of these modes of thought."[16]

6.3.6 THE POWER OF THE CLASSROOM

The public school classroom provides a forum for the dissemination of Secular Humanist sociological ideas. Collins explains the role of the teacher in this regard: "To me, teaching is much more than the passive transfer of technical skills from teacher to learner. Rather, teaching has political implications that reach far beyond the classroom."[17] Dunphy describes teachers as "ministers of another sort" in an article entitled "A Religion for a New Age" published in *The Humanist*. He calls on teachers to use their classrooms to "convey humanist values in whatever subject they teach."[18]

> We believe that the state should allow a wide plurality of moral values to coexist
>
> — HUMANIST MANIFESTO 2000

Secular Humanist documents appear to contradict Secular Humanist practice. John Dewey recognized the value of the classroom to promote Humanistic ideas. *Humanist Manifesto II*, however, defines the boundaries between religion and the classroom: "The separation of church and state and the separation of ideology and state are imperatives."[19] *Humanist Manifesto 2000* states that "Humanists everywhere have defended the separation of religion and state. We believe that the state should be secular, neither for nor against religion. . . . We believe that the state should allow a wide plurality of moral values to coexist."[20]

Dewey viewed Secular Humanism as a religion in his book *A Common Faith*. In fact, the American Humanist Association is a tax-exempt 501(c)3 religion organization. *Free Inquiry* printed the *Guide Star Page* that stated, "This organization [American Humanist Association] is not required to file an annual return with the IRS because it is a religious organization."[21] In a true sense, then, teachers promoting Secular Humanist ideology in the public classroom are in fact promoting the religion of Secular Humanism.

6.3.7 THE SELF-ACTUALIZING SOCIETY

Secular Humanist sociologists describe the new society in terms of human needs. Fromm defines his "sane society" as "that which corresponds to the needs of man—not necessarily to what he feels to be his needs, because even the most pathological aims can be felt subjectively

[15] Lawrence Casler, "Permissive Matrimony: Proposals for the Future," *The Humanist* (March/April 1974): 6.

[16] Ibid., 7.

[17] Collins, "Perceptivity and the Activist Potential of the Sociology Classroom," 341.

[18] John J. Dunphy, "A Religion for a New Age," *The Humanist* (January/February 1983): 26.

[19] *Humanist Manifesto II* (Buffalo, NY: Prometheus Books, 1980), 19.

[20] Paul Kurtz, *Humanist Manifesto 2000: A Call For A New Planetary Humanism* (Amherst, NY: Prometheus Books, 2000), 30.

[21] *Free Inquiry* (Fall 2002): 40. David A. Noebel, et. al., *Clergy in the Classroom: The Religion of Secular Humanism* contains 63 exhibits proving that Secular Humanism is a religion. Indeed, the U. S. *Supreme* Court in 1961(Torcaso vs. Watkins) listed Secular Humanism as a religion, and the 7th Circuit Court of Appeals identified atheism as a religion on August 19, 2005 (No. 04–1914). The Internal Revenue Service as of April 5, 2007 has the American Humanist Association listed as a 501 © 3 tax-exempt organization and "classified as a church."

as that which the person wants most; but to what his needs are objectively, as they can be ascertained by the study of man."[22]

Abraham Mazlow, although a psychologist, also entertained the goal of transforming society. He devised a hierarchy of human needs and taught that our highest need is self-actualization (reaching our full potential). Maurice R. Stein sees society evolving to better meet human needs when he says, "Humanist sociology views society as a historically evolving enterprise that can only be understood through the struggle to liberate human potentialities."[23] The linkage between the goals of Secular Humanist psychology and sociology is explicit in Glass and Staude's summation: "Just as the humanistic psychologist is concerned with individual change in a growthful direction, the humanistic sociologist is concerned with a society which would encourage and sustain such growth—a self-actualizing society, as it was."[24]

Joyce Milton wrote an account of the ideas and lives of the major theorists who shaped Secular Humanism. Entitled *The Road to Malpsychia:Humanistic Psychology and our Discontents*,[25] Milton illustrates how we are still suffering the effects of their ideas and innovations.

6.3.8 ECONOMICS AND THE NEW SOCIETY

Secular Humanist sociologists favor socialism as the economic system that best suits a self-actualized society. Many indorse a Marxist approach to economics. Secular Humanists hold society (rather than the individual) responsible for evil in the world. Since our culture was formed largely by Western and Christian influences, including capitalism, it needs to be transformed in order to allow individuals to realize their full potential. Fromm describes how capitalism alienates us from each other: "What is modern man's relationship to his fellow man? It is one between two abstractions, two living machines, who use each other."[26]

In the Secular Humanist worldview, socialism is more humane that capitalism. Fromm explains, "The only constructive solution is that of Socialism, which aims at a fundamental reorganization of our economic and social system in the direction of freeing man from being used as a means for purposes outside of himself, of creating a social order in which human solidarity, reason and productiveness are furthered rather than hobbled."[27] Secular Humanists not only espouse the ideas of socialism, but also encourage activism to bring about this change in social structure.

> What is modern man's relationship to his fellow man? It is one between two abstractions, two living machines, who use each other.
>
> — ERICH FROMM

6.3.9 CONCLUSION

Secular humanists believe social activism will bring about a culture of universal self-actualization. Reese says, "Informed and active people can make of society what they want it to become."[28] Optimism like Reese's tends to highlight the flaws in our current culture in

---

[22] Fromm, *The Sane Society*, 20.

[23] Glass and Staude, *Humanistic Society*, 165.

[24] Ibid., 271–2.

[25] Joyce Milton, *The Road to Malpsychia: Humanistic Psychology and our Discontents* (San Francisco, CA: Encounter Books, 2002).

[26] Erich Fromm, *Beyond the Chains of Illusion* (New York, NY: Simon and Schuster, 1962), quoted in Ross Ellenhorn, "Toward a Humanistic Social Work: Social Work for Conviviality," *Humanity and Society* (May 1988): 166.

[27] Fromm, *The Sane Society*, 277.

[28] Curtis W. Reese, "The Social Implications of Humanism," *The Humanist* (July/August 1961): 198.

contrast to the utopian society Humanists are working to effect. Secular Humanist disdain for modern society reflects an open distrust of all traditions and a desire to abandon or rework all existing social institutions.

The traditional institution of the church must be radically remodeled or eliminated altogether. To this end, Humanists have developed their own **non-traditional churches**, although these organizations go by different names, such as Ethical Societies. For example, the Council for Secular Humanism's website lists one of its purposes as providing the same kinds of support offered by traditional churches and religious organizations. Under the heading "Serving the Needs of Non-Religious People," it states, "The Council gives practical support and services to non-religious people. It runs courses and summer camps that educate children in critical thinking and ethical values. For rites of passage, such as marriage and death, it provides dignified non-religious celebrations and memorials. And it runs a national support network for secular families and parents."

> **NON-TRADITIONAL CHURCH:** An organization that provides the functions and services of a traditional religious organization while holding non-traditional beliefs

Two court cases in 1957 established secular humanist organizations as functioning as religious societies. One case involved a group of humanists calling themselves the Fellowship of Humanity. They were seeking tax exemption for using their property for religious worship, including weekly Sunday meetings, despite their non-theistic beliefs. The other group, the Washington Ethical Society, applied for tax-exempt status as a religious organization. In both cases, the courts ruled that these organizations functioned as traditional religious organizations, even though they held non-traditional beliefs.

Humanists also seek to use the institution of the state, especially the judiciary, to establish their agenda, including such non-traditional ideas as establishing state-run childcare centers, following a narrow interpretation of separation of church (meaning the Christian church) and state, and passing legislation for gay rights, same-sex marriage, abortion on demand, and animal rights. To this end, Humanists in the United States, with the assistance of the American Civil Liberties Union, call for the eradication of all Christian influence, traditions, and symbols in the public square and a complete overhaul of society. Only then will America be prepared to merge with other like-minded Humanist states to forge a new world order.

> **NON-TRADITIONAL STATE:** the political view that advocates non-traditional legislation for promoting social change

Sociology

Marxism-Leninism

> "With the transfer of the means of production into common ownership [communism], the single family ceases to be the economic unit of society . . . The care and education of the children becomes a public affair; society looks after all children alike, whether they are legitimate or not."[1]
>
> —— FREDERICK ENGELS

6.4.1 INTRODUCTION

While Secular Humanist sociologists sometimes refer to sociology as an art rather than a science, Marxists ground their social theory firmly in what they believe to be the scientific *fact* of Darwinian evolution. This scientific foundation for sociology is "Darwinism in its application to social science,"[2] according to G.V. Pkekhanov. Humanity is not only evolving biologically, but also socially. As humanity improves through the evolutionary chain of being, so does society. The scientific *fact* of biological evolution guarantees both the truth of Marxist social theory and the outcome of its practice: an international communist family.

---

[1] Frederick Engels, *The Origin of the Family, Private Property and the State* (New York, NY: International Publishers, 1942), 67.

[2] G.V. Plekhanov, *The Role of the Individual in History* (New York, NY: International Publishers, 1940), 200.

6.4.2 SOCIETY AS AN EVOLVING ENTITY

While Darwin described the evolution of species, Marx describes the evolution of society. Marxist sociologists refer constantly to the "development of society."

Marx and Lenin believed that we understand society only in the context of societal development. According to Marx, at a certain stage of social development, "the material productive forces of society come into conflict with the existing relations of production. . . . From forms of development of the productive forces these relations turn into their fetters. Then begins an era of social revolution. The changes in the economic foundation lead sooner or later to the transformation of the whole immense superstructure."[3]

In the Marxist system, economics determines the nature of society—its politics, religion, law, and culture. Our economic system (feudalism, capitalism, socialism, etc.) determines how we relate to others so that we operate efficiently within the system. In other words, the way goods are produced and distributed determines the way people relate to each other, which in turn determines the structure of society.

The stages in the development of society parallel the economic stages in our history. Marx divides the history of society into four stages: "In broad outline, the Asiatic, ancient, feudal and modern bourgeois modes of production may be designated as epochs marking progress in the economic development of society."[4]

The development of society continues past the bourgeois stage until it reaches a communist stage. The concept of the dialectic, however, requires that such development will also continue past the communist stage. The communist society becomes a new thesis, leading to antithesis, clash, and synthesis. In this view, then, the Communist society is also transitory.

6.4.3 SOCIETY IS PREDETERMINED BY ECONOMIC FORCES

> It is not the consciousness of men that determines their existence, but their social existence that determines their consciousness.
>
> — KARL MARX

According to Marx, "The mode of production of material life conditions the general process of social, political, and intellectual life. It is not the consciousness of men that determines their existence, but their social existence that determines their consciousness."[5] The economic system determines society, which determines our very consciousness. Economic forces thus supplant our free will.

The individual is insignificant in the face of powerful societal forces. Stalin believed that in order to understand history, we must rely "on the concrete conditions of the material life of society, as the determining force of social development; not on the good wishes of great men."[6] The evolution of society is too powerful a force to be affected by the actions of even the best individuals.

[3] Karl Marx and Frederick Engels, *The Individual and Society* (Moscow, USSR: Progress Publishers, 1984), 193.
[4] Ibid., 194.
[5] Ibid., 162.
[6] Joseph Stalin, *Problems of Leninism* (Moscow, USSR: Progress Publishers, 1947), 579. Cited in Gustav A. Wetter, *Dialectical Materialism* (Westport, CT: Greenwood Press, 1977), 217.

6.4.4 MANKIND'S CHANCE TO CREATE SOCIETY

Although Marxist sociologists deny that we have free will and believe that our social systems are determined by economic forces, they also believe a time will come when we can play a part in consciously working toward the next phase of social development—the overthrow of capitalism by the proletariat. Marxist sociology and psychology run parallel at this point: our individuality and usefulness are determined by society until the time when our free will is required to create the socialist society. At this point in history, the proletarian revolution will provide a position where we can control society by controlling the means of production.

In the Marxist worldview, the advent of the communist society is inevitable, so the individual is free to create the new society only by going along with the evolutionary process that leads toward communism.

6.4.5 THE ULTIMATE SOCIETY

Regardless of opposition, the march toward socialism and eventually communism is inevitable. Those who support these changes will become *free*, and those who resist will remain enslaved to capitalism. Social evolution based on biological conflict and survival of the fittest will bring about the spread of a communist society. Because economics is the foundation of society, Marxist sociologists see socialism as the first step toward communism. A socialist economic system will initiate the changes that will lead to the perfect communistic society.

> Only in Communist society when the resistance of the capitalists has been completely broken, when the capitalists have disappeared, when there are no classes . . . only then the State ceases to exist.
>
> — V.I. LENIN

Worldwide communism will abolish the class divisions and competition inherent in capitalistic societies, bringing about utopia and a better life for everyone. The need for government will eventually vanish. According to Lenin, "Only in Communist society when the resistance of the capitalists has been completely broken, when the capitalists have disappeared, when there are no classes . . . only then the State ceases to exist."[7] This idea of society running itself without the need for government is examined in the chapter on Marxist politics; the remainder of this chapter examines Marxist views of the church, education, and the family.

6.4.6 CHURCH IN MARXIST SOCIETY

Marxists have little patience with religion or any notion of God. They see religion as a stumbling block that slows the development of the **classless society**: "The influence of the church promotes the schism of the workers movement. Reactionary churchmen everywhere try to isolate religious workers from their class brothers by attracting them into separate organizations of a clerical nature. . . . and thus diverting them from the struggle against capitalism."[8]

CLASSLESS SOCIETY: The Marxists vision of a future society free from class antagonism, which will purportedly be brought about by the establishment of communism and the demise of oppressive capitalism

---

[7] V.I. Lenin, *The State and Revolution* (New York, NY: International Publishers, 1932), 73.
[8] *Fundamentals of Marxism-Leninism* (Moscow, USSR: Progress Publishers, 1959), 310. Cited in Raymond S. Sleeper, ed., *A Lexicon of Marxist-Leninist Semantics* (Alexandria, VA: Western Goals, 1983), 36.

In the former Soviet Union, Marxists used many different methods in their efforts to abolish religion. In the early days following the October Revolution, Marxists discriminated against priests in an effort to discourage anyone who wanted to be in the clergy. When discrimination failed to wipe out religion, Marxists tried to further restrict the church through state controls. On April 8, 1929, for example, the USSR enacted a law that forbade religious organizations from creating mutual assistance funds or providing aid to their members and from meeting at any time other than for religious services.

In effect, Marxist sociologists declared war against the church, a conflict that continues to the present day wherever Communists are in power.

6.4.7 EDUCATION IN MARXIST SOCIETY

Marxists believe that the means of production (the economic system) dictates a society's education system. Thus the educational system in modern capitalistic society reflects the evils of capitalism. Madan Sarup says, "The [modern] educational system thus meshes with capital to ensure the maintenance of women's oppression."[9] The working classes are also exploited within the current bourgeois system.

Prior to the proletarian revolt and the institution of socialism as the new means of production, the proletariat can only be educated in terms of the dialectical struggle. Once the struggle is over, however, and the proletariat has ushered in a socialist economic system, education will play a different role in creating the ultimate society of communism—the role of indoctrinating youth in the proletarian philosophy.

Education's role is delineated in *People's Education*: "The basic task of communist education and overcoming the survivals of religiousness in our present condition is to prove to the pupils the complete contrast and complete irreconcilability between science, the real and correct reflection of the objectively existing world in the consciousness of people—and religion as a fantastic, distorted and, consequently, harmful reflection of the world in the consciousness of the people."[10]

Thus, education is seen as a valuable tool for shaping ideology, a tool employed to create citizens more likely to cooperate with and fit into the Marxist notion of the ultimate society. Once capitalism and bourgeois society are destroyed, students will be educated to detest and distrust religion[11] and to embrace a materialistic view of the world.

William Z. Foster's *Toward Soviet America* published in 1932 provides a comprehensive view of Marxist ambitions for education in a future communist America. Foster writes, "Among the elementary measures the American Soviet government will adopt to further the cultural revolution are the following: the schools, colleges and universities will be coordinated and grouped under the National Department of Education and its state and local branches. The studies will be revolutionized, being cleansed of religious, patriotic and other features of the bourgeois ideology. The students will be taught on the basis of Marxian dialectical materialism, internationalism and the general ethics of the new Socialist society."[12]

Foster continues, "Science will become materialistic, hence truly scientific; God will be banished from the laboratories as well as from the schools."[13] Foster's view of the role of the

---

[9] Madan Sarup, *Education, State and Crisis* (London, UK: Routledge and Kegan, 1982), 91.

[10] *People's Education* (Moscow, USSR), April 1949. Cited in Sleeper, *A Lexicon of Marxist-Leninist Semantics*, 101.

[11] To judge the results of such an education see Stephane Courtois, et al., *The Black Book Of Communism*: *Crimes, Terror, Repression* (Cambridge, MA: Harvard University Press, 1999) and R. J. Rummel, *Death By Government* (New Brunswick, NJ: Transaction Publishers, 1994).

[12] William Z. Foster, *Toward Soviet America* (New York, NY: International Publishers, 1932), 316.

[13] Ibid., 317.

church in a communist America is equally chilling: "The churches will remain free to continue their services, but their special tax and other privileges will be liquidated. Their buildings will revert to the State. Religious schools will be abolished and organized training for minors prohibited. Freedom will be established for anti-religious propaganda."[14]

6.4.8 THE FAMILY IN MARXIST SOCIOLOGY

Marxist sociologists view the modern family created by bourgeois society as a great failure because its foundation is in capital and private wealth. Proletarians, however, are not tainted by the flaws in the bourgeois family and will never enter into family relations as they exist in present society. The proletariat is destined to usher in a new utopian society with a higher form of *family*. According to Kollontai, "The family deprives the worker of revolutionary consciousness"[15] and must, therefore, be shunned.

Engels predicts the kind of family that will evolve when the proletariat revolts and creates its perfect socialist society: "With the transfer of the means of production into common ownership, the single family ceases to be the economic unit of society. Private housekeeping is transformed into a social industry. The care and education of the children becomes a public affair; society looks after all children alike, whether they are legitimate or not. This removes all the anxiety about the consequences which today is the most essential social-moral as well as economic factor that prevents a girl from giving herself completely to the man she loves. Will not that suffice to bring about the gradual growth of unconstrained sexual intercourse and with it a more tolerant public opinion in regard to a maiden's honor and a woman's shame?"[16]

In the new social order premarital and extramarital sex and adultery cease to have the same meaning because within the context of community, there is no private property and everyone belongs to everyone.

In *The Communist Manifesto*, Marx and Engels argue that the idea of a "community of women" is not new, but "has existed almost from time immemorial."[17] To answer critics arguing that communism would "introduce a community of women," Marx and Engels respond, "Bourgeois marriage is in reality a system of wives in common and thus, at the most, what the Communists might possibly be reproached with, is that they desire to introduce, in substitution for a hypocritically concealed, an openly legalized community of women."[18]

The care of children also becomes a public affair in Marxist society. Children play an insignificant role in the family of the ultimate society since they become the entire community's responsibility. In effect, children are disengaged from the family in socialist society so the "school becomes literally a home."[19] Alienating children from their parents ensures that children formulate their worldview according to the education provided by the Marxist state rather than according to the outdated views regarding religion and the traditional family structure held by their parents.

---

[14] Ibid., 316.

[15] Aleksandra M. Kollontai, *Communism and the Family* (New York, NY: Andrade's Bookshop, 1920), 10. Cited in II. Kent Geiger, *The Family in Soviet Russia* (Cambridge, UK: Harvard University Press, 1970), 51.

[16] Engels, *The Origin of the Family, Private Property, and the State*, 67.

[17] Karl Marx and Frederick Engels, *Collected Works*, 40 vols. (New York, NY: International Publishers, 1976), 6:502.

[18] Ibid.

[19] V. Yazykova, *Socialist Life Style and the Family* (Moscow, USSR: Progress Publishers, 1984), 7.

6.4.9 CONCLUSION

Marxist sociology sees the economic system of a society as the determining factor for all its social institutions. Since the economic system is in a process of constant development, all institutions in society are also evolving. This development occurs regardless of the actions of individuals—in fact, it often occurs in spite of them.

Marxists believe the next step in economic and socio-cultural evolution will be a world socialist system (the abolishment of private property) and a new world order that will emerge as a result of the changed means of production. The new society will develop a proletarian system of education and family based on materialism, atheism, punctuated equilibrium, and communism. Marxist sociologists are confident this will occur because they believe their system of sociology is grounded in naturalistic science.

Lenin summarizes Marxist sociology's basis in science and the infallible nature of this approach: "Just as Darwin put an end to the view of animal and plant species being unconnected, fortuitous, 'created by God' and immutable, and was the first to put biology on an absolutely scientific basis by establishing the mutability and the succession of species, so Marx put an end to the view of society being a mechanical aggregation of individuals which allows [for] all sorts of modification at the will of the authorities (or, if you like, at the will of society and the government) and which emerges and changes casually, and was the first to put sociology on a scientific basis by establishing the concept of the economic formation of society as the sum-total of given production relations, by establishing the fact that the development of such formations is a process of natural history."[20]

The Pop Culture Connection

Enemy at the Gates (a 2001 film starring Jude Law, Joseph Fiennes, and Ed Harris)—During the WWII battle for Stalingrad, the Germans encountered fierce resistance from the Russians, who employed snipers to pick off German officers. Vassili (Jude Law) becomes famous as an ace Russian sniper, prompting the Germans to dispatch Major Konig (Ed Harris) to Stalingrad to track him down. In a scene late in the film, as Vassili waits for Konig to come into his sights, his friend Danilov (Joseph Fiennes) says,

"I've been such a fool, Vassili. Man will always be man. There is no new man. We tried so hard to create a society that was equal, where there would be nothing to envy your neighbor. But there is always something to envy. A smile, a friendship, something you don't have and want to appropriate. In this world, even a Soviet one, there will always be rich and poor—rich in gifts, poor in gifts; rich in love, poor in love."

Danilov's remarks reveal Marxism's basic flaw—a sociological system built on the failure to correctly assess humanity's true nature.

---

[20] V.I. Lenin, *Collected Works*, 45 vols. (Moscow, USSR: Progress Publishers, 1977), 1:142.

Sociology

Cosmic Humanism

"Communities, nations and cultures—all of our collective creations . . . reflect the decisions of our species to learn through fear and doubt."[1]

— GARY ZUKAV

6.5.1 INTRODUCTION

Cosmic Humanist sociology and psychology will merge into a single discipline once everyone has made the evolutionary leap to collective godhood. Both will study a society unified into one mind (the mind of God). In the meantime, Cosmic Humanist sociology is attempting to explode the limits of a society that inhibits our ability to achieve higher consciousness. According to Marilyn Ferguson, "Every society, by offering its automatic judgments, limits the vision of its members. From our earliest years we are seduced into a system of beliefs that becomes so inextricably braided into our experience that we cannot tell culture from nature."[2]

All social institutions should encourage us to seek inner truth from our perfectible human nature. Society must adopt a pantheistic perspective. David Spangler thus explains the New Age approach as looking at the objects, people, and events in our lives and saying, "You are sacred. In you and with you I can find the sacramental passages that reconnect me to the wholeness of creation." It is then to ask ourselves what kind of culture, what kind of institutions—be they political, economic, artistic, educational, or scientific—we need that can honor that universal sacredness.[3]

---

[1] Gary Zukav, *The Seat of the Soul* (New York, NY: Simon and Schuster, 1989), 162.

[2] Marilyn Ferguson, *The Aquarian Conspiracy* (Los Angeles, CA: J.P. Tarcher, 1980), 104.

[3] David Spangler, *Emergence: The Rebirth of the Sacred* (New York, NY: Delta/Merloyd Lawrence, 1984), 82.

6.5.2 BEYOND MARRIAGE AND FAMILY

Cosmic Humanists see marriage and family as outdated, unenlightened institutions. In their traditional Judeo-Christian forms, they are regarded as limiting—blind to the concept of universal sacredness and useless in helping us achieve full enlightenment. Vera Alder promotes a non-traditional perspective of family that sees "the idea that an unmarried person of either sex [having] to remain childless . . . far-fetched."[4]

Shakti Gawain believes we need to alter our attitude about divorce to create a society that is more conducive to our evolution to godhood: "People who divorce almost inevitably feel that they have failed, because they assume all marriages should last forever. In most such cases, however, the marriage has actually been a total success—it's helped each person to grow to the point where they no longer need its old form."[5]

Thus, attempting to maintain traditional versions of marriage and family is counter-evolutionary. Gawain continues, "Relationships and families as we've known them seem to be falling apart at a rapid rate. Many people are panicky about this; some try to re-establish the old traditions and value systems in order to cling to a feeling of order and stability in their lives. It's useless to try to go backward, however, because our consciousness has already evolved beyond the level where we were willing to make the sacrifices necessary to live that way."[6]

> An individual's sexual preference should be viewed as neither good nor evil—such preferences are but the functioning of the body's dialogue to and with another.
>
> — MARILYN FERGUSON

Sexual freedom, including homosexuality, is a part of going forward. In order to allow all humanity to achieve higher consciousness, society should not limit our options. According to Kevin Ryerson, "Sexuality, whether homosexual or heterosexual, is the exploring of the personalities of yourselves as incarnate beings, or as a spirit inhabiting the flesh. An individual's sexual preference should be viewed as neither good nor evil—such preferences are but the functioning of the body's dialogue to and with another."[7]

6.5.3 EDUCATING FOR THE NEW AGE

Cosmic Humanists are willing to work within the existing educational system to encourage a *limitless* society. In fact, Cosmic Humanists tend to choose careers within education. According to Ferguson, of all the New Age professionals she surveyed for *The Aquarian Conspiracy*, "more were involved in education than in any other single category of work."[8] By teaching children the proper attitudes toward themselves and their consciousness, New Age educators believe they can create a generation capable of ushering in the New Age.

In an article entitled "A Religion for the New Age," John Dunphy explains how Cosmic Humanist educators use their positions in the classroom to promote their worldview. He writes, "I am convinced that the battle for humankind's future must be waged and won in the public school classrooms by teachers who correctly perceive their role as proselytizers of a new faith: a religion of humanity that recognizes and respects the spark of what theologians call the Divinity in every human being. These teachers must embody the same selfless dedication as the

[4] Vera Alder, *When Humanity Comes of Age* (New York, NY: Samuel Weiser, 1974), 83–4.

[5] Shakti Gawain, *Living in the Light* (San Rafael, CA: New World Library, 1986), 110.

[6] Ibid., 3.

[7] Kevin Ryerson, *Spirit Communication: The Soul's Path* (New York, NY: Bantam Books, 1989), 172.

[8] Ferguson, *The Aquarian Conspiracy*, 280.

most rabid fundamentalist preachers."[9]

The implementation in public schools of Values Clarification, sex clinics, moral relativism, biological evolution, Cosmos, and globalism indicated that Cosmic Humanist proselytizers have succeeded in establishing a foundation for their new faith.

6.5.4 CONCLUSION

Cosmic Humanists believe that modern society's traditional views of family, church, and state hinder our evolution to godhood. In an effort to effect societal change, many Cosmic Humanists have chosen to work as educators so the next generation will learn to transcend traditional limits and achieve higher consciousness.

Because social institutions imply form and limits, Cosmic Humanists tend toward suspicion and rarely champion specific changes. Ultimately, meaningful change in society will occur only when sufficient meaningful change occurs in individuals. "Your decision to evolve consciously through responsible choice," says Gary Zukav, "contributes not only to your own evolution, but also to the evolution of all of those aspects of humanity in which you participate. It is not just you that is evolving through your decisions, but the entirety of humanity."[10]

Because each of us has God within, each of us individually has the power necessary to change society. Individual change is primary (psychology), while societal change is secondary (sociology). Societal institutions must refrain, however, from inhibiting our individual evolution to higher consciousness.

---

[9] *The Humanist* (January/February 1983): 26.

[10] Zukav, *The Seat of the Soul*, 164.

Sociology

Postmodernism

"I have been putting words like 'abnormal' and 'deviant' in quotes because those categorizations are under fire now, the boundary between normal and abnormal is as questionable now as are all the other boundaries that once defined social reality."[1]

—— WALTER TRUETT ANDERSON

6.6.1 INTRODUCTION

The Postmodern views of how we live together in society are nontraditional regarding family, church, and state. Foucault says, "the society in which we live, the economic relations within which it functions and the system of power which defines the regular forms and the regular permissions and prohibitions of our conduct...the essence of our life consists, after all, of the political functioning of the society in which we find ourselves."[2] Foucault thus sees the social order consisting of economics, law, and the state. Living within this order is "the essence of our life" since our culture determines who we are. Life is merely a summary of the cultural aspects of the social community since there is no unified self.

---

[1] Walter Truett Anderson, *The Future of the Self: Exploring the Post-Identity Society* (New York, NY: Tarcher/Putnam, 1997), 114.
[2] Michel Foucault, *History, Discourse and Discontinuity* (New York, NY: Semiotex (e), 1996), 48.

Foucault does not include the church in his view of societal institutions. Postmodernists, for the most part, want nothing to do with the church.[3] In *The Future of Religion*, Rorty replaces his atheism with "anticlericalism," contending that "congregations of the faithful" are socially unobjectionable, but "ecclesiastical institutions" are dangerous to the health of democratic societies. To Rorty, "religion is unobjectionable as long as it is privatized."[4] In other words, private religious views are acceptable, but the organized church is not.

6.6.2 SEXUAL EGALITARIANISM

> **SEXUAL EGALITARIANISM:** The belief that all sexual practices—which are based on preference and sexual identity (or polymorphous sexualities) and not physical characteristics—are equal

Many Postmodern socialists consider marriage the greatest of evils. Rorty is particularly harsh on Christian parents who teach their children about God, referring to them as "frightening, vicious, and dangerous."[5]

Other Postmodernists show their contempt for Christian concepts of love, sex, and marriage, preferring various forms of "free love" (hooking up, shacking up, living together, cohabitation, etc.). Postmodernist psychiatrist Adam Phillips precludes the possibility of contractual marriage and describes any relationship in harsh terms: "The only sane foregone conclusion about any relationship is that it is an experiment; and that exactly what it is an experiment in will never be clear to the participants. For the sane, so-called relationships could never be subject to contract."[6]

Acknowledging the traditional heterosexual family as the norm in Western society, Postmodernists decry that this "heterosexist norm" enables society "to marginalize some sexual practices as 'against nature,' and thereby [attempt] to prove the naturalness of the heterosexual monogamy and family values upon which mainstream society bases itself."[7]

Postmodernists encourage open conversation about the way we experience sexual relationships. Foucault maintains that talking about sex helps to create sexual diversity. He says, "The putting into discourse of sex, far from undergoing a process of restriction, on the contrary has been subjected to a mechanism of increasing incitement...the techniques of power exercised over sex have not obeyed a principle of rigorous selection, but rather one of dissemination and implantation of **polymorphous sexualities**."[8]

Talking about sex reveals "an ever expanding encyclopedia of preferences, gratifications and perversions. It creates a realm of perversion by

> **POLYMORPHOUS SEXUALITIES:** The belief that individuals can exist in more than one gender form—based upon one's sexual identity and preference—(including gay, bi-sexual, lesbian, transgendered, transsexual, etc.)

discovering, commenting on and exploring it. It brings it into being as an object of study and in doing so serves to categorize and objectify those who occupy what has been made into the secret underworld of 'deviance.'"[9] Foucault says, "We must . . . ask why we burden ourselves today with so much guilt for having once made sex a sin."[10] Foucault was "a disciple of the

---

[3] The French Postmodernists were particularly anti-Roman Catholic.

[4] Richard Rorty and Gianni Vattimo, *The Future of Religion* (New York, NY: Columbia University Press, 2005), 33. Cited in *Philosophia Christi*, vol. 7, no. 2 (2005): 525.

[5] Robert B. Brandom, ed., *Rorty and his Critics* (Oxford, UK: Blackwell Publishers, 2001), 22.

[6] *The Weekly Standard*, November 14, 2005, 41.

[7] Glenn Ward, *Postmodernism* (Chicago, IL: McGraw-Hill Companies, 2003), 145.

[8] Ibid., 146.

[9] Ibid.

[10] Ibid. Sourced to Paul Rabinow, ed., *The Foucault Reader: An Introduction to Foucault's Thought* (Eastbourne, UK: Gardners Books, 1991), 297.

Marquis de Sade,"[11] and like him embraced all sexual activity as permissible, including man/boy relationships (pederasty). Few boundaries exist in a socially constructed reality.

What used to be considered perverted, abnormal, or deviant sexual behavior is now viewed as personal preference, and no moral pronouncements are attached to the actions. The line between heterosexual and homosexual practices is blurred. **Walter Truett Anderson** says, "I have been putting words like 'abnormal' and 'deviant' in quotes because those categorizations are under fire now, the boundary between normal and abnormal as questionable now as are all the other boundaries that once defined social reality."[12]

Walter Truett Anderson

We use the term **"sexual egalitarianism"** to characterize the Postmodern view that allows each person to define his or her sexuality and proposes that all sexual preferences are equally valid.

6.6.3 POLITICALLY CORRECT EDUCATION

Anderson explains the goals and methods Postmodernists adopt in regard to education: "[Postmodernism] rejects the notion that the purpose of education is primarily to train a child's cognitive capacity for reason in order to produce an adult capable of functioning independently in the world. That view of education is replaced with the view that education is to take an essentially indeterminate being and give it a social identity. Education's method of molding is linguistic, and so the language to be used is that which will create a human being sensitive to its racial, sexual, and class identity."[13]

Anderson outlines major shifts in focus in the Postmodern classroom in contrast to the modern classroom: "Education should emphasize works not in the canon, it should focus on the achievements of non-whites, females and the poor;[14] it should highlight the historical crimes of whites, males, and the rich; and it should teach children that science's method has no better claim to yielding truth than any other method and, accordingly, that students should be equally receptive to alternative ways of knowing."[15]

Postmodern education teaches that all truth is relative,[16] all cultures are equally deserving of respect (although Western culture comes under severe criticism), and all values are subjective (although racism, sexism, classism, and homophobia are universally evil).

Course offerings at colleges and universities in the Postmodern age are also nontraditional, focusing on themes of race, sex, and gender. For example, Stanford University's Feminist Studies Department offers "Lesbian Communities and Identities." The catalog describes the course as "Scholarship and research on lesbian experience. Issues of homophobia, lesbian intimacy, and sexuality. Femme and butch roles, lesbian separatism, and diversity of lesbian communities and

---

[11] Mark Lilla, *The Reckless Mind: Intellectuals in Politics* (New York, NY: New York Review Books, 2001), 142. See the Postmodern Politics section for more on the Marquis de Sade.

[12] Walter Truett Anderson, 114.

[13] Ibid., 17.

[14] For example, see David Stoll, *Rigoberta Menchu and the Story of All Poor Guatemalans* (Oxford, UK: Westview Press, 1999).

[15] Ibid., 18.

[16] Allan Bloom, *The Closing of the American Mind* (New York, NY: Simon and Schuster, 1988), 25: "There is one thing a professor can be absolutely certain of: almost every student entering the university believes, or says he believes, that truth is relative."

identities."[17] Stanford's History Department offers a course entitled "Homosexuals, Heretics, Witches, and Werewolves: Deviants of Medieval Society." The catalog describes the course as answering the following question: "Why were medieval heretics accused of deviant sexual practices?"[18]

Every Ivy League school except Princeton offers more courses in Women's Studies than in Economics. Columbia's Women's Studies Department offers "The Invisible Woman in Literature: The Lesbian Literary Tradition," "Introduction to Gay and Lesbian Studies," and "Gendered Controversies: Women's Bodies and Global Contestations."

Dartmouth's Women's Studies Department offers "Shakespeare and Gender," described in the course catalog as answering the questions, "Is language gender-inflected? How is power exerted and controlled in sexual relationships?" Dartmouth's English Department offers a course called "Queer Theory, Queer Texts."[19]

Brown University offers these departments and courses: "Afro-American Studies—'Black Lavender: Study of Black Gay/Lesbian Plays;' Education—'The Psychology of Race, Class, and Gender;' English—'Unnatural Acts: Introduction to Lesbian/Gay Literature.'"[20]

Not only has the subject matter of courses and departments shifted dramatically away from traditional fare, Christianity is often viewed with contempt and ridicule. Richard Rorty, Professor of Comparative Literature at Stanford, writes, "When we American college teachers encounter religious fundamentalists . . . we do our best to convince these students of the benefits of secularization . . . I think these students are lucky to find themselves under . . . people like me, and to have escaped the grip of their frightening, vicious, dangerous parents."[21]

Not all new courses are met with enthusiasm. Richard Zeller, a sociology professor at Bowling Green State University in Ohio, attempted to introduce a new course that would examine the effects of political correctness in response to students' claims that they felt pressured to assume politically correct views in order to pass courses. BGSU's Director of Women's Studies, Kathleen Dixon, protested vehemently, saying, "We forbid any course that says we restrict free speech."[22] The course was voted down, and Zeller resigned in protest after twenty-five years of teaching at Bowling Green.

6.6.4 "NEW WAYS OF LIVING"

The Postmodern approach to restructuring society calls for "challenging power on a day-to-day level." Lyotard suggests we "gnaw away at the great institutionalized narrative apparatuses . . . by increasing the number of skirmishes that take place on the sidelines. That's what women who have had abortions, prisoners, conscripts, prostitutes, students, and peasants have been doing."[23]

Other "new ways of living" that might restructure society toward a Postmodern view could include any of the following "skirmishes on the sidelines:" pick a quarrel with your conservative neighbor; refuse to buy a certain brand of condensed milk; surf the net at work; deface billboards; sell pirated copies of CDs; buy fake designer labels; celebrate fragmentation, diversity and deviancy;[24] teach a "safe-sex" course in church or school; turn vices into virtues;

---

[17] *The Washington Times*, August 31, 1997, B2.

[18] Ibid., p. B2.

[19] Ibid.

[20] Ibid.

[21] Brandom, *Rorty and his Critics*, 21–22.

[22] Larry Elder, "Campus Gulag," *FrontPageMagazine.com*, October 2, 2000, http://www.frontpagemag.com/Articles/Printable.asp?ID=2711.

[23] Ward, *Postmodernism*, 176.

[24] See Anne Henderschott, *The Politics of Deviance* (San Francisco, CA: Encounter Books, 2002).

make the abnormal normal; legalize sodomy; decriminalize marijuana; legalize same-sex marriage; praise the concept of a "living" Constitution;[25] subscribe to MTV; attend art exhibits by Andy Warhol, a Madonna concert, a performance of *the V-Monologues*; view X-rated movies; protest Christian prayer in government schools; support the A.C.L.U; defend NAMBLA;[26] label Christians and conservatives as right-wing religious fanatics or Fascists; support the Green Party; protest "under God' in the Pledge; remove "In God We Trust" from U.S. money; support all tax increases; publicly burn your fur coat; drink French wine; help an illegal alien across the border; keep Intelligent Design out of the schools; join the anti-globalization protests; and so on. "None of these activities might strike you as particularly radical—they are perhaps not going to bring about a revolution—but from Lyotard's point of view they can be valued as disruptive skirmishes in the social system."[27]

6.6.5 SUBVERTING THE ARTS

Dada, a nihilistic movement in the arts that attempted to demolish aesthetic standards in the years after World War I, is sometimes linked to the more radical elements of Postmodernism. Ward explains, "Dada, especially, is often seen as the original prototype of how art should go about the business of being radical . . . Dada employed a number of tactics to disrupt bourgeois fantasies about art. Most prominent of these methods was the use of 'found' materials not conventionally associated with fine art. They took materials from the gutter, images from mass culture, and styles of presentation from shop window displays. Most famous of all, Marcel Duchamp exhibited signed Readymades—a urinal, a bottle rack, a comb, etc.—and eventually got them called art (or anti-art)."[28]

Stephen Hicks elaborates further on the link between Dada and Postmodernism in *Explaining Postmodernism*: "Dada's themes are about meaninglessness, but its works and manifestos are meaningful philosophical statements in the context in which they are presented. 'Art is -----' was, fittingly, the motto of the Dada movement. Duchamp's urinal was the fitting symbol. Everything is waste to be flushed away."[29]

Over the past thirty years, a number of popular recording artists have expressed elements of Postmodern thought in their style of music and in their lyrics. This nihilistic philosophy is expressed in the 1977 song by British band Ian Dury and the Blockheads. The opening stanza reads, "Sex and drugs and rock 'n' roll are all my brain and body needs." John Mayer's 2003 release *Any Given Thursday* expresses the meaninglessness of life in the lyrics, "I just found out there's no such thing as the real world. Just a lie you've got to rise above. I am invincible as long as I'm alive." The group Third Eye Blind's song "Horror Show," featured on the *Varsity Blues* soundtrack (1999), says:

> When gravity presses down like a lie
> We want wild sex
> But we don't wanna die
> Do you feel there's nowhere to go

---

[25] U. S. Supreme Court Justice Antonin Scalia says otherwise as reported in the Associated Press, February 14, 2006, "The Constitution is not a living organism, it is a legal document. It says something and doesn't say other things."

[26] NAMBLA stands for the North American Man/Boy Love Association, whose motto was once, "Eight is too late," meaning that boys under the age of eight should be allowed to engage in consensual sex with an older man.

[27] Ward, 176–177.

[28] Ibid., 51.

[29] Stephen R. C. Hicks, *Exploring Postmodernism: Skepticism and Socialism from Rousseau to Foucault*, (Tempe, AZ: Scholargy Publishing, 2004), 196.

We're the bait in a horror show
And we're all alone in a horror show
Yeah, we are all alone in a horror show.

6.6.6 CRITIQUE OF PERMISSIVE SEX

Postmodernists did not invent sexual liberation, but are riding the crest of the wave started by others. Many cultural observers consider Alfred Kinsey the father of the sexual revolution—the 1960s social tsunami that changed the way we think about sex. Kinsey's two reports, *Sexual Behavior in the Human Male* (1948) and *Sexual Behavior in the Human Female* (1953), presented evidence contradicting the traditional view of sex and marriage. The scientific format of these reports drowned out concerns of critics—who can argue with science? The result has been comprehensive sex education that introduces young children to *Heather Has Two Mommies* and teaches teens the virtues of "safer" sex.[30]

Now fifty years later, the startling discovery is that Kinsey's research turns out to be a house of cards resting on dishonest research, fraud, and outright lies. The fact is, he used faulty methods for gathering statistics. Kinsey's reports claim to be representative of a cross-section of the nation. In actuality, his team interviewed a disproportionate number of prisoners, pimps, prostitutes, pedophiles, and unmarried adults.

Second, the majority of those interviewed had *volunteered* to reveal their sexual histories to an interviewer. Well-known psychologist Abraham Maslow pointed out to Kinsey at the time that using volunteers would bias the results toward the non-normal end of the behavioral scale.

Third, some of the information Kinsey reported could have been gathered only through criminal activity! As it turns out, buried in the report, Kinsey admits that some of his statistics were taken from the personal diaries of pedophiles (although Kinsey did not use that term).

Fourth, and more telling, was the naturalistic worldview at the root of Kinsey's research (the same naturalism that is foundational to Postmodernism). Kinsey, like current-day Postmodernists, blurred the line between behavior and morality by assuming that human behavior is no different in kind than animal behavior. Based on this view, there is no moral value attached to the various kinds of sexual acts that are available to the human species. Thus, whatever a person does sexually is natural, whatever is natural is permissible, and whatever is permissible is good, even for children.

As we are fond of saying, "Ideas have consequences." And, as it turns out, the results of Kinsey's ideas have led many down a destructive path. One result has been the skyrocketing incidence of sexually transmitted diseases over the past 50 years. In Kinsey's day, there were only two known STD's, both of which were treatable with penicillin. But today, that number has blossomed to over 24, with over a dozen having no cure![31] The capstone of this proliferation of disease is HIV, a virus that can be passed on through homosexual sex acts which, thanks to Kinsey's mainstreaming of homosexuality, has also been on the increase.

In contrast to the view of sexual license that Kinsey promoted, a 1996 study published by researchers at The University of North Carolina supports the traditional view of sex. The study found that lower sexual activity among adolescents is correlated with higher levels of well-being. For example, sexually active girls are over three times as likely to report depressive

---

[30] *Heather Has Two Mommies* attempts to show grade school children that a lesbian couple can provide the same love and care as a heterosexual couple. "Safer" sex is now the term of choice when teaching teenagers the advantages of using a condom during intercourse, since this form of birth control and disease prevention was found *not* to be entirely "safe."

[31] For these and other statistics, see Meg Meeker, *Epidemic: How Teen Sex is Killing Our Kids* (Washington, DC: Lifeline Press, 2002).

symptoms than those who abstain, and sexually active boys are over twice as likely to report depressive symptoms. In fact, these two groups report higher incidence of suicide attempts; boys in particular are at 8 times the risk for a suicide attempt if they are sexually active.[32]

In addition, according to a study published in 2000 by Edward Laumann and colleagues, "a monogamous sexual partnership embedded in a formal marriage evidently produces the greatest satisfaction and pleasure."[33]

What we find, then, is a wholesale repudiation of Kinsey's assumption that humans are simply sexual animals living in an amoral world. On the contrary, true science confirms that sexual intimacy finds its highest fulfillment in a monogamous marital relationship with the prospect of producing children.

As the Bible eloquently states, "For this reason a man will leave his father and mother and be united to his wife, and they will become one flesh."[34] This is not only the religious view, but the one view that assures the ultimate happiness of individuals as well as a sure foundation for a healthy society.

6.6.7 CONCLUSION

While the Postmodern vision for Western culture may be taking hold, as Christians we need to take seriously the cultural commission God gave Adam and Eve in the Garden of Eden (Genesis 1:28), placing them in charge of His creation. The clear direction of this commission goes beyond tending the garden and naming animals. God commanded then to "multiply" and fill the earth with people.

> ## The Pop Culture Connection
>
> ***Kinsey*** (a 2004 film starring Liam Neeson) brought the issue of human sexuality again to the forefront of the national consciousness. Sex educator Dr. Gary Schubach praised the screenplay by commenting, "[W]e need more, not less, of the kind of straightforward sexual research that Kinsey stood for." The only problem with Schubach's assessment is that Kinsey's research was based on fraud and lies. For a critical expose' of Kinsey's reports, see *Kinsey, Sex, and Fraud* by Judith A. Reisman.[35]

The command implies taking charge of a growing social order as well. Jesus echoes this theme when He tells His disciples they are "salt and light" (Matthew 5:13–14). Jesus means that if our society is tasteless and dark, it is *our* fault for not providing the preserving and enlightening influences! Furthermore, Jesus' Great Commission (Matthew 28:18–20) speaks of the spiritual needs that we must address as well. Nowhere does Scripture rescind God's cultural commission—it is still our responsibility.

Christians should be involved in every area of society: in education as teachers, administrators, board members, and textbook selection committee members; in government as leaders at the local, state, and federal levels; as artists, developing the best art, recording the most inspiring music, and writing books and producing cutting edge movies with compelling storylines that capture the imagination of every reader or viewer; in families, as loving parents and role models; in communities, as business leaders and civic club members; in the media, as reporters and writers who are seen and read by millions. In the midst of these endeavors, we should share God's wonderful love story with those who will listen. When we participate in the Great Commission conjoined with the cultural commission, we are fulfilling God's purpose for us during our earthly sojourn.

[32] Robert E. Rector, et al. *Sexually Active Teenagers Are More Likely to Be Depressed and to Attempt Suicide*, http://www.heritage.org/Research/Family/cda0304.cfm.

[33] Edward O. Laumann, et al., *The Social Organization of Sexuality* (Chicago, IL: University of Chicago Press, 2000), 364.

[34] Genesis 2:24.

[35] http://www.doctorg.com/kinseyfilm.htm

 Law

Christianity

"To cut off Law from its ethical sources is to strike a terrible blow at the rule of law."[1]

— RUSSELL KIRK

7.1.1 INTRODUCTION

Christians believe that God gave us divine laws and the means of discovering them. Carl F.H. Henry says, "God is the only Legislator. Earthly rulers and legislative bodies are alike accountable to Him from whom stems all obligation—religious, ethical and civil"[2] (2 Chronicles 20:6; Acts 17:24–31).

The truth of Henry's summary of the Scripture passages mentioned above holds serious implications for all of us, and not just in the realm of law. We acknowledge this truth when we examine the assumptions and failings of all human-centered legal systems, especially those that deny God as Lawgiver. They fail because they recognize neither our dignity as God's image-bearers nor our fallen nature. The twentieth century alone proves both our fallen condition and the failure of human-based legal systems. The reigns of Lenin, Stalin, Hitler, and Tse-tung are gruesome examples of societies in which law was twisted by the state to allow the murder of millions of human beings, more than in all previous centuries combined.[3]

---

[1] Russell Kirk, "The Christian Postulates of English and American Law," *Journal of Christian Jurisprudence* (Tulsa, OK: O.W. Coburn School of Law/Oral Roberts University, 1980), 66.

[2] Carl F.H. Henry, *Twilight of a Great Civilization* (Westchester, IL: Crossway Books, 1988), 147.

[3] R.J. Rummel, *Death By Government* (New Brunswick, NJ: Transaction Publishers, 1994).

7.1.2 SYSTEMS OF MAN-CENTERED LAW

If God exists and imparts divine law, then any society that ignores His laws is risking untold consequences. People who ignore or deny the law of gravity by jumping out a ten-story window earn severe consequences. Societies that ignore or deny the prohibition against murder or theft also suffer severe consequences. A society that rejects God may pass arbitrary laws that result in a loss of respect for the law by its citizens. John Whitehead says that when fundamental principles of law are undermined, "public confidence in law and public willingness to abide by law are also sapped."[4]

When we fail to consider law as sacred, we also fail to consider it binding. If in our fallen condition we create our own laws, we are likely to revise them to better suit our selfish needs. A weak foundation for law creates a weak foundation for morality. We need laws that are unchanging and worthy of our obedience, but we cannot discover a consistent moral code within ourselves. If God does not exist, all things are permissible.

The bankruptcy of the world's legal and ethical codes demonstrates the need for a legal system based outside human interests. John Warwick Montgomery writes, "The horrors of our recent history [have] forced us to recognize the puerile inadequacy of tying ultimate legal standards to the mores of a particular society, even if that society is our own."[5] Most of the horrors can be traced back to positive law. As Christians, however, we believe that the omniscient, omnipotent, omnipresent, loving God is the world's Lawgiver (Psalm 127:1) and provides His own character as an absolute basis for law.

7.1.3 AN ABSOLUTE STANDARD

One aspect Christians find troubling about the theory of legal positivism is that it builds law on an ever-changing foundation—the whims of governmental authorities or political superiors. Legal positivists, though, view it from a different perspective. They believe a *flexible* system of law is desirable, since we and our laws are caught up in the process of evolution. Positivists believe laws are logically formulated by the state to best suit these evolving needs.

> Law has content in the eternal sense. It has a reference point. Like a ship that is anchored, law cannot stray far from its mooring.
>
> — JOHN WHITEHEAD

The failings of a system based on evolutionary processes are obvious, as A.E. Wilder-Smith points out: "Since humans are allegedly accidents, so are their laws."[6] Positive law is arbitrary and creates the profound danger of an all-powerful state (no matter how benevolent its purposes). Whitehead observes, "[I]f there is no fixity in law and no reference point, then law can be what a judge says it is. If, however, there is a fixity to law, there is some absolute basis upon which judgment can be made."[7]

Christians believe this *fixity* exists in the moral order in the form of divine law, which is grounded in the immutable nature of God, a firm foundation that does not flex or evolve. Whitehead explains the superiority of a fixed system of law over a flexible one: "Law has content in the eternal sense. It has a reference point. Like a ship that is anchored, law cannot stray far from its mooring."[8] The Christian view of law produces a legal system that does not

[4] John W. Whitehead, *The Second American Revolution* (Westchester, IL: Crossway Books, 1988), 80
[5] John Warwick Montgomery, *The Law Above the Law* (Minneapolis, MN: Dimension Books, 1975), 26.
[6] A.E. Wilder-Smith, *The Creation of Life* (Costa Mesa, CA: TWFT Publishers, 1970), ix.
[7] Whitehead, 21.
[8] Ibid., 73.

fluctuate according to our whims and preferences; rather, it remains constant and therefore just. This perspective provides law grounded on the absolute foundation of God as the ultimate Lawgiver.

Legal positivism cannot adequately explain the nature of law—why it is necessary and why human-determined law is not just. Christian legal theory, on the other hand, explains that law is necessary because we are universally in rebellion against God and His moral order, and we need earthly law based on His moral order to curb our rebellion. Further, our implementation of laws is always imperfect because our fallen nature prevents us from formulating and enforcing a totally just legal system. Christians believe that in spite of our corrupted, fallen nature we can, nevertheless, know God's laws through general and special revelation.

7.14 NATURAL AND BIBLICAL LAW

Natural law includes God's general revelation to us of both physical and moral laws. Christians believe that we can know God's will or natural law through our conscience, our inherent sense of right and wrong. The Apostle Paul says, "Indeed, when Gentiles, who do not have the [Mosaic] law, do by nature things required by the law, they are a law for themselves, even though they do not have the law . . . " (Romans 2:14).

> **NATURAL LAW:** Physical and moral laws revealed in general revelation and built into the structure of the universe (as opposed to the laws imposed by human beings)

William Blackstone, one of the most influential figures in the history of law, describes the Christian view of natural law this way: "Man, considered as a creature, must necessarily be subject to the laws of his creator, for he is an entirely dependent being. . . . And consequently as man depends absolutely upon his maker for every thing, it is necessary that he should in all points conform to his maker's will. This will of his maker is called the law of nature."[9]

Blackstone's view is consistent with the biblical account of creation, moral order, and divine law. The Apostle Paul explains the concept of natural law in Romans 1 and 2, claiming that we all have a fundamental knowledge of the existence of a transcendent law that we must obey, yet that we consciously fail to obey it. Our fallen, sinful nature does not destroy our awareness of this general revelation. We may "see through a glass darkly," yet we still see. We know intuitively that certain things are outside the moral order (Romans 1:26–32), such as homosexuality, hating God, spitefulness, pride, boasting, inventing evil, disobeying parental authority, breaking covenants, unnatural affections, and unmercifulness.

The general revelation of natural law is grounded in God. Understood properly, natural law explains why each of us is accountable to God for our actions: we know a transcendent law exists, yet we consciously flaunt it. This truth must be incorporated into any successful legal system.

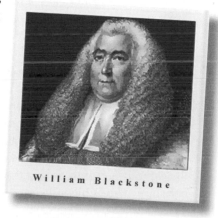

William Blackstone

In addition to natural law, Christian legal theory must take into account God's special revelation of His moral order and divine law, the Bible. Natural law gives us a general concept of right and wrong, while the Bible fleshes out that skeletal framework, telling us what God considers moral and lawful.

---

[9] William Blackstone, *Commentaries on the Laws of England*, in Blackstone's *Commentaries with Notes of Reference to the Constitution and Laws of the Federal Government of the United States and of the Commonwealth of Virginia*, 5 vols., ed., St. George Tucker (Philadelphia, PA: William Young Birch and Abraham Small, 1803; reprint, South Hackensack, NJ: Rothman Reprints, 1969), 1:38–9.

Leviticus 18 provides a good example. Here God tells Moses not to follow the legal structures either of Egypt, where the Israelites had been, or of Canaan, where they were going. God gave them clear laws that forbade certain practices: incest, adultery, infanticide (abortion), homosexuality, and bestiality. These practices continue to intrigue fallen people throughout history, from New Testament times up through today. God considers these practices abominations contrary to human nature (Romans 1:26–27), undermining the dignity and sanctity of His vision for the Christian home and family.

> Upon these two foundations, the law of nature and the law of revelation [the Bible], depend all human laws.
>
> — WILLIAM BLACKSTONE

God's general revelation and special revelation, considered together, allow for the implementation of a legal system that is independent of human wisdom. General and special revelation are accessible to everyone and provide the guidance necessary to create a reasonably just legal system. Blackstone summarizes, "Upon these two foundations, the law of nature and the law of revelation [the Bible], depend all human laws. . . ."[10]

7.1.5 DIVINE LAW

Divine law, based on these two foundations, provides a definite means for evaluating human laws. Legal positivists, however, have no criterion for judging the appropriateness of a law other than the sense of a perceived or evolving need. As Christians, we can and must refer to divine law as the basis for declaring a human law just or unjust. Whitehead argues that

> DIVINE LAW: Any law that comes directly from the character of God via special revelation

the very term *legislator* does not mean one who makes laws, but one who moves them "from the divine law written in nature or in the Bible into the statutes and law codes of a particular society."[11]

Thus governments exist not so much to create laws as to secure laws—to apply divine law to general and specific situations and to act as an impartial enforcer of such laws.

According to God's plan, the responsibility of governments is to encourage people to obey divine law by punishing wrongdoers and protecting those who live in accordance with God's laws (Romans 13:3–4). The Apostle Paul tells us that the righteous need not fear the law, but that the law is designed for those who do wrong. Rebels and lawbreakers need the law to keep them within the boundaries of acceptable behavior, thereby protecting the innocent from lawlessness.

The concern of courts, rather than the creation of laws, should be the application of laws so that God's justice is served. In the past, this concept was implicit in legal theory, although today that line is blurred. Whitehead emphasizes the need for a return to the original conception of the function of courts when he says, "The fact that courts were once seen as institutions of justice (not legislating bodies) cannot be underscored enough."[12] God does not condone false law making, including conceding to the largest factions or those with the loudest message as a basis for the legalization of abortion, homosexuality, pedophilia, or incest. A society that consciously turns away from divine law will suffer consequences. Montgomery says, "The clear pattern throughout Scripture is that those who do God's will live and those who flaunt His commands perish."[13] The Bible tells us clearly that the wages of sin is death.

---

[10] John Eidsmoe, *Christianity and the Constitution* (Grand Rapids, MI: Baker Book House, 1987), 58.

[11] Whitehead, 76.

[12] Ibid., 87–8.

[13] Montgomery, 47.

Grounding our legal system in divine law paves the way to true freedom because all disobedience results in personal and/or political enslavement. Paul asserts, "But now that you have been set free from sin and have become slaves to God, the benefit you reap leads to holiness, and the result is eternal life" (Romans 6:22).

Christian law consists of five basic precepts:

1) That the source of all divine law is the character and nature of God. Schaeffer says, "God has a character, and His character is the law of the universe."[14] Not all things are the same to God. Some things conform to His character and some do not.

2) That the moral order proceeds from and reflects the character of God—His holiness, justice, truth, love, and mercy. God's moral order is as real as the physical order.

3) That we are created in God's image and thus are significant. Our life is not an afterthought or an accident. God established human government to protect human life, rights, and dignity (Genesis 9:6; Romans 13).

4) That when Jesus Christ took on human form, human life assumed even greater significance. God the Creator became God the Redeemer (John 1:14).

5) That God through Christ will judge the whole human race according to His standard of good and evil (Acts 17:31; Romans 2:16; 2 Corinthians 5:10).

7.1.6 DUTIES AND RIGHTS

As Christians, we realize our guilt before an awesome God and flee to Jesus Christ for safety. The extent to which we as individuals or societies acknowledge and obey divine law powerfully affects our entire existence. Nowhere is this truth more important than in the area of human rights. According to Gary Amos, "The Biblical model of rights cannot be separated from the Biblical teaching about justice."[15] Christians believe the Bible is the only true source for discovering the rights that God confers on us. The Bible tells us we are created in God's image, making our life of inestimable worth and meaning. Our system of human rights must be built upon this foundation. Noah Webster clearly saw the implications of this truth: "The moral principles and precepts contained in the scriptures ought to form the basis of all our civil constitutions and laws . . . All the miseries and evils which men suffer from vice, crime, ambition, injustice, oppression, slavery, and war, proceed from their despising or neglecting the precepts contained in the Bible."[16]

> The Biblical model of rights cannot be separated from the Biblical teaching about justice.
>
> — GARY AMOS

In the Christian conception of law, human rights are derived from biblical principles. God commands us to obey divine law, and our obedience guarantees the protection of human rights for everyone. If we live biblically, everyone will enjoy the whole range of rights granted by God. If we disobey God, however, then the system of rights revealed in the Bible will suffer.

Webster explains the effects on human rights of ignoring divine law: "But as there is a God in heaven, who exercises a moral government over the affairs of this world, so certainly will the neglect of the divine command, in the choice of rulers, be followed by bad laws and a bad administration; by laws unjust or partial, by corruption, tyranny, impunity of crimes, waste of public money, and a thousand other evils. Men may devise and adopt new forms of government;

---

[14] Francis Schaeffer, *The Complete Works of Francis A. Schaeffer: A Christian Worldview*, 5 vols. (Westchester, IL: Crossway Books, 1982), 2:249.

[15] Gary T. Amos, *Defending the Declaration* (Brentwood, TN: Wolgemuth and Hyatt, 1989), 109.

[16] Noah Webster, *History of the United States*, 1883, Chapter XIX.

they may amend old forms, repair breaches, and punish violators of the constitution; there is, there can be, no effectual remedy, but obedience to the divine law."[17]

Divine law limits our rights as well. God commands us to act according to His universal order, not our own way. Amos delineates some limitations God gives us: "Men have rights, such as the right to life. But because a man has a duty to live his life for God, the right is unalienable. He can defend his life against all others, but not destroy it himself. No man has the right to do harm to himself, to commit suicide, or to waste his life."[18]

The Pop Culture Connection

Les Miserables (the 1979 film version starring Robert Jordan)—Set in 1800s France, the movie tells the story of escaped convict Jean Valjean (Richard Jordan), who is doggedly pursued for over twenty years by Inspector Javert (Anthony Perkins). At one point, Valjean has the opportunity to kill Javert, but lets him live. A short time later when the situation is reversed, Javert asks Valjean why he did not kill him when he had the chance. Valjean replies, "I had no choice ...Once, many years ago, a remarkable man bought my soul. He removed from it all evil thoughts and gave it to God." Javert responds, "There is no god, there is only the law. Guilt and innocence do not exist outside the law." "Then you must kill me," Valjean answers. As he waits for the bullet that will take his life, Javert vanishes. Later, unable to reconcile his atheism and legalism with Valjean's embodiment of God's grace, Inspector Javert commits suicide.

America's Declaration of Independence was built on just such an unchanging basis of our rights. Thomas Jefferson, its author, proclaimed the need for such a basis when he said, "God who gave us life gave us liberty. And can the liberties of a nation be thought secure when we have removed their only firm basis, a conviction in the minds of the people that these liberties are the gift of God? That they are not to be violated but with His wrath? Indeed, I tremble for my country when I reflect that God is just; that His justice cannot sleep forever."[19]

7.1.7 BIBLICAL APPLICATIONS

The Bible gives us guidelines for an ordered legal system. Judges were appointed to decide disagreements among people according to God's laws and teachings. (See Exodus 18:13–16; Deuteronomy 1:16–17; 19:15–21.) John Eidsmoe says, "The judges were commanded to be honest and not to take bribes or favor the rich (Exodus 23:1–8)."[20] These biblical examples of the judicial system demonstrate that God's ideal legal system is orderly and equitable. Each person has the right to be judged by the same standard of justice. One clear example of a biblical legal concept states, "Do not show partiality in judging; hear both small and great alike" (Deuteronomy 1:17).

The Bible addresses legal theory for assigning guilt as well. Simon Greenleaf explains, "The importance of extreme care in ascertaining the truth of every criminal charge, especially where life is involved, may be regarded as a rule of law. It is found in various places in the Mosaic Code, particularly in the law respecting idolatry; which does not inflict the penalty of death until the crime 'be told thee,' (viz. in a formal accusation), 'and thou hast heard of it,' (upon a legal trial), 'and inquire diligently, and behold to be true,' (satisfactorily proved), 'and the thing certain,' (beyond all reasonable doubt)."[21]

---

[17] Noah Webster, *Value of the Bible and Excellence of the Christian Religion for Use of Families & Schools*, 1834, 302.

[18] Amos, 117.

[19] Paul L. Ford, *The Writings of Thomas Jefferson* (New York, NY: G. P. Putnam's Sons, 1894), 3:267.

[20] John Eidsmoe, *God and Caesar* (Westchester, IL: Crossway Books, 1985), 197.

[21] Simon Greenleaf, "A Treatise on the Law of Evidence" (1824), Part V, Section 29, n. 1. Cited in Herbert Titus,

This illustration from the Mosaic code teaches us that earthly judges should not hastily condemn an accused person. Because of our fallen nature, our reason and our will are not perfect, making human error possible in meting out justice. We are taught that it is better for a judge to err in favor of the defendant than to punish an innocent person. Ultimately all lawbreakers will be judged by God on the final Day of Judgment.

The Bible also calls for a restoration of God's order and for restitution to be made to the offended person when laws are broken. C. S. Lewis writes, "[Christianity] thinks that a great many things have gone wrong with the world that God made and that God insists, and insists very loudly, in our putting them right again."[22]

7.1.8 LEGISLATING MORALITY

Every sin cannot be made explicitly illegal. Morality and legality are not synonymous—a specific law cannot enforce every moral action. A biblical legal system should attempt to legislate morality only to the extent that order is maintained and human rights are protected. The innocent should have nothing to fear from law, while the guilty should have everything to fear.

No legal system can cause every person to always act morally, just as no one is capable of living a completely lawful life. As Christians, we know the truth of this from our own violations of God's divine law, what we learn from Scripture, and what we know from earthly legal systems. A Christian system of law should stabilize society and promote justice (by protecting the innocent and punishing the guilty). It should also lead us to (or reinforce) an understanding of our fallen nature and desperate need for a Savior.

God uses law not only to ensure justice, but also to show us the folly of demanding our just desserts. God in His wisdom can use even earthly legal systems to show unbelievers their fallen nature and lead them to an understanding of its cause and remedy. Law can reveal our need to beg for God's mercy, turn to Christ for salvation, and become children of God (see Ephesians 2).

7.1.9 CONCLUSION

Christian law is based on God's unchanging character as an absolute foundation rather than on a foundation that evolves and changes over time based solely on societal concerns. Christian law ensures specific, absolute human rights that other worldviews that deny God's existence cannot guarantee. Christian human rights are based on specific duties prescribed in the Bible. God assigns us specific rights, and we are responsible for obeying God and protecting our rights as well as the rights of others.

The Bible provides specific instructions for establishing earthly legal systems and He requires such systems to be orderly and equitable. God expects our legal systems to hold individuals responsible for their actions and to work to restore God's order wherever possible. God does not expect legal systems to declare every sin illegal, but rather to maintain order and liberty by promoting justice.

The Bible tells us what God sees as good and what He requires of us: "to do justly, and to love mercy, and to walk humbly with thy God" (Micah 6:8). Our motivation to "do justly" comes from knowing that "the Lord is slow to anger, and great in power, and will not at all acquit the wicked" (Nahum 1:3). Our motivation to "love mercy" and to "walk humbly" comes

---

God, Man, and Law: The Biblical Principles, 2nd ed. (Oak Brook, IL: Institute in Basic Life Principles, 1983), 85.
[22] C.S. Lewis, *Mere Christianity* (New York, NY: Macmillan, 1974), 45.

from Jesus Christ, who said to the woman taken in adultery, "Neither do I condemn thee: go, and sin no more" (John 8:11). We know that we are not perfect, as Christ was, but we are assured that God's grace, mercy, and love will be shown to us on the final Day of Judgment.

Law

Islam

"The Qur'an deals with legal and social issues at a
secondary level and only to the extent necessary to
give some guide lines to pursue the higher principles,
purposes and policies of divine revelation, called
'Maqasid al-Shari'ah,' such as protection of human life,
human reason, offspring, right to property and freedom
of speech."[1]

— HAVVA G. GUNEY-RUEBENACKER

7.2.1 INTRODUCTION

The Islamic worldview has highly developed and detailed legal traditions. As we saw in the discipline of Theology, Islam affirms that God exists and that God is the ultimate Lawgiver. **Shari'ah** is the name of the body of laws Muslims believe are applicable, while *fiqh* is the human endeavor to understand and apply those laws.[2] "The goal" of Muslim jurists

> **SHARI'AH LAW:** Islamic law derived from the Qur'an and Hadith and applied to the public and private lives of Muslims within Islamic states. *Shari'ah law* governs many aspects of day-to-day life—politics, economics, banking, business, contracts, social issues, etc.

[1] Havva G. Guney-Ruebenacker, "Islamic Law: An Ever-Evolving Science Under The Light of Divine Revelation and Human Reason," http://www.averroes-foundation.org/articles/islamic_law_evolving.html.

[2] Malise Ruthven, *Islam: A Very Short Introduction* (Oxford, UK: Oxford University Press, 1997), 86. "The Shari'ah is divine, co-eternal with God. *Fiqh*, by contrast, is the product of human endeavor."

"is not law making, but *fiqh*—understanding or knowledge of a law deemed to exist already."[3] Some of the legal pronouncements encased in Shari'ah include the stoning of adulterers (though the Qur'an says the punishment should be whipping), cutting off the hands of thieves, and killing apostates.

7.2.2 SHARI'AH

In contrast to the Christian worldview that affirms that God reveals both His will *and* Himself, Islam holds that "God has not revealed Himself and His nature, but rather His law."[4] Indeed, "the *Shari'ah* itself is considered to be a timeless manifestation of the will of God, subject neither to history nor circumstance."[5] There are four main tributaries for Islamic *Shari'ah*: the Qur'an, the Sunnah, the *Ijma'*, and *Qiyas* (analogical reasoning).[6]

7.2.3 QUR'AN

The foremost source of *Shari'ah* is the Qur'an, which records "prohibitions on certain foods (pork, carrion, wine, animals slaughtered in pagan ceremonies), a number of legal rules concerning family law (marriage, divorce, and inheritance), criminal law (the *hudud* crimes, including penalties of highway robbery, illicit sexual activity, slander, and wine-drinking), rules about witnesses, and commercial regulation including the ban on *riba* (usury) and forms of contracts."[7] Yet several difficulties result from depending exclusively on the Qur'an: it simply does not speak to *all* (or even many) legal issues.[8]

In addition, many of its statements are ambiguous and addressed to specific historical situations. Ruthven comments, "As for the specific injunctions about the Muslims' struggles against and relationship with the non-Muslims, these varied according to situations and were too specific to be termed 'laws' in the strict sense." [9] While Ruthven may want to limit the applicability of these specific commands, throughout Islamic history many Muslims have read such commands as normative throughout time, for example those passages regarding aggression against non-Muslims. Modern Muslims, especially those educated in the West, perceive the difficulty inherent in failing to acknowledge the historically specific nature of such interactions and responses.

To illustrate the threatening nature of *Shari'ah* law, consider the case of Abdul Rahman. He was born a Muslim in Afghanistan. He converted to Christianity at the age of 25 while working with a group of Christians in Pakistan.[10] In 2002, at about the age of 41, he returned to Afghanistan in the hopes of gaining custody of his daughters who had been living with theizzthe authorities. Under Shari'ah law, a Muslim should be sentenced to death for

---

[3] Ibid., 81.

[4] Ibid., 73.

[5] Additionally, Ruthven observes, "By defining correct behavior or orthopraxy at the social level, the Shari'ah has left its distinctive imprint on a way of living that has evolved over time and varies from one country to another in accordance with local custom" (86).

[6] Ibid., 68: "The mutual relationship of these four principles is highly confusing and it is not at all easy to make it fully clear."

[7] Ibid., 75.

[8] Ibid., 69: "But still the strictly legislative portion of the Qur'an is relatively quite small. Besides the detailed pronouncement on the law of inheritance and laying down punishments for crimes such as theft and adultery, which are not defined legally, there is little in it that is, properly speaking, legislative."

[9] Ibid.

[10] Associated Press, "Afghan Man Faces Death for Allegedly Converting to Christianity" Associated Press, Sunday, March 19, 2006; online: http://www.foxnews.com/story/0,2933,188364,00.html (accessed 23 May 2006).

converting to another religion. He was put on trial for an "attack on Islam" and threatened with death.[11] Probably due to international pressure, the case was dropped "for lack of evidence" and he was granted asylum in Rome, a feat accomplished in part by Pope Benedict XVI.[12]

Also, the Islamic belief that some passages overrule (or abrogate) others has led to debate over which rulings still remain obligatory.[13] Thus Muslim jurists (legal scholars) historically have turned to the traditions regarding what Muhammad declared or practiced as having more practical significance than the Qur'an.

7.2.4 HADITH

Islamic traditions, or *Hadith*, contain records of Muhammad's practices and customs called *Sunnah*. Among these traditions we read of Muhammad's practices, significant actions or abstentions, rulings, and sayings. The Muslim approach to these records perceives Muhammad as expressing what should be normative among Muslims.[14] Because the Qur'an does not address all questions of law, Muslim legal scholars turn to the Sunnah to discern the shape of *Shari'ah*. This body of material contains many more legal rulings and examples than the Qur'an. A fundamental difficulty is that many of the Hadith present conflicting or contradictory rulings arising from different places and times. Because much of the historical context is unrecorded, examples and rulings are left open to debate.[15]

7.2.5 IJMA'

A third source for *Shari'ah* is the communal consensus, called *ijma'*, expressed among Muslim jurists of the first three centuries of Islam. An example of *Shari'ah* arising from this source is male circumcision, a practice not commanded in the Qur'an. In some areas, the practice of female "circumcision" (really female genital mutilation, often including a removal of part or the entire clitoris) is seen as demanded by *Shari'ah* as well. This illustrates how local customs sometimes rise to the level of *Shari'ah* in Muslim communities.

---

[11] "Apostasy (Irtidad) in Islam: The Case of Abdul Rahman, an Afghan Christian," online: http://www.religioustol-erance.org/isl_apos1.htm (accessed 23 May 2006).

[12] "World Briefing | Europe: Italy: Afghan Convert Thanks The Pope," *The New York Times*, 31 March 2006; online: http://query.nytimes.com/gst/fullpage.html?res=9B06E1DB1230F932A05750C0A9609 C8B63 (accessed 23 May 2006).

[13] Ibid.: "But, further, it had to be set out as to which specific command was earlier in time and which later." This briefly describes the Islamic teaching on "abrogation," i.e., the more recent commands or rulings supersede those earlier and remain obligatory.

[14] Ibid.: "The only natural method to be adopted in this comparative and interpretative procedure for a fresh ap-plication of the Qur'an to any given new situation was to see it as it had been actually worked in the lifetime of the Prophet, who was its most authoritative factual exponent and to whose conduct belonged a unique religious normativeness. This is the Sunna of the Prophet. . . . the doctrine of the sinlessness of the Prophet was formu-lated considerably later, but it was only the formal outcome of the inner logic of a process which goes back to the starting point of Islamic history . . . While he was alive, this authority was sufficient for and at any given point of time; the future remained open until it became present and was filled with decisive content by the Prophet bring-ing his authority to bear upon it. But after his death, that living authority was no longer available and had to be transformed formally into a doctrine of infallibility. This means that whatever decisions or pronouncements of the Prophet were authoritative during his lifetime became *infallible* after his death. This is the specific legal ground of the Prophetic infallibility. There is also a theological ground for a different, more general doctrine of infallibility, embracing all the Prophets, which is based on the consideration that a human who is a recipient of divine revela-tion cannot be expected to err grossly, especially in moral terms. . . . [A]fter his death his authority continued as it had been in his lifetime. . . . [N]o one person could claim authority except under the Prophet's aegis" (70).

[15] Ibid., 76.

7.2.6 QIYAS

The fourth source for *Shari'ah* arises from legal reasoning needed to address situations otherwise unaddressed in the Qur'an and the Hadith. But not all Muslims support this approach to legal rulings, giving rise to various legal traditions. One of the more pronounced differences regards the consumption of alcohol. Ruthven notes, "While some jurists would argue that only fermented products of the date-palm and vine are prohibited, others, basing their judgments on the *qiyas*, would insist that all alcoholic drinks are forbidden, since the effective cause or common denominator ('illa) behind the prohibition was the same in each case . . ."[16]

7.2.7 LEGAL SCHOOLS

Sunni Islam hosts four law traditions: Shafi'i, Hanifi, Asbahi, and Hanbal, with the Hanafi School being the most influential. "The differences between the four legal schools of Sunni Islam are mainly confined to questions such as marriage and guardianship, with the Hanafis taking a more liberal view of female rights . . . There are small differences in the ritual of prayer. The most significant are in the laws of inheritance and in an institution know as *muta'* . . . or temporary marriage."[17]

Shi'ite Muslims have their own legal school, Ja'fari, a school of legal tradition and thought that remains to this day. Shi'ite leaders such as the Ayatollahs are interpreters of the law, to which individual Shi'ites are to submit. In contrast to Sunni practice, the Shi'ite religious leaders are recipients of the religious taxes of the people. This results in granting their mosques financial independence from the government, as commonly is the case among the Sunni, and giving religious leaders great political power over government authorities. The legal traditions of the Shi'ites have given them "the edge over their Sunni counterparts in adapting the law to contemporary circumstances."[18]

7.2.8 FIVE CATEGORIES OF BEHAVIOR

The Islamic *Shari'ah*, as classically expressed, defines five categories of human behavior: that which is commanded, recommended, indifferent, disapproved, and forbidden.

1. Those acts that are *commanded* are required or obligatory. Disobedience is worthy of punishment (in this life and the next) and obedience is rewarded in eternity. These would include the five pillars of Islam as well as participation in *jihad*.
2. Those acts that are *recommended* are deemed commendable, but not required. Although failure to do them is not punishable, accomplishing recommended acts is worthy of reward (usually in paradise, though social commendation can be significant in this life). These include charitable acts above and beyond those commanded, extra prayers or fasting, and other good deeds.
3. Those acts that are *forbidden* are prohibited. To do them is to be worthy of punishment (most often in this life). To avoid them is to be worthy of reward (most often in paradise). Thievery, sexual immorality, and drinking wine are among the forbidden acts.

---

[16] Ibid., 79.
[17] Ibid., 82.
[18] Ibid., 83.

4. Those acts that are *disapproved* are discouraged to one degree or another. While doing them does not result in punishment, avoiding them may be worthy of reward in the afterlife. Many Muslims believe divorce is in this category.

5. Those acts that are *indifferent* are without either positive or negative consequences. Neither doing them nor refusing them gains punishment or reward.

7.2.9 CRITIQUE OF ISLAMIC LAW

Lord Acton coined the now famous phrase "Power tends to corrupt; absolute power corrupts absolutely."[19] Underlying this wise saying is the biblical notion that the sinful tendencies of humans are such that left to ourselves, we are not to be trusted with too much power. Thus in Western nations power is distributed among various facets of government. In the United States, for example, there are three branches of government: the Executive, the Legislative, and the Judicial. The division of power permits checks and balances on political power.

Islam stands in contrast both to the biblical revelation of human sinfulness and the importance of a division of powers. Malise Ruthven observes, "It is pessimism about human nature (a by-product, arguably, of the Christian doctrine of original sin) that leads to the liberal perception that all power corrupts, and that constitutional limitations must be placed on its exercise."[20] Yet Ruthven writes, "[B]ecause the Islamist model is predicated on the belief in government by morally impeccable individuals who can be counted on to resist temptation, it does not generate institutions capable of functioning autonomously by means of structural checks and balances. Political institutions function only as a result of the virtue of those who run them, but virtue can become widespread only if society is already Islamic."[21]

The result is that nations with a predominately Muslim population tend toward dictatorships or monarchies and in consequence lack personal freedom. In their report *Freedom in the World 2003*, Freedom House lists forty-eight nations that receive a rating of "Not Free." Of these, twenty-five in total have largely Islamic populations, and of the nine worst rated countries, six are Islamic (Iraq, Libya, Saudi Arabia, Sudan, Syria, and Turkmenistan.)[22]

Throughout the report, the authors insist that these facts "should not suggest some kind of inexorable link between Islam and tyranny." A few paragraphs later they again make clear that the lack of democratic reform in "large swaths of the world populated by Muslim majorities" is not "directly related to religious beliefs as such."[23]

Yet, even a casual look at Freedom House's own "Map of Freedom," which highlights the world's freest nations, reveals the link between freedom and worldview.[24] The nations that have the highest regard for basic human rights and the rule of law are those countries that have come under the influence of Christianity. In light of this, it seems that Freedom House is merely attempting to explain away the obvious conclusion that worldviews really do matter.

In contrast to a Biblical Christian view of the nature of man, the Muslim community cannot find a similar basis for individual freedom within its religion. On the one hand, Mawdudi, a prominent Pakistani Muslim scholar, states, "[A]ll non-Muslims will have the freedom of conscience, opinion, expression, and association as the one enjoyed by Muslims themselves,

---

[19] Lord Acton's letter to Bishop Mandell Creighton (1887). See John Bartlett's *Familiar Quotations*, 13th and centennial ed. (Boston, MA: Little Brown and Company 1955), 335.

[20] Malise Ruthven, 89–90.

[21] Ibid., 90.

[22] See Freedom House's 12-page report, "Freedom in the World 2003" at http://www.freedomhouse.org/research/freeworld/2002/webessay2003.pdf.

[23] Ibid., 5.

[24] To view Freedom House's "Map of Freedom 2001," go to http://www.freedomhouse.org/pdf_docs/research/freeworld/2001/map2001.pdf.

subject to the same limitations as are imposed by law on Muslims."[25] However, Samuel Shahid writes, "Mawdudi's views are not accepted by most Islamic schools of law, especially in regard to freedom of expression like criticism of Islam and the government. Even in a country like Pakistan, the homeland of Mawdudi, it is illegal to criticize the government or the head of state. Many political prisoners are confined to jails in Pakistan and most other Islamic countries. Through the course of history, except in rare cases, not even Muslims have been given freedom to criticize Islam without being persecuted or sentenced to death. It is far less likely for a *Zimmi* [Christian or Jew] to get away with criticizing Islam."[26]

The idea of freedom of expression is not part of Muslim legal tradition. Historically, Muslim countries operating under *Shari'ah* law and Muslim legal scholarship have allowed Muslim men a certain amount of freedom, but restricted the freedoms of women and non-Muslims.

In Saudi Arabia, for instance, churches are prohibited from being built. Christians must worship in the privacy of their own homes and refrain from even praying out loud, so that faithful Muslims can remain untainted by Christianity. In Algeria, a law passed in 2005 pronounces any means of enticing a Muslim to another religion criminal, including even producing, storing, or distributing "printed documents or audio-visual formats or any other format or means which seeks to shake the faith of a Muslim."[27] If convicted, the offender could be imprisoned for two to five years and fined as much as $14,000 (US). According to Arabic News reports, the new law "is an attempt to withstand the Christianizing campaign which had witnessed notable activity recently."[28]

7.2.10 CONCLUSION

Law cannot be discussed in isolation from other aspects of a worldview. In order to retain personal freedoms within a society, its legal system must have a solid, sustainable foundation. Only a biblical worldview provides a basis for law that respects both human dignity (that we are created in God's image) *and* human depravity (that we have fallen into sin). These two ideas also have implications in the area of politics and will be explored in more detail in that chapter.

[25] Samuel Shahid, *Rights of Non-Muslims in an Islamic State,*
http://www.answering-islam.org/NonMuslims/rights.htm.
[26] Ibid.
[27] Ibid.
[28] http://www.arabicnews.com/ansub/Daily/Day/060321/2006032108.html.

Secular Humanism

"As with laws, so with morals: human beings seem quite capable of making, on their own, sensible and sensitive decisions affecting conduct."[1]

— FREDERICK EDWORDS

7.3.1 INTRODUCTION

Secular Humanist legal theory is founded on the two basic assumptions that dictate all aspects of this worldview: 1) God does not exist; and 2) human beings are perfectible, evolving animals. Julian Huxley reinforces this conviction when he says, "Our present knowledge indeed forces us to the view that the world of reality is evolution—a single process of self transformation."[2] Our focus, according to this view, must be on creating an environment that encourages further evolutionary progress.

Secular Humanists also believe (as we saw in the sociology section) that the environment is the cause of any evil we do. Perfecting the environment will allow us to learn to choose consistently that which is morally correct. Secular Humanists see law as a tool that can manipulate our ability toward this end.

7.3.2 IF GOD DOES NOT EXIST

In denying the existence of God, Secular Humanists also deny the existence of an absolute moral code that must be obeyed. They view God's commands (traditionally understood to

---

[1] Frederick Edwords, "The Human Basis of Law and Ethics," *The Humanist* (May/June 1985): 12.
[2] J.R. Newman, ed., *What is Science?* (New York, NY: Simon and Schuster, 1955), 278.

be the absolute moral order) as harmful fiction. According to Paul Kurtz, "The traditional supernaturalistic moral commandments are especially repressive of our human needs. They are immoral insofar as they foster illusions about human destiny and suppress vital inclinations [i.e. in the sexual arena]."[3]

Secular Humanists believe that we are capable of devising our own moral code in regard to both behavior and law. Frederick Edwords notes, "It should be obvious from the most casual observation that human beings are quite capable of setting up systems and then operating within them."[4] Thus, the Secular Humanist system of law requires a human-centered ethics that we discover in the nature of our relations with each other, rather than in the nature of God. Morality is also an evolving process. V.M. Tarkunde explains, "Moral behavior of a rudimentary type is found in the higher animals and can be traced even to lower forms of life. This fact is enough to establish that the source of morality is biological and not theological."[5]

7.3.3 Do Rights Evolve?

Oliver Wendell Holmes

Darwin's evolutionary theory had a profound impact on the Secular Humanist conception of law. Huxley explains, "There proceeded during the 19th Century under the influence of the evolutionary concept, a thoroughgoing transformation of older studies like . . . Law."[6] An example of how this transformation affected the field of law comes from **Oliver Wendell Holmes, Jr.**: "I see no reason for attributing to man a significance different in kind from that which belongs to a baboon or a grain of sand."[7] Holmes' philosophy of law shines a light on both Secular Humanist and Postmodernist law.[8]

A moral as well as a legal dilemma arises from the belief that we are evolving animals on an equal footing with baboons—why should we (humans) enjoy rights that other animals do not enjoy? Morris B. Storer states the dilemma this way: "What is there that's different about a human being that dictates the right to life for all humans (unarguably in most circumstances) where most people acknowledge no such right in other animals? That justifies equal right to liberty where we fence the others in, equal justice under law where the other animals are not granted any trial at all."[9] This position logically leads to the assumption that since mankind, society, morality, and laws all evolve, human rights also evolve.

7.3.4 NATURAL LAW

Secular Humanist Paul Kurtz, however, does not take that logical step. He explains, "There are common human rights that must be respected by everyone."[10] He and other Humanists attempt to use the concepts of natural law and natural rights to provide a standard that transcends

---

[3] Paul Kurtz, ed., *The Humanist Alternative* (Buffalo, NY: Prometheus Books, 1973), 50.

[4] Edwords, 11.

[5] Morris B. Storer, ed., *Humanist Ethics* (Buffalo, NY: Prometheus Books, 1980), 156.

[6] Cited in John W. Whitehead, *The Second American Revolution* (Elfin, IL: David C. Cook, 1982), 46.

[7] Richard Hertz, *Chance and Symbol* (Chicago, IL: University of Chicago Press, 1948), 107.

[8] See Albert W. Alschuler, *Law Without Values: The Life, Work, and Legacy of Justice Holmes* (Chicago, IL: University of Chicago Press, 2000). Holmes admits his decisions were based on the fact that humanity is an evolving animal and that the concept of "survival of the fittest" was important to him.

[9] Storer, 291.

[10] Paul Kurtz, *Eupraxophy: Living Without Religion* (Buffalo, NY: Prometheus Books, 1989), 158.

humans and governments. The concept of natural law assumes one true morality that we are capable of discerning. Natural law exists independent of us much like the law of gravity does, but we can know it and exact laws in conformity with it.

Christians believe that God implanted laws in the universe and inscribed natural law on our hearts, but Secular Humanists are kept from accepting this explanation for the source of natural law by their vehement denial of God. Instead, they must fall back on evolutionary theory for their explanation.

Julian Wadleigh asserts that evolution is just as good an explanation for natural law as is a Creator. In keeping with the Secular Humanist stance on biological evolution, Wadleigh believes that natural law is basic and instinctive in human beings because we are evolving social animals. He says, "The Declaration [of Independence] speaks of natural law as an endowment by a creator, whereas I speak of it as the result of humankind's evolution as a social animal. There is a difference, but that difference concerns the questions of how and why we have natural law—not whether or not natural law exists. Regardless of its origin, it is the same natural law."[11]

To integrate the concepts of evolution and natural law, Wadleigh explains, "Natural law is not a set of precise rules but a guide that must be followed using plain common sense."[12] In saying this, Wadleigh is conceding that he sees natural law as an unstable, evolving guide, a stark contrast to the view the authors of the Declaration of Independence had in mind of natural law as a stable foundation for moral behavior.

7.3.5 NATURAL LAW DENIED

Natural law and natural rights are therefore incompatible with the ideology of Secular Humanism. Delos McKown asks the pointed question, "When, one wonders, in evolutionary history did hominids first acquire natural rights?"[13]

Kurtz denies natural rights entirely when he says, "Am I not bringing in a doctrine of natural rights that are prior to political policy? No, I reject any such fiction."[14] For Kurtz, rights come into being through human systems: "Most . . . rights have evolved out of the cultural, economic, political, and social structures that have prevailed."[15]

Secular Humanism's denial of natural rights leads to a denial of natural law. This denial stems from the Humanist belief that we are not subservient to any force apart from our own human understanding. Law must be human-centered, rather than God-centered. John Herman Randall, Jr., explains, "The Humanist temper has always protested against any subservience to an external law, whether religious or mechanical, imposed upon man from without."[16]

Kurtz also denies the existence of natural law, saying, "How are these principles [of equality, freedom, etc.] to be justified? They are not derived from a divine or natural law, nor do they have any special metaphysical status. They are rules offered to govern how we shall behave. They can be justified only by reference to their results."[17] Secular Humanists, then, approach law from the standpoint that laws are not derived from natural law, but from our own reasoning and judgment.

---

[11] Julian Wodleigh, "What is Conservatism?" *The Humanist* (Nov./Dec. 1989): 21.

[12] Ibid.

[13] Delos McKown, "Demythologizing Natural Human Rights," *The Humanist* (Nov./Dec. 1989): 22

[14] Paul Kurtz, *The Fullness of Life* (New York, NY: Horizon Press, 1974), 162.

[15] Paul Kurtz, *Forbidden Fruit* (Buffalo, NY: Prometheus Books, 1988), 196.

[16] Kurtz, *The Humanist Alternative*, 59.

[17] Kurtz, *The Fullness of Life*, 162.

7.3.6 HUMANIST POSITIVE LAW

Approaching legal theory from a belief in human reason is known as legal positivism. In its strict sense, legal positivism claims that the state is the ultimate authority for creating law. Because God is a myth and natural law a legal fiction, we must rely on human reason to discern what is legal. Those who determine the law are those who are in power

Humanism's rejection of natural law leads to the understanding that humans are therefore responsible for the creation of all laws. According to Max Hocutt, "Human beings may, and do, make up their own rules. All existing moralities and all existing laws are human artifacts, products of human society, social conventions."[18] Government, then, is the ultimate source of legal truth since the state, not individuals, enacts laws.

The state thus becomes the source of human rights, which are no longer called *natural rights* but constitutional rights. McKown explains the difference: "Natural human rights exist only among human beings; that is, one holds natural rights only against other natural rights holders. Maintaining this point, however, begs the question of natural rights and leaves us wondering how such rights differ from constitutional or legal rights."[19] From this, McKown concludes that legal rights are all that exist. He says: "Our eyes and our idealism ought to be focused, rather, on the only kind of rights that can be realized: legal rights . . ."[20]

A system of legal positivism results in an arbitrary legal code. When legal positivism is combined with evolution, Humanist legal theory grows capricious. Kurtz describes the result: "Laws . . . provide us only with general guides for behavior; how they work out depends upon the context."[21]

Roscoe Pound explains the unanswerable dilemma of grounding laws in nothing but the state and yet convincing citizens to obey them without question: "From the time when lawgivers gave over the attempt to maintain the general security by belief that particular bodies of human law had been divinely dictated or divinely revealed or divinely sanctioned, they have had to wrestle with the problem of proving to mankind that the law was something fixed and settled, whose authority was beyond question, while at the same time enabling it to make constant readjustments and occasional radical changes under the pressure of infinite and variable human desires."[22]

The real problem created by Humanist legal theory, however, is not the potential disobedience of its citizens; rather, it is the government's potential to take advantage of its position as the

---

The Pop Culture Connection

The Cider House Rules (a 1999 film starring Tobey Maguire which won 2 Academy Awards)—The movie follows Homer Wells (Maguire), born at a Maine orphanage in the 1940s, through his "coming-of-age" journey from innocence to adulthood. After working for several seasons picking apples, Homer, the only literate man among the workers, is asked to read the list of rules nailed to the bunkhouse wall. The rules, such as *Do not sleep on the bunkhouse roof*, seem overly restrictive and arbitrary. When Homer finishes, one worker comments, "That don't mean nothing at all. And all this time I've been wondering about 'em." The crew boss adds, "These rules ain't for us. We're the ones that are supposed to make our own rules, and we do, every single day. Ain't that right, Homer?" Symbolically, the scene concludes with Homer burning the paper rules in the stove.

---

[18] Storer, *Humanist Ethics*, 137.

[19] McKown, "Demythologizing Natural Human Rights," 23–24.

[20] Ibid., 34

[21] Kurtz, *The Fullness of Life*, 163.

[22] Roscoe Pound, *An Introduction to the Philosophy of Law* (New Haven, CT: Yale University Press, 1969), 3.

ultimate source of legal truth. Tibor Machan, recognizing the danger, says, "If there were no moral, humanistic foundations for the legal rights we ought to have, we would face the prospect of governments that exist without any limits, without any standards by which to ascertain whether or not they are just and morally legitimate."[23] Thus Secular Humanist **positive law** creates a state with the authority of a god, wielding all power and placing individuals at its mercy.[24]

> **POSITIVE LAW [OR LEGAL POSITIVISM]:** The Humanistic legal school of thought that claims laws are rules made by human beings and that there is no inherent or necessary connection between law and morality

7.3.7 CONCLUSION

In order to be consistent with their worldview (that God does not exist and that humans are mere evolving perfectible animals), Secular Humanists must embrace a legal theory that is both atheistic and evolving. Their legal system must also deny any external or supernatural source of ethics, rights, or laws, including natural law and natural rights. Secular Humanists, therefore, cannot sincerely embrace statements such as, "We hold these Truths to be self-evident, that all Men are created equal, that they are endowed by their Creator with certain unalienable Rights, that among these are Life, Liberty, and the Pursuit of Happiness—That to secure these Rights, Governments are instituted among Men, deriving their just Powers from the Consent of the Governed."[25]

To fit their evolutionary beliefs, some Secular Humanists simply redefine natural law as an inner guide. Yet to maintain consistency between their worldview and their legal theory, they must fully embrace legal positivism, which centers the creation of law within the state. Alistair Hannay explains the dilemma of a theory of law that rejects the Lawgiver: "Humanists naturally want to believe that we have moral obligations, duties in some virtually legalistic sense but not the product of arbitrary legislation, to one another. But on what can the belief be based?"[26] Because its base is evolutionary theory (and the whims of the state), legal positivism results in an arbitrary legal system that discourages obedience and grants the state virtually unlimited authority.

In stark contrast to Hannay's dilemma, John Adams, the second president of the United States, says this about our legal foundation: "May that Being who is supreme over all, the Patron of Order, the Fountain of Justice, and the Protector in all ages of the world of virtuous liberty, continue His blessing upon this nation and its Government and give it all possible success and duration consistent with the ends of His providence."[27] Humanist law, therefore, faces a bitter choice: an inconsistent legal theory that embraces natural law, or a consistent legal positivism with its accompanying problems.

---

[23] Tibor Machan, "Are Human Rights Real?" *The Humanist* (Nov./Dec. 1989): 28.

[24] Robert Bork uses the term "Olympianism" to describe the belief that activist judges are an intellectual elite class ordained to shape a nation's destiny by their decisions from the bench. (From a speech delivered to the Council on National Policy on May 13, 2006).

[25] From the *Declaration of Independence*, July 4, 1776.

[26] Storer, *Humanist Ethics*, 187.

[27] John Adams, "Inaugural Address," City of Philadelphia, March 4, 1797.

Law

Marxism–Leninism

"Law, morality, religion, are to [the proletariat] so many bourgeois prejudices, behind which lurk in ambush just as many bourgeois interests."[1]

— KARL MARX

7.4.1 INTRODUCTION

The assumptions basic to Marxist legal theory—first, that God does not exist; and second, that humans are evolving animals—deny both the possibility of an absolute moral code and the existence of any law grounded in any authority other than human authority. V. I. Lenin says, "In what sense do we repudiate ethics and morality? . . . In the sense in which it was preached by the bourgeoisie, who derived ethics from God's commandments. We, of course, say that we do not believe in God."[2]

L.S. Jawitsch, a modern-day Marxist legal theorist, maintains Lenin's denial of anything supernatural, saying, "There are no eternal, immutable principles of law."[3] Therefore, Marxist law cannot be based on anything other than human rationality. In Lenin's words, "We repudiate all morality taken apart from human society and classes."[4]

---

[1] Karl Marx and Frederick Engels, *Collected Works*, 40 vols. (New York, NY: International Publishers, 1976), 6:494–5.

[2] V.I. Lenin, *On Socialist Ideology and Culture* (Moscow, USSR: Foreign Languages Publishing House, 1981), 51–2. Cited in James D. Bales, *Communism and the Reality of Moral Law* (Nutley, NJ: The Craig Press, 1969), 2.

[3] L.S. Jawitsch, *The General Theory of Law* (Moscow, USSR: Progress Publishers, 1981), 160.

[4] Lenin, *On Socialist Ideology and Culture*, 51–2.

7.4.2 THE ORIGIN OF LAW

Marxists explain that law and human rights arise from the interactions of human beings within social structures that contain economic class distinctions. Class divisions within societies create conflict and disorder and therefore law (and the state) comes into existence to deal with this conflict. According to Engels, "In order that these . . . classes with conflicting economic interests, may not annihilate themselves and society in a useless struggle, a power becomes necessary that stands apparently above society and has the function of keeping down the conflicts and maintaining 'order.' And this power, the outgrowth of society, but assuming supremacy over it and becoming more and more divorced from it, is the State."[5]

The state that rises to maintain order within society perpetuates the conflict as a dominant class wielding power over classes with less power. Lenin explains, "The State is an organ of class domination, an organ of oppression of one class by another; its aim is the creation of 'order' which legalizes and perpetuates this oppression by moderating the collisions between the classes."[6] Laws are thus imposed by the state to quell these disturbances.

7.4.3 BOURGEOIS LAW AND THE PROLETARIAT

In the Marxist worldview, the bourgeoisie and the proletariat are the two classes involved in the struggle for power. Societies that allow the bourgeoisie to make moral decisions and formulate laws are unjust societies.

In the *Communist Manifesto*, Marx denounces bourgeois law as nothing more than a reflection of the desires of that class. Speaking to the bourgeois, he says, "[Y]our jurisprudence is but the will of your class made into a law for all, a will, whose essential character and direction are determined by the economic conditions of existence of your class."[7]

Bourgeois law is oppressive because it is based on the concept of private property, and thus laws are created that promote unequal rights. Capitalism cannot create equal rights for all because the very nature of the economic system creates *haves* and *have-nots*. Cornforth states, "There cannot be equality between exploiters and exploited."[8]

A capitalist society that creates unequal rights based on property and class leads those with fewer rights to protest in the form of lawlessness. Engels explains, "The contempt for the existing social order is most conspicuous in its extreme form—that of offences against the law."[9] Society, therefore, is more responsible than the individual for lawlessness. Indeed, criminals need not feel remorse for their actions because the unjust bourgeois society leaves them no alternative but to lash out against it.

The Marxist solution to the unjust society and lawlessness is to overthrow the bourgeoisie, thus allowing the proletariat to make the laws. The legal system that promotes the interests of the working class is called **proletariat law.** Jawitsch believes, "Complete success in the masses' struggle for their democratic rights and liberties can only be achieved

> **PROLETARIAT LAW:** A legal system established by state authority that favors the interests of the working people

---

[5] Frederick Engels, *The Origin of the Family, Private Property and the State* (Chicago, IL: Kerr, 1902), 206.

[6] V.I. Lenin, *The State and Revolution* (New York, NY: International Publishers, 1932), 9.

[7] Marx and Engels, *Collected Works*, 6:501.

[8] Maurice Cornforth, *The Open Philosophy and the Open Society* (New York, NY: International Publishers, 1976), 290.

[9] Frederick Engels, *The Condition of the Working Class in England* (Moscow, USSR: Progress Publishers, 1973), 168. Cited in R.W. Makepeace, *Marxist Ideology and Soviet Criminal Law* (Totowa, NJ: Barnes and Noble, 1980), 30.

by overcoming monopoly capital's economic and political domination and establishing a state authority that expresses the interests of the working people."[10]

According to Marxist legal theory, the working class may break capitalistic law if such an action is in pursuit of equality. According to Lenin, "The revolutionary dictatorship of the proletariat is won and maintained by the use of violence by the proletariat against the bourgeoisie, rule that is unrestricted by any laws."[11]

> The revolutionary dictatorship of the proletariat is won and maintained by the use of violence by the proletariat against the bourgeoisie, rule that is unrestricted by any laws.
>
> — V.I. LENIN

7.4.4 LAW AND SOCIALIST ECONOMICS

Once the revolution of the proletariat has succeeded, the new socialistic law will reflect the desires of the working people rather than those of the bourgeoisie. Law based on the will of the proletariat will create a society that is less exploitative than that based on capitalist bourgeois law. According to Jawitsch, "An anti-exploiter tendency is what characterizes the special features of all the principles of the law of socialist society in most concentrated form."[12]

The will of the proletariat becomes the basis for all rights, laws, and judgments, thereby negating natural law, God, or any absolute moral code. Howard Selsem explains, "Marxism, which has been so often accused of seeking to eliminate moral considerations from human life and history emphasizes rather the moral issues involved in every situation. It does so, however, not by standing on a false platform of absolute right, but by identifying itself with the real needs and interests of the workers and farmers."[13]

Marxists see law based on the will of the proletariat as flexible rather than inconsistent, a flexibility that denies a need for a comprehensive legal system. Pashukanis writes, "We require that our legislation possess maximum elasticity. We cannot fetter ourselves by any sort of system."[14]

7.4.5 LEGAL POSITIVISM

An elastic legal system is consistent with the Marxist view of human evolution. Humans are constantly evolving; law is based on the will of the proletariat; therefore law is also constantly changing. Marxist laws and human rights are arbitrary, based on the will of the ruling class, the proletariat. Jawitsch describes law in a Marxist society this way: "As a component of the legal superstructure law is closely linked with the political superstructure and with the state."[15] Lenin agrees, saying, "A court is an organ of state power. Liberals sometimes forget that. It is a sin for a Marxist to forget it."[16] Courts, in other words, determine and dispense justice through the will of the ruling class, the state.

Any system of law based on the will of those in power—the state—is legal positivism. Marxists, however, do not recognize or admit that their approach to law is from a legal positivist perspective.

[10] Jawitsch, *The General Theory of Law*, 46.

[11] V.I. Lenin, *Collected Works*, 45 vols. (Moscow, USSR: Progress Publishers, 1981), 28:236.

[12] Jawitsch, *The General Theory of Law*, 160.

[13] Howard Selsam, *Socialism and Ethics* (New York, NY: International Publishers, 1943), 13.

[14] E.B. Pashukanis in a 1930 speech regarding the Soviet State and the Revolution of Law (Moscow).

[15] Jawitsch, *The General Theory of Law*, 290.

[16] Lenin, *Collected Works*, 25:155. Cited in John Hazard, *Settling Disputes in Soviet Society* (New York, NY: Columbia University, 1960), 3.

7.4.6 LAW AS AN EXTENSION OF PARTY POLITICS

Because Marxism bases much of its legal theory on economics, its version of legal positivism differs in one sense from the Secular Humanist approach. In Marxism, the proletariat must gain control of the state and formulate new laws in order to create a truly just society. Therefore, Marxist-Leninist legal positivism requires a class-consciousness that Secular Humanist positivism does not emphasize. The working class must lead the Marxist state.

However, Marxists believe the political party functions as the guiding force for the working class once it attains power. In actuality, then, the entity that determines justice is not the working class, but the Marxist-Leninist political party. Vyshinsky explains, "There might be collisions and discrepancies between the formal commands of laws and those of the proletarian revolution. . . . This collision must be solved only by the subordination of the formal commands of law to those of party policy."[17]

7.4.7 MARXIST LAW AND THE ENEMIES OF THE PROLETARIAT

In the Marxist system, those who disagree with the Marxist-Leninist party are guilty of lawlessness. Since the party decides what is legal and illegal, it wields tremendous power in dispensing its form of justice to those who disagree with it.

The 1936 Soviet Constitution affirmed that all citizens are granted certain rights "in conformity with the interests of the working people, and in order to strengthen the socialist system."[18] Thus, citizens are granted certain rights, but they cannot exercise them in ways that would undermine the advance of socialism and communism. Citizens whose actions are deemed unacceptable by the Marxist-Leninist party find themselves without any rights. Alexander Solzhenitsyn in *The Gulag Archipelago*[19] and Stephane Courtois (et al.) in *The Black Book Of Communism: Crimes, Terror, Repression*[20] document the loss of rights by those who are deemed enemies of the state.

Vyshinsky believes legal discrimination by the party should be relentless against those who disagree with its political agenda: "The task of justice . . . is to assure the precise and unswerving fulfillment of . . . laws by all the institutions, organizations, officials, and citizens of the [state]. This the court accomplishes by destroying without pity all the foes of the people in whatsoever form they manifest their criminal encroachments upon socialism."[21] Those who create and enforce laws within a specific ideology cannot tolerate actions that oppose the ideology.

7.4.8 LAW WITHERS AWAY

Because Marxists believe law arises from class conflicts caused by property, the need for law itself will dissolve once a communist society is established. Since only one class (the proletariat) will then exist, the need to promote order between classes will no longer remain—in effect law will have become unnecessary.

---

[17] Andrei Y. Vyshinsky, *Judiciary of the USSR*, 2nd ed. (Moscow, USSR: Progress Publishers, 1935), 32. Cited in Berman, *Justice in the USSR: An Interpretation of Soviet Law*, (New York, NY: Vintage, 1963), 42–3.

[18] Cited in John Hazard, *Law and Social Change in the USSR* (London, UK: Stevens and Sons, 1953), 79.

[19] Alexander Solzhenitsyn, *The Gulag Archipelago*, 3 vols. (New York, NY: Harper and Row, 1973–1978).

[20] Stephane Courtois, et al., *The Black Book Of Communism: Crimes, Terror, Repression* (Cambridge, MA: Harvard University Press, 1999). Also, R.J. Rummel, *Death By Government* (New Brunswick, NJ: Transaction Publishers, 1994).

[21] Andrei Y. Vyshinsky, *The Law of the Soviet State* (New York, NY: Macmillian, 1948), 13. Cited in Raymond S. Sleeper, ed., *A Lexicon of Marxist-Leninist Semantics* (Alexandria, VA: Western Goals, 1983), 147.

Marxists believe that when classes are abolished, all people will create and live in an environment that promotes harmony. Criminal activity will be almost nonexistent since the catalysts for anti-social activity—injustice and inequality—will no longer exist. Plamenatz says that in a communist society crime will be "virtually unknown" because "motives will be less urgent and frequent, and the offender will be more easily brought to his senses by the need to regain the good opinion of his neighbors."[22] Unfortunately, more than 5,000 years of recorded history disproves the probability of such a utopian plan working.

7.4.9 CONCLUSION

Both Marxist and Secular Humanist legal theory are grounded in a denial of the existence of God and a belief that we and our social systems are evolving. These assumptions require Marxists and Secular Humanists to rely on legal positivism as the basis for law. The Marxist version of legal positivism adds the unique feature of class-consciousness to the state's role as the will of the ruling proletarian class. Furthermore, the working class must rule under the guidance of the Marxist-Leninist political party, giving the party final authority on morality and law.

When those adhering to a specific ideology arbitrarily determine a system of law, laws will be created that are prejudiced against those with opposing views. In such a society, freedom disappears, as each citizen is held hostage by the arbitrary laws of the state.

The Pop Culture Connection

Animal Farm (a 1999 film based on the book by George Orwell)—This political satire is set on a small farm where the prized boar, Old Major, describes his dream of "Animal Freedom" from the lazy, drunken owners. The animals lead a revolt (think 1917 Bolshevik revolution) against the humans to take back the farm. After the revolution, the pigs, who are the cleverest animals, rule the new roost and every animal seems to be getting a fair share. The only problem is the pigs begin acting more and more like men! They lie and manipulate to remain in power and exploit those below them. Orwell's story describes how the Communist dream in Russia quickly began to sour, as those in Stalin's government became corrupt—just like the leaders they had overthrown in the name of revolution. A famous slogan from the book/film: "All animals are equal, but some animals are more equal than others."

---

[22] John Plamenatz, *Man and Society*, 2 vols. (London, UK: Longmans, 1963), 2:374. Cited in Makepeace, *Marxist Ideology and Soviet Criminal Law*, 35.

Law

Cosmic Humanism

"As extensions of God, we are ourselves the spirit of compassion, and in our right minds, we don't seek to judge but to heal."[1]

— MARIANNE WILLIAMSON

7.5.1 INTRODUCTION

Cosmic Humanists do not spend a lot of time discussing law. They prefer to concentrate on personal inner development, getting in touch with the God within. Yet, this primary goal of Cosmic Humanists has implications for the field of law.

In Cosmic Humanist law, all authority resides within the individual. If each of us is God and God is each of us, we can decide the legality of an action only be getting in touch with our inner God. Thus, each of us acts as our own legal authority, and any manifestation of outside authority hinders our communication with our godhood.

Shakti Gawain explains the problem of imposition of outside authority when he says, "The real problem with commitment to an external form is that it doesn't allow room for the inevitable changes and growth of people and relationships. If you promise to feel or behave by a certain set of rules, eventually you are going to have to choose between being true to yourself and being true to those rules."[2]

If we choose to honor a set of rules other than inner truth, we sacrifice our godhood. Gawain reiterates what happens when we look to authority outside ourselves: "When we consistently suppress and distrust our intuitive knowingness," writes Gawain, "looking instead for [external]

---

[1] Marianne Williamson, *A Return to Love* (New York, NY: Harper Collins, 1989), 37.
[2] Shakti Gawain, *Living in the Light* (San Rafael, CA: New World Library, 1986), 110.

authority, validation, and approval from others, we give our personal power away."[3] There is, therefore, a desire in Cosmic Humanist thinking for an abandonment of externally imposed laws to govern society.

7.5.2 "FREEDOM" OR LEGAL ABSOLUTES?

Only after achieving higher consciousness by connecting with the God within can Cosmic Humanists act under proper authority. Their actions are lawful when they conform to the reality they are creating. Gawain explains, "As each of us connects with our inner spiritual awareness, we learn that the creative power of the universe is within us. We also learn that we can create our own reality and take responsibility for doing so."[4]

> **SELF LAW:** The legal perspective that actions are lawful if they come from the God within and unlawful if imposed by an outside authority

The New Age concept of **self law** states that any action we choose is lawful as long as it is true to our inner reality, and by way of contrast, actions are unlawful if imposed by an outside authority. Additionally, once we achieve collective consciousness, we will act as co-creators of reality, where everyone works by his or her own authority.

The Cosmic Humanist reliance on the God within stands in stark contrast to the Christian belief in the authority of the Bible. David Spangler, through the voice of a channeled spirit, disdains the Christian worldview as well as others opposed to Cosmic Humanism. He says, "Their world (of darkness) is under the law and shall disappear."[5] Cosmic Humanists need no such outside authority because "mankind, and all life, is basically good," according to Kevin Ryerson.[6] If humanity is basically good, then law only keeps us from being totally free to achieve godhood.

Cosmic Humanists believe (incorrectly) that the Bible teaches individual autonomy and personal freedom that allows individuals to communicate with their godhood. Ryerson believes that over the centuries the church has twisted biblical truth, which actually teaches that each soul has "responsibility for its own behavior in the realization of its own divinity."[7] Christians, therefore, should abandon law and focus on achieving higher consciousness.

7.5.3 CONCLUSION

In the Cosmic Humanist worldview, laws and authority are counter-evolutionary, preventing us from achieving godhood. Mark Satin says, "Getting in touch with our selves would appear to be, not just fun (though it can be that), and not self-indulgence at all, but an imperative for survival that's built right in to the structure of the universe. (Maybe even an evolutionary imperative.)"[8] Joseph Campbell agrees, saying, "I always tell my students [to] go where your body and soul want to go. When you have the feeling, then stay with it, and don't let anyone throw you off."[9]

[3] Ibid., 37.

[4] Ibid., 3.

[5] David Spangler, *Revelation: The Birth of a New Age* (Middleton, WI: Lorain Press, 1976), 65.

[6] Shirley MacLaine, *Out on a Limb* (New York, NY: Bantam Books, 1989), 204.

[7] Ibid.

[8] Mark Satin, *New Age Politics* (New York, NY: Dell Publishing, 1978), 103.

[9] Joseph Campbell, *The Power of Myth* (New York, NY: Doubleday, 1988), 118.

Postmodernism

"[Postmodernism] is a powerful and coherent mindset. It provides a philosophical outlook (social constructionism), a legal reform program, and a set of governing metaphors, all in one convenient package. This package has the added benefit of resonating with ideas that are popular in other parts of the academy. If one has doubts about the social construction of truth or merit, one can rest assured that the matter has been settled in the impenetrable prose of some esteemed French philosophers."[1]

— DANIEL A. FARBER AND SUZANNA SHERRY

7.6.1 INTRODUCTION

Before exploring the topic of Postmodern law, it may be helpful to give the discussion an historical context. No one does this better than Harold J. Berman, former professor of law at Harvard Law School. Berman maintains that there is currently a major debate over our

---

[1] Daniel A. Farber and Suzanna Sherry, *Beyond All Reason: The Radical Assault on Truth in American Law* (Oxford, UK: Oxford University Press, 1997), 124.

understanding of law. The West's legal system is rooted in certain beliefs, he writes, including "the structural integrity of law, its ongoingness, its religious roots, [and] its transcendent qualities."[2]

However, Berman explains that today these foundational beliefs are rapidly disappearing, not only from the minds of philosophers, but from "the minds of lawmakers, judges, lawyers, law teachers . . . [and] from the consciousness of the vast majority of citizens. . . . The law is becoming fragmented, more subjective, geared more to expediency and less to morality, concerned more with immediate consequences and less with consistency or continuity. Thus the historical soil of the Western legal tradition is being washed away in the twentieth century, and the tradition itself is threatened with collapse."[3]

Declaring that the Western legal tradition is on the verge of collapse is a bold statement, but not too strong for the situation we are facing in the early years of the twenty-first century. Berman notes the historical background for this dramatic shift in ideology. In many ways, Western civilization has never recovered from the utter destruction and slaughter of World War I (1914–1918). That war, fought within the Western powers and traditions, cast grave doubts about the viability and desirability of Western traditions, as the most enlightened, best educated, most scientifically astute of all peoples proceeded to mow themselves down in frightening numbers. This led, Berman says, to a "loss of confidence in the West itself, as a civilization . . . and in the legal tradition which for nine centuries has helped to sustain it."[6]

The current crisis in Western civilization has paved the way for a new approach to legal theory. This is where Postmodernism finds a foothold to enter the debate over the place and substance of law.

7.6.2 REJECTION OF ENLIGHTENMENT IDEAS

Postmodernists view the European Enlightenment as a white male undertaking that elevated reason and empirical data. It focused on objective knowledge of a real world, such as the scientific method for discovering objective facts about the universe, and the concept of justice in relation to law.

> As to the rule of law, it is an article of [Postmodern] faith that legal rules are indeterminate and serve only to disguise the law's white male bias.
>
> — FARBER AND SHERRY

From a Postmodern perspective, the source of knowledge and justice is at the root of the problem. Postmodernists insist that Western law, which grew out of Christianity and the Enlightenment, reflects white male bias. They attack "the concepts of reason and objective truth, condemning them as components of white male domination. They prefer the more subjective 'ways of knowing' supposedly favored by women and minorities, such as storytelling. As to the rule of law, it is an article of [Postmodern] faith that legal rules are indeterminate and serve only to disguise the law's white male bias."[4] For this reason, Postmodernists are intent on eliminating religious roots and transcendent qualities from Western law. They desire more fragmentation and subjectivity, and less objective morality than the Judeo-Christian tradition demands. In the end, they are intent on creating and using their own brand of social justice merely for left-wing political purposes.

---

[2] Quoted in Daniel A. Farber and Suzanna Sherry, *Beyond All Reason: The Radical Assault on Truth in American Law* (Oxford, UK: Oxford University Press, 1997), 39.

[3] Ibid., 40.

[4] Ibid., 5.

7.6.3 CRITICAL LEGAL STUDIES

At the center of this assault on traditional Western law is the **Critical Legal Studies** movement. Critical Legal Studies (CLS) publishes "critiques of law focused on progressive— even radical—political change rather than on efficient government."[5] In fact, the CLS slogan is "critique is all there is." Using Derrida's deconstruction principle, they dissect a law to discover its subjective meaning, no matter what the law objectively states.

> **CRITICAL LEGAL STUDIES:**
> The deconstruction of law used to discover its subjective meaning and biased intent

"While CLS and the newer movements share a left-leaning or progressive outlook, the new movements tend to have a narrower focus. . . . [T]he new radicals concentrate on race and gender issues, and particularly on how the law creates or contributes to unequal power relations,"[6] according to Farber and Sherry.

The Postmodern thesis is that "reality is socially constructed by the powerful in order to perpetuate their own hegemony [power over other people]. As one radical feminist puts it, 'Feminist analysis begins with the principle that objective reality is a myth.'"[7] To amplify the focus on the legal inequalities imposed on women and minorities by those in power, CLS includes the core ideas of "the thought of French postmodernists such as Michel Foucault and Jacques Derrida. This meant extending the insight that law is socially constructed into an argument that everything is socially constructed."[8] From Foucault, Postmodern legal radicals draw the assertion that what counts for objective knowledge "is a power relation, one category of people benefiting at the expense of another category of people."[9] Foucault sees all relationships between people as power relationships. Universal standards of legal judgment, common to all, do not exist. Any claim to universal truth is merely a mask for gaining political power over women and minorities.

Stanley Fish, professor of Law and English, argues, "the name of the game has always been politics."[10] One example of the Postmodern focus on politics over objective knowledge has been provided by Susan Estrich, Professor of Law and Political Science at the University of Southern California Law School and a syndicated columnist who has worked with many liberal politicians and appeared on numerous television talk shows. Estrich was asked why she supported Anita Hill when Hill charged Clarence Thomas (during his confirmation hearings for the Supreme Court) with sexual harassment but opposed Paula Jones when she made sexual harassment allegations against President Clinton. Ms. Estrich replied, "You believe in principle; I believe in politics."[11]

Estrich, like Marx, Nietzsche, and Foucault, sees law simply as a tool for political power. According to Marx, "Political power, properly so called, is merely the organized power of one class for oppressing another."[12] Estrich implies that she uses the law in any way necessary to get what she wants. Thus, the law is no longer a God-ordained, objective standard by which to judge behavior and maintain an ordered society, but a weapon to beat political opponents into submission to a point of view.

---

[5] Ibid., 19.

[6] Ibid., 21.

[7] Ibid., 23.

[8] Ibid., 22.

[9] Ibid., 24.

[10] Quoted in Dennis McCallum, ed., *The Death of Truth* (Minneapolis, MN: Bethany House, 1996), 170. See Stanley Fish, *There's No Such Thing As Free Speech: And It's a Good Thing, Too* (Oxford, UK: Oxford University Press, 1993).

[11] Susan Estrich in an online letter to Stuart Taylor Jr., http://www.slate.com/id/3628/entry/23734/.

[12] Karl Marx and Friedrich Engels, *The Communist Manifesto* (New York, NY: Pocket Books, 1964), 95.

7.6.4 STORIES AND THE LAW

In place of objective reasoning, Postmodernists use storytelling as a better way to arrive at equitable law, since it is open to multiple points of view and varied interpretations. Stories are easier to manipulate to meet a political end than are empirical facts. Farber and Sherry explain the way Postmodernists rely on story: "Because the scholarship of women and people of color reflects their distinctive knowledge [gained from listening to and telling stories], the radical multiculturalists argue, it cannot be judged or tested by traditional standards. Instead, they imply, it should be judged according to its political effect: it should be judged 'in terms of its ability to advance the interests of the outsider community,' because 'outsider scholarship is often aimed not at understanding the law, but at changing it.'"[13]

The Pop Culture Connection

Batman Begins (a 2005 film)–"The principle rule of law plays out against the idea of vigilante justice. The bad guys turn out to be members of the League of Shadows, from whom Wayne learned to fight. They credit themselves with bringing down Rome and Constantinople, and even London, by loading cargo holds with plague-infected rats. This time, Henri Ducard, the group's ringleader, claims to employ economics and fear to destroy Gotham, lamenting that the only thing that kept him from achieving victory was Thomas Wayne's example of virtue. Ultimately, Bruce's tenacious belief in societal institutions as the proper avenues for justice becomes the key breaking point between he and the League."*

One current issue that illustrates the Postmodern use of stories is global warming. Although empirical scientific data show no significant temperature increases worldwide,[14] pressure from the radical left has been exerted on the United States to sign an international global warming treaty. Some of the pressure comes from creating stories that appeal to the emotions. For example, the film *The Day After Tomorrow* is an emotion-charged story about what will happen *when* global warming gets out of control.

The film does not deal with facts about whether global warming is an actual threat to the planet; it simply assumes it is and builds the story from there.

This illustrates the Postmodern focus on rhetoric rather than logic. Since logic and dispassionate reasoning are seen as tools of white male bias, rhetoric and story are used to effect political change, regardless of scientific arguments to the contrary. Farber and Sherry illustrate how this shift is impacting legal theory: "Rather than relying solely on legal or interdisciplinary authorities, empirical data, or rigorous analysis, legal scholars have begun to offer stories, often about their own real or imagined experiences."[15]

The emotional impact of story can be used to replace rationality in the courtroom and in the media. Faber and Sherry cite the case of Tawana Brawley as an example of how racially motivated attorneys and politicians could manipulate a story to undermine legal facts in the courtroom. Brawley, a fifteen-year-old black girl, claimed she was abducted, raped, and tortured by a group of white men that included a state district attorney and two police officers. It was

[13] Farber and Sherry, *Beyond All Reason*, 30.
[14] See Michael Crichton, *State of Fear* (New York, NY: HarperCollins, 2004), for a fictionalized look at the global warming issues along with their political and scientific implications. For a scholarly look at the issue, see the website for Oregon Institute of Science and Medicine.
[15] Farber and Sherry, 39.
*"Business and Virtue in *Batman Begins*," by Ben Sikma, Advancement Associate, http://www.acton.org/ppolicy/comment/print.php?id=273

later shown that she had made up the entire story as a distraction to get her stepfather to forgive her for running away from home. However, even though the grand jury found that no crime had been committed, the following was written about the case: "Tawana Brawley has been the victim of some unspeakable crime . . . no matter who did it to her—and even if she did it to herself. Her condition was clearly the expression of some crime against her." Farber and Sherry continue, "In other words, whether it was true or false, Tawana Brawley's story tells us something about the condition of black women."[16]

In this case, the story's power to create an emotional backlash against the dominant culture of white males took precedence over the truth that those accused were innocent and that police officers and district attorneys protect women and minorities from danger more often than not regardless of race, age, or ethnicity.

7.6.5 CONCLUSION

Even if all knowledge were socially constructed, the matter of truth would remain important. Brawley's story was false—not just in one community but in all communities—because truth is universal. If law is not based on objective truth, we can only look forward to authoritarianism and totalitarianism. Justice and truth must go hand in hand.

Trial lawyer Gary Saalman predicts the results of a Postmodern focus on racial, gender, and cultural politics becoming an integral part of the legal system: "Postmodern legal theory trickles down to breed cynicism toward all government and the entire criminal justice system. This, then, is the real issue. No one questions the fact that law requires interpretation, or that judges or juries may have acted unfairly, sometimes based on race or gender bias. The question is this: How do we view such unfairness? Do we accept that all people must inevitably be unfair and subjective, as postmodernists claim? Or do we recognize such unfairness as the evil it is and resist it? When we accept what postmodernism preaches, we lose all basis for calling the system to fairness. We instead challenge minority populations to pursue power so they can take their turn."[17]

---

[16] Ibid., 96.
[17] McCallum, 175.

Politics

Christianity

> "Everyone must submit to the governing authorities, for there is no authority except that which God has established."
>
> — ROMANS 13:1

> "Render therefore unto Caesar the things which are Caesar's; and unto God the things that are God's."
>
> — MATTHEW 22:21

8.1.1 INTRODUCTION

The Christian worldview sees government as an institution established by God (Genesis 9:6; Romans 13) for the primary purpose of promoting justice for its citizens — protecting the innocent from the aggressor and the lawless. Without security, every other function of government (protecting life, liberty, property, reputation, etc.) is meaningless.

As Christians we recognize government as a sacred institution whose rulers are ministers of God for good (Romans 13). God ordained the state to practice godly justice and commands us to obey its rules and laws. Peter instructs us to "submit . . . for the Lord's sake to every authority instituted among men, whether to the king, as the supreme authority, or to governors, who are sent by him to punish those who do wrong and to commend those who do right" (1 Peter 2:13–14). As long as government is serving the

> JUSTICE, FREEDOM, ORDER: Human governments are instituted by God to protect the innocent and punish the guilty, and to preserve the rights of all people against our sinful tendencies to destroy those rights

purpose for which God created it, we must show our allegiance to God by submitting to human government.

8.1.2 LIMITED GOVERNMENT RESPONSIBILITIES

We expect the state to accomplish limited, God-ordained tasks. Its two principle roles are to protect the innocent and punish the guilty (Romans 13:3–4). Government should adhere to the principle "Let all things be done decently and in order" (1 Corinthians 14:40; Exodus 18:19f) because order reflects God's character.

We know that power tends to corrupt, so a government that disperses power is better than one that gathers power into the hands of a few. As Christians, we should welcome opportunities to participate in government with the goal of influencing the state to conform to God's will for it as a social institution (Proverbs 11:11). The Christian worldview does not single out any one form of government as acceptable, although a constitutional form is more likely to conform to biblical principles and respond to its citizens than are less democratic forms.

One significant aspect of the United States' government that conforms to biblical ideals is the division of power into three branches—executive, legislative, and judicial—along with its system of checks and balances. The three-branch model was patterned after Isaiah 33:22: "For the Lord is our judge [judicial], the Lord is our lawgiver [legislative], the Lord is our king [executive]."

8.1.3 CREATION AND ORIGINAL SIN

Perhaps the Christian concept our founding fathers best understood was the Christian understanding that although we are created in God's image, we nevertheless have a fallen, sinful nature. Because they understood these opposing aspects of our nature, the founding fathers tailored a government suited to our rightful place in God's creative order.

Human government is necessary because of sin. Our evil inclinations toward sin must be kept in check by laws and a government capable of enforcing such laws. Thus, government protects us from our own sinful nature. But our founding fathers also grappled with the problem of protecting ordinary citizens from the sinful inclinations of those in authority. The result of their efforts is our system of checks and balances among the branches of government. Each branch wields unique powers that prevent the focus of governmental power and authority from falling into the hands of a select few. By broadly distributing power and responsibility, the American system of government minimizes the possibility of an abuse of power because of our fallen nature. James Madison says, "If men were angels, no government would be necessary. If angels were to govern men, neither external nor internal controls on government would be necessary."[1]

The Pop Culture Connection

Fellowship of the Ring (2001, directed by Peter Jackson; the film won four Oscars, with another 68 wins from other organizations)—Early in the story, Frodo understands the significance of the ring in his possession and pleads with Gandalf to take it from him. Gandalf responds, "Don't touch me, Frodo. I dare not take it, even to keep it safe. Understand me Frodo. I would use this ring from a desire to do good, but through me, it would wield a power too great and terrible to imagine." Working from a Biblical worldview, Tolkien presents the view that power tends to corrupt, and since the ring represents absolute power, the corrupting influence would also be total, even for a good wizard.

---

[1] See no. 51 in Alexander Hamilton, et al., *The Federalist Papers* (New York, NY: Pocket Books, 1964), 122.

8.1.4 THE SOURCE OF HUMAN RIGHTS

A Christian worldview also understands God as the source and guarantee of our basic human rights. Because we believe we are created in the image of God (Genesis 1:26), we know that we are valuable. (This becomes doubly clear when we remember that Christ took upon Himself human flesh and died for humanity.) God grants all individuals the same rights based on an absolute moral standard. The Declaration of Independence proclaims, "All men are created equal . . . [and] endowed by their Creator with certain unalienable rights." Two assumptions are inherent in this declaration: 1) we were created by a supernatural Being; and 2) this Being provides the foundation for all human rights.

The knowledge that human rights are based on an unchanging, eternal Source is crucial in our understanding of politics. If our rights were not tied inextricably to God's character, then they would be arbitrarily assigned according to the whims of each passing generation or political party—rights are "unalienable" only because they are based on God's unchanging character. Therefore, human rights do not originate with human government, but with God Himself, who ordains governments to secure these rights.

Our founding fathers understood this clearly. John Adams, in a letter to Thomas Jefferson in 1813, says, "The general principles, on which the Fathers achieved Independence, were the only Principles in which that beautiful Assembly of young Gentlemen could Unite . . . And what were these general Principles? I answer, the general Principles of Christianity, in which all these Sects were United . . . Now I will avow, that I then believe, and now believe, that those general Principles of Christianity, are as eternal and immutable, as the Existence and Attributes of God."[2]

John Winthrop says that the best friend of liberty is one who is "most sincere and active in promoting true and undefiled religion and who sets himself with the greatest firmness to bear down on profanity and immorality of every kind. Whoever is an avowed enemy of God, I scruple not to call him an enemy of his country."[3]

Noah Webster wrote "The moral principles and precepts found in the scriptures ought to form the basis of all our civil constitutions and laws. These principles and precepts have truth, immutable truth, for their foundation."[4]

Alexis de Tocqueville says, "There is no country in the world where the Christian religion retains a greater influence over the souls of men than in America; and there can be no greater proof of its utility, and of its conformity to human nature, than that its influence is most powerfully felt over the most enlightened and free nation on the earth."[5]

George Washington, in his inaugural address as first president of the United States, referred to "the propitious smiles of Heaven" that fall only on that nation that does not "disregard the eternal rules of order and right which Heaven itself has ordained."[6]

> The moral principles and precepts found in the scriptures ought to form the basis of all our civil constitutions and laws.
>
> — NOAH WEBSTER

[2] Lester J. Cappon, ed., *The Adams-Jefferson Letters* (Chapel Hill, NC: University of North Carolina Press, 1987), 339-40.

[3] Winthrop's speech at Princeton, May 17, 1776.

[4] Noah Webster, *History of the United States*, "Advice to the Young" (New Haven: CT, Durrie & Peck, 1832), 338-340.

[5] Alexis de Tocqueville, *Democracy in America* (New York, NY: Vintage Classics, 1990), 303.

[6] George Washington, First Inaugural Address, New York City, April 30, 1789. http://www.bartleby.com/124/pres13.html.

8.1.5 THE PURPOSE OF GOVERNMENT

According to the Biblical Christian worldview, human government was instituted by God to protect our unalienable rights from our own selfish tendencies (Genesis 9:6; Romans 13:1–7). Human nature is capable of both vice and virtue. We know our tendency to infringe on our neighbor's rights in an effort to improve our own life. Therefore, we know government and political systems must exist to protect our rights and to keep our evil tendencies at bay.

Protecting human rights of life, liberty, property, work, rest, worship, a free press, etc., from those who would diminish them means promoting justice. E. Calvin Beisner says justice and truth are interrelated, for justice is the practice of truth in human relationships; he concludes, "[J]ustice is rendering to each his due according to a right standard."[7] The right standard is God's moral order, which is based on the very character of God. This standard insists that the innocent citizens of society be protected from evil—rapists, murderers, child molesters, thieves, liars, drug runners, sex traffickers, dishonest tax collectors, adulterers, etc.

> Justice is rendering to each his due according to a right standard.
>
> — E. CALVIN BEISNER

Christians see justice as the principal reason for the state's existence. The Christian view of justice is founded on a belief in God as the absolute guarantor of our unalienable rights. Thus, promoting justice becomes more important than any other aspect of government. R.J. Rushdoony is correct in his assertion that whether we "can vote or not is not nearly as important as the question of justice: does the law leave [us] secure in [our] governmental spheres, as an individual, a family, church, school, or business?"[8]

Government, therefore, has limited responsibility. The state must never assume the responsibilities of other institutions, including those of church and family. The church's responsibility is to manifest God's love and grace on the earth. The family's responsibility is to manifest God's community and creativity, including procreativity. These three God-ordained institutions—government, church, and family—are limited by their own definition as well as the definitions of the other two. Because government is an institution of justice, not of grace, community, or creativity, it should not interfere with freedom of religion, attempt to dispense grace through tax-funded handouts, control family size, interfere in the raising of children (including their education), or control the economy. Government has its role, and it should allow other God-ordained institutions the freedom to perform their roles as well.

8.1.6 SOVEREIGNTY APART FROM GOD

Human governments almost always wind up overstepping their God-ordained role. Today, many political leaders, as well as leaders in other disciplines, do not understand their place in God's universe. Their false perspectives often result in the usurpation of God's sovereignty, which covers everyone and everything everywhere for all time (Psalm 103:19). Trusting individuals or the state rather than God results in a power-hungry and abusive state. Charles Colson says, "Excise belief in God and you are left with only two principals: the individual and the State. In this situation, however, there is no mediating structure to generate moral values and, therefore, no counterbalance to the inevitable ambitions of the State."[9] William

---

[7] E. Calvin Beisner, *Prosperity and Poverty: The Compassionate Use of Resources in a World of Scarcity* (Westchester, IL: Crossway Books, 1988), 45.

[8] R.J. Rushdoony, *Politics of Guilt and Pity* (Fairfax, VA: Thoburn Press, 1978), 239.

[9] Charles Colson, *Kingdoms in Conflict* (Grand Rapids, MI: Zondervan, 1987), 226.

Penn concludes, "If we are not governed by God, then we will be ruled by tyrants."[10]

Today, some worldviews (such as Secular Humanism, Marxism, and to a lesser extent Postmodernism) advocate global government to serve as the ultimate political and economic authority to advance humanity's evolution. If they prevail in their movement toward "a new world order"[11] and a complete abandonment of God, we may well experience the coming of the Anti-Christ.

8.1.7 UTOPIANISM

Utopianism provides a prime example of our willingness to deny God and place absolute sovereignty in the hands of the government. This mistake results from a deliberate disregard of God's ultimate authority and a misconception about human nature. Marxists and Secular Humanists espouse the utopian belief in humanity's collective perfectibility, as well as the perfectibility of our environment through evolutionary processes that will be brought about through the auspices of the state. This belief in our perfectibility, which Colson calls "the most subtle and dangerous delusion of our times,"[12] is evident today in the widespread denial of individual responsibility.

Denying individual responsibility for our actions separates us from God and our only means of salvation—individually knowing and accepting Christ's atonement for sins. Denying individual responsibility condemns us to an endless search for utopia. Utopianism, however, offers no salvation except through the hope that the state will perfect us and our environment. Colson goes on to say, "While Christian teaching emphasizes that each person has worth and responsibility before God, utopianism argues that salvation can only be achieved collectively."[13] Reliance on the state ultimately results in the individual being trampled underfoot.

Infringements on human rights by governments based on the sovereignty or whim of those in power speak eloquently of the need for a transcendent law that is impartial to all. The lack of legitimate authority caused by the denial of God reinforces our belief that God must be recognized as Ruler in every sphere, including politics.

8.1.8 A QUESTION OF OBEDIENCE

The Christian view of politics accounts for God's sovereignty and our dependence on Him. We understand that God instituted government to promote His justice. We also understand our God-given obligation to respect, obey, and participate in governments that serve His will (Romans 13:1–2). Our obedience minimizes the need for increased governmental authority. Our duty to promote justice and preserve order, however, does not require that we blindly follow leaders who stray from their responsibility to God. Rather, we must hold them accountable by our participation in government—voting, petitioning if necessary, running for political office,

---

[10] Francis A. Schaeffer, *A Christian Manifesto* (Westchester, IL: Crossway Books, 1982), 34.

[11] See Georgi Shakhnazarov, *The Coming World Order* (Moscow, USSR: Progress Publishers, 1981).

[12] Charles Colson, *Who Speaks for God?* (Westchester, IL: Crossway Books, 1988), 144.

[13] Colson, *Kingdoms in Conflict*, 77. For an understanding of the ideas presently in the mix of modern-day utopianism consult Stewart Justman, *Fool's Paradise: The Unreal World of Pop Psychology* (Chicago, IL: Ivan R. Dee, 2005). Says Justman, "The German expatriate who served as perhaps the foremost intellectual patron of the student revolt of the 1960s, Herbert Marcuse, wrote in 1970 that 'the new theory of man . . . implies the genesis of a new morality as the heir and the negation of the Judeo-Christian morality which up to now has characterized the history of Western civilization.'" Marcuse, a Marxist and fellow of the Frankfurt School, contended that Christian morality is repressive, self-defeating, and obsolete (p. 133). And the abolition of morality is just one of the ideas of present day utopianism. Before William Morris wrote *News from Nowhere* "he wrote the *Manifesto of the Socialist League*" (p. 171). That should give an idea of what ideas are being bandied about the university campus.

or serving in non-elected positions where we may be able to influence those in power (Proverbs 29:2).

However, the Bible clearly instructs us to obey God even when His commands conflict with the state. For example, when Peter and John were commanded by the Sanhedrin to stop teaching about Jesus, they replied, "Judge for yourselves whether it is right in God's sight to obey man rather than God" (Acts 4:19). We are required to obey God even when our reform efforts through political channels fail. If the system of government remains unjust, we may be required to engage in civil disobedience in order to remain obedient to God. Francis Schaeffer says, "The bottom line is that at a certain point there is not only the right, but the duty, to disobey the State."[14] Our disobedience to the state may even result in death, but in such instances it is better to die than to live. Daniel understood this truth and chose death over worshiping a king (Daniel 6:1–10). God honors such commitment.

8.1.9 CONCLUSION

God ordains governments to administer His justice. When government rules within the boundaries of its role in God's order, we submit to the state's authority willingly because we understand that God has placed it in authority over us. However, when the state abuses its authority or claims to be sovereign, we must acknowledge God's transcendent law rather than that of the state. Our loyalty to God may call us to political involvement in an effort to create good and just government. The involvement of righteous people can significantly influence government for the better.

Our ongoing struggle to create and maintain just government may or may not be effective. We must, however, remain obedient to God in all circumstances. Colson says, "Christians are to do their duty as best they can. But even when they feel that they are making no difference, that they are failing to bring Christian values to the public arena, success is not the criteria. Faithfulness is."[15]

---

[14] Schaeffer, *A Christian Manifesto*, 93. An example of the proper time for disobedience recently arose when the American government (through its public health services) advised churches to amend their attitude toward homosexuality. The Bible clearly dictates the proper Christian response to homosexuality (see Romans 1 and Jude 1), and the church must stand firm in her commitment to obey God's commands even when they conflict with the State's. Later the U. S. Supreme Court placed its stamp of approval on sodomy in the Lawrence and Garner v. Texas decision (Case no. 02–0102), overturning an earlier Court decision in Bowers v. Hardwick.

[15] Colson, *Kingdoms in Conflict*, 291.

Politics

Islam

"Jihad has been made obligatory, which means that the individual should, when the occasion arises, offer even his life for the defense and protection of Islam and the Islamic state."[1]

— KHURSHID AHMAD

"Islam is international in its outlook and approach and does not admit barriers and distinctions based on color, clan, blood or territory . . . It wants to unite the entire human race under one banner."[2]

— KHURSHID AHMAD

8.2.1 INTRODUCTION

One of the most controversial aspects of Islam is the concept of *jihad*, or "holy war." Since September 11, 2001, many Muslims have sought to soften *jihad*, relegating it to the realm of the personal struggle with sin. While the Qur'an does allow for this view of *jihad* that is not *all* the Qur'an has to say about it. Most passages in the Qur'an teach that *jihad* is warfare against peoples who oppose the Islamic faith.

---

[1] Khurshid Ahmad, *Islam: Its Meaning and Message*, 3rd ed. (Leicester, UK: The Islamic Foundation, 1999), 39.
[2] Ibid., 40–41.

A Muslim is one whose outlook on life is permeated with this consciousness [of the pillars of Islam]. He is committed to the values of life given by the Qur'an and the *Sunnah*. He tries to live according to the guidance given by God and His Prophet and he strives to promote the message of Islam through his word and actions. This striving is known as *Jihad* which means a striving and a struggle in the path of God. It consists in exerting one's self to the utmost in order to personally follow the teachings of Islam and to work for their establishment in society. *Jihad* has been described in the Qur'an and the *Sunnah* as the natural corollary of these pillars of faith. Commitment to God involves commitment to sacrifice one's time, energy and wealth to promote the right cause. It may be necessary at times to give one's life in order to preserve Truth. *Jihad* implies readiness to give whatever one has, including his life, for the sake of Allah.[3]

8.2.2 ISLAMIC THEOCRACY

Islam, as with Christianity, is a worldview with the vision to encompass the entire world. Whereas Christians hold to the Great Commission—the call to make disciples of *all* nations (Matthew 28:18-20) and proclaim the ministry of reconciliation to the whole world (2 Corinthians 5:18-19)—Muslims hold to the call of global Islam, a goal accomplished if need be through the force of *jihad*. Global Islam means that all nations would be ruled under an **Islamic theocracy**. "Islam is international in its outlook and approach and does not admit barriers and distinctions based on color, clan, blood or territory," explains Khurshid Admad. "It wants to unite the entire human race under one banner. To a world torn by national rivalries and feuds, it presents a message of life and hope and of a glorious future."[4]

> **ISLAMIC THEOCRACY:**
> A national government set up under the rule of Allah's divine sanction as expressed in the Qur'an and Shari'ah law

Zaki Badawi speaks to the reality that many Muslims exist with minority status in non-Muslim countries. While it is a struggle some Muslims have always faced, it is not a satisfactory situation in their eyes. He explains,

> As we know, the history of Islam as a faith is also the history of a state and a community of believers living by Divine law. The Muslims, jurists and theologians, have always expounded Islam as both a Government and a faith. This reflects the historical fact that Muslims, from the start, lived under their own law. Muslim theologians naturally produced a theology with this in view— it is a theology of the majority. Being a minority was not seriously considered or even contemplated. The theologians were divided in their attitude to the question of minority status. Some declared that it should not take place; that is to say that a Muslim is forbidden to live for any lengthy period of time under non-Muslim rule. Others suggested that a Muslim living under non-Muslim rule is under no obligation to follow the law of Islam in matters of public law. Neither of these two extremes is satisfactory. Throughout the history of Islam some pockets of Muslims lived under the sway of non-Muslim rulers, often without an alternative. They nonetheless felt sufficiently committed to their faith to attempt to regulate their lives in accordance with its rules and regulations in so far as their circumstances permitted. In other words, the practice of the community rather than the theories of the theologians provided a

---

[3] Ibid., 23.
[4] Ibid., 40–41.

solution. Nevertheless Muslim theology offers, up to the present, no systematic formulation of the status of being a minority. The question is being examined. It is hoped that the matter will be brought to focus and that Muslim theologians from all over the Muslim world will delve into this thorny subject and allay the conscience of the many Muslims living in the West and also to chart a course for Islamic survival, even revival, in a secular society.[5]

Muslim minorities in Western countries often place themselves in positions where they seek to govern themselves under *Shari'ah* law, while simultaneously maintaining citizenship in their respective countries. To this end, many Muslims seek advancement in politics, education, and law, all with the hope of being better able to make their case. Typically they seek to implement *Shari'ah* in regard to education and family law, seeing Islamic law—in additions to being an obligation for Muslims—as superior to other law systems. Additionally, these Muslims seek to squelch any and all public criticisms of their faith. In our current politically correct culture, Muslims sometimes join hands with the political Left in opposing traditional Western values. Both are critical of the Christian faith and the Christian history of their respective countries. But at other points, especially with regard to family values, Muslims and leftists find little common ground.

Currently this situation is a reality in Canada and Australia. The Muslim population in Canada has gained a significant voice regarding the implementation of *Shari'ah* within their communities. In Australia, Christian apologists are regularly hassled in courts, sometimes being forced into silence regarding their critique of Islam. Recent court decisions are very troubling in this regard. While Muslims may continue their critique of the Christian faith, standing alongside the political and anti-Christian leftist movements, Christians in turn are threatened with loss of income or home as Muslims sway the courts to rule in their favor.

8.2.3 JIHAD THROUGH HISTORY

The teachings of Jesus and Muhammad about the implementation of violence differ fundamentally: Jesus taught His disciples not to take up arms against those who opposed Him, but Muhammad taught his disciples to conquer anyone who opposed them or who refused to become Muslims. Afif A. Tabbarah recounts an example of Muhammad's teachings in action: "Muhammad sent his delegates to eight neighboring rulers with messages calling them to embrace Islam. The appeal was rejected. Some of them even killed the Prophet's delegates, and some tore the message and threatened the delegates who had brought it. In that case, Moslems found no other alternative but fighting, after being certain that those rulers had slain the Prophet's delegates, misled their people, and ruled them in oppression and tyranny."[6] The message the delegates carried was "Convert to Islam or we will battle with you." Peace with Muhammad was impossible if unbelievers did not adopt Islam or submit to Muslim rule.

8.2.4 THE DHIMMIS

Those who submitted to Muslim authority only (not in Muhammad himself) were called *dhimmis*. *Dhimmis* were expected to express their submission to their Muslim rulers by paying a tax called *jizya*. The Qur'an explains their situation. "Fight those who believe not in God nor the Last Day, nor hold that forbidden which hath been forbidden by God and His Apostle, nor acknowledge the Religion of Truth, (even if they are) of the People of the Book, until they pay the *jizya* with willing submission, and feel themselves subdued" (9:29). Those who paid

---

[5] Colin Chapman, *Cross and Crescent: Responding to the Challenge of Islam* (Downers Grove, IL: InterVarsity Press, 2003), 149–150.

[6] Afif. A. Tabbarah, *The Spirit of Islam: Doctrine and Teachings* (Beirut, Lebanon: Dar El-llm Lilmalayin, 1978), 384.

the tax illustrated that they "did not accept Islam, but were willing to live under the protection of Islam," explains Abu Yusuf Ali, "and were thus tacitly willing to submit to its ideals being enforced in the Muslim State, saving only their personal liberty of conscience as regarded themselves." As a tax levied against all men of military age, "it was in a sense a commutation for military service."[7]

Some Muslims have viewed such a tax as of relatively little consequence when compared to the advantages of living under Muslim rule and protection. Afif A. Tabbarah explains, "The poll tax is a small sum of money indeed when compared to the services the Moslem State offers to protect the *Dhimmis* and support the army in charge to keep them safe from others' assaults."[8] One of the inherent problems with this practice, however, is that there "was no amount fixed for it,"[9] according to Abu Yusef Ali. Thus it often became extremely burdensome, relegating non-Muslims to virtual slavery.

"All taxes on trade and transport paid by Muslims were generally doubled for *dhimmis*," observes Bat Ye'or. "In addition, the population—but particularly the *dhimmi* communities—were subject to ruinous extortions designed to cover the financing of incessant wars."[10] Because Muslims have often been at war, to finance such activities the non-Muslims who dare to remain in Muslim lands are fleeced to finance Muslim aggression (or, more rarely, defense). Most troubling is how these non-Muslims are treated when they cannot pay the *jizyah*. Churches have been destroyed, houses dispossessed, and children taken and sold into slavery, not to mention dismemberment, torture, and death.[11]

8.2.5 ATTEMPTS TO SOFTEN JIHAD

Contemporary Muslim apologists, especially following the shocking attacks on the United States on September 11, 2001, attempt to soften the concept of *jihad* in two ways: 1) they assert that *jihad* is focused on the internal spiritual struggle of the individual or community; and 2) they often assert that the early conquests of Muhammad and his companions were purely defensive.

While the first assertion—that *jihad* concerns the internal spiritual struggle of Muslims—is true, this interpretation is only one of its two sides. It seems a purely rhetorical maneuver to emphasize only one facet of the definition. In a post-9/11 historical context, Muslims, especially those living in Western nations, naturally may want to downplay jihadist aggression lest their non-Muslim neighbors and friends fear the worst. But it is inaccurate and misleading to mute the historical primacy of wars in the name of *jihad*.

The second assertion—that *jihad* was purely defensive—simply does not fit the historical facts. Fazlur Rahman writes, "The most unacceptable [explanation] on historical grounds, however, is the stand of those modern Muslim apologists who have tried to explain the *jihad* of the early Community in purely defensive terms."[13] Early *jihad*, and *jihad* ever since, has never been purely defensive, but rather it has been characteristically *offensive*, as the history of Islam clearly reveals.[14]

---

[7] A. Yusuf Ali, *The Holy Qur'an: Text, Translation and Commentary* (Washington, DC: American International Printing Company, 1946), 447, n. 1281.

[8] Tabbarah, *The Spirit of Islam*, 396.

[9] *The Holy Qur'an*, 447, n. 1281.

[10] Bat Ye'or, *Islam and Dhimmitude: Where Civilizations Collide*, trans. Miriam Kochan and David Littman (Madison, NJ: Fairleigh Dickinson University Press, 2002), 71.

[11] See the discussion in Stuart Robinson, *Mosques and Miracles: Revealing Islam and God's Grace*, 2nd ed. (Upper Mt. Gravatt, AUS: City Harvest Publications, 2004), 202. Robinson records that even as recent as 1997, almost fifty Christians were killed, several in a Sunday School class, apparently because they failed to pay *jizyah*.

[12] * http://www.christianitytoday.com/movies/reviews/munich.html

[13] Fazlur Rahman, *Islam*, 2nd ed. (Chicago, IL: University of Chicago Press, 1966, 1991), 37.

[14] An extensive discussion of the theory and history of *jihad* is presented in Serge Trifkovic, *The Sword of the Prophet: Islam: History, Theology, Impact on the World* (Boston, MA: Regina Orthodox Press, 2002).

8.2.6 JIHAD REVIVED TODAY

The activities of contemporary Muslim terrorists illustrate the aggressive nature of *jihad*. While the majority of Muslims do not directly support most terrorist activities, the rationale for such activities is persuasive to many Muslim minds. That such forms of *jihad* are intended to be in force until Islam is a global reality can best be understood with reference to the Muslim beliefs in 1) the nature of the world as a creation of Allah, 2) the nature of all prophets as having taught Islam, 3) the nature of every human at birth as in a state of Islam, and 4) the intent to return the world to its original state of Islam.

1) CREATION AND ORIGINAL ISLAM. Muslims believe that when Allah created the world, the first humans (Adam and Eve) were Muslims. Indeed, Adam himself was a prophet of Islam. Although Adam and Eve disobeyed Allah's original prohibition and ate from the forbidden tree, their mistake (not sin) was quickly forgiven. And though their action resulted in the world not being as it should be (with humans rebelling against God), Allah's intent ever since has been to bring the world back to the original state of Islam—the original state of submission to Allah.

2) PROPHETS OF ISLAM. Muslims believe that ever since the beginning of time Allah has provided prophets for every nation. All the prophets, it is claimed, taught Islam, just as did Muhammad. Allah's intent was for these prophets to draw humans back into submission to Islam. Some people believed and obeyed while others rejected the message of the prophets. Indeed, though Allah gave special books to Moses, David, and Jesus (as well as to Muhammad) these books have since been tampered with and confused so that they now contradict history, science, and the Qur'an. The Qur'an is the only book to remain throughout history unchanged and perfect. Thus all humans should submit to the Qur'an and the teachings of Muhammad found in the Hadith.

3) BORN MUSLIMS. Muslims believe every human being is born a Muslim in a state of submission to Allah. But from very young ages, humans are led astray to worship false gods or to deny that there is a God. Additionally, humans are taught false religious practices. Therefore, prophets of Allah to speak to all the nations of the world to correct these errors of belief and practice are needed in every age.

4) GLOBAL ISLAM. In conjunction with the first three beliefs, Muslims hope and expect that all nations will eventually submit to Allah and become Muslim nations. This is accomplished as Muslims bear witness to Allah's revelation in the Qur'an and the teachings of Muhammad. Consider the words of the famous Arab historian, Ibn Kjaldun (A.D. 1333–1406): "In the Muslim community, the holy war is a religious duty, because of the universalism of the (Muslim) mission and (the obligation to) convert everybody to Islam either by persuasion or force."[15]

When a person refuses to believe the message of Islam, then that person's well-being is brought into question. While there is some provision for non-Muslims living in Islamic territories, they often are harassed, persecuted, oppressed, and sometimes killed. The *jizyah* (the tax upon unbelievers) sometimes is so great that non-Muslims can do little more than live as slaves to Muslims.

> In the Muslim community, the holy war is a religious duty, because of the universalism of the (Muslim) mission and (the obligation to) convert everybody to Islam either by persuasion or force.
>
> — IBN KJALDUN

8.2.7 GLOBAL ISLAMIC STATES

The vision of Muslims is that Islam will one day be global in extent and authority. Yet some people refuse to convert to Islam or to submit to Muslim conquest and rule. When this occurs,

---

[15] Chapman, *Cross and Crescent*, 293.

these individuals are deemed aggressors against Islam and are seen as legitimate targets for *jihad* if they seek to stop Islamic practice and growth.

When we understand this Muslim vision, especially in light of the fact that most Western nations have refused Islamic demands to establish *Shari'ah* (or even to permit Muslim ghettos to practice *Shari'ah* among their Muslim populations), then we cannot fail to see that Muslims view such refusals as aggressive toward Islam. These nations are deemed aggressors against Islam because they refuse to permit Muslims to live as they please—not only in regard to ruling their own subcultures, but also because of a refusal to adopt and propagate Islam (as Muslims believe they are commanded to do).

> **GLOBAL ISLAMIC STATES:** The vision of many Muslims to bring all nations under *Shari'ah* law, whether accomplished through peaceful means or *jihad*

More fundamentally, though, because the world was created in submission to Allah and every human being is born a Muslim, to refuse Allah's demands to seek to restore the world and its inhabitants to that state is to perpetuate rebellion against Allah. This sets such people or nations up in opposition to Islam itself and causes them to become a legitimate target for *jihad*. *Jihad*, while being called "defensive," is nothing less than the offensive posture of Muslims intent on seeing the world Islamicized.

Thus when a modern Muslim claims that *jihad* is only a defensive action, the typical non-Muslim understands that in terms quite different than Islam teaches. What the typical non-Muslim understands as military aggression, especially as expressed in the early conquest history of Islam, is seen by Muslims as a defensive action against those who oppose Islam. But if this Islamic viewpoint of the world is not understood, then it is easy and natural for us to take modern Muslim statements (that Islam is a religion of peace or that *jihad* is only defensive) quite differently than how this has been understood throughout Islamic history.

8.2.8 JIHAD AND THE CRUSADES

The Crusades of the Middle Ages are a questionable blot on institutional Christianity.[16] The Crusades began as a *response* to Muslim aggression. Muslim armies had moved north, taken Jerusalem, and made several incursions into the Christian Byzantine Empire. Eastern Christians called on Western Christians for aid in the face of Muslim aggression. The later Spanish crusades, with the aim of driving Muslim armies from Spain, were intended to *take back* land and free those captive to Muslim intruders.

However, there was a very unfortunate disorganization in the Crusader movement that led some to rush off to war without proper training and strategy. The resultant tragedies included many Crusaders wasting their efforts and their lives as well as the lives of others. This is particularly apparent in the Fourth Crusade, where the grand vision of recapturing Muslim-conquered lands mutated into the sack of the Eastern Christian capital of Constantinople. Another misfortune was the so-called Children's Crusade through which many children were drowned in the Mediterranean Sea or sold into slavery in North Africa.

8.2.9 CONCLUSION

Although there is some diversity among Muslims regarding Islamic political theory, the historical patterns and precedent support the self-ascribed agenda of more traditional Muslims. Early Islam spread largely through force; the radical Muslims of the twenty-first century desire to return to that golden age.

---

[16] See Alvin J. Schmidt's *The Great Divide* (Boston, MA: Regina Orthodox Press, 2004) for his understanding of the Crusades.

*www.telegraph.co.uk/news/main.jhtml?xml=/news/2004/01/18/wcrus18.xml&sSheet=/news/2004/01/18/ixworld.html.

The Pop Culture Connection

Kingdom of Heaven (2005; directed by Sir Ridley Scott)—"The £75 million film, which stars Orlando Bloom, Jeremy Irons and Liam Neeson, is described by the makers as being 'historically accurate' and designed to be 'a fascinating history lesson.' Academics, however—including Professor Jonathan Riley-Smith, Britain's leading authority on the Crusades—attacked the plot of *Kingdom of Heaven*, describing it as 'rubbish', 'ridiculous', 'complete fiction' and 'dangerous to Arab relations'...Prof Riley-Smith...said the plot was 'complete and utter nonsense.' He said that it relied on the romanticized view of the Crusades propagated by Sir Walter Scott in his book *The Talisman*, published in 1825 and now discredited by academics ...'which depicts the Muslims as sophistica-ted and civilized, and the Crusaders are all brutes and barbarians. It has nothing to do with reality.'...Dr Jonathan Philips, a lecturer in history at London University and author of *The Fourth Crusade and the Sack of Constantinople*, agreed that the film relied on an outdated portrayal of the Crusades and could not be described as 'a history lesson.' Prof Riley-Smith added that Sir Ridley's efforts were misguided and pandered to Islamic fundamentalism. 'It's Osama bin Laden's version of history. It will fuel the Islamic fundamentalists.'"*

Politics

Secular Humanism

"All those who share the vision of the human community as part of one world should be willing to take any measures that will awaken world opinion to bring it about."[1]

— LUCILE W. GREEN

8.3.1 INTRODUCTION

Secular Humanists embrace democracy as the most acceptable form of government. Paul Kurtz declares, "The Humanist is also committed to democracy, particularly in the present epoch, as an ideal and a method for maximizing happiness and achieving the good society."[2] Rudolf Dreikurs concurs, saying, "We believe sincerely in democracy."[3]

However, the Humanist conception of democracy differs significantly from more commonly held attitudes. For Secular Humanists, democracy extends far beyond the realm of government. In fact, Secular Humanists believe democracy should color every aspect of life. Corliss Lamont explains, "Humanist principles demand the widest possible extension of democracy to all relevant aspects of human living."[4] Secular Humanists' motivation for the application of democracy to all of life is to change human relationships. Dreikurs explains the rationale, "In an autocratic order all relations between individuals and between groups are those of superiors and inferiors. One is dominant, the other submissive. In contrast, the process of democratization

---

[1] Lucile W. Green, "The Call for a World Constitutional Convention," *The Humanist* (July/August 1968): 13.

[2] Paul Kurtz, ed., *The Humanist Alternative* (Buffalo, NY: Prometheus Books, 1973), 179.

[3] Rudolf Dreikurs, "The Impact of Equality," *The Humanist* (Sept./Oct. 1964): 143.

[4] Corliss Lamont, *The Philosophy of Humanism* (New York, NY: Frederick Ungar, 1982), 262.

LIBERALISM: A political tradition based on a secular ethic and a high degree of government control

entails a process of equalization."[5] This concept of equalization influences much of Secular Humanist political theory.

Liberalism is a term often associated with a Secular Humanist approach to politics.[6] **Liberalism** is a political tradition based on a secular ethic and a high degree of government control. Specific policies include moral issues such as a woman's right to an abortion and promotion of same-sex marriage, as well as equality issues like equal rights for women, redistribution of wealth to help the poor, heavy regulation of business, and affirmative action.[7]

8.3.2 OUR ROLE IN EVOLUTION

Julian Huxley

In the Secular Humanist worldview, we are evolving animals, continually progressing onward and upward toward some form of biological and social perfection. **Julian Huxley** believes that "all reality is a single process of evolution."[8] Secular Humanists believe that we are capable of controlling our own evolutionary development. Huxley writes, "Today, in twentieth-century man, the evolutionary process is at last becoming conscious of itself and is beginning to study itself with a view to directing its future course."[9]

If we are truly capable of controlling our own evolution, and the possibilities of this evolution seem virtually limitless, then this is the most important task we face. For Humanists, then, the political arena becomes very significant, because government is one of our most powerful agents for effecting the changes necessary to further our evolution. Walt Anderson believes the evolutionary perspective "urges us to see political development itself as an advance for biological evolution, to look at humanity not as a cog in a vast social machine but rather as (in Julian Huxley's phrase) evolution becomes conscious of itself."[10]

8.3.3 SECULAR WORLD GOVERNMENT

Humans, according to Secular Humanists, are the highest form of evolved animals, yet we are still just one among many aspects of the world's single ecosystem. When we attempt to divide the world into states and nations, we are violating our place in nature. Timothy J. Madigan says, "Humanism holds that the planet Earth must be considered a single ecosystem, which is to say it is no longer feasible to arbitrarily divide it into separate states and hope that each one can satisfactorily manage itself."[11]

---

[5] Dreikurs, "The Impact of Equality," 143.

[6] Liberalism as we are using it in this text refers to how the term is used in the United States. In other Western nations, the term carries different connotations.

[7] "Affirmative action" means giving certain preferences to "under-represented' groups, such as when a government building project is required to hire a certain number of minority-owned sub-contractors, or when a university policy requires a certain percentage of minority students must be accepted each year, regardless of the students ability to perform on a college level.

[8] Julian Huxley, *The Humanist Frame* (New York, NY: Harper and Brothers, 1961), 15.

[9] Ibid., 7.

[10] Walter Truett Anderson, *Politics and the New Humanism* (Pacific Palisades, CA: Goodyear Publishing Company, 1973), 83

[11] Timothy J. Madigan, "Humanism and the Need for a Global Consciousness," *The Humanist* (March/April 1986):

The notion that humanity is one part of a single ecosystem has concrete ramifications for Secular Humanist concepts of community. They believe that everyone should live in one community, without national borders and differing state policies.

Secular Humanists believe that a world community necessitates a **secular world government**. Systems of national government are destined to fail; thus world government is an inevitable step forward in the evolutionary process. Kurtz says that "today there are powerful forces moving us toward a new ethical global consciousness."[12] To no one's surprise, the worldview that will most encourage the creation of this world community (according to the Humanist) is Secular Humanism. Kurtz says, "Humanism, we believe, can play a significant role in helping to foster the development of a genuine world community."[13]

> **SECULAR WORLD GOVERNMENT:**
> A non-religious political body that would make, interpret, and enforce a set of international laws

We are perfectible, and Humanism provides a framework for channeling our inherent goodness in the right direction. *Humanist Manifesto II* proclaims, "What more daring a goal for humankind than for each person to become, in ideal as well as practice, a citizen of a world community. It is a classical vision; we can now give it new vitality. Humanism thus interpreted is a moral force that has time on its side. We believe that humankind has the potential intelligence, good will, and cooperative skill to implement this commitment in the decades ahead."[14] Thus, peaceful world government is inevitable in the Secular Humanist worldview.

8.3.4 DISARMAMENT AND THE UNITED NATIONS

Most Humanists call for universal disarmament and expanded power for the United Nations as two steps necessary for the implementation of a democratic world community. "The first steps in avoiding a nuclear cataclysm and preserving democracy are to agree on universal disarmament,"[15] according to Erich Fromm. Linus Pauling believes, "The only hope for the world lies in achieving control of the methods of waging war and ultimately to reach the goal of total and universal disarmament."[16] Once disarmed, nations will be more willing to cooperate, less intent on enforcing nationalistic boundaries, and ready to merge into a global community. At present, the only organization that is truly global in scope is the United Nations. Thus, Secular Humanists support expanded power for this institution. William Carleton says, "Our hopes for political internationalism may have to center around the United Nations."[17]

In *Humanist Manifesto 2000*, Kurtz argues for a World Parliament "and elections to it based on population—which will represent the people, not their governments."[18] He goes on to say, "The idea of a World Parliament is similar to the evolution of the European Parliament, still in its infancy. The current UN General Assembly is an assembly of nations. This new

17–18.

[12] Paul Kurtz, *Forbidden Fruit* (Buffalo, NY: Prometheus Books, 1988), 146. Among these forces are Marxism-Leninism, Postmodernism, the New Age movement, Secular Humanism, and various Internationalist and Trans-nationalists organizations, including the Council for Foreign Relations, Club of Rome, Bilderburgers, Trilateral Commission, and the United Nations. Biblical Christianity constitutes one major opposition to one-world government; Revelation 13 declares that the head of a man-made world government will be the Beast or Anti-Christ. For a fairly complete list of organizations and movements striving for a world order, see Malachi Martin, *The Keys of This Blood* (New York, NY: Simon and Schuster, 1990), 275f.

[13] Paul Kurtz, "A Declaration of Interdependence: A New Global Ethics," *Free Inquiry* (Fall 1988); 6.

[14] *Humanist Manifesto II* (Buffalo, NY: Prometheus Books, 1980), 23.

[15] Erich Fromm, *May Man Prevail?* (Garden City, NY: Double Day, 1961), 248.

[16] Linus Pauling, "Humanism and Peace," *The Humanist* no. 2 (1961), 75.

[17] William G. Carleton, *Technology and Humanism* (Nashville, TN: Vanderbilt University Press, 1970), 22.

[18] Paul Kurtz, *Humanist Manifesto 2000* (Amherst, NY: Prometheus Books, 2000), 57.

World Parliament would enact legislative policies in a democratic manner. Perhaps a bicameral legislature is the most feasible with both a Parliament of peoples and a General Assembly of nations."[19]

Humanists have consistently worked in conjunction with the United Nations to bring the world closer to globalism. Julian Huxley served as the first Director General of the United Nations Educational, Scientific, and Cultural Organization (UNESCO). Lamont says, "Ever since I was an undergraduate at Harvard, I have been active in endeavors to establish enduring world peace. I backed the League of Nations, and since World War II, I have vigorously supported the United Nations."[20]

8.3.5 IDEOLOGIES AND ETHICS

Before the world can move beyond these two general recommendations (global disarmament and expansion of the UN), however, both nations and individuals will have to make ideological and ethical compromises. *Humanist Manifesto II* demands ideological compromise in the form of "international cooperation in culture, science, the arts, and technology across ideological borders. We must learn to live openly together or we shall perish together."[21]

The need for compromise between ideologies is rooted in a Humanist definition of democracy as not only a form of government, but also an overall means of equalization. Proponents of specific ideologies perceive other ideologies as unequal (and inferior) to their own. Humanists believe this denial of equality creates tensions that cannot exist in a democratic world government. The fact that some ideologies are perceived as more right than others is contrary to the Secular Humanist definition of democracy.

This idea can best be understood by exploring the Secular Humanist attitude toward the role of ethics in establishing the world community. Dreikurs believes that "the task of our generation [is] to explore the means by which we can reach agreement, the basis for co-operation between equals. No pressure or 'being right' will accomplish this."[22] It is better to agree to begin agreeing rather than continue arguing about which worldview is ethically right.

According to Secular Humanism, no ethical system holds all the answers, and no system is totally sinister—instead, we are asked to take a more egalitarian view of ideologies and their ethical systems. Since ideologies are continually evolving, we must simply embrace the newest, most highly developed ideology. Huxley puts it this way: "[M]ajor steps in the human phase of evolution are achieved by breakthroughs to new dominant patterns of mental organization, of knowledge, ideas and beliefs—ideological instead of physiological or biological organization."[23]

Secular Humanists believe that their worldview is capable of promoting tolerance, compromise, and cooperation in a world community. Huxley says, "A world organization cannot be based on one of the competing theologies of the world but must, it seems, be based on some form of humanism . . . a world humanism . . . a scientific humanism . . . an evolutionary humanism."[24]

Francis Williams calls for us "to stop thinking politically as Capitalists, or Communists, Christians, Muslims, Hindus or Buddhists, and think as Humanists . . . A world in which men

---

[19] Ibid.

[20] Corliss Lamont, *Voice in the Wilderness* (Buffalo, NY: Prometheus Books, 1975), 318.

[21] *Humanist Manifesto II*, 22.

[22] Dreikurs, "The Impact of Equality," 146.

[23] Huxley, "The Humanist Frame," 16.

[24] Morris B. Storer, ed., *Humanist Ethics* (Buffalo, NY: Prometheus Books, 1980), 2.

have both hydrogen bombs and closed minds is altogether too dangerous."[25] In other words, world democracy will flourish only when all nations embrace Humanism.

8.3.6 MORALS AND POLITICS

Secular Humanists recognize that politics cannot be separated from ethical considerations. Sidney Hook believes the proper means for developing moral codes and re-examining standards lies in the practical application of political theory. Thus, once world government is established, the need to reach consensus about morality must be addressed although it must not rely on religious belief. Hook says, "The democratic open society must be neutral to all religious overbeliefs; but no matter how secular it conceives itself to be, it cannot be neutral to moral issues. It seeks to draw these issues into the area of public discussion in the hope that a reasonable consensus may be achieved."[26]

Achieving a universal moral awareness through consensus rather than from absolutes outside ourselves may be difficult, if not impossible, to accomplish. Mark Reader tells us that "In the end politics is the place of public happiness."[27] The problem arises from the fact that "The 'good life' or 'quality of life' is relative to each individual's preferences, desires, and needs."[28] The state cannot democratically provide happiness for every world citizen if happiness is relative to individual desires, tastes, and standards.

Thus, if Secular Humanists succeed in their goal of establishing a system of global ethical standards by eliminating all existing ideologies and their related ethical systems (other than Humanism), all they will offer the democratic world community is open-mindedness, which in theory is conducive to cooperation and equalization.

8.3.7 HUMANISM AND ECONOMIC DEMOCRACY

The Secular Humanist goal of equalization extends from politics to economics. V.M. Tarkunde says, "A genuine political democracy is not possible in the absence of economic democracy."[29] Many Humanists are socialists who favor the redistribution of wealth since the unequal distribution of goods hinders the process of evolution. Anderson says that "when people are deprived of the fundamental necessities, as are millions of Americans and even more millions of human beings in other countries, their capacity for development is frustrated at the most basic level."[30] Thus, Secular Humanists see the redistribution of wealth as a necessary step toward further evolutionary development.

Lamont defines economic democracy as "the right of every adult to a useful job at a decent wage or salary, to general economic security and opportunity, to an equitable share in the material goods of this life, and to a proportionate voice in the conduct of economic affairs."[31]

Kurtz proposes a rationale for economic democracy and a means to achieve it: "We believe . . . that the more affluent nations have a moral obligation to increase technological and economic assistance so that their less developed neighbors may become more self-sufficient. We need to work out some equitable forms of taxation on a worldwide basis to help make this

[25] Huxley, "The Humanist Frame," 107.
[26] Sidney Hook, *Religion in a Free Society* (Lincoln, NE: University of Nebraska Press, 1967), 36.
[27] Mark Reader, "Humanism and Politics," *The Humanist* (Nov./Dec. 1975): 38.
[28] Storer, *Humanist Ethics*, 130.
[29] V.M. Tarkunde, "An Outline of Radical Humanism," *The Humanist* (July/Aug. 1988): 13.
[30] Walter Truett Anderson, *Politics and the New Humanism*, 141.
[31] Lamont, *The Philosophy of Humanism*, 267.

a reality."[32] Tarkunde suggests "a cooperative economy in which the workers in an undertaking will be the owners of the means of production employed in that undertaking is undoubtedly the most democratic economic institution conceived so far."[33]

8.3.8 CONCLUSION

Secular Humanist politics, biology, economics, ethics, and law are linked to the belief that human beings are the highest rung on the evolutionary ladder and that the establishment of world politics is necessary to advance to the next evolutionary stage. In this perspective, humans are part of one ecosystem—the world—and should be working toward a democratic world government. Universal disarmament and increased power for the United Nations are two intermediate steps crucial to the advancement of a global government.

A Secular Humanist world government is problematic for Christians. In the United States alone, such a world government would seek to eradicate Christian symbols and content from the public square by removing the Ten Commandments from public schools, removing "under God" from the nation's Pledge of Allegiance, replacing Christian ethics with values clarification, replacing divine law with legal positivism, replacing the celebration of Christmas with winter holiday, standardizing sex education and alternative lifestyles into the public school curriculum, and disregarding references in the Declaration of Independence to God-given rights.

The Secular Humanist concept of equalization precludes the Christian belief that God created human beings in His image, subject to His laws and commands that take precedence when human authority conflicts with it. Equalization strives for a democracy that supports moral relativism rather than absolute moral standards. Kurtz unwittingly summarizes the Secular Humanist dilemma in equalization and democratic world government when he says, "The essential ingredient in this new world of planetary humanism depends on the cultivation of ethical wisdom."[34]

C.S. Lewis was prophetic in this regard. In his book, *The Abolition of Man*, he refers to "the Conditioners" who have a utopian vision for recreating society. He writes, "Man's conquest of himself means simply the rule of the Conditioners over the conditioned human material, the world of post-humanity which, some knowingly and some unknowingly, nearly all men in all nations are at present labouring to produce."[35] He develops this theme further, writing, "But the man-molders of the new age will be armed with the powers of an omnicompetent state and an irresistible scientific technique: we shall get at last a race of conditioners who really can cut out all posterity in what shape they please."[36]

We stand at a crossroads, with one path leading to individual liberty and the other to a future lived under the rule of the Conditioners. Which path our society takes depends on the choices we make today and whether those choices are based on God's principles of life, or that of secular man.

---

[32] *Humanist Manifesto II*, 22.
[33] Tarkunde, "An Outline of Radical Humanism," 13.
[34] Kurtz, *Forbidden Fruit*, 176.
[35] C.S. Lewis, *The Abolition of Man* (New York, NY: Macmillan, 1952), 86.
[36] Ibid., 73.

Politics

Marxism—Leninism

"In reality . . . the State is nothing more than a
machine for the oppression of one class by another."[1]

— FREDERICK ENGELS

8.4.1 INTRODUCTION

In Marxism, the struggle to control the forces of production is the dynamic force behind
human development. The economic system determines other features of a society, including its

V.I. Lenin

political structure. To Karl Marx, the "economic structure of
society [is] the real foundation on which rise moral, legal and
political superstructures and to which definite forms of social
consciousness correspond."[2]

Thus, to a Marxist, particular political systems are
grounded in and arise from particular economic systems. A
socialist economy, therefore, lays the foundation for *genuine*
democracy (although an "impure" form of democracy does
exist in capitalist nations). Genuine democracy is not the aim
of Marxist politics, and in fact Marxists view democracy
as little more than a necessary evil. V.I. Lenin explains,
"Democracy is a state which recognizes the subordination
of the minority to the majority, i.e., an organization for the

[1] Karl Marx, *Civil War in France* (New York, NY: International Publishers, 1937), 19.
[2] Karl Marx, *A Contribution to the Critique of Political Economy* (Chicago, IL: C.H. Kerr, 1911), 11.

systematic use of force by one class against another, by one section of the population against another."[3] This definition of democracy is consistent with Marxist emphasis on class struggle.

8.4.2 CLASS ANTAGONISM

> COMMUNISM: A dream of future utopia brought about by a proletariat revolution and ultimately leading to a classless society in which all property is publicly shared and each person works and is paid according to his or her abilities and needs

Marxists see the world as a struggle between the bourgeoisie (owners of private property and the means of production) and the proletariat (workers), with economics as the foundation on which the rest of society is built. Marxists believe the state is an arena in which the *haves* and the *have-nots* struggle. Thus, Marxists see a democratic state or republic, especially in a capitalist economic system, as undesirable. According to Engels, "The modern state, no matter what its form, is essentially a capitalist machine."[4] This "machine" is an unacceptable state since it so clearly focuses on exploiting its citizens.

In a socialist society, the mode of production does not exploit its citizens to the extent that capitalism does and thus encourages a less exploitative political system. Socialist governments tend to discourage class antagonism since they are founded on economic systems that are close to abolishing class distinctions. This less exploitative nature of government makes the democracy more *genuine* and socialism more appealing than capitalism. Socialism, however, still lacks several factors of the ideal state of communism.

The ideal state for the Marxist is no state at all, since any government (whether a democracy or a dictatorship) is a vehicle for maintaining class antagonism. Marx says, "Political power is merely the organized power of one class for oppressing another."[5] The state exists, therefore, because class antagonism exists. Once class antagonism is eradicated, the state will no longer be necessary. Lenin

> Political power is merely the organized power of one class for oppressing another.
>
> — Karl Marx

says, "According to Marx, the State could neither arise nor maintain itself if a reconciliation of classes were possible."[6]

8.4.3 THE DICTATORSHIP OF THE PROLETARIAT

In the transition from capitalism to communism, however, the state remains a necessary evil. The concentration of all the means of production in the hands of the state, termed statism, is the first step in the Marxist formula to abolish all classes. Marx writes, "Between

> STATISM: A political system in which the concentration of economic controls and planning are placed completely in the hands of a highly centralized government

capitalist and communist society lies the period of the revolutionary transformation of the one into the other. Corresponding to this is also a political transition period in which the state can be nothing but the revolutionary dictatorship of the proletariat."[7]

---

[3] Karl Marx, Frederick Engels, and V.I. Lenin, *On the Dictatorship of the Proletariat* (Moscow, USSR: Progress Publishers, 1984), 243.

[4] Ibid., 124.

[5] Ibid., 59.

[6] V.I. Lenin, *The State and Revolution* (New York, NY: International Publishers, 1932), 9.

[7] Marx, Engels, and Lenin, *On the Dictatorship of the Proletariat*, 122.

Marxists perceive democracy as the propertied classes oppressing those without property or the majority oppressing the minority. They see democracy as similar to a dictatorship in that one class (the majority) dictates government policy and laws to another class (the minority). In capitalism, the bourgeoisie uses the state to oppress the proletariat. In socialism, the opposite is true— the proletariat operates as the powerful authoritarian. In this sense, Marxists use the term "dictatorship of the proletariat."

Democracy in Marxist terms, then, is simply the means to an end, a necessary tool for maintaining the early stages of socialism. Democracy is useful in establishing the dictatorship of the proletariat, a crucial facet of Marxist political development.

> Whoever expects that socialism will be achieved without social revolution and a dictatorship of the proletariat is not a socialist. Dictatorship is state power, based directly upon force.
>
> — V.I. Lenin

The dictatorship of the proletariat is crucial for two major reasons. First, dictatorship is necessary because it consolidates the means of production in the hands of the state, which in turn leads toward the abolition of classes. Second, dictatorship is necessary because the proletariat, which seized power through revolution, will need the might of the state to thwart bourgeois efforts to reclaim power. Lenin says, "Whoever expects that socialism will be achieved without social revolution and a dictatorship of the proletariat is not a socialist. Dictatorship is state power, based directly upon force."[8]

8.4.4 THE FATE OF THE BOURGEOISIE

Marxist-Leninist politics explicitly calls for the proletariat to suppress the bourgeoisie by violence and force. Lenin writes, "The state is a special organization of force . . . an organization of violence for the suppression of some class. What class must the proletariat suppress? The exploiting class, i.e., the bourgeoisie."[9] In a similar vein, Lenin says, "We must crush [the bourgeoisie] in order to free humanity from wage-slavery; their resistance must be broken by force."[10] In addition, the dictatorship of the proletariat will require confiscation of property. All of this will be accomplished through the guidance and governance of the Marxist party.

8.4.5 THE ROLE OF THE MARXIST PARTY

The Marxist political party will assist the workers in their efforts to establish the dictatorship of the proletariat. According to the authors of *Socialism as a Social System*, "Marxist/Leninist theory and the experience of history show conclusively that the working class can carry out its historic mission only if led by a strong, well-organized party."[11] Stalin writes, "Our Party guides the government. The Party supervises the work of the administration . . . and tries to secure for them the support of the masses, since there is not any important decision taken by them without the direction of the Party."[12]

---

[8] Lenin, "O lozunge razoruzheniia," October 1916. Cited in Elliot R. Goodman, *The Soviet Design for a World State* (New York, NY: Columbia University Press, 1968), 287.

[9] Claire Sterling, *The Terror Network: The Secret War of International Terrorism* (New York, NY: Berkley Books, 1982), 203.

[10] V.I. Lenin, *Selected Works*, 38 vols. (New York, NY: International Publishers, 1938), 7:81.

[11] V.V. Zagladin, ed., *The World Communist Movement* (Moscow, USSR: Progress Publishers 1973), 159.

[12] Joseph Stalin, "Beseda s pervoi amerikanskoi rabochei delegatsiei," Sept. 9, 1927. Cited in Goodman, *The Soviet Design for a World State*, 191.

Thus, the dictatorship of the proletariat is in essence the dictatorship of the Marxist party. The state will rule by the majority of the proletariat guided by the principles of Marxism. Those opposed to the Party will be considered bourgeois or reactionary. Eventually, all in opposition to Marxism will be eliminated, rendering the dictatorship of the proletariat unnecessary. Once classes cease to exist, everyone will be of like mind, and no state will be needed to enforce one class' oppression of another.

8.4.6 The State Withers Away

In Marxist perception of human social development, the state evolved at a point in history when it was necessary, and it will cease to exist when it is no longer necessary for society. It is a mere transitory phenomenon. Engels says, "The State is . . . simply a product of society at a certain stage of evolution."[13]

Lenin supports the idea that the state is necessary only in a capitalist society because it is responsible for engendering class antagonisms. He stresses the necessity of eliminating the bourgeoisie, which in turn will eliminate the need for the state: "Only in communist society, when the resistance of the capitalists has been completely crushed, when the capitalists have disappeared, when there are no classes . . . only then 'the state . . . ceases to exist,' and 'it becomes possible to speak of freedom.'"[14] Since freedom to Marxists means no government at all, until the classless society is established freedom is an illusion. Lenin continues, "So long as the state exists, there is no freedom. When there is freedom, there will be no state."[15]

Marxists believe "only communism makes the state absolutely unnecessary, for there is nobody to be suppressed . . ."[16] Communism must be established worldwide in order for Marxists to consider their political ends achieved, and at that time in history, the state will wither away completely. If the state exists anywhere in the world, then classes still exist as a threat to a completely classless society.[17]

8.4.7 New World Order

The establishment of global communism as a new world order and the dissolution of the state are inevitable evolutionary steps. In the same sense that humans, societies, economies, and politics are evolving, so the new world order is an evolutionary advance over former nations, states, tribes, and other race or class distinctions.

Georgi Shakhnazarov, a top aide to former Soviet President Mikhail Gorbachev, writes, "Our epoch is the epoch of the revolutionary transformation of capitalist society into communist."[18] In tracing the beginnings of the revolution, he says, "the building of a new world order . . . was begun in October 1917 by revolutionary Russia, proclaiming socialist principles."[19] The establishment of world communism, the ultimate aim of Marxism, puts the means of production in the hands of the people, abolishes classes, abolishes the state, and leads to a world society of cooperation and consensus.

[13] Frederick Engels, *The Origin of the Family, Private Property and the State* (Chicago, IL: Kerr, 1902), 206.

[14] Marx, Engels, and Lenin, *On the Dictatorship of the Proletariat*, 249-50.

[15] Ibid., 256.

[16] Ibid., 251.

[17] In reality there will never be a "classless" society, only a one-class society. According to the dialectical view of history this one-class (synthesis) will become the new thesis, draw to itself an antithesis, and renew the struggle. Remember, this is evolutionary or process philosophy and is never-ending. In reality, the murder of millions of human beings was for a transitory moment in history.

[18] Georgi Shakhnazarov, *The Coming World Order* (Moscow, USSR: Progress Publishers, 1981), 18.

[19] Ibid., 201.

8.4.8 CONCLUSION

In the Marxist worldview, all forms of government are ugly reflections of the fact that class antagonism exists. Marxists advocate a form of democracy they call the "dictatorship of the proletariat" as the first step toward socialism. When socialist society evolves into communism, class distinctions will no longer exist, which will eliminate the need for the state in any form.

Until world communism is a reality, however, conflict between socialist societies (whose states are in the process of withering away) and capitalist societies will be a reality. This conflict will include wars as an extension of class antagonism. Just as the bourgeoisie and the proletariat clash, so nations controlled by capitalists and nations controlled by socialists will clash. Thus, the establishment of global communism and the abolition of all forms of government are the unabashed goals of Marxists. To this end they are willing to suppress, persecute, and wage war against the enemy.

The political and military history of Marxism from the October Revolution of 1917 to the Tiananmen Square student uprising of 1989 is one of the most ruthless, efficient killing machines the world has ever witnessed. The death toll of this "scientific socialism" experiment has exceeded the 100 million mark, according to University of Hawaii professor R.J. Rummel, author of *Death By Government*. Rummel summarizes the period by saying it is "as though our species has been devastated by a modern Black Plague."[20]

> ## The Pop Culture Connection
>
> ***Good Night and Good Luck*** (a 2005 film written by George Clooney)—"In the early 1950s, the threat of Communism created an air of paranoia in the United States and exploiting those fears was Senator Joseph McCarthy of Wisconsin. However, CBS reporter Edward R. Murrow and his producer Fred W. Friendly decided to take a stand and challenge McCarthy and expose him for the fear monger he was. However, their actions took a great personal toll on both men, but they stood by their convictions and helped to bring down one of the most controversial senators in American history." While the film portrays Senator George McCarthy as wrong for seeking to "out" Communists, the facts came to light in the 1990s that McCarthy was on the right track! After the breakup of the Soviet Union in 1991, the Secret Service archives were opened to the public, where researchers found evidence that over 340 Communist spies and sympathizers had indeed infiltrated a number of State Department positions in the U.S. government during the Cold War.[21]

---

[20] R.J. Rummel, *Death by Government* (New Brunswick, NJ: Transaction Publishers, 1994), 9.

[21] Quoted from http://www.imdb.com/title/tt0433383/plotsummary. For additional information on how right McCarthy was, see Daniel J. Flynn. "The Hidden Truth About Joseph McCarthy," http://www.academia.org/campus_reports/2000/january_2000_5.html. Flynn writes, "Documents from the Soviet Union's archives, USSR spy messages deciphered by the U.S. government's Venona program, and declassified FBI files and wiretaps all prove that hundreds of U.S. officials were agents of an international Communist conspiracy. If these previously inaccessible documents shed light on only a few of McCarthy's specific charges, they certainly vindicate his general charge that security in the U.S. government was lax and that large numbers of Communists penetrated positions of great importance.

"Alger Hiss, Roosevelt's foreign policy advisor and first secretary general of the United Nations; Harry Dexter White, assistant secretary of the Treasury and Truman's appointee as director of the International Monetary Fund; and Lauchlin Currie, administrative assistant to Presidents Roosevelt and Truman, have all been confirmed, among hundreds of others, to have been agents of the USSR. In addition to the multitudes of executive branch agents, we also know of at least three Congressmen working clandestinely for the Soviet Union during this time period."

Politics

Cosmic Humanism

"[T]he New Age solution does not call for top-down bureaucratic government, but for much more local autonomy than we have at the present, and much more planetary cooperation."[1]

— MARK SATIN

8.5.1 INTRODUCTION

Cosmic Humanists believe that humanity is evolving toward a collective consciousness that will transcend all material and individual boundaries, including national and political boundaries. World government is a natural evolutionary step in this dissolution of boundaries. According to Donald Keys, humanity is "on the verge of something entirely new, a further evolutionary step unlike any other: the emergence of the first global civilization."[2]

The Cosmic Humanist desire for global government is based less on political theory than on the concept that "all is one" and that evolution and other scientific principles are leading humanity into global unity. World government has the potential to remove barriers

> [Humanity is] on the verge of something entirely new, a further evolutionary step unlike any other: the emergence of the first global civilization.
>
> — Donald Keys

[1] Mark Satin, *New Age Politics* (New York, NY: Dell Publishing, 1978), 22.

[2] Donald Keys, *Earth at Omega: Passage to Planetization* (Boston, MA: Branden Press, 1982), iii.

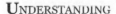

and limits and is thus important for Cosmic Humanists. David Spangler explains, "Unlike many historical expressions of the one-world idea, which focus in particular upon the establishment of a world government, the vision of the New Age qua planetary civilization arises less out of politics than out of what is called the holistic vision. This is the awareness that all life is interrelated and interdependent, that the formative elements of creation are not bits of matter but relationships, and that evolution is the emergence of ever more complex patterns and syntheses of relationships."[3]

Since Cosmic Humanists think in terms of understanding the world as a whole instead of the parts, the next pattern to emerge is global civilization, a unity that will demand a one-world government.

8.5.2 Evolution's Guarantee

Cosmic Humanists believe evolution guarantees the disintegration of political boundaries and the advent of a global civilization (just as it guarantees the merging of humanity into the mind of God). Evolution is seen as a process not merely of physical development but total spiritual development as well. As we evolve into higher species, so we evolve into higher consciousness. Integrated into this move toward higher consciousness is the dissolution of political and national boundaries.

> **NEW WORLD ORDER:** The New Age belief that (given each person's evolution toward collective consciousness) humanity will eventually develop the capacity for worldwide self-government

Randall Baer describes how scientific evolution supports the Cosmic Humanist belief that global civilization is inevitable: "I read that startling advances in such diverse scientific fields as genetic engineering, telecommunications, supercomputers, nuclear fusion technology, artificial intelligence, solid state physics, quantum physics, advanced holography, laser optics, astrophysics, and others were to be combined with New Age spiritual philosophy in creating a utopian **New World Order**.[4]

Mark Satin says, "New Age politics is uncompromisingly evolutionary . . . though it does believe that evolution can be speeded up . . ."[5] The Cosmic Humanist, by achieving higher consciousness, may speed mankind's evolutionary ascent toward the New World Order.

8.5.3 Autonomy or Anarchy?

Cosmic Humanists rarely specify the political nature of the coming global civilization, but they believe that each individual is evolving the capacity for **self-government**. Marilyn Ferguson explains, "The new political awareness has little to do with parties or ideologies. Its constituents don't come in blocs. Power that is never surrendered by the individual cannot be brokered. Not by revolution or protest but by autonomy, the old slogan becomes a surprising fact: Power to the people. One by one by one."[6] Thus in Cosmic Humanist terms, world government is self-government. Centralized national governments will not be necessary. Each individual will be autonomous, deciding what is right for him or her without reference to institutional limits.

> **SELF-GOVERNMENT:** The New Age political perspective that maintains that each divine individual is evolving the ability to govern himself or herself

---

[3] David Spangler, *Emergence: The Rebirth of the Sacred* (New York, NY: Delta/Merloyd Lawrence, 1984), 42.

[4] Randall N. Baer, *Inside the New Age Nightmare* (Lafayette, LA: Huntington House, 1989), 34.

[5] Satin, *New Age Politics*, 20–21.

[6] Marilyn Ferguson, *The Aquarian Conspiracy* (Los Angeles, CA: J.P. Tarcher, Inc., 1980), 240.

The dangerous potential for such a system of individual autonomy, however, is that it will disintegrate into **anarchy**. Cosmic Humanists, however, emphasize the concept of community as having the capacity to overcome the dangers of anarchy. Satin says, "In New Age society we would learn to make our own decisions and not to hang on others. But that wouldn't isolate us from others . . . it would make us more attractive to others and more confident about being in community with them."[7] Cosmic Humanists propose communities largely lacking in any political or legal form.

> **ANARCHY:** The complete absence of government and law

8.5.4 CONCLUSION

Cosmic Humanists see the world evolving toward a New World Order in which individuals are free to follow their whims uninhibited by law or government. The New World Order will be reached when everyone (or a majority) achieves a state of higher consciousness. Individual autonomy will make it easier for everyone to reach higher consciousness.

One aspect of personal freedom that the Cosmic Humanist worldview discourages is in the area of faith and traditional religion. Former United Nations Assistant Secretary General Robert Miller says, "Religions must actively cooperate to bring to unprecedented heights a better understanding of the mysteries of life and of our place in the universe. 'My religion, right or wrong,' . . . must be abandoned forever in the Planetary Age."[8]

This attitude toward religion stems from the understanding that some religions, such as Christianity and Islam, are incompatible with the Humanist belief that we are evolving toward our own godhood. Christianity will always threaten the New Age emphasis on higher consciousness and hence must be stifled. In the New World Order you may follow your inclinations only as long as they are not found in obedience to Jesus Christ.

---

[7] Satin, *New Age Politics*, 106.

[8] Robert Muller, *The New Genesis: Shaping a Global Spirituality* (New York, NY: Image Books, 1984), 164.

Politics

Postmodernism

"I see the 'orthodox' (the people who think that
hounding gays out of the military promotes traditional
family values) as the same honest, decent, blinkered,
disastrous people who voted for Hitler in 1933. I see
the 'progressives' as defining the only America I care
about."[1]

— RICHARD RORTY

8.6.1 INTRODUCTION

As keen observers of the Postmodern condition, Steven Best and Douglas Kellner comment on the current status of Postmodern politics: "As with postmodern theory, there is no one 'postmodern politics,' but rather a conflicting set of propositions that emerges from the ambiguities of social change and multiple postmodern theoretical perspectives."[2] Postmodern politics takes a variety of forms. On one end of the spectrum is the "anti-politics" of Baudrillard, a "cynical, despairing rejection of the belief"[3] that politics can be used to change society. On the other side of Baudrillard's negative, nihilistic approach is a more affirmative one, outlined by Foucault, Lyotard, and Rorty, who suggest that the way to "enhance individual freedom" and bring about "progressive change"[4] is to concentrate on the local level.

---

[1] Richard Rorty, "Trotsky and the Wild Orchids" (1992), http://www.philosophy.uncc.edu/mleldrid/cmt/rrtwo.html.
[2] Steven Best and Douglas Kellner, "Postmodern Politics and the Battle for the Future," (http://uta.edu/huma/illuminations/kell28.htm).
[3] Ibid.
[4] Ibid.

Although there is a lack of consensus surrounding much of Postmodern politics, most agree Postmodernists fall on the left side of the political spectrum. Barbara Epstein, a self-proclaimed "moderate" Postmodernist, writes, "Many people, inside and outside the world of Postmodernism, have come to equate Postmodernism with the left."[5] Stephen R.C. Hicks agrees, writing, "Of the major names in the Postmodernist movement there is not a single figure who is not leftwing in a serious way."[6]

> Many people, inside and outside the world of Postmodernism, have come to equate Postmodernism with the left.
>
> —— BARBARA EPSTEIN

Most of the early French Postmodernists emerged from the Marxist tradition—some grew up in families supportive of leftist causes, and others were former Stalinists. Foucault initially joined the Maoist Gauche Proletarienne and the French Communist Party but left once he discovered the Marxist stance toward homosexuality. As time went on, Foucault moved further away from Marxism, particularly the "state-centered focus" of classic Marxism. Foucault would later write, "Marxism exists in nineteenth century thought as a fish exists in water; that is, it ceases to breathe anywhere else."[7] Anthony Thomson claims that Postmodernism is generally "fueled by the failure of Marxian-inspired State socialism."[8]

However, in spite of his aversion to some aspects of Marxism, Foucault does not abandon Marxist thought altogether. Specifically, Foucault remained under "the profound influence of Marxist analyses of power relations and the role of economic inequality in determining social structures."[9] Mark Lilla notes that Foucault felt he needed something "more radical" than classic Marxism, so he turned to "Nietzsche and Heidegger, but also avant-garde writers and Surrealists whose hostility to bourgeois life took more aesthetic and psychological forms."[10]

8.6.2 LEFTIST POLITICS

For Postmodernists, politics is not centered around political parties, utopian visions, or an ultimate *telos*; rather, it is a tool of experimentation that involves a radical critique of the existing systems of power in a society, the identification of oppressed groups, and the remedy for bringing those identified groups out of oppression to achieve a sense of social justice.

Some Postmodernists, including Foucault and Rorty, use terms such as leftism and progressivism to describe their approach to politics. For Foucault, progressive politics outlines the "possibilities for transformation and the play of dependencies between those transformations, whereas other politics rely upon the uniform abstraction of change or the . . . presence of genius."[11] This means that "rather than seeing politics as being centered around individual great leaders who have utopian visions of the future . . . Foucault is more concerned to develop and describe a politics which takes account of the transformative possibilities within the present."[12]

---

[5] Barbara Epstein, "Postmodernism and the Left," *New Politics* vol. 6, no. 2 (new series), whole no. 22 (Winter 1997). Available online at http://www.wpunj.edu/~newpol/issue22/epstei22.htm.

[6] Stephen R.C. Hicks, *Explaining Postmodernism: Skepticism and Socialism from Rousseau to Foucault* (Tempe, AZ: Scholargy Publishers, 2004), 85.

[7] Michel Foucault, *The Order of Things: An Archaeology of the Human Sciences* (New York, NY: Vintage Books, 1994), 262.

[8] Anthony Thomson, "Post-Modernism and Social Justice," http://ace.acadiau.ca/soci/agt/constitutivecrim.htm. He references Stuart Henry and Dragan Milovanovic, *Constitutive Criminology: Beyond Postmodernism*, (London, UK: Sage, 1996), 4.

[9] Robert Eaglestone, ed., *Routledge Critical Thinkers*, (New York, NY: Routledge, 2003), 15.

[10] Mark Lilla, *The Reckless Mind: Intellectuals in Politics* (New York, NY: New York Review Books, 2001), 142.

[11] Cited in David Macey, *The Lives of Foucault* (New York, NY: Vintage, 1994), xix.

[12] Simon Malpas, *Jean-Francois Lyotard*. Cited in Robert Eaglestone, ed., *Routledge Critical Thinkers*, 16.

Foucault assumes that in the same way there is no ultimate purpose (*telos*) to life, there is no ultimate purpose for politics or what he refers to as "the themes of meaning, origin . . . [or] the deep teleology of a primeval destination."[13] Sara Mills writes, "Foucault seems to be trying to establish a basis for productive political activity without necessarily having to agree with a whole range of problematic assumptions about progress and the role of individuals bringing about political change"[14]

Mills suggests that Foucault "does not seem to have felt it necessary to have a fully worked-out political position, since in some ways it was precisely this sense of having to hold to a party line which he was reacting against."[15] In other words, there is no right way to approach politics since there is no unifying story that is true for life or politics. Lyotard explains, "With the destruction of the grand narratives, there is no longer any unifying identity for the subject or society. Instead, individuals are the sites where ranges of conflicting moral and political codes intersect, and the social bond is fragmented."[16]

Foucault expresses his range of political leanings this way: "I think I have in fact, been situated in most of the squares on the political checkerboard, one after another and sometimes simultaneously: as anarchist, leftist, ostentatious or disguised Marxist, explicit or secret anti-Marxist, technocrat in the service of Gaullism, new liberal, etc . . . It's true, I prefer not to identify myself and that I'm amused by the diversity of the ways I've been judged and classified."[17]

Foucault claims to have been in "most of the squares on the political checkerboard," and along with most of Postmodernism's founders, they played their game on the far left of the political game board! **Leftism** is therefore an appropriate term to summarize the Postmodern approach to politics.

> **LEFTISM:** An ideological approach to politics emphasizing the state's role in bringing about social justice, with a special focus on helping the poor or those oppressed due to race, gender, or sexual orientation

8.6.3 IDENTITY POLITICS

Barbara Epstein explains where the early Postmodern movement began: "The constellation of trends that I am calling Postmodernism has its origins in the writings of a group of French intellectuals of the '60s, most preeminently Michel Foucault, Jacques Derrida, Jacques Lacan, and Jean-Francois Lyotard. Those who developed Postmodernism tended to be associated with the radicalism of the '60s."[18]

The sexual and feminist revolutions that began in the sixties were intent on correcting the wrongs perpetuated by Western culture, especially the "puritanical" United States.[19] What was wrong was identified as white, European, male, heterosexual, and Judeo-Christian. Epstein observes that "one reason that Postmodernism has taken hold so widely is that it is much easier to be critical than to present a positive vision."[20] In their desire to tear down socio-political structures that they deemed oppressive, radical, or revolutionary, agitators developed the concept of identity politics to correct the social and political wrongs they deemed Western civilization had perpetuated.

---

[13] Michel Foucault, *Discipline and Punishment* (New York, NY: Vintage, 1991), 64–5.
[14] Eaglestone, *Routledge Critical Thinkers*, 17.
[15] Ibid., 15.
[16] Ibid., 29.
[17] Cited in Macey, *The Lives of Foucault*, xix.
[18] Epstein, "Postmodernism and the Left."
[19] Allan Bloom, *Closing of the American Mind* (New York, NY: Simon and Schuster, 1988), 97f.
[20] Epstein, "Postmodernism and the Left."

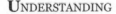

Identity politics seeks to advance the interests of particular groups in society that are perceived as victims of social injustice. The identity of the oppressed group gives rise to a political basis around which they can unite.[21] For example, radical feminists identified all women as victims of male oppression. Once they had established their case, whatever was needed to free women from male domination was considered *politically correct*.

> **IDENTITY POLITICS:**
> A political ideology that seeks to advance the interests of particular groups in society that are perceived as victims of social injustice

Alan Sokol quotes feminist Kelly Oliver: "[I]n order to be revolutionary, feminist theories should be political tools, strategies for overcoming oppression in specific concrete situations. The goal then, of feminist theory, should be to develop strategic theories—not true theories, not false theories, but strategic theories."[22] Since there are no true theories, the revolutionary way is to promote a theory that strategically accomplishes what needs to be accomplished.

For radical feminists, the ultimate goal became women's equality with men, which means, among other things, total sexual freedom. To bring this about, the strategic theory proclaimed children a burden and marriage a form of slavery, counterproductive to a woman's self-fulfillment. Abortion was declared a political right and women's only means for sexual equality with men—since men can engage in sexual intercourse without the consequences of bearing children, women must have the same freedom and political right.

Likewise, homosexuals were viewed as having been oppressed by a heterosexual majority who had forced their puritanical sexual mores onto society. The strategic theory marketed the homosexual lifestyle as normal, moral, healthy through television sit-coms about likeable homosexual characters, gay-themed movies, and public education that introduced very young children to appealing homosexual families.[23]

Similarly, Postmodernists claim that white Europeans had dominated people of color for hundreds of years. The strategic theory claimed blacks and other minorities suffered an unfair disadvantage in admission to higher education. The concept of affirmative action was developed to guarantee minorities access to higher education, often at the expense of more qualified white applicants. In this way, years of minority subservience to white oppression is remedied and social justice is affirmed.

The strategies of identity politics have succeeded in changing the beliefs of a growing number of people throughout Western society, demonstrating the power of the Postmodern approach for shaping the terms of the debate.

8.6.4 MANIPULATION OF LANGUAGE

Another strategy Postmodernists use in pursuit of their political goals is the manipulation of language. Someone once noted that we will either master words or be mastered by those who do. Postmodernists have mastered the manipulation of language to such an extent that what used to be considered shameful, immoral, or bad behavior is now heralded as progressive. Postmodernists have succeeded in gaining public acceptance of the following:

- Believing in the sanctity of heterosexual marriage is a mark of backwardness, while favoring legalization of same-sex marriage is a mark of broadmindedness.

---

[21] "Identity politics," *Wikipedia, The Free Encyclopedia*, http://en.wikipedia.org/w/index.php?title=Identity_ politics&oldid=47299218. (Accessed 6 Apr 2006.)

[22] Epstein, "Postmodernism and the Left."

[23] See, for example, the following books written for children and taught in many school districts across America: *Heather Has Two Mommies, Daddy's Roommate, Gay Pride Parade, The King and King,* etc.

- Expressing belief in a male Christ is a mark of bigotry, while preferring the female Christ (Christa) is a mark of discernment.
- Campaigning for abstinence education is restrictive, while promoting "free love" and revolution is a mark of liberation.
- Not allowing children to be taught about the homosexual lifestyle is a throwback to religious narrow-mindedness, bigotry, and the ultimate negative label, "intolerant," while teaching students to embrace homosexuality as a healthy lifestyle is a mark of inclusion and tolerance. [24]

These kinds of language games contribute to reorienting the masses to an acceptance of the Postmodern political agenda for changing society.

8.6.5 THE GOAL OF SOCIAL JUSTICE

Postmodernists long for a time when all of society's ills and abuses will be eliminated and **social justice** will prevail. Richard Rorty elaborates his vision for America: "[Walt] Whitman and [John] Dewey tried to substitute hope for knowledge. They wanted to put shared utopian dreams—dreams of an ideally decent and civilized society—in the place of knowledge of God's Will, Moral Law, the Laws of History, or the Facts of Science . . . As long as we have a functioning political left, we still have a chance to achieve our country, to make it the country of Whitman's and Dewey's dreams."[25]

Rorty's language is idealistic—the goal is nothing less than "an ideally decent and civilized society." Rorty further develops this idea: "[Whitman and Dewey] wanted utopian America to replace God as the unconditional object of desire. They wanted the struggle for social justice to be the country's animating principle, the nation's soul."[26] Elsewhere Rorty reiterates the desire to substitute "social justice for individual freedom as our country's principal goal."[27]

> **SOCIAL JUSTICE:** An ambiguous term used to denote a wide range of meaning, from basic social equality to the equalization of wealth and special rights for minority groups

The Postmodern understanding of social justice revolves around the "other." Derrida's phrase "the singularity of the Other" and Rorty's term "otherness" refer to those who are marginalized by society—the poor, unemployed, migrants, Hispanics, blacks, women, gays and lesbians.[28] This is equivalent to the Marxist idea that virtue resides only among the oppressed and forms the foundation for identity politics.

Social justice in the Postmodern sense means giving oppressed groups their due in society. Oppressed groups have traditionally been identified according to their race, sex, or gender as well as their economic level. To achieve economic equality requires governmental redistribution of wealth—take from the rich and give to the poor—a common theme among leftists. Rorty refers to Dewey's utopian dream, and while Dewey was not a Postmodernist, Rorty draws from

---

[24] Alan Sears and Craig Osteen, *The Homosexual Agenda: Exposing The Principal Threat To Religious Freedom Today* (Nashville, TN: Broadman and Holman Publishers, 2003). Postmodernists approve homosexuality along with polymorphous perversity and sexuality of any kind.

[25] Richard Rorty, *Achieving Our Country: Leftist Thought in Twentieth-Century America* (Cambridge, MA: Harvard University Press, 1999), 106–7.

[26] Ibid.

[27] Ibid., 101.

[28] Women's Studies, Black Studies, Gay/Queer Studies, et. al., are taught from the Postmodernist point of view. For example, see F. Carolyn Graglia, *Domestic Tranquility: A Brief Against Feminism* (Dallas, TX: Spence Publishing, 1998).

Dewey's pragmatism to express his own political hopes. In that light, it is noteworthy that Dewey was himself the head of the League for Industrial Democracy, the American counterpart to the British Fabian Society, a socialistic organization founded in 1883.[29] Both of these organizations attempted to influence their governments toward socialism.

8.6.6 CONCLUSION

To achieve their vision for the West, Postmodernists must dismantle the present socio-political-economic system, replacing the foundational ideas of individual liberty and the rule of law based on God's moral order with the concepts of identity politics and social justice.

---

[29] For an in-depth study of the British Fabian Society, see Sister M. Margaret Patricia McCarran, *Fabianism In The Political Life Of Britain, 1919-1931* (Chicago, IL: The Heritage Foundation, 1954). For an in-depth look at John Dewey's role bringing his brand of socialism into America's public schools, see B.K. Eakman, *Cloning of The American Mind: Eradicating Morality Through Education* (Lafayette, LA: Huntington House Publishers, 1998).

Economics

Christianity

> "Better a little [wealth] with righteousness than much gain with injustice."
>
> — PROVERBS 16:8

> "Let him that stole steal no more: but rather let him labor, working with his hands the thing which is good, that he may have to give to him that needeth."
>
> — EPHESIANS 4:28

9.1.1 INTRODUCTION

Christians hold different views about which economic system is most in line with biblical teaching. Some believe the Bible encourages a system of private property and individual responsibilities and initiatives (citing Isaiah 65:21–2; Jeremiah 32:43–4; Acts 5:1–4; Ephesians 4:28). Others support a socialist economy (citing Acts 2:44–45). Still others, who are called liberation theologians, believe the Bible teaches a form of Marxism and that some form of socialism will usher in the Kingdom of God.

No economic system, however, is capable of saving us or bringing in the Kingdom of God. Nor is any single economic system perfect. Yet one is more compatible with biblical teaching and our imperfect, sinful world.

9.1.2 SOCIALISM OR FREE ENTERPRISE?

The Christian worldview must embrace either **socialism** (centralized control) or some form of **capitalism** (free enterprise or open markets). No economic system exists in its pure form in the real world—all capitalist systems contain some elements of socialism, and vice versa.

> **CAPITALISM:** An economic system in which all or most of the means of production and distribution (land, factories, railroads, etc.) are privately owned and operated for profit
>
> **SOCIALISM:** An economic system in which the ownership and operation of the means of production and distribution are controlled by the government. In Marxist thinking, socialism (i.e., abolition of private property) is the transitional phase between capitalism and communism

Ronald Nash outlines the distinctions between free market capitalism and socialism: "One dominant feature of capitalism is economic freedom, the right of people to exchange things voluntarily, free from force, fraud, and theft. Capitalism is more than this, of course, but its concern with free exchange is obvious. Socialism, on the other hand, seeks to replace the freedom of the market with a group of central planners who exercise control over essential market functions."[1]

Christians who believe socialism (or communism) is a more desirable system than capitalism do so trusting that centralized control or command economy will create a more just means of sharing scarce resources. Those who call for a socialist economic system do so on the basis of Acts 2:44–45 that describes Christians in the early church sharing all things in common. They fail to consider, however, the implications of Acts 2:46–47 that describes Christians eating with others in their homes and Acts 5:1–4 that tells of their freedom to own and sell private property.

Ronald Nash

The Bible as a whole supports an economic system that respects private property and the work ethic. (See especially Proverbs 31, Isaiah 65:21–22, Jeremiah 32:43–44, Acts 5:1–4 and Ephesians 4:28.) Rodney Stark's definition of capitalism is biblically sound: "Capitalism is an economic system wherein privately owned, relatively well-organized, and stable firms pursue complex commercial activities within a relatively free (unregulated) market, taking a systematic, long-term approach to investing and reinvesting wealth (directly or indirectly) in productive activities involving a hired workforce, and guided by anticipated and actual returns."[2]

Stark argues that capitalism centers around property rights, free markets, free labor, cash/credit, management, and a work ethic that looks upon work as a virtue, not a vice. He maintains that capitalism began in the early Christian monasteries, long before the Protestant Reformation and Adam Smith.[3]

9.1.3 PRIVATE PROPERTY

Those Christians who believe socialism is a more just economic system than capitalism argue that public ownership of property prevents the greed and envy that private ownership

[1] Ronald H. Nash, *Poverty and Wealth: The Christian Debate Over Capitalism* (Westchester, IL: Crossway Books, 1987), 63.
[2] Rodney Stark, *The Victory of Reason: How Christianity Led to Freedom, Capitalism, and Western Success* (New York, NY: Random House, 2005), 56.
[3] Ibid., 55f.

tends to create. This way of thinking, though, is incompatible with biblical teachings. Irving E. Howard says, "The commandment 'Thou shalt not steal' is the clearest declaration of the right to private property in the Old Testament."[4]

Both the Old and New Testament teach about private property and good **stewardship** of property (Genesis 23:13–20; Deuteronomy 8; Ruth 2; Isaiah 65:21–22; Jeremiah 32:42–44; Psalms 112; Proverbs 31; Micah 4:1–4; Luke 12:13–15; Acts 5:1–4; Ephesians 4:28). E. Calvin Beisner asks the pointed question,

> STEWARDSHIP: The science, art, and skill of responsible and accountable management of resources. Christians believe that God is the ultimate owner of everything and that human beings have been given the responsibility to manage and care for His creation

"Why does Scripture require restitution, including multiple restitution, in cases of theft, even if paying the restitution requires selling oneself into slavery (Exodus 22:1ff)?"[5] Ownership of property is a God-given right, and stewardship is a God-given responsibility.

Our right to own property stems from our duty to work. After God thrust Adam and Eve out of the Garden of Eden, He decreed that they (and we) would face a lifetime of hard work (Genesis 3:17–19). However, God mercifully allows our hard work to reward us with property. The very existence of private property encourages our diligence and fruitfulness: "Lazy hands make a man poor, but diligent hands bring wealth" (Proverbs 10:4).

We are accountable to God for how we use the property He allows us to own, and we are responsible to exercise wisdom in our stewardship not only of property but also of God's creation. Beisner says, "Biblical stewardship views God as Owner of all things (Psalm 24:1) and man—individually and collectively—as His steward. Every person is accountable to God for the use of whatever he has (Genesis 1:26–30; 2:15). Every person's responsibility as a steward is to maximize the Owner's return on His investment by using it to serve others (Matthew 25:14–30)."[6] We can use our property to serve others only in a society that permits private ownership.

> Biblical stewardship views God as Owner of all things, and man individually and collectively as His steward.
>
> — E. Calvin Beisner

When we understand private property in the context of godly stewardship, we are better able to concentrate on our need to work and serve others rather than accumulate more and more for our selfish purposes. In this sense, private property encourages our wise use of scarce resources, whereas publicly owned property provides no such incentive.

9.1.4 ECONOMIC COMPETITION

The Bible teaches that workers deserve their pay, and those that work hard are rewarded, while those who are lazy remain poor (Proverbs 10:4, 14:23; Luke 10:7). These teachings imply that competition in the workplace leads to fruitfulness. However, Christians who believe a socialist economic system is more biblical than a capitalist system contend that competition is evil in that it leads to greed and envy, and competition for limited resources is counterproductive.

Competition encourages cooperation in a capitalist society when we act in accordance with the *principle of comparative advantage*. This principle states that individuals in a free market economy can produce valuable goods or services by specializing in an area where there is the

---

[4] Irving E. Howard, *The Christian Alternative to Socialism* (Arlington, VA: Better Books, 1966), 4

[5] E. Calvin Beisner, *Prosperity and Poverty: The Compassionate Use of Resources in a World of Scarcity* (Westchester, IL: Crossway Books, 1988), 66.

[6] Ibid., xi–xii.

least absolute disadvantage. In other words, focusing on producing goods or services through cooperation benefits society as a whole. This in turn creates more goods and services that can benefit the poor.

Competition through comparative advantage also reinforces our worth and dignity in the sense that our work and diligence contribute to the welfare of society as a whole. Comparative advantage allows us the opportunity to become the best producer of a service or product. Thus, competition that leads to cooperation and the recognition of individual worth harmonizes with the Christian worldview, which sees human beings as image-bearers of God.

9.1.5 THE PRINCIPLE OF SOCIAL JUSTICE

Christian socialists believe that social justice to the poor demands that everyone share limited resources equally and that this principle takes precedence over all other considerations. Reconciling this principle with biblical teachings, however, is problematic. Paul teaches the relationship between work and property when he says, "For even when we were with you, we gave you this rule: 'If a man will not work, he shall not eat'" (2 Thessalonians 3:10).

God teaches us that fairness consists of not showing special favor to the rich or to the poor (Leviticus 19:15). Beisner counters the socialist interpretation of social justice when he says, "God is not 'on the side of the poor,' despite protests to the contrary. Any law, therefore, that gives an advantage in the economic sphere to anyone, rich or poor, violates Biblical justice."[7] Justice requires equality before the law rather than equality of income or ability. Justice will in fact lead to economic inequality. Beisner continues, "The Bible demands impartiality, which—because people differ in interests, gifts, capacities, and stations in life—must invariably result in conditional inequality."[8]

Biblical justice is based on equal opportunity rather than on equal distribution of wealth. Michael Novak explains, "Given the diversity and liberty of human life, no fair and free system can possibly guarantee equal outcomes. A democratic system depends for its legitimacy, therefore, not upon equal results but upon a sense of equal opportunity."[9] Equal opportunity does not mean that everyone possesses the same skills, interests, or social contacts, but that the law should prohibit no one from competing equally in the marketplace (Proverbs 31).

9.1.6 THE RICH AND THE POOR

Christian socialists believe in the equal distribution of wealth because they assume that poverty is created when the rich exploit the poor. The Bible, however, teaches many causes for poverty. Nash says, "It is certainly true that Scripture recognizes that poverty sometimes results from oppression and exploitation. But Scripture also teaches that there are times when poverty results from misfortunes that have nothing to do with exploitation. These misfortunes include such things as accidents, injuries, and illness. And of course the Bible also makes it plain that poverty can result from indigence and sloth (Proverbs 6:6–11; 13:4; 24:30–34; 28:19)."[10]

Another argument socialists make against a free market economy is that the wealthy hoard limited resources. Wealth in a free market economy, however, usually creates wealth, which can then be used to multiply goods and services that create opportunities for rich and poor alike. George Gilder explains, "Under capitalism, when it is working, the rich have the anti-Midas

---

[7] Ibid., 52.
[8] Ibid.
[9] Michael Novak, *The Spirit of Democratic Capitalism* (New York, NY: Simon and Schuster, 1982), 15.
[10] Nash, *Poverty and Wealth*, 71.

touch . . . turning gold into goods and jobs and art."[11]

The rich, then, aid the poor by constantly expanding the pool of wealth and opportunity. Gilder goes on to explain, "Most real wealth originates in individual minds in unpredictable and uncontrollable ways. A successful economy depends on the proliferation of the rich, on creating a large class of risk-taking men who are willing to shun the easy channels of a comfortable life in order to create new enterprise, win huge profits, and invest them again."[12]

9.1.7 SOURCES OF WEALTH

Socialists tend to ignore the fundamental truth that wealth comes more from the creativity and hard work fostered by free enterprise than from resources themselves. A free market economy encourages the wealthy to invest their wealth in productive enterprises, thus making jobs, goods, and services available to others.

> The only way to arrive at equal fruits is to equalize behavior and that requires robbing men of liberty, making them slaves.
>
> — E. CALVIN BEISNER

In the same sense, natural resources or raw materials, in and of themselves, are not productive. They require the application of human thought, ingenuity, and energy to make them useful. Land by itself produces only weeds and limited food, but with human work and creativity, it can produce enough fruits and vegetables to feed the entire community.

Theodore Dalrymple, in his book *Life at the Bottom: The Worldview That Makes the Underclass*, graphically illustrates the causes and psychology of poverty. Dalrymple worked as a physician and psychiatrist in the poorest areas of London, and contends that poverty is caused more by people's worldview than their lack of material goods or money. He says, "[M]ost of the social pathology exhibited by the underclass has its origin in ideas that have filtered down from the intelligentsia. Of nothing is this more true than the system of sexual relations that now prevails in the underclass, with the result that 70 percent of the births in my hospital are now illegitimate."[13] He continues, "If blame is to be apportioned, it is the intellectuals who deserve most of it. They should have known better but always preferred to avert their gaze. They considered the purity of their ideas to be more important than the actual consequences of their ideas. I know of no egotism more profound."[14] The ideas Dalrymple cites as causing the abject poverty of the inner city are ideas about sexual freedom. He says, "Intellectuals in the twentieth century sought to free our sexual relations of all social, contractual, or moral obligations and meaning whatsoever, so that henceforth only raw sexual desire itself would count in our decision making."[15] The poor bought into the package and suffer accordingly.

9.1.8 FREEDOM AND ECONOMICS

The fundamental difference between a capitalist and a socialist economic system is that capitalism trusts free markets while socialism requires a planned economy and state control of pricing, production, and distribution of goods and services. Socialism relies on increased political power and a powerful central government to achieve the goals of economic equality

[11] George Gilder, *Wealth and Poverty* (New York, NY: Basic Books, 1981), 63.

[12] Ibid, 245. For further discussion of the role of mind in economics, see Warren Brookes' work *The Economy in Mind* (New York, NY: Universe Books, 1982).

[13] Theodore Dalrymple, *Life at the Bottom: The Worldview That Makes the Underclass* (Chicago, IL: Ivan R. Dee, 2002), x.

[14] Ibid., xv.

[15] Ibid., x–xi.

and a planned economy. A case in point in the United States is the mass of counterproductive bureaucracies created by the welfare system.

In a pure capitalist economic system, far less political power is necessary because the government does not control incomes, prices, and production. Citizens are free to determine how they will spend their money and use their resources.

In a socialist economy, individuals must relinquish a great deal of control over their lives to the government. Beisner says, "The only way to arrive at equal fruits is to equalize behavior, and that requires robbing men of liberty, making them slaves."[16] Economic freedoms and the right to private property are crucial in maintaining political freedom.

9.1.9 Conclusion

The Christian worldview embraces a form of democratic capitalism that allows for the peaceful and free exchange of goods and services without fraud, theft, or breech of contract as the biblical view. First, the Bible grants us the right to private property and calls us to be good stewards of our resources. Second, a free enterprise system affords the greatest opportunity to steward our resources responsibly by creating wealth and opportunity. Third, the competition in a free market system works according to the principle of comparative advantage, which affirms our inherent worth as individuals.

The thousands of years of experiments with socialist economic systems have resulted in nothing but failure and tragedy—Fascism, Nazism, and Communism relied on the

The Pop Culture Connection

Batman Begins (a 2005 film)—"[O]ne of the most gratifying aspects of this film is its affirmation of the value of traditional institutions more generally, such as the family, rule of law, and private ownership of the means of production...What about private property?...Bruce gives his father's philanthropic vision a real entrepreneurial touch as he actively seeks to root out corruption and serve as a paragon of virtue for Gotham. Is Batman himself a microcosm for the corporate entity? Probably not purposely, but as he lays out his idea for fighting injustice as Batman, he explains to Alfred, "A man is just flesh-and-blood, and can be ignored or destroyed. But a symbol...as a symbol I can be...everlasting." Corporations, too, are symbolic. Their names represent legally distinct entities that exist indefinitely and operate independently of human conventions. This is at once a strength and weakness, primarily the former, as long as the human persons who comprise them are committed to solidarity with their neighbors, as Thomas Wayne believed. Granted that a business mogul who by night wears a cape and fights crime is far-fetched and meant to be fantastic, such films nonetheless exert a powerful influence over the popular imagination. The depiction of a morally responsible citizen who is devoted to the common good serves not only to challenge entrenched stereotypes with respect to business; it challenges us all to pursue virtue—even heroically."[17]

faulty ideas of socialism and Darwinian evolution. Their catastrophic failings are documented in Igor Shafarevich's *The Socialist Phenomenon*,[18] Ludwig von Mises' *Socialism*,[19] and Joshua Muravchik's *Heaven On Earth: The Rise And Fall Of Socialism*.[20]

[16] Beisner, *Prosperity and Poverty*, 54.

[17] "Business and Virtue in *Batman Begins*," by Ben Sikma, Advancement Associate, http://www.acton.org/ppolicy/comment/print.php?id=273.

[18] Igor Shafarevich, *The Socialist Phenomenon* (New York, NY: Harper and Row, 1980).

[19] Ludwig von Mises, *Socialism* (Indianapolis, IN: Liberty Fund Classics, 1981).

[20] Joshua Muravchik, *Heaven On Earth: The Rise And Fall Of Socialism* (San Francisco, CA: Encounter Books,

Socialism's call for economic equality is countered by capitalism's call for the biblical requirement of equality before law. The biblical view does not cause the rich to get richer and the poor poorer as socialists contend. Rather, the biblical view encourages the rich to create more wealth, thereby aiding all of society. Policies of redistribution of wealth, including welfare systems, only multiply problems for the poor by creating needless bureaucracies and concentrating too much power in the hands of the government. Capitalism, on the other hand, encourages freedom in the political sphere, minimizing the danger of granting sovereignty to the state instead of to God.

The biblical Christian worldview supports private property and free enterprise. Christians see work as a virtue, not a vice. The Greeks and Romans, in contrast, grounded their case for slavery in the idea that work is a vice, a view endorsed by both Aristotle and Plato.[21] The Bible does not teach socialism or communism, a truth evident even to Engels, who writes, "[I]f some few passages of the Bible may be favourable to Communism, the general spirit of its doctrines is, nevertheless, totally opposed to it."[22]

2002).

[21] Stark, *The Victory of Reason*, 26–7.

[22] Karl Marx and Frederick Engels, *Collected Works*, 40 vols. (New York, NY: International Publishers, 1976), 3:399.

Economics

Islam

"Islamic economics is rooted in Islam's particular worldview and derives its value-premises from the ethico-social teachings of the Quran and Sunnah."[1]

— KHURSHID AHMAD

9.2.1 INTRODUCTION

Islamic and Christian approaches to economics bear some similarities as well as some differences. As a facet of the Islamic approach to sociology, Islamic economics is "an evolving discipline" in the modern world.[2] While Islam ruled parts of the world for centuries, in more recent times Muslims have faced the trials of Western colonialism. "The Muslim society of today is not yet a society on its own," explains Syed Nawab Haider Naqvi. "It is still under the shadow of the Western system: and, as such, it is doubtful how 'representative' of the Islamic ethos its current behavior can be."[3] Naqvi implies that the contemporary economic practices and systems in Muslim nations might not finally accord with Islamic scripture, the Qur'an, or tradition.

Muslims insist that human nature, motivation, and work must reflect the ethical convictions of Islam. Thus, as Naqvi explains, "Islamic economy is part of the religion of Islam which covers the various branches of life."[4] Because of this, Muslim scholars insist that their approach to economics is superior to both the capitalism of the West and the socialism or communism of the East, precisely because both systems lack a sound religious ethic. In Islam there is neither separation nor distinction between religious and secular facets of life.

---

[1] Syed Nawab Haider Naqvi, *Islam, Economics, and Society* (London, UK: Kegan Paul International, 1994), xiii.
[2] Ibid., xiv.
[3] Ibid.
[4] Ibid., 2.

9.2.2 UNDER GOD

Muslims believe that human beings are created by God, were delegated authority over creation, and one day will give an accounting of how they have used the good resources God has provided (see Genesis 1:28). Abdalati explains, "The actual and real owner of things is God alone of Whom any proprietor is simply an appointed agent, a mere trustee."[5] Like the Christian view of economics, we term this approach to economics as stewardship of one's property and resources.

> The actual and real owner of things is God alone of Whom any proprietor is simply an appointed agent, a mere trustee.
>
> — HAMMUDA ABDALATI

The belief in final judgment, one of the five pillars of Islam, places all actions under divine scrutiny: no action is hidden from God (Qur'an 9:105), and he is the most just of all (95:8). God expects Muslims to feed the poor, give alms, help orphans, provide loans without interest (to Muslims), not hoard food, and not gamble. Islamic economics, however, is not just a series of prohibitions. Muslims are to work hard and share their wealth with fellow Muslims in need. They can earn income, amass wealth, and enjoy all good things.

9.2.3 FOUR FOUNDATIONAL PRINCIPLES

Naqvi, the National Professor in Economics of Pakistan, presents four foundational principles for the Islamic approach to economics (several of which are discussed at greater length in other disciplines, as we will note): unity, equilibrium, free will, and responsibility.

9.2.4 UNITY

In Islamic theology, God is a stark unity, a single divine person without partners. He is the Creator of all things, the one to whom all humans will give account. As such, all humans should submit to God, which is nothing other than being a Muslim (i.e., one in submission to God). This submission entails aligning all desires, ambitions, and actions with God's will, a will expressed in His commands. "My service and sacrifice, my life and my death, are all of them for God, the creator and Lord of all the worlds" (6:162). Corresponding to the unity of God is the unity of humanity. Though divided by national boundaries, fractured by war, distinguished by religious convictions, all humans are intended to be Muslims and the whole world an Islamic state. Thus, a Muslim's actions toward others bear on his or her status in the final judgment. Economic resources must never be used contrary to this vision of universal unity of the *Ummah*, the Muslim community.

9.2.5 EQUILIBRIUM

"Verily God has enjoined justice and kindness" (16:90). Muslims must reflect justice and kindness in all social institutions, including economic life. Justice and kindness relate not only to economic transactions but also to the care of the less fortunate members of society. As such, "the needs of all the least-fortunate members in Muslim society constitute the first charge on the real resources of the society," observes Naqvi.[6] Islam affirms the value of private property, as well as the inevitable economic disparity among people. But Islam also affirms that there is

---

[5] Hammuda Abdalati, *Islam in Focus* (Indianapolis, IN: American Trust Publications, 1977), 128.
[6] Ibid., 27–8.

a basic standard of living (e.g., food, clothing, shelter) due to all people. Thus regular warnings are given to the wealthy (59:7; 70:24–25).

9.2.6 FREE WILL

Muslims believe we are responsible for our beliefs and actions. Such responsibility presupposes that we have wills that allow us to choose to do right or wrong. Muslims see free will as a gift from God to be used only for good. Muslims deny that we are born with a sinful nature, but affirm that we are capable of virtue as well as of vice. Thus greed, selfishness, gluttony, exaggerated materialism and the like are expressions of our nature gone astray. Naqvi summarizes the role of free will in the following way: "In the final analysis, we can say that, notwithstanding the differences of emphasis, there has been a tacit agreement among theologians that man is responsible for his acts, and that God, by His very nature, is just in deciding man's fate according to his deeds. Concomitantly, therefore, man must have freedom of will in shaping his destiny."[7]

9.2.7 RESPONSIBILITY

Corresponding to free will is responsibility. Not only are we responsible to God, we are also responsible to our fellow humans. Almsgiving is central to being responsible in our economic activities and "mostly takes the form of giving to the poor and the needy."[8] Hoarding our wealth at the expense of the well-being of other Muslims is prohibited. "You will never come to piety unless you spend of things you love" (3:92). Muslims believe that by giving we become better people and fulfill our moral responsibility to God, ourselves, and our fellow human beings. Some even believe that generosity can atone for sins.

The Pop Culture Connection

Syriana (a 2006 film starring George Clooney and Matt Damon)—"The true distinction of Syriana's script is the near-incomprehensible plot—a muddled mix of story lines about a corrupt Kazakh oil deal, a succession struggle in an oil-rich Arab kingdom, and a giant Texas oil company that pulls the strings at the CIA....[O]nly two things are absolutely clear and coherent: the movie's one political hero and one pure soul. The political hero is the Arab prince who...intends to modernize his country by bringing the rule of law, market efficiency, women's rights, and democracy. What do you think happens to him? He, his beautiful wife, and beautiful children are murdered . . . [as] his evil younger brother, the corrupt rival to the throne and puppet of the oil company, is being [honored] at a suitably garish 'Oilman of the Year' celebration populated by fat and ugly Americans ....The most pernicious element in the movie is the character at the moral heart of the film: the beautiful, modest, caring, generous Pakistani who becomes a beautiful, modest, caring, generous . . . suicide bomber.... Syriana [presents] a pathological variety [of leftism] that burns with the certainty of its malign anti-Americanism. Osama bin Laden could not have scripted this film with more conviction."*

[7] Ibid., 35.

[8] Ibid., 32.

*Charles Krauthammer, "Oscars for Osama," *The Washington Post*, Friday, March 3, 2006; A17, http://www.washingtonpost.com/wp-dyn/content/article/2006/03/02/AR2006030201209_pf.html.

9.2.8 NEITHER CAPITALISM NOR SOCIALISM

Muslims attempt to distinguish their approach to economics from both capitalism and socialism, alleging that their view is a mediating approach. Naqvi defines socialism as centered in the abolition of private property (which was Karl Marx's definition in *The Communist Manifesto*).[9] In turn, Naqvi defines capitalism as the unlimited freedom of private property with near absolute rights, insisting that as such it divorces ethics from economics. While Naqvi acknowledges that modern capitalism may derive from Protestant ethics, he insists that capitalism is a "dedicated and unlimited pursuit of wealth through unremitting industry, rigid limitations of expenditures on personal consumption or charity, concentration of time and attention on the pursuit of one's business affairs, avoidance of distraction through intimate friendship with others, systematic and pitiless exploitation of labor and strict observance of honesty in one's relations with others within the limits set by "formal legality."[10]

> As to the ownership of private property, especially of land ownership, it has been restricted in various ways. For instance, individuals cannot own uncultivated lands, forests, grazing grounds, mines, etc. All these must be owned by the public authority for public welfare.
>
> — SYED NAWAB HAIDER NAQVI

Strangely, Naqvi here quotes a former Socialist (Heilbroner) and approves of his skewed description of capitalism. Of course, a fair definition of capitalism would have been *the free and peaceful exchange of goods and services without theft and fraud*, but such a definition would not have served Naqvi's purpose of painting capitalism in such negative tones. In reality, Naqvi is here portraying not capitalism but *libertarianism*: "Obviously, free markets run by self-interest-maximizing economic agents, who may otherwise be productively efficient, fail in many important cases to maximize social welfare."[11]

Nevertheless, Naqvi contends that Islamic economics rejects socialism's negation of private property, but also rejects capitalism's alleged absolute view of private property. "Within the framework of a set of ground rules, individual (economic) freedom should be guaranteed, but the state should be allowed to regulate it in cases where the exercise of individual freedom becomes inconsistent with social welfare."[12] Naqvi also insists that, "As to the ownership of private property, especially of land ownership, it has been restricted in various ways. For instance, individuals cannot own uncultivated lands, forests, grazing grounds, mines, etc. All these must be owned by the public authority for public welfare."[13]

Elsewhere he summarizes the Islamic view of property, noting that "Islam recognizes private property rights when acquired through one's own labor, but it has reservation with respect to the right of an individual to hold that which is not due to his labor and, with respect to landed property, which he does not cultivate himself. According to an influential view, work is the sole basis of private property holding, and that the fact of cultivation is the only justification for the private ownership of land, which as a rule should be in public ownership. One implication of this principle is that private holdings of land not being self-cultivated arenot allowed in Islam."[14]

---

[9] Karl Marx and Frederick Engels, *Collected Works*, 40 vols. (New York, NY: International Publishers, 1976), 6:498.

[10] Naqvi, *Islam, Economics, and Society*, 77.

[11] Ibid., 64.

[12] Ibid., 55.

[13] Ibid., 91.

[14] Ibid., 100–1.

To insure that all facets of Islamic economics are carried out according to Islamic principles, "the state will have to play a very important role in the Islamic economy,"[15] not merely in terms of instituting justice in economic dealings, but even meddling in the ways and means of production, distribution, and risk.

9.2.9 REDISTRIBUTING WEALTH

Economic justice requires economic well-being for all believers. To accomplish this, instituted within Islam are *zakat* (almsgiving for the sake of the poor), *jizrah* (taxes levied against unbelievers within the Islamic community), and laws regarding inheritance.

9.2.10 ZAKAT (ALMSGIVING)

The giving of alms (one of the pillars of Islam) speaks directly to the needs of the poor within the Muslim community. Every Muslim is required to give 2.5 percent ($1/40^{th}$) of his or her annual net income (income after expenses, taxes, etc.)[16] to the poor, either directly or through charities. Many mosques have boxes to receive the alms. Through the *zakat,* wealth is redistributed to the poor (including widows, orphans, the sick, and the otherwise unfortunate) for they have a fundamental right to the provisions necessary for life: food, clothing, and shelter. Some Muslims may give more than this: 2.5 percent is the minimum.[17] In some Muslim countries, the *zakat* is enforced by law, while it remains voluntary and unaccounted in others.[18] Nevertheless, it is a duty prescribed by God in the Qur'an and will be investigated at the final judgment.

The alms are to be given to Muslims only. Muslims are not mandated to help needy non-Muslims with their alms. Hammudah Abdalati lists eight groups worthy of receiving help from the *zakat*: poor Muslims, needy Muslims, new Muslim converts, Muslim prisoners of war, Muslims in debt, Muslim employees appointed by a Muslim governor for the collection of *zakat* to pay their wages, Muslims in service of the cause of God, and Muslim wayfarers.[19]

The practice of *zakat* is spoken of as a lofty vision, one that Muslim scholars and apologists present in grand terms. Abdalati expresses the effects of *zakat* on both the giver and the receiver in such language: "Zakat does not only purify the property of the contributor but also purifies his heart from selfishness and greed for wealth. In return, it purifies the heart of the recipient from envy and jealousy, from hatred and uneasiness; and it fosters in his heart, instead, good will and warm wishes for the contributor. As a result, the society at large will purify and free itself from class warfare and suspicion, from ill feelings and distrust, from corruption and disintegration, and from all such evils."[20]

While this vision is ideal—no hatred between the *haves* and the *have nots*—it also is naïve in that it fails to appreciate our fundamental sinful nature as human beings who naturally and normally expresses envy for the possessions of others. While being fed, housed, and clothed by *zakat*, it is doubtful that recipients would relinquish all envy for the larger house, finer

---

[15] Ibid., 106.

[16] Abdalati, *Islam in Focus*, 97: "His personal expenses, his family allowances, his necessary expenditures, his due credits—all are paid first, and Zakat is for the net balance."

[17] Ibid., 96.

[18] George W. Braswell, Jr., *Islam: Its Prophet, Peoples, Politics and Power* (Nashville, TN: Broadman and Holman, 1996), 65.

[19] Abdalati, *Islam in Focus*, 97–8. Alms are only for the poor, the needy, the officials charged with the duty of collection, those whose hearts are inclined to truth [i.e., Muslims], the ransoming of captives, those in debt, in the way of Allah, and the wayfarer [i.e., a traveling Muslim, especially one on pilgrimage] (Qur'an, ix 60).

[20] Abdalati, *Islam in Focus*, 95–6.

foods, and nicer clothing of others. Selfishness and greed, jealousy and envy, are part of our inherent sinful disposition that we must overcome; basic economic provisions cannot provide a complete solution.

The primary motive of *zakat* is religious and spiritual, while the social and economic aspects are subservient to it. *Zakat* is a form of worship, not a mere tax. In Islam, however, *zakat* or *sadaqa* is not a voluntary act of charity. Rather it is an obligatory act that every Muslim is enjoined to perform if he is sincere in his belief in God and the afterlife. The one who receives *zakat* feels no sense of burden or obligation, but the one who gives it is rewarded with a sense of thankfulness and gratitude to the recipient who enables him or her to discharge an obligation to God and to society.[21]

9.2.11 JIZYAH

Unbelievers in Muslim communities are called *dhimmis*. While they may be monotheists (e.g., Jews or Christians), they are not Muslims. As such, they do not enjoy the same privileges as Muslims, and they are taxed at much higher rates, rates unspecified in the Qur'an (9:29). Usually this extra tax is supposed to be in return for protection and provision as non-Muslim citizens within these communities. But how this has worked throughout history has brought much difficulty to non-Muslims.

"All taxes on trade and transport paid by Muslims were generally doubled for *dhimmis*," observes Bat Ye'or. "In addition, the population—but particularly the *Dhimmi* communities— was subject to ruinous extortions designed to cover the financing of incessant wars."[22] Because Muslims have often been at war, the non-Muslims who dare to remain in Muslim lands are fleeced to finance Muslim aggression (or, more rarely, defense). Most troubling is how these non-Muslims are treated when they cannot pay the *jizyah*. Churches have been destroyed, people have been disposed of their houses, and children have been taken and sold into slavery, as well as personal atrocities such as dismemberment, torture, and death.[23]

9.2.12 INHERITANCE

While Islam respects the individual's right to own property, that right terminates on the owner's death and the property is distributed over the next two generations.[24] Upon death, a Muslim's estate is to be divided up among relatives (2:180). Upon the death of a wife, the husband is to receive one-half of her estate, while upon the death of a husband, the wife is to receive one-quarter of his estate (4:7–12). Such practices, unequal though they are, are understood as a divine command and a way to redistribute wealth in the *Ummah*.

---

[21] Hadith Sahih Muslim, Book 5, Zakat, Introduction.

[22] Bat Ye'or, *Islam and Dhimmitude: Where Civilizations Collide*, trans. Miriam Kochan and David Littman (Madison, NJ: Fairleigh Dickinson University Press, 2002), 71.

[23] See the discussion in Stuart Robinson, *Mosques and Miracles: Revealing Islam and God's Grace*, 2nd ed. (Upper Mt. Gravatt, AUS: City Harvest Publications, 2004), 202. Robinson records that even as recent as 1997 almost fifty Christians were killed, several in a Sunday School class, apparently because they failed to pay *jizyah*.

[24] This wasn't the case when Abraham purchased a piece of property to bury his wife Sarah (Genesis 23:12–20). Abraham certainly expected "deeded property" would last more than two generations!

9.2.13 INTEREST

A distinctive feature of Islamic economics regards disallowing interest on loans (2:274–276; 3:130–131; 30:39; 2:278–279; 83:1–6). This is commonly understood to mean that when loaning money to fellow Muslims, interest on that loan is forbidden. But some Muslims wonder whether the prohibition pertains to any interest at all or to excessive or unfair interest. "Nearly all English translations of the Quran translate *riba* as usury,"[25] Naqvi observes, which suggests that excessive interest (usury), not simple interest, is what is prohibited. Nevertheless, Naqvi records that some Muslims are seeking to replace all forms of interest with something they refer to as Profit-and-Loss Sharing (PLS). These financial instruments would be commercial bank transactions offering customers an opportunity to invest in stocks and bonds and also take the risk that goes with such financial instruments. Naqvi also observes, though, that these PLS bank transactions are not doing well and perhaps the state will have to step in and make sure customer losses are not too severe.[26]

9.2.14 CONCLUSION

While the principles underlying Islamic economics are well-noted and set forth by Muslim scholars such as Abdalati and Naqvi, current economic policies and practices in Muslim nations might not (indeed, do not) bear out the ideal vision presented. "A small wealthy class rules many Muslim nations while the masses are extremely poor," observes George Braswell, Jr. "In some countries the government collects zakat; many people resent the zakat and question how the money is used. Islam prohibits usury, yet this prohibition is seldom followed either on an individual or national level." But even if these conditions are not supposed to pertain in Muslim societies, the oppression, alienation, terror, and death, and expulsion of non-Muslims remains characteristic among almost all Muslim nations.[27]

---

[25] Naqvi, *Islam, Economics, and Society*, 117.

[26] Ibid., 141–3.

[27] The Voice of the Martyrs illustrates this observation with impressive regularity (www.voiceofthemartyrs.com).

Economics

Secular Humanism

"We socialists are not ashamed to confess that we have a deep faith in man and in a vision of a new, human form of society."[1]

— ERICH FROMM

9.3.1 INTRODUCTION

Secular Humanists do not agree about the ideal economic system although most support socialism in one form or another. Robert Schaeffer writes, "Many humanists see socialism as a vital element of humanism; indeed, at one time, most humanists believed this."[2] Some former socialists, however, have realized its impracticality. Paul Kurtz has turned from socialism to free enterprise. Sidney Hook, a lifetime socialist, now acknowledges, "I no longer believe that the central problem of our time is the choice between capitalism and socialism but the defense and enrichment of a free and open society against totalitarianism."[3]

Nevertheless, Secular Humanists on the whole embrace some form of socialism because they believe in the inherent goodness of humanity and in human ability to overcome evil— theoretically the only thing that prevents a socialist economy from succeeding.

---

[1] Erich Fromm, *On Disobedience and Other Essays* (New York, NY: Seabury Press, 1981), 90.

[2] Robert Scheaffer, "Socialism is Incompatible with Humanism," *Free Inquiry* (Fall 1989): 19.

[3] Sidney Hook, *Out of Step* (New York, NY: Harper and Row, 1987), 600–1.

9.3.2 SOCIALISM AND INTERVENTIONISM

Humanist Manifesto I (1933) and *Humanist Manifesto II* (1973) call for a socialistic redistribution of wealth.[4] Many early Humanists in the United States openly proclaim the need for socialism. Corliss Lamont championed socialism for more than half a century: "I became a convinced believer in socialism as the best way out for America and the world . . . about 1931 or 1932."[5] John Dewey, a former leader of the socialistic League for Industrial Democracy, also believed socialism was the best economic system. He claims that "social control of economic forces is . . . necessary if anything approaching economic equality and liberty is to be realized."[6] Dewey's worldview coincides with that of Karl Marx in the belief that we must embrace socialism to be truly free.

> Social control of economic forces is . . . necessary if anything approaching economic equality and liberty is to be realized.
>
> — JOHN DEWEY

Erich Fromm also supported socialism: "We are not forced to choose between a managerial free-enterprise system and a managerial communist system. There is a third solution, that of democratic, humanistic socialism which, based on the original principles of socialism, offers the vision of a new, truly human society."[7]

On the other hand, John Kenneth Galbraith, a former Humanist of the Year, supports only a limited socialism, saying, "In an intelligently plural economy, a certain number of industries should be publicly owned."[8] As author of *Humanist Manifesto 2000,* Paul Kurtz calls for a free-market economy although he does not give a ringing endorsement of capitalism.[9]

One reason given for abandoning socialism is that it has never worked wherever it has been tried. Robert Sheaffer says, "[N]o intellectually honest person today can deny that the history of socialism is a sorry tale of economic failure and crimes against humanity."[10] Since Humanists are also pragmatists, they prefer an economic system that truly serves the people. Marvin Zimmerman writes, "I contend that the evidence supports the view that democratic capitalism is more productive of human good than democratic socialism."[11]

> **INTERVENTIONISM:** Political activity undertaken by a state to influence aspects of the economy usually in order to uphold certain moral values

Secular Humanists, whether leaning toward capitalism or socialism, favor some degree of government intervention in the economy in the form of a redistribution of wealth. **Interventionism** expresses the belief that the state has a responsibility to manage and direct some aspects of the economy in order to uphold certain moral values.

---

[4] Socialists love to distribute wealth that they have not created! See Igor Shafarevich, *The Socialist Phenomenon* (New York, NY: Harper and Row, 1980); Ludwig von Mises, *Socialism* (Indianapolis, IN: Liberty Classics, 1981); Tom Bethell, *The Noblest Triumph*: *Property and Prosperity Through the Ages* (New York, NY: St. Martin Press, 1998); Joshua Muravchik, *Heaven on Earth: The Rise and Fall of Socialism* (San Francisco, CA: Encounter Books, 2002).

[5] Corliss Lamont, *Voice in the Wilderness* (Buffalo, NY: Prometheus Books, 1975), 1

[6] John Dewey, *Liberalism and Social Action* (New York, NY: G.P. Putnam's Sons, 1935), 356–7.

[7] Fromm, *On Disobedience and Other Essays*, 74.

[8] John Kenneth Galbraith, *Economics, Peace and Laughter* (Boston, MA: Houghton Mifflin, 1971), 101.

[9] In fact, Kurtz doesn't mention the word capitalism. Ever since Karl Marx made the word a "forbidden" expression, liberals like Kurtz have shied away from it. See Paul Kurtz, *Humanist Manifesto 2000: A Call for a New Planetary Humanism* (Amherst, NY: Prometheus Books, 2000), 60.

[10] Sheaffer, "Socialism is Incompatible with Humanism," 19.

[11] Paul Kurtz, ed., *Sidney Hook: Philosopher of Democracy and Humanism* (Buffalo, NY: Prometheus Books, 1983), 80.

9.3.3 THE MORAL BASIS FOR SOCIALISM

Most Secular Humanists embrace socialism on moral grounds. Hook says, "In my case, as in so many others, allegiance to socialism at first appeared to be primarily the articulation of a feeling of moral protest against remediable evils that surrounded us."[12] Both Lamont and Dewey also chose socialism on ethical grounds. Lamont writes, "My own path to socialism, therefore, was that of analysis through reason, combined with belief in a humanist ethics and a deep attachment to democracy in its broadest sense."[13] Dewey's concept of liberty implies a moral ground for choosing socialism: "But the cause of liberalism will be lost for a considerable period if it is not prepared to go further and socialize the forces of production, now at hand, so that the liberty of individuals will be supported by the very structure of economic organization."[14] Dewey adopts an "ends justify the means" approach to economics, stating that a "socialized economy is the means of free individual development as the end."[15]

> ## The Pop Culture Connection
>
> ***John Q*** (a 2002 film starring Denzel Washington)—This movie presents an emotional case for governmental healthcare coverage for all its citizens. John's son needs a heart transplant, but since he has no health insurance and no money to pay for it, the hospital administrator and surgeon refuse to treat the boy. Although this movie highlights some of the flaws of the current health insurance system, it is by no means guaranteed that a government-run system would provide for the needs of its citizens more efficiently or more equitably.

Humanists believe socialism is more ethical than other economic systems because it allows greater freedom and it is more concerned with the common good. Fromm explains, "The aim of socialism is an association in which the full development of each is the condition for the full development of all."[16] Because Secular Humanists use humanity rather than God as the measure of morality, the common good of humanity is paramount. The utilitarian concept of "the greatest amount of happiness for the greatest number of people" can best be achieved through the equal distribution of work and wealth, allowing more people to reach the Humanist goal of self-actualization.

9.3.4 THE FAILURE OF CAPITALISM

Besides embracing socialism on moral grounds, Secular Humanists choose socialism because of the evils they see inherent in capitalism. Fromm explains, "The giant corporations which control the economic, and to a large degree the political, destiny of the country constitute the very opposite of the democratic process; they represent power without control by those submitted to it."[17] Fromm not only believes that socialism is a more democratic economic system, he also believes it has the potential to reduce our focus on consumption and restore our damaged humanity.

Lamont cites the "tremendous waste inherent in the capitalist system and its wanton exploitation of men and natural resources"[18] as reason for embracing socialism. His distrust

---

[12] Hook, *Out of Step*, 30.

[13] Lamont, *Voice in the Wilderness*, 164.

[14] Dewey, *Liberalism and Social Action*, 88.

[15] Ibid., 90.

[16] Fromm, *On Disobedience and Other Essays*, 75–6.

[17] Ibid., 62.

[18] Lamont, *Voice in the Wilderness*, 166.

of capitalism runs so deep that he says: "Since fascism is simply capitalism stripped of all democratic pretenses and other unessentials—capitalism in the nude, as it were—the danger of fascism remains as long as the capitalist system is with us."[19]

Dewey believes that capitalism must create artificial scarcity to operate successfully, and this contrived scarcity is the cause of poverty and hunger. He says, "There is an undoubted objective clash of interests between finance-capitalism that controls the means of production and whose profit is served by maintaining relative scarcity, and idle workers and hungry consumers."[20] He views this as a blatant infringement on individual liberty.

Humanists believe that capitalism promotes materialism, strips us of our humanity, and creates artificial scarcity. The implication is that socialism has the potential to ameliorate these flaws inherent in a capitalist economy.

9.3.5 SPECIFICS FOR THE TRANSITION TO SOCIALISM

Secular Humanists who advance socialism as the preferred economic system acknowledge some of the hurdles that must be overcome before full-fledged socialism becomes a reality in the United States. Hook, for example, realizes the need to engineer each job so that it grants value to the worker. He says, "But until some way can be found to organize a society in which everyone's way of earning a living is at the same time a satisfactory way of living his or her life, there will always be a problem of incentive."[21]

Lamont recommends a government purchase of all the means of production through a process that would compensate the rightful owners and honor the United States Constitution. He specifies neither how a fair price would be determined nor the source of the purchase money, however.

Once these and other intermediate problems are solved, Secular Humanists Lamont, Dewey, Fromm, and Sellars all agree that a redistribution of wealth in the form of a guaranteed income for everyone is the means to achieve a more equal society. A guaranteed income conforms to Dewey's concept of liberty in that it would grant us economic independence and at the same time restore our lost humanity.

9.3.6 CONCLUSION

A socialist system of economics is consistent with the Secular Humanist worldview. Although some support a free market economy, many of those who shaped Secular Humanist thought in the last century were socialists.

If we deny our fallen nature, some form of socialism becomes the most attractive economic system for creating a heaven on earth. If original sin does not exist, then a community of mutual cooperation and sharing of work and wealth becomes a possibility. Socialism or some degree of interventionism becomes the economic system best suited to promote the ethics of Secular Humanism and rectify the evils of capitalism.

> If we deny our inherent fallen nature, some form of socialism becomes the most attractive economic system for creating a heaven on earth.

---

[19] Ibid., 169. Lamont is clearly confused about economic theories. In reality, fascism is more closely akin to socialism than to capitalism, for while fascism leaves titular ownership of productive property in private hands, it insists that only the central government should control productive property. Capitalist philosophy has always held that control is an essential element of ownership. The only difference between fascism and socialism, therefore, is that the former allows people to hold legal title to capital, but neither allows them to control it.

[20] Dewey, *Liberalism and Social Action*, 79–80.

[21] Hook, *Out of Step*, 600.

Over the past century, socialism has been instituted in the former Soviet Union, China, Cuba, North Korea, and a host of other Latin American, South American, and African countries. Socialism has failed in every case to change human nature for the better. Yet because of a commitment to evolution, Secular Humanists believe that socialism is part of the next step in humanity's advancement. Many believe the move to socialism in the United States is inevitable. Dewey predicts, "We are in for some kind of socialism, call it by whatever name we please, and no matter what it will be called when it is realized."[22]

Nothing illustrates Dewey's prediction better than a careful reading of Jonah Goldberg's Liberal Fascism: The Secret History of the American Left from Mussolini to the Politics of Meaning. The expression "politics of meaning" refers to "all of society's institutions [family, school, church, workplace] are wrapped around the state." Indeed, as Goldberg says, "The politics of meaning is ultimately a theocratic doctrine because it seeks to answer the fundamental questions about existence, argues that they can only be answered collectively, and insists that the state put those answers into practice."[23]

---

[22] John Dewey, *Individualism, Old and New* (Amherst, NY: Prometheus Books, 1999), 119.

[23] Jonah Goldberg, *Liberal Fascism: The Secret History of the American Left from Mussolini to the Politics of Meaning* (New York, NY: Doubleday, 2007), 336.

Economics

Marxism—Leninism

"Communist society means that everything—the land, the factories—is owned in common. Communism means working in common."[1]

— V.I. LENIN

9.4.1 INTRODUCTION

The economic system plays a much larger role in the Marxist worldview than in that of either Christianity or Secular Humanism. For Marxists, the economic system determines laws, the type of government, and the role of society in day-to-day life. While most would agree that an economic system affects these areas to some extent, Marxists claim that it dictates their precise character. With this in mind, Marxists conclude that undesirable economic systems create backward, undesirable societies. They point to the evils in a capitalist society and conclude that capitalism, based on private property, is a bad economic system that must be replaced with a more humane system, one that abolishes private property and the free and peaceful exchange of goods and services (a free market).

According to Marx, the key problem with capitalism is that it breeds exploitation of the workers. Marx says that in a capitalist society, the bourgeoisie (property-owners) equate personal worth with exchange value, leading to "naked, shameless, direct, brutal exploitation."[2]

---

[1] V.I. Lenin, *Selected Works*, 38 vols. (New York, NY: International Publishers, 1937), 9:479.

[2] Karl Marx and Frederick Engels, *Collected Works*, 40 vols. (New York, NY: International Publishers, 1976), 6:487.

9.4.2 THE EVILS OF CAPITALISM

For Marx, two flaws necessarily cause capitalism to be a system of exploitation. The first flaw is the problem of surplus labor. According to this concept, the bourgeoisie profit not by selling their product at a price above the cost of materials plus labor, but rather by paying the worker less than the value of their labor. This ability of the bourgeoisie to manipulate workers allows them to devalue labor, thereby creating profit for themselves by lowering the price of labor. Marxists see capitalism as creating a vicious circle that causes workers to be exploited more and more. Marx explains, "Accumulation of wealth at one pole is, therefore, at the same time accumulation of misery, agony of toil, slavery, ignorance, brutality, mental degradation, at the opposite pole . . . "[3]

The second flaw in capitalism is its chaotic nature. Whereas the state can control every aspect of socialism from production to distribution, capitalism is controlled by the free market. (Technically, capitalism is known as a market-directed economy and social-ism as a centrally planned economy although in practice most economies are a mixture of both.) In a socialistic system, economic decisions regarding price, production, and consumption are made by central planners affiliated with the government. In a capitalistic system, economic decisions are made by every producer and every consumer—a housewife with a shop-ping list, for example, is an economic planner in a capitalistic system. Marxism stresses this difference, claiming that only a planned economy can truly discover the best methods of production and distribution. Marxists believe that capitalist economies thrive on crises that tend to stimulate them. Marx believed this reliance on crises would create economic havoc in the long run, and therefore advocated that a planned community replace such a spontaneous, erratic, freewheeling system.

> ### The Pop Culture Connection
>
> ***Batman Begins*** (a 2005 film)—"Like a hideous gargoyle believed to protect ancient institutions from evil, the motionless silhouette of Batman stands out against Gotham's dark cityscape. This arresting image from *Batman Begins* suggests that the bad guys are in for another hard time from the Dark Knight. But what is peculiar about this latest foray into comic book film noir is that Batman's alter ego, Bruce Wayne, represents what would usually be an inviting object of attack by film writers and producers: Bruce is fabulously rich, the "prince of Gotham," and his wealth was inherited. Instead, the unlikely hero uses all his resources—virtue, physical prowess, and capital—to fight injustice, even to the point of engaging in a hostile takeover of a publicly traded company. Although the central theme of *Batman Begins* is how Bruce controls his own phobia (bats) and redirects it to fight fear (personified in the villain Scarecrow), the film also presents a picture of a businessman...that overcomes stereotypes about such people as almost inevitably corrupt, unethical, and heartless ....The film seems to present the view that the wealthy Wayne family can be highbrow, have and enjoy their status symbols—essentially live the bourgeois lifestyle—and still be virtuous people. Karl Marx must be rolling in his grave."

---

[3] Karl Marx, *Capital* (London, UK: Sonnenschein, 1982), 660–1. Cited in Harry W. Laidler, *History of Socialism* (New York, NY: Thomas Y. Crowell, 1968), 152–3.

[4] Ben Sikma, "Business and Virtue in *Batman Begins*," http://www.acton.org/ppolicy/comment/print.php?id=273.

9.4.3 THE SELF-DESTRUCTION OF CAPITALISM

Marxists believe that capitalism eventually destroys itself as it exploits more and more people until everyone has been reduced to worker status. Engels explains the process: "Whilst the capitalist mode of production more and more completely transforms the great majority of the population into proletarians, it creates the power which, under penalty of its own destruction, is forced to accomplish this revolution. [Eventually] The proletariat seizes political power and turns the means of production into state property."[5]

In this way, the proletariat acts as a catalyst for the downfall of capitalism and the rise of the new socialist system. "The extremely sharp class conflict between the exploiters and the exploited constitutes the basic trait of the capitalist system. The development of capitalism inevitably leads to its downfall. However, the system of exploitations does not disappear of itself. It is destroyed only as the result of the revolutionary struggle and the victory of the proletariat."[6]

The concept of the dialectic illustrates that the downfall of capitalism and the subsequent rise of socialism and eventually communism are inevitable. The bourgeoisie (thesis) and the proletariat (antithesis) clash to create socialism (synthesis) that guarantees the advent of communism. The dialectic, if carried forward, also guarantees that communism cannot be the final synthesis.

9.4.4 DIFFERENCES BETWEEN SOCIALISM AND COMMUNISM

Socialism and communism are not identical. Marxists believe that socialism is the first phase or first step in the transition to communism, the perfect economic system. The *Political Dictionary* explains the difference between the two systems: "Socialism is the first phase of communism. The principle of socialism is: from each according to his abilities, to each according to his work . . . Under communism the basic principle of society will be: from each according to his abilities, to each according to his needs."[7]

Socialism is the phase in history when the proletariat seizes both the means of production and the state. The arrival of communism will occur when the government has withered away because classes have ceased to exist and no one owns the means of production (it is owned in common). Lenin describes communism as "means working in common."[8] In this perfect economic system, the ideal is that everyone will freely work together to produce the necessary goods and services.

> Socialism is the first phase of communism. The principle of socialism is: from each according to his abilities, to each according to his work . . . Under communism the basic principle of society will be: from each according to his abilities, to each according to his needs.
>
> — POLITICAL DICTIONARY

---

[5] Frederick Engels, *Socialism: Utopian and Scientific* (New York, NY: International Publishers, 1935), 69.
[6] Raymond Sleeper, ed., *A Lexicon of Marxist-Leninist Semantics* (Alexandria, VA: Western Goals, 1983), 30.
[7] Ibid., 249.
[8] Lenin, *Selected Works*, 9:479.

9.4.5 The Transition to Pure Communism

Engels explains why the transition from socialism to communism must be gradual. Because private property cannot be abolished all at once, "the proletarian revolution . . . will transform existing society only gradually, and be able to abolish private property only when the necessary quantity of the means of production has been created."[9] Marx says, "Between capitalist and communist society lies a period of revolutionary transformation from one to the other."[10] Lenin explains that the transitional phase of socialism will be a blend of capitalism and communism: "Theoretically, there can be no doubt that between capitalism and communism there lies a definite transition period which must combine the features and properties of both these forms of social economy."[11] Engels describes the features of the inevitable communist society: "Finally, when all capital, all production, and all exchange are concentrated in the hands of the nation, private ownership will automatically have ceased to exist, money will have become superfluous, and production will have so increased and men will be so much changed that the last forms of the old social relations will also be able to fall away."[12]

9.4.6 The Transition in Practice

The transition to a communist society in actuality has not been smooth. In 1918, Marxists attempted to rapidly institute socialism in Russia by seizing land from its owners. The Soviet constitution proclaimed "all private property in land is abolished, and the entire land is declared to be national property and is to be apportioned among agriculturists without any compensation to the former owners, in the measure of each one's ability to till it."[13]

Lenin realized quickly that the Russian economy would never survive such a rapid move to socialism. In 1921, he declared, "We are no longer attempting to break up the old social economic order, with its trade, its small-scale economy and private initiative, its capitalism, but we are now trying to revive trade, private enterprise, and capitalism, at the same time gradually and cautiously subjecting them to state regulation just as far as they revive."[14]

> One out of every ten idlers will be shot on the spot.
>
> — V.I. Lenin

Lenin was also quick to justify his reasons for this move backwards toward capitalism. He says, "Capitalism is an evil in comparison with socialism, but capitalism is a blessing in comparison with medievalism, with small industry, with fettered small producers thrown to the mercy of bureaucracy."[15] Lenin explained that before Russia could arrive at pure communism, it must revert to capitalism and advance through its stages.

During the transition period, Lenin experimented with a number of social methods to hasten the arrival of socialism and communism. In trying to find the best method for dealing with those who did not do their fair share of the work, he suggested imprisonment, forced labor, and "one out of every ten idlers will be shot on the spot."[16]

[9] Marx and Engels, *Collected Works*, 6:350.

[10] Cited in Kenneth N. Cameron, *Marxism: The Science of Society* (Boston, MA: Bergin & Garvey, 1985), 97.

[11] V.I. Lenin, *Collected Works*, 45 vols. (Moscow, USSR: Progress Publishers, 1980), 30:107.

[12] Marx and Engels, *Collected Works*, 6:351.

[13] Laidler, *History of Socialism*, 384.

[14] *Pravda*, Nov. 7, 1921.

[15] Laidler, *History of Socialism*, 390.

[16] Lenin, *Collected Works*, 26:414–5.

9.4.7 THE COMMUNIST UTOPIA

Worldwide communism will usher in a number of benefits. Marxists claim that communism provides more freedom than other economic systems. Humanity will have achieved perfection, making the law and government moot. The redistribution of wealth will solve many problems. The text *Political Economy* explains some of them: "Once the exploiting classes with their parasitic consumption have been abolished, the national income becomes wholly at the disposal of the people. Working conditions are radically altered, housing conditions in town and country substantially improved and all the achievements of modern culture made accessible to the working people."[17]

Another advantage of communism has to do with the motivation of workers: "Can capitalist society with its chronic unemployment ensure each citizen the opportunity to work, let alone to choose the work he likes? Clearly, it cannot. But the socialist system makes the right to work a constitutional right of a citizen, delivering him from the oppressive anxiety and uncertainty over the morrow."[18]

In short, Marxists believe communism is the ideal economic system and the foundation for utopia in all aspects of society.

9.4.8 CONCLUSION

The move from capitalism to socialism to communism and the classless society is inevitable, according to the dialectic. Capitalism contains its own fatal flaw, and it cannot stop its advance toward socialism just as socialist countries such as the People's Republic of China cannot stop their advance toward communism. When communism becomes the world's economic system, the dialectical march toward utopia will have reached its zenith. Kenneth Neill Cameron explains, "Marx and Engels expected that communist society would be the last form of human society, for once the world's productive forces were communally owned no other form could arise."[19]

In the Marxist worldview, nothing could be more ideal, and according to Lenin nothing else will allow the survival of the human race. He says, "Outside of socialism, there is no salvation for mankind from war, hunger and the further destruction of millions and millions of human beings."[20]

In reality, however, the Marxist system itself is responsible for the destruction of millions of human beings at the hands of its political parties and dictators, making it the greatest killing machine of all time.[21]

---

[17] G.A. Kozlov, ed., *Political Economy: Socialism* (Moscow, USSR: Progress Publishers, 1977), 55.

[18] Sleeper, *A Lexicon of Marxist-Leninist Semantics*, 302.

[19] Cameron, *Marxism: The Science of Society*, 85.

[20] John Strachey, *The Theory and Practice of Socialism* (New York, NY: Random House, 1936), title page.

[21] Stephane Courtois, et al., *The Black Book Of Communism* (Cambridge, MA: Harvard University Press, 1999) and R.J. Rummel, *Death By Government* (New Brunswick, NJ: Transaction Publishers, 1994).

Economics

Cosmic Humanism

> "Like everything else, money is either holy or unholy,
> depending on the purposes ascribed to it by the mind.
> We tend to do with money what we do with sex: we desire
> it but we judge the desire. It is the judgment that then
> distorts the desire, turning it into an ugly expression."[1]
>
> — MARIANNE WILLIAMSON

9.5.1 INTRODUCTION

Cosmic Humanist economic theory is shaped by the need for a world system of self-government. In this light, some Cosmic Humanists call for a universal system of exchange. Vera Alder describes the monetary system of the future: "As . . . individual needs would largely be supplied on the ration-card system, the need for handling of money would dwindle. There would, of course, be a universal currency the world over. There would be a central bank."[2]

Because of their belief in individual autonomy, Cosmic Humanists do not discuss specifics of a world economic system just as they avoid concrete political declarations or definitive legal systems. Marilyn Ferguson believes, "Both capitalism and socialism, as we know them, pivot on material values. They are inadequate philosophies for a transformed society."[3]

---

[1] Marianne Williamson, *Return to Love: Reflections on the Principles of "A Course in Miracles"* (New York, NY: HarperCollins, 1989), 168.

[2] Vera Alder, *When Humanity Comes of Age* (New York, NY: Samuel Weiser, 1974), 48–9.

[3] Marilyn Ferguson, *The Aquarian Conspiracy* (Los Angeles, CA: J.P. Tarcher, 1980), 326–7.

All concern with the marketplace will be moot in the coming transformed New Age. People of the future will not be concerned with choosing vocations that will meet their needs or those of their neighbors. Rather, people will choose vocations in accordance with their inner voice, the voice of God. Coupled with a reliance on our inner voice is the belief that positive thought creates wealth, often called **universal enlightened production**.

> **UNIVERSAL ENLIGHTENED PRODUCTION:** The belief that positive thought creates wealth

9.5.2 HIGHER CONSCIOUSNESS = HIGHER INCOME

Cosmic Humanists believe that if we all allow our inner voice to lead us, no one in society will want for anything. Shakti Gawain says, "We make a contribution to the world just by being ourselves in every moment. There are no more rigid categories in our lives—this is work, this is play. It all blends into the flow of following the universe and money flows in as a result of the open channel that's created. You no longer work in order to make money. Work is no longer something you have to do in order to sustain life. Instead, the delight that comes from expressing yourself becomes the greatest reward.[4] Gawain also says, "The more you are willing to trust yourself, and take the risks to follow your inner guidance, the more money you will have. The universe will pay you to be yourself and do what you really love!"[5]

Randall Baer concurs with Gawain on the results of positive thinking. In New Age success philosophy, "the more attuned a person is to the 'Universal Mind' the more the universe will demonstrate this level of enlightenment by mirroring more 'god-money in action.' The more enlightened a person is, the more money and success will naturally occur in life."[6]

To Cosmic Humanists, God wants us to prosper materially, and by getting in touch with our higher consciousness, we are able to ensure ourselves a high income. Williamson believes that if we want something and focus on it, we will probably attain it. But God may want us to have something even better, so our focus should be more on attaining higher consciousness than on material blessings. Williamson believes that we can trust the world to grant us material blessings because we, as part of God, ultimately control reality. She believes that "[o]ur purpose on this earth is to be happy."[7] In a similar vein, Kevin Ryerson says, "God does not work for you; God works through you."[8]

9.5.3 CONCLUSION

Cosmic Humanists tend not to be concerned with economic theory because economic systems are only applicable in unenlightened societies. When people achieve higher consciousness, the God within will lead them to make wise economic decisions, and economic systems will cease being necessary.

People who are led by their higher consciousness will achieve material success and need not be concerned about the success or failure of particular economic systems. Poverty will thus gradually disappear as more and more people are led by the God within.

Since human nature is basically good, we can solve our economic dilemmas as we get in touch with our goodness. Cosmic Humanists believe Christians are wrong to believe that we have a sinful nature. According to Shirley MacLaine, greed, envy, slander, theft, covetousness,

---

[4] Shakti Gawain, *Living in the Light* (San Rafael, CA: New World Library, 1986), 110.

[5] Ibid., 142.

[6] Randall N. Baer, *Inside the New Age Nightmare* (Lafayette, LA: Huntington House, 1989), 140.

[7] Ibid., 171.

[8] Kevin Ryerson, *Spirit Communication: The Soul's Path* (New York, NY: Bantam Books, 1989), 160.

etc., are only "a manifestation of the need for human love"[9]

In the New Age, greed and poverty will cease to exist. People will work together harmoniously to increase and share wealth. Williamson says that "God does not require sacrifice."[10] Rather, the God within wants to bless us with happiness and material success.

---

[9] Shirley MacLaine, *Out on a Limb* (New York, NY: Bantam Books, 1989), 291.
[10] Williamson, *Return to Love*, 158.

Economics

Postmodernism

"It is possible to choose (and to persuade others of the advantages of) socialism over capitalism."[1]

— DAVID F. RUCCIO AND JACK AMARIGLIO

"Just about the only constructive suggestion Marx made, the abolition of private property, has been tried. It did not work."[2]

—RICHARD RORTY

9.6.1 INTRODUCTION

The quotations above by Rorty and Ruccio and Amariglio illustrate one of the hurdles to understanding Postmodern economics—a lack of consensus among Postmodernists. Another hurdle is that Postmodernists tend not to use traditional language associated with economics—wages, pensions, interest rates, inflation, Social Security, retirement, etc. Instead, they use obscure words and phrases such as fragmentation, differentiation, chronology, pastiche, anti-foundationalism, and pluralism. More terminology that obscures meaning includes "the undecidability of meaning, the textuality of discursivity of knowledge, the inconceivability of

---

[1] David F. Ruccio and Jack Amariglio, *Postmodern Moments in Modern Economics* (Princeton, NJ: Princeton University Press, 2003), 299.
[2] Richard Rorty, *Philosophy and Social Hope* (New York, NY: Penguin Books, 1999), 214.

pure 'presence,' the irrelevance of intention, the insuperability of authenticity, the impossibility of representation, the celebration of play, difference, plurality, chance, inconsequence, and marginality."[3]

Confusion even surrounds the meaning of the word *person* in Postmodern economic terms. Postmodern economists Ruccio and Amariglio, authors of *Postmodern Moments in Modern Economics*, explain, "The Postmodern condition opens up a very different research agenda for economic scientists should they choose to disown (what many regard as a necessary fiction) the unified self and move, instead to a fiction supposedly more in tune with contemporary reality, the decentered self."[4]

Ruccio and Amariglio expose the heart of Postmodern economics—and to understand them, we must define *unified self* and *decentered self* and why they are said to be fictions.

9.6.2 THE BASIC ECONOMIC UNIT: THE DECENTERED SELF

Economics flows from our understanding of the human person. Postmodern psychology sees human beings as fictions—meaning there is no unified, rational self and no permanent understanding of who we are. Rather, what we call human beings Postmodernists call social constructions.

Ruccio and Amariglio say there is "no singular and unique 'I.'"[5] In other words, there is no self-identity and no permanent soul or mind. Postmodernists refer to human beings not as persons, but as subjects, bodies, or units. *Person* suggests the existence of a *singular and unique I* who possesses a personality or *human nature*. To Postmodernists, there is no human nature. There is only an ever evolving, highly sexual, social animal with multiple subjective interests crying out for recognition and acceptance. Ruccio and Amariglio admit they have "no interest in determining or representing what the body [subject] 'really' looks like."[6]

Our common understanding of self corresponds to our perception of gender and sex. However, in the Postmodern view, these two terms are not synonymous. Being born with a male or female anatomy thus does not make us male or female because these concepts are socially constructed fictions. Ruccio and Amariglio say, "Regardless of biological sex," human beings can be "gendered in different ways."[7] Thus, according to the Postmodernist way of seeing things, there are no longer only two sexes—male and female–but a multiplicity of genders, including, but not limited to, heterosexual, homosexual, bi-sexual, trans-sexual, etc. All sexualities are socially and economically constructed and must be considered in any emerging economic theory and practice.[8]

One of the major goals of Postmodern economics is to eliminate the distinction between men and women, a distinction that has been "inculcated by an oppressive patriarchal society."[9] The goal is to eliminate patriarchal society itself and elevate the economic realities of gendered subjects (women, homosexuals, bisexuals, etc.). The goal includes creating more equitable work environments for all subjects in fields that are viewed to be presently monopolized by heterosexual males—the military and the clergy, for example.

Postmodern economics is built on several interlocking concepts. First, every subject's perception of self is shaped by the surrounding culture. Second, these perceptions are *fictions*

---

[3] Ruccio and Amariglio, *Postmodern Moments in Modern Economics*, 17–8.

[4] Ibid., 14.

[5] Ibid., 167.

[6] Ibid., 134.

[7] Ibid., 169.

[8] Ibid., 129.

[9] *The Washington Times*, April 21, 2005, A2.

in the sense that they are stories we have been told by our society. Third, these stories do not correspond to anything objective or eternal, and they vary from culture to culture and over time.

9.6.3 SOCIALISM OVER CAPITALISM

Building on the conviction that human units are interchangeable, Postmodernists critique our understanding of gender in Western culture as oppressive and outmoded. Historically, Western economic systems were based on a male-dominated society. Men are said to have had an upper hand because they constructed society and its corresponding economic structure to their advantage. Therefore, in order to create a society with equal opportunities for all subjects, this male-dominated system must be dismantled. Since men will not willingly relinquish their economic power to women and the poor, the government must intervene to see that economic justice is available to all. Socialism, or a state-planned economy, is such an intervention.

Postmodernists thus denounce male-dominated capitalism because it produces "one-sided" individuals who lack the ability to perceive the whole. Socialism, by contrast, "allows potentially all of its members to see the whole."[10] In other words, capitalism speaks primarily to heterosexual maleness, while socialism speaks to the "total" decentered subjects of numerous genders with its "many different subjectivities simultaneously none of which is given privilege as representing the subject's real essence, whether natural or historical . . . and without a goal or end to which they are moving."[11]

Some Postmodernists prefer to replace the term *socialism* with *everyday economics*.[12] An older term is collectivism. Whatever name is used, there is a consistent denunciation of capitalism, while Postmodernists criticize in several ways: 1) "profits seem to have a higher priority than people; 2) stress on workers is grueling; and 3) U.S. citizens are being fleeced by banks and pharmaceutical companies and utilities and energy companies and HMOs and big, international companies in general [numbers added]."[13]

Stephen Hicks provides perspective to the Postmodern view of economics: "Postmodern thinkers inherit an intellectual tradition that has seen the defeat of all of its major hopes, but there was always socialism. As bad as the philosophical universe became in metaphysics, epistemology, and the study of human nature, there was still the vision of an ethical and political order that would transcend everything and create the beautiful collectivist society."[14]

9.6.4 INTERVENTIONISM OVER SOCIALISM

While many Postmodernists advocate a whole-hearted socialist agenda, others are critical of how socialism has been implemented in the past. Some Postmodern theorists go so far as to claim that Postmodernism is "fueled by the failure of Marxian-inspired State socialism."[15] In this regard, Mills writes that Foucault reacted against ". . . the purely economic and State-centered focus [of socialism and nationalism] . . . stressing that power needs to be reconceptualized and

---

[10] Ruccio and Amariglio, *Postmodern Moments in Modern Economics*, 250.

[11] Ibid., 249.

[12] Ibid., 270.

[13] Ibid., 269.

[14] Stephen R.C. Hicks, *Explaining Postmodernism: Skepticism and Socialism from Rousseau to Foucault* (Tempe, AZ: Scholargy Publishing, 2004), 197.

[15] Anthony Thomson, "Post-Modernism and Social Justice," citing Stuart Henry and Dragan Milovanovic, *Constitutive Criminology: Beyond Postmodernism* (London, UK: Sage, 1996), 4. Available online at http://ace.acadiau.ca/soci/agt/constitutivecrim.htm.

the role of the State, and the function of the economic, need a radical revisioning."[16] Toward the end of his life, Foucault even began encouraging his students to read "libertarian authors on the right like Friedrich A. Hayek and Ludwig von Mises."[17]

Richard Rorty looked at the history of socialism and came to the conclusion that, practically speaking, it was a failure. Rorty writes, "Just about the only constructive suggestion Marx made, the abolition of private property, has been tried. It did not work."[18]

While the utopian promise of socialism has much emotional appeal, the actual results where socialism has been implemented were increased poverty and greater class division, in addition to the millions of citizens slaughtered in the attempt to maintain a state-run monopoly. Rorty criticizes socialism and offers an alternative. He writes, "Most people on my side of this . . . cultural war have given up on socialism in light of the history of nationalization enterprises and central planning in Central and Eastern Europe. We are willing to grant that welfare-state capitalism is the best we can hope for. Most of us who were brought up Trotskyite now feel forced to admit that Lenin and Trotsky did more harm than good."[19]

Rorty is suggesting that an interventionist approach to economics works best. Interventionism is not a totally state-planned economy or a completely free market economy, but a combination of the two, where the state plays a role in redistributing wealth created in a partially or mostly free market environment. Rorty refers to this as *welfare-state capitalism*.

While most Postmodernists repudiate any references to purpose or goals, Rorty is different. He believes that economic theory should have the goal of alleviating human suffering. Rorty is so committed to this goal that he calls it the "transcultural imperative."[20] He sees an interventionist economy as the best way to decrease human suffering. As he told a college audience in 1999, "The non-West has a lot of justified complaints to make about the West, but it does owe a lot to Western ingenuity. The West is good at coming up with devices for lessening human suffering . . . These devices are used to prevent the strong from having their way with the weak and, thereby, to prevent the weak from suffering as much as they would have otherwise."[21]

9.6.5 THE NEED FOR EXPERIMENTATION

Other Postmodernists, however, believe Rorty is too optimistic. They are convinced that every economic system to date has failed in one way or another. Iain Grant writes, ". . . if the tools of the past—Marxism, the Enlightenment project, market liberalism and so on—have been tried and found wanting, then [as Lyotard suggested] experiment is demanded."[22] Here, Postmodernists acknowledge that all economic theories have failed, and therefore the best we can do is keep experimenting as we go. Maybe, by chance, we will invent some new economic idea that will better serve the people. Yet Postmodernists offer no concrete alternative to build upon. Epstein observes correctly that "one reason that Postmodernism has taken hold so widely

---

[16] Robert Eaglestone, ed., *Routledge Critical Thinkers* (New York, NY: Routledge, 2003), 15

[17] Mark Lilla, *The Reckless Mind: Intellectuals in Politics* (New York, NY: New York Review Books, 2001), 153. Foucault's biographer, Didier Eribon, wrote, Foucault "had been seen with an iron rod in his hands, ready to do battle with militant Communists; he had been seen throwing rocks at the police." See Eribon's *Michel Foucault* (Cambridge, MA: Harvard University Press, 1992), 209.

[18] Rorty, *Philosophy and Social Hope*, 214.

[19] Richard Rorty, "Trotsky and Wild Orchids," in *Wild Orchids and Trotsky: Messages from American Universities*, ed., Mark Edmundson (New York, NY: Penguin Books, 1993), 47.

[20] Ibid.

[21] Richard Rorty, "The Communitarian Impulse," http://www.coloradocollege.edu/academics/anniversary/Transcripts/RortyTXT.htm.

[22] Stuart Sim, ed., *The Routledge Companion to Postmodernism* (London, UK: Routledge, 2004), 40.

is that it is much easier to be critical than to present a positive vision."[23]

Even Ruccio and Amariglio seem to have low expectations of Postmodern *everyday economics*. They say, "We don't envision (or for that matter, seek to promote) a separate Postmodern economic theory."[24] In fact, they are "hesitant to argue that Postmodernism shows the way forward,"[25] and are content with conversations and encounters "rather than a new [economic] home." Since there is no truth about the real world or the nature of humanity, it is hard to arrive at a correct view of economics. Such is the Postmodern dilemma.

9.6.6 CONCLUSION

Postmodern economics is a mixed bag of conflicting ideas and theories. While most Postmodernists favor socialism, others opt for some milder form of interventionism. Still others harshly critique both socialism and capitalism, and some are critical of *all* economic theories.

In the final analysis, while Postmodernists are not in total agreement in every detail, they are committed to the leftist side of the economic spectrum, favoring, to varying degrees, some form of government intervention. This intervention may be more overt, as with Ruccio and Amariglio, or less so, as with Rorty. But in either case, there is agreement that capitalism is the enemy of social justice. Yet based on the Postmodern aversion to metanarratives, most hesitate to offer concrete solutions, preferring instead to experiment with some degree of socialism for an economic alternative that best suites an ever-changing social structure.

[23] Barbara Epstein, "Postmodernism and the Left," *New Politics* vol. 6, no. 2 (new series), whole no. 22 (Winter 1997). Available online at http://www.wpunj.edu/~newpol/issue22/epstei22.htm.
[24] Ruccio and Amariglio, *Postmodern Moments in Modern Economics*, 295.
[25] Ibid., 299.

History

Christianity

"Paul regarded the resurrection as an event in history supported by the strongest possible eyewitness testimony, including his own (1 Corinthians 15:5-8). For Paul, the historicity of the resurrection was a necessary condition for the truth of Christianity and the validity of Christian belief."[1]

— RONALD H. NASH

10.1.1 INTRODUCTION

The basis for the Christian worldview appeared in human history about two thousand years ago in the person of Jesus Christ. While "Christ died for our sins" is solid orthodox Christian theology, "Christ died" is history. Shattering Christianity's historical underpinnings would surely shatter its doctrine and thus the entire worldview.

Christians also believe that the Bible is God's revealed Word in the form of a trustworthy book grounded in history. Thus, for Christians, history is supremely important. Either Christ is a historical figure and the Bible is a historical document that describes God's communications with humanity and records events in the life of Christ or the Christian faith is bankrupt (1 Corinthians 15:14).

If the Christian perspective is correct, history has already revealed the worldview that fits the facts of reality. Christians believe redemption was offered to humanity two thousand years ago and that it works as powerfully today as it did then.

---

[1] Ronald H. Nash, *Christian Faith and Historical Understanding* (Dallas, TX: Probe Books, 1984), 112.

10.1.2 THE BIBLE AND HISTORY

When considering the claims of Christianity, we must ask, "Can we trust the Bible to tell us the truth about God's actions in history?" Most of the negative criticism of the Bible, as Norman L. Geisler says, "is pre-archaeological based on unproven philosophical presuppositions that have subsequently been antiquated by archaeology. As with the Old Testament, the positive case for the historical reliability of the New Testament is based on two main points: the reliability of the New Testament manuscripts and the reliability of the New Testament witnesses."[2]

The first area we must explore when judging the historicity of the Bible is the question of authorship. Was the Bible written by eyewitnesses of historical events, or were some books written many years after the fact by men who had only heard vague accounts of the events they attempted to describe? For example, did one of Christ's apostles write the book of Matthew, or did some unknown scribe with no firsthand knowledge of Christ's life write the book to strengthen the case for Christianity?

Today's scholars have little doubt that the books of the Bible were written largely by eyewitnesses. William F. Albright, a leading twentieth-century archaeologist, writes, "In my opinion, every book of the New Testament was written by a baptized Jew between the forties and the eighties of the first century (very probably sometime between about A.D. 50 and 75)."[3]

Even H.G. Wells, a confirmed atheist, acknowledges that "the four gospels . . . were certainly in existence a few decades after [Christ's] death."[4] The evidence concludes that the historical accounts in the Bible were written by men living in that historical period.[5]

However, a second objection arises. Perhaps, say the critics, the Bible was an accurate historical document as it was originally written, but inevitable mistakes made by copyists over hundreds of years have rendered it inaccurate and unreliable. At first glance, this objection seems plausible. But one archaeological discovery made nearly half a century ago shattered this theory. Gleason L. Archer, Jr. explains: "Even though the two copies of Isaiah discovered in Qumran Cave 1 near the Dead Sea in 1947 were a thousand years earlier than the oldest dated manuscript previously known (A.D. 980), they proved to be word for word identical with our standard Hebrew Bible in more than 95 per cent of the text. The 5 per cent of variation consisted chiefly of obvious slips of the pen and variations in spelling."[6] That is, a manuscript one thousand years older than the oldest copy of the Bible previously known to exist proved the transmission over that time span to be virtually error-free.

> Archaeology has consistently supported the assertion that the Bible is a trustworthy historical document.

In fact, archaeological discoveries have consistently supported the veracity of the Bible. Nelson Gluck says, "It may be stated categorically that no archaeological discovery has ever controverted a biblical reference."[7] Harvard's Simon Greenleaf (the greatest nineteenth-century authority on the law of evidence in the common law) believes "that the competence of the New Testament documents would be established in any court of law."[8]

---

[2] Norman L. Geisler, *Systematic Theology*, 4 vols. (Minneapolis, MN: Bethany House, 2002), 1:461.

[3] W.F. Albright, "Toward a More Conservative View," *Christianity Today*, Jan. 18, 1963, 4.

[4] H.G. Wells, *The Outline of History* (Garden City, NY: Garden City Publishing, 1921), 497.

[5] For a full accounting of the historicity of both Old and New Testaments, see Norman L. Geisler, *Systematic Theology*, 1:438f. For an accounting of the Old Testament's historicity, see K. A. Kitchen, *On The Reliability Of The Old Testament* (Grand Rapids, MI: Eerdmans, 2003).

[6] Gleason L. Archer, Jr., *A Survey of Old Testament Introduction* (Chicago, IL: Moody Press, 1968), 1

[7] Nelson Glueck, *Biblical Archaeologist*, vol. 22 (Dec. 1959): 101.

[8] John Warwick Montgomery, *Human Rights and Human Dignity* (Dallas, TX: Probe Books, 1986), 137.

10.1.3 HISTORICITY OF CHRIST

If the Bible is a reliable historical document, then we cannot intellectually deny that a man named Jesus actually lived and taught at that point in history. Indeed, Christ is treated as a historical figure by early secular historians as well. Around A.D. 93, the Jewish historian Josephus refers to Jesus at least twice in his *Antiquities of the Jews*. In one instance, he recorded that the high priest Annas "assembled the Sanhedrim of the judges, and brought before them the brother of Jesus, who was called Christ, whose name was James . . ."[9]

Another early historian, Cornelius Tacitus, writes circa A.D. 112 about "the persons commonly called Christians," and also states, "Christus, the founder of the name, was put to death by Pontius Pilate, procurator of Judea in the reign of Tiberius: but the pernicious superstition, repressed for a time broke out again, not only through Judea, where the mischief originated, but through the city of Rome also."[10]

These references and others provide sufficient evidence for the historicity of Christ, even if we ignore the New Testament. Bruce Metzger writes that "the early non-Christian testimonies concerning Jesus, though scanty, are sufficient to prove (even without taking into account the evidence contained in the New Testament) that he was a historical figure who lived in Palestine in the early years of the first century, that he gathered a group of followers about himself, and that he was condemned to death under Pontius Pilate. Today no competent scholar denies the historicity of Jesus."[11]

Even Secular Humanist historian Will Durant accepts the historicity of Jesus. He asks, "What evidence is there for Christ's existence? The earliest non-Christian reference occurs in Josephus' *Antiquities of the Jews* (A.D. 93): 'At that time lived Jesus, a holy man, if man he may be called, for he performed wonderful works, and taught men, and joyfully received the truth. And he was followed by many Jews and many Greeks. He was the Messiah.'"[12] Durant's chapter about Jesus speaks more highly of Him than all liberal Protestant writings combined! He admits that "Christ was in this spiritual sense the greatest revolutionist in history."[13] Nor does he deny the resurrection of Jesus Christ.[14] He treats the Gospel records as historical and allows them to tell what happened.

10.1.4 RESURRECTION AND HISTORY

The Bible goes out of its way to place its message and major figures in history (see Luke 3:1–2). This is especially true in regard to Christ's resurrection. Luke mentions Pilate, Caesar, Herod, Barabbas, "Joseph, counselor," "Arimathaea, a city of the Jews," and then describes Christ's resurrection as a real event in history (Luke 24:1–7).

More than five hundred people witnessed the resurrected Christ (1 Corinthians 15:6), including Mary, Peter, and ten other apostles. These witnesses were so moved by the resurrection that they committed their lives to it and to the One whose divinity and righteousness it vindicated. The disciples did not abandon Christ, but were willing to die for the gospel they were proclaiming.

---

[9] Josephus, *Antiquities of the Jews*, XX.ix.1.

[10] Cornelius Tacitus, *Annals* XV. 44. Cited in Josh McDowell, *Evidence that Demands a Verdict* (San Bernardino, CA: Campus Crusade for Christ International, 1972), 84

[11] Bruce M. Metzger, *The New Testament: Its Background, Growth, and Content* (Nashville, TN: Abingdon Press, 1965), 78.

[12] Will Durant, *Caesar and Christ* (New York, NY: Simon and Schuster, 1944), 554.

[13] Ibid., 566.

[14] Ibid., 573.

Indeed, the resurrection of Christ took a group of scared (Mark 16:8; John 20:19) and skeptical (Luke 24:38; John 20:25) men and transformed them into courageous evangels who proclaimed the Resurrection in the face of threats on their lives (Acts 4:21; 5:18). If the disciples did not consider Christ's resurrection a historical event, would they have been willing to die in order to maintain a lie?

Josh McDowell says, "After more than seven hundred hours of studying this subject and thoroughly investigating its foundation, I have come to the conclusion that the resurrection of Jesus Christ is one of the most wicked, vicious, heartless hoaxes ever foisted upon the minds of men, OR it is the most fantastic fact of history."[15] McDowell concludes that it is one of the most fantastic facts of history.[16]

N.T. Wright comes to this conclusion as well. Covering over eight hundred pages and looking at resurrections in general and the resurrection of Jesus Christ in particular, Wright concludes that the resurrection of Jesus is a fact of history.[17]

The faith of Christians today should be no less secure than that of the apostles—it is grounded in historical fact. Through the resurrection, God reveals His plan for humanity by conquering sin and guaranteeing a just end to human history. D.W. Bebbington says that, since Jesus won the battle against evil on the cross, "The outcome of world history is therefore already assured. God will continue to direct the course of events up to their end when the outcome will be made plain."[18]

Christians learn from history that Christ offered Himself up as a perfect sacrifice for us. Christians also discover another important truth: God is active throughout history and plans to lead it to a triumphant conclusion. While the course of history may seem tragic to some people, Christians understand that all history is working together for good. Because God became man and died for our sins, the final chapter of history will conquer sin for the rest of eternity. Thus, Christians are prepared to face a difficult, sometimes pain-filled life, because we understand that the sin that causes death has been erased from our future. Christians hold no unreasonable expectations for our earthly lifetime—in fact, we anticipate persecution and trials—but we do expect to be triumphant in the end because God has come into history to save us from our own sinful inclinations.

The Pop Culture Connection

Amistad (a 1997 film directed by Steven Spielberg) retells the true story of fifty-three Africans who mutinied on a slave ship in 1839, ending up on the shores of America to stand trial. Evangelical Christians had a major role in helping the slaves win their freedom, yet in the film these Christians are depicted as hypocritical and indifferent to the lives of the Africans. Brian Godawa writes, "The historically dominant force of liberation [for slaves], the Quakers, are relegated to the role of kooky protesters in the background chanting irrelevant slogans and remaining blatantly unconnected to their modern world." But in spite of the revisionist history, "*Amistad* contains one of the most thorough descriptions of the gospel from Genesis to John that has ever been shown in a movie."[19]*

---

[15] Josh McDowell, *The New Evidence That Demands A Verdict* (Nashville, TN: Thomas Nelson Publishers, 1999), 203.

[16] Ibid., 203f.

[17] N.T. Wright, *The Resurrection Of The Son Of God* (Minneapolis, MN: Fortress Press, 2003).

[18] D.W. Bebbington, *Patterns in History* (Downers Grove, IL: InterVarsity Press, 1979), 169.

[19]* Brian Godawa, *Hollywood Worldviews* (Downers Grove, IL: InterVarsity Press, 2002), 133-134. For additional material on black slavery, see Thomas Sowell, *Black Rednecks and White Liberals* (New York, NY: Encounter Books, 2005).

From the Christian perspective, history is a beautiful unfolding of God's ultimate plan for all humanity. Knowing that God has been active throughout history helps us to understand our own role in the day-to-day history of our lives. "It is always a 'Now,'" writes Herbert Butterfield, "that is in direct relation to eternity—not a far future; always immediate experience of life that matters in the last resort—not historical constructions based on abridged text-books or imagined visions of some posterity that is going to be the heir of all the ages."[20] Christians understand that all of history is ordained for a purpose.

10.1.5 PURPOSE IN HISTORY

Christians view history through the concepts of **creation, fall,** and **redemption**, a progression of events beginning with God's good creation, humanity's rebellion against God, and God's ultimate plan for divine intervention, redemption, and restoration. Thus, all of creation is sacred and stands under the blessing, judging, and redeeming purposes of God. This belief of creation/fall/redemption/restoration has vast ramifications for humanity. If the Christian philosophy of history is correct, then not only is the overall story of humanity invested with meaning, but every moment that we live is charged with purpose. C.S. Lewis explains, "Where a God who is totally purposive and totally foreseeing acts upon a Nature which is totally interlocked, there can be no accidents or loose ends, nothing whatever of which we can safely use the word 'merely.' Nothing is 'merely a by-product' of anything else. All results are intended from the first."[21]

Indeed, understanding how God works in our lives helps us understand how God directs the course of history. Butterfield explains, "[T]here are some people who bring their sins home to themselves and say that this is a chastisement from God; or they say that God is testing them, trying them in the fire, fitting them for some more important work that he has for them to do. Those who adopt this view in their individual lives will easily see that it enlarges

> **CREATION, FALL, REDEMPTION:** The progression of events in God's creation: that all was created good, but humanity rebelled against God and requires divine redemption. Thus, all of creation is sacred and stands under the blessing, judging, and redeeming purposes of God.

and projects itself onto the scale of all history."[22] Therefore, purpose and meaning saturate every aspect of a Christian's life.

In order to speak accurately about purpose, however, Christians must speak not only of God's activity throughout history but also of the ultimate goal toward which He is leading us. Purpose implies constant supervision by God, a direction for the course of human events, and an ultimate end or goal. For Christians, history is moving toward a specific climax—the Day of Judgment (Acts 17:31; Romans 2:11–16). At that point, Christ's victory over sin will become apparent to all and Christians throughout history will be allowed to share in His triumph. This is the good news of Christianity, the truth that makes all earthly trials bearable. Paul sums up this faith: "I consider that our present sufferings are not worth comparing with the glory that will be revealed in us" (Romans 8:18; 2 Corinthians 4:11–18). The ultimate direction of history is toward a triumphant close. Even at this very moment, God is moving human history closer to that end—which, in a very real sense, is only the beginning.

---

[20] Herbert Butterfield, *Christianity and History* (New York, NY: Charles Scribner's Sons, 1950), 66.

[21] C.S. Lewis, *Miracles. A Preliminary Study* (London, UK: Geoffrey Bles, 1952), 149. Norman Geisler says of Lewis's work on miracles, "The best overall apologetic for miracles written in this century" (*Miracles and Modern Thought* [Dallas, TX: Probe Ministries International, 1982], 167). Geisler's work is part of the Christian Free University Curriculum and self-published.

[22] C.T. McIntire, ed., *God, History, and Historians* (Oxford, UK: Oxford University Press, 1977), 201.

10.1.6 LINEAR CONCEPTION OF HISTORY

This belief about the direction of history is known as a linear conception of history. That is, Christians believe that human history had a specific beginning (creation) and is being directed by God toward a specific end (restoration), and that historic events follow a non-repetitive course toward that end.

Most of Western society has a linear view of history, a view founded on the Judeo-Christian perspective. Prior to this Christian description of history, classical thought supported a cyclical view in which historical events were repeated over and over by consecutive societies. Thus, the directional view of history given by Christians created a unique conception of the movement of humanity through time. John Warwick Montgomery says, "The importance of the Biblical conception cannot be overstressed. Here for the first time Western man was presented with a purposive, goal-directed interpretation of history. The Classical doctrine of recurrence had been able to give a 'substantiality' to history, but it had not given it any aim or direction."[23] Direction, as always, comes from God.

10.1.7 CONCLUSION

Christian history centers in the reliability of the Bible. The historical foundation of the Bible, as recorded in both Testaments and substantiated by archaeology and secular writings, has stood the test of time.

Because of the biblical understanding of the fallen nature of humanity, Christians are able to form a consistent view regarding the past, the present, and the future as well as our role in history. We may freely choose to obey or disobey God, but it is only when we obey that we can affect history positively. Regardless of our choices—for good or for evil—God will work through our actions to direct history toward His ultimate end: a Day of Judgment, the restoration of the heavens and earth (1 Timothy 6:13–19; 2 Peter 3:13), and the new age to come with Jesus Christ as King of Kings and Lord of Lords. This belief in a climactic conclusion causes Christians to adopt a linear conception of history that reflects the vast meaning with which God has endowed history. Wise men still seek Him, and for good reason, for He is the only source of meaning in history and in life.

---

[23]   John Warwick Montgomery, *The Shape of the Past* (Minneapolis, MN: Bethany Fellowship, 1975), 42.

History

Islam

"Islam is the only future hope of humanity; and its victorious emergence out of the present ideological warfare is the only guarantee of man's salvation."[1]

— MUHAMMAD QUTB

10.2.1 INTRODUCTION

Muhammad, the founder and prophet of Islam, was born in circa A.D. 570 into a culture characterized by polytheism and animism. Yet, throughout his merchant career, he likely came into contact with Jewish and Christian monotheism. Muhammad was a spiritual man and encountered many visions. At first he thought they were satanic visions, but his wife, Khadija, persuaded him that the visions were from God. In A.D. 610, Muhammad claimed he had been visited by the angel Gabriel and commissioned to be a prophet of God. His basic message was simple and elegant: There is one God to whom all people must submit and there will be a day of judgment in which all humans will be judged according to their deeds, both good and evil.

10.2.2 A.D. 622

Mecca was a great religious, economic, and political power center on the Arabian peninsula in Muhammad's day. It boasted the **Ka'ba** (a large black box-like building) that hosted 360 tribal deities. Tribes would make regular pilgrimages to the city, thus bringing great economic wealth to the city's merchants. But Muhammad's message contradicted the pantheism of his

---

[1]Khurshid Ahmad, ed., *Islam: Its Meaning and Message* (Leicester, UK: The Islamic Foundation, 1999), 253.

day: rather than many gods, there was only one, Allah. Inevitably, Muhammad's teaching led to a clash with Meccan leaders, and the Muslims fled to Medina (then called Yathrib) in A.D. 622. This event is called the *Hijra*, the migration that began the Muslim era, and forms the starting point for the Islamic calendar.

From early days Muslims began raiding merchant caravans seeking to deliver their wares to Mecca. The raids led to a number of battles, the most famous of which was the Battle of *Badr* (A.D. 624) in which 324 Muslims defeated a Meccan force three times their number. Naturally, such a victory added to the perception that Islam was indeed God's will. Two years later, Muslims repelled a Meccan attack on Medina in the Battle of *Ahzab* (A.D. 627). The following year brought a treaty with Meccan leaders, permitting Muhammad to enter the city as a pilgrim. On January 11, A.D. 629, Muhammad and about 10,000 Muslim warriors captured Mecca without a battle, thus permitting Muhammad to cleanse the Ka'ba of its idols and establish Islam.

Today Islam is a major world religion, boasting a membership of nearly one-fourth of the world's population. The majority of Muslims, which come from numerous ethnic backgrounds and reside in every country, are not Arabs.

10.2.3 ISLAMIC DIVERSITIES

Islam is a religion and worldview as diverse as Christianity, Judaism, Buddhism, or Hinduism. Throughout its history various factions with differing convictions and levels of commitment have existed in Islam.

10.2.4 SUNNI AND SHI'ITE

Shortly after Muhammad died (A.D. 632) his followers faced the immediate question of who should succeed him. The conflict resulted in the two major factions of Islam. Those who insisted the successor should be elected by popular vote became the Sunni Muslims, which currently comprise about 80 percent of Muslims worldwide. The Shi'ite Muslims, however, believed that the successor should be someone from the bloodline of Muhammad, a family member or descendant. The Shi'ites, though outnumbered worldwide, are a powerful force among Muslims, especially following the 1979 Iranian revolution when the Ayatollah Khomeini (died 1989) gained control of the country. Shi'ites remain a majority in Iran, and significant communities of Shi'ites persist in Iraq and other countries. While agreeing that no prophets succeed Muhammad, Shi'ites believe in a leader, the *Imam*, who is gifted by God to guide Muslims. While the Sunnis and Shi'ites agree on the importance of the Qur'an, they have different collections of the *Hadith* (the traditional actions and sayings of Muhammad and his followers).

10.2.5 SUFISM

Sufi Islam historically has expressed the more spiritual side of Islam. While existing from Islam's earliest days, it was not considered mainstream until the famous Sufi Muslim scholar Al-Ghazali sought spiritual renewal among the Muslim peoples. While orthodox Islam holds that Allah does not reveal himself but merely his will, Sufism advocates seeking a personal experience and oneness with Allah (some even adopt a pantheistic theology). Sufis protested the worldliness of Islam at a time when wealth had been gained through many conquests and religion in general was dry. The Sufis promote a lively religion, invested with spiritual ways and means, and a less legalistic form of Islam. Sufism has been and continues to be a major force in the spread of Islam throughout the world. Jalal al-Din Rumi (died A.D. 1273) is the most well known Sufi poet.

10.2.6 SOME SMALLER UNORTHODOX GROUPS

Islam has many religious offshoots. While orthodox Islam holds that Muhammad was the final prophet in a long succession of prophets, some groups claim that other prophets since Muhammad have come. The Baha'i World Faith was established in 1844 and boasts the prophet Baha'u'allah. The Baha'i claim that their religion is the fulfillment of all religions and that all religions are essentially one. The Nation of Islam (a.k.a., The Black Muslims) also holds that there has been a modern-day prophet: **Elijah Muhammad** (died A.D. 1975). Beyond this, they teach a polytheistic and racist theology.

Elijah Muhammad

10.2.7 ISLAM IS A WORLDVIEW

Islam is a comprehensive worldview, as Salam Azzan, the Secretary General of the Islamic Council of Europe, explains,

> Islam is a complete way of life. It integrates man with God, awakens in him a new moral consciousness and invites him to deal with all the problems of life—individual and social, economic and political, national and international—in accord with his commitment to God. Islam does not divide life into domains of the spiritual and the secular. It spiritualizes the entire existence of man and produces a social movement to reconstruct human life in the light of principles revealed by God. Prayer and worship in Islam are means to prepare man to fulfill this mission. Islam aims at changing life and producing a new man and a new society, both committed to God and the welfare of mankind. That is why Islam is not a religion in the limited sense of the word; rather it is a complete code of life and a culture-producing factor. Muslim culture profits from all available sources, local and international, but its unique characteristic is that it grows from the foundations of the Qur'an and *Sunnah*. Hence the distinctiveness of Muslim culture and life in Europe and elsewhere.[2]

> HISTORICAL DETERMINISM: The Islamic belief that history is not made up of a series of chance happenings, but that Allah superintends history throughout time

10.2.8 HISTORICAL DETERMINISM

Like the Christian worldview, Islam affirms that history is not made up of a series of chance happenings. Rather, because Allah created the world, he superintends it throughout time, guiding it toward an expression of his will. Hammuda Abdalati explains, "The world is

---

[2] Ibid., 5–6.

JIHAD: An Arabic word meaning "striving in the way of God." This striving can take a number of forms, including the daily inner struggle to be a better person. However, jihad is most often used to refer to an armed struggle with the enemies of Islam

a becoming entity, created by the will of a Designer and sustained by Him for meaningful purposes. Historical currents take place in accordance with His will and follow established laws. They are not directed by blind chance, nor are they random and disorderly incidents."[3] The phrase **historical determinism** captures the essence of the Islamic approach to history.

10.2.9 THE VISION OF GLOBAL ISLAM

In concert with historical determinism is the Muslim hope that Islam one day will span the globe with all peoples and nations being Muslim. *The Concise Encyclopedia of Islam*, for example, states that *jihad* is "a Divine institution of warfare to extend Islam into the Dar al-harb (the non-Islamic territories which are described as the 'abode of struggle,' or of disbelief) or to defend Islam from danger."[4]

10.2.10 ISLAM AND BIBLICAL HISTORY

While there are some common affirmations of biblical history between Muslims and Christians, there are also stark and fundamental differences. Muslims deny that Jesus died on the cross or was resurrected from the dead. They also deny that the Bible is reliable.

10.2.11 CONTINUING THREAT OF ISLAM

While there are many opinions within global Islam regarding the definition of *jihad*, it would be naïve and deadly to deny the record of history.[5] On the one hand, many Muslims express a moderate view in which the aggressive nature of Islamic teaching and practice has been curbed by such realities as the western value of civic tolerance and pluralism.[6] On the other hand, the Islamic worldview retains the essential hope that all humanity will one day bow to Allah freely or by force. While it may be that only a fraction of Muslims are expressive militants, a much larger number manifest emotional, vocal, and monetary support of *jihad*. The negative reaction expressed by some Muslims when witnessing the collapse of the World Trade Center towers is unable to erase doctrinally engrained and historically buttressed Islamic hope that arises from the fall of the infidel.

---

[3] Hammuda Abdalati, *Islam in Focus* (Indianapolis, IN: American Trust Publications, 1975), 51.

[4] Cyril Glasse, *The Concise Encyclopedia of Islam* (New York, NY: Harper Collins, 1991), 209. Cited in Alvin J. Schmidt, *The Great Divide: The Failure of Islam and the Triumph of the West* (Boston, MA: Regina Orthodox Press, 2004), 222.

[5] One of the more sobering analyses and recollections of the threat of Islam's inherent militancy is found in Serge Trifkovic, *The Sword of the Prophet: Islam, History, Theology, and Impact on the World* (Boston, MA: Regina Orthodox Press, 2002). See also the Bat Ye'or, *Islam and Dhimmitude: Where Civilizations Collide*, trans. Miriam Kochan and David Littman (Madison, NJ: Fairleigh Dickinson University Press, 2002).

[6] See, for example, Bassam Tibi, *The Challenge of Fundamentalism: Political Islam and the New World Disorder* (Berkeley, CA: University of California Press, 1998). Tibi, a Muslim, distinguishes between what he describes as the religion of Islam, as a personal and corporate practice, and what he called "Islamic fundamentalism," which he believes opposes worldwide security and stability.

10.2.12 ATTACK ON AMERICA

On September 11, 2001,[7] four commercial airliners were mutated into flying missiles in the service of radical Islamist ideology and the world changed. On each of the flights, the hijackers had used knives or box cutters, mace or pepper spray, as well as deceptively reporting to the passengers that they had bombs and needed to return to their respective airports. Nobody dreamed (except perhaps the military/suspense novelist extraordinaire, Tom Clancy[8]) that the "bombs" were *not* brought aboard in checked luggage or other cargo, but were in fact the aircraft themselves. Initiating their flights in Boston, Washington Dulles, and Newark, they were intended for destinations on the West Coast, Los Angeles, and San Francisco—destinations they never reached.

The Pop Culture Connection

Munich (a 2005 film directed by Steven Spielberg) "The film begins in September 1972, when Palestinian terrorists captured and murdered 11 Israeli athletes at the Summer Olympics in Munich, Germany. . . . . The bulk of the film, however, takes place *after* the Olympics, when the Israeli government responds to the incident by sending a counter-terrorist team to Europe and other points around the Mediterranean to find and execute 11 Palestinian leaders. . . . While the film *is* ambivalent on the question of whether Israel ought to exist, its critique of counter-terrorism is expressed in very Jewish terms, and the fact that it is the Jews who wrestle with their consciences actually reflects rather well on them. In contrast, the few Arab terrorists we meet never question their methods—methods which are, of course, much worse, even if the film isn't as clear on that point as it should be."*

Around 8:14 that fateful morning, American Airlines Flight 11, a nonstop flight to Los Angeles, was the first to be hijacked. Five armed men, all committed to live and die for Allah, murdered several people on the flight before ramming the plane into the North Tower of the World Trade Center in New York City thirty-two minutes later. United Airlines Flight 175, also bound for Los Angeles, was similarly hijacked at 8:45 am. It was a horrendous and frightening ordeal for the passengers and crew. At 9:00 am, one brave passenger, Peter, called his father, Lee.

> It's getting bad, Dad — A stewardess was stabbed — They seem to have knives and Mace — They said they have a bomb — It's getting very bad on the plane — Passengers are throwing up and getting sick — The plane is making jerky movements — I don't think the pilot is flying the plane — I think we are going down — I think they intend to go to Chicago or someplace and fly into a building — Don't worry, Dad — If it happens, it'll be very fast — My God, my God.[9]

---

[7] On September 11, 1683, the "Muslims were turned away at the gates of Vienna" at the Battle of Vienna. This loss resulted in the demise of Islam in the West, which Muslims have never forgotten or forgiven. See "Battle of Vienna" on Wikipedia.

[8] The scenario of a commercial airliner crashing into the Capital Building and killing many politicians, including the president, is played out in the final pages of Tom Clancy's *Debt of Honor* (New York, NY: Putnam, 1994), as well as at the beginning of *Executive Orders* (New York, NY: Putnam, 1996). The latter story tells of a terrorist disbursal of the Ebola virus in the U.S., the assassination of the Iraqi president, and a move by Iranian militants to take Saudi Arabia.

* Peter T. Chattaway, "Munich," http://www.christianitytoday.com/movies/reviews/munich.html.

[9] *The 9/11 Commission Report* (Washington, DC: National Commission on Terrorist Attacks Upon the United States, 2004), 8.

As the phone connection abruptly ended, Lee witnessed Flight 175 crash into the South Tower of the World Trade Center at 9:03, instantly disintegrating all on board and untold numbers in the building.

American Airlines Flight 77, departing from Washington Dulles and also intended for Los Angeles, was hijacked minutes before 9:00. It was the passengers on this flight who relayed the detail that the hijackers were using box cutters to strike their first victims. A harrowing half-hour later, the plane's autopilot was disengaged at 7000 feet. Officials on the ground

suspected it was headed for the White House and alerted the Secret Service. The plane then descended and began a 330-degree turn, pointing the plane at downtown Washington. At 9:37 the plane crashed into the Pentagon traveling at a velocity of 530 miles per hour, annihilating all on board and several civilian and military personnel in the Pentagon.

United Airlines Flight 93, departing Newark and bound for San Francisco, met a similar fate, though not in the manner originally intended by the hijackers. The flight departed twenty-five minutes behind schedule and the passenger load was a scant thirty-seven souls. Also, the supposed fifth member of the terrorist team was being held by immigration officers in Orlando. Given the destruction of the other planes in quick succession that morning, authorities knew full well that a worst-case scenario was playing out on America soil. At 9:23 a warning message was transmitted to Flight 93. Unfortunately, the pilot somehow failed to grasp the message and requested clarification. Five minutes later the hijackers attacked. The airplane suddenly dropped 700 feet. "Mayday," the pilot cried. Then the air traffic controllers heard a three-fold, "Hey, get out of here."

A number of passengers and members of the flight crew began making calls to loved ones and friends, when they were informed of the fates of Flights 11 and 175. The passengers eventually voted to storm the cockpit and attempt to recover control of the plane. They had no other reasonable choice. At 9:57 they surged toward the front of the plane. The cockpit voice recorder vividly captured the commotion as the hijackers rolled the plane, attempting to jumble the passengers. When that failed to suffice, they then pitched the plane up and down. Thumps, crashes, and shouts were captured on the recording. At 10:00 the plane stabilized, though the hijackers seemed to realize they too would fail to reach *their* intended destination.

The hijacker pilot asked another terrorist, "Is that it? Shall we finish it off?" But his cohort said they should wait for the next assault from the passengers. He pitched the plane up and down again but the passengers were still battling away for their lives. "Allah is greatest! Allah is greatest!" cried one of the terrorists.

> The passengers continued their assault and at 10:02:23, a hijacker said, "Pull it down! Pull it down!" The hijackers remained at the controls but must have judged that the passengers were only seconds from overcoming them. The airplane headed down; the control wheel was turned hard to the right. The airplane rolled onto its back, and one of the hijackers began shouting "Allah is the greatest. Allah is the greatest." With the sounds of the passenger counterattack continuing, the aircraft plowed into an empty field in Shanksville, Pennsylvania, at 580 miles per hour, about 20 minutes' flying time from Washington, D.C.[10]

---

[10] Ibid., 14.

10.2.13 CONCLUSION

While not all Muslims praised these vicious and diabolical tactics, millions did. All of the hijackers were Muslims, as were some of their victims in the World Trade Center towers. The events of September 11, 2001, provide an unmistakable example of the Islamic call for *jihad*—a call to Muslims to expend their efforts, their money, and even their lives in the cause of establishing global Islam in the name of Allah.

In the name of Allah, Islam is, according to Mark Steyn, "the fastest-growing religion in Europe and North America: in the United Kingdom, more Muslims than Christians attend religious services each week. Meanwhile, in areas of traditionally moderate Islam, from the Balkans to Indonesia, Muslims are becoming radicalized and fiercer in their faith."[11] Of course, al Qaeda is only one of the "more radicalized" groups serving Islam today. Its English counterpart is an Islamic missionary society entitled Tablighi Jamaat that "has announced that it plans to build a mosque in the East End—right next door to the new Olympic stadium." Christened the London Markaz it will be, according to Steyn, "the biggest house of worship in the United Kingdom: it will hold 70,000 people—only 10,000 fewer than the Olympic stadium, and 67,000 more than the largest Christian facility (Liverpool's Anglican cathedral)."[12] Steyn also notes that "Tablighi Jamaat is an openly Islamist organization of global reach and, according to the FBI, an al Qaeda recruiting front for terrorists."[13]

Islamic countries are among the most vociferous persecutors of Christians, presenting probably the greatest missionary challenge to the church and exhibiting the most prominent external threat to the biblical values of freedom, justice, and order. The Christian response must be one that embodies the grace and love of the gospel of Christ coupled with an eternal and vigilant defense of the truth which would certainly entail a thoughtful and prayerful study of such writers as Stuart Robinson and his *Mosque and Miracles*.[14]

---

[11] Mark Steyn, *America Alone: The End of the World As We Know It* (Washington, D.C.: Regnery Publishing, Inc. 2006), 15.

[12] Ibid., 95.

[13] Ibid., 95.

[14] Stuart Robinson, *Mosque and Miracles: Revealing Islam and God's Grace* (Upper Mt. Gravett Qld, Australia: City Harvest Publications, 2004).

History

Secular Humanism

"Man's destiny is to be the sole agent for the future evolution of this planet."[1]

— JULIAN HUXLEY

10.3.1 INTRODUCTION

In 1933, Secular Humanists were positively elated about human potential. *Humanist Manifesto I*, released that year, described history as one long story of humanity's progress to paradise. Then came World War II, followed by the discovery of the atrocities of Joseph Stalin. Suddenly the unbounded optimism of the Humanists seemed farcical. *Humanist Manifesto II* (published in 1973) admitted, "Nazism has shown the depths of brutality of which humanity is capable. Other totalitarian regimes have suppressed human rights without ending poverty. Science has sometimes brought evil as well as good."[2]

Today, it seems impossible that Humanists view history with optimism although *Humanist Manifesto 2000* certainly tries. Assuming an atheistic stance, Secular Humanists must view history as a bumbling, uncertain, often immoral enterprise, with little hope for improvement in the future. *Humanist Manifesto II* seems to describe modern Humanism's rejection of historical optimism in some places, yet follows with a declaration of incomparable historical optimism: "Using technology wisely, we can control our environment, conquer poverty, markedly reduce disease, extend our life-span, significantly modify our behavior, alter the course of human evolution and cultural development, unlock vast new powers, and provide humankind with unparalleled opportunity for achieving an abundant and meaningful life."[3]

---

[1] Julian Huxley, *Essays of a Humanist* (London, UK: Chatto and Windus, 1964), 77.
[2] *Humanist Manifesto II* (Buffalo, NY: Prometheus Books, 1980), 13.
[3] Ibid., 14.

Humanism claims to take a realistic view of history, but this is belied by statement after statement reflecting an insistence that our future will outshine our past.

10.3.2 HUMANISTS MUST BE OPTIMISTIC

Secular Humanists remain unrealistically optimistic for two reasons. The first and most telling is the *belief* that all life evolved from non-life and has been evolving upward and onward for 3.6 billion years.[4] This evolutionary perspective colors Humanism's attitude toward all reality, especially history. If, as Humanists believe, all reality is an evolutionary pattern that moves upward step by step to create rational thought and morality in the highest species, then our history also must be a progressive march toward a better world. As the evolutionary process continues, so must progress continue. History is the story of development from non-life to life, from simple to more complex, from mindless to mind, from animal to human, from amoral to moral.

> [The] rise and fall of empires and cultures is a natural phenomenon, just as much as the succession of dominant groups in biological evolution.
>
> — JULIAN HUXLEY

John Dietrich explains, "There never has been any Garden of Eden or perfect condition in the past, there never has been any fall, and there has been a constant rise. Man has been climbing slowly up the ages from the most primitive condition to the present civilization."[5] Secular Humanism sees the whole process of history as the evolution of people, cultures, and civilizations into more advanced people, cultures, and civilizations. Julian Huxley insists that the "rise and fall of empires and cultures is a natural phenomenon, just as much as the succession of dominant groups in biological evolution."[6] The future will improve on the past and the present because evolution demands progress.

The second reason Humanists adhere to an optimistic view of history is because they deny the existence of God. Huxley best summarizes this sentiment: "In the evolutionary pattern of thought there is no longer either need or room for the supernatural."[7] Leaving no room for the supernatural greatly reduces the importance of human actions since in this view, as Bertrand Russell notes, "The universe is vast and men are but tiny specks on an insignificant planet."[8]

HISTORICAL EVOLUTION: The belief that history is to be understood in terms of unguided evolution and the guidance of human ingenuity and intelligence

Secular Humanist atheism, instead of leading into the trap of nihilism, creates dependence on the progress of human history to provide meaning for life. Secular Humanists believe that the progress of **historical evolution** is inevitable.

10.3.3 HUMANISM AND THE BIBLE

Ironically, Secular Humanists use the discipline of history to support their atheism by claiming that a scientific approach to history exposes the mythological nature of the Bible, especially the miracles of Christ. Paul Kurtz declares, "There is no evidence that Yahweh

---

[4] There is absolutely no scientific support for the theory of spontaneous generation.

[5] Roger E. Greeley, ed. *The Best of Humanism* (Buffalo, NY: Prometheus Books, 1988), 174.

[6] Huxley, *Essays of a Humanist*, 33.

[7] Ibid., 78.

[8] Robert E. Egner and Lester E. Denon, eds., *The Basic Writings of Bertrand Russell* (New York, NY: Simon and Schuster, 1961), 685.

spoke to Abraham, Moses, Joseph, or any of the Old Testament prophets."[9] Harry Elmer Barnes equally distrusts the accuracy of the Bible: "Biblical criticism, applied to the New Testament, has removed the element of supernaturalism from the biographies of its founders as thoroughly as Old Testament criticism has from those of its heroes."[10] Secular Humanists regard the Bible, and especially its historical account of Christ's resurrection and ascension, as historically inaccurate.[11] Indeed, Humanism's atheistic theology and naturalistic philosophy disallow the existence of the supernatural altogether.

10.3.4 WHO SHAPES HISTORY?

Some Humanists believe that our social environment plays the greatest role in shaping history. Barnes writes, "History is a record of man's development as conditioned by his social environment."[12] At first glance, this view seems consistent with the Secular Humanist worldview. Humanist psychology describes humans as inherently good animals driven to do evil by environmental stimuli. However, Humanism does not accept the conclusion that history is the story of our response to our environment over the years because this conclusion denies that we hold any power to control our destiny. Secular Humanists believe that we possess the free will to shape our environment

> History is a record of man's development as conditioned by his social environment.
>
> — HARRY BARNES

and our history. Corliss Lamont explains, "Within certain limits prescribed by our earthly circumstances and by scientific law, individual human beings, entire nations, and mankind in general are free to choose the paths that they truly wish to follow. To a significant degree they are the molders of their own fate and hold in their own hands the shape of things to come."[13]

Humanist Manifesto II also teaches that humanity is a dynamic force in history: "While there is much that we do not know, humans are responsible for what we are or will become. No deity will save us; we must save ourselves."[14] Secular Humanists thus maintain both an optimistic view of history and a belief that humanity has some purpose.

10.3.5 IDEOLOGIES SHAPE HISTORY

However, in the Secular Humanist view of history, humans in and of themselves do not shape history; rather their ideologies do. Ideologies evolve, and certain ideologies are more effective than others in realizing change at different stages of history. Huxley says, "Major steps in the human phase of evolution are achieved by breakthroughs to new dominant patterns of mental organization, of knowledge, ideas and beliefs—ideological instead of physiological or biological organization."[15]

The implication is that Christianity, an ideology that effectively shaped history at some time in the past, is now outdated and outmoded and cannot address modern problems. The ideology of Secular Humanism is the breakthrough ideology for today.

---

[9] Paul Kurtz, *Eupraxophy: Living Without Religion* (Buffalo, NY: Prometheus, 1989), 33–4.

[10] Harry Elmer Barnes, *The New History and the Social Studies* (New York, NY: Century, 1925), 21.

[11] See volume 1, chapters 25 and 26 of Norman L. Geisler, *Systematic Theology*, 4 vols. (Minneapolis, MN: Bethany House, 2002), for a defense of the historicity of the Bible.

[12] Harry Elmer Barnes, *Living in the Twentieth Century* (Indianapolis, IN: Bobbs-Merrill, 1928), 32.

[13] Corliss Lamont, *The Philosophy of Humanism* (New York, NY: Frederick Ungar, 1982), 282.

[14] *Humanist Manifesto II*, 16.

[15] Huxley, *Essays of a Humanist*, 76.

10.3.6 HUMANITY'S ROLE IN SHAPING THE FUTURE

Lamont boldly claims, "Humanism assigns to man nothing less than the task of being his own savior and redeemer."[16] Erich Fromm explains the Secular Humanist view of our role in history by saying, "Man creates himself in the historical process."[17] Fromm describes our role as our own redeemer when he says, "The messianic time is the next step in history, not its abolition. The messianic time is the time when man will have been fully born. When man was expelled from Paradise he lost his home; in the messianic time he will be at home again—in the world."[18]

Secular Humanists strive to affect our redemption by creating a heaven on earth. Lamont's view sees an evolving species even more advanced than humans: "Men can find plenty of scope and meaning in their lives through . . . helping to evolve a new species surpassing Man."[19] In this vein, Victor J. Stenger also sees the possibility of a species higher than humans—computers created by humans. He says this new species will not come about "by the painfully slow and largely random process of biological evolution," but through the rapid and guided advances of technology. "This new form of 'life' I will call, for historical reasons, the computer."[20] Stenger believes that computers will eventually prove more capable than humans in every meaningful realm of life, saying, "If there is anything we do that computers cannot, be patient. In time they will do it better, if it is worth doing at all."[21]

> ## The Pop Culture Connection
>
> A.I. (a 2002 film directed by Stephen Spielberg and starring Haley Joel Osment and Jude Law)—The film reveals a future where all living things have died out, including the human race. The only survivors are sophisticated, intelligent robots. One robot comments, "I've often felt a sort of envy of human beings of that thing they call spirit. Human beings have created a million explanations of the meaning of life, in art, poetry, and mathematical formula. Certainly, human beings must be the key for the meaning of existence. But human beings no longer existed."

When Secular Humanists speak of human beings controlling their own evolution, they are not speaking of common humans, but of elite humans, called "the Conditioners"[22] by C.S. Lewis in *The Abolition of Man*. Lewis comments about those who believe they can create their own destiny: "Either we are rational spirit obliged forever to obey the absolute values of the *Tao* [moral order], or else we are mere nature to be kneaded and cut into new shapes for the pleasures of masters who must, by hypothesis, have no motive but their own 'natural' impulses . . . The Conditioners, then, are to choose what kind of artificial *Tao* they will, for their own good reason, produce in the human race. It is not that they are bad men. They are not men at all. Stepping outside of the *Tao* they have stepped into the void."[23]

---

[16] Lamont, *The Philosophy of Humanism*, 283.

[17] Erich Fromm, *You Shall Be as Gods* (New York, NY: Rinehart, and Winston, 1966), 88.

[18] Ibid., 123.

[19] Lamont, *The Philosophy of Humanism*, 107–8.

[20] Victor J. Stenger, *Not By Design* (Buffalo, NY: Prometheus Books, 1988), 186.

[21] Ibid., 188.

[22] See chapter 3 of C.S. Lewis, *The Abolition of Man* (New York, NY: Macmillan, 1952).

[23] Stenger, *Not By Design*, 188

10.3.7 CONCLUSION

In the Secular Humanist worldview, history is not only about the past; it also concerns a future heaven on earth. Secular Humanism declares that at some future time, humanity will redeem itself by creating the ultimate social order, and eventually humans will perfect themselves (possibly in some form of computer technology). This optimistic view is consistent with the evolutionary perspective Secular Humanists employ that sees humans moving ever closer to perfection.

In their denial of God as the guide to history, Secular Humanists see instead humanity's emerging ideology as the dynamic force in history, and the elite who embrace Humanist ideology as the one who will lead us to save and perfect ourselves. The creed of Secular Humanism seems to be that Secular Humanism is the plan of salvation to ensure a future heaven on earth in the form of a global community.

Richard Carrier actually ends his book with a chapter entitled "The Secular Humanist's Heaven." He says that one of the first orders of business will be to abolish death or as he puts it, "We might even make immortality possible. It may even happen that, in the fullness of time, we will be able to transfer our minds, by transferring the patterns of our brains, into computer-simulated worlds that are in even more perfect regulation than the physical world, a true paradise…It is possible it will never die."[24]

[24] Richard Carrier, *Sense and Goodness Without God: A Defense of Metaphysical Naturalism* (Bloomington, IN: AuthorHouse, 2005), 406.

Marxism–Leninism

> "Whatever is the mode of production of a society, such in the main is the society itself, its ideas and theories, its political views and institutions. Or, to put it more crudely, whatever is man's manner of life, such is his manner of thought."[1]
>
> — JOSEPH STALIN

10.4.1 INTRODUCTION

Marxists-Leninists believe their historical perspective is based strictly on a scientific view of the world, incorporating the science of evolution and the dialectic path of thesis, antithesis, and synthesis. Marxist evolution shapes its view of history based on the belief that humanity, as well as other living things, is constantly improving and will continue to do so.

The Marxist view of history is termed **historical materialism**, meaning that only matter exists, so history is merely the account of matter in motion. In this view, neither God nor angels nor human souls act as the basis for the working of history; rather, matter obeying specific laws is the source of progress in the world.

> HISTORICAL MATERIALISM: The methodological approach to the study of society, economics, and history that looks for the causes of developments and changes in human societies through economic analysis (e.g., social classes, political structures, ideologies, etc.)

---

[1] Joseph Stalin, *Dialectical and Historical Materialism* (New York, NY: International Publishers, 1977), 29.

10.4.2 ECONOMICS AS THE BASIS FOR THE SOCIAL SUPERSTRUCTURE

Karl Marx says, "It is not the consciousness of men that determines their existence, but, on the contrary, their social existence determines their consciousness."[2] Thus, the driving force behind history is the material world. The historian must examine the means of production and exchange to understand the basis for all historical progress, making economics in specific the most powerful force of history. Marx says, "With the change of the economic foundation the entire immense superstructure is more or less rapidly transformed."[3]

Marxists believe in **economic determinism**, which states that economics acts as the foundation for the whole social superstructure, including the thoughts of individuals. Frederick Engels declares that "in every historical epoch, the prevailing mode of economic production and exchange, and the social organization necessarily following from it, form the basis upon which is built up, and from which alone can be explained, the political and intellectual history of that epoch."[4]

ECONOMIC DETERMINISM: The belief that economics is the major driving force in history

In Marxism, governments, courts, philosophies, and religions are based on a society's economic system and therefore affect history only to the extent that economics shapes their ability to guide human development. Economics is the only dynamic force in history, and all other aspects of humanity and society are determined by it.

10.4.3 ECONOMIC DETERMINISM AND FREE WILL

Marx believes that we can still possess free will within this framework, but he carefully distinguishes between being totally free and being free within the constraints placed on us by all outside material influences. He writes, "Men make their own history, but they do not make it just as they please; they do not make it under circumstances chosen by themselves, but under circumstances directly encountered, given and transmitted from the past."[5]

Marx seems to admit the apparent contradiction in granting us free will while stating that economics alone drives history. He says, "Are men free to choose this or that form of society for themselves? By no means . . . Assume particular stages of development in production, commerce and consumption and you will have a corresponding social structure, a corresponding organization of the family, of orders or of classes, in a word, a corresponding civil society . . . It is superfluous to add that men are not free to choose their productive forces—which are the basis of all their history . . ."[6]

> In every historical epoch, the prevailing mode of economic production and exchange, and the social organization necessarily following from it, form the basis upon which is built up, and from which alone can be explained, the political and intellectual history of that epoch.
>
> — FREDERICK ENGELS

[2] Karl Marx, *A Contribution to the Critique of Political Economy* (New York, NY: International Publishers, 1904), 11. Marx's view here is identical to that of existentialists, who insist that existence precedes essence. This viewpoint is thus attractive to Marxists and Postmodernists.

[3] Marx, *Contribution to the Critique of Political Economy*, 12.

[4] Karl Marx and Frederick Engels, *The Communist Manifesto* (Chicago, IL: Henry Regnery Publishers, 1954), 5.

[5] Karl Marx, Frederick Engels, and V.I. Lenin, *On Historical Materialism* (New York, NY: International Publishers, 1974), 120.

[6] Karl Marx, *The Poverty of Philosophy* (New York, NY: International Publishers, 1936), 152–3.

But if we may not choose our society, its superstructure, or its mode of production, and if these things in turn determine our mode of thought, then what *can* we choose? It would seem that our only option is to follow the flow of history as determined by the economic structure.

This conclusion seems even more inescapable in light of the Marxist belief that history is governed by certain scientifically discoverable laws. V.I. Lenin believes Marx drew attention "to a scientific study of history as a single process which, with all its immense variety and contradictoriness, is governed by definite laws."[7]

The belief in such laws has a sinister implication—it allows Marxists to abandon both morality and reason because they can justify whatever they do as being predetermined by the "hidden laws" that govern historical events. Joseph Stalin claims, "Hence the practical activity of the party of the proletariat must not be based on the good wishes of 'outstanding individuals,' not on the dictates of 'reason,' 'universal morals,' etc., but on the laws of development of society and on the study of these laws."[8]

10.4.4 COMMUNISM AS INEVITABLE

Such laws will guide history through a series of economic systems to a founding system on which the perfect society can be built. This redemption is guaranteed, regardless of the action or inaction of individuals. The paradise to which all of history is leading is a socialist/communist society. Salvation for the Marxist lies in the consummation of the historical process in a one-world utopia. Lenin proclaims, "Communists should know that the future belongs to them . . . [I]n all cases and in all countries communism is becoming steeled and is spreading, its roots are so deep that persecution does not weaken it, does not debilitate it, but strengthens it."[9]

The laws leading the world toward communism are inexorable, and no amount of human will can stop the collapse of capitalism, the rise of socialism, and the steady transition from socialism to communism. Maurice Cornforth declares, "From the point of view of the capitalist class, Marx's theory is certainly 'fatalistic.' It says: You cannot contrive a managed capitalism, you cannot do away with the class struggle, and you cannot keep the system going indefinitely."[10]

Marxists believe that scientific laws are directing the evolution of economic systems toward a paradisiacal end. Marxism perceives human efforts working toward any other end as useless and insignificant, and declares that humanity will achieve utopia (a communist society) despite all efforts and desires to the contrary.

10.4.5 DIALECTIC APPLIED TO HISTORY

For Marxists, free will is drastically truncated: we are free in the sense that we may influence history by striving to achieve communism, but we are determined in the sense that we can affect history in no other way than toward communism. Communism is inevitable, as dictated by the laws of history, which, in turn, are governed by the dialectic.

Marxists believe that the dialectic has guided society through certain phases (all based on economic structures) in a constant upward spiral. They believe that human society began with primitive communism, but thesis and antithesis collided, giving birth to societies based on slavery, which in turn developed into feudalism. This phase progressed into capitalism,

---

[7] Marx, Engels, and Lenin, *On Historical Materialism*, 461.

[8] Stalin, *Dialectical and Historical Materialism*, 19.

[9] V.I. Lenin, *Collected Works*, 45 vols. (Moscow, USSR: Progress Publishers, 1980), 2:57.

[10] Maurice Cornforth, *The Open Philosophy and the Open Society* (New York, NY: International Publishers, 1976), 159.

which is now moving toward socialism. The continued clash of the bourgeoisie (the present thesis) with the proletariat (the present antithesis) will lead society into a transitional phase—socialism—and when the clash is resolved due to the abolition of classes, society will have achieved communism. Thus, history must obey the laws of the dialectic, and these laws declare that economic structures will eventually evolve into communism, on which the perfect societal superstructure will arise.

The part of the dialectic that Marxists emphasize when discussing free will is the clash. Because the dialectic requires a clash (revolution) to instigate progress, the activity of classes becomes important. The individual is still insignificant in the Marxist view of history, but classes of humanity (in modern times, the bourgeoisie and the proletariat) can play a role in human development. Cornforth states, "Historical development is not determined by the personal decisions of public men, but by the movement of classes."[11]

> Historical development is not determined by the personal decisions of public men, but by the movement of classes.
>
> — MAURICE CORNFORTH

Thus, the dialectic appears to maintain a degree of human free will—our actions matter, but only in regard to our movements as a class, and even then only if we are working in accordance with the laws of history. In other words, in modern times, only the proletarian can work as a progressive force, and even then only under the guidance of the Marxist party (because only the party truly understands the historical process). Our ability to shape history according to this view is limited, but Marxists emphasize this ability as much as possible.

In fact, Marxism requires the participation of the masses to such an extent (from a practical standpoint) that it often describes the revolutionary's role as the most critical in history. Lenin proclaims, "According to the theory of socialism, i.e., of Marxism . . . the real driving force of history is the revolutionary class struggle."[12]

10.4.6 THE FUTURE ACCORDING TO MARX

The Marxist view of history fails to address two potentialities. First, if classes act as the catalyst for the dialectic, then what becomes of the dialectic when classes cease to exist? Under communism all class distinctions will be abolished. But without classes, what will act as the thesis and the antithesis to drive the dialectic toward a clash and ultimately to a new synthesis? What will keep the wheels of history turning?

Second, theoretically the dialectic has improved our economic structures (and consequently, our societies and ideas) throughout history, but as soon as the dialectic forces the whole world to communism, the ultimate mode of production and exchange will have been achieved and the need for the dialectic will be erased. How can the dialectic lead us beyond communism? No better economic structure (and therefore, no better basis for society and ideas) exists.

10.4.7 CONCLUSION

Marxists view history from an atheistic and evolutionary perspective and therefore believe human history will always progress, just as the development of life constantly progresses. Consequently, Marxists perceive that the historical process guarantees our redemption through the future establishment of a communist utopia.

---

[11] Maurice Cornforth, *Historical Materialism* (New York, NY: International Publishers, 1972), 68.
[12] Lenin, *Collected Works*, 11:71.

Marxism sees history operating according to specific, discoverable laws of the dialectic, which change economic structures and thereby revolutionize societies and ideas.

Marxists try to re-establish humans as a driving force in history by declaring the revolution of the oppressed classes to be the catalyst for the dialectical process. According to this view, only people who act in accordance with the laws of history and the course of development have any impact. Thus, in the Marxist view of history, we are much like fans at a fixed boxing match. No matter how long and loud we cheer, no matter how hard we clap and stomp our feet, the boxer "taking a dive" will undoubtedly lose. We might as well clap and cheer for the predetermined winner, encouraging him to win the bout more decisively.

In Marxist terms, whether we take a direct route or zigzag back and forth, the final outcome of history remains the same. Marxists believe their worldview alone adheres to the scientific conception of history and that natural laws guarantee inevitable progress. Marxism grants all power to the historical/dialectical process

The Pop Culture Connection

Good Will Hunting (a 1997 film)—Giving a nod to radical Marxist personalities, Will Hunting (Matt Damon) informs his psychiatrist of his interest in Howard Zinn's book, *A People's History of the United States.* In response, the psychiatrist (Robin Williams) praises Noam Chomsky as well. However, both writers are Marxists who hate America and everything it stands for. Zinn once wrote, "Objectivity is impossible and it is also undesirable...because if you have any kind of a social aim...then it requires that you make your selection on the basis of what you think will advance causes of humanity."* *A People's History* is a revisionist tale with outrageous remarks and factual errors parading as history, yet is required reading on many campuses. For example, Zinn portrays the founding of the United States as a "diabolically creative way to ensure oppression." Noam Chomsky, also a radical leftist, "ranks with Marx, Shakespeare, and the Bible as one of the ten most quoted sources in the humanities." In a 2003 interview, he said "the U.S. government is an extreme radical and nationalist group with some similarities to European Fascism."[14]

and calls for individuals to work only in submission to this omnipotent force. Marx says, "History is the judge—its executioner, the proletarian."[13]

---

[13] Marx, Engels, and Lenin, *On Historical Materialism*, 135.

[14] Interview with Howard Zinn," DigressMagazine.com, www.digressmagazine.com/zinn/zinn1. Quotes cited in Daniel Flynn, *Intellectual Morons: How Ideology Makes Smart People Fall for Stupid Ideas* (New York, NY: Crown Forum, 2004), 102, 107, 109.

Cosmic Humanism

"For the first time in history, humankind has come upon
the control panel of change—an understanding of how
transformation occurs. We are living in the change of
change, the time in which we can intentionally align
ourselves with nature for rapid remaking of ourselves
and our collapsing institutions."[1]

— MARILYN FERGUSON

10.5.1 INTRODUCTION

The Cosmic Humanist trusts cosmic evolution to guide humanity unswervingly toward perfection. In a very real sense, members of the New Age movement place their faith in evolution as humanity's savior.

Faith in evolution causes the Cosmic Humanist to view human history as an ascent—a development from lower to higher levels of consciousness. Evolution is upward because the God-force within the universe pulls it upward. Benjamin Ferencz and Ken Keyes explain, "We have seen that humankind is not simply moving in a vicious killing circle; it is on an upward climb toward completing the governmental structure of the world. We are inspired by our great progress toward planethood."[2] Elsewhere they declare that their "optimism is justified by the facts."[3]

[1] Marilyn Ferguson, *The Aquarian Conspiracy* (Los Angeles, CA: J.P. Tarcher, 1980), 71
[2] Benjamin B. Ferencz and Ken Keyes, Jr., *Planethood* (Coos Bay, OR: Vision Books, 1988), 141.
[3] Ibid., 33.

In the Cosmic Humanist worldview, history is progressive because of the force of evolution. Even the Second Law of Thermodynamics does not discourage their optimistic view of history. Indeed, physicist Paul Davies writes, "Far from sliding towards a featureless state, the Universe is progressing from featurelessness to states of greater organization and complexity. This cosmic progress defines a global arrow of time that points in the opposite way to the thermodynamic arrow."[4]

10.5.2 IRRELEVANCE OF CHRISTIANITY

Part of "cosmic progress" is the evolution from religion to religion. Certain religions, according to the Cosmic Humanist, were beneficial for the evolution of humanity at certain times in history—until humanity "outgrew" them. Thus, the Christian worldview might have helped us in our quest for godhood a thousand years ago, but today it is hopelessly outdated. Joseph Campbell says, "The old-time religion belongs to another age, another people, another set of human values, another universe. By going back you throw yourself out of sync with history."[5] In order to continue evolving, we must abandon biblical Christianity.

The New Age movement is quick to ascribe a number of faults to Christianity. Its most serious failing, of course, is its dogma—the Christian insistence that Christ is the only Savior (John 14:6). Various Cosmic Humanists also attack Christianity on the grounds that it is nationalistic, racist, or promotes feelings of guilt. These failings among others "disqualify [Christianity] for the future,"[6] according to Campbell. Christianity is no longer relevant, let alone true. Cosmic Humanism is the only appropriate religion for our modern age and it alone can foster an evolutionary leap into higher consciousness.

10.5.3 FUTURE OF MANKIND: EVOLUTIONARY GODHOOD

Evolution guarantees that everyone will eventually embrace Cosmic Humanism and usher in the New Age. Faith in this sustained progress into the New Age has been demonstrated by a number of Cosmic Humanists, most notably M. Scott Peck, who says, "God wants us to become Himself (or Herself or Itself). We are growing toward godhood. God is the goal of evolution. It is God who is the source of the evolutionary force and God who is the destination. This is what we mean when we say that He is the Alpha and the Omega, the beginning and the end."[7]

Evolutionary Godhood describes the historical trajectory of Cosmic Humanism. Human history began because of the actions of an Ultimate Cause and it has been marked by a reliable, though bloody, evolution toward the New Age. In the New Age, all humanity will achieve a unity of consciousness with God. Marianne Williamson believes, "When love reaches a critical mass, when enough people become miracle-minded, the world will experience a radical shift."[8]

EVOLUTIONARY GODHOOD: The belief that the divine is the source of evolutionary force and that we are growing toward godhood

This shift has been revealed through the channeled work *A Course in Miracles*. Every person will be absorbed into a "Divine Abstract," where there are "no distinctions, where no words are communicated, and

---

[4] Paul Davies, "Great Balls of Fire," *New Scientist* 24/31 December 1987, 64
[5] Joseph Campbell, *The Power of Myth* (New York, NY: Doubleday, 1988), 18.
[6] Ibid.
[7] M. Scott Peck, *The Road Less Traveled* (New York, NY: Simon and Schuster, 1978), 269–70.
[8] Marianne Williamson, *A Return to Love: Reflections on the Principles of "A Course in Miracles"* (New York, NY: Harper Collins, 1989), 71.

where there are no events—only a static, eternal now."[9]

Some members of the New Age movement, unsatisfied with the concept of evolution as the redemptive force in history, have postulated the appearance of a spiritual Savior who will guide humanity to higher consciousness and utopia. Thus, Donald H. Yott suggests that a "Savior appears every two thousand years (more or less) for the different ages. Each Savior brings the tone or key-note for the age."[10] A spirit channeled by Levi H. Dowling proclaims, "But in the ages to come, man will attain to greater heights. And then, at last, a mighty Master Soul will come to earth to light the way up to the throne of perfect man."[11]

These predictions are not intended to deny the influence of evolution on our

The Pop Culture Connection

What Dreams May Come (a 1998 film)—Chris Nielsen (Robin Williams) dies and goes to heaven—only to find that it looks like a painting done by his wife. Heaven, as it turns out, is a creation of his own will. When Nielsen notices a bird painted in the sky, he asks his spiritual guide, Albert Lewis (Cuba Gooding, Jr.) why it's not moving. Lewis says it's completely up to him; if he wants it to fly, it will. So Nielson wills the bird to life, and it begins to fly wherever he wants it to go. At one point, Albert says, "Thought is real. Physical is the illusion. Ironic, huh?"—indicating that our thoughts control reality. The underlying theme is that ultimate happiness is to have all our wishes and desires fulfilled, whether in the here-and-now or the future.

development. Rather, they simply add a "supernatural" dimension to human progress. While not every Cosmic Humanist would agree with the idea that a new Savior will appear in the future, all would agree with the assertion that throughout history humanity evolves from lower to higher consciousness.

10.5.4 CONCLUSION

A historical perspective that embraces evolution as the vehicle for change—that expects it is only a matter of time until humanity achieves perfection—might be expected to lean toward complacency. If we believe that the evolutionary process will determine how and when we achieve godhood, we should not bother working toward godhood in our lifetime. Cosmic Humanists circumvent this apathetic attitude by stressing that we have already achieved a level of consciousness that allows us to work in harmony with evolution to hasten the advent of the New Age. This view not only encourages Cosmic Humanists to act on their beliefs but also allows those with a higher consciousness to catapult the "backward" part of humanity into godhood.

Shakti Gawain explains, "Every individual's consciousness is connected to, and is a part of, the mass consciousness. When a small but significant number of individuals have moved into a new level of awareness and significantly changed their behavior, that change

> When a small but significant number of individuals have moved into a new level of awareness and significantly changed their behavior, that change is felt in the entire mass consciousness.
>
> — SHAKTI GAWAIN

[9] Dean C. Halverson, *Crystal Clear: Understanding and Reaching New Agers* (Colorado Springs, CO: NavPress, 1990), 77.
[10] Donald H. Yott, *Man and Metaphysics* (New York, NY: Weiser, 1980), 74.
[11] Levi H. Dowling and Eva H. Dowling, *The Aquarian Gospel of Jesus the Christ* (Los Angeles, CA: DeVorss & Co., 1972), 24.

is felt in the entire mass consciousness."[12] This is the goal that all Cosmic Humanists work toward in an effort to hasten the full-blown evolution of all things. David Spangler describes this as the "individual's sense of being a co-creator with history, of being involved in a process of conscious and participatory evolution."[13]

---

[12] Shakti Gawain, *Living in the Light* (San Rafael, CA: New World Library, 1986), 179.
[13] David Spangler, *Emergence: The Rebirth of the Sacred* (New York, NY: Delta/Merloyd Lawrence, 1984), 12.

Postmodernism

> "I am well aware that I have never written anything but fictions. I do not mean to say, however, that truth is therefore absent. It seems to me that the possibility exists for fiction to function in truth. One 'fictions' history on the basis of a political reality that makes it true, one 'fictions' a politics not yet in existence on the basis of a historical truth."[1]
>
> — MICHEL FOUCAULT

10.6.1 INTRODUCTION

The Postmodern approach to history differs dramatically from that of all other worldviews.[2] For example, a Christian worldview sees history as the grand unfolding of God's divine plan to redeem a fallen humanity (see Paul's speech in Acts 17). In contrast, the more radical

---

[1] Michel Foucault, *Power/Knowledge: Selected Interviews and Other Writings 1972–1977*, Colin Gordon, ed. (New York, NY: Pantheon Books, 1980), 193. Cited in Keith Windschuttle, *The Killing of History: How Literary Critics and Social Theories Are Murdering Our Past* (San Francisco, CA: Encounter Books, 1996), 151.

[2] See Mark Goldblatt's article "Can Humanists Talk to Poststructuralists?" in *Academic Questions,* Spring 2005, Vol. 18, No. 2. Goldblatt's answer: "This is why humanists, in the end, cannot talk to poststructuralists." Goldblatt levels at Derrida the following charge: "For Derrida winds up his analysis with another logical throw-away: 'Neither/nor, that is, simultaneously either/or.' In other words, whatever Derrida is affirming, he is also simultaneously denying. From a humanist perspective, the only way to read Derrida on his own terms is mentally to insert the phrase 'or not' after every one of his statements" (59).

HISTORICISM: The view that past beliefs, morals, and truths can only be understood in relation to the cultural/historical periods in which they arose

Postmodernists see no ultimate purpose in history, advocating instead a *nihilist* perspective. Less radical Postmodernists advocate the view that history is what we make of it. They believe that historical facts are inaccessible, leaving the historian to his or her imagination and ideological bent to reconstruct what happened in the past.

Postmodernists use the term **historicism** to describe the view that all questions must be settled within the cultural and social context in which they are raised. Both Lacan and Foucault argue that each historical period has its own knowledge system and individuals are unavoidably entangled within these systems. Answers to life's questions cannot be found by appealing to some external truth, but only to the norms and forms within each culture that phrase the question.

10.6.2 HISTORY AS FICTION

The traditional approach to history holds that by sifting through the evidence at hand (texts, artifacts, etc.), we may arrive at a more or less accurate understanding of past events and their significance. This means that not all descriptions of history are equally valid. Some accounts may be more true to the actual events than others. As new information comes to light, any narrative of history could be revised or supplemented.

However, most Postmodernists doubt that an accurate telling of the past is possible because they blur the difference between fact and fiction—some even claim that *all* historical accounts are fiction.[3] Foucault is one of the originators of this Postmodern approach to history, which offers a profound challenge to the norm. Professor John Coffey, in a biography of Foucault, provides insight into how Foucault's background influenced his views on history:

The Pop Culture Connection

A Knight's Tale (a 2001 film)—is a postmodern fusion of episodes from different historical time periods and fictional characters and events. Hollywood screenwriter Brian Godawa explains how this blending of actors and action, past and present, reveals a postmodern self-consciousness. He writes, "*A Knights Tale* is Brian Helgeland's fictional medieval story about jousting. . . . In this movie, medieval jousting tournaments are staged like modern sports contests, complete with the crowd clapping to the song 'We Will Rock You' by the modern band Queen, as well as a royal dance breaking out into modern choreography to a David Bowie song, 'Golden Years.' Here is self-conscious storytelling about stories with no pretense to reality."[4]

In 1948 Michel Foucault attempted to commit suicide. He was at the time a student at the elite Parisian university, the Ecole Normale. The resident doctor there had little doubt about the source of the young man's distress. Foucault appeared to be racked with guilt over his frequent nocturnal visits to the illegal gay bars of the French capital. His father, a strict disciplinarian who had previously sent his son to the most regimented Catholic school he could find, arranged for Michel to be admitted to a psychiatric hospital for evaluation. Yet Foucault remained obsessed with death, joked about hanging himself and made further attempts to end his own life. This youthful experience of

---

[3] Christopher Butler, *Postmodernism: A Very Short Introduction* (Oxford, UK: Oxford University Press, 2002), 32–36.

[4] Brian Godawa, *Hollywood Worldviews: Watching Films with Wisdom and Discernment* (Downers Grove, IL: InterVarsity Press, 2002), 93.

himself as homosexual, suicidal and mentally disturbed proved decisive for Foucault's intellectual development. The subject matter of many of his later books arose from his own experience—*Madness and Civilization* (1961), *The Birth of the Clinic* (1963), *Discipline and Punish* (1975), and *The History of Sexuality* (3 Vols. 1976-1984) all dwell on topics of deep personal concern to their author. Foucault's intellectual career was to be a lifelong crusade on behalf of those whom society labeled, marginalized, incarcerated and suppressed.[5]

Thus Foucault was intent on liberating himself and others from all constraints: theological, moral, and social. Mark Poster observes, "Foucault offers a new way of thinking about history, writing history and deploying history in current political struggles. Foucault is an anti-historian, one who in writing history, threatens every canon of the craft."[6] Indeed, one of Foucault's major theses was that *truth* and *knowledge* were nothing other than claims to power.

For Foucault, truth and knowledge were constructions we offer to persuade others. They need not correspond to reality, for we construct our own reality in such a way as to give us power over others. With this in mind, his admission in *Knowledge/ Power* is revealing: "I am well aware that I have never written anything but fictions. I do not mean to say, however, that truth is therefore absent. It seems to me that the possibility exists for fiction to function in truth, for a fictional discourse to induce effects of truth, and for bringing it about that a true discourse engenders or 'manufactures' something that does not as yet exist, that it 'fictions' it. One 'fictions' history on the basis of a political reality that makes it true, one 'fictions' a politics not yet in existence on the basis of a historical truth."[7]

> Foucault is an anti-historian, one who in writing history, threatens every canon of the craft.
>
> — MARK POSTER

10.6.3 REVISING HISTORY

While the history of humanity itself may not have a purpose, the writing of historical accounts does. Resonating with Foucault's approach to history is the view that the writing of history should promote an ideology. If, as Foucault declares, a claim to knowledge really is nothing but an attempt to overpower others, then retelling history serves the purpose of gaining power for some repressed group.

Thus, according to the Postmodern condition the discipline of history has turned away from the study of significant individuals and the struggles between nations to focus on social groups and institutions. Tom Dixon writes, "Social historians are often driven by activist goals. Historical research becomes not an attempt to understand the past but a propaganda tool for use in modern political and social power struggles."[8] Dixon also notes, "Postmodern cultural historians consider bias unavoidable in whole or even in part. As a result we see a growing willingness to arrange and edit facts in a way

> Historical research becomes not an attempt to understand the past but a propaganda tool for use in modern political social power struggles.
>
> — TOM DIXON

[5] John Coffey, *Life After the Death of God: Michel Foucault and Postmodern Atheism* (Cambridge, UK: Cambridge Papers, 1996), 1. Online at http://jubilee-centre.org/online_documents/LifeafterthedeathofGod.htm (September 2005).

[6] Mark Poster, *Foucault, Marxism and History: Mode of Production versus Mode of Information* (Cambridge, UK: Polity Press, 1984), 73. Cited in Windschuttle, *The Killing of History*, 132.

[7] Foucault, *Power/Knowledge*, 193. Cited in Windschuttle, *The Killing of History*, 151.

[8] Cited in Dennis McCallum, ed., *The Death of Truth* (Minneapolis, MN: Bethany House, 1996), 133.

that supports the message of particular historians."[9] This is precisely where the line between recording history and revising history is crossed.

This rewriting of the past to serve a purpose, known as **revisionist history**, contributes to empowering oppressed social minorities. Thus feminist histories attempt to expose a male-dominated, patriarchal past and point the way for empowering women. Likewise, homosexual

> REVISIONIST HISTORY:
> Rewriting the past to serve an ideological purpose and to empower oppressed social groups

histories are put forward (in response to homophobic repressions) to provide equality for homosexuals. Black histories emphasize the horrors of slavery to redress past maltreatment of African Americans. Every repressed group—minorities of all colors, ethnicities, nationalities, and sexualities—has an injustice that must be exposed in order to rectify the abuses of the past.

Take as one example Rigoberta Menchu, who won the Nobel Prize in 1992 for her autobiography, *I, Rogoberta Menchu: An Indian Woman in Guatemala*. Her book became an instant success on college campuses, where professors used her story to demonstrate the plight of the impoverished Guatemalans languishing under government death squads. Menchu maintains that she personally witnessed the Guatemalan army burn her brother alive in her town's public square. However, when doctoral student David Stoll went to Guatemala to verify Menchu's story, he discovered no villager had a memory of such a slaughter by the Guatemalan Army.[10] In fact, the key struggle in the book, between her father and a light-skinned landowner, was actually an argument between her father and his in-laws.

As it turns out, Menchu had told her story to French leftist Elisabeth Burgos-Debray, who actually wrote the autobiography, misrepresenting many "facts" in her book. Burgos-Debray claimed that Menchu, as a female, was denied school, yet she actually attended two Catholic boarding schools through seventh grade. The book states that she worked on a plantation under horrible conditions, yet she never set foot on a plantation as a child. Also, the author claimed that the local villagers saw the Marxist guerrillas as liberators, when in actuality the villagers were terrified of them.

Kevin J. Kelley comments, "U.S. leftists who give his [Stoll's] arguments a full hearing—and who have not been deafened by their own dogma—will find Stoll's analysis difficult to dismiss."[11] Yet, in response to Stoll's research, Professor Marjorie Agosin of Wellesley College stated bluntly, "Whether her book is true or not, I don't care. We should teach our students about the brutality of the Guatemalan military and the U.S. financing of it."[12] Ideology therefore trumps integrity.

Some feminist historians assert that men cannot write histories of women, first because men simply cannot understand women, and second because men have masculine ideologies and women have feminine ideologies. The same is said about a person attempting to write the history of a different race. It cannot be done since all people are presumed to be under a cloud of racial bias.

[9] Ibid., 138, 139.

[10] See David Stoll, *Rigoberta Menchu and the Story of All Poor Guatemalans* (Oxford, UK: Westview Press, 1999).

[11] Ibid., back cover.

[12] Robin Wilson, "Anthropologist Challenges Veracity of Multicultural Icon," *The Chronicle of Higher Education*, 1999. http://chronicle.com/colloquy/99/menchu/background.htm

10.6.4 MARXIST DERIVATIVES AND DEPARTURE

A Postmodernist approach to history in some ways mimics Marxism, which is understandable since the fountainheads of Postmodernism have Marxism in their intellectual genealogies. A distinct residue of Marxist critique remains in their work, providing them with the dichotomizing perspective so blatant in the Marxist vision of class struggle. Derrida admits that his deconstruction is a radicalization "within the tradition of a certain Marxism, in a certain spirit of Marxism."[13]

Specifically the Postmodern historian mimics Marxist understanding of the ideological nature of writing history. While Marxists focus on the proletariat rising against the bourgeoisies, Postmodernists focus on one gender, race, or socially identifiable group in a struggle for dominion over another. Gene Veith explains, "Post-Marxist radicalism constructs new revolutionary ideologies by replacing Marx's concern for the oppressed working class with other oppressed groups (blacks, women, gays). Status and moral legitimacy come from being 'excluded from power.' The victim has the favored role. . . . To be black, female or gay is to enjoy a sort of secular sainthood. But even these categories are segmenting into ever-smaller sects of victim hood."[14] Such an approach does little to draw society together toward harmonious civility. Rather, it engenders a new tribalism, pitting every group against the other in an attempt to gain moral standing by becoming the greatest victim.

One significant difference between Postmodernist and Marxist approaches to history concerns whether history has an inherent meaning. Marxists advocate *historical materialism*, complete with the vision that human history eventually will arrive at a purely communistic (i.e., classless) society. In a similar way Secular Humanists hope for evolutionary progress throughout history and Cosmic Humanists spiritualize those evolutionary hopes for bringing about a "New Age." But the Postmodernist view of history is distinctly *a*teleological (i.e., without a purpose). For them, mankind is an evolving animal but not necessarily at the top of the species list. Homo sapiens are simply one among many species. We have arrived at this point in evolutionary history by chance, not design, and therefore have no purpose or destiny.

A world without meaning or purpose results in nihilism. Stephen Hicks suggests that Derrida clearly understood the kind of world Postmodernism was bringing and declared his intention not to be among those who let their queasiness get the better of them. Derrida proclaimed that Postmodernists "do not turn their eyes away" when faced with the prospect that ours is "the species of the nonspecies, in the formless, mute, infant, and terrifying form of monstrosity."[15] This is a strong rejection of a meaningful past. Given a naturalistic approach to life, one without the bold assertions of Marxism or the sentimental hopefulness of Humanism, a Postmodern view of history is devoid of ultimate meaning or purpose.[16]

---

[13] Jacques Derrida, *Moscou aller-retour* (Saint Etienne, France: De l' Aube, 1995). Cited in Stephen R.C. Hicks, *Explaining Postmodernism: Skepticism and Socialism from Rousseau to Foucault* (Tempe, AZ: Scholargy Publishing, 2004), 186.

[14] Gene Edward Veith, *Postmodern Times: A Christian Guide to Contemporary Thought and Culture* (Wheaton, IL: Crossway Books, 1994), 161.

[15] Jacques Derrida, *Writing and Difference* (Chicago, IL: University of Chicago Press, 1978), 293. Cited in Hicks, *Explaining Postmodernism*, 195.

[16] See Elizabeth A. Clark, *History, Theory, Text: Historians and the Linguistic Turn* (Cambridge, MA: Harvard University Press, 2004), 42-43 for a discussion of early Postmodern theories and Marxist historical teleology.

10.6.5 CONCLUSION

Because ideas have consequences, we cannot afford to overlook the consequences of the more radical Postmodern approaches to history. If history is mere fiction, or even largely so, then those who deny, for example, the Nazi holocaust are validated in their attempts to diminish the numbers of Jews imprisoned, tortured, starved, shot, cremated, or buried in mass graves. Indeed, if history is (largely) fiction, then Mother Teresa and Adolph Hitler cannot be used as examples of good and evil. There are no "facts." There are only various degrees of fiction.

Conclusion

Part One

> "I now believe that the balance of reasoned considerations tells heavily in favor of the religious, even of the Christian view of the world."[1]

— C.E.M. JOAD

11.1.1 INTRODUCTION

"Come now, let us reason together," God says (Isaiah 1:18).

"Always be prepared to give an answer to everyone who asks you to give the reason for the hope that you have. But do this with gentleness and respect," says the Apostle Peter (1 Peter 3:15, NIV).

Acting in accordance with these exhortations, Christians must meet the challenges posed by non-Christian worldviews that claim Biblical Christianity is irrational, unhistorical, and unscientific. This concluding chapter speaks to many of these challenges.

All non-Christian worldviews contain some truth. Secular Humanism, for example, does not deny the existence of the physical universe and our ability to know it. Marxism accepts the significance and relevance of science. Postmodernism acknowledges the importance of texts and words. Islam acknowledges a created universe. Cosmic Humanism teaches there is more to reality than matter. All five non-Christian worldviews, to one extent or another, understand

---

[1] C.E.M. Joad, *The Recovery of Belief* (London, UK: Faber and Faber, 1955), 22.

> A major dividing line separates the non-Christian worldviews from Christianity, and that is what each one believes about Jesus Christ.

the importance of "saving" the human race.

However, a major dividing line separates the non-Christian worldviews from Christianity—that is, what each one believes about Jesus Christ. Christianity views Jesus Christ as the true and living Way (John 14:6) and the key to reality itself (Colossians 1:16, Hebrews 1:1–3, John 1:1–3). Early Christians were known as members of The Way (Acts 9:2). All other major worldviews reject Jesus Christ as Savior, Lord, King—indeed, some deny His very existence. Thus, an insurmountable difference exists between Christianity and its worldview competitors.

11.1.2 OUT OF TOUCH WITH REALITY

Who is Jesus? Did Jesus Christ live on this earth two thousand years ago? Was He God in flesh? Did He come to earth to reveal God's will for us and to save the human race from sin? These are important questions. Biblical Christianity lives or dies on the answers, as Paul points out: "If Christ be not risen, your faith is in vain" (1 Corinthians 15:14).

For example, if Postmodernists are correct in their belief that there are no metanarratives, Christianity is doomed, for it depends on the truths that all human beings have sinned and come short of the glory of God; that God loved the whole human race (John 3:16); and that Christ died for our sins (I John 2:2). If these universal claims are false, Christianity is false.

Whether we choose to believe biblical Christianity, Islam, Secular Humanism, Marxism-Leninism, Cosmic Humanism, or Postmodernism, we are accepting a worldview that describes the others as hopelessly distorted. Only one view depicts things as they really are; all other perspectives must be out of step with human nature and the universe.

> Whether one chooses to believe biblical Christianity, Islam, Secular Humanism, Marxism-Leninism, Cosmic Humanism, or Postmodernism, we are accepting a worldview that describes the others as hopelessly distorted.

Adherents to secular religious worldviews understand that if their assumptions are correct, any worldview that permits the supernatural to exist must be dangerous. For instance, Marxists and Humanists are quick to describe Christians as out of touch with reality. Marx viewed all religion as a drug that deluded its adherents—an "opiate of the masses." Postmodernists like Richard Rorty view Christians as intolerant, frightening, bigoted, homophobic, fanatic, vicious, and dangerous.[2]

Some Humanists even portray Christians as mentally imbalanced. James J.D. Luce, the assistant executive director of Fundamentalists Anonymous, claims that "the fundamentalist experience can be a serious mental health hazard to perhaps millions of people."[3] His organization works to "heal" Christians of their "mental disorder"—their Christian worldview. Harvard's Edward O. Wilson takes this a step further, describing Christianity as "one of the unmitigated evils of the world."[4] On the other end of the spectrum, Cosmic Humanists reject the personal God of the Bible as a dangerous myth that separates people into religious factions, claiming for themselves a unified consciousness instead.

---

[2] Robert B. Brandom, ed., *Rorty and his Critics* (Oxford, UK: Blackwell Publishers, 2001), 22.

[3] James J.D. Luce, "The Fundamentalists Anonymous Movement," *The Humanist* (Jan/Feb 1986): 11.

[4] Edward O. Wilson, "The Relation of Science to Theology," *Zygon,*(Sept/Dec 1980). Cited in Henry M. Morris, *The Long War Against God* (Grand Rapids, MI: Baker Book House, 1990), 34.

Either Christians correctly describe reality when they speak of a loving, wise, just, personal, creative God or they are talking nonsense. We cannot blend the basic tenets of the Bible with non-Christian claims that we are inherently good and require no savior outside ourselves. Only one view describes the facts of a universe that Christians believe was created by God and was important enough that He sent His son to redeem it. These differences exist and, since there can be no reconciliation between Christianity and opposing worldviews, everyone must examine the evidence to arrive at the truth.

To this end, this concluding section focuses on the fundamental concepts of these six worldviews. We are not interested in hair-splitting. Secular Humanism, for example does not stand or fall according to its position on gun control. It does stand or fall, however, on its theology, philosophy, ethics, and biology. Our emphasis is foundational—we desire to evaluate and separate wheat from chaff, truth from fiction. It is here, we believe, that Christianity stands tall, looming over its competition.

11.1.3 CHRISTIANITY SHINES BRIGHTLY

Christianity best explains the existence of the universe and all things related to it. In a systematic analysis of the ten major components of a worldview, Christianity claims the following:

- **Theology**—the evidence for the existence of a personal and holy God, a designed universe, and an earth prepared for human life outweighs any argument for atheism or pantheism.
- **Philosophy**—the notion that mind (*logos*) precedes matter is superior to the atheistic stance of matter preceding mind.
- **Ethics**—the concept that right and wrong are objective absolutes based on the nature and character of a personal, loving God is superior both theoretically and practically to any concept of moral relativism.
- **Biology**—the concept of a living God creating life fits the evidence better than any hint of spontaneous generation and macroevolution.
- **Psychology**—understanding human beings as being body and soul, yet sinful, imperfect, and in need of a Savior, far outweighs expecting humans to be guilt-free and ultimately perfectible.
- **Sociology**—the biblical definition of a family, with father, mother, and child, transcends any experiments in trial marriage, open marriage, or same-sex marriage.
- **Law**—the notion that God hates the perversion of justice provides a firmer foundation than legal theories that cradle criminals or abort unborn human beings.
- **Politics**—the Christian belief that human rights are a gift from God protected by government is more logically persuasive, morally appealing, and politically sound than any atheistic theory that maintains human rights are derived from the state.
- **Economics**—the concept of private property and using resources responsibly to glorify God is nobler than the notion of state ownership that destroys individual responsibility and incentives to work.
- **History**—the Bible's promise of a future kingdom ushered in by Jesus Christ is far more hopeful than any utopian schemes dreamed up by sinful, mortal humans.

In other words, in every discipline the Christian worldview shines brighter than its competition. It better explains our place in the universe, is more realistic, is more scientific, is more intellectually satisfying and defensible, and best of all, is in keeping with and faithful to the one person who has the greatest influence in heaven and on earth—Jesus Christ.

We cannot imagine one category in which a non-Christian worldview outshines the Christian position. For example, putting Christian economics into practice results in prosperity for the greatest number of people, while all forms of socialism, including the interventionist welfare state, guarantee various levels of poverty. Putting Christian sociology into practice encourages strong families and guards against widespread drug-use, crime, unemployment, poverty, and disease, whereas secular views contribute to the breakdown of the family unit and the disintegration of society. Putting Christian law into practice guarantees human rights as God-ordained, while the history of positive law—in France for two centuries, in the Soviet Union for seventy years, and in the U.S. for the last half-century—has been a history of carnage.[5] Most importantly, of course, putting Christian theology and philosophy into practice results in salvation of the soul (Matthew 16:26), enlightenment of the mind, and purpose in life.

11.1.4 SETTING THE STAGE

Some of the weaknesses in each of the five non-Christian worldviews have been alluded to in the body of this text, while many of their flaws should have become apparent in reading the sections on Biblical Christianity. But we have saved the bulk of our criticism for this final section. Here we evaluate in more detail how the non-Christian worldviews fail to persuade that they are true and fail to correctly interpret the world in which we live.

We begin with a critique of Islam written by Dr. Norman L. Geisler, who contrasts Jesus and Muhammad. We then critique Secular Humanism and Marxism-Leninism[6] together, since these two worldviews agree on many fundamental points. Next, we offer a brief evaluation of Cosmic Humanism and an assessment of some of the major points of Postmodernism. A final challenge to Christian students concludes the text.

---

[5] Yes, carnage in the United States: 1.2 million unborn babies killed every year by abortion.

[6] In spite of the fall of the Berlin Wall and the U.S.S.R. in the early 1990s, it is still relevant to understand Marxism because of its advances in Central and South America, China, Vietnam, Cuba, and various African nations.

Conclusion

Part Two

11.2.1 JESUS AND MUHAMMAD IN THE QUR'AN (BY DR. NORMAN L. GEISLER)

Islam is the second largest and the fastest growing religion in the world. One out of every four persons on earth is a Muslim–some 1.6 billion human beings. As such, it presents one of the greatest challenges to Christianity in the world today. It behooves us then to understand it better. And there is no better way to understand Islam than through their Holy Book, the Qur'an. We begin with a comparison of Jesus and Muhammad in the Qur'an.

11.2.2 A BRIEF COMPARISON OF JESUS AND MUHAMMAD IN THE QUR'AN

Jesus in the Qur'an	Muhammad in the Qur'an
Virgin born	Not virgin born
Sinless	Sinful
Called "Messiah"	Not called "Messiah"
Called "Word of God"	Not called "Word of God"
Performed miracles	Did not perform miracles
Ascended bodily into heaven	Did not ascend bodily into heaven

Now let us examine the Qur'anic texts that support the above comparison.[1] This will be extremely helpful for witnessing to Muslims about the Christian faith.

---

[1] All citations from the Qur'an come from the Ali translations: Abdullah Yusuf Ali, *The Meaning of the Glorious Qur'an*, 3rd ed. (Cairo, Egypt: Dar Al-Kitab Al-Masri Publisher, 1938).

11.2.3 An Examination of the Qur'anic Texts on Jesus and Muhammad

Those not familiar with the Qur'an and Muslim teaching about Jesus may be surprised at the honored place Jesus is given among the prophets of Islam. Consider this text alone:

> "Behold! the angels said: "O Mary! God giveth thee glad tidings of a Word from Him: his name will be Christ Jesus, the son of Mary, held in honor in this world and the Hereafter and of (the company of) those nearest to God; "He shall speak to the people in childhood and in maturity. And he shall be (of the company) of the righteous." She said: "O my Lord! How shall I have a son when no man hath touched me?" He said: "Even so: God createth what He willeth: When He hath decreed a plan, He but saith to it, 'Be,' and it is! "And God will teach him the Book and Wisdom, the Law and the Gospel, "And (appoint him) an apostle to the Children of Israel, (with this message): "'I have come to you, with a Sign from your Lord, in that I make for you out of clay, as it were, the figure of a bird, and breathe into it, and it becomes a bird by God's leave: And I heal those born blind, and the lepers, and I quicken the dead, by God's leave; and I declare to you what ye eat, and what ye store in your houses. Surely therein is a Sign for you if ye did believe; "'(I have come to you), to attest the Law which was before me. And to make lawful to you part of what was (Before) forbidden to you; I have come to you with a Sign from your Lord. So fear God, and obey me" (Sura 3:45–50).

11.2.4 Jesus Was Virgin Born and Muhammad Was Not

It is noteworthy that this text affirms the virgin birth of Christ for Mary said: "O my Lord! How shall I have a son when no man hath touched me?" He said: "Even so: God createth what He willeth: When He hath decreed a plan, He but saith to it, 'Be,' and it is!" (3:45–47). Sura 19 also affirms that Jesus was born of a virgin. "He [the angel] said: "Nay, I am only a messenger from thy Lord, (to announce) to thee the gift of a holy son. She said: "How shall I have a son, seeing that no man has touched me, and I am not unchaste?" He said: "So (it will be): Thy Lord saith, 'that is easy for Me: and (We wish) to appoint him as a Sign unto men and a Mercy from Us': It is a matter (so) decreed." (Sura 19:19–21).

Nowhere in the Qur'an is a supernatural conception of Muhammad recorded. In fact, both his father (Abdullah) and mother (Aminah) are known from the history of Islam. Muhammad's birth was a natural as any mortal since Adam.

11.2.5 Jesus Is Sinless and Muhammad Is Not

In the nearly one hundred references to Jesus in the Qur'an never once does it refer to Him as committing a sin. Indeed, He is called a "righteous" prophet (Sura 6:85). His sinless nature can be inferred from His virgin birth which the Qur'an affirms (implies Jesus' sinlessness, as does His title of "Messiah" (cf. Isa. 53:5, 9). Further, the "Book" or Bible[2] to which Muhammad referred (see Suras 4:171; 5.46) speaks of Christ as sinless (2 Corinthians 5:21; Hebrews 4:15; 1 Peter 1:19; 1 John 3:3).

By contrast with the sinlessness of Jesus, Muhammad is repeatedly said to have sinned. In Sura 47 the prophet is told to ask God to forgive his faults. We read: "Know, therefore, that there is no god but God, and ask forgiveness for thy fault, and for the men and women who

---

[2] Muslims are inconsistent in admitting the Bible of Muhammad's day was a valid source of truth from God and yet claiming, on the other hand, that the Bible has been corrupted. We have abundant manuscript evidence going back centuries before Muhammad demonstrating that the text of the Bible today is substantially the same as it was in Muhammad's day (see chapter 22 in Norman L. Geisler and William Nix, *General Introduction to the Bible* [Chicago, IL: Moody Press, 1986]).

believe: for God knows how ye move about and how ye dwell in your homes" (47:19). Again, we read of God saying to Muhammad: "That God may forgive thee thy faults of the past and those to follow; fulfill His favour to thee; and guide thee on the Straight Way" (Sura 48:2). In fact, Muhammad is rebuked by God for his sin in Sura 36 which affirms: "It is not fitting for a Believer, man or woman, when a matter has been decided by God and His Apostle to have any option about their decision: if any one disobeys God and His Apostle, he is indeed on a clearly wrong Path." But "thou didst hide in thy heart that which God was about to make manifest: thou didst fear the people, but it is more fitting that thou shouldst fear God . . . And God's command must be fulfilled" (Sura 33:36–38).

11.2.6 JESUS IS CALLED THE "MESSIAH" AND MUHAMMAD IS NOT

Jesus is called Messiah (Christ) eleven times in the Qur'an. Sura 3:45 declares: "Behold! the angels said: "O Mary! God giveth thee glad tidings of a Word from Him: his name will be Christ [Messiah] Jesus, the son of Mary, held in honour in this world and the Hereafter and of (the company of) those nearest to God." Again we read: "That they said (in boast), We killed Christ [Messiah] Jesus the son of Mary, the Apostle of God; but they killed him not, nor crucified him, but so it was made to appear to them . . . " (Sura 4:157). Later, verse 171 it adds, "O People of the Book! Commit no excesses in your religion: Nor say of God aught but the truth. Christ [Messiah] Jesus the son of Mary was (no more than) an apostle of God . . ." (see also 5:72, 75; 9:30, 31).

Nowhere in the Qur'an is Muhammad called Messiah. He is merely called an "apostle" or "prophet" of God. For example, "And remember, Jesus, the son of Mary, said: `O Children of Israel! I am the apostle of God (sent) to you, confirming the Law (which came) before me, and giving Glad Tidings of an Apostle to come after me, whose name shall be Ahmad [Muhammad]'" (Sura 61:6). Elsewhere Muhammad is called a "prophet" (cf. 7:158; 33:45). Indeed, he is considered the last of the prophets: "Muhammad is not the father of any of your men, but (he is) the Apostle of God, and the Seal of the Prophets: and God has full knowledge of all things" (Sura 33:45). Thus, he is affectionately labeled "the prophet" by Muslims. Nowhere is Muhammad honored with the title "Messiah" as Jesus is.

11.2.7 JESUS IS CALLED THE "WORD OF GOD" AND MUHAMMAD IS NOT

In the Qur'an Jesus is referred to as the "Word of God." It speaks of "Christ Jesus the son of Mary" who was "His [God's] Word" (Sura 4:171). Again, "Likewise, Behold! the angels said: "O Mary! God giveth thee glad tidings of a Word from Him: his name will be Christ Jesus, the son of Mary, held in honor in this world and the Hereafter and of (the company of) those nearest to God". Of course, Muslims do not believe He is the eternal Word of God as Christians do (John 1:1; cf. Revelation 19:13) since they believe it is untenable to affirm God has an eternal Son. For "Behold! Allah will say: `O Jesus the son of Mary! Didst thou say unto men, worship me and my mother as gods in derogation of Allah.?' He will say: `Glory to Thee! never could I say what I had no right (to say). Had I said such a thing, thou wouldst indeed have known it' (Sura 5:116). Again, "They say: `God hath begotten a son!'—Glory be to Him! He is self-sufficient! His are all things in the heavens and on earth! No warrant have ye for this! say ye about God what ye know not?" (Sura 10:68).

Muslims believe that it is not only spiritually repugnant (Sura 5:17; 9:30)[3] but also rationally incoherent to speak of an eternal Father and an eternal Son. Repeatedly the Qur'an declares "Allah has no partners" (Sura 7:145; 41:47). However, there is an inherent inconsistence here since many Muslims believe that the Qur'an is eternal and yet is not identical to Allah. Why then cannot Jesus be the eternal Word, a perfect expression of God, and yet not identical to the Father? For example, they believe the Qur'an is the eternal Speech of God, existing in the Mind of God from all eternity. Sura 85:21–22 declares, "Nay, this is A Glorious Qur'an, (Inscribed) in A Tablet Preserved! [in heaven]." And in Sura 43:3–4, we read, "We have made it A Qur'an in Arabic, That ye may able To understand (and learn wisdom). And verily, it is In the Mother of the Book, In Our Presence, high (In dignity), full of wisdom" (cf. Sura 13:39). This eternal Original is the template of the earthly book we know as the Qur'an. So, while Muslims insist the Qur'an is uncreated and perfectly expresses the mind of God, yet they acknowledge that the Qur'an is not identical to the essence of God.

Some Muslim scholars even liken the Qur'an to the Divine Logos view of Christ held by orthodox Christians. As Professor Yusuf K. Ibish stated of the Qur'an, "It is not a book in the ordinary sense, nor is it comparable to the Bible, either the Old or New Testaments. It is an expression of Divine Will. If you want to compare it with anything in Christianity, you must compare it with Christ Himself." He adds, "Christ was the expression of the Divine among men, the revelation of the Divine Will. That is what the Qur'an is."[4] But if this is so, then it is not incoherent to speak about Christ the "Word of God" as also being God. However understood, no such special title as "Word of God" is given to Muhammad in the Qur'an.

11.2.8 JESUS PERFORMED MIRACLES AND MUHAMMAD DID NOT

The Jesus of the Qur'an performed many miracles including resurrecting the dead. Sura 3:49 declares of Jesus: "And (appoint him) an apostle to the Children of Israel, (with this message): "'I have come to you, with a Sign from your Lord, in that I make for you out of clay, as it were, the figure of a bird, and breathe into it, and it becomes a bird by God's leave: And I heal those born blind, and the lepers, and I quicken the dead, by God's leave." Again we read, "And remember, Jesus, the son of Mary, said: "O Children of Israel! I am the apostle of God (sent) to you, confirming the Law (which came) before me, and giving Glad Tidings of an Apostle to come after me, whose name shall be Ahmad." But when he came to them with Clear Signs, they said, "this is evident sorcery!" (Sura 61:6).

While Jesus' "signs" included everything from creating life to raising the dead, Muhammad did none of these. Indeed, many Qur'anic texts inform us that Muhammad refused to perform miracles, even though he acknowledged that other prophets before him had done so to prove their prophetic credentials. Sura 3 records, "They (also) said: "God took our promise not to believe in an apostle unless He showed us a sacrifice consumed by Fire (From heaven)." Say: "There came to you apostles before me, with clear Signs and even with what ye ask for: why then did ye slay them, if ye speak the truth?" Then if they reject thee, so were rejected apostles before thee, who came with Clear Signs, Books of dark prophecies, and the Book of Enlightenment" (3:183–184 cf. 4:153; 6:8–9; 17:90–93).

---

[3] Muslim moral and spiritual repugnance to the deity of Christ is based largely on a misunderstanding of what it means for Christ to be a "son" of God. They understand it in a physical sense of resulting from a sexual union between God and Mary (see Sura 10:68), rather than in a spiritual sense. There are two Arabic words for "son," one meaning son in a physical sense (*walad*) and one meaning son in a metaphorical or relational sense (*ibn*). In dialogue with Muslims, Christians should use the latter when referring to Christ to avoid misunderstanding.
[4] Charis Waddy, *The Muslim Mind* (London, UK: Longman, 1976), 14.

Muhammad even admitted that God performed miracles through prophets like Moses before him, saying, "To Moses We did give Nine Clear Signs" (Sura 7:101). And, of course, Muhammad acknowledged that Jesus even created life and raised the dead, but his response was the same: Read the Qur'an; this is my sign from God (see Sura 17: 102–108). But there is nothing miraculous about the Qur'an as a book that could not also be said about other books, like the Bible, that claim to come from God.[5] Truth is not determined by how beautifully it is expressed.

In one place Muhammad used the excuse that he did not do miracles because the people who saw miracles did not believe anyway. He said, "We refrain from sending the signs, only because the men of former generations treated them as false" (Sura 17:59). He added elsewhere, "They swear their strongest oaths by God, that if a (special) sign came to them, by it they would believe. Say: `Certainly (all) signs are in the power of God: but what will make you (Muslims) realize that (even) if (special) signs came, they will not believe?'"

But this is an insufficient response since: 1) Some did believe because of Jesus' miracles; 2) Even those who do not believe are even more responsible for not doing so because they saw miracles (Mt. 12:40–41); 3) If miracles do not work, then why did Muhammad offer another alleged miracle (the Qur'an) to them as proof his message was from God?

Even more strange, in another place Muhammad's extreme "Calvinism" shows through when he calls those who reject his "signs" persons who are "dumb" because God "willeth" them to be so: "They say: `Why is not a sign sent down to him from his Lord?' Say: `God hath certainly power to send down a sign: but most of them understand not.... Those who reject our signs are deaf and dumb, in the midst of darkness profound: whom God willeth, He leaveth to wander: whom He willeth, He placeth on the way that is straight'" (Sura 6:37).

11.2.9 JESUS ASCENDED BODILY INTO HEAVEN AND MUHAMMAD DID NOT

According to the Qur'an, Jesus is also said to have ascended bodily into heaven. This is based on text like Sura 3:55 which affirms that "Behold! God said: "O Jesus! I will take thee and raise thee to Myself and clear thee (of the falsehoods) of those who blaspheme; I will make those who follow thee superior to those who reject faith, to the Day of Resurrection". Sura 4:157–158 adds: "That they said (in boast), "We killed Christ Jesus the son of Mary, the Apostle of God"; but they killed him not, nor crucified him, but so it was made to appear to them, and those who differ therein are full of doubts, with no (certain) knowledge, but only conjecture to follow, for of a surety they killed him not: Nay, God raised him up unto Himself; and God is Exalted in Power, Wise". Jesus did not die on the Cross. Rather, God "raised him up unto Himself," that is He ascended bodily into heaven without dying. After Jesus returns to earth He will die and then rise in the general resurrection with all other people. In Sura 19:33, Jesus (Isa) says, "So peace is on me the day I was born, the day that I die, and the day that I shall be raised up to life (again)"!

Unlike Jesus, Muhammad never bodily ascended into heaven. Some mistakenly believe that He did based on Sura 17:1 which says, "Glory to (God) Who did take His servant for a Journey by night from the Sacred Mosque to the farthest Mosque, whose precincts We did

---

[5] The Muslim claim that the miraculous nature of the Qur'an as found in its beautiful style is insufficient as a test of its divine origin because: 1) Parts of the Qur'an are poorly constructed (see Ali Dashti, *Twenty Years: A Study of the Prophetic Career of Muhammad* [London, UK: George Allen & Unwin, 1985], 48–9); 2) There was other literature produced in Arabic which equals the Qur'an in beauty (e.g., Mu'allaqat, Maqamat, and Hariri), yet Muslims do not consider them inspired. Further, by the same argument Shakespeare should be canonized; 3) Muslims would not accept another book as inspired that opposed monotheism and Muhammad, even if it were more beautiful Arabic; 4) Parts of the Bible (like Isaiah), which Muslims reject, are beautiful literature.

bless, in order that We might show him some of Our Signs." However, even some noted Muslim scholars reject this interpretation, pointing out that this "Journey by night" was only as "vision" as the text says it was (Sura 17:60). Both Yusuf Ali and Muhammad Ali, noted Muslim commentators, understand it as a vision.[6] In any event, it is indisputable that Muhammad never had a permanent bodily ascension since his body is entombed in Mecca where faithful Muslims make their life-time pilgrimage to pay homage to him.

Further, his "night journey" was called a "Miraj" from which we get our word "mirage." The great Muslim scholar and translator of the Qur'an calls it a "mystic Vision" and "mystic story."[7] If Muhammad had ascended bodily, he would have to have had an immortal body that cannot die, as the Qur'an says he will when he returns (Sura 19:33).

11.2.10 OTHER UNIQUE FEATURES OF JESUS

Jesus spoke at His birth (Sura 19:29, 30). He had supernatural knowledge (Sura 3:49). He is Blessed (Sura 19:31). He was endowed with the Holy Spirit (Sura 4:171). He is called "Spirit of Him [God]," meaning not the Holy Spirit but (as Ali translates it, "a Spirit proceeding from Him [God]" (Sura 4:171). But even so, this is a distinctive designation of Christ, indicating that He was a being of special spiritual significance who was sent from God. He also was to be given "honour in this world and the Hereafter and of (the company of) those nearest to God; an honored place in heaven among those closest to God" (Sura 3:45).

11.2.11 AN EVALUATION OF THE EVIDENCE FROM THE QUR'AN

We begin our evaluation by noting the many common teachings between Muslims and Christians about Christ. Then, we will note the tension between the superiority granted to Muhammad by Islam (by claiming he is the last and "seal" of the prophets) in light of the obvious superiority given to Christ in character, titles, and actions in the Qur'an.

11.2.12 THE COMMON GROUND

There is indeed much common ground in communicating with Muslims. Among the more important common doctrines are the following: 1) the belief in one God; 2) the creation of heaven and earth; 3) the sinfulness of humanity; 4) the need for forgiveness; 5) belief in moral absolutes; 6) acknowledgment of revelation from God in the Law (taurat), Psalms (Zabur), and Gospels (injil); 7) the belief in prophets of God (including Adam, Noah, Abraham, and Jesus); 8) the Virgin Birth of Christ; 9) the sinlessness of Christ; 10) that Christ was called the "Messiah"; 11) Christ's bodily ascension into heaven; 12) Christ's second coming. In light of these, it is ironic that evangelicals have far more in common with orthodox Muslims than we do with liberal Christians!

Of course, there are many significant differences, since Muslims reject crucial orthodox Christian beliefs such as the Trinity, the Deity of Christ, His atoning death,[8] and His bodily resurrection. And since these are at the heart of the Gospel which is alone the power of God unto salvation (Rom. 1:16) and without which no one can be saved (Rom. 10:9; 1 Cor. 15:1–7, 17), it follows that we cannot neglect the importance of communicating this message with

---

[6] See Joseph Gudel, *To Every Muslim an Answer*, unpublished thesis at Simon Greenleaf School of Law, 1982, 80.
[7] Abdullah Yusuf Ali, *The Meaning of the Glorious Qur'an*, 691, and "Introduction" to Sura 1.
[8] Muslims reject the death of Christ on *a priori* grounds, not on *a posteriori* evidence which is abundant (see chapter 11 in Norman L. Geisler, *Answering Islam*, 2nd ed. [Grand Rapids, MI: Baker Book House, 2002]).

Muslims. For "there is no other name [than Jesus) under heaven, given among men, whereby we must be saved" (Acts 4:12). And in the presentation of this unique message of salvation, we are aided considerably by the many things the Qur'an affirms about Christ.

11.2.13 A SUMMARY OF THE EVIDENCE

A summation of the comparison between Jesus and Muhammad will help focus the superiority of the former. According to the Qur'an, Jesus is sinless and Muhammad is not. Jesus is Virgin Born and Muhammad is not. Jesus is called "Messiah" and Muhammad is not. Jesus is called the "Word of God" and Muhammad is not. Jesus is also called "Spirit of [from] God" but Muhammad is not. Further, Jesus is said to be strengthened by the Holy Spirit. And perhaps most important of all, Jesus performed miracles including raising the dead, while Muhammad refused to do such miracles. Finally, unlike Muhammad, Jesus ascended bodily into heaven and Muhammad is entombed in Mecca.

11.2.14 OTHER COMPARISONS BETWEEN JESUS AND MUHAMMAD

There are a number of other unusual or supernatural things about Christ mentioned in the Qur'an that are not true of Muhammad. Several of these stand out.

JESUS SPOKE AT HIS BIRTH

Naturally speaking, no one speaks naturally from the moment of birth. But according to the Qur'an Jesus did. Sura 19 declares: "At length she brought the (babe) to her people, carrying him (in her arms). They said: `O Mary! truly an amazing thing hast thou brought!'" But as she pointed to the baby, "They said: `How can we talk to one who is a child in the cradle?' He said: `I am indeed a servant of God: He hath given me revelation and made me a prophet; And He hath made me blessed wheresoever I be, and hath enjoined on me Prayer and Charity as long as I live' . . . Such (was) Jesus the son of Mary: (it is) a statement of truth, about which they (vainly) dispute" (Sura 19:28–35).

JESUS CREATED LIFE

Another incredible thing the Qur'an attributes to Jesus is the creation of life–something only God can do. Twice we read that Jesus gave life to clay birds. Sura 3 records: "And (appoint him) an apostle to the Children of Israel, (with this message): "'I have come to you, with a Sign from your Lord, in that I make for you out of clay, as it were, the figure of a bird, and breathe into it, and it becomes a bird by God's leave" (3:49). Likewise, Sura 5 asserts: "Then will Allah say: "O Jesus the son of Mary!... Behold! I taught thee the Book and Wisdom, the Law and the Gospel and behold! thou makest out of clay, as it were, the figure of a bird, by My leave, and thou breathest into it and it becometh a bird by My leave, and thou healest those born blind, and the lepers, by My leave" (5:110).

While this kind of miracle is not found in the canonical Gospels but only in the Apocrypha, nevertheless, the fact that the Qur'an attributes such supernatural powers to Jesus is amazing. How then can Muhammad, who admittedly never performed any such act, be considered in the same class as Jesus?

JESUS RAISED THE DEAD

What is more, according to the Qur'an, Jesus raised the dead. We read, "And (appoint him) an apostle to the Children of Israel, (with this message): "'I have come to you, with a Sign from your Lord, in that... I quicken the dead, by God's leave" (Sura 3:49). Again, "Then will Allah say: "O Jesus the son of Mary! Recount My favour to thee and to thy mother. Behold! I strengthened thee with the holy spirit, so that thou didst speak to the people in childhood and in maturity. Behold! . . . And behold! thou bringest forth the dead by My leave" (Sura 5:110). Even though it is by God's permission that Jesus does this miracle of resurrection, nevertheless, God never gave Muhammad any such powers. Indeed, given the fact that Jesus alone is able to do such feats it reveals that the traditions about Jesus passed on to Muhammad portray someone who is more than a prophet, but is truly the "Messiah" who was confirmed by incredible miracles.

11.2.15 SOME CONCLUDING COMMENTS

We conclude our study with quotations from three noted persons: Blaise Pascal, William Paley, and Muhammad himself.

FROM BLAISE PASCAL

The famous French mathematician and philosopher Blaise Pascal summarized the superiority of Christ over Muhammad succinctly:

> "The Mahometan religion has for a foundation the Qur'an and Mahomet. But has this prophet, who was to be the hope of the world, been foretold? What sign has he that every other man has not, who chooses to call himself a prophet? What miracle does he himself say that he has done? What mysteries has he taught, even according to his own tradition? Any man can do what Mahomet has done; for he performed no miracles,[9] he was not foretold. No man can do what Christ has done."[10]

It is important to notice in this connection that Jesus was predicted by nearly one hundred thirteen prophecies,[11] but Muhammad by none. [12] Jesus had no earthly father, but Muhammad had two natural parents. Jesus' name is mentioned ninety-seven times in the Qur'an and Muhammad's name only twenty-five times. Jesus taught peace, and Muhammad waged

---

[9] The Muslim claim that Muhammad performed many miracles lacks credibility because 1) It contradicts the Qur'an in which Muhammad refused to do miracles (3:181–185; 4:153; 6:8–9); 2) It is based on apocryphal stories from the Hadith (traditions) composed one hundred to two hundred years after the time of Muhammad; 3) Even many Muslim scholars admit that most of these stories are not true (See Joseph Horowitz, "The Growth of the Mohammed Legend" *The Moslem World* vol X [1920]: 49–58). Of the 300,000 stories collected by Muslim Hadith scholar Bukhari, he admitted there were errors in over 290,000 of them; 4) None of these alleged miracles fit all the nine criteria laid down by Muslims scholars for a genuine miracle to confirm a prophet's claim; 5) the origin of the miracle claims of Islam are suspect since the stories arose as a result of Christian apologists demonstrating the superiority of Jesus to that of Muhammad by way of Jesus' miracles (Daniel J. Sahas, "The Formation of Later Islamic Doctrines as a Response to Byzantine Polemics: The Miracles of Muhammad," *The Greek Orthodox Theological Review* vol. 27, nos. 2 and 3 [Summer/Fall 1982]: 312).

[10] Quoted in Gudel, *To Every Muslim an Answer*, 82.

[11] J. Barton Payne's *Encyclopedia of Biblical Prophecy* (London, UK: Hodder & Stoughton, 1973), 665–8, lists 113 Old Testament predictions that were fulfilled at Christ's first coming.

[12] Muslims have offered some alleged predictive prophecies in the Qur'an, but none are really predictive (see chapter 9 in Geisler, *Answering Islam*) nor do they measure up to the biblical standard of numerous, clear predictions made hundreds of years in advance that were literally fulfilled.

war. Jesus motivated by love and Muhammad by fear. Jesus ordered the death of no one, but Muhammad commanded the assassination of hundreds.[13] Jesus never married, and Muhammad had as many as fifteen wives.[14] Jesus established only a spiritual kingdom while on earth (John 18:36), and Muhammad established an earthly empire. The early growth of Muhammad's religion was by using the sword on others, while the early growth of Christianity was by others using the sword on it. When Jesus' alleged followers used the sword (in the Crusades) it was contrary to the teaching and example of their Leader, but when Muslims use the sword it is consistent with the teaching and example of their leader.

FROM WILLIAM PALEY

The famous Christian apologist William Paley shows the contrast between Jesus and Muhammad in these words:

> For what are we comparing? A Galilean peasant accompanied by a few fishermen with a conqueror at the head of his army. We compare Jesus, without force, without power, without support, without one external circumstance of attraction or influence, prevailing against the prejudices, the learning, the hierarchy, of his country, against the ancient religious opinions, the pompous religious rites, the philosophy, the wisdom, the authority, of the Roman empire, in the most polished and enlightened period of its existence, with Mahomet making his way amongst Arabs; collecting followers in the midst of conquests and triumphs, in the darkest ages and countries of the world, and when success in arms not only operated by that command of men's wills and persons which attend prosperous undertakings, but was considered as a sure testimony of Divine approbation. That multitudes, persuaded by this argument, should join the train of a victorious chief; that still greater multitudes should, without any argument, bow down before irresistible power—is a conduct in which we cannot see much to surprise us; in which we can see nothing that resembles the causes by which the establishment of Christianity was effected.[15]

FROM MUHAMMAD

According to the popular contemporary Muslim biographer Haykal, here is how Muhammad originally understood his alleged "revelations":

> Stricken with panic, Muhammad arose and asked himself, "What did I see? Did possession of the devil which I feared all along come to pass?" Muhammad looked to his right and his left but saw nothing. For a while he stood there trembling with fear and stricken with awe. He feared the cave might be haunted and that he might run away still unable to explain what he saw.[16]

Haykal notes that Muhammad had feared demon possession before, but his wife Khadijah talked him out of it. For "as she did on earlier occasions when Muhammad feared possession

---

[13] In the earliest and most authoritative book on the topic, *The Life of Muhammad*, written by Ibn Ishaq in the second century of the Islamic era, he relates many stories of Muhammad's bloodshed, including the orchestration of the execution of 600 to 900 Jews (trans. A. Guillaume [Oxford, UK: Oxford University Press, 1955], 464).

[14] See Geisler, *Answering Islam*, 171, for documentation from Muslim sources.

[15] William Paley, *Evidence of Christianity* (London, UK: W. Clowes and Sons, 1851), 257. Muslim critics argue that the spread of Christianity in many lands was certainly not always due to peaceful proclamation of the Gospel but also through the use of wars. While this may be true of some later periods, such as the Crusades (11th and 12th centuries), it certainly was not true of early Christianity (1st to 3rd centuries) when it grew from 120 (Acts 1–2) to the dominant spiritual force in the Roman world before Constantine was converted in A. D. 313.

[16] Muhammad Husayn Hasykal, *The Life of Muhammad* (Burr Ridge, IL: North American Trust Publications, 1976), 74–5, emphasis added.

by the devil, so now stood firm by her husband and devoid of the slightest doubt." Thus "respectfully, indeed reverently, she said to him, 'Joy to my cousin! Be firm. By him who dominates Khadijah's soul I pray and hope that you will be the Prophet of this nation. By God, He will not let you down.'"[17]

Herein is a final contrast between Muhammad and Jesus. On the one hand, we have Muhammad who at first believed he was demon possessed and was later talked out of it by the voice of his wife who was no doubt ambitious for her husband's success. On the other hand, we have Jesus who knows from the beginning where He came from (Luke. 2:49 cf. John. 17:5) and was later confirmed three times to be the Son of God by the voice of God (Matthew 3:17; 17:5; John 12:28).

[17] Ibid.

Conclusion

Part Three

"[T]he clash that is coming—and that has, indeed, already begun . . . [is] between those who claim the Judeo-Christian worldview and those who have abandoned that worldview in favor of the "isms" of contemporary American life—feminism, multiculturalism, gay liberationism, lifestyle liberalism—what I here lump together as a family called 'the secularist orthodoxy.'"[1]

— ROBERT P. GEORGE

11.3.1 INTRODUCTION

This critique does not treat Marxism and Secular Humanism as mutually exclusive for the simple reason that "Marxism is humanism."[2] The body of this text makes it clear that most of the foundational or theoretical assumptions of Secular Humanism and Marxism are virtually indistinguishable, with the notable exception being that Marxism treats economics as primary, while Secular Humanism tends to concentrate on philosophy and biology.

Both worldviews are, in the main, atheistic, naturalistic, evolutionary, positivistic, monistic, utopian, and relativistic; but Marxism, thanks to its dialectic and well-developed economic theory, provides a better-defined perspective. Thus, there will be places in this critique where

---

[1] Robert P. George, *The Clash of Orthodoxies* (Wilmington, DE: ISI Books, 2001), 3.
[2] Erich Fromm, *On Disobedience and Other Essays* (New York, NY: Seabury Press, 1981), 24.

we address only the flaws of Marxist theory, but for the most part, our criticism applies to both worldviews as well as to the atheism of Postmodernism.

We contend that Marxism and Secular Humanism are incapable of describing the universe from start to finish. Therefore, we contrast these views with Christianity using a model that begins with the beginning and works chronologically toward the future. This is to reinforce what this entire text should make clear: only Biblical Christianity presents an accurate view of the world and our place in it.

11.3.2 GENESIS

In the beginning, one of two things existed: mind or matter. Either a supreme mind has always existed and created matter and the universe at a specific point in time, or matter is eternal and formed the universe by itself. Either mind created matter, or matter created mind.

> Either a supreme mind has always existed and created matter and the universe at a specific point in time, or matter is eternal and formed the universe by itself.

The Bible, of course, declares that God is eternal and that He created the physical universe and its inhabitants (Genesis 1). The Bible goes on to say that the physical universe was well thought out in the mind of God before creation ever took place (John 1:1–3). Marxists and Secular Humanist deny the very possibility that Scripture accurately accounts for the beginning of the universe. They therefore must hold that matter is eternal and has moved from a disordered state to an ordered state guided by chance. That is, matter previously packed into a mathematical point (called a "singularity") and scattered by an incredible explosion ordered itself into such remarkable entities as supernovas, diamonds, beagles, DNA—and the human mind.

Non-Christian worldviews (excluding Islam) believe that the universe was once dead and yet brought forth life—that inorganic matter, given enough time and the proper recipe for primordial soup, brought forth amoebas and hummingbirds, squids, and prairie dogs. Further still, Marxists and Secular Humanists believe that dead, disordered matter eventually organized human beings capable of inventing bicycles, jokes, and Hamlet. The faith of Christians pales in comparison to the credulity required to believe that such diversity and complexity arose by chance.

This is one of the most glaring flaws of Marxist and Secular Humanist theory—it asks us to believe in a reality that currently moves from order to disorder (according to the Second Law of Thermodynamics) moved in exactly the opposite direction for billions of years in the past. Of course, Marxists and Secular Humanists ignore, or at least downplay, the teleological nature of the universe and the wonder of human beings in an effort to mask this inconsistency— Stephen Jay Gould describes humans as an "afterthought"[3]—but they cannot hope to sway any individual with an open mind about the mysteries and manifest intelligence of the universe.

Chesterton says, "Man is a very strange animal . . . Not that there is anything particularly queer about our physical equipment; this is all quite reasonable. But gorillas have hands as we do, yet use them for very little, and never to play the piano or skip stones or whittle or write letters. Dolphins have bigger brains than we do, but you seldom hear them discoursing on nuclear physics. Chihuahuas are more hairless than we, but have never thought to wear clothes. . . . Man alone weeps for cause, and 'is shaken with the beautiful madness called laughter.'"[4]

---

[3] Cited in Daniel S. Levy, "Interview: Evolution, Extinction and the Movies," *Time*, May 14, 1990, 19.
[4] Cited in George Roche, *A World Without Heroes* (Hillsdale, MI: Hillsdale College Press, 1987), 103.

Secular worldview adherents would like to ignore the unmistakably unique character of human beings because their ideologies cannot adequately account for it. A worldview that asserts the primacy of matter has a difficult time explaining this unique creature so distinct from the rest of the animal kingdom.

The Christian worldview, by contrast, accounts for the unique character of humanity from the first chapter of Scripture. In Genesis 1:26, God declares, "Let us make man in our image, in our likeness, and let them rule over the fish of the sea and the birds of the air, over the livestock, over all the earth, and over all the creatures that move along the ground." Likewise, the Christian view accounts for the rest of the design found in nature; because it begins with a Designer. Whereas Secular Humanist and Marxists must rely on chance and matter to explain birds capable of astronomical navigation and bees that communicate through dance, Christians posit an omniscient God who chose to order the universe into a beautiful symphony of light, life, sound, and color.

"The heavens declare the glory of God; the skies proclaim the work of His hands" (Psalm 19:1). "Everywhere we look in nature (whether in living or non-living matter)," say Percival Davis and Dean Kenyon, "design and material organization are on display."[5] Evolutionist Paul Amos Moody echoes Davis and Kenyon: "The more I study science the more I am impressed with the thought that this world and universe have a definite design—and a design suggests a designer. It may be possible to have design without a designer, a picture without an artist, but my mind is unable to conceive of such a situation."[6]

The Pop Culture Connection

I, Robot (a 2004 sci-fi action thriller set in the year 2035)—Robots are everywhere, serving people with very human-like qualities. Homicide detective Del Spooner (Will Smith) is called to investigate the suicide of Dr. Alfred Lanning (James Cromwell), the scientist mastermind behind the robotics industry giant, U.S. Robotics. In scene 27 ("The Ghost in the Machine"), a robot is about to be reprogrammed after being accused of Dr. Lanning's death. As the procedure is taking place, we hear Dr. Lanning's voiceover: "There have always been ghosts in the machine: random segments of code that have grouped together to form unexpected protocols. Unanticipated, these free radicals engender questions of free will, creativity, and even the nature of what we might call the soul. Why is it that when some robots are left in darkness, they will seek out the light? Why is it that when robots are stored in an empty space, they will group together rather than stand alone? How do we explain this behavior? Random segments of code, or is it something more?"

It comes down to this: did life and intelligence and humor and design come from a living, intelligent God who loves order and joy, or did they arise randomly from dead matter? Christians believe that a lawfully designed reality demands an origin that provides the groundwork for such attributes.

Thus, Christians find the key in John 1:1–5: "In the beginning was the Word, and the Word was with God, and the Word was God. He was with God in the beginning. Through Him all things were made; without Him nothing was made that has been made. In Him was life, and that life was the light of men. The light shines in the darkness, but the darkness has not understood it."

---

[5] Percival Davis and Dean H. Kenyon, *Of Pandas and People* (Dallas, TX: Haughton, 1989), 55.
[6] Paul Amos Moody, *Introduction to Evolution* (New York, NY: Harper and Row, 1962), 497.

11.3.3 MIND OVER MATTER?

In the area of origins, the ultimate problem faced by Secular Humanists and Marxists is the existence of the mind (the overarching term we will use for all the supernatural qualities of people, including heart, conscience, ideas, soul, and spirit). A naive student might be persuaded that life and order arose from nonliving matter, but even the most gullible cannot swallow that the human mind, which has pierced the atom and conceived *The Brothers Karamazov*, came about by the chance workings of matter. It truly is a question of mind creating matter or matter creating mind—did the Supreme Mind or "eternal" nonliving matter instill in people the capacity for reason, appreciation of aesthetic qualities, and a conscience?

Clearly, this is a fatal flaw of Marxist and Secular Humanist philosophy. While both naturalistic worldviews claim that matter is primary or ultimate reality and mind is a pale reflection of this reality, they are faced again and again with the magnificent workings of the human mind.

> Either we are rational spirit obliged forever to obey the absolute values of the Tao [moral order], or else we are mere nature to be kneaded and cut into new shapes for the pleasures of masters who must, by hypothesis, have no motive but their own natural impulses.
>
> — C.S. Lewis

Further, experience suggests that mind acts creatively on matter, rather than vice versa. Warren Brookes speaks of economy in the mind as preceding the physical transfer of money, goods, and services. If people conceive things in their minds and then act creatively, it does not seem irrational to believe that the universe began in a similar fashion—we would expect an uncreated supreme mind to precede created matter.

C.S. Lewis speaks to this point when he says, "Either we are rational spirit obliged forever to obey the absolute values of the *Tao* [moral order], or else we are mere nature to be kneaded and cut into new shapes for the pleasures of masters who must, by hypothesis, have no motive but their own natural impulses."[7]

Altruism is another concept that we cannot account for naturally. "It is a metaphysical reality that is simply un-accountable to a materialist philosophy."[8] That is, Christians expect heroism from others—after all, we are made in the image of the God who sacrificed His own life so that we might live. Secular religious worldviews, by contrast, only speak of self-preservation and species-preservation instincts, which provide an inadequate explanation for a young person's diving into an icy river to save an octogenarian. Indeed, Secular Humanists, Marxists, and Postmodernists must ignore such nonmaterial activity because it demands more than a materialist explanation. No scientist, including the world's finest neurosurgeon, has ever held the idea of altruism in his or her hands for inspection or dissection. The same can be said for the idea of love, justice, or a scientific theory.

The only time secular worldviews care to treat the mind as important is in reference to theories devised by their own minds. But as we have stressed throughout this text, it is irrational to consistently portray the mind as random chemical firings of synapses in the brain and a mere reflection of the physical universe and then expect one's own mind to comprehend and process reality accurately. No less of an authority than Charles Darwin recognized the problem faced by adherents to atheistic, naturalistic explanations of mind: "With me, the horrid doubt always arises whether the convictions of man's mind, which has been developed from the mind of

---

[7] C.S. Lewis, *The Abolition of Man* (New York, NY: Macmillan, 1952), chapter 3.
[8] Roche, *A World Without Heroes*, 245.

lower animals, are of any value or at all trustworthy. Would any one trust in the convictions of a monkey's mind, if there are any convictions in such a mind?"[9] But Secular Humanists go behind the monkey. S. Matthew D'Agostino writes, "Based on current knowledge we can only assume that life is one of the many inherent capabilities that matter happens to possess, a capability that actualized or developed under some still largely unknown set of initial conditions. We're not absolutely sure what life looked like once the process was fully underway: something like algae, the biologists suggest: a foamy blue-green pond scum."[10]

Furthermore, no one trusts a mind whose ancestral roots trace back beyond monkeys' minds to amoebas and even to mindless, inorganic, chaotic matter. Naturalistic theologies and philosophies that begin with matter are incapable of explaining not only the teleological nature of the universe but also the capabilities of human minds and souls. Perhaps it sounds more manageable to simplify or reduce all reality to an ultimate material substance, but in the end this oversimplified worldview leads to hopeless complications because of its inability to explain reason. It is all well and good to declare, as Carl Sagan does in his book *Cosmos*, that matter (or nature, or the Cosmos) is all that has ever existed or ever will, but it leaves the naturalists with a number of inexplicable phenomena to sweep under the rug.

What can naturalists do with mind, soul, altruism, creativity, rationality, conscience, song, and laughter? They can try to ignore them, but they find this impossible. Indeed, they depend on them. It sounds learned to describe them as secondary, derivative, mere reflections of material reality, but how can the thought processes that formulated the notion of dialectical materialism be described as reflections, as cranial illusions, when they seem to be (at least for Marxists) the most powerful facet of reality?

> What can a naturalist do with mind, soul, altruism, creativity, rationality, conscience, song, and laughter?

The questions of origins and ultimate substance provide an excellent starting point for a serious critique of Secular Humanism and Marxism because they highlight the glaring weaknesses in the theology and philosophy of these worldviews. Christians expect people to be the most intricate part of an infinitely intricate creation, because they begin with a personal God, who specially created a world for men and women. Humanists should expect very little—should, indeed, be awed by ordered matter—and should recognize that people are completely inexplicable in naturalist terms.

In *Does God Exist? The Great Debate*, Dallas Willard, a professor of philosophy at the University of Southern California, raises an important point. Every great philosopher—Plato, Aristotle, St. Augustine, St. Thomas, William of Occam, Rene Descartes, Baruch Spinoza, Gottfried von Leibniz, John Locke, George Berkeley, Immanuel Kant, and Georg W.F. Hegel— was a theist, in one form or another. Even David Hume, a man Secular Humanists embrace as one of their own, declares, "The whole frame of nature bespeaks an intelligent author; and no rational enquirer can, after serious reflection, suspend his belief a moment with regard to the primary principles of genuine Theism and Religion."[11] The conclusion is obvious: Christian theology and philosophy are more intellectually defensible than those of secular worldviews.

[9] Francis Darwin, ed., *The Life and Letters of Charles Darwin*, 2 vols. (London, UK: J. Murray, 1888), 1:316.
[10] *Free Inquiry* vol. 22, no. 1 (Winter 2001/02): 39.
[11] Cited in J.P. Moreland and Kai Nielsen, *Does God Exist? The Great Debate* (Nashville, TN: Thomas Nelson, 1990), 211.

11.3.4 THE EVOLUTION OF EVOLUTION

From the Secular Humanists and Marxist-Leninist perspective, our discussion of mankind and all other life forms is premature. While the Christians and Muslims can begin talking about human beings virtually from the beginning of time, secular worldviews must postulate an immense amount of time (ca. 13.6 billion years) between the formation of the universe and the development of life and human. In order to do justice to the Secular Humanist and Marxist view of humans and their institutions, we must back up and examine the cornerstone of their worldview: the theories of spontaneous generation and evolution.

> Neither of the two fundamental axioms of Darwin's macroevolutionary theory...[has]been validated by one single empirical discovery or scientific advance since 1859.
>
> — MICHAEL DENTON

We do, of course, discuss the theory of evolution at length in the section on biology. We note that there has been no directly observed development of any new fundamental kind/type of animal by means of natural selection or mutation (genetic mistakes) and we also note microbiologist Michael Denton's charge that Darwinism lacks empirical verification: "Neither of the two fundamental axioms of Darwin's macroevolutionary theory...has...been validated by one single empirical discovery or scientific advance since 1859."[12]

We highlight most of the flaws in evolutionary theory, but by no means all. Evolutionary theory is marked with more inconsistencies and contradictions than we can discuss here, including the argument based on the peppered moth, the beak of the finch, and the Cambrian explosion—sometimes referred to as biology's Big Bang.[13] Thus, in this critique, we focus on two distinct aspects of the theory that we touched on briefly in the body of the text: the amount of faith required to believe in spontaneous generation, and the evolution of the theory of evolution.

11.3.5 SPONTANEOUS GENERATION

One of the most fundamental beliefs that humanists must cling to is that somewhere, somehow, at sometime, life arose from nonlife. Without spontaneous generation, something living must always have existed, namely an eternal God. Therefore, in order to be a consistent atheist, Secular Humanists and Marxists must trust fervently in the ability of inorganic matter to self-organize toward life. But they must also ignore the scientific experiments conducted by Francesco Redi and Louis Pasteur, who, in the mid 1800s, disproved spontaneous generation!

George Wald provides an excellent example of the dogmatic tenacity with which naturalistic evolutionists cling to the concept of spontaneous generation. He speaks of believing in spontaneous generation as a "philosophical necessity" and declares, "Most modern biologists, having reviewed with satisfaction the downfall of the spontaneous generation hypothesis, yet

[12] Michael Denton, *Evolution: A Theory in Crisis* (Bethesda, MD: Adler and Adler, 1986), 345.

[13] For a professional discussion on the Cambrian period and its difficulties for all evolutionary theories, see John Angus Campbell and Stephen C. Meyer, *Darwinism, Design and Public Education* (East Lansing, MI: Michigan State University Press, 2003). The rest of the books mentioned here speak to all aspects of the evolutionist's arguments: Jonathan Wells, *Icons Of Evolution: Science Or Myth?* (Washington, DC: Regnery Publishing, 2000; Judith Hooper, *An Evolutionary Tale Of Moths And Men: The Untold Story Of Science And The Peppered Moth* (New York, NY: W.W. Norton, 2002); Geoffrey Simmons, *What Darwin Didn't Know: A Doctor Dissects the Theory of Evolution* (Eugene, OR: Harvest House Publishers, 2004); Richard Milton, *Shattering the Myths of Darwinism* (Rochester, VT: Park Street Press, 1997); William A. Dembski, ed., *Uncommon Dissent: Intellectuals Who Find Darwinism Unconvincing* (Wilmington, DE: ISI Books, 2004).

unwilling to accept the alternative belief in special creation, are left with nothing. I think a scientist has no choice but to approach the origin of life through a hypothesis of spontaneous generation."[14]

In an effort to bolster their faith in spontaneous generation, proponents of secular religious worldviews have encouraged numerous experiments in which sparks are introduced into carefully concocted primordial soups in an effort to duplicate the first jump from nonlife to life. A.I. Oparin made these experiments famous and remains an icon of evolutionists. But the hard fact remains that neither Oparin nor any other scientist has succeeded in coaxing life from primordial soup. Nor is such a miracle likely to occur.

"The step from simple compounds to the complex molecules of life, such as protein and DNA, has proved to be a difficult one," say Davis and Kenyon. "Thus far it has resisted all efforts by the scientists working on the problem."[15] Elsewhere these authors state, "Without intelligence using selected chemicals and control conditions, amino acids have not been collected in the laboratory. Doubtless the same is true in nature."[16] All of these experiments seeking to create life in a test tube were conducted in the absence of oxygen because oxygen would destroy any organic compounds. "Yet scientists now know," say Davis and Kenyon, "that oxygen was present on the earth from the earliest ages."[17]

> The step from simple compounds to the complex molecules of life, such as protein and DNA, has proved to be a difficult one. Thus far it has resisted all efforts by the scientists working on the problem.
>
> — MICHAEL DENTON AND DEAN KENYON

Fred Hoyle, for years a leading atheist spokesman, has seen the error of his thinking and now argues there is a better chance of producing a Boeing 747 via an explosion in a junkyard than there is to arrive at life by accident. He believes there is no way of producing DNA by chance processes, noting that merely lining up the necessary enzymes by chance would consume 20 billion years. Three respected scientists—Charles Thaxton, Walter Bradley, and Roger Olsen—write in *The Mystery of Life's Origin* that "the undirected flow of energy through a primordial atmosphere and ocean is at present a woefully inadequate explanation for the incredible complexity associated with even simple living systems, and is probably wrong."[18]

This conclusion, however, is unacceptable for humanists. To admit that life cannot arise from nonlife would shake their worldviews to the very foundations. Adherents of these secular worldviews are fond of labeling Christians dogmatic, but they neglect to mention that the doctrine of spontaneous generation is every bit as sacred to atheists as the doctrine of the Incarnation is to Christians. Humanist Keith Parsons, for example, states, "With the environment operating to remove nonviable variations, the appearance of life on earth becomes a certainty rather than an extreme improbability."[19] Thus, we discover in secular religions a faith more profound and more unfounded than that of the most rudimentary religions.

Further, this blind faith[20] encompasses the entire discipline of biology. In the introduction to

---

[14] George Wald, "The Origin of Life," *Scientific American* (August 1954): 33.

[15] Davis and Kenyon, *Of Pandas and People*, 3.

[16] Ibid., 56.

[17] Ibid., 4.

[18] Charles Thaxton, Walter Bradley, and Roger Olsen, *The Mystery of Life's Origin: Reassessing Current Theories* (New York, NY: Philosophical Library, 1984), 186. Students particularly interested in biological origins should also read Davis and Kenyon, *Of Pandas and People*.

[19] Cited in Moreland and Nielsen, *Does God Exist?*, 185.

[20] Norman L. Geisler and Frank Turek, *I Don't Have Enough Faith To Be An Atheist* (Wheaton, IL: Crossway Books, 2004).

the 1971 edition of Darwin's *Origin of Species*, L.H. Matthews admits, "The fact of evolution is the backbone of biology, and biology is thus in the peculiar position of being a science founded on an unproved theory—is it then a science or a faith? Belief in the theory of evolution is thus exactly parallel to belief in special creation—both are concepts which believers know to be true but neither, up to the present, has been capable of proof."[21]

In examining our changing attitude toward evolutionary theory, it becomes obvious that evolution has been reduced to an insupportable dogma embraced by secular worldviews. But it has not always been this way. Evolution began as just another scientific theory. Darwin, knowing he was going contrary to most scientists of his day, treated his theory as subject to falsification. He believed that there would be a "rich bed" of fossils "beneath the lowest Cambrian strata,"[22] and if there were not, science "[would] rightly reject the whole theory."[23] Geology has not uncovered this "rich bed" of fossils. Darwin also insisted that unless numerous transitional forms appeared in the fossil record, his theory broke down. He wrote, "The number of intermediate varieties which have formerly existed on the earth, [must] be truly enormous. Why then is not every geological formation and every stratum full of such intermediate links? Geology assuredly does not reveal any such finely graduated organic chain; and this, perhaps, is the most obvious and gravest objection which can be urged against my theory."[24]

> Evolution . . . came into being as a kind of secular ideology in explicit substitute for Christianity. It stressed laws against miracles and, by analogy, it promoted progress against providence.
>
> — MICHAEL RUSE

Darwin's embarrassment over his theory's conflict with the fossil record is evidenced by the fact that in *The Descent of Man*, "[He] did not cite a single reference to fossils in support of his belief in human evolution."[25] Despite Darwin's own reservations, however, atheists everywhere proclaimed evolution to be fact. Julian Huxley declared that Darwin "rendered evolution inescapable as a fact . . . all-embracing as a concept."[26]

Perhaps in 1960 Huxley could get away with such a rash claim. But today, as we demonstrate in this text, it is generous to label evolution as a scientific theory, and one is sorely tempted to label it a myth. In modern times the theory has become a religious dogma that is counter-rational and therefore demands great resources of faith. "Evolution is a religion," says evolutionist Michael Ruse. "This was true of evolution in the beginning, and it is true of evolution still today." Ruse further says, "Evolution, therefore, came into being as a kind of secular ideology in explicit substitute for Christianity. It stressed laws against miracles and, by analogy, it promoted progress against providence."[27]

11.3.6 IN THE BEGINNING: EVOLUTION

In the beginning, evolution was a working hypothesis; later it was championed as theory; today it is touted as fact. Now it is such a remarkable fact that it can contradict all the factual findings of paleontology, homology, and molecular biology and still be labeled absolute truth.

---

[21] L.H. Mathews, "Introduction," in Charles Darwin, *The Origin of Species* (London, UK: J.M. Dent and Sons, 1971), x–xi. Cited in Luther D. Sunderland, *Darwin's Enigma* (San Diego, CA: Master Books, 1984), 30–1.

[22] Charles Darwin, *The Origin of Species*, 2 vols. (New York, NY: D. Appleton and Company, 1898), 2:121.

[23] Ibid., 125.

[24] Ibid., 49.

[25] Davis and Kenyon, *Of Pandas and People*, 108.

[26] Julian Huxley, *Essays of a Humanist* (London, UK: Chatto and Windus, 1964), 9.

[27] Michael Ruse, "How Evolution Became A Religion," *The [Canadian] National Post*, May 13, 2000, B1.

Atheists cling to evolution despite the findings of modern science: they blind themselves to all facts that contradict evolution, or they abandon Darwinian evolution and postulate a theory that circumvents the absence of supportive facts. The theory of punctuated evolution is the first "scientific" theory ever postulated that claims to be true not because any facts support it but because no fact can be conceived that disputes it. Believing such a theory requires absolute blind faith.

Modern Darwinists exhibit a similar blind faith. They blind themselves to the entire fossil record in order to maintain their belief in evolution. For example, Secular Humanist Chris McGowan points to a few fossils and concludes, "These intermediate fossils falsify the creationists' claim that transitional fossils linking major groups do not exist, and provide compelling evidence for evolution."[28]

The plain fact from which McGowan is shielding his eyes is this: the more honest members of his own camp admit that not one transitional fossil exists. It would be one thing if only a few rabid creationists were proclaiming the absence of transitional fossils—but it is quite another when noncreationist paleontologists declare it. In fact, no less august an authority than the late Colin Patterson, a paleontologist with the London Museum of Natural History, admits that he does not know of any evidence, "fossil or living" that provides "direct illustration of evolutionary transitions." He writes, "I will lay it on the line—there is not one such fossil [that is ancestral or transitional] for which one could make a watertight argument."[29]

The flaws in evolutionary theory have become so glaring that even some reputable evolutionists are abandoning ship. Patterson explains his awakening:

> "One of the reasons I started taking this anti-evolutionary view, or let's call it a non-evolutionary view, was that last year I had a sudden realization. For over twenty years I was working on evolution in some way. One morning I woke up and something had happened to me in the night, and it struck me that I had been working on this stuff for more than twenty years, and there was not one thing new about it. It's quite a shock to learn that one can be misled for so long. So either there was something wrong with me or there was something wrong with evolutionary theory. Naturally I know there is nothing wrong with me, so for the last few weeks I've been putting a simple question to various people and groups. Question is; can you tell me anything you know about evolution? Any one thing, any one thing that is true?...One person said, 'Yes, I do know one thing. It ought not to be taught in high schools.'"[30]

11.3.7 THE DEMISE OF NEO-DARWINISM

It is startling to realize that evolutionists cannot point to one aspect of their theory that they know to be true. Clearly, scientists should be abandoning the theory of evolution. But few evolutionists can summon the courage to completely break away from their discredited theory. As the *Encyclopedie Française* (written in cooperation with the leading biologists of France) says, "It follows from this presentation that the theory of evolution is impossible... Evolution is a kind of dogma in which its priests no longer believe but which they keep presenting to their people."[31]

We pray for a drastic change in the twenty–first century. To argue as Sagan does that we are the children of the stars may be good poetry, but it is terrible theology and even worse science. We agree with Soren Lovtrup's observation: "I believe that one day the Darwinism myth will

[28] Chris McGowan, *In the Beginning* (Amherst, NY: Prometheus Books, 1984), 141.

[29] Tom Bethel, *The Politically Incorrect Guide to Science* (Washington, DC: Regnery Publishing, 2005), 218.

[30] Ibid., 217.

[31] Carl Sagan, *The Dragons of Eden* (New York, NY: Random House, 1977), 93.

be ranked the greatest deceit in the history of science."[32] Why is Darwinism a deceit? Because, as Geoffrey Simmons writes, "Darwin knew little of genetics, hardly anything about human physiology, and nothing of conception. He could not tell the difference between a kidney cell and a liver cell, nor did he know they existed.... No such scientific article would be accepted for publication nowadays."[33]

The Pop Culture Connection

Salvation comes through the scientific method and a little luck in the film *Independence Day* (1996). After killing the aliens with a nuclear bomb and computer virus, a scientist and pilot strut across the desert signaling that science and technology wins. Contrast this theme of human arrogance with the 1953 version of *War of the Worlds*, where germs in the air kill the Martian invaders. The final scene has a voice-over, "After all that men could do failed, the Martians were destroyed and humanity was saved by the littlest things—which God in His wisdom had put upon this earth."

The neo-Darwinian position (evolution via genetic mistakes) does not seem to be doing much better. Simmons notes, "Once in every ten million cell divisions, a cell makes a copying mistake. The chance of the mistake passing into the next generation is one in two. The odds are six to one that it will disappear by the tenth generation and fifty to one that it will be gone by the hundredth generation.

According to F.B. Livingston, it would take approximately 20,000 generations, or 400,000 years, for an advantageous gene to spread among the hominid populations of the Pleistocene Era. If we are descendants of the famous Lucy, the australopithecine skull found in Ethiopia in 1974 and thought to be three million years old, then there would have been time for only seven advantageous genes to have changed, barely enough of a change to tell a difference, let alone make a monkey into a person.

But the theory of evolution dies hard. All atheistic positions must trust in it blindly and defend it to the death. Their willingness to cling to such a poor explanation should not surprise us. G.K. Chesterton says that if man will not believe in God, the danger is not that he will believe in nothing, but that he will believe in anything. What should surprise us is that so much of the world and, tragically, so many Christians, swallowed the entire theory and allowed it to gain such ascendancy among worldviews.

Christianity is a worldview that is capable of changing the world, and yet many Christians turned their backs on creationism and bought into evolutionary theory, a theory that conflicts with the Bible and is gradually proving to conflict with modern science.

11.3.8 THE BUCK STOPS ... WHERE?

The atheistic assumptions about human nature are a prime example of the damage evolution has wrought. An erroneous explanation of human origin distorts the view of human nature. The Christian model of human nature is based on the book of Genesis. We believe that Adam and Eve lived in the Garden of Eden until they chose to disobey God and that the human race has suffered the consequences of their disobedience ever since, including a universally shared sin nature. Ironically, Sagan acknowledges that the Genesis account explains a number of things, including the fact that "childbirth is generally painful in only one of the millions of species on Earth: human beings."[34] However, his evolutionary preconceptions do not allow him to accept the Bible as a trustworthy document; therefore, he explains this phenomenon by postulating,

---

[32] Soren Lovtrup, *Darwinism: The Refutation of a Myth* (London, UK: Croom Helm, 1987), 422.

[33] Geoffrey Simmons, *What Darwin Didn't Know: A Doctor Dissects the Theory of Evolution* (Eugene, OR: Harvest House Publishers, 2004), 302.

[34] Carl Sagan, *The Dragons of Eden* (New York, NY: Random House, 1977), 92.

"Childbirth is painful because the evolution of the human skull has been spectacularly fast and recent."[35]

Genesis provides a better overall explanation for overall human nature than does Islam, Secular Humanism, Marxism, Cosmic Humanism, or Postmodernism. We stress this distinction because our view of human nature colors one's attitude toward many other aspects of life. In fact, Joad's conversion to Christianity resulted largely from his recognition that the Christian explanation of human nature better fits the facts of experience and allows a more comprehensible view of the world. He says his "changed view of the nature of man . . . led to a changed view of the nature of the world."[36] That is, once we understand that we possess a sin nature, we understand our need for Christ's atoning death and the significance of His resurrection. We must first understand that we are dead in Adam, before we can desire to be alive in Christ. But the theory of evolution, by doing away with Adam and Eve, regards this central point of Christianity as nonsense.

Most atheists shudder at such a "guilt-ridden" description of man. The consistent evolutionist perceives human nature as morally perfect in its pristine state. Unfortunately, they cannot deny that we act immorally, so they must find a scapegoat for our sinful actions. Their scapegoat is society and its institutions. They claim that the environment encourages the wrong kind of actions and that people would stop doing wrong if the right society were created. But this only compounds the problem since society is made up of people.

11.3.9 ATTACK ON FAMILY

We are not responsible for our wrong-doings—we are only automatons that respond to the stimuli forced on us by society. For this reason, Secular Humanists and Marxists believe the most humane thing they can do is to usher in a socialistic society. The most desirable goal for the proponents of these worldviews is the creation of a utopian society in which our perfect nature can flourish. Toward this end, they call for major revisions to the traditional family unit. *The Communist Manifesto* derides as bourgeois the traditional unit of father, mother, and child. Acting on this mandate, communist Russia established free love associations and sanctioned lax divorce and abortion laws to break down the basic family unit. Secular and Cosmic Humanists as well as Postmodernists opt to move the same way, attacking the traditional family and encouraging experimentation, including bisexuality, homosexual marriage, open marriage, pederasty, and abortion as a means of birth control.

Christians believe that such attacks on the traditional family form the groundwork for many of our social ills, including AIDS, drug abuse, and crime. The family is the glue that holds society together. As the family goes, so goes society. Examples of the cause-and-effect role the family plays in society are everywhere: poverty is epidemic among families headed by single women; young men and women between 17 and 24 years old are far more likely to abuse drugs or commit crimes if they come from fatherless homes; legalized abortion has cheapened human life to the point that many are no longer shocked by euthanasia, and child abuse rates have risen in tandem with abortion rates. According to the Biblical view, these destructive social tendencies can only be corrected as children are raised in loving familes. Thus, Christians call for a return to the traditional family unit of father and mother (married to each other for life) and children and to traditional family values including love, fidelity, and respect.

Non-Christians cling to the hope that one day society will evolve to the point where men and women are "free" of the constraints of such tradition. But the question arises: How do we

---

[35] Ibid., 93.
[36] C.E.M. Joad, *The Recovery of Belief* (London, UK: Faber and Faber, 1955), 46.

know whom to trust as an architect of this perfect society, since all people are theoretically tainted by their present environment? Can we trust Marx or B.F. Skinner since they were both influenced by their respective societies? Is Corliss Lamont's belief that the perfect society will be socialistic fostered by his inherent goodness or a reflection of the negative impact American society has had on him? We cannot know. It is impossible to find a perfect person to shape a perfect society.

Why? Because when we are honest with ourselves, when we ask ourselves whether our inclinations are really toward good or toward evil and if it is fair to blame society for our urge to steal, lust, or tell a lie, we must face the fact that we have an inherent tendency toward sin. As Joad says, "Is it not obvious that human arrogance and love of power, that human brutality and cruelty, that, in a word, man's inhumanity to man, are responsible for . . . [tragic events such as the Holocaust]; obvious, too, that it is precisely these characteristics that have written their melancholy record upon every page of human history?"[37]

Deep down we all know this is true. We understand that "our righteous acts are unclean" (Isaiah 64:6). A simple adherence to the ancient admonition "Know thyself" reveals the folly of the non-Christian view of human nature.

Marxism-Leninism provides some of the most powerful examples of sinful human nature in the twentieth century. The record stretches from Marx's consistent dishonesty and misrepresentation of facts in his writings[38] to the slaughter of millions of innocent citizens by Marxist-Leninist dictators. The *Moscow News* speaks of "the horrors of Stalinism" and admits that Joseph Stalin was responsible for the mass murder of 15,000 Polish officers in the Katyn Forest. Robert Conquest documents Stalin's systematic annihilation of 14.5 million Ukrainians; Ronald Nash reveals that Rumanian Communist Nicolae Ceausescu ordered the deaths of some 60,000 people during his reign of terror. Jung Chang and Jon Halliday write that "Mao Tse-tung, who for decades held absolute power over the lives of one-quarter of the world's population, was responsible for well over 70 million deaths in peacetime, more than any other twentieth-century leader."[39] R.J. Rummel and Stephane Courtois document Communism's twentieth-century slaughter of millions more.[40]

Christianity knows that people are capable of such inhumanity. The Bible never waxes romantic about human nature; instead, it graphically depicts our utter sinfulness (Jeremiah 17:9; Romans 3:10–23). The historical fruits of both Marxism (e.g., Soviet and Chinese atrocities, the Cambodian killing fields) and Secular Humanism, Cosmic Humanism, and Postmodernism (e.g., the murder of forty-six million unborn children worldwide every year) confirm the Bible's perspective. G.K. Chesterton is right: our penchant for vice is ubiquitous. The Bible is certainly right: our heart is deceitful and desperately wicked.

11.3.10 ANOTHER SOCIALIST EXPERIMENT

In their quest for the ultimate society, Marxists believe that economics and the forces of production play the primary role, while Secular Humanists trust world government to lead us to the Promised Land. The worldviews picture a world order based on atheism, evolution, and socialism.

Marxists believe that the dialectic has worked throughout history to lead society through a series of syntheses, from primitive communism to slavery to feudalism to capitalism and,

---

[37] Ibid., 64

[38] Paul Johnson, *Intellectuals* (New York, NY: Harper and Row, 1988), 52f.

[39] Jung Chang and Jon Halliday, *Mao: The Unknown Story* (New York, NY: Alfred A. Knopf, 2005), 3.

[40] R.J. Rummel, *Death By Government* (New Brunswick, NJ: Transaction Publishers, 1994) and Stephane Courtois, et al., *The Black Book of Communism: Crimes, Terror, Repression* (Cambridge, MA: Harvard University Press, 1999).

recently, to socialism. Socialism itself is a transition between capitalism and communism. Marxist theory trusts that the worker (the antithesis) will clash with the capitalist (the thesis), creating a revolution leading to world socialism and, eventually, a utopian state of communism (the synthesis). A dictatorship of the proletariat (under the guidance of the Marxist-Leninist party) will be necessary initially to enforce such a world order, but it will wither away with the advent of communism. Likewise, law is now necessary to move us toward communism, but eventually the need for law will also disappear.

> The Communist revolution, conducted in the name of doing away with classes, has resulted in the most complete authority of any single new class.
>
> — MILOVAN DJILAS

As with the rest of the Marxist worldview, there are a number of inconsistencies in its theories regarding civilization and her institutions. If people are but helpless pawns of the dialectic, why bother to encourage workers to revolt—won't societal change happen inevitably when the dialectic demands it? Further, does the dialectic just stop working once the perfect society (i.e., communism) is attained? Or will communism draw a new antithesis to itself and clash to form another synthesis? In other words, because the synthesis is transitory, even utopia will be transitory and must logically give way to another social order.

A larger problem is created by the Marxist insistence that socialism is an improvement over capitalism. Perhaps some credence might have been given to this claim a century ago, before the grand socialist experiment in Soviet Russia, but the constant failings of the Soviet economy unambiguously demonstrated the impracticality of socialism.[41] As Biblical Christianity declared all along, socialism robs us of any incentive to better ourself because it is contrary to human nature's built-in sense of justice. Those who are lazy and do not produce—whether grades in school or cars on an assembly line—should not receive an equal result with those who do. A student who studies hard and earns an "A" should not be required to share his or her grade with someone who studies little, sleeps a lot, or shoots cocaine. Socialism discriminates against the competent, the hardworking, the productive, and encourages envy and laziness among poor men and women who might, in a capitalist society, achieve productivity and cultivate feelings of self-worth rather than jealousy.[42]

Further, socialism does not hasten the abolition of class distinctions (as Marxists claim it will), but creates a new elite. Hoover Institute Research Fellow Arnold Beichman points out that socialism in the former Soviet Union created a class known as the nomenklatura (also referred to as the "state bourgeois" or the "class of privileged exploiters"). This class, according to Beichman, is the prime example of the inequality spawned by socialism. Its members "own everything, the auto factories, the dachas, the food markets, the pharmacies, the transport system, the department stores. Everything."[43] Instead of destroying class distinctions, socialism created a completely authoritarian class. Milovan Djilas says, "The Communist revolution, conducted in the name of doing away with classes, has resulted in the most complete authority of any single new class."[44] This elite, founded on political connections and applied communist ideology, ran the Soviet economic sector into the ground.

After being confronted with the tragic results of applied socialism, why would anyone be interested in attaining advanced socialism? The Marxist attitude toward private property

---

[41] For an in depth look at socialism, see Joshua Muravchik, *Heaven on Earth: The Rise and Fall of Socialism* (San Francisco, CA: Encounter Books, 2002).

[42] Theodore Dalrymple, *Life At The Bottom: The Worldview That Makes The Underclass* (Chicago, IL: Ivan R. Dee, 2001).

[43] Arnold Beichman, "Immune From the Shortages," *The Washington Times*, December 31, 1990, G3.

[44] Ibid.

removes the incentive to work and replaces it with governmental coercion—causing production to grind to a virtual halt—and then wants to remove the coercion! Somehow, we are told, the dialectic will lead us into a glorious society in which we work according to our ability, and takes according to our need. But the economies in China, Cuba, and every other Marxist country in the world demonstrate that even the pale shadow of such a socialist society creates an environment in which we are less and less willing to demonstrate ability and more and more willing to demonstrate need.

This is the same problem faced by Secular Humanists and Postmodernists who call for wealth redistribution. They ignore the fact that redistribution encourages recipients to work not to earn a living but to demonstrate need, i.e., to get the biggest piece of the redistributed pie. Further, socialistic Secular Humanists and Marxists refuse to recognize that free enterprise and private property (a New Testament concept; Acts 5:1–4), actually work to produce wealth. In capitalism, property and skills can be used to produce more, thereby creating a wealthier society. In contrast, wealth redistribution programs merely spread wealth around, encouraging a consumptive, rather than productive, mindset. The question becomes not "How can I produce more?" but "How can I get more?" This attitute is evident even in the United States, a country that should have learned from the practical failures of socialism around the world but is instead embracing more and more plans for wealth redistribution.

11.3.11 THE CENTRAL PLANNERS

The greatest flaw in Marxist and Secular Humanist socialistic schemes was pinpointed by economist and social philosopher Ludwig von Mises years ago. Socialists expect to replace the precise free market mechanism with that of central planners. They trust that enough economists can make correct decisions about what to produce and how much of it to produce and assign the right prices as efficiently as the constant adjustments made by the laws of supply and demand. Not only does this claim appear unworkable in theory, it has been proven totally unworkable in practice in numerous socialist countries. Black markets thrive in such settings because they supply the goods and services people actually want— something the central planners have never shown themselves able to accomplish.

Trust in central planners, although impractical, is a logical extension of non-Christian thought. Because these worldviews believe that we are inherently good, they expect that, given enough control over our environment, we can create the perfect society. By reshaping the economy to grant inherently good people more control, we should be able to move steadily toward a more desirable society.

Centrally planned economies create enormous bureaucracies, but Marxists and Secular Humanists hesitate to discuss this aspect of their political theory because bureaucracy is an unpopular term. Marxists actually deny the major role that government plays in their worldview, claiming that the state will wither away in communist society. The question arises, then: When, exactly, can we expect to see the state begin to wither away? Which Marxist leader will show him or herself willing to abandon power rather than garner more? These questions are unanswerable for the simple reason that no one who has tasted power is interested in abandoning it. Power, as Lord Acton said long ago, tends to corrupt. The more power one gets, the more it tends to corrupt. And this problem is by no means restricted to the Marxist worldview— Secular Humanists must answer variations of the same questions. When will government be big enough? Until every problem faced by the human race—from famine to slander—is solved, Secular Humanists and Marxists will blame society and cry for more government to correct the flaws of our environment. Their desire is to establish one world government to direct the evolution of the human race toward utopia

11.3.12 WORLD PLANNERS

The call for world government is a cause for much concern among Christians. After witnessing Secular Humanism's systematic eradication of Christianity from the public square in America over the past thirty years, Christians are justified in opposing a world government that would surely work toward the same goal on a global scale. Such an order would be based on naturalistic values because those promoting world government (Secular Humanists, Marxist-Leninists, Cosmic Humanists, etc.) are anti-Christian.

Christians recognize the false assumptions that form the basis for bloated governmental power, understanding that the blame lies not on faulty societal structures but on the inherent sinfulness of every human heart. Thus, Christianity postulates a cure—the gospel of transformation by Christ—that actually treats the disease. By acknowledging our responsibility for our actions, Christianity grants every individual the opportunity to break the bonds of sin rather than saddling him or her with the quiet desperation of trusting the government to solve the world's problems. "Christianity," says John Warwick Montgomery, "asserts that man, being radically self-centered, can only be saved and transformed so as to treat his neighbor with proper dignity when he admits that he cannot 'do his duty' or save himself—and relies entirely on God in Christ for salvation."[45]

> Christianity, asserts that man, being radically self-centered, can only be saved and transformed so as to treat his neighbor with proper dignity when he admits that he cannot 'do his duty' or save himself—and relies entirely on God in Christ for salvation
>
> — JOHN WARWICK MONTGOMERY

Marxism and Secular Humanism's false ideas of politics and economics trace back to their false assumptions of human nature, which in turn stem from their false beliefs about our origins. By declaring that God does not exist and that matter organized itself into human beings, the secular worldviews strip sovereignty from God and find themselves forced to bestow sovereignty on the state. Secular Humanists and Marxists are usually unwilling to admit that their views grant sovereignty to government, but the simple fact remains that, barring anarchy, human beings require an absolute basis on which to judge individual actions. If God is denied, the state must usurp His role. Thus, absolute power falls into the hands of politicians—persons who are not, despite optimism to the contrary, infallible.

Ironically, one of the men Secular Humanists most frequently point to as a proponent of Humanist thought, Thomas Jefferson, strongly opposed big government. He believed that good government is government "which shall restrain men from injuring one another, shall leave them otherwise free to regulate their own pursuits of industry and improvement, and shall not take from the mouth of labor the bread it has earned. This is the sum of good Government."[46] Jefferson's portrait of government is remarkably similar to the biblical government Paul describes in Romans 13:1–5. It is also common sense if we understand the true role of government and our responsibility for our own actions.

11.3.13 THE EVOLUTION OF LAW

Secular Humanists and Marxists do not accept human sinfulness, and thus create another problem. When we deny our responsibility and declare the state sovereign, we also destroy justice—perhaps the most dangerous aspect of the utopian vision. When government becomes

---

[45] John Warwick Montgomery, *Human Rights and Human Dignity* (Dallas, TX: Probe Books, 1986), 123.

[46] Thomas Jefferson, First Inaugural Address, 1801.

> [T]here is no objective rationale for elevating our species into a category separate from the rest of the animals with whom we share the presence of a nervous system, the ability to feel pain, and behaviors aimed at avoiding pain. Thus, the fundamental rights we accord ourselves must be equally applicable to any other organism with these same characteristics.
>
> — KENNETH L. FEDER AND ALAN PARK

our only guide, then only legal positivism can result. Legal positivism and the sovereignty of the state (statism) are inseparable—either theory assumes the other.

If we recall that the three most tyrannical dictators of the twentieth century, Adolph Hitler, Joseph Stalin, and Mao Tse-tung, all advocated statism and practiced positive law, we should find no comfort in knowing that the law on which the "new world order" will be founded is positivist. The legal structures proposed by world government proponents are based on the naturalistic interpretation of humanity and government. Human rights are assigned according to what will assist humanity's evolutionary climb to perfection. The design of this whole legal and political superstructure, as Malachi Martin points out, "is built on the presumption that we ourselves are the authors of our destiny. Man is exalted. The God-Man is repudiated; and with him, the idea of man's fallenness is rejected. Evil is a matter of malfunctioning structures, not in any way a basic inclination of man."[47]

Secular Humanists and Marxists advocate positive law because they deny the existence of God and His law. Thus, we are either a law unto ourselves or we must trust the sovereign state to manufacture law. Cosmic Humanists tend toward making every individual a law unto himself or herself. But Secular Humanists and Marxists understand that this leads to anarchy, and therefore choose to grant the state sovereignty. Trusting the state as the absolute basis in law leads to legal relativism because government is an ever-changing entity. But for law to remain constant, for the word justice to mean anything in a rational, legal sense, law must have an unchanging basis. Only an absolute foundation can create absolute laws (i.e., It is always unlawful and morally wrong for a judge to take a bribe; It is always and universally wrong for an adult to sexually molest and torture a child for fun). Systems of law based on relativism can declare only, "It is unlawful, in the present circumstances, to take a bribe" or "Thou shalt not commit bribery . . . ordinarily."

Legal positivism leads to rampant relativism, as demonstrated by Sidney Hook: "The rights of man depend upon his nature, needs, capacities, and aspirations, not upon his origins. Children have rights not because they are our creatures but because of what they are and will become. It is not God but the human community that endows its members with rights."[48]

This is the height of relativism! Because our nature is always in evolutionary flux and every individual differs from his fellow human beings in terms of needs and capacities, it naturally follows that individual's rights must vary in proportion to these differences. Does this mean, then, that I have fewer rights than a concert pianist because he is more capable than I? Do I have more rights than the needy in Ethiopia? Clearly, it is no good founding rights on human capacities or governmental policies. Rights and laws must be based on the character of God, or they will be humanly arbitrary, and consequently, most often in favor of the rich and powerful. God's laws, on the other hand, do not vary for the rich and poor; they apply to everyone equally!

A prime example of consistent humanistic evolutionary thinking is found in the animal

[47] Malachi Martin, *The Keys of This Blood* (New York, NY: Simon and Schuster, 1990), 656.
[48] Sidney Hook, "Solzhenitsyn and Secular Humanism: A Response," *The Humanist* (Nov/Dec 1978): 6.

rights movement quest for species equality: Kenneth L. Feder and Michael Alan Park write, "[T]here is no objective rationale for elevating our species into a category separate from the rest of the animals with whom we share the presence of a nervous system, the ability to feel pain, and behaviors aimed at avoiding pain. Thus, the fundamental rights we accord ourselves must be equally applicable to any other organism with these same characteristics."[49]

Consistent with their atheistic bias, these Secular Humanists see no distinction between humans and the rest of the animal kingdom—people and rats are viewed as equals and with no favoritism displayed in the realm of rights. But this view strips us of our dignity as created in the image of God and denies God's will that we rule over His creation (Genesis 1:28). It renders human rights transitory and as meaningless as the rights we bestow on toads and Tasmanian devils.

Will lions have the right to pursue happiness even if that entails depriving jackals of their right to life? Will we bestow rights on plants as well (after all, they are also living evolutionary relations), thereby starving the human race for fear of "murdering" a fellow organism? The absurdity is apparent—as obvious as the absurdity of animal rights advocates displaying more affection for embryonic bald eagles than for human babies in the womb. But the absurdity follows necessarily from worldviews that base human rights on temporal, changeable institutions and ideologies.

The danger of legal relativism should be obvious to all. When the state is the only basis for law, any law may be conceived. Examples of this truth are seen throughout history. Hitler, Stalin, and many others used positive law to murder millions—passing laws to eliminate Jews, gypsies, the sick, landowners, Christians, or anyone they had an urge to destroy—which fundamentally means anyone who stood in the way of their absolute domination of every person and action in society.

In the West, laws that many people considered inconceivable a few years ago are now the standards by which we must live. Abortion is legal because the state decided that a baby in the womb is not a baby. Perhaps, twenty years from now infanticide will be legal because the state will decide that a baby is not a human being until it can walk or talk. The distinction between right and wrong is tenuous in a society that subscribes to legal positivism. Yesterday homosexual marriages were illegal; today homosexual marriages are the cry of political and moral liberals everywhere.

Conversely, Christian law applied to society results in practical and just legal structures. Christian law is based on the character of God and His absolute moral order. It is grounded in an understanding that although we are created in the image of God, we are imperfect and prone to evil, and because of our sin, Jesus Christ came to earth as a man to die for the sins of the world. Christian law has produced the concept of common law, the Magna Charta, the Declaration of Independence, and the Constitution of the United States.

The Magna Charta resulted in a just government in England; likewise, the application of Christian law to the U.S. Constitution positively shaped America. Because her founding fathers read human nature correctly and divided power properly, America instituted a system of law that protects human rights and human dignity. "America is still the place," said Alexis de Tocqueville, "where the Christian religion has kept the greatest real power over men's souls; and nothing better demonstrates how useful and natural it is to man, since the country where it now has widest sway is both the most enlightened and the freest."[50]

Contrast such legal history with the history of positive law in the first half of the twentieth

---

[49] Kenneth L. Feder and Michael Alan Park, "Animal Rights: An Evolutionary Perspective," *The Humanist* (July/August 1990): 44.

[50] Alexis de Tocqueville, *Democracy in America* (New York, NY: Harper and Row, 2000), 291. This observation was made circa 1840.

century: "No half-century ever witnessed slaughter on such a scale," said Robert Jackson, "such cruelties and inhumanities, such wholesale deportations of peoples into slavery, such annihilations of minorities." Ideas have consequences. Bad ideas have bad consequences, and the consequences of legal positivism are tragic.[51]

11.3.14 WHOSE SCIENCE?

The closely related disciplines of politics, economics, and law—are aspects of Marxist and Secular Humanist worldviews that do not adequately take into account the workings of the real world. Both worldviews try to circumvent the problems of statism by claiming that the real basis for the state's guidance of society lies in the scientific method. That is, we are able to use science to discern the proper direction for society, and science provides a foundation that is not subject to the whims of people. Science is the force that will lead us to utopia. Paul Kurtz says bluntly, "Science is the ultimate source of our knowledge of value. . . . It discovers and creates ideal systems which contribute to the homeostatic expansion of life. Therefore, the extension of science is perhaps the chief practical good for humankind to achieve."[52]

If the atheistic and naturalistic assumptions of Secular Humanism and Marxism were correct, we would live in a disorderly universe that follows no discernible pattern and subscribes to no unalterable laws. We would not have seasons, the law of gravity, or the migration of swallows to the same area year after year. Only in the Christian model of the universe—a universe created by a rational, personal God—can we expect to find such magnificent order. And only an ordered and intelligible universe allows room for science.

The fact that science arose at all is powerful testimony to the truth of Christianity.[53] Yet, as Louis Victor de Broglie says, "We are not sufficiently astonished by the fact that any science may be possible." [54] This is especially true of Marxists and the Secular Humanists who do not understand that orderly science could never have been conceived in a society dominated by naturalistic worldviews.

Historian and philosopher of science Stanley Jaki says that "the belief in a personal rational Creator . . . as cultivated especially within a Christian matrix . . . supported the view for which the world was an objective and orderly entity investigable by the mind because the mind too was an orderly and objective product of the same rational, that is, perfectly consistent Creator." We can believe science is possible because we believe in a God of reason and order.[55]

The supreme irony is that modern public school classrooms, using the arbitrary power of positive law, bar the Christian worldview while welcoming both the Marxist and Secular Humanist perspectives. It is an irony that Jefferson would have been quick to condemn:

> "Was the government to prescribe to us our medicine and diet, our bodies would be in such keeping as our souls are now. Thus in France the emetic was once forbidden as a medicine, and the potato as an article of food. Government is just as infallible, too, when it fixes systems in physics. Galileo was sent to the Inquisition for affirming that the earth was a sphere; the government had declared it to be as flat as a trencher, and Galileo was obliged to abjure his error. This error, however, at length prevailed, the earth became a globe, and Descartes declared

---

[51] Cited in Montgomery, *Human Rights and Human Dignity*, 107.

[52] Paul Kurtz, *Philosophical Essays in Pragmatic Naturalism* (Amherst, NY: Prometheus Books, 1990), 163.

[53] See chapter 2 of Rodney Stark, *For the Glory of God* (Princeton, NJ: Princeton University Press, 2003).

[54] Quoted in Roche, *A World Without Heroes*, 289.

[55] Stanley L. Jaki, *The Road of Science and the Ways to God* (Chicago, IL: University of Chicago Press, 1978), 242. We also recommend Norman L. Geisler and J. Kerby Anderson, *Origin Science: A Proposal for the Creation-Evolution Controversy* (Grand Rapids, MI: Baker Book House, 1987), and J.P. Moreland, *Christianity and the Nature of Science* (Grand Rapids, MI: Baker Book House, 1989).

it was whirled round its axes by a vortex. The government in which he lived was wise enough to see that this was no question of civil jurisdiction, or we should all have been involved by authority in vortices. In fact, vortices have been exploded, and the Newtonian principle of gravitation is now more firmly established, on the basis of reason, than it would be were the government to step in, and to make it an article of necessary faith. Reason and experiment have been indulged, and error has fled before them. It is error alone which needs the support of government. Truth can stand by itself."[56]

11.3.15 THE DANGERS OF SCIENTISM

Atheist worldviews have expanded on the concept of science to the point of distortion, assigning science the ability to grant man knowledge of everything, including value and truth. Tonne declares, "Seeking the nearest approximation to truth that we can attain is an endless struggle. It is probably the most important study we undertake. That is what 'science' is all about."[57] Secular worldviews have invested science with an almost supernatural quality—even speaking of its "omnipotence"—trusting the scientific method to provide the correct answer to virtually any question.

But such attitudes toward science are false. Science has natural limits, including the fact that it can only provide us with knowledge about the material, observable universe. Any attempt to expand science beyond these natural limits leads not to better science but to scientism. Trusting science for an entire epistemology leads either to frustration or to methods of obtaining knowledge that are labeled scientific but are unfounded. Humanists and Marxists are usually guilty of the latter error, describing utopian social programs and ethical codes with no basis in science as "scientific." This approach actually hinders true scientific progress. Jaki explains, "Scientism is never a genuine reverence for science but a harnessing of science for a nonscientific purpose. Since that purpose is fixed, science can only serve it by remaining fixed, namely, by remaining in its supposedly final stage."[58]

Scientism is yet another flaw that taints both Marxist and Secular Humanist theory. It is unreasonable to demand that science provide us with all knowledge. Even Julian Huxley, in one of his more candid moments, recognized the limited nature of the scientific method: "Science has removed the obscuring veil of mystery from many phenomena, much to the benefit of the human race: but it confronts us with a basic and universal mystery—the mystery of existence in general, and of the existence of mind in particular. Why does the world exist? Why is the world-stuff what it is? Why does it have mental or subjective aspects as well as material or objective ones? We do not know."[59]

11.3.16 EXPERIMENTING WITH THE OBJECTIVE MORAL ORDER

Unfortunately, Secular Humanists and Marxists ignore Huxley's startling admission and cling tenuously to their scientism. Without science for their epistemology, they would have to revert to the "trust the voice within you" mentality of Cosmic Humanism and Postmodernism. That is, their theory of knowledge would be based only on individual experience or community standards respectively. But by clinging to science, they find themselves trusting an epistemology

---

[56] Cited in John P. Foley, ed., *The Jeffersonian Cyclopedia*, 2 vols. (New York, NY: Russell and Russell, 1967), 1:386.

[57] Herbert Arthur Tonne, *Scribblings of a Concerned Secular Humanist* (Northvale, NJ: Humanists of New Jersey, 1988), 40.

[58] Jaki, *The Road of Science and the Ways to God*, 218.

[59] Huxley, *Essays of a Humanist*, 107.

unqualified to speak to a number of disciplines, including ethics. Science cannot tell the world what is right and what is wrong. In fact, ethics precedes science because honesty and truthfulness must be a part of the scientist's vocabulary of sciences.

Marxists and Secular Humanists apply the theories of evolution and the dialectic to morality and conclude that ethics evolves as humanity evolves and that we have not yet established the perfect ethical code to govern us in utopian society. Indeed, Marxists go so far as to declare all present moral codes "bourgeois" and therefore sinister. Given these beliefs, proponents of Marxism and Secular Humanism see ethics as relative. They reject all ethical absolutes and even view claims of unchangeable ethical codes as horrible deceptions. Tonne warns that "the notion that there is an absolute truth etched into the eternal heavens as so many of us were brought up to believe is not only a falsehood, it is a menace to human development."[60]

However, people who make blanket statements like this are not being consistent with how they live. It is doubtful, for example, that Tonne believes it is morally right for an adult male to sexually molest and torture a child for fun. If there is no place on earth where this is right, then Mr. Tonne should be honest and call it what it is—a moral absolute.

Moral absolutes abound: It is always wrong to steal from a blind man's tin cup. It is always right to be kind to the homeless. It is never right to murder a professor because of his or her atheism, etc. Even Jurgen Habermas, a Secular Humanist, admits that some sort of universally agreed upon framework is both possible and necessary in order to ensure that freedom and justice are achieved.[61]

> The notion that there is an absolute truth etched into the eternal heavens as so many of us were brought up to believe is not only a falsehood, it is a menace to human development.
>
> — HERBERT TONNE

In reality, Tonne's ideas are a menace to civilized society. Trusting evolutionary theory to provide a framework for ethics leads down a number of paths—all of which are hopelessly twisted. For example, Hitler applied Darwin's theory of natural selection to morality and concluded, "There is absolutely no other revolution but a racial revolution. There is no economic, no social, no political revolution. There is only the struggle of lower races against the higher races."[62] As Richard Weikart notes, "Darwinism delivered a death-blow to the prevailing Judeo-Christian ethics, as well as Kantian ethics and any other fixed moral code. If morality was built on social instincts that changed over evolutionary time, then morality must be relative to the conditions of life at any given time. Darwinism—together with other forms of historicism ascendant in the nineteenth century—thus contributed to the rise of moral relativism."[63]

Others who applied Darwinism to ethics were Karl Marx and Frederick Engels, who concluded that the ends justified the means. This, in turn, was used by Stalin to justify "the dictatorship of the proletariat . . . over the bourgeoisie, untrammeled by the law and based on violence and enjoying the sympathy and support of the toiling and exploited masses."[64] Likewise, following his 1949 conquest of China, Mao Tse-Tung's first lectures to villagers were not about Marxist theory; they were about Darwin's theory.

If ethical and cultural relativism are true, then human beings ultimately determine their own moral conduct, which means that Hitler, Stalin, and Mao never acted unethically (at least

[60] Tonne, *Scribblings of a Concerned Secular Humanist*, 40.

[61] Glenn Ward, *Postmodernism* (Chicago, IL: McGraw-Hill Companies, 2003), 179.

[62] Quoted in Roche, *A World Without Heroes*, 248.

[63] Richard Weikart, *From Darwin To Hitler: Evolutionary Ethics, Eugenics, and Racism in Germany* (New York, NY: Palgrave MacMillan, 2004), 229.

[64] Joseph Stalin, *J. Stalin Works*, (Moscow, USSR: Foreign Languages Publishing House, 1953, 6:118

not according to their subjective standards). In fact, if these men succeeded in moving the evolutionary timetable forward, then Secular Humanists and Marxists should be consistent and applaud them for the work. But Secular Humanists and Marxists do not applaud; rather they condemn. This brings to light a glaring flaw in the fabric of their ethics: the inability to live with the logical conclusions of their worldview.

11.3.17 SCIENTISM AND MORALS

Still another frightening conclusion of applying scientism to ethics can be seen in the example of Harry Elmer Barnes. He assumes that an intelligent individual can use the scientific method to determine morals. He then draws the logical conclusion that there is no truly intelligent person who is not at the same time moral in the scientific sense of that term. "It should be absolutely clear to any thoughtful and informed person," writes Barnes, "that morality, far from being divorced from intelligence, depends more thoroughly and completely upon intelligence and scientific information than any other phase of human thought."[65]

> The new morality, makes it quite possible to be a passionate lover of humanity, like a Marx or a Lenin, and to be a passionate hater of actual human beings.
>
> — WILLIAM STANMEYER

This theory takes on a sinister character when we realize that whoever society labels "intelligent" has free reign to dictate morals. Further, it allows intelligent people to dictate right and wrong for every member of society with a lower IQ. Barnes admits as much: "Wide variations in capacity appear to be the most important single fact about the human race. It would seem to follow that there will be certain kinds of conduct which will not be harmful for the abler members of society; which, indeed, may be positively desirable and beneficial."[66]

The belief that some people will always know better than others, regardless of actual concern with morality, has already severely wounded our world. It has allowed dictators to commit unspeakable acts of violence. It has encouraged the attitude in America that a mother knows what is right for her unborn baby, even if it means abortion; that doctors know when a fatally ill person would like to die; and that Planned Parenthood knows the proper means of sex education for all. The results of such morality range from the slaughter of Ukrainians and the unborn to a raging AIDS epidemic. "The new morality," says William Stanmeyer, "makes it quite possible to be a passionate lover of humanity, like a . . . Marx or a Lenin, and to be a passionate hater of actual human beings."[67]

According to this ethical vision, it makes sense to kill millions of bourgeoisie or millions of babies because they are obstacles to our march toward utopia. Secular Humanists and Marxists do not like to talk about the devastating consequences of their ethics. When discussing morality, they prefer positive terms like justice, love, and courage. But when asked for the specific basis for such concepts, they flounder. Science can no more reveal a meaningful foundation for these terms than it can explain a man and a woman falling in love. So, despite railing against absolute codes and traditional morality, secular worldviews must fall back on some form of Christian ethics when postulating specific moral suggestions.

Secular Humanist H. J. Eysenck warns, "In rejecting religion altogether, Humanism may be throwing out the ethical baby with the supernatural bathwater."[68] Lamont also tries to borrow

---

[65] Harry Elmer Barnes, *The New History and the Social Studies* (New York, NY: Century, 1925), 543.
[66] Ibid., 539.
[67] William Stanmeyer, *Clear and Present Danger* (Ann Arbor, MI: Servant Books, 1983), 167.
[68] Paul Kurtz, ed., *The Humanist Alternative* (Amherst, NY: Prometheus Press, 1985), 92.

Christian ethics while snubbing their foundation: "Any humane philosophy must include such New Testament ideals as the brotherhood of man, peace on earth and the abundant life. There is much ethical wisdom, too, in the Old Testament and its Ten Commandments. Without accepting any ethical principle as a dogmatic dictum never to be questioned, the Humanist certainly adheres in general to a Biblical commandment such as, 'Thou shalt not bear false witness against thy neighbor.'"[69]

Lamont surely knows, however, that if God is denied, everything is permissible. Without its foundation in the absolute nature of God, morality is set adrift. Will Durant admits, "[W]e shall find it no easy task to mold a natural ethic strong enough to maintain moral restraint and social order without the support of supernatural consolations, hopes and fears."[70] Francis Schaeffer responds: "It is not just difficult, it is impossible."[71]

Science had nothing to do with forming the foundation for biblical morality. God's character is the foundation for Christian law and ethics—and as a result, Christian legal and ethical systems fit the facts of reality and provide genuine guidance for those who seek to act rightly. Schaeffer remarks that one of the distinctive things about God is that "He is a God with character. Everything is not equally right before God, and because of this we have our absolutes."[72]

Marxists and Humanists have built ethical systems on shifting sand and tolerate any action they believe brings the human race closer to utopia. Christians base morality on the unchanging nature of God, a moral order reflecting God's character and the understanding that our highest calling is to love and serve others (Mark 10:43–45; Romans 7:4–6).

11.3.18 "I COULDN'T HELP MYSELF"

Ethics is not the only realm in which humanistic scientism creates unsolvable problems. Marxist and Secular Humanist psychology is also distorted by faulty theoretical assumptions. Because they assume that science is the only means of discerning truth, they abandon all "unscientific" notions like mind, idea, conscience, soul, and spirit. Wilson declares, "A scientific humanist . . . is someone who suggests that everything in the universe has a material basis. And that means everything, including the mind and all its spiritual products."[73] Humanist psychology is ontological monism in that mind and brain are considered identical (materialistic events or entities).

Before Darwin's *Origin of Species by Means of Natural Selection, or The Preservation of Favored Races in the Struggle for Life*, people would have scoffed at the completely behaviorist theories of Pavlov and Skinner who carried their secular worldviews to its logical conclusion. Many early atheists, of course, had suggested that mind and soul did not exist, but none had the audacity to draw the logical conclusion: without mind, our actions are but a series of responses to various external stimuli; therefore, they are completely determined.

Their conclusion should not shock us. Behaviorism is the logical extension of naturalism. What should shock us is that Marxists and Secular Humanists expect us to believe that this model accurately describes reality. A model that strips us of free will can lead only to nonsensical conclusions such as, "it means you literally have no choice about reading this book at this moment; your doing so was, as it were, determined by the stars. Nor have I any choice in what

[69] Corliss Lamont, *A Lifetime of Dissent* (Amherst, NY: Prometheus Books, 1988), 55.

[70] Cited in Francis A. Schaeffer, *The Complete Works of Francis A. Schaeffer: A Christian View of the West*, 5 vols. (Westchester, IL: Crossway Books, 1982), 5:439.

[71] Schaeffer, *Complete Works*, 5:439.

[72] Ibid., 4:30.

[73] Edward O. Wilson, "Biology's Spiritual Products," *Free Inquiry* (Spring 1987): 14.

I'm writing, being, as it were, merely a stenographer for what is dictated by the dance of the atoms. Consequently, if I were to write that all naturalists were ugly useless cockroaches, the naturalist would have to agree that Nature herself forced me to say so."[74]

Behaviorism absolves us of responsibility for our actions. In real life, Secular Humanists and Marxists do hold people responsible for their actions (when someone steals their car, they demand prosecution), but when they do so, they are acting inconsistently. True adherence to secular philosophy, theology, psychology, and biology requires never blaming (or praising for that matter) any individual for his or her actions.

Further, true adherence to the behavioral view of man negates the meaningfulness of the behaviorist's findings. "We must use our will to study the world. If we conclude that the world is of a character that does not allow free will, we destroy our credentials for saying so."[75] Only if our mind is more than a receptor and processor of stimuli can we trust it to devise meaningful theories. Only if our will is our own, and not slave to the changeable winds of society, can we arrive at a rational conclusion.

11.3.19 I Can Help Myself

Secular Humanists and Marxists are embarrassed by these problems—thus, they presently downplay the behavioral aspect of their worldviews. Both secular worldviews also treat people as if they possess free will when encouraging them to choose to support their particular revolution or utopian vision. In a very real sense, Secular Humanists and Marxists want to have their cake and eat it, too. They desire a universe without God, made entirely of matter and evolving toward perfection, but they wish to retain concepts negated by these presuppositions, including mind, ideas, and free will. Secular Humanist Wayne L. Trotta provides an example of this mentality: "It may be prudent to assume that all behavior is governed by causal laws. But reducing human conduct to a set of mechanistic—'if this happens then that happens'— formulae would ultimately reduce therapy to nothing more than a set of techniques."[76]

The Secular Humanist and Marxist worldviews describe the universe one way, but their adherents cannot live in accordance with their views. Secular worldview proponents leave their atheism and materialism on the shelf and embrace the concept of absolutes and free will when interacting with the community. However, when Secular Humanist psychology is put into practice, the outcome has been horrendous. Joyce Milton describes Humanist psychology in action in her work *The Road to Malpsychia: Humanistic Psychology and Our Discontents*.[77] The rage was to debunk "the old value system" and replace it with 'a sexually liberated lifestyle.'"[78]

Why do Secular Humanists and Marxists continue to cling to worldviews that they must be abandoned when faced with cold hard facts. If love "comes from a pure heart and a good conscience and a sincere faith," (1 Timothy :5) why do proponents of secular worldviews insist on denying the existence of the supernatural? Why, when Marxist regimes are crumbling throughout the world, do Western (and especially American) professors still believe that Marxism is a workable worldview? Why do Secular Humanists deny the existence of the conscience and the divinity of Christ and then proclaim, as Bertrand Russell does, that the world needs more "Christian love"? The answer is that both secular worldviews are religions built upon an unreasonable faith.

---

[74] Roche, *A World Without Heroes*, 116.

[75] Ibid., 106.

[76] Wayne L. Trotta, "Why Psychotherapy Must Be, and Cannot Be, a Science," *The Humanist* (Sept/Oct 1989): 42.

[77] Joyce Milton, *The Road to Malpsychia: Humanistic Psychology and Our Discontents* (San Francisco, CA: Encounter Books, 2002).

[78] Ibid., 161–2.

11.3.20 THE KINGDOM OF UTOPIA

Secular Humanists and Marxists base their attitudes about history and the future on the belief that evolution (either neo-Darwinian or punctuated) is a fact. Accordingly, all of life is on a grand march forward, progressing toward perfection (Marxism makes doubly sure of this progress by postulating a near-divine, teleological dialectic that moves us through various means of production toward the most desirable society). The belief that evolution virtually guarantees the eventual perfection of life is as old as Darwin, who suggested that because "natural selection works solely by and for the good of each being, all corporeal and mental endowments will tend to progress towards perfection."[79]

Clearly, Marxist and Secular Humanist worldviews offer incentives for their faithful. Not only do they promise an "inevitable" ascent into paradise, they also promise a heaven without the uncomfortable concept of a holy and just God. We do not have to be responsible for our actions, yet we can still achieve paradise! This belief about history and the future provides the incentive for men and women to cling to worldviews that are otherwise untenable.

Sadly, even the paradise that provides hope for so many Secular Humanists and Marxists is a pale and inadequate concept. If the supernatural does not exist, then individuals pass away with their bodies. Paradise is a fleeting state, and all those who have already died will never experience it. William Kirk Kilpatrick points out, "What good does it do to the billions who have already passed through this life in wretchedness, that scientific humanism will one day create a world without suffering? For that matter what good does it do to those who are right now dying miserable and lonely deaths all over the world? All that a strict humanism has to say to most of the human race living and dead is 'Too bad you were born too early' and 'Too bad about your suffering.' The bulk of the world's pain is written off as a bad expense." [80]

Such a callous, tenuous paradise is hardly paradise at all. Some Secular Humanists and Marxists try to circumvent the fact of our mortality in an effort to create a more appealing notion of utopia. By granting the evolutionary process a state of wisdom usually reserved for God, they say that progress will one day guide humanity to an evolutionary form that fosters immortality. For example, Victor Stenger claims that computers are the next step in the evolutionary ladder that because their memory banks are basically immortal, people "also can become immortal. It should be possible in the future to save the accumulated knowledge of an individual human being when he or she dies. Perhaps even those thoughts which constitute consciousness will also be saved, and the collective thoughts of all human beings will be continued in the memory banks of computers."[81]

We are rightly appalled by the naiveté of Stenger's faith in evolution and his trust that change always denotes progress. As a keen observer notes, "We have to sweep away the trashy modern superstition that history is on some sort of grand, unstoppable march to human betterment . . . In its thrall, we automatically assume that 'new' is better. The ceaseless anti-heroic murmur for 'change' is a statement that everything past is evil, and any change is better. This is not only idiocy but moral defection. Does anybody really believe Germany was the better for Hitler? Change for the worse, both personal and social, is more the rule than the exception. Humans are born backsliders."[82]

Thus, one of the biggest flaws in the view of history founded on evolution and the dialectic is there is no evidence that humanity and society are moving toward perfection. In fact, the evidence is to the contrary. Secular Humanists and Marxists cannot dispute this, but neither

[79] Cited in Roche, *A World Without Heroes*, 238.

[80] William Kirk Kilpatrick, *Psychological Seduction* (Nashville, TN: Thomas Nelson, 1983), 185.

[81] Victor Stenger, *Not By Design* (Amherst, NY: Prometheus Books, 1988), 188.

[82] Roche, *A World Without Heroes*, 87.

can they accept the logical implication: the truth of the Biblical Christian worldview. Because they begin with the assumption that God does not exist, they must ignore all evidence to the contrary and make not one but numerous irrational leaps of faith to cope with their theology, philosophy, ethics, biology, etc.

Their entire perspective is distorted and causes them to discount the one historical Person who truly holds the key to a paradise in our future—"the kingdom of God's dear Son" (Colossians 1: 13), open to anyone who accepts, trusts, believes the Lord Jesus Christ (Acts 16:31; Matthew 7:21; Ephesians 2:8–10) and what He says He has done for the human race (e.g., John 3:16). By opting for a paradise that does not require our responsibility to God, Marxists and Secular Humanists turn their backs on the One who says He is the fount of all wisdom and knowledge (Colossians 2: 3) and the true and living Way (John 14:6) for the whole human race.

Marxists and Secular Humanists turn their backs on reality. They choose to deal in distortions, shadows and epiphenomena, advancing theories that deny the most important aspects of existence: God, the moral order, soul, mind, conscience, ideas, free will, and altruism. Their denial leads to inhuman theories and concepts, including "survival of the fittest" and the morality of violence against an entire class of people (the bourgeoisie). It leads to moral nonsense like "Thou shalt not commit murder . . . ordinarily," and a whole host of sexual perversions, disease, and death. Stewart Justman is correct—theirs is a Fool's Paradise.[83]

[83] Stewart Justman, *Fool's Paradise: The Unreal World of Pop Psychology* (Chicago, IL: Ivan R. Dee, 2005).

UNDERSTANDING
THE TIMES

465

Conclusion

Part Four

11.4.1 INTRODUCTION

When defending a biblical worldview in the marketplace of ideas—whether it takes the form of a letter to the editor of your local paper or a face-to-face dialogue with a neighbor—Christians must keep two things in mind. According to 2 Timothy 2:24–26, we must present the truth in order to set free those who have been captured by deceptive philosophies, and secondly, we must be kind and gentle as we do so. Both our content and our character are important. Since New Age adherents place a premium on peace and harmony, this approach is especially needed when seeking to lead them to God's truth.

The influence of Cosmic Humanist theology is seen in the number of people who believe that all religions lead to the same God. According to Barna's research, 44 percent of American adults agree that the Bible, the Koran, and the Book of Mormon are all different expressions of the same spiritual truths, and 30 percent of teens believe that all religions pray to the same God.[1]

A much larger percentage of Americans, including over 80 percent of those claiming to be "born again," have adopted the New Age and Postmodern idea of relativism in truth and ethics. Therefore, Christians need to understand why relativism is logical nonsense and know the key questions to ask their friends to guide them out of the relativistic fog. To counter these growing trends, this section explores religious pluralism, relativism, and New Age psychology with specific ways Christians can engage these ideas.

---

[1] See Barna's website: www.barna.org/cgi-bin/PagePressRelease.asp?PressReleaseID=122&Reference=A and // www.barna.org/cgi-bin/PageCategory.asp?CategoryID=37.

11.4.2 RELIGIOUS PLURALISM: A LOGICAL IMPOSSIBILITY

One particularly attractive component of New Age theology to its devotees is its non-judgmental approach to religion. Neale Donald Walsch says God communicated to him that "No path to God is more direct than any other path. No religion is the 'one true religion' . . . ."[2] In an interview with Bill Moyers, filmmaker George Lucas said, "The conclusion I've come to is that all the religions are true."[3]

Lucas' and Walsch's conviction is shared in the wider population, even among many Christians. According to George Barna, 63 percent of the teenagers surveyed agree that "Muslims, Buddhists, Christians, Jews, and all other people pray to the same god, even though they use different names for their god."[4]

Although in our rush to be non-judgmental many may choose to believe "all the religions are true," the idea is actually a logical impossibility. The first law of logic, the law of non-contradiction, states specifically what we know intuitively: Two things cannot be the same and different at the same time and in the same way. In other words, something cannot be both true and false at the same time.

> While it is possible all the religions of the world are false, it is a certainty that they cannot all be true.

When we apply the law of non-contradiction to the religions of the world, we find that Hindus, Buddhists, Jews, and Muslims deny what Christians affirm: that Jesus is God incarnate, the third person of the Trinity. Either Jesus is, in fact, a member of the Trinity, or He is not. If He is not, then Christians are wrong and people of other religions are right. On the other hand, if Christians are right, then the other religions are wrong. It cannot be both ways. While it is *possible* all the religions of the world are false, it is a *certainty* that they cannot all be true.

So the first step in setting free those who have been captured by New Age theology is to point out the illogic of their beliefs. They will likely counter that logic and rational thought cannot be trusted and we must instead trust our feelings. If they raise this objection, then ask this simple question: Did you just make a rational statement concerning what can be trusted? Since the answer to your questions is "yes," you can point out that their statement is self-refuting since they made a rational statement that says rational statements cannot be trusted.

Logic cannot be denied. God has designed our minds to operate rationally, so even when someone rejects rationality, we can use it to our benefit to shed light on the reality of clear thinking. And once again, this affirms the reality of the biblical view of God.

11.4.3 THE ELEPHANT IN THE ROOM

Since Cosmic Humanists insist that all religions contain partial truth about God. they are prone to single out a variety of religious traditions to assimilate into their worldview. This habit, however, brings up the legitimate question *How do you know you are selecting the correct beliefs from each religion?* The principle problem of picking and choosing is that there is no way to be sure when you have selected the right ideas. Although a common New Age response

---

[2] Neale Donald Walsch, *The New Revelations: A Conversation with God* (New York, NY: Artia Books, 2002), 97.
[3] "Of Myth and Men: A Conversation between Bill Moyers and George Lucas on the meaning of the Force and the true theology of *Star Wars*," *Time*, April 26, 1999, 92.
[4] Barna Research Group, *Third Millennium Teens* (Ventura, CA: The Barna Research Group, 1999), 48. It should be noted that of the teenagers surveyed, 70 percent were active in a church youth group and 82 percent identified themselves as Christians.

is that each person *knows* the right answers instinctively (again, according to *feelings*), such an answer fails to pass the test of logic. Even devout Cosmic Humanists hold conflicting views as to the nature of God, and every view cannot be right at the same time.

As a defense of the belief that all religions are equal, Cosmic Humanists often cite a Hindu parable. In this illustration, six blind men come into contact with an elephant. One handles the tail and exclaims that an elephant is like a rope. Another grasps a leg and describes the elephant as a tree trunk. A third feels the tusk and says the animal is similar to a spear, and so on. Since each feels only a small portion of the whole elephant, all six men give correspondingly different descriptions of their experience. Cosmic Humanists apply this illustration to religion. They conclude that although the various religions are describing the same God, each one depicts Him in different terms simply because each faith touches only a small part of the whole.

But this begs the question, *How do we know the blind men are all touching the same elephant?* The parable assumes (1) that each man can discern only part of the truth about the nature of the elephant and (2) that *we* know something the blind men don't—there is a real elephant everyone is touching.

While the first assumption relies on the belief that no one possesses complete knowledge, the second presupposes that objective knowledge about the nature of God does exist and that *someone* knows what the elephant (or God) is really like. But here we find a contradiction. On the one hand, the story claims that we—the blind men—have only limited knowledge. But if everyone is blind, no one can know the ultimate shape of the elephant. We need the perspective of someone who is not blind, a privileged position that the New Ager claims for herself or himself. But how is it that the New Age adherent knows the truth and the rest of us do not?

As it turns out, this story does not prove the point it is trying to make—it is merely an illustration of what Cosmic Humanists already believe to be the case. From their own admissions, they simply feel this is the right way to understand God. But without an objective source of truth as a plumb line, there is no way to determine whose feelings are correct, theirs or ours.

> When it comes to the nature of God and reality, the Christian worldview offers a confidence not found in Cosmic Humanism. Hebrews 11:1 explains that biblical faith is not based on intuition or subjective feelings, but upon evidence and substance.

After pointing to the faulty thinking of such beliefs, we can explain that Christianity, rather than assuming a blind search for God, begins with the idea that God has revealed Himself in the objective revelation found in the Bible. In the section on Biblical Christian philosophy, we offer several reasons for the Bible's reliability and the historicity of Christ's resurrection. In the section on Biblical Christian theology, we say that although the Bible describes God as a Being who cannot be known fully, that is, we cannot comprehensively understand all that God is, we can know certain things, such as His transcendence, imminence, holiness, love, mercy, faithfulness, and judgment of sin.

When it comes to the nature of God and reality, the Christian worldview offers a confidence not found in Cosmic Humanism. Hebrews 11:1 explains that biblical faith is not based on intuition or subjective feelings, but upon evidence and substance. In contrast to the idea that "all roads lead to God," the historical evidence maps out only *one* road leading to God. This road passes through the life, teachings, death, and resurrection of Jesus Christ. Based on the historical eye-witness accounts of Jesus' life and resurrection, we can know with certainty the truth of His claims to be "the way, the truth, and the life." (See John 8:31–32; Colossians 2:2; 2 Peter 1:16–18; and 1 John 5:20.)

11.4.4 No One Is a Moral Relativist

The foremost problem with moral relativism is that it is inconsistent with how we actually live. People everywhere (even ethical relativists) cannot get away from the idea that they ought to be treated with compassion, justice, and truthfulness—values that presuppose a universal, transcendent, objective moral law.

> People everywhere (even ethical relativists) cannot get away from the idea that they ought to be treated with compassion, justice, and truthfulness—values that presuppose a universal, transcendent, objective moral law.

Yet, in the Cosmic Humanist worldview, the moral code has no knowable source. Starting from the pantheist position, where nature is all there is, we find no "moral law" written into the universe of molecules in motion. In the pantheist view of reality, if God is everything, evil is as much a part of God as is good. Thus, there is no standard of goodness by which to evaluate evil. Moral judgments are impossible to make in the Cosmic Humanist worldview.

Whether they recognize it or not, ethical relativists cannot live consistently with their own moral position. The first step in defending a Christian view of ethics requires showing how other views are not valid. When someone says all morals are relative, the simplest way to deflate that idea is to ask, "Relative to what?" As soon as anyone attempts to answer that question by giving a fixed reference point, he or she has just provided an "absolute" standard and thus ceases to be a relativist!

Another way to help people realize they actually do believe in moral absolutes is to take from them something they value, like a wallet or Mp3 player. When they object to this, turn the tables and ask, "Why are you upset? You're not trying to force *your* morality on *me*, are you?" When it comes to things people hold dear, everyone becomes a moral absolutist! While some claim not to know what is always just, right, or fair, they seem to know innately what is not just, right, and fair when it affects them personally.

This chink in relativists' armor can be used to pry open their minds and let in a glimmer of the reality of a moral law given by a transcendent moral Lawgiver. A biblical worldview informs us of a knowledge of right and wrong that is built deep into the structure of our minds. Paul says as much in Romans 2:15: "[Non-believers] show that the work of the law is written on their hearts. Their consciences testify in support of this, and their competing thoughts either accuse or excuse them." As Professor J. Budziszewski succinctly says that there are some things "we can't not know."[5]

As image-bearers of God, all people have an innate sense of right and wrong, an *oughtness* associated with behavior that accounts for the goodness we observe in others acts of kindness and generosity. But on the other hand, we find people ignoring these absolute standards of goodness, resulting in acts of hatred and violence. Only the biblical worldview explains what we actually see lived out in the world around us, the moral lapses as well as the moral heroism. We know instinctively it is wrong to murder fellow human beings, to steal their spouses, or to

---

[5] J. Budziszewski, *The Revenge of Conscience: Politics and the Fall of Man* (Dallas, TX: Spence Publishing, 1999), xv.

covet their homes or cars! It is wrong to steal from a blind man's cup and torture children. On the other hand, we know it is morally right to love our neighbor as ourselves and to be the good Samaritan instead of the thief or Pharisee. It is right to love our Creator who gave us a rational mind and a moral conscious.

Christians understand that everyone's view of morality rests ultimately on a theological foundation. Secular Humanists, Marxists and Postmodernists begin with atheism, and Cosmic Humanists begin with pantheism, but all three worldviews lead to various forms of moral relativism. Christianity, on the other hand, begins with theism and a moral order based on the nature of God. The Christian God is not silent, but expresses His nature through moral imperatives such as "love God and your neighbor as yourself" (Luke 10:27).

11.4.5 COUNTERING NEW AGE PSYCHOLOGY

Concerning the grip of New Age ideas on Americans, a 2002 survey by Barna Research Group found that 35 percent of adults believe it is possible to communicate with the deceased. This is up from 18 percent just twelve years earlier. Similarly, a Gallup poll found belief in reincarnation grew from 21 to 24 percent among a cross-section of all age groups. These numbers indicate that New Age ideas are gaining influence across our society. So how does a Christian present the truth in love in the face of these trends?

Our first approach in countering non-Christian ideas is to start with the assumptions of a biblical worldview. We follow the logic that, beginning with a personal God, all people are created in God's image and have stamped upon their consciousness the knowledge of Him, even though this knowledge has been suppressed (Romans 1:18–20). Because of their refusal to embrace the truth, many fall prey to deceptive philosophies (Colossians 2:8). To rescue those who have been captured by these philosophies, we remind non-Christians of the truth they know but have suppressed, pointing out areas where they have been deceived in their thinking, then moving to the good news of God's forgiveness through Jesus Christ. You may recall that the Apostle Paul proceeded through these steps as he spoke to the atheistic and pagan philosophers in Athens (Acts 17).

When talking to someone who has been captured by the New Age worldview, we can affirm his or her desire for greater spirituality in the midst of our materialistic culture. Their longing for inspiration and wonder in life is legitimate as well as their craving for a sense of personal worth. Yet we also need to explain that they are selling themselves short by seeking personal fulfillment in a nonpersonal source—the New Age cosmic-energy-force-God. Only a personal God can meet their deepest need for love and unconditional acceptance.

In addition, we can agree with the New Age concern for karma as it reflects our innate sense of justice—the idea of reaping what we sow, as the Bible mentions in Galatians 6:7. Yet, the idea of karma does not measure up to the Bible's assertion that our past faults can be forgiven and cleansed and that we can be united with the God who created us to have a relationship with Him.

Here are some additional questions related to psychology that may help stimulate discussion with a New Age devotee:

- "Help me understand how *you*, a person, can come from an *It*, an impersonal force?" (A person has a mind, will, emotions, etc., while an impersonal force, by definition, does not. Of course, there is no answer to this important question from a New Age perspective. This shows the New Age view of humanity to be a contradiction in terms, thus undermining the foundation of the New Age worldview.)

- "How can love come from an impersonal force?" (Recall Walsch's claim that God is impersonal energy, but our first nature is "unconditionally loving." The law of cause and effect tells us that an effect cannot be greater than its cause. So how can we arrive at love by starting with non-love, for how can an impersonal force love?)

- "If reincarnation is the system whereby we pay off our past karmic failings, how did this process get started?" (New Age reincarnation assumes that evil and suffering in life are ultimately the result of our free choices in previous lives, and that individuality itself is a result of ignorance—a form of suffering and evil. But if you were originally a part of "the one," why did you become individualized into this illusion of life in the first place? This question raises a major contradiction for reincarnation. If we go back in past lives far enough, we must come to a *first* incarnation. But in this first life, there is no karmic debt to pay because there were no prior lives, hence, no reason to exist as an individual in the first place.)

The Pop Culture Connection

Gandhi (a 1982 film which won eight Oscars and the Academy Award for Best Picture)—"the film ignores Gandhi's own very real vacillations and contradictions with regard to nonviolence as an absolute. It makes no mention, for example, of the fact that Gandhi endorsed three British wars and himself attempted to enlist (he led an ambulance corps to support the war when the British refused to have Indians as soldiers in South Africa). The most troubling issue raised by *Gandhi*, of course, is the effectiveness of nonviolence in confronting a Hitler, to which the film devotes a single line. Asked how nonviolence could stop the armies of Nazi Germany, the film responds simply that evil must be opposed wherever it is found, and disappears from the screen. The historical Gandhi remained unable to come to grips with the Hitler question and at various times advised the British to surrender and the Jews to commit collective suicide (In 1941, Gandhi insisted to the British that Hitler is not a bad man). The film concludes with the moral of the story spelled out, in case anyone should miss it. 'Tyrants and murderers can seem invincible at the time, but in the end they always fall. Think of it. Always.' The message is repeated twice. These are the last words of the film, and they are never questioned. It is an uplifting thought, but poor history . . . ignoring the reality of places like Indochina, Afghanistan, and Central America."*

- "Do you believe in animal rights? (If yes, then ask . . .) What is the source of 'rights'?" ("Rights," as in animal rights, implies there is a difference between a right way to act toward animals and a wrong way to act. In a pantheistic system, where all is ultimately "one," there is no difference between right and wrong, good or evil, cruelty or noncruelty. Pantheism cannot account for these concepts. Therefore, there is no such thing as legal "rights," animal or human.)

- "Should you help a person in need? (If yes, then ask . . .) Wouldn't that interfere with a person's karma?"

(The traditional Hindu idea is that one should *never* interfere with someone else's karma, which is why Hindus and Buddhists did not found hospitals. Hospitals were begun by Christians who were following Jesus' teaching about loving one's neighbor, as in the Good Samaritan, and His instruction that sickness is not the result of sin (see John 9:1–5). Some may point to **Mahatma Gandhi**, a Hindu and humanitarian who was concerned with the needs of the poor. Yet Gandhi acknowledges that Christian missionaries, not his own religion, "awakened in him a revulsion for the caste system and for the maltreatment of outcastes."[6] Gandhi acted *inconsistently* with his Hindu presuppositions and instead, incorporated a biblical system of ethics. The same is true for most New Agers—they cannot live consistently with the implications of their worldview when it comes to helping others.)

- "How do you know if you are following your inner truth? What if you feel like murdering someone? Should you follow that inner truth?" (There must be an external standard of truth and morality, as discussed in the last chapter, in order to answer these questions. Otherwise, we are left only with our subjective feelings. But an objective, external standard undermines the notion of getting in touch with the god within.)

After focusing on the weaknesses of New Age psychology, we can present a biblical understanding of how, beginning with a personal Creator, there is a solid foundation for building a psychology of personhood, as one created in God's image. Only in the Bible do we find an adequate basis for our personhood, with a soul comprised of will, intellect, and emotions. Biblical psychology answers the question of why we sense an awareness of a spiritual dimension to life as well as a distinctiveness from the rest of the created world. The psalmist helps our understanding in this regard:

> What is man that You remember him,
> the son of man that You look after him?
> You made him little less than God
> and crowned him with glory and honor.
> You made him lord over the works of Your hands;
> You put everything under his feet:
> all the sheep and oxen,
> as well as animals in the wild,
> birds of the sky,
> and fish of the sea
> passing through the currents of the seas.
> O LORD, our Lord,
> how magnificent is Your name throughout the earth![7]

The Bible also explains why there is evil in the world. The fall into sin provides a rational explanation for why there is hate in our hearts (Jeremiah 17:9), and indeed, why the entire universe "groans" (Romans 8:20–22). On a personal as well as a cosmic level, the biblical account resonates with what we actually observe about our world and ourselves.

In the Bible, we also find hope and healing in the midst of our fallenness. Unlike other worldviews where there is no purpose to life, love actually makes sense from a Christian worldview, for the Bible presents a God who acts with unconditional love to bring us out of our sinful state of rebellion and brokenness. His love is supremely displayed through the willing sacrifice of His son, Jesus Christ (Romans 5:6–8).

By acknowledging God's love through Jesus Christ, those seeking spiritual unity with God can turn their belief in the continuing cycle of reincarnation to the one-time rebirth as a child of God (1 Peter 1:23).

---

[6] John Warwick Montgomery, *Human Rights and Human Dignity* (Grand Rapids, MI: Zondervan, 1986), 113.
*"Why Gandhi Drives The Neoconservatives Crazy," by Jason DeParle, The *Washington Monthly*, September 1983. Posted at http://groups.google.com/group/soc.culture.indian/msg/38b451bdbfbefb61?)
[7] Psalm 8:4–9.

Once that rebirth takes place, our growth in understanding God develops as we engage our minds, as Paul tells believers in Rome to "renew their minds," not their feelings (Romans 12:1–2). And to Timothy, Paul instructs, "Be diligent to present yourself approved to God, a worker who doesn't need to be ashamed, correctly teaching the word of truth" (2 Timothy 2:15). As Christians, we can do no better than to heed Paul's admonitions.

Conclusion

Part Five

11.5.1 INTRODUCTION

In this section we provide an overall critique of Postmodernism. Atheism and evolution are addressed in the critique on Secular Humanism and Marxism and are not repeated here. While we offer some assessment within several of the Postmodern worldview disciplines, we provide an in-depth critique. As with the other worldviews, we focus on the major themes that are the distinguishing features of this worldview. For Postmodernism, these primary areas are philosophy (the nature of reality and truth), politics, and history.

11.5.2 SUBJECTIVE TRUTH, DECONSTRUCTION, AND ANTI-REALISM

Postmodernists most likely have difficulty living with their view of reality. They claim that "reality" is constructed by language. On one level, the statement "the train is coming" may convey a multitude of interpretations to different people. To some it may even simulate a train. But if people fail to get off the tracks, the result of their interpretation could prove fatal because there are indeed objective, non-verbal referents to words and texts. Real life is not open to infinite interpretations. At any particular moment in time, either a train is coming down the track or a train is not coming down the track. This real world fact is not a matter of our personal interpretation. Regardless of the word games Postmodernists play, there is an actual reality! Postmodernists have a hard time escaping the correspondence theory of truth.

For example, Postmodernist Melville Herskovits writes, "Even the facts of the physical world are discerned through the enculturative screen, so that the perception of time, distance, weight, size, and other 'realities' is mediated by the conventions of any group."[1] To which Hadley Arkes responds, "Happily for us all, this argument is fatally vulnerable to the recognition, accessible to the educated, the uneducated—and even, at times, to the overeducated—that there is a material world out there. That world happens to be filled with facts [truths] that do not depend for their existence as facts on the 'experience' or the subjective 'perceptions' of individuals. Even if the 'enculturative screen' of Jersey City affected its natives with fanciful 'perceptions' of 'distance,' the actual distance between Jersey City and Paris is very likely to remain the same."[2]

Or consider the well-worn Postmodern phrase, "That's just *your* interpretation." As D. A. Carson points out, there is a problem with this view. Carson says he has never met a deconstructionist who would be pleased if a reviewer misinterpreted his work. He notes, " . . . in practice deconstructionists implicitly link their own texts with their own intentions."[3] In other words, deconstructionists believe in authorial intent when they are the authors, but deny authorial intent when it comes to works by others!

Likewise, we recognize a dilemma with the popular Postmodern slogan, "That may be true for you but not for me." If the person making that statement means that it applies only to him, then who cares what he says. He is only talking to himself! On the other hand, if the person means to apply his statement also to *you*, then you can respond, "I get the impression that you think I should believe what you just said. If that is the case, why are you trying to impose your concept of what is true on me?" Either way, the Postmodernist has made a statement he cannot live with himself. It is a self-defeating position, one that is totally absurd. If you try to apply the Postmodernist view of truth to day-to-day life, the result is a total breakdown in the ability to communicate.

11.5.3 WHO DECIDES?

Another serious problem arises from a Postmodern philosophy of language. If each community determines what is true through its use of language, which community gets to decide between rival communities when it comes to conflicting ideas (such as suttee, the Hindu practice of burning a widow on her deceased husband's pyre, exterminating the Jewish race, or abolishing private ownership of property). Since no community can claim to be "right" on any of these or other issues, the result is an increased competition for which group will dominate the others. We are witnessing this kind of escalation between warring factions in many areas of society, from the college campus to the political arena to the international scene.

Paul Kurtz elaborates on this problem. He describes Postmodernism as a nihilistic "philosophical-literary movement," meaning that since objective truth does not exist, we can neither know nor communicate anything. To balance the idea that objective truth is unknowable, Kurtz claims that science offers "reasonably objective standards for judging its truth claims." He continues, "Science has become a universal language, speaking to all men and women no matter what their cultural backgrounds."[4]

While we agree with Kurtz that scientific knowledge can lead to truth concerning the physical universe, our Biblical Christian philosophy of knowledge also emphasizes revealed truth as a means for understanding other truths, including our relationship to God.

---

[1] Melville Herskovits, *Cultural Relativism* (New York, NY: Vintage Books, 1972), 15.

[2] Hadley Arkes, *First Things: An Inquiry into the First Principles of Morals and Justice* (Princeton, NJ: Princeton University Press, 1986), 145.

[3] D.A. Carson, *The Gagging of God: Christianity Confronts Pluralism* (Grand Rapids, MI: Zondervan, 1996), 103.

[4] Paul Kurtz, *Humanist Manifesto 2000: A Call For A New Planetary Humanism* (Amherst, NY: Prometheus Books, 2000), 22.

The negative consequences of a Postmodern approach to language cannot be overstated. For a telling example of applying deconstruction to law, go back to 1973. In handing down their decision in the *Roe v Wade* case, the majority of the Supreme Court chose to look at the Constitution as a "living document"— that is, open to many interpretations (polysemy). As a result, they invented new meanings from the original text— meanings that are not openly stated— and came up with a novel interpretation regarding a woman's reproductive rights. The conse-quence of their decision is that, since 1973, over 40 million unborn children have been murdered at the request of their mothers.

Postmodernists are correct about one thing—interpretation is important. Confucius says, "When words lose their

> ## The Pop Culture Connection
>
> **Revolutions** (a 2003 film starring Keanu Reeves and Hugo Weaving.) Late in the film, after a prolonged fight with Agent Smith (Hugo Weaving), Neo (Keanu Reeves), lying in the mud, refuses to surrender. Smith responds with a Postmodern tirade: "Why do you do it? Why keep fighting? You believe you're fighting for something, for more than your survival. Can you tell what it is? Do you even know? Is it freedom, or truth, perhaps peace? Could it be for love? Illusions, Mr. Anderson, vagaries of perception. Temporary constructs of a feeble human intellect trying desperately to justify an existence that is without meaning or purpose. And all of them as artificial as the Matrix itself. . . . Why do you persist?" Neo replies, "Because I choose to." The conversation reflects a nihilistic philosophy on the part of both men.

meanings, people lose their freedom."[5] In reality, however, when words lose their meaning, people lose not only their freedom, but their lives!

11.5.4 THE TRUTH ABOUT TRUTH

In stark contrast to Postmodern ideas that language is fluid and open to varying interpretations, the Christian worldview says that objective truth exists. In contrast to Postmodern ideas that our particular community determines truth, nearly everything about Christianity is *universal* in scope and application. God created the whole universe, including men and women. Sin is a *universal* condition affecting every human being. God loved the *whole world*, including every human being. Christ died for the sins of the *whole world*, not just one or two particular communities. Christians are to love God with all their heart and mind and their fellow human beings around the *whole world*.

God chose to communicate the truth about Himself and His world through words contained in the Scriptures along with the language of the heavens (Psalm 19). God's words do not depend upon a reader's interpretation. Instead, the reader is to interpret the Bible according to God's intention. The Apostle Peter is clear when he writes, "Above all, you must understand that no prophecy of Scripture came about by the prophet's own interpretation. For prophecy never had its origin in the will of man, but men spoke from God as they were carried along by the Holy Spirit" (2 Peter 1:19–21).

> God's words do not depend upon a reader's interpretation. Instead, the reader is to interpret the Bible according to God's intention.

To correctly understand the meaning of any text of Scripture, we should heed Paul's advice to Timothy: "Do your best to present yourself to God as one approved, a workman who does not need to be ashamed and who correctly handles the word of

---

[5] F.A. Hayek, *The Fatal Conceit: The Errors of Socialism* (Chicago, IL: University of Chicago Press, 1989), 106.

truth" (2 Timothy 2:15). By acknowledging that God has communicated in language true things about the real world, and by diligently studying the Bible, you can know the truth that sets you free (John 8:32).

11.5.5 PROGRESSIVE POLITICS AND SOCIAL INJUSTICE

Postmodernists seem to contradict themselves in identifying their political stance. An assessment of the Postmodernist approach to politics reveals a glaring contradiction. While Foucault maintains a seeming detachment regarding various political systems and says he is all over the political checkerboard, he undeniably holds leftist political views. Postmodernists may refer to their views as *progressive*, and some, like Rorty, may be more "moderate" than others, but the fact remains that they are all huddled together on the political left. Foucault stated publicly, "When the proletariat takes power, it may be quite possible that the proletariat will exert toward the classes over which it has triumphed a violent, dictatorial, and even bloody power. I can't see what objection could possibly be made to this."[6]

> In reality, when a Postmodernist calls for justice or fairness, he is borrowing this idea from a Christian worldview and trying to make it fit into his own, since there is no such thing as fairness found within his own worldview.

Another difficulty is that Postmodernists fail to act consistently with their worldview. On the one hand, they say no metanarrative can capture the essence of truth. Yet, at the same time they say that a leftist vision of social justice is "right" for the world. Denying all metanarratives, how do they know their view is correct? Why do they try to rescue the oppressed? Why is oppression wrong? Why do they try to impose their views on others? These are questions Postmodernists cannot answer according to their own view of reality and truth. The best they can say is "We don't like it."

Although they do not know it, their desire to change the plight of the oppressed is an appeal to something basic, a sense of the moral order. Only a biblical worldview can answer the question of why Postmodernists sense that everyone should be treated fairly. It is because God has written on their hearts the requirements of His moral law (Romans 2:14–15). In reality, when a Postmodernist calls for justice or fairness, he is borrowing this idea from a Christian worldview and trying to make it fit into his own, since there is no such thing as fairness found within his own worldview.

When it comes to social justice, Postmodernists begin with the wrong theology (atheism), which leads to a wrong philosophy (anti-realism), which in turn results in a wrong understanding of human nature (we are a product of social forces). Therefore, Postmodernists fall into a badly aimed approach to politics—trying to force an outward change upon society under the guise of social justice.

Those who invest in learning from history and observing human nature are aware of problems inherent in the quest for social justice. Milton Friedman wrote, "A society that puts equality—in the sense of equality of outcome—ahead of freedom will end up with neither equality nor freedom. The use of force to achieve equality will destroy freedom, and the force, introduced for good purposes, will end up in the hands of people who use it to promote their own interests."[7]

Thomas Sowell refers to this desire for the perfect society as "The Quest for Cosmic

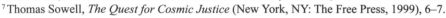

[6] Mark Lilla, *The Reckless Mind: Intellectuals in Politics* (New York, NY: New York Review Books, 2001), 150.
[7] Thomas Sowell, *The Quest for Cosmic Justice* (New York, NY: The Free Press, 1999), 6–7.

Justice." Sowell explains that traditionally, justice is "characteristic of a *process*." [8] He then illustrates his point: "A defendant in a criminal case would be said to have received justice if the trial were conducted as it should be, under fair rules and with the judge and jury being impartial. After such a trial, it could be said that "justice was done'—regardless of whether the outcome was an acquittal or an execution."[9]

In contrast to the traditional definition of justice, the Postmodern concept of social justice seeks to "eliminate undeserved disadvantages for selected groups."[10] This they consider "fair." Sowell explains, "Note how the word 'fair' has an entirely different meaning in this context. Cosmic [social] justice is not about the rules of the game. It is about putting particular segments of society in the position that they would have been in but for some undeserved misfortune. This conception of fairness requires that third parties must wield the power to control outcomes, over-riding rules, standards, or the preferences of other people."[11]

Sowell points out that social justice can never be achieved because it demands vastly more knowledge then anyone has available. In reality, every individual has advantages or disadvantages in life. Some have beauty but lack intelligence, others are born into wealth but lack emotional stability, while others may have athletic ability but are crippled by a quick temper. The point is, how can anyone else be in a position to judge which advantages should be disregarded and which disadvantages should be remedied? The answer is that no one possesses the necessary insight. There are too many variables. Therefore, the idea that government can bring about a forced equality among all people is unreasonable and unattainable.

Another problem with social justice is that it fails to consider the overall cost to society as a whole. Social justice focuses on one segment of the population but "disregards the interests of others who are not the immediate focus of discussion, but who nevertheless pay the price of the decisions made."[12]

For example, when a certain class of students is given preference for admittance to college in spite of low test scores, the additional cost to the college for providing scholarships to students who will eventually drop out is being overlooked. Other groups not considered in the decision are the alumni supporting their school with donations for such scholarships, as well as other students who were better qualified academically but not admitted. The result is not fairness but further state-sanctioned "unfairness." As former radical David Horowitz writes, "The regime of social justice, of which the Left dreams, is a regime that by its very nature must crush individual freedom."[13]

11.5.6 FAITH-BASED JUSTICE

When it comes to helping the poor, while a worthy goal, Socialism's vision of economic equality is a false hope. History is replete with the failed attempts of such schemes. Nowhere has socialism been tried that it succeeded. That is because the idea is based on a wrong psychology, one that assumes that humanity is basically good. On the other hand, acknowledging our sinfulness leads to a free market economy that provides the greatest amount of opportunity and economic progress. Furthermore, helping the poor is accomplished through actions, not mere words. Richard John Neuhaus offers a critique of Postmodern rhetoric in contrast to the actions of faith-based groups: "In cities across the country and generally under conservative auspices, such street-level

[8] Ibid., 8.
[9] Ibid., 9.
[10] Ibid.
[11] Ibid., 12.
[12] Ibid., 13.
[13] David Horowitz, *The Politics of Bad Faith* (New York, NY: The Free Press, 1998), 183.

programs of personal and community renewal are rapidly multiplying. Nothing comparable is happening on the left."[14] In other words, "faith-based organizations" (generally religious and conservative in nature) are helping the poor, families with no father, and communities overrun with drugs and crime. Postmodern organizations are few and far behind in these efforts to practice what they preach.

The founders of Western civilization rejected the utopian vision of social justice and opted instead for traditional justice. Specifically, those who formed the United States sought to create a nation based on realistic ideals—individual liberty and opportunity. Because they also understood our sinful nature, they sought to put "chains" (their term) around government to check its tendency to abuse power. They wrote the ultimate check on the politics of power into the Declaration of Independence—an appeal to the "laws of nature and Nature's God" as well as the opening phrase of the Constitution: "We, the people . . ." Their wisdom placed political power ultimately in the hands of the citizens, who themselves were trained by Christian religion and biblical morality. If we do not take our responsibility seriously, then we have only ourselves to blame when we lose our liberty to those who would seek to impose their brand of social justice on us.

Yet, the task at times seems overwhelming. What can we do to make a difference? J.R.R. Tolkien provides an answer. In a scene from *The Two Towers*, Pippin and Merry entreat the peace-loving Ents (ancient trees that walk and talk) to join the battle against the forces of the evil Sauron. When the trees refuse, Pippin tries to solace Merry by saying, "Maybe Treebeard is right. We don't belong here, Merry. This is too big for us. What can we do in the end? We've got the Shire. Maybe we should go home." Merry replies with desperation in his voice, "The fires of Isengard will spread, and the woods of Tribru and Buckland will burn. And all that was once great and good in this world will be gone."

What Merry understood is a lesson for contemporary Christians. If we fail to act while we still have the freedom to speak our minds, there will come a day when the power-plays of political correctness will eliminate our liberties, and all that was once "great and good" about Western civilization will be gone. The land of the free will cease to exist.

11.5.7 WHAT CAN WE KNOW ABOUT HISTORY?

Postmodernists claim that all historical accounts are merely fictions created for a political purpose and that all historians are biased, confined within their own social setting. Historians, of course, have a worldview, some vision of political improvement, and a host of emotional investments. This always has been the case, and it is well known. Dixon writes, "In earlier times, historians acknowledged and resisted personal bias as antithetical to good historical research."[15]

Nevertheless, some historical events have been grossly mischaracterized, such as when some claimed that the terrorist attacks of September 11, 2001, were a Jewish plot to encourage America to pursue a more aggressive policy against Muslims.[16] Clearly, history can be both misidentified as well as mischaracterized. While it is true that some historians have misconstrued history to convince others of a certain perspective of past events, the fact that we can even know this has occurred illustrates that history is not entirely inaccessible. That narratives of the past can be corrected illustrates that history should not be equated with fictional accounts such as imaginative novels.

---

[14] *First Things* (March 1999): 63.

[15] Dennis McCallum, ed., *The Death of Truth* (Minneapolis, MN: Bethany House, 1996), 138–9.

[16] See "9-11 Conspiracy Theories: Claims Related to Jews and Israel," http://www.answers.com/topic/9-11-con-spiracy-theories.

Should we accept the Postmodern feminist approach to history that claims everyone has an insurmountable bias? The problem here is that the feminist historian's ideology is very much like the feminists' objections to pro-life arguments against abortion. When confronting a man who is pro-life, feminists decry, "But you're a man!" It is as though our gender determines the legitimacy of our argument. On the other hand, if a woman presents a similar pro-life argument, is she taken seriously? No! Feminists retort that such women are intellectually incarcerated by the dominant male ideology. Pro-life women are considered dupes, pawns in the struggle for male dominance. To assert that only participants in particular groups can write the histories of those groups is to imply that the oppressed can never write the histories of their oppressors. Yet, such histories would be very appropriate, revealing what the oppressors might otherwise overlook as mundane.

Today, many people are ignorant of history, which plays into the hands of film-makers with particular agendas. By weaving together fact and fiction in entertaining ways, with engaging story-lines and attractive actors, screenwriters, directors, and producers can manipulate the understanding of the average viewer because most are ill equipped to sort out historical events from imaginative interpretations. Films such as *Braveheart, Good Night and Good Luck, The Last Temptation of Christ,* or *The Da Vinci Code* leave viewers with a compelling story of the past, yet with no way to decipher where history ends and embellishment begins. [17]

It goes without saying that we should not believe everything we read or see. We must retain a certain degree of skepticism as we listen to various claims, for not all claimants intend to tell the truth. This is especially true in our Postmodern world, where ideology is considered more important that telling the truth.

It is also clear that individuals, communities, and governments have misconstrued history for the purpose of either gaining power or covering up their

> ## The Pop Culture Connection
>
> Author J.R.R. Tolkien understood the danger of uniting good intentions with political power. In an early scene of **Lord of the Rings: The Fellowship of the Ring**, Tolkien presents a dialogue between Frodo, the Hobbit, and Gandalf, the wizard. Frodo, learning of the power of the "one ring" he possesses, frantically attempts to give it to Gandalf. The wise wizard refuses to take it, saying, "Understand me, Frodo. I would use this ring from a desire to do good, but through me, it would wield a power too great and terrible to imagine." Tolkien knew what those on the left side of the political spectrum do not—because of our sinful nature, no man or group can be trusted with unchecked power.

misdeeds. For example, the former Soviet Union controlled the writing of textbooks and taught children that Joseph Stalin was the epitome of virtue when in reality he was a mass murderer. [18] The truth was discovered when eyewitnesses came forward speaking of the atrocities and when the mass graves of the slaughtered were found. Continued research into history revealed the truth about Stalin, Lenin, Mao Tse-Tung, [19] Pol Pot, and others.

Revelations of truth concerning Stalin and others are not mere social constructions or the political biases of present-day historians. Rather they form the consensus of scholarly reflection based on the assumption that we can have access to truth about the past. While this is something that Postmodernists are not willing to admit, it is the only sensible approach to understanding history.

---

[17] See Ben Witherington III, *The Gospel Code: Novel Claims about Jesus, Mary Magdalene and Da Vinci* (Downers Grove, IL: InterVarsity Press, 2004).

[18] Stephane Courtois, et al., *The Black Book of Communism: Crimes, Terror, Repression* (Cambridge, MA: Harvard University Press, 1999).

[19] For example, Jung Chang and Jon Halliday's *Mao: The Unknown Story* (New York, NY: Alfred A. Knopf, 2005), is a definitive study and story of Mao's life and times along with his crimes.

Conclusion

Part Six

11.6.1 A Call to Dedication

The Christian communities acceptance of many humanistic distortions is one of our greats areas of shame. Countless Christians accept evolutionary theory, many so firmly that they no longer welcome creationists. Some Christian colleges that have finally recognized the scientific weaknesses of neo-Darwinian evolution still shun special creationism, moving instead toward punctuated evolution. Other Christians embrace various forms of Marxism and socialism, calling it "Liberation Theology." Some have bought into concepts and practices such as self-actualization, behaviorism, feminism, abortion on demand, homosexuality, Eastern meditation, and world government.

11.6.2 POSTMODERN CHRISTIANS?

In more recent years, a growing group of evangelical Christians is toying with the idea of becoming "Postmodern Christians." The assumption is that Postmodernism provides a new approach to the world that is compatible with Christianity. These are signs for concern. These have been outlined in *Becoming Conversant with the Emerging Church: Understanding a Movement and its Implications*.

Theologian D.A. Carson makes the following observations:

> "Christian postmodernism will acknowledge, in general terms, that they believe the Bible and want to espouse the doctrinal verities of historic confessionalism, but whenever a preacher or teacher lays the same stress on truth that the Bible does, or the same stress on the exclusiveness of Jesus Christ that the New Testament does, they are instantly nervous. For they are still operating with the fundamental axiom shared by

both modernism and postmodernism: it is appropriate to begin with the finite 'I.'

"This is profoundly mistaken. An omniscient, talking God changes everything. It does not change the fact that I will always be finite and that my knowledge of him and about him will always be partial. But once I know that he exists, that he is the Creator and my Savior and Judge, it is improper, even idolatrous, to try to think of my knowing things without reference to him. All of my knowledge, if it is true knowledge, is necessarily a subset of his." [1]

While the Postmodern movement within the church is just getting started, already Rorty and Derrida are appearing on some Christian websites. At one Christian conference, the spokesman said he favored both homosexual marriages and abortion.

There is a growing tendency among some Christians in the emergent church to split the human personality into mind—understood as what we can know—and heart—defined as our emotional self. The Scriptures do not make this distinction. The term used for "heart" in Scripture encompasses both the knowing as well as feeling aspects of personhood—in fact, it refers to the entire self (Psalm 14:1; Hebrews 4:12). Christianity combines mind, heart, soul, spirit, and consciousness in a unified person who is responsible to God.

There are also signs of restraint in that two prominent spokesmen in the emergent church movement, Brian McLaren and Leonard Sweet, have both rejected mainstream Postmodernism. McLaren says, "Postmodernism is the latest in a long series of absurdities."[2] Carson continues, "Although some writers in the emergent movement continue to praise Postmodernism and denigrate modernism in absolute terms, the movement's better thinkers occasionally warn against absolutizing Postmodernism. Thus Leonard Sweet, for example, rightly warns his readers not to embrace Postmodernism."[3]

11.6.3 CHRISTIANITY IN RETREAT

In some ways non-Christians are more consistent than Christians. For instance, there are no Postmodernists, Secular Humanists, Cosmic Humanists or Marxist-Leninists who believe in creation. No New Ager believes in ethical absolutes. No Muslim accepts the Trinity. Yet, while Christians should be the first to recognize the bankruptcy of secular religious views, all too often they are the first to embrace bits and pieces of them!

> While Christians should be the first to recognize the bankruptcy of secular religious views, all too often, they are the first to embrace bits and pieces of them!

Too many Christians ignore Paul's admonition to not be taken captive "through vain and deceitful philosophy" (Colossians 2:8). The superiority of the Christian position in theology, philosophy, ethics, economics, politics, law, biology, history, psychology, and sociology is described and expounded throughout this text. The non-Christian worldviews have, in their own words, declared their position as irreconcilable with Christianity. The battle lines have been drawn. As Christians armed with the truth—the revelation of Truth Himself (John 14:6)—we are more than equipped to shatter the myths of all opposing worldviews.

The Apostle Paul summarizes the Christian position and responsibility: "For though we live in the world, we do not wage war as the world does. The weapons we fight with are not the weapons of the world. On the contrary, they have divine power to demolish strongholds. We demolish arguments and every pretension that sets itself up against the knowledge of God, and we take captive every thought to make it obedient to Christ." (2 Corinthians 10:3-5, NIV)

---

[1] D.A. Carson, *Becoming Conversant With The Emerging Church* (Grand Rapids, MI: Zondervan, 2005), 123.
[2] Ibid., 127.
[3] Ibid., 126.

Yet we are not honoring our responsibility. The Christian worldview is in retreat in nearly every arena of life—including our universities, media, arts, music, law, business, medicine, psychology, sociology, public schools, and government. "The humanistic system of values has now become the predominant way of thinking in most of the power centers of society,"[4] claim Dr. James C. Dobson and Gary L. Bauer. According to Dobson and Bauer, the Christian worldview has only two power centers remaining in America—the church and the family—and both of them are under tremendous pressure to surrender.

11.6.4 WHAT ARE WE TO DO?

Go on the offensive! Light a candle. Pray (2 Chronicles 7:14; Colossians 1:9-14). Study (2 Timothy 2:15). Understand the times (1 Chronicles 12:32). Rebuild the foundations (Psalm 11:3). Spread the word.

Truth is our greatest weapon. Philosophy students at Charles University in Prague, Czechoslovakia, told their professors they had had enough of Marxist-Leninist dialectics. Other students can say the same to their humanistic professors.

When a few Christian students at Harvard University lightly protested that a class on Freud needed balance, the professor changed the course by combining the study of Christian author C.S. Lewis with the study of Freud—changing the course into one of the most popular on campus![5]

Standing for Christianity will require a rebirth of morality, a revival of spiritual interests, a renewal of intellectual honesty, and a recovery of courage. It will take a shoring up of the family and a reawakening in our churches. It will take strenuous effort on the part of Christians to re-establish the influence of Christianity on our culture, but it can be done. It must be done!

> ## The Pop Culture Connection
>
> ***Bruce Almighty*** (a 2003 film directed by Tom Shadyac)—"What does it mean to be a Christian artist? What is the relationship between faith and art? Shadyac believes it is his faith in God that differentiates him as a director. "Shadyac says that *Bruce Almighty* is about the theme of personal responsibility. 'A lot of people blame God. This movie is about that. It's about blaming God [and saying,] 'Why don't You fix my life?'" He points to the old story of the nun who asks God, 'Why don't you do something about these starving people?' and God says, 'I did. I made you.' With a laugh, Shadyac says, 'That's ultimately what we're saying in this movie—that God lives in us and gave us hands and feet. We're to walk the walk.'"*

Perhaps most importantly, Christians must shore up our knowledge of our worldview and teach it to the younger generation. We must immerse ourselves in Christian theology, Christian philosophy, Christian ethics, Christian politics, Christian economics, Christian psychology, Christian sociology, Christian biology, Christian law, and Christian history.

Some progress has been made in this direction. Alvin Plantinga, a leading Christian philosopher challenges the Christian community to discover its worldview. Philosophers like Plantinga, Nicholas Woltersdorf, Dallas Willard, J.P. Moreland, William Lane Craig, Ronald Nash, Walter Alston, and Norman Geisler have gone to great lengths to defend Christianity from its Secular Humanist and Postmodernist opponents.

---

[4] James C. Dobson and Gary L. Bauer, *Children at Risk* (Dallas, TX: Word, 1990), 22.

[5] The book that came out of that class should be read by every Christian student. See Armand M. Nicholi, Jr, *The Question of God: C.S. Lewis and Sigmund Freud Debate God, Love, Sex, and the Meaning of Life* (New York, NY: The Free Press, 2002).

*Excerpt from "Bruce Almighty's Tom Shadyac is not your Average Hollywood Director," by Dan Ewald. http://www.ccmmagazine.com/features/2280.aspx.

Henry Morris, Duane Gish, Ken Cummings, A.E. Wilder-Smith, Stephen Meyer, Paul Nelson, and a whole host of Christian men and women of science have demonstrated the veracity of the creationist position. Wendell Bird's *Origin of Species Revisited* contains enough scientific data to sink evolutionary theory. Thaxton, Bradley, and Olson's *The Mystery of Life's Origins* and Davis and Kenyon's *Of Pandas and People* encourage the position that science and Christianity are allies. Rodney Stark's *For The Glory Of God* and *The Victory of Reason* relate the birth of modern science within the biblical worldview. Still, much more needs to be accomplished to remind the world of the truth of Christianity and give encouragement to God's people for the future.

We need Christian young people, strong in the faith, to follow Cal Thomas, Brit Hume and Fred Barnes into the media, to take charge of the universities, to run for Congress and school boards, and to take up Christian sociology (with a strong emphasis on traditional family values)[6]. We need Christian artists challenging us with something that feeds the spirit and fuels the imagination.

Christians can reclaim law, history, politics, economics, and all other disciplines. Understanding ourselves to be men and women created to serve God, we can know and feel the call to excellence more profoundly than proponents of any other worldview.

The first and last words Christ spoke to Peter were, "Follow me." He speaks the same to us. To follow Christ means, at a minimum, taking every idea captive for Christ (2 Corinthians 10:5) and not allowing humanistic worldviews to take us captive (Colossians 2:8). Then we must set our hearts and minds on fire for God, His creation, and coming again–hearts open to God's calling and minds open to receive His wisdom and instruction; hearts willing to love truth, God's creation, and each other as fallible fellow human beings.

---

[6] Alexis de Tocqueville, *Democracy in America* (New York, NY: Harper and Row, 2000), 291: "In Europe almost all the disorders of society are born around the domestic hearth and not far from the nuptial bed."

This textbook has been the trip of a lifetime for me personally—on a roadway marked "worldview studies." As on any journey, however, there are wrong turns, dead ends, and even speed bumps to contend with. Which reminds me of C.S. Lewis' observation—"If you are on the wrong road, progress means doing an about-turn and walking back to the right road; and in that case the man who turns back soonest is the most progressive."

While there may be many who insist I've made wrong turns and hit dead ends, I wish to state for the record that I am not against progress. If I have seriously misread someone or something, I am more than willing to walk back to the right road. At one time, Christians roasted each other over various religious rituals and dogmas. I believe we have progressed past that point, and that's good, that's progress! I'm also not against tolerance as long as it means respecting other points of view (unless tolerance results in the death of millions via genocide, abortion, etc.) and not having to accept or condone them. The truth is some ideas are just plain dumb, some are evil, and others need exposure that may not be considered "tolerant" by today's standards.

This fifty-year trip started in a chapel service at Hope College in Holland, Michigan, and is now nearing its end at Summit Ministries in Manitou Springs, Colorado. The chapel speaker that particular day was Dr. Fred Schwarz who turned on a light in an inquiring young mind, and the road trip was off and running.

Along the way, I have experienced much help from family and friends (even my wife enjoyed much of the trip), so as my thoughts are put into print I want to express my profound thanks and appreciation for those whose help made this undertaking possible. First, those who helped me with the early edition of *Understanding The Times* (1991) upon which this present edition is built (and which has already seen nineteen printings and numerous foreign language translations): J.P. Moreland, John Hannah, Ron Jensen, Randy Rodden, Carl F.H. Henry (who looking over the outline of the book told me, "I've always wanted to do something like that"), Ronald Nash, John Stormer, Herb Titus, Virginia Armstrong, Duane Gish, Mark Hartwig, Mike McGuire, Connie Willems, Cal and Debbie Beisner (Cal did a professional job of editing), Jim and Carol Bowers, Clark Bowers, Ken Gasper, and finally Jeff Baldwin, a Summit and Westmont graduate who was willing to interrupt his graduate studies to help me research and write the original text.

Second, those who have had a direct hand in making this revised and updated edition (2006) possible include: Michael Bauman, Norman Geisler, Nancy Hay, Chuck Edwards, Kevin Bywater, Clark Bowers, Todd Cothran, Jason Graham, Sara Witherow, Micah and Sonne Wierenga, Josh Wierenga, Amanda Lewis, Jennifer Honken, and Trudy Friesma. If I have forgotten someone, please forgive me.

In spite of all the excellent help and advice, however, there may still be mistakes, errors, and misjudgments discovered by the most demanding critics, but these all rest solely with me. I have sincerely tried to be conscientious, level headed, fair-minded, open-ended, Spirit-led, etc., but like everyone else I, too, am a fallen human being with limited insight and discernment, weak points, and blind spots. My prayer is that our great God of this magnificently designed universe will use this work to encourage His people and to give His enemies something to chew on and think over—maybe even digest.

Now may the love of God the Father, the grace and truth of Jesus Christ and the peace and wooing of the Holy Spirit rest upon all of us until we no longer see in a glass darkly, but face to face with the One who came into this world to shed the light of the knowledge of God in the face of Jesus Christ (2 Corinthians 4:6).

For Further Reading

CHRISTIAN THEOLOGY

Augustine. *The Confessions of Augustine in Modern English*. Grand Rapids, MI: Zondervan, 1986.

Bauman, Michael. *Pilgrim Theology: Taking the Path of Theological Discovery*. Manitou Springs, CO: Summit Press, 2007.

Chesterton, G.K. *Orthodoxy*. Garden City, NY: Image Books, 1955.

D'Souza, Dinesh. *What's So Great About Christianity*. Washington, D.C.: Regnery Publishing, Inc., 2007.

Erickson, Millard. *The Postmodern World*. Wheaton, IL: Crossway Books, 2002.

Erickson, Millard. *Truth or Consequences: The Promise and Perils of Postmodernism*. Downers Grove, IL: InterVarsity Press, 2002.

Flew, Antony. *There Is A God*. New York, NY: Harper One, 2007.

Geisler, Norman L. *Systematic Theology*. 4 vols. Minneapolis, MN: Bethany House, 2005.

————. *Baker Encyclopedia of Christian Apologetics*. Grand Rapids, MI: Baker Book House, 1999.

Geisler, Norman L., and William E. Nix. *A General Introduction to the Bible*. Chicago, IL: Moody Press, 1968.

Henry, Carl F.H. *God, Revelation and Authority*. 6 vols. Waco, TX: Word, 1983.

Lewis, C.S. *Mere Christianity*. New York, NY: Macmillan, 1974.

————. *Christian Reflections*. Grand Rapids, MI: Eerdmans, 1967.

McGrath, Alister. *The Twilight of Atheism*. New York, NY: Doubleday, 2004.

————. *The Dawkins Delusion: A Theist Fundamentalism and the Denial of the Divine*. London, UK: SPCK (Society for Promoting Christian Knowledge), 2007.

Moreland, J.P., and Kai Nielsen. *Does God Exist?* Nashville, TN: Thomas Nelson, 1990.

Nash, Ronald H. *The Concept of God.* Grand Rapids, MI: Zondervan, 1983.

Nicholi, Armand M., Jr. *The Question of God: C. S. Lewis and Sigmund Freud Debate God, Love, Sex, and the Meaning of Life.* New York, NY: Free Press, 2002.

Orr, James. *The Christian View of God and the World.* Grand Rapids, MI: Kregel, 1989.

Overman, Dean L. *A Case Against Accident and Self-Organization.* New York, NY: Rowman and Littlefield, 1997.

Packer, J.I. *Knowing God.* Downers Grove, IL: InterVarsity Press, 1973.

Schaeffer, Francis A. *The Finished Work of Christ.* Wheaton, IL: Crossway Books, 1998.

Thielicke, Helmut. *A Little Exercise for Young Theologians.* Grand Rapids, MI: Eerdmans, 1962.

CHRISTIAN PHILOSOPHY

Arkes, Hadley. *First Things: An Inquiry into the First Principles of Morals and Justice.* Princeton, NJ: Princeton University Press, 1986.

Beckwith, Francis J., William Lane Craig, and J.P. Moreland, eds. *To Everyone an Answer: A Case for the Christian Worldview.* Downers Grove, IL: InterVarsity Press, 2004.

Clark, Gordon H. *Thales to Dewey*, 2nd ed. Jefferson, MD: Trinity Foundation, 1989.

Craig, William Lane. *Reasonable Faith.* Wheaton, IL: Crossway Books, 1994.

Geisler, Norman L. *Christian Apologetics.* Grand Rapids, MI: Baker Book House, 1976.

Geisler, Norman L., and Paul D. Feinberg. *Introduction to Philosophy.* Grand Rapids, MI: Baker Book House, 1980.

Geisler, Norman L., and Frank Turek. *I Don't Have Enough Faith to Be an Atheist.* Wheaton, IL: Crossway Books, 2004.

Groothuis, Douglas. *Truth Decay.* Downers Grove, IL: InterVarsity Press, 2000.

Jaki, Stanley L. *The Road to Science and the Ways to God.* Chicago, IL: University of Chicago Press, 1978.

Joad, C.E.M. *The Recovery of Belief.* London, UK: Faber and Faber, 1955.

Johnson, Phillip E. *Reason in the Balance: The Case Against Naturalism in Science, Education and Law.* Downers Grove, IL: InterVarsity Press, 1955.

Lennox, John C. *God's Undertaker: Has Science Buried God?* Oxford, UK: Lion, 2007.

Moreland, J.P., and William Lane Craig. *Philosophical Foundations for a Christian Worldview.* Downers Grove, IL: InterVarsity Press, 2003.

Moreland, J.P. *Christianity and the Nature of Science.* Grand Rapids, MI: Baker Book House, 1989.

Nash, Ronald H. *Life's Ultimate Questions: An Introduction to Philosophy.* Grand Rapids, MI: Zondervan, 1999.

Pearcey, Nancy. *Total Truth: Liberating Christianity from Its Cultural Captivity.* Wheaton, IL: Crossway Books, 2004.

Plantinga, Alvin. *Warranted Christian Belief.* New York, NY: Oxford University Press, 2000.

Smith, R. Scott. *Truth and the New Kind of Christian.* Wheaton, IL: Crossway Books, 2005.

Willard, Dallas. *Logic and the Objectivity of Knowledge.* Athens, OH: Ohio University Press, 1984.

Willard, Dallas. "How Concepts Relate the Mind to Its Objects: The 'God's Eye View' Vindicated. *Philosophia Christi*, Series 2, 1:2 (1999): 5-20.

Willard, Dallas. "A Crucial Error in Epistemology." *Mind*, (October 1967): 513-523.

CHRISTIAN ETHICS

Arkes, Hadley. *First Things: An Inquiry into the First Principles of Morals and Justice.* Princeton, NJ: Princeton University Press, 1986.

Anderson, Kerby. *Christian Ethics in Plain Language.* Nashville, TN: Thomas Nelson, 2005.

———. *Moral Dilemmas.* Dallas, TX: Word, 1998.

Beckwith, Francis J., and Gregory Koukl. *Relativism: Feet Firmly Planted In Mid-Air.* Grand Rapids, MI: Baker Book House, 1998.

Bonhoeffer, Dietrich. *The Cost of Discipleship.* New York, NY: Macmillan, 1963.

———. *Ethics.* New York, NY: Simon and Schuster, 1995.

———. *Life Together: A Discussion of Christian Fellowship.* New York, NY: Harper and Row, 1954.

Chamberlain, Paul. *Can We Be Good Without God?* Downers Grove, IL: InterVarsity Press, 1996.

Colson, Charles, and Nancy Pearcey. *How Now Shall We Live?* Wheaton, IL: Tyndale House, 1999.

Copan, Paul. *True for You, But Not for Me.* Minneapolis, MN: Bethany House Publishers, 1998.

Geisler, Norman L. *Christian Ethics.* Grand Rapids, MI: Baker Book House, 1990.

Geivett, Douglas. *Evil and the Evidence for God.* Philadelphia, PA: Temple University Press, 1993.

Harris, James. *Against Relativism.* Peru, IL: Open Court, 1992.

Heimbach, Daniel R. *True Sexual Morality: Recovering Biblical Standards for a Culture in Crisis.* Wheaton, IL: Crossway Books, 2004.

Henry, Carl F.H. *The Christian Mindset in a Secular Society.* Portland, OR: Multnomah, 1984.

Kilpatrick, William. *Why Johnny Can't Tell Right From Wrong: Moral Illiteracy and the Case for Character Education.* New York, NY: Simon and Schuster, 1992.

Klusendorf, Scott. *Pro-Life 101.* Signal Hill, CA: Stand to Reason Press, 2002.

Lewis, C.S. *The Screwtape Letters.* New York, NY: Macmillan, 1982.

———. *God in the Dock.* Grand Rapids, MI: Eerdmans, 1972.

McDowell, Josh, and Norm Geisler. *Love is Always Right.* Dallas, TX: Word, 1996.

McDowell, Josh, and Bob Hostetler. *Right From Wrong.* Dallas, TX: Word, 1994.

McDowell, Sean. *Ethix: Being Bold in a Whatever World.* Nashville, TN: Broadman and Holman, 2006.

Moreland, J.P., and Norman L. Geisler. *The Life And Death Debate: Moral Issues of our Time.* Westport, CT: Praeger, 1990.

Pojman, Louis P. *Ethics: Discovering Right and Wrong.* Belmont, MA: Wadsworth, 1990.

Reed, Gerard. *C.S. Lewis Explores Vice and Virtue.* Kansas City, MO: Beacon Hill Press, 2001.

Schaeffer, Francis. *How Should We Then Live?* Old Tappan, NJ: Revell, 1976.

CHRISTIAN BIOLOGY

Ankerberg, John, and John Weldon. *Darwin's Leap of Faith.* Eugene, OR: Harvest House, 1998.

Behe, Michael J. *Darwin's Black Box: The Biochemical Challenge to Evolution.* Rev. Ed., New York, NY: Free Press, 2006.

Behe, Michael J. *The Edge of Evolution: The Search for the Limits of Darwinism.* New York, NY: Free Press, 2007.

Brown, Walt. *In The Beginning: Compelling Evidence for Creation and the Flood*, 7th ed. Phoenix, AZ: Center for Scientific Creation, 2001.

Dembski, William, ed. *Uncommon Dissent: Intellectuals Who Find Darwinism Unconvincing.* Wilmington, DE: ISI Books, 2004.

Dembski, William A. and Jonathan Wells. *The Design of Life.* Dallas, TX: Foundation for Thought and Ethics, 2007.

Denton, Michael. *Evolution: A Theory in Crisis.* Bethesda, MD: Adler and Adler, 1986.

DeYoung, Don. *Thousands...Not Billions: Challenging an Icon of Evolution.* Green Forest, AR: Master Books, 2005.

Johnson, Phillip E. *Darwin on Trial*, 2nd ed. Downers Grove, IL: InterVarsity Press, 1993.

Martin, Jobe. *The Evolution of a Creationist.* Rockwall, TX: Biblical Discipleship Publishers, 2004.

Milton, Richard. *Shattering the Myths of Darwinism.* Rochester, VT: Park Street Press, 1997.

Moore, John N., and Harold S. Slusher. *Biology: A Search for Order in Complexity.* Grand Rapids, MI: Zondervan, 1970.

Moreland, J.P., ed. *The Creation Hypothesis: Scientific Evidence for an Intelligent Designer.* Downers Grove, IL: InterVarsity Press, 1994.

Morris, Henry. *The Long War Against God.* Grand Rapids, MI: Baker Book House, 1990.

Pearcey, Nancy R., and Charles B. Thaxton. *The Soul of Science: Christian Faith and Natural Philosophy.* Wheaton, IL: Crossway Books, 1994.

Sanford, John C. *Genetic Entropy and the Mystery of the Genome.* Lima, NY: Ivan Press, 2005.

Simmons, Geoffrey. *What Darwin Didn't Know.* Eugene, OR: Harvest House, 2004.

————. *Billions of Missing Links: A Rational Look at the Mysteries Evolution Can't Explain.* Eugene, OR: Harvest House Publishers, 2007.

Spetner, Lee. *Not By Chance: Shattering the Modern Theory of Evolution.* Brooklyn, NY: Judaica Press, 1998.

Starkey, Walter L. *The Cambrian Explosion: Evolution's Big Bang or Darwin's Dilemma?* Dublin, OH: WLS Publishing, 1998.

Stove, David. *Darwinian Fairy Tales: Selfish Genes, Errors of Heredity, and Other Fables of Evolution.* New York, NY: Encounter Books, 1995.

Thaxton, Charles B., Walter L. Bradley, and Roger L. Olsen. *The Mystery of Life's Origin.* New York, NY: Philosophical Library, 1984.

Wells, Jonathan. *Icon of Evolution: Science or Myth?* Washington, DC: Regnery Publishing, 2000.

————. *The Politically Incorrect Guide to Darwinism and Intelligent Design.* Washington, DC: Regnary Publishing, Inc., 2006.

CHRISTIAN PSYCHOLOGY

Cooper, John W. *Body, Soul, and Life Everlasting.* Grand Rapids, MI: Eerdmans, 1989.

Custance, Arthur. *Man in Adam and in Christ.* Grand Rapids, MI: Zondervan, 1975.

————. *The Mysterious Matter of Mind.* Grand Rapids, MI: Zondervan, 1980.

Delitzsch, Franz J. *A System of Biblical Psychology.* Grand Rapids, MI: Baker Book House, 1966.

Dembski, William, ed. *The End of Materialism.* to be published in 2007.

Justman, Stewart. *Fool's Paradise: The Unreal World of Pop Psychology.* Chicago, IL: Ivan R. Dee, 2005.

Kilpatrick, William Kirk. *Psychology Seduction*. Nashville, TN: Thomas Nelson, 1983.

Lewis, C.S. *Screwtape Letters*. New York, NY: HarperCollins, 2001.

———. *The Great Divorce*. New York, NY: HarperCollins, 2001.

Machen, J. Gresham. *The Christian View of Man*. London, UK: Banner of Truth, 1965.

Milton, Joyce. *The Road to Malpsychia: Humanistic Psychology and our Discontents*. San Francisco, CA: Encounter Books, 2002.

Moreland, J.P., and Scott B. Rae. *Body and Soul: Human Nature and the Crisis in Ethics*. Downers Grove, IL: InterVarsity Press, 2000.

Nicholi, Armand M., Jr. *The Question of God: C.S. Lewis and Sigmund Freud Debate God, Love, Sex and the Meaning of Life*. New York, NY: Free Press, 2003.

Orr, James. *God's Image in Man*. Grand Rapids, MI: Eerdmans, 1948.

Penfield, Wilder. *The Mystery of the Mind*. Princeton, NJ: Princeton University Press, 1975.

Schaeffer, Francis. *The Complete Works of Francis Schaeffer*. Vol. 3, bk. 2. *True Spirituality*. Westchester, IL: Crossway Books, 1982.

Sokoloff, Boris. *The Permissive Society*. New Rochelle, NY: Arlington House, 1972.

Vitz, Paul. *Psychology as Religion*. Grand Rapids, MI: Eerdmans, 1985.

CHRISTIAN SOCIOLOGY

Armstrong, John H., ed. *The Compromised Church: The Present Evangelical Crisis*. Wheaton, IL: Crossway Books, 1998.

Baehr, Ted. *The Media-Wise Family*. Colorado Springs, CO: Cook Communications, 1998

Bennett, William J. *The Devaluing of America: The Fight for Our Culture and Our Children*. New York, NY: Simon and Schuster, 1992.

Blankenhorn, David. *Fatherless America*. New York, NY: Basic Books, 1995.

Carlson, Allan C., and Paul T. Mero. *The Natural Family: A Manifesto*. Rockford, IL: Howard Center for Family, Religion and Society, 2005.

Dalrymple, Theodore. *Life at the Bottom: The Worldview That Makes the Underclass*. Chicago, IL: Ivan R. Dee, 2001.

———. *Our Culture, What's Left Of It*. Chicago, IL: Ivan R. Dee, 20005.

de Tocqueville, Alexis. *Democracy in America*. New York, NY: HarperCollins, 2000.

Dobson, James C. *Bringing Up Boys: Practical Advice and Encouragement for Those Shaping the Next Generation of Men*. Wheaton, IL: Tyndale House, 2001.

———. *The New Dare To Discipline*. Wheaton, IL: Tyndale House, 1992.

Dobson, James C. and Gary L. Bauer. *Children at Risk*. Dallas, TX: Word, 1990.

Gaede, S.D. *Where Gods May Dwell*. Grand Rapids, MI: Zondervan, 1985.

Gairdner, William D. *The War Against The Family*. Toronto, Canada: Stoddart Publishing, 1993.

George, Robert P., and Jean Bethke Elshtain, eds. *The Meaning of Marriage*. Dallas, TX: Spence Publishing, 2006.

Gilder, George. *Men and Marriage*. Gretna, LA: Pelican, 1986.

Grant, George. *Grand Illusions: The Legacy of Planned Parenthood*. Franklin, TN: Adroit Press, 1992.

Levin, Michael. *Feminism and Freedom*. New Brunswick, NJ: Transaction Books, 1998.

Medved, Michael, and Diane Medved. *Saving Childhood. Protecting Our Children From The National Assault On Innocence*. New York, NY: HarperCollins, 1998.

Piper, John, and Wayne Grudem, eds. *Recovering Biblical Manhood and Womanhood: A Response to Evangelical Feminism*. Wheaton, IL: Crossway Books, 1991.

Reisman, Judith A. *Kinsey: Crimes and Consequences*. Arlington, VA: Institute for Media Education, 1998.

Schlafly, Phyllis. *Feminist Fantasies*. Dallas, TX: Spence Publishing, 2003.

Schweizer, Peter, and Rochelle Schweizer. *Disney the Mouse Betrayed: Greed, Corruption, and Children at Risk*. Washington, DC: Regnery Publishing, 1998.

Short, Bruce N. *The Harsh Truth About Public Schools*. Vallecito, CA: Chalcedon Foundation, 2004.

Stark, Rodney. *For the Glory of God*. Princeton, NJ: Princeton University Press, 2003.

CHRISTIAN LAW

Amos, Gary T. *Defending the Declaration*. Brentwood, TN: Wolgemuth and Hyatt, 1989.

Arkes, Hadley. *First Things: An Inquiry into the First Principles of Morals and Justice*. Princeton, NJ: Princeton University Press 1986.

Barton, David. *Original Intent: The Courts, the Constitution, and Religion*. Aledo, TX: WallBuilder Press, 1997.

Bastiat, Frederick. *The Law*. Irvington-on-Hudson, NY: Foundation for Economic Education, 1990.

Blackstone, William. *Commentaries on the Laws of England*. 4 vols. Chicago, IL: University of Chicago Press, 1979.

Budziszewski, J. *Written on the Heart: The Case for Natural Law*. Downers Grove, IL: InterVarsity Press, 1997.

Geisler, Norman L. *Creation and the Courts: Eighty Years of Conflict in the Classroom and the Courtroom*. Wheaton, IL: Crossway Books, 2007.

Holzer, Henry Mark. *The Keeper of the Flame: The Supreme Court Opinions of Justice Clarence Thomas*. Bangor, ME: Booklocker.com, 2006.

House, Wayne H., ed. *Restoring the Constitution*. Dallas, TX: Probe, 1987.

Montgomery, John Warwick. *Human Rights and Human Dignity*. Dallas, TX: Probe, 1986.

Ring, Kevin A. *Scalia Dissents: Writings of the Supreme Court's Wittiest, Most Outspoken Justice*. Washington, DC: Regnery Publishing, 2004.

Schlafly, Phyllis. *The Supremacists: The Tyranny of Judges*. Dallas, TX: Spence Publishing, 2004.

Sears, Alan and Craig Osten. *The ACLU Vs. America*. Nashville, TN: Broadman and Holman Publishers, 2005.

Stormer, John A. *Betrayed By the Bench*. Florissant, MO: Liberty Bell Press, 2005.

Titus, Herbert W. *God, Man, and Law: The Biblical Principles*. Oak Brook, IL: Institute in Basic Life Principles, 1994.

Whitehead, John W. *The Second American Revolution*. Westchester, IL: Crossway Books, 1988.

CHRISTIAN POLITICS

Belmonte, Kevin C., ed., *A Practical View of Christianity: Personal Faith as a Call to Political Responsibility*. Peabody, MA: Hendrickson Publishers, Inc., 1996.

Clark, Gordon H. *Essays on Ethics and Politics*. Unicoi, TN: The Trinity Foundation, 1992.

Colson, Charles. *Kingdoms in Conflict*. Grand Rapids, MI: Zondervan, 1987.

Coulter, Ann. *Godless: The Church of Liberalism*. New York, NY: Crown Forum, 2006.

Crippen, Alan R. *Christianity and Politics: William Wilberforce, Member of Parliament*. Washington, D.C.: Family Research Council, 2001.

DeMar, Gary. *America's Christian History: The Untold Story*, 2nd ed. Atlanta, GA: American Vision, 1995.

Evans, M. Stanton. *The Theme is Freedom: Religion, Politics, and the American Tradition.* Washington, DC: Regnery Publishing, 1994.

Geisler, Norman L., and Frank Turek. *Legislating Morality: Is it Wise? Is it Legal? Is it Possible?* Minneapolis, MN: Bethany House, 1998.

Goldberg, Jonah. *Liberal Fascism: The Secret History of the American Left from Mussolini to the Politics of Meaning.* (New York, NY: Doubleday), 2007.

Hart, Benjamin. *Faith and Freedom.* Dallas, TX: Lewis and Stanley, 1988.

Henry, Carl F.H. *Twilight of a Great Civilization.* Westchester, IL: Crossway Books, 1988.

Horowitz, David. *The Politics of Bad Faith.* New York, NY: Free Press, 1998.

Neuhaus, Richard J. *The Naked Public Square.* Grand Rapids, MI: Eerdmans, 1984.

Siedentop, Larry. *Tocqueville.* New York, NY: Oxford University Press, 1994

Sowell, Thomas. *A Conflict of Visions: Ideological Origins of Political Struggles.* New York, NY: William Morrow and Company, 1987.

CHRISTIAN ECONOMICS

Alcorn, Randy. *Money, Possessions and Eternity.* Wheaton, IL: Tyndale House, 2003.

Bastiat, Frederic. *Economic Harmonies.* New York, NY: D. Van Nostrand, 1964.

Bauer, P.T. *Equality, the Third World, and Economic Delusion.* Cambridge, MA: Harvard University Press, 1981.

Bauman, Michael, ed. *Morality and the Marketplace.* Hillsdale, MI: Hillsdale College Press, 1994.

Beisner, E. Calvin. *Prosperity and Poverty: The Compassionate Use of Resources in a World of Scarcity.* Westchester, IL: Crossway Books, 1988.

Bethell, Tom. *The Noblest Triumph: Property and Prosperity Through the Ages.* New York, NY: St. Martin's Press, 1998.

Brooks, Arthur C. *Who Really Cares: America's Charity Divide—Who Gives, Who Doesn't, and Why It Matters.*

Gilder, George. *Wealth and Poverty.* New York, NY: Basic Books, 1981.

Nash, Ronald H. *Poverty and Wealth: The Christian Debate Over Capitalism.* Westchester, IL: Crossway Books, 1987.

Novak, Michael. *The Spirit of Democratic Capitalism.* New York, NY: Simon and Schuster, 1982.

Robbins, John W. *Freedom and Capitalism: Essays on Christian Economics and Politics.* Unicoi, TN: The Trinity Foundation, 2006.

Schaeffer, Franky, ed. *Is Capitalism Christian?* Westchester, IL: Crossway Books, 1986.

Shafarevich, Igor. *The Socialist Phenomenon.* New York, NY: Harper and Row, 1980.

Stark, Rodney. *The Victory of Reason: How Christianity Led to Freedom, Capitalism, and Western Success.* New York, NY: Random House, 2005.

von Mises, Ludwig. *Socialism: An Economic and Sociological Analysis.* Indianapolis, IN: Liberty Classics, 1981.

CHRISTIAN HISTORY

Amos, Gary, and Richard Gardiner. *Never Before in History.* Richardson, TX: Foundation for Thought and Ethics, 1998.

Barton, David. *Benjamin Rush: Signer of the Declaration of Independence.* Aledo, TX: WallBuilder Press, 1999.

Blomberg, Craig L. *The Historical Reliability of the Gospels*. Downers Grove, IL: InterVarsity Press, 1987.

———. *The Historical Reliability of John's Gospel*. Downers Grove, IL: InterVarsity Press, 1998.

Butterfield, Herbert. *Christianity and History*. New York, NY: Charles Scribner's Sons, 1950.

Durant, Will. *Caesar and Christ*. New York, NY: Simon and Schuster, 1944.

Habermas, Gary R., and Michael Licona. *The Case for the Resurrection of Jesus*. Grand Rapids, MI: Kregel Publications, 2004.

Habermas, Gary, and Antony Flew. *Did Jesus Rise From The Dead?* New York, NY: Harper and Row, 1987.

Himmelfarb, Gertrude. *The Roads to Modernity: The British, French, and American Enlightenments*. New York, NY: Alfred A. Knopf, 2004.

Hutson, James H. *Religion and the Founding of the American Republic*. Washington, DC: Library of Congress, 1998.

Johnson, Paul. *Intellectuals*. New York, NY: Harper and Row, 1990.

———. *A History of the American People*. New York, NY: HarperCollins, 1998.

———. *Modern Times: The World from the Twenties to the Nineties*, rev. ed. New York, NY: HarperCollins, 1991.

Kennedy, D. James, and Jerry Newcombe. *What if Jesus Had Never Been Born?* Nashville, TN: Thomas Nelson, 1994.

Kirk, Russell. *The Roots of American Order*. Washington, DC: Regnery Gateway, 1991.

Marshall, Peter and David Manuel. *Sounding Forth the Trumpet: God's Plan for America in Peril*. Grand Rapids, MI: Baker Book House, 1998.

Mascall, E. L. *The Secularization of Christianity*. New York, NY: Holt Rinehard Winston, 1965.

McDowell, Josh. *The New Evidence That Demands a Verdict*. Nashville, TN: Thomas Nelson, 1999.

Nash, Ronald H. *Christian Faith and Historical Understanding*. Dallas, TX: Probe, 1984.

———. *The Meaning of History*. Nashville, TN: Broadman and Holman, 1998.

Pearce, Meic. *The Gods of War: Is Religion the Primary Cause of Violent Conflict*. Downers Grove, IL: InterVarsity Press, 2007.

Roberts, Mark D. *Can We Trust the Gospels?* Wheaton, IL: Crossway Books, 2007.

Schlossberg, Herbert. *Idols for Destruction: The Conflict of Christian Faith and American Culture*. Wheaton, IL: Crossway Books, 1993.

Schmidt, Alvin J. *How Christianity Changed the World*. Grand Rapids, MI: Zondervan, 2004.

Solzhenitsyn, Aleksandr I. *The Gulag Archipelago*. New York, NY: HarperCollins, 2002.

Sowell, Thomas. *The Quest for Cosmic Justice*. New York, NY: Free Press, 1999.

Wilkins, Michael J., and J.P. Moreland, eds. *Jesus Under Fire: Modern Scholarship Reinvents the Historical Jesus*. Grand Rapids, MI: Zondervan, 1995.

Wright, N.T., *The Resurrection Of The Son Of God*. Minneapolis, MN: Fortress Press, 2003.

------------------------ A ------------------------

A.C.L.U.: (American Civil Liberties Union) Originally founded in 1920 as a socialist front group by Roger Baldwin, a noted Marxist and lifelong pacifist; the organization is the largest non-profit that purports to defend the rights of all Americans. It supports, among others, separation of church and state, reproductive rights, full civil rights for homosexuals, and affirmative action.

Agnosticism: The philosophical belief that evidence for the existence of God is lacking or inconclusive.

Anarchy: The belief that government, by its very nature, is oppressive, and should be abolished.

Anthropic Principle: Either of two principles in cosmology: (a) conditions that are observed in the universe must allow the observer to exist; or, (b) the universe must have properties that make inevitable the existence of intelligent life.

Antirealism: The belief that reality is subjectively constructed by human thought.

Apologetics: The branch of theology concerned with defending Christianity as a reasonable and practical faith.

Atheism: A denial of the existence of a supernatural God.

------------------------ B ------------------------

Bourgeoisie: The social/economic class who owns private property and the means of production. In Marxist economic theory, the bourgeoisie exploit the labor of the poorer proletariat class. See Proletariat.

------------------------ **C** ------------------------

Capitalism: An economic system based on the peaceful and free exchange of goods and services, where all or most of the means of production and distribution are privately owned and operated for profit.

Christian: A follower of Jesus Christ who has personally accepted Christ's death and resurrection as the only means for salvation.

Collectivism: The ownership and control of the means of production and distribution by the people collectively—not necessarily government owned or administered.

Communism: The Marxist goal of a future utopia in which all resources for production are owned in common by a classless society.

Correspondence theory of truth: A philosophical belief that a statement is true if it corresponds to the facts of reality. See Truth.

Cosmic Evolution: The progression of collective humanity toward an age of higher consciousness.

Cosmology: The study of the structure, origin, and design of the universe.

Cosmological argument: A proof for the existence of God based on the necessity of a First Cause, i.e. God. An explanation of the origin of the universe, often taking the form: 1) Whatever begins to exist has a cause. 2) The universe began to exist. 3) Therefore, the universe had a cause.

Creationism: A scientific theory that God was directly involved in creating the universe and all the various kinds of plants and animals, including mankind as created in God's image.

Cultural Relativism: The belief that truth and morals are relative to one's culture.

------------------------ **D** ------------------------

Darwinism: The theory proposed by Charles Darwin that species gradually evolve into new species over time due to natural selection. See also Evolution and Neo-Darwinism.

Decalogue: The Ten Commandments given to Moses by God as recorded in Exodus 20.

Deconstruction: A theory of literary criticism that seeks to expose the hidden assumptions and prejudices of the author of any written text, emphasizing the underlying racist, sexist, homophobic, or bourgeois bias of authors from the Western philosophic tradition.

Deism: The belief, based solely on reason, that God created the universe but now stands completely detached from it, giving no supernatural revelation.

Despotism: A form of government in which the ruler is an absolute dictator.
Determinism: The belief that events, actions, or decisions are inevitable consequences of proceeding events or natural laws, denying freedom of the human will.

Dialectic: A Hegelian process involving thesis, antithesis, and synthesis with the synthesis being a higher form of truth.

Dialectical materialism: In Marxist philosophy, the theory that the primary functioning of nature involves a continuous process of a thesis coming in conflict with its antithesis, resulting in a new synthesis.

Divine law: Any law that comes directly from the character of God via special revelation.

Divine revelation: God revealing Himself and His character through nature, the Bible, and the person and work of Jesus Christ.

Dualism: The theory that reality is composed of two basic and distinct elements—mind and matter. Related to psychology, the belief that mind (soul/spirit) and matter (body) exist as separate entities, i.e., the mind is not mere matter.

------------------------ E ------------------------

Economic determinism: The belief that economics (the modes of production and exchange) determines the entire course of history, including the social, political, and moral processes of life.

Egalitarianism: The belief that both sexes are equal; men and women should have equal rights politically, socially, and economically.

Empiricism: The view that the five senses (touch, sight, hearing, taste, and smell) are the only accurate and true sources of knowledge.

Epistemology: The study of the origin, nature, methods, and limits of knowledge.

Ethical relativism: The belief that no absolute moral code exists and therefore man determines what is right in each situation according to his private judgment.

Ethics: A set of principles for determining what is good and evil or right and wrong behavior. See Morality.

Evolution: In biology, the idea that life on earth originated from inanimate matter and proceeded to change over time into the diversity of plants and animals as evidenced by fossils and currently living organisms. See Darwinism and Neo-Darwinism.

------------------------ F ------------------------

Fascism: A political system based on national socialism and Darwinian evolution; favors strong centralized government and rejects a free economy and individual liberty.

Feminism: The belief that women are the victims of male domination, and the demand for equal status of women economically, politically, and socially.

Free market economy: See Capitalism.

Freedom: Liberty of a person from slavery, oppression, or incarceration; the ability to make free choices.

Free will: The ability of a human being to make genuine choices free from coercion.

------------------------- **G** -------------------------

General revelation: God's revelation of Himself and His will through nature, history, and the human conscience to all persons at all times and in all places.

Globalism: An outlook or policy that is worldwide in scope; sometimes used for world government.

Golden Rule: Do unto others as you would have them do to you.

------------------------- **H** -------------------------

Hedonism: The belief that pleasure is the highest good for individuals and society.

Higher consciousness: The ever-increasingt awareness of one's spiritual essence and the underlying spiritual nature in all things.

Historicism: The view that past beliefs, morals, and truths can only be understood in relation to the cultural/historical periods in which they arose.

Homosexuality: Sexual activity between two people of the same gender.

------------------------- **I** -------------------------

Idealism: The theory that ideas are the ultimate reality, and external perceptions consist only of ideas, not matter.

Ideology: The doctrines, opinions, or way of thinking of an individual or group.

Integrity: The quality or state of being of sound moral principle; uprightness, honesty, sincerity.

Intelligent Design: The scientific hypothesis that irreducible complexity observed in every level of life cannot be explained by Neo-Darwinian theory and, instead, is best explained by the agency of an intelligent designer.

Interventionism: An economic approach seeking a middle path between socialism and capitalism. Interventionists do not seek to abolish private property but to highly regulate it by taxation and government regulation of businesses and wages.

Irreducible complexity: The philosophical concept that considers the complexity of living organisms—if any part is removed, the system loses function.

------------------------- **J** -------------------------

Justice: Fair and impartial handling; due reward or treatment.

------------------------- **K** -------------------------

Karma: The total effect of a person's actions and conduct during each phase of existence, determining the person's destiny.

------------------------- **L** -------------------------

Law: The measure of right and wrong; Christians understand that the God of the universe has established what is right and what is wrong, which makes law and ethics co-equal.

Leftism: An ideological approach to politics emphasizing the state's role in bringing about social justice, with a special focus on helping the poor or those oppressed due to race, gender, or sexual orientation.

Legal positivism: The Humanistic legal school of thought that claims laws are rules made by human beings and that there is no inherent or necessary connection between law and morality.

Liberalism: An educational system based on a Secular Humanist Worldview. A political tradition emphasizing personal liberties and equality over traditional moral concerns; specific policies include a woman's right to an abortion, promotion of same-sex marriage, equal rights for women, and redistribution of wealth to help the poor.

------------------------- **M** -------------------------

Macroevolution: The origin of fundamentally new organisms from prior life forms over time.

Maoism: The communistic teachings of Mao Tse-Tung.

Marxism: The worldview developed by Karl Marx centered around atheism, dialectical materialism, evolution, and socialism.

Materialism: The belief that reality consists only of material elements.

Metanarrative: Any overarching, all-encompassing story that seeks to define the whole of reality.

Metaphysics: The study of ultimate reality.

Microevolution: Small changes within the species of a gene pool.

Miracle: An event brought about by a special act of God.

Monism: The belief that there is only one fundamental reality. In psychology, the theory that the physical brain and mind (thoughts, ideas, feelings) are one substance; mental events are reducible to chemical firings in the brain.

Morality: The system of ideas that distinguishs between right and wrong thoughts and behavior.

Moral absolutes: The belief that an absolute ethical standard exists for all individuals regardless of era or culture; also known as the eternal moral order.

Moral law: That part of natural law that defines the consequences for the moral choices made by men and women.

Moral relativism: See Ethical Relativism.

------------------------ **N** ------------------------

Natural law: The theory that both physical and moral laws are discovered through studying the natural world.

Naturalism: The belief that all reality is fundamentally material and all phenomena can be explained in terms of natural causes.

Nihilism: The belief that life has no ultimate meaning.

Nazism: A political system based on national socialism (German Workers National Socialist Party) and Darwinian evolution.

Neo-Darwinism: The theory that new species arise from natural selection acting over vast periods of time on chance genetic mutations in reproductively isolated populations.

------------------------ **O** ------------------------

Olympianism: The belief that activist judges are an intellectual elite class ordained to shape a nation's destiny.

Ontology: The study of the existence of being.

Open theism: The belief that God does not know the future.

------------------------ **P** ------------------------

Pantheism: A belief that identifies the forces/energy of nature with god; god is everything and everything is god.

Philosophy: Literally, "the love of wisdom or knowledge." A study of the processes governing thought, conduct, and ultimate reality.

Polygamy: The practice of having more than one wife or husband.

Positive Law: A legal system that insists all law is of human origin.

Postmodernism: The "anti-worldview" worldview characterized by skepticism of absolute truth and morality.

Proletariat: The blue-collar working class, generally property-less.

Property: A possession, whether tangible or intangible, to which its owner has legal title.

Punctuated Evolution: The theory of evolution that proposes that evolutionary changes occur over a relatively quick period of time, followed by periods of little to no evolutionary change.

---------------------- **R** ------------------------

Realism: The theory that objects in the world exist independently of human thought.

Relativism: The belief that "truth" is relative to the individual and the time and place in which one acts; there are no absolute or objective truths.

Religion: Any system of beliefs used to guide one's life and conduct, whether that system includes a belief in the existence of God or not. Note: on this definition of religion, an atheistic worldview such as Secular Humanism is *religious*.

Religious Pluralism: The conviction that one should be tolerant of all religious beliefs because no one religion is true.

Resurrection: A rising from the dead; returning to life following death.

Revisionist History: Rewriting the past to serve an ideological purpose and to empower oppressed social groups.

---------------------- **S** ------------------------

Scientism: The belief that the scientific method provides the only means for arriving at the truth. The harnessing of empirical science for a non-scientific purpose. e.g., making use of physics, chemistry, or biology to enforce conclusions about morality, politics, or metaphysics.

Second law of thermodynamics: A natural law that states that although the total energy in the cosmos remains constant, the amount of energy available to do useful work is always decreasing.

Secular Humanism: A worldview based on atheism and naturalism in which "man is the measure" of all things; man, not God, is the ultimate norm by which truth and morals are to be determined.

Self-actualization: The highest level of a person's potential and the ultimate goal of Maslow's "hierarchy of needs" (a theory contending that as we meet our basic needs, we seek to satisfy successively higher needs).

Special revelation: God's revelation of Himself and His character to certain persons at various times and places. In Christianity, this revelation is found in miraculous events (e.g. the Exodus), is recorded in the Scriptures (Psalm 19:7-11, 2 Timothy 3:14-17), is found supremely in Jesus Christ (John 1:1-18), and is the means by which man comes to know of salvation.

Socialism: An economic system in which private property is transferred to the state and operation of the means of production and distribution are controlled by the government. In Marxist theory, socialism is the transitional phase between capitalism and communism.

Social justice: The belief that government has a moral duty to bring about economic and social equality by taxing the wealthy and redistributing it to the poor.

Spontaneous generation: The belief that life originated from non-living matter through a purely naturalistic process, without supernatural intervention from God.

State: The political body organized for supreme civil rule.

Statism: The concentration of economic controls and planning in the hands of a highly centralized government.

Stewardship: The science, art, and skill of responsible and accountable management of resources. Christians believe that God is the ultimate owner of everything and that human beings have been given the responsibility to manage and care for His creation.

Supernaturalism: The belief that reality is more than nature, allowing a transcendent agent to intervene in the natural realm.

------------------------ **T** ------------------------

Theism: A belief in the existence of a supernatural God.

Theistic evolution: The belief that God works through the natural process of evolution.

Theocracy: Government by a ruling power that claims Divine sanction.

Theology: The study of God and the relations between God, man, and the universe.

Totalitarianism: See Statism.

Truth: When a statement or belief corresponds to fact, reality, or logic. See Correspondence Theory of Truth.

------------------------ **U** ------------------------

Utilitarianism: An ethical framework that posits that all action should be directed toward achieving the greatest utility for the greatest number of people.

Utopianism: A visionary scheme for a man-made, perfect society on earth.

------------------------ **W** ------------------------

Worldview:
1) Any ideology, philosophy, theology, movement, or religion that provides an overarching approach to understanding God, the world, and man's relationship to God and the world (see metanarrative);
2) A comprehensive system for recognizing the inter-relationship between theology, philosophy, ethics, biology (origins), psychology, sociology, politics, law, economics, and history;
3) A framework for answering life's major questions—Who is God? How did I get here? Why am I here? How do I know? How should I behave? How should I treat others? Where am I going?
4) A set of ideas, beliefs, convictions, values, and virtues for guiding one's life.

507